Accounting for Derivatives

For other titles in the Wiley Finance series
please see www.wiley.com/finance

Accounting for Derivatives

Advanced Hedging under IFRS 9

Second Edition

JUAN RAMIREZ

WILEY

This edition first published 2015
© 2015 Juan Ramirez
First edition published 2007 by John Wiley & Sons, Ltd.

Registered office
John Wiley & Sons Ltd, The Atrium, Southern Gate, Chichester, West Sussex, PO19 8SQ, United Kingdom

For details of our global editorial offices, for customer services and for information about how to apply for permission to reuse the copyright material in this book please see our website at www.wiley.com.

Wiley publishes in a variety of print and electronic formats and by print-on-demand. Some material included with standard print versions of this book may not be included in e-books or in print-on-demand. If this book refers to media such as a CD or DVD that is not included in the version you purchased, you may download this material at http://booksupport.wiley.com. For more information about Wiley products, visit www.wiley.com.

Designations used by companies to distinguish their products are often claimed as trademarks. All brand names and product names used in this book are trade names, service marks, trademarks or registered trademarks of their respective owners. The publisher is not associated with any product or vendor mentioned in this book.

Limit of Liability/Disclaimer of Warranty: While the publisher and author have used their best efforts in preparing this book, they make no representations or warranties with the respect to the accuracy or completeness of the contents of this book and specifically disclaim any implied warranties of merchantability or fitness for a particular purpose. It is sold on the understanding that the publisher is not engaged in rendering professional services and neither the publisher nor the author shall be liable for damages arising herefrom. If professional advice or other expert assistance is required, the services of a competent professional should be sought.

Library of Congress Cataloging-in-Publication Data

Ramirez, Juan.
  Accounting for derivatives : advanced hedging under IFRS 9 / Juan Ramirez. – Second edition.
      pages cm. – (The wiley finance series)
   Includes bibliographical references and index.
  ISBN 978-1-118-81797-1 (hardback)
1. Financial instruments–Accounting–Standards. 2. Derivative securities–Accounting. 3. Hedging (Finance)–Accounting.
I. Title.
  HF5681.F54R35 2015
  657′.7–dc23
                                    2014045650
Cover Design: Wiley
Top Image: ©iStock.com/nikada
Bottom Image: ©iStock.com/doockie

Set in 10/12pt Times by Laserwords Private Limited, Chennai, India
Printed in Great Britain by TJ International Ltd, Padstow, Cornwall, UK

To my wife Marta and our children Borja, Martuca and David

Table of Contents

Preface

The main goal of IFRS is to safeguard investors by achieving uniformity and transparency in the accounting principles. One of the main challenging aspects of the IFRS rules is the accounting treatment of derivatives and its link with risk management. Whilst it takes years to master the interaction between IFRS 9 (the main guidance on derivatives accounting) and the risk management of market risks using derivatives, this book accelerates the learning process by covering real-life hedging situations, step-by-step. Because each market risk – foreign exchange, interest rates, inflation, equity and commodities- has its own accounting and risk management peculiarities, I have covered each separately to address their particular issues.

Banks have developed increasingly sophisticated derivatives that have increased the gap between derivatives for which there is a consensus about how to apply IFRS 9 and derivatives for which their accounting is unclear. This gap will remain as long as the resources devoted to financial innovation hugely exceed those devoted to accounting interpretation. The objective of this book is to provide a conceptual framework based on an extensive use of cases so that readers can come up with their own accounting interpretation of any hedging strategy.

This book is aimed at professional accountants, corporate treasurers, bank financial engineers, derivative salespersons at investment banks and credit/equity analysts.

CHANGES TO THE PREVIOUS EDITION

The previous edition of *Accounting for Derivatives* was based on IAS 39. This second edition is based on IFRS 9, the accounting standard replacing IAS 39. IFRS 9 has incorporated a large number of new concepts including new hedge effectiveness assessment requirements, rebalancing and hedge ratio determination, a wider eligibility of hedged items, and a special treatment for options, forwards and cross currency swaps. New cases have been incorporated, especially in the chapters covering commodities and equity risk management. In addition three new chapters have been incorporated to the book: a chapter that provides a summary of IFRS 13 *Fair Value Measurement* with a special emphasis on credit/debit valuation adjustments (CVA/DVA), a chapter addressing hedging of share-based compensation plans and another chapter covering inflation risk.

CHAPTER 1

The Theoretical Framework – Recognition of Financial Instruments

IFRS 9 *Financial Instruments* is a complex standard. IFRS 9 replaced IAS 39 *Financial Instruments: Recognition and Measurement*. It establishes accounting principles for recognising, measuring and disclosing information about financial assets and financial liabilities. The objective of this chapter is to summarise the key aspects of financial instrument recognition under IFRS 9.

IFRS 9 is remarkably wide in scope and interacts with several other standards (see Figure 1.1). When addressing hedging there are, in addition to IFRS 9, primarily three standards that have an impact on the way a hedge is structured: IAS 21 *The Effects of Changes in Foreign Exchange Rates*, IAS 32 *Financial Instruments: Disclosure and Presentation* and IFRS 13 *Fair Value Measurement*.

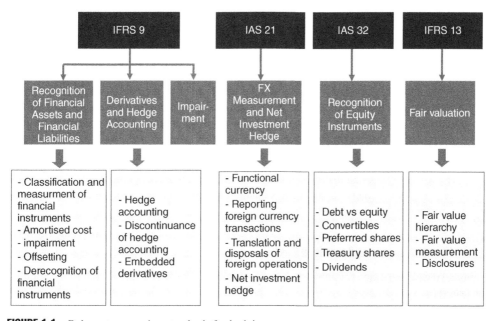

FIGURE 1.1 Relevant accounting standards for hedging.

Whilst the International Accounting Standards Board (IASB) is responsible for setting the IFRS standards, jurisdictions may incorporate their own version. For example, entities in the European Union must apply the version of IFRS 9 endorsed by the EU, which might differ from the IASB's IFRS 9 standard.

1.1 ACCOUNTING CATEGORIES FOR FINANCIAL ASSETS

Under IFRS 9, a financial instrument is any contract that gives rise to both a financial asset in one entity and a financial liability or equity instrument in another entity.

IFRS 9 does not cover the accounting treatment of some financial instruments – for example, own equity instruments, insurance contracts, leasing contracts, some financial guarantee contracts, weather derivatives, loans not settled in cash (or in any other financial instrument), interests in subsidiaries/associates/joint ventures, employee benefit plans, share-based payment transactions, contracts to buy/sell an acquiree in a business combination, contracts for contingent consideration in a business combination, and some commodity contracts are outside the scope of IFRS 9.

1.1.1 Financial Asset Categories

A financial asset is any asset that is cash, a contractual right to receive cash or some other financial asset, a contractual right to exchange financial instruments with another entity under conditions that are potentially favourable, or an equity instrument of another entity. Financial assets include derivatives with a fair value favourable to the entity.

IFRS 9 considers three categories of financial assets (see Figures 1.2 and 1.3):

- At **amortised cost**. This category consists of debt investments that meet both the **business model test** (i.e., the investment is managed to hold it in order to collect contractual cash flows) and the **contractual cash flow test** (the contractual terms give rise on specified dates to cash flows that are solely payments of principal and interest on the principal amount outstanding), and for which the fair value option (FVO) is not applied.
- At **fair value through other comprehensive income** (FVOCI). This category consists of debt investments that meet both the business model test and the contractual cash flow test, but that are managed to sell them as well. It also consists of equity investments not held for trading for which the entity chooses not to classify them at fair value through profit or loss.
- At **fair value through profit or loss** (FVTPL). This category consists of financial assets that are neither measured at amortised cost nor at FVOCI.

The classification of an instrument is determined on initial recognition. Reclassifications are made only upon a change in an entity's business model, and are expected to be very infrequent. No other reclassifications are permitted.

1.1.2 Financial Assets at Amortised Cost

A financial asset qualifies for amortised cost measurement only if it meets both of the following criteria:

- **Business model test**. The asset is held within a business model whose objective is to hold assets in order to collect contractual cash flows.
- **Contractual cash flows test**. The contractual cash flows of the financial represent solely payments of principal and interest.

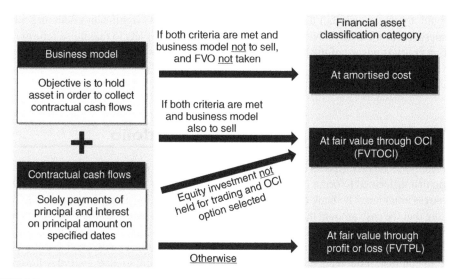

FIGURE 1.2   IFRS 9 financial assets classification categories – summary flowchart.

This is a mandatory classification, unless the fair value option is applied. Financial assets in the amortised cost category include non-callable debt (i.e. loans, bonds and most trade receivables), callable debt (provided that if it is called the holder would recover substantially all of debt's carrying amount) and senior tranches of pass-through asset-backed securities.

If a financial asset does not meet any of the two conditions above it is measured at FVTPL. If both conditions are met but the sale of the financial asset is also integral to the business model, it is recognised at FVOCI.

Even if an asset is eligible for classification at amortised cost or at FVOCI, management also has the option – the FVO – to designate a financial asset at FVTPL if doing so reduces or eliminates a measurement or recognition inconsistency (commonly referred to as "accounting mismatch").

Business Model Test   If the entity's objective is to hold the asset to collect the contractual cash flows, then it will meet the first criterion to qualify for amortised cost. The entity's business model does not depend on management's intentions for the individual asset, but rather on the basis of how an entity manages the portfolio of debt instruments. Examples of factors to consider when assessing the business model for a portfolio are:

- the way the assets are managed;
- how performance of the business is reported to the entity's key management personnel;
- how management is compensated (whether the compensation is based on the fair value of the assets managed); and
- the historical frequency, timing and volume of sales in prior periods, the reasons for these sales (such as credit deterioration), and expectations about future sales activity.

IFRS 9 indicates that sales due to deterioration of the credit quality of the financial assets so that they no longer meet the entity's documented investment policy would be consistent with the amortised cost business model. Sales that occur for other reasons may also be consistent with the amortised cost business model if they are infrequent (even if significant) or insignificant (even if frequent), or if the sales take place close to the maturity of the financial asset and the proceeds from the sale approximate the collection of the remaining contractual cash flows. For example, an entity could sell one financial asset that results in a large gain and this would not necessarily fail the business model test due to its significant effect on profit or loss unless it was the entity's business model to sell financial assets to maximise returns.

If an entity is unsure of the business model for the debt investments, the default category would be at FVTPL.

Example: Liquidity portfolio

A bank holds financial assets in a portfolio to meet liquidity needs in a "stress case" scenario that is deemed to occur only infrequently. Sales are not expected except in a liquidity stress situation. The bank also monitors the fair value of the assets in the portfolio to ensure that the cash amount that would be realised if a sale is required would be sufficient to meet liquidity needs. In this case (i.e., where the "stress case" is deemed to be rare), the bank's business model is to hold the financial assets to collect contractual cash flows.

In contrast, if the bank holds financial assets in a portfolio to meet everyday liquidity needs and that involves recurring and significant sales activity, the objective is not to hold to collect the contractual cash flows. However, if the objective of the regulator is for the bank to demonstrate liquidity, the bank could consider other ways to demonstrate liquidity that would allow the portfolio to still qualify for amortised cost (e.g., entering into a repurchase agreement for the debt investments)

In addition, if the bank is required by the regulator to routinely sell significant volumes of financial assets in a portfolio to demonstrate the assets are liquid, the bank's business model is not to hold to collect contractual cash flows (the fact that this requirement is imposed by a third party is not relevant to the analysis).

Example: Financial assets backing insurance contracts

An insurer holds financial assets in a portfolio to fund insurance contract liabilities. The insurer uses the proceeds from the contractual cash flows to settle the insurance liabilities as they come due. There is also rebalancing of the portfolio on a regular basis as estimates of the cash flows to fund the insurance liabilities are not always predictable.

The objective of the insurer's business model is both to hold the financial assets to collect contractual cash flows to fund liabilities as they come due and to sell to maintain the desired profile in the asset portfolio. In this case, the insurer holds financial assets with a dual objective to fund insurance liabilities and maintain the desired profile of the asset portfolio. This portfolio would fail the business model test of holding to collect contractual cash flows but would likely qualify for FVOCI subject to the contractual cash flow test.

Contractual Cash Flows Test   If the financial asset's contractual terms give rise on specified dates to cash flows that are "solely payments of principal and interest on the principal amount outstanding" (SPPI), then it will meet the second criterion to qualify for amortised cost.

 Interest is defined as "consideration for the time value of money and for the credit risk associated with the principal amount outstanding during a particular period of time". The assessment as to whether cash flows meet this test is made in the currency of denomination of the financial asset.

Contractual Cash Flows Test – Modified Economic Relationship   IFRS 9 also refers to the case of "modified economic relationships". For example, a financial asset may contain leverage or an interest rate that is resettable, but the frequency of the reset does not match the tenor of the interest rate (an "interest rate mismatch"). In such cases, the entity is required to assess the modification to determine whether the contractual cash flows represent solely payments of principal and interest on the principal amount outstanding. To do this, an entity considers cash flows on a comparable or **benchmark** financial asset that does not contain the modification. The benchmark asset is a contract of the same credit quality and with the same contractual terms (including, when relevant, the same reset periods), except for the contractual term under evaluation (i.e., the underlying rate).

 If the modification results in cash flows that are more than insignificantly different from the benchmark cash flows, or if the entity is unable to reach a conclusion, then the financial asset does not satisfy the SPPI test (see Figure 1.3).

 In making this assessment the entity only considers reasonable possible scenarios rather than every possible scenario. If it is clear with little or no analysis whether the cash flows on the financial asset could or could not be more than insignificantly different from the benchmark cash flows, then an entity does not need to perform a detailed assessment.

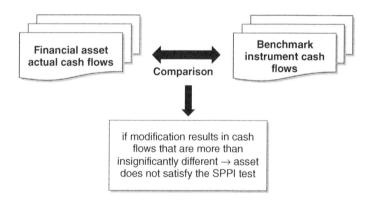

FIGURE 1.3   Contractual cash flows modification test.

Example: Constant maturity swap

A constant maturity bond with a 5-year term pays a variable rate that is reset semiannually linked to the 5-year swap rate. The benchmark cash flows are those of an otherwise identical bond but linked to the 6-month rate. At the time of initial recognition, the difference between the 6-month rate and the 5-year swap rate is insignificant. This bond does not meet the SPPI requirement because the interest payable in each period is disconnected from the term of the instrument (except at origination). In other words, the relationship between the 6-month rate and the 5-year swap rate could change over the life of the instrument so that the asset and the benchmark cash flows could be more than insignificantly different.

1.1.3 Financial Assets at Fair Value through Other Comprehensive Income

This category consists of debt investments that meet the contractual cash flows test, for which their business model is held to collect and for sale. This is a mandatory classification, unless the FVO is applied. This category is intended to acknowledge the practical reality that an entity may invest in debt instruments to capture yield but may also sell if, for example, the price is considered advantageous or it is necessary to periodically adjust or rebalance the entity's net risk, duration or liquidity position.

This category also consists of equity investments which are not held for trading. An entity can choose to classify non-trading equity investments in this category on an instrument-by-instrument basis. This is an irrevocable election.

1.1.4 Financial Assets at Fair Value through Profit or Loss

The FVTPL category is in effect the "residual category" for instruments that do not qualify for the amortised cost or FVOCI categories. The following financial assets would be included in the FVTPL category:

- financial assets held for trading;
- financial assets managed on a fair value basis to maximise cash flows through the sale of financial assets such that collecting cash flows is only incidental;
- financial assets managed, and whose performance is evaluated, on a fair value basis;
- financial assets where the collection of cash flows is not integral to achieving the business model objective (but only incidental to it); and
- financial assets that fail the SPPI test.

Derivatives are recognised at FVTPL unless they are a hedging instrument in cash flow hedge or net investment in foreign operation. Therefore, derivatives undesignated or being hedging instruments in fair value hedging relationships are classified at FVTPL. Recognition of derivatives is covered in detail in Chapter 2.

1.1.5 Financial Assets – Initial and Subsequent Recognition

An entity recognises a financial asset when and only when the entity becomes a party to the contractual provisions of a financial instrument. The initial measurement of the financial asset is its fair value, which normally is the consideration given, including directly related transaction costs.

Debt Instruments at Amortised Cost   Debt instruments classified at amortised cost are subsequently recognised at amortised cost less impairment in the statement of financial position. Interest income and impairment are recognised in profit or loss. Interest income is recognised using the effective interest rate method. Impairment charges can be reversed through profit or loss. Foreign exchange gains and losses are recognised in profit or loss.

Debt Instruments at FVOCI   A debt instrument classified at FVOCI is presented in the statement of financial position at fair value. The entity also keeps an amortised cost calculation (i.e., an effective interest rate) to recognise interest income in profit or loss.

Interest income and impairment are recognised in profit or loss, using the same methodology as for amortised cost. Interest income is recognised using the effective interest rate method. Impairment charges can be reversed through profit or loss. Likewise, foreign exchange gains and losses are recognised in profit or loss as if the instrument were carried at amortised cost. The difference between amortised cost (in the currency of denomination) and fair value (in the currency of denomination) is recognised in OCI and recycled when the instrument is sold.

Equity Instruments at FVOCI   Gains and losses on equity investments in this category are recognised in OCI with no recycling of gains and losses into profit or loss. If an equity investment is so designated, then dividend income generally is recognised in profit or loss. No impairment is recognised.

Instruments at FVTPL   Gains and losses on instruments in this category are recognised in profit or loss. No impairment is recognised.

Summary   The table below gives an overview of the accounting treatment of each category of financial assets:

Asset category	Measurement	Fair value changes
At amortised cost	Initial recognition at fair value Subsequent recognition at amortised cost less impairment. Any premium or discount is amortised to profit or loss	Not relevant unless impaired Interest income, impairment and foreign exchange gains/losses recognised in profit or loss. Impairment can be reversed through profit or loss
At FVTPL	Fair value	Changes in fair value recorded in profit or loss No impairment recorded
At FVOCI	Fair value	Changes in fair value recorded in OCI For debt instruments: interest revenue, credit impairment and foreign exchange gains or losses recognised in profit or loss. On derecognition any cumulative gains and losses in OCI reclassified to profit or loss For equity investments: no impairment is recorded. Dividends recorded in profit or loss

Leveraged Financial Assets   In order to meet the contractual cash flows criterion, there should be no leverage of the contractual cash flows. Leverage increases the variability of the contractual cash flows, with the result that they do not have the economic characteristics of interest.

Non-recourse Financial Assets   IFRS 9 contains specific guidance on classifying non-recourse (or limited recourse) financial assets. These assets represent an investment in which the investor's claims are limited to specified assets, which may be financial or non-financial assets. IFRS 9 states that the fact that a financial asset is non-recourse does not mean in itself that the SPPI criterion is not met.

- If, for instance, the underlying assets meet the SPPI criterion, it may be possible to conclude that the non-recourse asset also meets the criterion.
- If, for example, the non-recourse asset is a vehicle whose only asset is an equity investment, it will not meet the SPPI criterion.

Contractually Linked Instruments – Tranches of Securitisations   IFRS 9 contains specific guidance on classifying contractually linked instruments that create concentrations of credit risk (e.g., securitisation tranches). The right to payments on more junior tranches depends on the issuer's generation of sufficient cash flows to pay more senior tranches. The standard requires a look-through approach to determine whether the SPPI criterion is met. Otherwise, the tranche would be recognised at fair value.

A tranche meets the SPPI criterion only if all the following conditions are met:

Principal and interest test. The contractual terms of the tranche itself have only SPPI characteristics.

Look-through test. The underlying pool of financial instruments:

contains one or more instruments that meet the SPPI criterion;

also may contain instruments that:

reduce the cash flow variability of the instruments under (i) and the combined cash flows meet the SPPI criterion (e.g., interest rate caps and floors, credit protection), or

align the cash flows of the tranches with the cash flows of the instruments under (i) arising as a result of differences in whether interest rates are fixed or floating or the currency or timing of cash flows.

Credit risk test. The exposure to credit risk inherent in the tranche is equal to, or lower than, the exposure to credit risk of the underlying pool of financial instruments. The standard states as an example that this condition would be met if, in all circumstances in which the underlying pool of instruments loses 50% as a result of credit losses, the tranche would lose 50% or less.

The look-through approach is carried through to the underlying pool of instruments that create, rather than pass through, the cash flows. For example, if an entity invests in a tranched note issued by SPE 2 whose only asset is an investment in another tranched note issued by SPE 1, the entity looks through to the assets of SPE 1 in performing the assessment.

Example: Tranched issuance

Suppose that a special-purpose entity (SPE) has bought mortgage assets with a notional amount of USD 800 million and issued three tranched notes (A, B and C) that are contractually linked. All assets in the pool meet the SPPI criterion. The underlying mortgage assets pay fixed rates of interest on a monthly basis. The vehicle holds an interest rate swap that swaps the underlying mortgages monthly fixed interest for 3-month Libor. The weighted average credit spread of the assets in the mortgage pool is 400 basis points.

- Tranche A pays a quarterly interest of 3-month Libor plus 50 basis points on a principal of USD 300 million.
- Tranche B pays a quarterly interest of 3-month Libor plus 400 basis points on a principal of USD 200 million.
- Tranche C pays a quarterly interest of 3-month Libor plus 500 basis points on a principal of USD 100 million.

If the underlying pool of instruments were to lose 50% as a result of credit losses, a loss of USD 400 million would arise (= 800 million × 50%), and the effect on the tranches would be as follows:

- The overcollateralisation would absorb the first USD 200 million losses.
- Tranche C would lose USD 100 million, representing 100% of its total principal.
- Tranche B would lose USD 100 million, representing 50% of its total principal.
- Tranche A would not experience any losses.

In addition to the tranches and the asset pool, the vehicle contains another financial instrument, an interest rate swap, but it only aligns the cash flows of the underlying pool with those of the tranches, and consequently it does not affect the tranches' SPPI eligibility. Whilst all the three tranches meet two of the SPPI conditions (i.e., the underlying mortgage pool meets the SPPI criterion and the tranches pay cash flows that only represent principal and interest), only tranches A and B are eligible for amortised cost recognition, subject to meeting the business model criterion, as a 50% loss in the underlying asset pool would not cause these tranches to experience losses exceeding 50% of their principal amounts. As a result, the larger the level of overcollateralisation (i.e., the excess of the underlying pool size relative to the size of the issued tranches), the higher the likelihood of meeting the credit risk test.

Item	Look-through test	Principal and interest test	Credit risk test	Amortised cost eligibility (*)
Tranche A	Pass	Pass	Pass	Yes
Tranche B	Pass	Pass	Pass	Yes
Tranche C	Pass	Pass	Fail	No

(*) Subject to the business model criterion being met

When the tranche held by the investor is prepayable contingent upon a prepayment occurring in the pool of underlying assets, it may meet SPPI even if the following features exist in the structure (assuming the three primary conditions for the tranche as a whole are met):

- The tranche is prepayable contingent on repayment occurring in the underlying pool. Because SPPI must be met for the underlying pool, it is assumed the underlying prepayment risk on the pool is consistent with SPPI.
- Even if the collateral underlying the pool does not meet the qualifying conditions for amortised cost, the underlying collateral can be disregarded unless the instrument was acquired with the intention of controlling the collateral.

1.1.6 Reclassifications

IFRS 9 requires an entity to reclassify financial assets if and only if the objective of the entity's business model for managing those assets changes. Such changes are expected to be infrequent, and need to be determined by the entity's senior management as a result of internal or external modifications. These modifications have to be significant to the entity's operations and demonstrable to external parties. Reclassification is applied prospectively from the start of the first reporting period following the change in business model.

Both the amortised cost and FVOCI categories require the effective interest rate to be determined at initial recognition. Therefore, when reclassifying a financial asset between the amortised cost and the FVOCI categories, the recognition of interest income would not change and the entity would continue to use the effective interest rate determined at initial recognition. A financial asset reclassified out of the FVOCI category to the amortised cost category would be measured at amortised cost as if it had always been so classified. This will be effected by transferring the cumulative gain or loss previously recognised in OCI out of equity, with an offsetting entry against the fair value carrying amount at the reclassification date.

However, for financial assets at FVTPL, and entity is not required to separately recognise interest income. When reclassifying a financial asset out of the FVTPL category, the effective interest rate would be determined based on the fair value carrying amount at the reclassification date.

	Reclassification to		
Asset category	Amortised cost	FVOCI	FVTPL
From: At amortised cost	N/A	Remeasure at fair value with any difference in OCI	New carrying amount is the fair value on reclassification date
		The effective interest rate determined at initial recognition remains unchanged	Any difference between amortised cost and fair value is recognised in profit or loss
From: At FVOCI	Accumulated OCI recycled out of equity, with offsetting entry against fair value carrying amount	N/A	Accumulated OCI amount recycled to profit or loss

	Reclassification to		
Asset category	Amortised cost	FVOCI	FVTPL
	Adjusted carrying amount is existing amortised cost		Asset continues to be measured at fair value
			Subsequent changes in fair value recognised in profit or loss
	The effective interest rate determined at initial recognition remains unchanged		
From: At FVTPL	New amortised cost is the fair value on reclassification date	Asset continues to be measured at fair value	N/A
		Subsequent changes in fair value recognised in OCI	
	The effective interest rate is calculated	The effective interest rate is calculated	

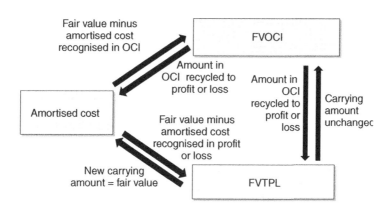

FIGURE 1.4   Reclassification of financial assets.

1.2 THE AMORTISED COST CALCULATION: EFFECTIVE INTEREST RATE

It was mentioned earlier that some assets and liabilities are measured at amortised cost. The amortisation is calculated using the **effective interest rate** (EIR). This rate is applied to the carrying amount at each reporting date to determine the interest expense for the period. The EIR is the rate that exactly discounts the stream of principal and interest cash flows to the initial net outlay (in the case of assets) or proceeds (in the case of a liability). In this way, the contractual interest expense in each period is adjusted to amortise any premium, discount or transaction costs over the life of the instrument.

The carrying amount of an instrument accounted for at amortised cost is computed as:

- the amount to be repaid at maturity (usually the principal amount); plus
- any unamortised original premium, net of transaction costs; or less
- any unamortised original discount including transaction costs; less
- principal repayments; less
- any reduction for impairment or uncollectability.

Transaction costs include fees, commissions and taxes paid to other parties. Transaction costs do not include internal administrative costs.

1.2.1 Example of Effective Interest Rate Calculation – Fixed Rate Bond

Suppose that an entity issues a bond with the following terms:

Nominal amount:	EUR 1,250
Maturity:	5 years
Issue proceeds:	EUR 1,250
Coupons:	First year: 6% (75)
	Second year: 8% (100)
	Third year: 10% (125)
	Fourth year: 12% (150)
	Fifth year: 16% (200)

$$1,250 = \frac{75}{1+EIR} + \frac{100}{(1+EIR)^2} + \frac{125}{(1+EIR)^3} + \frac{150}{(1+EIR)^4} + \frac{1,250+200}{(1+EIR)^5}$$

The EIR is computed as the rate that exactly discounts estimated future cash payments through the expected life of the financial instrument:
Solving this equation, we get EIR = 9.96%. The amortised cost of the liability at each accounting date is computed as follows:

Year	Amortised cost at beginning of year (a)	Interest (b) = (a) × 9.96%	Cash flow (c)	Amortised cost at end of year (d) = (a) + (b) – (c)
1	1,250	125	75	1,300
2	1,300	129	100	1,329
3	1,329	132	125	1,336
4	1,336	133	150	1,319
5	1,319	131	200	1,250

1.2.2 Effective Interest Rate Calculation – Floating Rate Debt

IFRS 9 does not specify how the EIR is calculated for floating rate debt instruments. The EIR of a floating rate instrument changes as a result of periodic re-estimation of determinable cash flows to reflect movements in market interest rates. Two approaches can be used to calculate the EIR in a floating rate debt instrument:

- calculation based on the actual benchmark rate that was set for the relevant period; or
- calculation using the method employed for fixed rate debt (i.e., estimating the EIR at the beginning of each interest period taking into account the expected interest rates in each future interest period).

When the floating rate instrument is recognised at an amount equal to the principal receivable or payable on maturity, this periodic re-estimation does not have a significant effect on its carrying amount. Therefore, for practical reasons the first approach is used, and in such cases the carrying amount is usually not adjusted at each repricing date, because the impact is generally insignificant. According to this method, the interest income for the period is calculated as follows:

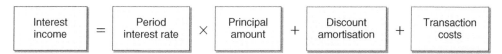

Similarly, for floating rate debt liabilities, the following method is used to calculate interest expense for the period:

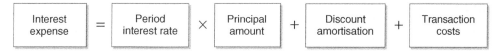

The treatment of an acquisition discount or premium on a floating rate instrument depends on the reason for that discount or premium. For example:

- When the discount (or premium) reflects changes in market rates since the last repricing date, it is amortised to the next repricing date.
- When the discount (or premium) results from a change in the credit spread over the floating rate as a result of a change in credit risk, it is amortised over the expected life of the instrument.

IFRS 9 does not prescribe any specific methodology for how transaction costs should be amortised for a floating rate instrument. Any consistent methodology that would establish a reasonable basis for amortisation of the transaction costs may be used. For example, it would be reasonable to determine an amortisation schedule of the transaction costs based on the interest rate in effect at inception. In my view, this approach also could be applied for a floating rate instrument recognised at amortised cost with an embedded derivative that is not separated (e.g., a floating rate bond with a cap). Another reasonable approach would be to linearly amortise the transaction costs over the life of the instrument.

1.3 EXAMPLES OF ACCOUNTING FOR FIXED RATE BONDS

Suppose that an investor bought, at a discount, a fixed rate bond with the following terms:

	Bond terms
Purchase price	EUR 98 million
Purchase date	1-Jan-X0
Notional	EUR 100 million
Maturity	Three years (31-Dec-X2)
Notional	USD 100 million
Coupon	5% annually, 30/360 basis

1.3.1 Example of a Fixed Rate Bond at Amortised Cost

$$98 = \frac{5}{1 + EIR} + \frac{5}{(1 + EIR)^2} + \frac{105}{(1 + EIR)^3} \, .$$

Let us assume that the bond was recognised at amortised cost, and that no impairments were recognised. The calculation of the effective interest rate was performed as follows (in EUR millions):

EIR was 5.7447%.

Year	Amortised cost beginning of year (a)	Interest (b) = (a) × EIR	Cash Flow (c)	Amortised cost end of year (d) = (a) + (b) − (c)
1	98,000,000	5,630,000	5,000,000	98,630,000
2	98,630,000	5,666,000	5,000,000	99,296,000
3	99,296,000	5,704,000	5,000,000	100,000,000

The related accounting entries were as follows:

Entries on 1-Jan-X0:		
Bond (Asset)	98,000,000	
Cash (Asset)		98,000,000
Entries on 31-Dec-X0:		
Cash (Asset)	5,000,000	
Bond (Asset)	630,000	
Interest income (Profit or loss)		5,630,000
Entries on 31-Dec-X1:		
Cash (Asset)	5,000,000	
Bond (Asset)	666,000	
Interest income (Profit or loss)		5,666,000

Entries on 31-Dec-X2:		
Cash (Asset)	105,000,000	
Bond (Asset)		105,000,000
Interest income (Profit or loss)		5,704,000

1.3.2 Example of a Fixed Rate Bond Recognised at FVOCI

Let us assume that the bond was recognised at FVOCI, and that no impairments were recognised. Let us assume further that the fair value of the bond on 31 December 20X0 and 31 December 20X1 was EUR 97 million and EUR 101 million, respectively. The change in the bond's clean fair at each reporting date was:

Year	Clean fair value (a)	Previous clean fair value (b)	Change (c) = (a) – (b)
1	97,000,000	98,000,000	<1,000,000>
2	101,000,000	97,000,000	4,000,000
3	100,000,000	101,000,000	<1,000,000>

In order to account for the bond the investor had to keep track of both the bond's amortised cost and its fair value. The bond's amortised cost profile, which was identical to that in the previous example, determined the interest expense to be recognised at each period.

Any difference between the bond's clean fair value (i.e., excluding accrued interest) and its amortised cost was recognised in the FVOCI reserve in OCI.

Year	Clean fair value (a)	Amortised cost end of year (b)	FVOCI reserve (c) = (a) – (b)	Previous FVOCI reserve (d)	New FVOCI entry (c) – (d)
1	97,000,000	98,630,000	<1,630,000>	-0-	<1,630,000>
2	101,000,000	99,296,000	1,704,000	<1,630,000>	3,334,000
3	100,000,000	100,000,000	-0-	1,704,000	<1,704,000>

The related accounting entries were as follows:

Entries on 1-Jan-X0:		
Bond (Asset)	98,000,000	
Cash (Asset)		98,000,000
Entries on 31-Dec-X0:		
Cash (Asset)	5,000,000	
FVOCI reserve (Equity)	1,630,000	
Bond (Asset)		1,000,000
Interest income (Profit or loss)		5,630,000

Entries on 31-Dec-X1:			
Cash (Asset)		5,000,000	
Bond (Asset)		4,000,000	
	Interest income (Profit or loss)		5,666,000
	FVOCI Reserve (Equity)		3,334,000
Entries on 31-Dec-X2:			
Cash (Asset)		105,000,000	
FVOCI reserve (Equity)		1,704,000	
Bond (Asset)			101,000,000
	Interest income (Profit or loss)		5,704,000

1.4 ACCOUNTING CATEGORIES FOR FINANCIAL LIABILITIES

1.4.1 Financial Liability Categories

A financial liability is any liability that is a contractual obligation to deliver cash or some other financial asset to another entity or to exchange financial instruments with another entity under conditions that are potentially unfavourable.

Under IFRS 9 there are only two categories of financial liabilities (see Figure 1.5): at amortised cost and at FVTPL. The following table summarises the accounting treatment of each category of financial liabilities:

Liability category	Measurement	Fair value changes
At amortised cost	Amortised cost. Any premium or discount is amortised to profit or loss	Not relevant by virtue of not being fair valued
At FVTPL	Fair value	Changes in fair value attributable to changes in credit risk presented in OCI (unless it creates or increases accounting mismatch) Remaining changes in fair value recorded in profit or loss

The category of financial liabilities at FVTPL has two sub-categories: liabilities held for trading and those designated to this category at their inception using the FVO. Financial liabilities classified as held for trading include:

- financial liabilities acquired or incurred principally for the purpose of generating a short-term profit (i.e., held for trading);
- a derivative not designated in a cash flow or net investment hedging relationship, or the ineffective part if designated;
- obligations to deliver securities or other financial assets borrowed by a short seller;

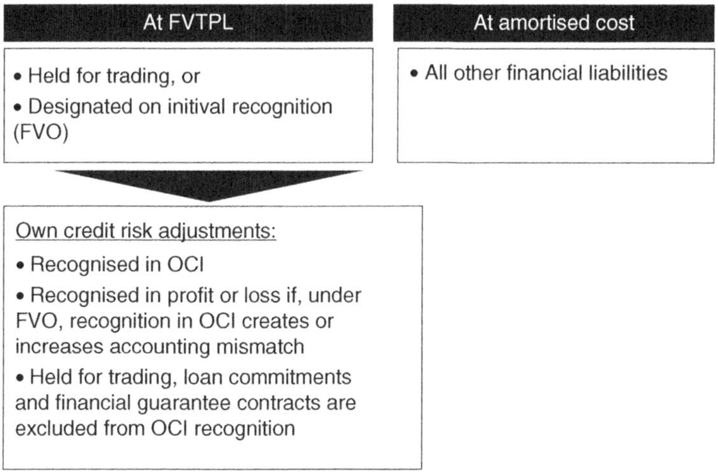

At FVTPL	At amortised cost
• Held for trading, or • Designated on initival recognition (FVO)	• All other financial liabilities

Own credit risk adjustments:

• Recognised in OCI

• Recognised in profit or loss if, under FVO, recognition in OCI creates or increases accounting mismatch

• Held for trading, loan commitments and financial guarantee contracts are excluded from OCI recognition

FIGURE 1.5 IFRS 9 financial liabilities classification categories.

- financial liabilities that are part of a portfolio of identified financial instruments that are managed together and for which there is evidence of a recent actual pattern of short-term profit taking.

The following instruments are measured under specific guidance in IFRS 9:

- financial guarantee contracts; and
- commitments to provide a loan at a below market interest rate.

1.4.2 Partial Repurchases of Financial Liabilities

When an entity repurchases own financial liabilities, the repurchased part is derecognised. According to IFRS 9, "if an entity repurchases a part of a financial liability, the entity shall allocate the previous carrying amount of the financial liability between the part that continues to be recognised and the part that is derecognised based on the relative fair values of those parts on the date of the repurchase. The difference between (a) the carrying amount allocated to the part derecognised and (b) the consideration paid, including any non-cash assets transferred or liabilities assumed, for the part derecognised shall be recognised in profit or loss."

1.4.3 Changes in Credit Risk in Financial Liabilities at FVTPL

The amount of change in the fair value of a liability designated at FVTPL under the FVO that is attributable to changes in credit risk must be presented in other comprehensive income (OCI), unless:

- Presentation of the fair value change in respect of the liability's credit risk in OCI would create or enlarge an accounting mismatch in profit or loss. In this case, the fair value change attributable to changes in credit risk must be recognised in profit or loss. This determination is made at initial recognition of the individual liability and will not be reassessed.

The remainder of the change in fair value is presented in profit or loss.

To determine whether the treatment would create or enlarge an accounting mismatch, the entity must assess whether it expects the effect of the change in the liability's credit risk to be offset in profit or loss by a change in fair value of another financial instrument. In reality, such instances are expected to be rare, unless an entity, for example, holds an asset whose fair value is linked to the fair value of the liability.

The changes in credit risk recognised in OCI are *not* recycled to profit or loss on settlement of the liability.

The following instruments, when recognised at FVTPL, are not required to isolate the change in fair value attributable to credit risk (i.e., all gains and losses are presented in profit or loss):

- financial guarantee contracts; and
- loan commitments.

Measurement of a Liability's Credit Risk   IFRS 9 largely carries forward guidance from IFRS 7 on how to determine the effect of changes in credit risk. An entity determines the amount of the fair value change that is attributable to changes in its credit risk either:

- as the amount of change in its fair value that is not attributable to changes in market conditions that give rise to market risk (e.g., a benchmark interest rate, the price of another entity's financial instrument, a commodity price, a foreign exchange rate or an index of prices or rates); or
- using an alternative method, if it provides a more faithful representation of the changes in the fair value of the liability attributable to the changes in its credit risk.

IFRS 9 clarifies that this would include any liquidity premium associated with the liability.

If the only significant relevant changes in market conditions for a liability are changes in an observed (benchmark) interest rate, under IFRS 9 the amount of fair value changes that is attributable to changes in credit risk may be estimated using the so-called **default method** as follows:

1) The entity first calculates the liability's internal rate of return at the start of the period using the liability's fair value and contractual cash flows at that date. It then deducts from this internal rate of return the observed (benchmark) interest rate at the start of the period so as to arrive at an "instrument-specific component" of the internal rate of return.
2) Next, the entity computes a present value of the cash flows of the liability at the end of the period using the liability's contractual cash flows at that date and a discount rate equal to the sum of (i) the observed (benchmark) interest rate at that date and (ii) the instrument-specific component of the internal rate of return determined in 1).
3) The entity then deducts the present value calculated in 2) from the fair value of the liability at the end of the period. The resulting difference is the change in fair value that is not attributable to changes in the observed (benchmark) interest rate and which is assumed to be attributable to changes in credit risk.

This default method is appropriate only if the only significant relevant changes in market conditions for a liability are changes in an observed (benchmark) interest rate and that, when other factors are significant, an alternative measure that more faithfully measures the effects of changes in the liability's credit risk should be used. For example, if the liability contains an embedded derivative, the change in fair value of the derivative would be excluded in calculating the fair value change amount attributable to changes in credit risk.

1.5 THE FAIR VALUE OPTION

The **fair value option** is an option to designate financial assets or financial liabilities at FVTPL. The election is available only on initial recognition and is irrevocable. In the case of **financial assets**, the FVO is available for instruments that would otherwise be mandatorily recognised at amortised cost or at FVOCI, being permitted only if:

- it eliminates or significantly reduces a measurement or recognition inconsistency (an **accounting mismatch**).

In the case of **financial liabilities**, the FVO is available for instruments that would otherwise be mandatorily recognised at amortised cost, being permitted only if:

- it eliminates or significantly reduces an accounting mismatch; or
- a group of financial liabilities (or financial assets and financial liabilities) is managed and its performance is evaluated on a fair value basis, in accordance with a documented risk management or investment strategy, and the information about the group is provided internally on that basis to the entity's key management personnel; or
- a contract contains one or more embedded derivatives and the host is not a financial asset, in which case an entity may designate the entire hybrid contract at FVTPL unless the embedded derivative is insignificant or it is obvious that separation of the embedded derivative would be prohibited.

The FVO is only available on initial recognition of the financial asset or liability. This requirement may create a problem if the entity enters into offsetting contracts on different dates. A first financial instrument may be acquired in the anticipation that it will provide a natural offset to another instrument that has yet to be acquired. If the natural hedge is not in place at the outset, IFRS 9 would not allow the first financial instrument to be recorded at FVTPL, as it would not eliminate or significantly reduce a measurement or recognition inconsistency. Additionally, to impose discipline, an entity is precluded from reclassifying financial instruments in or out of the fair value category, unless (in the case of financial assets) the business model for those assets changes.

Accounting Mismatch Sometimes a particular market risk that affects a financial asset or a financial liability is hedged with another financial instrument that behaves in an opposite way to movements in such market risk (i.e., an increase in the market variable would increase the fair value of one of the two items while decreasing that of the other item). In this case, the entity would be interested in measuring the financial asset or financial liability at FVTPL to benefit from their natural offsetting. The entity could apply the FVO because it will eliminate or significantly reduce the measurement or recognition inconsistency that would otherwise arise from measuring these assets or liabilities, or recognising the gains and losses on them, on different bases.

1.6 HYBRID AND COMPOUND CONTRACTS

1.6.1 Embedded Derivatives in Assets or Liabilities – Hybrid Instruments

Sometimes, a derivative is "embedded" in an instrument – called a **hybrid instrument** or **hybrid contract** – in combination with a host contract. The embedded derivative causes some

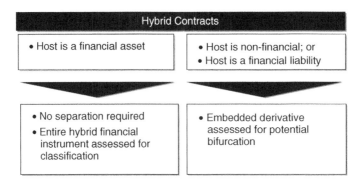

FIGURE 1.6   IFRS 9 hybrid contracts accounting treatment.

or all of the contractual cash flows to be modified based on a specified interest rate, a security price, a commodity price, a foreign exchange rate, index of prices or rates, or other variables. The accounting treatment depends on whether the host is a financial asset or a financial liability (see Figure 1.6).

A derivative that is attached to a financial instrument but is contractually transferable independently of that instrument (e.g., an equity warrant attached to a bond), or has a different counterparty, is not an embedded derivative, but a separate financial instrument.

Host Contract is a Financial Asset   When the host contract is a financial asset within the scope of IFRS 9, the hybrid financial instrument is *not* bifurcated; instead it is assessed in its entirety for classification under the standard.

Existence of a derivative feature in a hybrid instrument might not preclude amortised cost. This may be the case when the economic risks and characteristics of the instrument are closely related to the host contract.

Example: Investment in an convertible bond

An entity invests in a convertible bond. Under the terms of the bond, the entity has the right to convert the bond into a fixed number of shares of the bond's issuer. From a structuring perspective, the bond can be split between a debt instrument and an equity option. From an accounting perspective, the convertible bond would be classified at FVTPL in its entirety as the conversion right causes the instrument to fail the SPPI test.

Host Contract is a Financial Liability or a Non-financial Host   When the host contract is either (i) a financial liability within the scope of IFRS 9 or (ii) an instrument not within the scope of IFRS 9, an assessment is performed to determine whether the embedded derivative must be separated from the host (i.e., whether the embedded derivative should be accounted for separately).

IFRS 9 does not require the separation of the embedded derivative (see Figure 1.7):

- if the derivative does not qualify as a derivative if it were free-standing; or
- if the host contract is accounted for at fair value, with changes in fair value recorded in profit and loss; or
- if the economic characteristics and risks of the embedded derivative are closely related to those of the host contract.

Contracts with embedded derivatives to be separated include:

- options to extend the maturity date of fixed rate debt, except when interest rates are reset to market rates;
- any derivative that "leverages" the payments that would otherwise take place under the host contract;
- credit-linked notes, convertible bonds, equity or commodity indexed notes, notes with embedded currency options.

Examples of contracts not requiring separation include:

- debt without leveraged interest rates;
- debt without leveraged inflation;
- debt with vanilla interest rate options (i.e., caps and floors);
- debt with cash flows linked to the creditworthiness of a debtor.

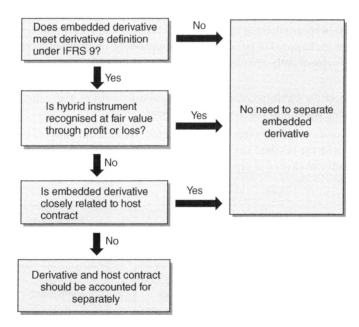

FIGURE 1.7   Bifurcation of embedded derivative in financial liabilities – decision tree.

Example: Issuance of an exchangeable bond

An entity might issue a low coupon bond that is exchangeable for shares in another listed company. Under IFRS 9, the amount received for the exchangeable bond is split between:

- a liability component – an obligation to pay the scheduled coupons and, when the bond is not converted, the principal; and
- an embedded derivative – the conversion right by the bondholders (a sold call option on the third-party shares).

1.6.2 Liability Compound Instruments

The concept of compound instruments is similar to that of hybrid instruments (see Figure 1.8). A hybrid instrument is comprised of a liability component (the host contract) and an embedded derivative, while a compound instrument is comprised of a liability component (the host contract) and an equity component. An example of a compound instrument is a bond issued by the entity that is convertible into a fixed number of shares of the entity, which can be split between:

- a **liability component** – an obligation to pay the scheduled coupons and, when the bond is not converted, the principal; and
- an **equity component** – the conversion right by the bondholders (a sold call option on own shares).

Compound instruments are defined in IAS 32. The liability and equity components of a compound instrument are required to be accounted for separately, upon initial recognition, and the separation is not subsequently revised. The split between the two components is implemented in two steps:

The fair value of the liability component is calculated, and this fair value establishes the initial carrying amount of the liability component,

The fair value of the liability component is deducted from the fair value of the instrument in its entirety, with the residual amount being an equity component.

I have included several cases that cover the accounting of convertible bonds in Chapter 9.

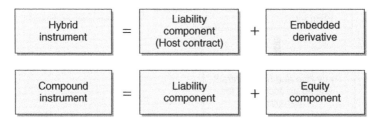

FIGURE 1.8   Hybrid and compound instruments.

CHAPTER **2**

The Theoretical Framework –
Hedge Accounting

The objective of this chapter is to summarise the key theoretical issues surrounding hedge accounting under IFRS 9. This chapter also covers the fair valuation of derivatives under IFRS 13 *Fair Value Measurement*, a standard that has a substantial effect on hedge accounting.

2.1 HEDGE ACCOUNTING – TYPES OF HEDGES

Whilst other instruments (e.g., a loan denominated in a foreign currency) may also be used, derivatives are the most common instruments transacted to reduce or mitigate exposures to market risks.

2.1.1 Derivative Definition

Under IFRS 9, a derivative is a financial instrument (or other contract within the scope of IFRS 9) with *all* of the following characteristics:

1) Its value changes in response to changes in a specified "underlying" interest rate, financial instrument price, commodity price, foreign exchange (FX) rate, index of prices or rates, credit rating or credit index, or other variable, provided in the case of a non-financial variable that the variable is not specific to a party to the contract.
2) It requires no initial investment, or an initial net investment that is smaller than would be required for other types of contracts that would be expected to have a similar response to changes in market factors.
3) It is settled at a future date.

Some commodity-based derivatives are not considered derivatives under IFRS 9. See Chapter 10 for a detailed discussion regarding which commodity contracts can be treated as IFRS 9 instruments.

2.1.2 Hedge Accounting

The objective of hedge accounting is to represent, in the financial statements, the effect of an entity's risk management activities that use financial instruments to manage market risk exposures that could affect profit or loss (or OCI in the case of equity investments at FVOCI).

Hedged Item and Hedging Instrument In a hedging relationship there are two elements: the hedged item and the hedging instrument.

- The **hedged item** is the item that exposes the entity to a market risk(s). It is the element that is designated as being hedged.
- The **hedging instrument** is the element that hedges the risk(s) to which the hedged item is exposed. Frequently, the hedging instrument is a derivative.

For example, an entity hedging a floating rate loan with a pay-fixed receive-floating interest rate swap and applying hedge accounting would designate the loan as the hedged item and the swap as the hedging instrument.

Hedge Accounting Hedge accounting is a technique that modifies the normal basis for recognising gains and losses (or revenues and expenses) associated with a hedged item or a hedging instrument to enable gains and losses on the hedging instrument to be recognised in profit or loss (or in OCI in the case of hedges of equity instruments at FVOCI) in the same period as offsetting losses and gains on the hedged item. Hedge accounting takes two forms under IFRS 9:

- **Fair value hedge** – recognising gains or losses (or revenues or expenses) in respect of both the hedging instrument and hedged item in earnings in the same accounting period.
- **Cash flow hedge** or **net investment hedge** – deferring recognised gains and losses in respect of the hedging instrument on the balance sheet until the hedged item affects earnings.

The following example compares the timing of the impacts on profit or loss when applying, or not applying, hedge accounting. Assume that an entity enters in 20X0 into a derivative to hedge a risk exposure of an item that is already recognised in the balance sheet. The derivative matures in 20X1 and the hedged item settles in 20X2. It can be observed that only the fair value hedge provided a perfect synchronisation between the hedging instrument and hedged item recognitions.

Without hedging

	20X1	20X2	Total
Hedging instrument	1,000		1,000
Hedged item (realised gain)		<1,000>	<1,000>
Net profit/(loss)	1,000	<1,000>	-0-

With fair value hedge

	20X1	20X2	Total
Hedging instrument	1,000		1,000
Hedged item (unrealised gain)	<1,000>		<1,000>
Net profit/(loss)	-0-	-0-	-0-

With cash flow hedge

	20X1	20X2	Total
Hedging instrument (after deferral in equity)		1,000	1,000
Hedged item (realised gain)		<1,000>	<1,000>
Net profit/(loss)	-0-	-0-	-0-

To be able to apply hedge accounting, the hedge must meet remarkably strict criteria at inception and throughout the life of the hedging relationship, which I will cover below.

2.1.3 Accounting for Derivatives

I mentioned earlier that all derivatives are recognised at fair value on the balance sheet, no matter whether or not they are part of a hedge accounting relationship. Fluctuations in the derivative's fair value can be recognised in different ways, depending on the type of hedging relationship:

- undesignated or speculative;
- fair value hedge;
- cash flow hedge;
- net investment hedge.

2.1.4 Undesignated or Speculative

Some derivatives are termed "undesignated" or "speculative". They include derivatives that do not qualify for hedge accounting. They also include derivatives that the entity may decide to treat as undesignated even though they could qualify for hedge accounting. These derivatives are recognised as assets or liabilities for trading. The gain or loss arising from their fair value fluctuation is recognised directly in profit or loss.

2.2 TYPES OF HEDGES

Under IFRS 9 there are three types of hedging relationships: fair value, cash flow and net investment hedges. This section describes the main accounting mechanics of each type of hedge.

2.2.1 Fair Value Hedge

The objective of the fair value hedge is to reduce the exposure to changes in the fair value of an asset or liability already recognised in the balance sheet, or a previously unrecognised firm commitment (or a component of any such item), that is attributable to a particular risk and could affect reported profit or loss. Therefore, the aim of the fair value hedge is to offset in profit or loss the change in fair value of the hedged item with the change in fair value of the hedging instrument (e.g., a derivative). See Figure 2.1.

If the hedged item is an equity instrument designated at FVOCI, the hedged exposure must be one that could affect OCI.

The recognition of the **hedging instrument** is as follows:

- Losses or gains from remeasuring the hedging instrument at fair value are recognised in profit or loss (or in OCI, including hedge ineffectiveness, if the hedged item is an equity instrument classified at FVOCI).
- If the hedging instrument is a non-derivative hedging the foreign currency risk component of a hedged item, the amount recognised in profit or loss related to the hedging instrument is the gain or loss from remeasuring, in accordance with IAS 21, the foreign currency component of its carrying amount.

The recognition of the **hedged item** is as follows:

- If the hedged item is measured at amortised cost or a debt instrument at FVOCI, the hedging gain or loss on the hedged item adjusts the carrying amount of the hedged item (if applicable) and is recognised in profit or loss. The adjustment of the carrying amount is amortised to profit or loss. Amortisation may begin as soon as an adjustment exists and shall begin no later than when the hedged item ceases to be adjusted for hedging gains and losses. In theory the amortisation is based on a recalculation of the effective interest rate for the hedged item. In practice, to ease the administrative burden of amortising the adjustment while the hedged item continues to be adjusted for changes in fair value attributable to the hedged risk, it may be easier to defer amortising the adjustment until the hedged item ceases to be adjusted for the designated hedged risk. An entity must apply the same amortisation policy for all of its debt instruments. In other words, an entity cannot defer amortising on some items and not on others.
- If the hedged item is an equity instrument at FVOCI, the hedging gain or loss on the hedged item shall remain in OCI.
- If the hedged item is an unrecognised firm commitment (or a component thereof), the subsequent cumulative change in the fair value of the unrecognised firm commitment attributable to the hedged risk is recognised as an asset or a liability with a corresponding gain or loss recognised in profit or loss. If the firm commitment is to acquire an asset or assume a liability, the initial carrying amount of the asset or liability that results from the entity meeting the firm commitment is adjusted to include the cumulative change in the fair value of the commitment attributable to the hedged risk that was recognised in the statement of financial position.

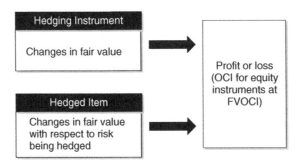

FIGURE 2.1   Accounting for fair value hedges.

A hedge of the FX risk of a firm commitment may be accounted for as a fair value hedge or a cash flow hedge.

2.2.2 Cash Flow Hedge

A cash flow hedge is a hedge of the exposure to variability in cash flows that:

- is attributable to a particular risk associated with all, or a component, of a recognised asset or liability (such as all or some future interest payments on variable rate debt), or a highly probable forecast transaction; and
- could affect reported profit or loss.

A hedge of the FX risk of a firm commitment may be accounted for as a fair value hedge or as a cash flow hedge.

Effective and Ineffective Parts The change in the hedging instrument fair value is split into two components (see Figure 2.2): an effective and an ineffective part.

The **effective part** represents the portion that is offset by a change in fair value of the hedged item and is calculated as the lower of the following (in absolute amounts):

- the cumulative gain or loss on the hedging instrument from inception of the hedge; and
- the cumulative change in fair value (present value) of the hedged item (i.e., the present value of the cumulative change in the hedged expected future cash flows) from inception of the hedge.

The **ineffective part** represents the hedge ineffectiveness, or in other words, the portion of the change in fair value of the hedging instrument that has not been offset by a change in fair value of the hedged item. It is calculated as the difference between the cumulative change in fair value of the hedging instrument and its effective part.

The ineffective part includes specific components excluded, as documented in the entity's risk management strategy, from the assessment of hedge effectiveness. Common sources of ineffectiveness for a cash flow hedge are (i) the time value of an option or the forward points of a forward or the foreign currency basis spread included in the hedging relationship (this situation is quite unusual as commonly these elements are excluded from the hedging relationship), (ii) structured derivative features embedded in the hedging instrument, (iii) changes in timing of the highly probable forecast transaction, (iv) credit/debit valuation adjustments and (v) differences between the risk being hedged and the underlying of the hedging instrument.

Accounting Recognition of the Effective and Ineffective Parts The recognition of the change in fair value of the hedging instrument is as follows:

- The effective portion of the gain or loss on the hedging instrument is recognised directly in a separate reserve in OCI –the "cash flow hedge reserve".
- The ineffective portion of the fair value movement on the hedging instrument is recorded immediately in profit or loss.

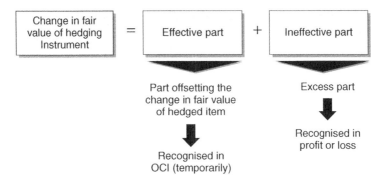

FIGURE 2.2 Recognition of effective and ineffective parts of the change in fair value of a hedging instrument.

THE TEMPTATION TO UNDERHEDGE

An entity may be tempted to "underhedge" its cash flow exposure to increase the likelihood that the cumulative change in fair value of the hedged instrument for the risk being hedged does not exceed the cumulative change in fair value of the hedged item for the risk being hedged, and consequently lessen the possibility of recording ineffectiveness. IFRS 9 precludes the voluntary use of underhedging by requiring a hedge ratio "that is the same as that resulting from actual amounts of hedged items and hedging instruments that the entity uses to hedge that quantity of hedged item to meet the risk management objective".

An "underhedging" decision does not bring any benefits in a fair value hedge because both gains and losses on the hedged item and the hedging instrument are recognised in profit or loss. Therefore, both the effective part and the ineffective part would be recorded in profit or loss.

The amount that has been accumulated in the cash flow hedge reserve of OCI is reclassified, or "recycled", as follows (see Figure 2.3):

- If the hedged item is a forecast transaction that will result in the recognition of a non-financial asset or non-financial liability (e.g., a purchase of raw material or inventory), or a firm commitment, the entity removes the amount from the cash flow hedge reserve and includes it directly in the initial cost or other carrying amount of the asset or the liability (e.g., within "inventories").
- For cash flow hedges other than those covered in the previous paragraph, the amount that has been accumulated in the cash flow hedge reserve of OCI is reclassified to profit or loss in the same period or periods during which the hedged expected future cash flows affect profit or loss, therefore offsetting to the extent that the hedge is effective. For example, if the hedged item is a variable rate borrowing, the reclassification to profit or loss is recognised in profit or loss within "finance costs", therefore offsetting the borrowing's interest cost.

To take another example, if the hedged item is an export sale, the reclassification to profit or loss is recognised in the profit or loss statement within "sales", therefore adjusting the revenue amount.

■ If the amount accumulated in the cash flow hedge reserve of OCI is a loss and the entity expects that all or a portion of that loss will not be recovered in one or more future periods, it immediately reclassifies the amount that is not expected to be recovered into profit or loss in the same way as in the previous paragraph.

Discontinuance of Hedge Accounting   When an entity discontinues hedge accounting for a cash flow hedge it shall account for the amount that has been accumulated in the cash flow hedge reserve of OCI as follows:

■ If the hedged future cash flows are still expected to occur, that amount remains in the cash flow hedge reserve until the future cash flows occur or, as mentioned above, until the amount accumulated in the cash flow hedge reserve of OCI is a loss that will not be recovered in one or more future periods.

■ If the hedged future cash flows are no longer expected to occur, that amount is immediately reclassified from the cash flow hedge reserve to profit or loss as a reclassification adjustment. A hedged future cash flow that is no longer highly probable to occur may still be expected to occur.

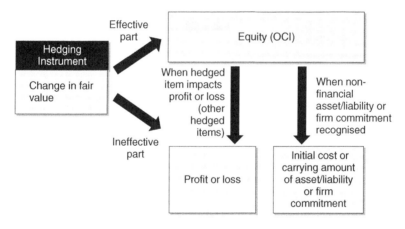

FIGURE 2.3   Accounting for a cash flow hedge.

2.2.3 Net Investment Hedge

A net investment hedge, or hedge of a net investment in a foreign operation, is a hedge of the foreign currency exposure arising from the reporting entity's interest in the net assets of a foreign operation. The hedging instrument may be either a derivative or a non-derivative financial instrument (e.g., a borrowing denominated in the same currency as the net investment). Figure 2.4 highlights the accounting treatment of net investment hedges.

■ The effective portion of the gain or loss on the hedging instrument is recognised in the "foreign currency translation reserve" of OCI. As the exchange difference arising on the net investment is also recognised in OCI, the objective is to match both exchange rate differences.

■ The ineffective portion of the gain or loss on the hedging instrument is recognised immediately in profit or loss.

■ On disposal (or partial disposal) or liquidation of the foreign operation, the cumulative balance in the foreign currency translation reserve of OCI related to its hedge and its related net investment exchange differences are simultaneously transferred from OCI to profit or loss.

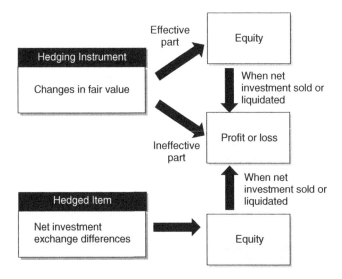

FIGURE 2.4   Accounting for net investment hedges.

2.3 HEDGED ITEM CANDIDATES

In a hedging relationship there are two elements: the hedged item and the hedging instrument. The hedged item is the element that is designated as being hedged. The fundamental principle is that the hedged item creates an exposure to risk that could affect profit or loss (or OCI in the case of equity instruments investments at FVOCI).

2.3.1 Hedged Item Candidates

The following can be designated as hedged items:

■ A **recognised asset or liability** (or a component thereof).
■ An **unrecognised firm commitment** (or a component thereof). A firm commitment is a legally binding agreement for the exchange of a specified quantity of resources at a specified price on a specified future date or dates.
■ A **highly probable forecast** transaction (or a component thereof). A forecast transaction is an anticipated transaction that is not yet legally committed.
■ A net investment in a foreign operation (on a consolidated basis only).

- A group of the above items.
- An aggregated exposure that is a combination of an exposure that could qualify as **a hedged item and a derivative**, if the aggregated exposure creates a different aggregated exposure that is managed as one exposure for a particular risk (or risks). For example, a utility with the EUR as functional currency may designate as hedged item the combination of highly probable crude oil purchases and USD-denominated crude oil futures (i.e., a string of fixed amounts of EUR–USD FX risk). The items that constitute the aggregated exposure remain accounted for separately.

An entity may hedge the foreign currency risk for the entire term of a 10-year fixed rate debt denominated in GBP. However, the entity requires fixed rate exposure in its functional currency (the EUR) only for 2 years and floating rate exposure in EUR for the remaining term to maturity. At the end of each of the 2-year intervals (i.e., on a 2-year rolling basis) the entity fixes the next 2 years' interest rate exposure (if the interest level is such that the entity wants to fix interest rates). In such a situation an entity may enter into a 10-year GBP fixed-to-EUR floating cross-currency interest rate swap that swaps the fixed rate GBP debt into a variable rate EUR exposure. This is overlaid with a EUR 2-year interest rate swap that swaps EUR variable rate debt into EUR fixed rate debt. In effect, the fixed rate GBP debt and the 10-year fixed-to-floating cross-currency interest rate swap in combination can be designated as a hedged item, viewed as a EUR 10-year variable rate debt exposure for risk management purposes.

The way in which a derivative is included as part of an aggregated exposure must be consistent with the designation of that derivative as the hedging instrument at the level of the aggregated exposure. For example, if an entity excludes the forward element of a derivative from its designation as the hedging instrument for the hedging relationship between the items that constitute the aggregated exposure, it must also exclude the forward element when including that derivative as a hedged item as part of the aggregated exposure. Otherwise, the aggregated exposure shall include a derivative, either in its entirety or a proportion of it.

- The **FX risk component of an intragroup monetary item** (e.g., a payable/receivable between two subsidiaries) in the consolidated financial statements if it results in an exposure to FX rate gains or losses that are not fully eliminated on consolidation in accordance with IAS 21 (i.e., when the intragroup monetary item is transacted between two group entities that have different functional currencies).
- The **FX risk component of a highly probable forecast intragroup transaction** in the consolidated financial statements provided that the transaction is denominated in a

currency other than the functional currency of the entity entering into that transaction and the foreign currency risk will affect consolidated profit or loss. For this purpose an entity can be a parent, subsidiary, associate, joint arrangement or branch. The relevant period or periods during which the FX risk of the hedged transaction affects profit or loss is when it affects consolidated profit or loss.

An example of this sort of transactions is a forecast sale or purchase of inventory between members of the same group (including parent, subsidiary, associate, joint venture or branch) if there is an onward sale of inventory to party external to the group.

Another example is a forecast intragroup sale of equipment from the group entity that manufactured it to a group entity that will use the equipment in its operations (it affects profit or loss because the equipment will be depreciated by the purchasing entity, and the amount initially recognised may change if it is denominated in a currency other than the functional currency of the purchasing entity).

If the foreign currency risk of a forecast intragroup transaction does not affect consolidated profit or loss, the intragroup transaction cannot qualify as a hedged item. This is usually the case for royalty payments, interest payments or management charges between members of the same group, unless there is a related external transaction.

Components of an Item Eligible for Designation as a Hedged Item   An entity may designate an eligible item (or group of eligible items) **in its entirety** as the hedged item in a hedging relationship. An entire item comprises all changes in the cash flows or fair value of an item.

A **proportion** of an eligible item (or group of eligible items) provided that designation is consistent with the entity's risk management objective. An example would be 50% of the contractual cash flows of a loan.

An entity may designate a **risk component** of an eligible item (or group of eligible items) as the hedged item in a hedging relationship. A component comprises less than the entire fair value change or cash flow variability of an item. In that case, an entity may designate only the following types of components (including combinations) as hedged items:

(**a**) Only changes in the cash flows or fair value of an item attributable to a specific risk or risks (risk component), provided that, based on an assessment within the context of the particular market structure, the risk component is **separately identifiable** and the changes in the cash flows or the fair value of the item attributable to changes in that risk component must be **reliably measurable**. For example, it is possible to hedge only the USD Libor 6-month interest rate component in a loan with interest calculated as USD Libor 6-month plus a margin on its notional amount. Risk components include a designation of only changes in the cash flows or the fair value of a hedged item above or below a specified price or other variable (a one-sided risk).

(**b**) One or more selected contractual cash flows.

(**c**) Components of a nominal amount (i.e., a specified part of the amount of an item).

When identifying what risk components qualify for designation as a hedged item, an entity assesses such risk components within the context of the particular market structure to which the risk or risks relate and in which the hedging activity takes place. Such a determination requires an evaluation of the relevant facts and circumstances, which differ by risk and market.

When designating risk components as hedged items, an entity considers whether the risk components are explicitly specified in a contract (**contractually specified** risk components) or whether they are implicit in the fair value or the cash flows of an item of which they are a part (**non-contractually specified** risk components). Non-contractually specified risk components can relate to items that are not a contract (e.g., forecast transactions) or contracts that do not explicitly specify the component (e.g., a firm commitment that includes only a single price instead of a pricing formula that references different underlyings).

For example, an entity has a long-term supply contract for natural gas that is priced using a contractually specified formula that includes references to crude oil prices, fuel oil prices and other components such as transport charges. The entity hedges the crude oil component in that supply contract using a crude oil futures contract. Because the crude oil component is specified by the terms and conditions of the supply contract it is a contractually specified risk component, and therefore the entity concludes that the gas oil price exposure is separately identifiable. At the same time, there is a market for crude oil futures and forward contracts. Hence, the entity concludes that the crude oil price exposure is reliably measurable. Consequently, the crude oil price exposure in the supply contract is a risk component that is eligible for designation as a hedged item.

An entity may also designate only changes in the cash flows or fair value of a hedged item above or below a specified price or other variable (a "one-sided risk").

CAP

An entity may buy a 6% cap to hedge the variability of the Libor-linked flows of a floating rate liability. The entity can designate the hedged risk as the variability of future cash flow outcomes resulting from a Libor increase above 6%.

COMBINATION OF A CAP AND A FLOOR

An entity buys a 6% cap to hedge the variability of the Libor-linked flows of a floating rate liability. The entity simultaneously sells a 4% floor to avoid paying a premium.

Assuming that the combination of the cap and the floor (i.e., a collar) is an eligible hedging instrument, the entity can designate the hedged risk as the variability of future cash flow outcomes resulting from a Libor increase above 6% and a Libor decline below 4%.

CAP SPREAD

An entity buys a 6% cap to hedge the variability of the Libor-linked flows of a floating rate liability. The entity simultaneously sells an 8% cap to reduce the overall premium to be paid. Assuming that the combination of both caps (i.e., a cap spread) is an eligible hedging instrument, the entity can designate the hedged risk as the variability of future cash flow outcomes resulting from a Libor increase between 6% and 8%.

A **layer component** of an overall group of items (e.g., a bottom layer) only if:

(a) it is separately identifiable and reliably measurable;
(b) the risk management objective is to hedge a layer component;
(c) the items in the overall group from which the layer is identified are exposed to the same hedged risk (so that the measurement of the hedged layer is not significantly affected by which particular items from the overall group form part of the hedged layer);
(d) for a hedge of existing items (e.g., an unrecognised firm commitment or a recognised asset) an entity can identify and track the overall group of items from which the hedged layer is defined (so that the entity is able to comply with the requirements for the accounting for qualifying hedging relationships); and
(e) any items in the group that contain prepayment options meet the requirements for components of a nominal amount.

A layer component may be specified from a defined, but open, population, or from a defined nominal amount. Examples include:

(a) A part of a monetary transaction volume denominated in foreign currency. For example, related to a sale denominated in USD, the next USD 10 cash flows after the first USD 20 in March 201X.
(b) A part of a physical volume. For example, the bottom layer, measuring 5 million cubic metres, of the natural gas stored in location XYZ.
(c) A part of a physical or other transaction volume. For example, the first 100 barrels of the oil purchases in June 201X or the first 100 MWh of electricity sales in June 201X.
(d) A layer from the nominal amount of the hedged item. For example, the last EUR 80 million of a EUR 100 million firm commitment, the bottom layer of EUR 20 million of a EUR 100 million fixed rate bond or the top layer of EUR 30 million from a total amount of EUR 100 million of fixed rate debt that can be prepaid at fair value (the defined nominal amount is EUR 100 million).

Items Not Eligible for Designation as Hedged Items   A derivative alone cannot be designated as a hedged item. The only exception is an embedded purchased option that is hedged with a written option.

An entity's own equity instrument cannot be a hedged item because it does not expose the entity to a particular risk that could impact profit or loss. Similarly, a forecast dividend payment by the entity cannot be a hedged item as its distribution to equity holders is debited directly to equity and therefore does not impact profit or loss.

A firm commitment to acquire a business in a business combination cannot be a hedged item, except for foreign currency risk, because the other risks being hedged cannot be specifically identified and measured. Those other risks are general business risks.

An equity method investment cannot be a hedged item in a fair value hedge. This is because the equity method recognises in profit or loss the investor's share of the investee's profit or loss, rather than changes in the investment's fair value.

An investment in a consolidated subsidiary cannot be a hedged item in a fair value hedge. This is because consolidation recognises in profit or loss the subsidiary's profit or loss, rather than changes in the investment's fair value. A hedge of a net investment in a foreign operation is different because it is a hedge of the foreign currency exposure, not a fair value hedge of the change in the value of the investment.

A **layer component** that includes a prepayment option is not eligible to be designated as a hedged item in a fair value hedge if the prepayment option's fair value is affected by changes in the hedged risk, unless the designated layer includes the effect of the related prepayment option when determining the change in the fair value of the hedged item.

Other Restrictions   IFRS 9 imposes the following restrictions or conditions regarding the hedge item:

- The hedged item must be **reliably measurable**.
- The party to the hedged item has to be **external** to the reporting entity. Hedge accounting can be applied to transactions between entities in the same group only in the individual or separate financial statements of those entities and not in the consolidated financial statements of the group, except for the consolidated financial statements of an investment entity, as defined in IFRS 10, where transactions between an investment entity and its subsidiaries measured at fair value through profit or loss will not be eliminated in the consolidated financial statements. The only exceptions to this external condition are the intragroup transactions mentioned above.

2.3.2 Forecast Transaction versus Firm Commitment

Commonly, a transaction before becoming a firm commitment is a forecast transaction. A forecast transaction itself typically is expected to occur before it becomes highly expected to occur, as shown in Figure 2.5.

- A **forecast transaction** is an anticipated transaction that is not yet legally committed. In assessing "highly probable" the entity must consider, among other things, the frequency of similar past transactions.
- A **firm commitment** is a legally binding agreement for the exchange of a specified quantity of resources at a specified price on a specified future date or dates.

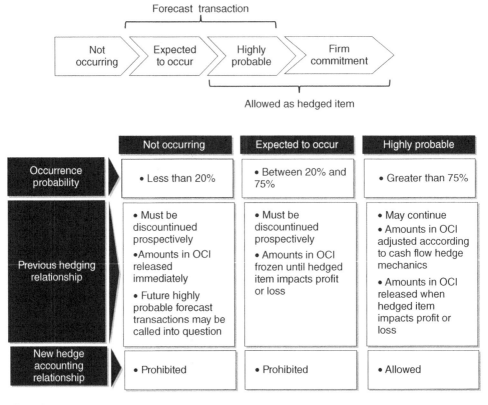

FIGURE 2.5 Scale of probability of a forecasted transaction.

2.4 HEDGING INSTRUMENT CANDIDATES

The following can be designated as hedging instruments:

- A derivative that involves an external party (i.e., external to the reporting entity). A written option does not qualify as a hedging instrument unless it is designated as an offset to a purchased option, including one that is embedded in another financial instrument (e.g., a call option sold to hedge a callable liability). Derivatives that are embedded in hybrid contracts, but that are not separately accounted for, cannot be designated as separate hedging instruments.
- The intrinsic value element of an option contract (i.e., excluding the time value element).
- The spot element of a forward contract (i.e., excluding the forward element)
- The elements of a contract excluding its foreign currency basis spread (e.g., a cross-currency swap, excluding its basis).
- An external non-derivative financial asset or an external non-derivative liability measured at FVTPL unless it is a financial liability designated as at FVTPL for which the amount of its change in fair value that is attributable to changes in the credit risk of that liability is presented in OCI. For hedges other than hedges of foreign currency risk, an entity may only designate the non-derivative financial instrument in its entirety or a proportion of it.

■ The foreign currency risk component of an external non-derivative financial asset or an external non-derivative financial liability in a hedge of foreign currency risk provided that it is not an equity instrument investment at FVOCI. The foreign currency risk component of a non-derivative financial instrument is determined in accordance with IAS 21.

■ A proportion of the entire hedging instrument. The proportion must be a percentage of the entire derivative (e.g., 40% of the notional). It is not possible to designate a hedging instrument only for a portion of its life.

■ Two or more derivatives, or proportions of their nominal, can be viewed in combination as the hedging instrument only if, in combination, they are not, in effect, a net written option at the time of designation.

■ Any combination of the following (including those circumstances in which the risk or risks arising from some hedging instruments offset those arising from others): (i) derivatives or a proportion of them; and (ii) non-derivatives or a proportion of them.

■ A single hedging instrument may be designated as a hedging instrument of more than one type of risk, provided that there is a specific designation (i) of the hedging instrument and (ii) of the different risk positions as hedged items. Those hedged items can be in different hedging relationships.

■ An entity's own equity instruments are not financial assets or financial liabilities of the entity and therefore cannot be designated as hedging instruments.

2.5 HEDGING RELATIONSHIP DOCUMENTATION

One of the three requirements for a hedging relationship to qualify for hedge accounting is that "at the inception of the hedging relationship there is formal designation and documentation of the hedging relationship and the entity's risk management objective and strategy for undertaking the hedge". The formal documentation must include the following:

■ The entity's risk management objective and strategy for undertaking the hedge: an explanation of the rationale for contracting the hedge. This should include evidence that the hedge is consistent with the entity's risk management objectives and strategies.

■ The type of hedge: fair value, cash flow, or net investment hedge.

■ The nature of the risk being hedged: foreign exchange risk, interest rate risk, inflation risk, equity price risk or commodity price risk.

■ The identification of the hedging instrument: its terms and how it will be fair valued.

■ The identification of the hedged item: a sufficiently detailed explanation of the hedged item.

■ For fair value hedges, the document must include the method for recognising in earnings the gains or losses in the fair value of the hedged item.

■ If the hedged item is a forecasted transaction, the documentation should also include reference to the timing (i.e., the estimated date), the nature, and amount of the forecasted transaction. It also should include the rationale for the forecasted transaction being highly probable to occur and the method for reclassifying into profit or loss amounts deferred in equity (if the hedged item is other than an equity instrument at FVOCI).

■ How the entity will assess whether the hedging relationship meets the hedge effectiveness requirements, including the method (or methods) used, its analysis of the sources of hedge ineffectiveness and how it determines the hedge ratio. The documentation shall be updated for any changes to the method, its hedge ratio, etc.

The following is an example of hedging relationship documentation for a highly expected foreign currency export transaction hedged with an FX forward.

Hedging relationship documentation	
Risk management objective and strategy for undertaking the hedge	The objective of the hedge is to protect the EUR value of the USD 100 million highly expected sale of finished goods against unfavourable movements in the EUR–USD FX rate. This hedging objective is consistent with ABC's overall FX risk management strategy of reducing the variability of its profit or loss statement using FX forwards and FX options
Type of hedge	Cash flow hedge
Risk being hedged	FX risk. The variability in EUR of the cash flow related to the highly expected transaction denominated in USD
Hedging instrument	The FX forward contract with reference number 012345. The main terms of this contract are a USD 100 million notional, a EUR 80 million notional, a 1.2500 forward rate and a 6-month maturity. The counterparty to the forward is XYZ Bank and the credit risk associated with this counterparty is considered to be very low
Hedged item	USD 100 million sale of finished goods expected to be delivered on 31 March 20X5 and to be paid on 30 June 20X5. Rationale for the forecast transaction being highly probable: negotiations with the US client are at an advanced stage; the client has a consistent previous history of purchasing similar items; and the entity is able to produce the goods by its expected delivery date
Hedge effectiveness assessment	A hedge effectiveness assessment will be performed at inception, at each reporting date and upon occurrence of a significant change in the circumstances of the hedging relationship. To assess whether there is an economic relationship between the hedged item and the hedging instrument, a qualitative assessment will be performed: the critical terms method will be applied as the critical terms of the hedged item and the hedging instrument match. The credit risk of the counterparty of the hedging instrument will be continuously monitored. The hedge's effective and ineffective parts will be determined by comparing changes, since the start of the hedging relationship, in the fair value of the hedging instrument to changes in the fair value of a hypothetical derivative. The terms of the hypothetical derivative will match those of the forecast cash flow. The effective part of the hedge will be accumulated in the cash flow hedge reserve of OCI and reclassified to profit or loss when the hedged item impacts profit or loss. The ineffective part of the hedge will be recognised in profit or loss. Hedge effectiveness assessment will be performed on a forward-forward basis. In other words, the forward points of both the hedging instrument and the expected cash flow are included in the assessment

2.6 HEDGE EFFECTIVENESS ASSESSMENT

2.6.1 Qualifying Criteria for Hedge Accounting

To qualify for hedge accounting, there are three requirements that a hedging relationship must meet (see Figure 2.6):

1) The hedging relationship consists only of **eligible hedging instruments** and **eligible hedged items**.
2) At the inception of the hedging relationship there is **formal designation and documentation** of the hedging relationship and the entity's risk management objective and strategy for undertaking the hedge. That documentation shall include identification of the hedging instrument, the hedged item, the nature of the risk being hedged and how the entity will assess whether the hedging relationship meets the hedge effectiveness requirements (including its analysis of the sources of hedge ineffectiveness and how it determines the hedge ratio).
3) The hedging relationship meets all three **hedge effectiveness requirements**.

The three hedge effectiveness requirements are as follows:

1) There is an **economic relationship** between the hedged item and the hedging instrument.
2) The effect of **credit risk** does not dominate the value changes that result from that economic relationship.
3) The weightings of the hedged item and the hedging instrument (i.e., the hedge ratio of the hedging relationship) are the same as those resulting from the quantity of the hedged item that the entity actually hedges and the quantity of the hedging instrument that the entity actually uses to hedge that quantity of hedged item. However, that designation shall not reflect an imbalance between the weightings of the hedged item and the hedging instrument that would create hedge ineffectiveness (irrespective of whether recognised or not) that could result in an accounting outcome that would be inconsistent with the purpose of hedge accounting.

The first effectiveness requirement means that the hedging instrument and the hedged item must be expected to move in opposite directions as a result of a change in the hedged risk (i.e., there is an economic relationship and not just statistical correlation). For example, it would be possible to hedge a West Texas Intermediate (WTI) crude oil exposure using a Brent crude oil forward instrument. A perfect correlation between the hedged item and the hedging instrument is not required and, indeed, would not be sufficient on its own.

The second requirement indicates that the impact of changes in credit risk should not be of a magnitude such that it dominates the value changes, even if there is an economic relationship between the hedged item and hedging derivative. This implies that when the creditworthiness of the entity or the counterparty to the hedging instrument notably deteriorates, the hedging relationship may not qualify for hedge accounting going forward because the change in the credit risk may be the largest factor affecting the hedging instrument's fair value change.

The third requirement indicates that the actual hedge ratio used for accounting should be the same as that used for risk management purposes, unless the ratio is inconsistent with the purpose of hedge accounting. IFRS 9 tries to avoid deliberate underhedging, either to minimise recognition of ineffectiveness in cash flow hedges or the creation of additional fair value adjustments to the hedged item in fair value hedges.

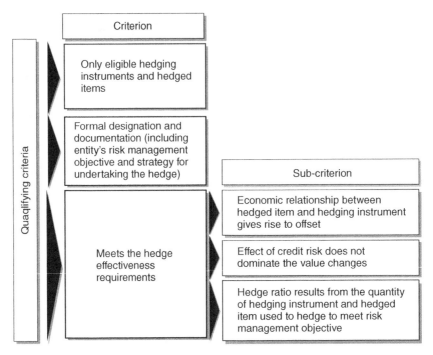

FIGURE 2.6   Qualifying criteria for hedge accounting.

2.6.2 Hedge Ratio

IFRS 9 does not define the term **hedge ratio**, but I have assumed throughout this book that it is the designated amount (i.e., notional) of the hedged item compared with the designated amount (i.e., notional) of the hedging instrument within the hedging relationship (alternatively, it may be defined the other way around).

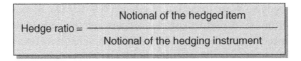

In most simple hedges, where the underlyings of the hedging instrument and the hedged item match, the hedge ratio is 1:1. For example, a highly probable forecast sale denominated in USD of an entity whose functional currency is the EUR hedged with a EUR–USD FX forward will result in a 1:1 hedge ratio.

In other hedging relationships the hedge ratio may differ from 1:1, especially where the underlyings of the hedged item and the hedging instrument differ. This is the case where there is an underlying for which its market is notably more liquid than that of the hedged item underlying, and both underlyings are highly correlated (a "proxy hedge"). For example, an entity whose functional currency is the EUR may decide to hedge a highly probable forecast sale denominated in Norwegian krone (NOK) with a more liquid Swedish krona (SEK) proxy: a SEK–EUR FX option. The entity may decide that 1 NOK is best hedged with 0.94 SEK, and as a result, the hedge ratio is set at 1:0.94. Such an assessment is usually made by considering historical and current market data for the hedged item and hedging instrument where possible, taking into account their relative performance in the past.

2.6.3 Effectiveness Assessment

Periodically the entity shall assess whether the hedging relationship meets the hedge effectiveness requirements – **hedge effectiveness assessment**. This assessment is probably the most operationally challenging aspect of applying hedge accounting. At a minimum, whichever comes first, IFRS 9 requires that hedge effectiveness be evaluated (see Figure 2.7):

- at the inception of the hedge;
- at each reporting date, including interim financial statements; and
- upon a significant change in the circumstances affecting the hedge effectiveness requirements.

Each effectiveness assessment relates to future expectations about hedge effectiveness and is therefore only forward-looking.

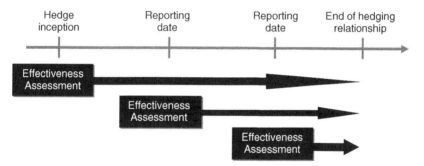

FIGURE 2.7   Frequency of hedge effectiveness assessments.

2.6.4 Effectiveness Assessment Methods

One of the effectiveness requirements is that an economic relationship exists between the hedging instrument and the hedged item, or in other words, that the hedging instrument and the hedged item have values that will generally move in opposite directions. IFRS 9 does not specify a method for assessing whether an economic relationship exists between a hedging instrument and a hedged item. However, an entity shall use a method that captures the relevant characteristics of the hedging relationship, including its sources of hedge ineffectiveness.

IFRS 9 states that an entity's risk management is the main source of information to perform the assessment of whether a hedging relationship meets the hedge effectiveness requirements. This means that the management information (or analysis) used for decision-making purposes can constitute a basis for assessing whether a hedging relationship meets the hedge effectiveness requirements.

The effectiveness requirement of an existence of an **economic relationship** between the hedged item and the hedging instrument (the "economic relationship requirement") is commonly assessed by applying one of the following methods:

- The **critical terms** method. This is a qualitative method (i.e., no numerical analysis is performed).
- The **simple scenario** analysis method: assessing how the hedging relationship would behave under various future scenarios. This is a quantitative method.
- The **linear regression** method: assessing, using historical information, how the hedging relationship would have behaved if it had been entered into in the past. This is a quantitative method.
- The **Monte Carlo simulation** method: assessing how the hedging relationship would behave under a large number of future scenarios. This is a quantitative method.

IFRS 9 requires an entity to specify at hedge inception, in the hedge documentation, the method it will apply to assess the hedge effectiveness requirements and to apply that method consistently during the life of the hedging relationship. The method chosen by the entity has to be applied consistently to all similar hedges unless different methods are explicitly justified.

If there are changes in circumstances that affect hedge effectiveness, an entity may have to change the method for assessing whether a hedging relationship meets the hedge effectiveness requirements in order to ensure that the relevant characteristics of the hedging relationship, including the sources of hedge ineffectiveness, are still captured.

A quantitative method may also be used to assess whether the hedge ratio used for designating the hedging relationship meets the hedge effectiveness requirements. An entity can use the same method as that used to assess the economic relationship requirement, or a different method.

2.6.5 The Critical Terms Method

The critical terms method is the simplest way to assess whether the economic relationship requirement is met. Under IFRS 9, an entity may conclude that there is an economic relationship between the hedged item and the hedging instrument if the critical terms of the hedged item and hedging instrument match or are closely aligned. At a minimum, the following critical terms must be the same or closely aligned:

- the notional amounts;
- the maturity and interim periods (e.g., interest periods); and
- the underlying (e.g., Euribor 3-month rate).

This conclusion is valid while the credit risk associated with the entity or the counterparty to the hedging instrument is considered to be very low.

2.6.6 The Simple Scenario Analysis Method

The simple scenario analysis method is the simplest quantitative method to assess whether a hedging relationship meets the economic relationship requirement. The goal of this method is to reveal the behaviour of changes in fair value of both the hedging item and the hedging instrument under specific scenarios.

Normally a few scenarios (e.g., four) are simulated. Each scenario assumes that the underlying risk being hedged will move in a specific way over a certain period of time.

The main drawback of the scenario analysis method is the subjectivity in selecting the scenarios. The scenarios chosen may not be followed by the underlying hedged risk once the hedge is in place, and therefore the conclusions of the analysis may not depict the realistically expected behaviour of the hedge. As a result, this method is used to assess hedging relationships in which the critical terms method cannot be used but it is quite clear that the changes in fair value of the hedge item and hedging instrument will almost fully offset each other.

For example, assume that an entity, with the EUR as its functional currency, enters into a 12-month GBP–EUR FX forward with a forward rate of 0.8015 to hedge a highly expected GBP-denominated sale expected to occur in 15 months. The spot rate was 0.8000 at the time. The significantly different maturities of the hedged item (15 months) and the hedging instrument (12 months) make the use of the critical terms method inappropriate. However, the entity concludes that a scenario analysis captures the relevant characteristics of the hedging relationship. The economic relationship requirement can be assessed under the following three scenarios:

1) a two-standard deviation depreciation of the GBP relative to the EUR during the next 12 months;
2) an unchanged 0.80 spot rate in 12 months' time;
3) a two-standard-deviation appreciation of the GBP relative to the EUR during the next 12 months.

Establishing the FX Rate of a Scenario   At the moment of the analysis, a currency pair is trading at its spot rate. However, it is impossible to know with certainty what would be the FX spot rate at the end of the analysis horizon. Assuming a normal distribution of FX rate, it is possible to calculate a range in which, with a specific probability, the FX rate is expected to be on a specific date in the future. The boundaries of the range can be calculated according to the following formula:

$$\text{Shifted FX spot rate} = (\text{Current FX spot rate}) \times e^{\sigma \times N \times T}$$

where:

   σ is the standard deviation. Normally, σ is set at the volatility of an option with strike at-the-money forward with term coinciding with the analysis horizon and a currency pair coinciding with that of the hedge item.

   N is the number of standard deviations. Figures based on a 95% confidence interval of require $N = 1$ and $N = -1$. For a 99% confidence interval, $N = 2$ and $N = -2$ are used.

   T is the number of years elapsed from the current date to the end of the analysis horizon.

In our example, assuming a 12% volatility of the GBP–EUR FX rate, the FX spot rates at the end of the 12-month period would be:

   ▪ under the first scenario, 1.0170 ($= 0.8000 \times \exp(2 \times 12\% \times 1)$);
   ▪ under the second scenario, 0.8000;
   ▪ under the third scenario, 0.6293 ($= 0.8000 \times \exp(-2 \times 12\% \times 1)$).

The movements under the first and third scenario are very large . The entity expected the GBP–EUR FX rate to be between 0.8293 and 1.0170 with a 99% probability.

2.6.7 The Regression Analysis Method

The regression analysis method is typically applied when a proxy hedge is used (i.e., when the underlying of the hedged item and that of the hedging instrument differ). The idea is to analyse the behaviour of the hedging relationship using historical market rates. Regression analysis is a statistical technique that assesses the level of correlation between one variable (the dependent variable) and one or more other variables (known as the independent variables). In the context of hedge effectiveness testing, the primary objective is to determine whether changes in the fair value of the hedged item and the hedging instrument attributable to a particular risk were highly correlated in the past, and thus supportive of the assertion that there will be a high degree of offset in changes in the fair value of the hedged item and the hedging instrument in the future. The regression analysis is a process that can be divided into three major steps, as shown in Figure 2.8.

The first step in the regression analysis is to obtain the inputs to the analysis: the X and Y observations. Figure 2.9 outlines this process. This step is quite complex and requires a computer program (e.g., Microsoft Excel) to perform it. The idea is to go back to a specific date (the simulation period start date), assume that the hedging relationship started on that date and observe the behaviour of the hedging relationship using the historical market data of the simulation period. The simulation period ends on a date such that the term of the simulation is equal to the term of the actual hedge. This process is repeated several times.

The second step of the regression analysis is to plot the values of the X and Y variables and to estimate a line of best fit. A pictorial representation of the variables in the standard regression equation is shown in Figure 2.10.

Regression analysis uses the "least squares" method to fit a line through the set of X and Y observations. This technique determines the slope and intercept of the line that minimises the size of the squared differences between the actual Y observations and the predicted Y values. The linear equation estimated is commonly expressed as:

$$Y = \alpha + \beta X + \varepsilon$$

where

X is the change in the fair value (or cash flow) of the hedging instrument attributable to the risk being hedged;

Y is the change in the fair value (or cash flow) of the hedged item attributable to the risk being hedged;

α is the intercept (where the line crosses the Y axis);

β is the slope of the line;

ε is the random error term.

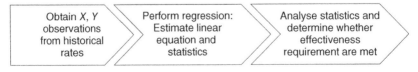

FIGURE 2.8   Phases in the regression analysis method.

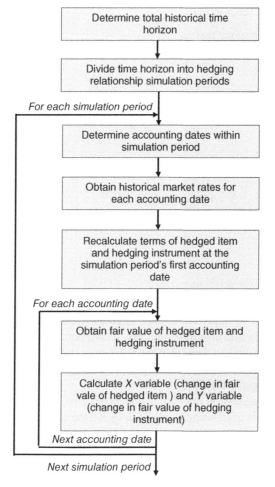

FIGURE 2.9   Process to obtain X and Y observations.

The third step of the regression process is to interpret the statistical results of the regression and determine whether the regression suggests that there is an economic relationship between the hedged item and the hedging instrument. The following three statistics must achieve acceptable levels to provide sufficient evidence for such a conclusion:

- R-squared, or the coefficient of determination, measures the degree of explanatory power or correlation between the dependent and the independent variables in a regression. R-squared indicates the proportion of variability in the dependent variable that can be explained by variation in the independent variable. By way of illustration, an R-squared of 95% indicates that 95% of the movement in the dependent variable is "explained" by variation in the independent variable. R-squared can never exceed 100% as it is not possible to explain more than 100% of the movement in the independent variable. IFRS 9 does not provide a minimum reference R-squared level, but an R-squared greater than or equal to 80% may probably indicate a high correlation between the hedged item and the hedging instrument. In my view, and this is notably subjective opinion, an R-squared

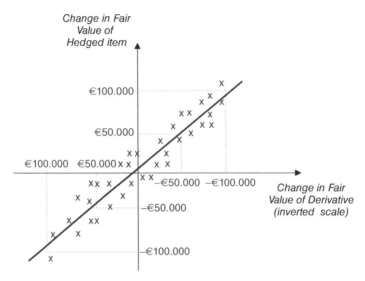

FIGURE 2.10   Regression line of best fit.

below 70% is likely to imply an absence of economic relationship between the hedged item and the hedging instrument. In any case, it is important to remember that a pure high correlation is not sufficient; there also has to be an economic justification for such a high correlation. Moreover, from a statistical perspective, R-squared by itself is an insufficient indicator of hedge performance.

▪ The slope β of the regression line. There is no bright line for the slope. Under the previous financial instruments accounting standard (IAS 39) the slope was required to be between -0.80 and -1.25. Judgement is required to decide whether a given slope means that the economic relationship requirement has been met. The slope can provide an indication of the appropriate hedge ratio.

▪ The t-statistic or F-statistic. These two statistics measure whether the regression results are statistically significant. The t-statistic or F-statistic must be compared to the relevant tables to determine statistical significance. A 95% or higher confidence level is generally accepted as appropriate for evaluating the statistical validity of the regression.

2.6.8   The Monte Carlo Simulation Method

One way to draw meaningful conclusions about an economic relationship assessment is to test the behaviour of the changes in fair value of both the hedging item and the hedging instrument under a very large number of scenarios of the underlying risk being hedged. For some highly structured products, the use of the scenario analysis method may miss a potential scenario that has a substantial effect in the hedging instrument's payout. Monte Carlo simulation is a tool that provides multiple scenarios by repeatedly estimating hundreds of different paths of the risk being hedged, based on the probability distribution of the risk. In my view, a well-performed Monte Carlo simulation can be very effective in assessing hedge effectiveness when the payout of the hedging instrument is highly dependent on the behaviour of the underlying risk during the life of the instrument.

2.6.9 Suggestions Regarding the Assessment Methods

The entity shall use the method that captures the relevant characteristics of the hedging relationship, including the sources of hedge ineffectiveness. What follows is just my own personal recommendation (remember that an entity's external auditors always have the last word) regarding which method to use (see Figure 2.11):

- Use the **critical terms method** when the critical terms of the hedged item and the hedging instrument perfectly match. Remember, the critical term method is a qualitative assessment and therefore relatively simple to document.
- Use the **critical terms method** coupled with a **single scenario analysis** when there is a slight mismatch between the critical terms of the hedged item and the hedging instrument – for example, where there is a relatively short time lag between the interest periods of a swap and those of a hedged loan.
- Use the **scenario analysis method** when there is a mismatch in dates or notionals of the hedged item and the hedging instrument, and the latter is a vanilla hedging instrument (e.g., a swap, a forward, a standard option).
- Use the **regression analysis method** when there is a mismatch in underlyings of the hedged item and the hedging instrument (i.e., a proxy hedge has been used), and this instrument is a vanilla hedging instrument (e.g., a swap, a forward, a standard option).
- Use the **Monte Carlo simulation method** when the hedging instrument is complex and/ or when its payout is highly dependent on the behaviour of the underlying risk during the life of the instrument (e.g., a range accrual with knock-out barriers).

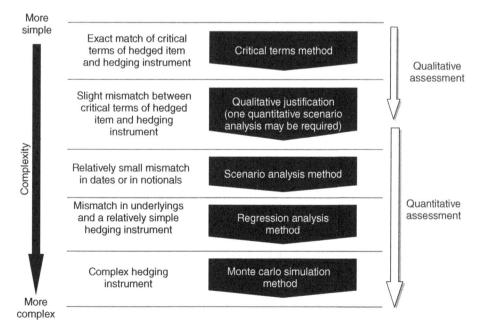

FIGURE 2.11 Recommended decision tree of hedge effectiveness assessment methods.

2.7 THE HYPOTHETICAL DERIVATIVE SIMPLIFICATION

The hypothetical derivative approach is a useful simplification when assessing whether a **cash flow** (or a net investment) hedge meets the effectiveness requirements and when measuring hedge effectiveness/ineffectiveness. Whilst IFRS 9 does not preclude the use of the hypothetical derivative in fair value hedges, in my view, auditors will not allow its use in fair value hedges as a hypothetical derivative does not fully replicate the fair value changes of a hedged item. Therefore, I will use the hypothetical derivative simplification only in cash flow and net investment hedges throughout this book.

IFRS 9 allows determining the changes in the fair value of the hedged item using the changes in fair value of the hypothetical derivative. The hypothetical derivative replicates the hedged item and hence results in the same outcome as if that change in fair value was determined by a different approach. Hence, using a hypothetical derivative is not an assessment method in its own right but a mathematical expedient that can only be used to calculate the fair value of the hedged item.

The hypothetical derivative is a derivative whose changes in fair value perfectly offset the changes in fair value of the hedged item for variations in the risk being hedged. The changes in the fair value of both the hypothetical derivative and the real derivative (i.e., the hedging instrument) are then used to assess whether the hedge effectiveness requirements are met and to calculate a hedge's effective and ineffective parts. The terms of the hypothetical derivative are assumed to be the following:

- Its critical terms match those of the hedged item (notional, underlying, maturity, interest periods).
- For hedges of risks that are not one-sided, the hypothetical derivative is a non-option instrument (e.g., a forward, a swap) and its rate (or price) is the at-the-money rate (or price) at the time of designation of the hedging relationship. For one-sided risks (i.e., a risk hedged from a certain value), the hypothetical derivative is an option with strike determined in accordance with the risk being hedged (e.g., the strike of the hypothetical derivative –a cap – is 6% when the hedged risk in a floating rate loan is a potential movement in the Euribor rate above 6%). Similarly, for two-sided risks (i.e., risks that are hedged up to a certain level and from another level) the strike of the hypothetical derivative – a combination of a bought and sold options – is determined by the ranges of the risk being hedged. The hypothetical derivative strike cannot be in-the-money.
- Its counterparty is free of credit risk (i.e., the counterparty will always pay any settlement amounts due to the entity).
- The hypothetical derivative has no time value, in the case of it being a single option or a combination of options.

For example:

- When hedging the FX exposure of a highly expected foreign currency cash flow, the hypothetical derivative would be an FX forward rate with an FX rate that gives the forward an initial zero cost, a currency pair that equals the entity's functional currency and the currency in which the hedged cash flow is denominated, a notional that equals the amount of the expected cash flow, and a maturity that represents the date on which the cash flow is expected to occur.

- When hedging the interest rate exposure of a bullet floating rate liability (i.e. its principal is repaid at maturity only and its periodic interest is linked to a short-term interest rate such as the 3-month Euribor), the hypothetical derivative would be an interest rate swap with a notional equal to that of the debt, interest periods matching those of the debt and a fixed interest rate that gives the swap an initial zero cost.

Ineffectiveness will be measured as the difference between changes in fair value of the hypothetical derivative and the hedging instrument. Ineffectiveness will in principle arise due to differences in their terms and the presence of counterparty credit risk in the hedging instrument.

2.8 REBALANCING

Rebalancing refers to adjustments to the hedge ratio, or in other words, to adjustments in the designated quantities of the hedged item or the hedging instrument of an already existing hedging relationship for the purpose of maintaining a hedge ratio that complies with the hedge effectiveness requirements (see Figure 2.12).

An entity at each assessment date must evaluate whether an existing hedging relationship needs rebalancing. Rebalancing is required when maintaining the existing hedge ratio would reflect an imbalance that would **create hedge ineffectiveness** that could result in an accounting outcome that would be inconsistent with the purpose of hedge accounting (i.e., an entity must not create an imbalance by omitting to adjust the hedge ratio).

Adjusting the hedge ratio allows an entity to respond to changes in the relationship between the hedging instrument and the hedged item that arise from their underlyings or risk variables, and to continue the hedging relationship. The adjustment to the hedge ratio can be effected in different ways:

- increasing (or decreasing) the quantity of the hedged item; or
- increasing (or decreasing) the quantity of the hedged instrument.

If a hedging relationship ceases to meet the hedge effectiveness requirement regarding the hedge ratio but the risk management objective for that designated hedging relationship remains the same, an entity shall adjust the hedge ratio of the hedging relationship so that it meets the qualifying criteria again. Rebalancing does not apply (or is not required) if:

- The risk management objective for a hedging relationship has changed. Instead, hedge accounting for that hedging relationship shall be discontinued (notwithstanding that an entity might designate a new hedging relationship that involves the hedging instrument or hedged item of the previous hedging relationship).
- Fluctuation around a constant hedge ratio (and hence the related hedge ineffectiveness) cannot be reduced by adjusting the hedge ratio in response to each particular outcome. Hence, in such circumstances, the change in the extent of offset is a matter of measuring and recognising hedge ineffectiveness but does not require rebalancing.

EXAMPLE: Hedging a HKD–EUR exposure

A EUR-based entity hedges a highly expected HKD 500 million cash flow using a EUR–USD FX forward with a USD notional of USD 65 million, when the HKD is pegged to the USD in a 7.75:1 ratio. If the Chinese authorities decide to devalue the HKD by changing the USD–HKD peg to a 10:1 exchange rate, rebalancing the hedging relationship to reflect the new exchange rate would ensure that the hedging relationship would continue to meet the hedge effectiveness requirement regarding the hedge ratio in the new circumstances. The entity may either reduce the amount of hedging instrument to USD 50 million notional (the excess 15 million would be considered speculative) or, less likely, increase the amount of hedged item to HKD 650 million.

In contrast, if there were a default on the FX forward, changing the hedge ratio could not ensure that the hedging relationship would continue to meet that hedge effectiveness requirement. Hence, rebalancing does not facilitate continuing a hedging relationship in situations where the relationship between the hedging instrument and the hedged item changes in a way that cannot be compensated for by adjusting the hedge ratio.

When rebalancing a hedging relationship, an entity shall update its analysis of the sources of hedge ineffectiveness that are expected to affect the hedging relationship during its remaining life. The documentation of the hedging relationship shall be updated accordingly.

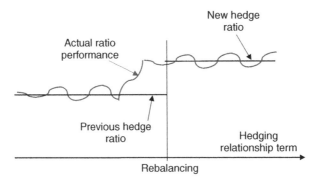

FIGURE 2.12   Rebalancing of a hedging relationship.

2.8.1 Accounting for Rebalancings

Rebalancing is accounted for as a continuation of the hedging relationship. On rebalancing, the hedge ineffectiveness of the hedging relationship is determined and recognised immediately before adjusting the hedging relationship.

EXAMPLE (Part 1)

Suppose that an entity determined, based on historical data, that in order to hedge 100 tonnes of a future purchase of commodity A it should transact 120 tonnes of notional value of derivatives on benchmark commodity B. The entity designated this as a cash flow hedging relationship.

On the next reporting date, the effectiveness assessment demonstrated that the basis for benchmark commodity B had changed such that only 110 tonnes were required to hedge 100 tonnes of commodity A. The entity believed this was part of a trend leading away from the hedge ratio rather than just a temporary fluctuation. To rebalance the hedge ratio, the entity could:

- de-designate 10 tonnes of the hedging derivative (i.e., decreasing the volume of the hedging instrument to 110 tonnes); or
- designate an additional 9.1 (= 100 × 120/110 – 100) tonnes of the hedged item (i.e., increasing the volume of the hedged item to 109.1 tonnes), if highly probable to occur.

Adjusting the Hedge Ratio by Decreasing the Volume of the Hedging Instrument   Adjusting the hedge ratio by decreasing the volume of the hedging instrument does not affect how the changes in the value of the hedged item are measured. The measurement of the changes in the fair value of the hedging instrument related to the volume that continues to be designated also remains unaffected.

However, from the date of rebalancing, the volume by which the hedging instrument was decreased is no longer part of the hedging relationship (by 10 tonnes in our previous example). The entity may decide whether to unwind the excess hedge or retain it. If the excess hedge is retained, such a proportion of the hedging instrument would be designated as speculative and, as a result, its fair value change recognised in profit or loss (unless after the rebalancing it was designated in a different hedging relationship).

Adjusting the Hedge Ratio by Increasing the Volume of the Hedged Item   Rebalancing by increasing the volume of the hedged item does not affect how the changes in the fair value of the hedging instrument are measured. The measurement of the changes in the value of the hedged item related to the previously designated volume also remains unaffected. However, from the date of rebalancing, the changes in the value of the hedged item also include the change in the value of the additional volume of the hedged item.

These changes are measured starting from, and by reference to, the date of rebalancing instead of the date on which the hedging relationship was designated. In our previous example, the entity would designate an additional 9.1 tonnes of the hedged item.

EXAMPLE (Part 2)

Based on our previous example, let us assume that instead the effectiveness assessment demonstrated that the basis for benchmark commodity B had changed such that 130 tonnes, rather than 120 tonnes, were required to hedge 100 tonnes of commodity A. To adjust the hedge ratio, the entity had two main alternatives:

- Enter into an additional 10 tonnes of the hedging derivative (i.e., increasing the volume of the hedging instrument to 130 tonnes from 120 tonnes); or
- De-designate 7.7 tonnes ($=100 - 100 \times 120/130$) of the hedged item (i.e., decreasing the volume of the hedged item to 92.3 tonnes from 100 tonnes).

Adjusting the Hedge Ratio by Increasing the Volume of the Hedging Instrument   Adjusting the hedge ratio by increasing the volume of the hedging instrument does not affect how the changes in the fair value of the hedged item are measured.

The measurement of the changes in the fair value of the hedging instrument related to the previously designated volume also remains unaffected. However, from the date of rebalancing, the changes in the fair value of the hedging instrument also include the changes in the value related the additional volume of the hedging instrument. The changes are measured starting from, and by reference to, the date of rebalancing instead of the date on which the hedging relationship was designated. In our previous example, one of the alternatives available to the entity was to designate on rebalancing an additional 10 tonnes of the hedging derivative so its total volume would comprise 130 tonnes. From the date of rebalancing the change in the fair value of the hedging instrument was the total change in the fair value of the derivatives that make up the total volume of 130 tonnes. It is likely that the entity would have entered into the additional volume at a different price.

Adjusting the Hedge Ratio by Decreasing the Volume of the Hedged Item   Adjusting the hedge ratio by decreasing the volume of the hedged item does not affect how the changes in the fair value of the hedging instrument are measured.

The measurement of the changes in the value of the hedged item related to the volume that continues to be designated also remains unaffected. However, from the date of rebalancing, the volume by which the hedged item was decreased is no longer part of the hedging relationship. In our previous example, one of the alternatives available to the entity was to reduce on rebalancing 7.7 tonnes of the hedged item, to 92.3 tonnes. The 7.7 tonnes of the hedged item that are no longer part of the hedging relationship would be accounted for in accordance with the requirements for the discontinuation of hedge accounting. In a fair value hedge, for instance, the entity would begin amortising the amount within the separate line item in the statement of financial position related to the amount that is no longer part of the hedging relationship. This means that entities have to keep track of the accumulated gains or losses for the risk being hedged related to the individual hedged items.

2.9 DISCONTINUATION OF HEDGE ACCOUNTING

In certain circumstances, an entity may be interested in discontinuing a hedging relationship. IFRS 9 **prohibits voluntary discontinuation** of a hedging relationship when the qualifying criteria are still met, after taking into consideration rebalancing of the hedging relationship. That is:

- the hedging relationship still meets the risk management objective on the basis of which it qualified for hedge accounting (i.e., the entity still pursues that risk management objective); and
- the hedging relationship continues to meet all other qualifying criteria (after taking into account any rebalancing of the hedging relationship, if applicable).

Otherwise (see Figure 2.13), it is required for an entity to discontinue prospectively hedge accounting from the date on which the qualifying criteria are no longer met. However, if an entity discontinues a hedging relationship, then it can designate a new hedging relationship that involves the hedging instrument or the hedged item, but that designation constitutes the start of a new hedging relationship, not the continuation of the old one.

Risk Management Strategy versus Risk Management Objective   It is important to distinguish between risk management strategy and risk management objective. A **risk management strategy** is established at the highest level at which an entity determines how it manages its risk. This strategy is normally set out in a general document identifying the risks to which the entity is exposed and setting out how the entity responds to them, and may include some flexibility to react to changes in circumstances that occur while that strategy is in place (e.g., different interest rate or commodity price levels that result in a different extent of hedging). This document is commonly cascaded down through the entity by way of policies containing more specific guidelines.

In contrast, the **risk management objective** for a hedging relationship applies at the level of a particular hedging relationship. It relates to how the particular hedging instrument that has been designated is used to hedge the particular exposure that has been designated as the hedged item. Hence, a risk management strategy can involve many different hedging relationships whose risk management objectives relate to executing that overall risk management strategy. Thus, a risk management objective may change while its related risk management strategy remains unchanged.

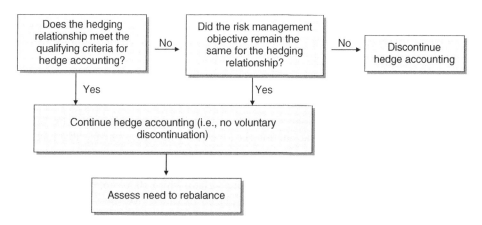

FIGURE 2.13   Decision tree for discontinuation of a hedging relationship.

EXAMPLE

The risk management strategy of an entity set targets regarding the proportion of fixed relative to floating interest rate bearing liabilities for different levels of interest rates. The strategy is to maintain between 20% and 40% of the debt at fixed rates. If interest rates are low the entity fixes the interest for more debt than when interest rates are high.

The entity's debt is EUR 100 million of variable rate debt of which EUR 30 million is converted into a fixed rate exposure through an interest rate swap. Following a substantial fall in interest rates, the entity takes advantage of the low interest rates to issue a EUR 50 million fixed rate bond. In light of the low interest rates, the entity decides to set its fixed interest rate exposure to 40% of the total debt by unwinding EUR 20 million (= 30 mn – 40% × 150 mn + 50 mn) of the interest rate swap, resulting in EUR 60 million (= 40% × 150 mn) of fixed rate exposure. In this situation the risk management strategy itself remains unchanged. However, the entity's execution of that strategy has changed and this means that, for EUR 20 million of variable rate exposure that was previously hedged, the risk management objective has changed (i.e., at the hedging relationship level). Consequently, hedge accounting must be discontinued for EUR 20 million of the previously hedged variable rate exposure. The entity would then need to decide whether to unwind EUR 20 million of the original swap, or to keep it. If the excess EUR 20 million notional is kept, it will be designated as speculative unless designated as hedging instrument in a different hedging relationship. Hedge accounting would have to be continued for EUR 10 million of its previously hedged variable rate exposure.

Alternatively, if, instead of unwinding EUR 20 million of the interest rate swap, the entity swapped into variable EUR 20 million of its new fixed rate bond, hedge accounting would have to be continued for its EUR 30 million previously hedged variable rate exposure.

The discontinuation of hedge accounting can affect:

- a hedging relationship in its entirety; or
- a part of a hedging relationship (which means that hedge accounting continues for the remainder of the hedging relationship, or in other words, when only a part of the hedging relationship ceases to meet the qualifying criteria).

A hedging relationship is discontinued in its entirety when as a whole it ceases to meet the qualifying criteria. For example:

- The hedging relationship no longer meets the risk management objective on the basis of which it qualified for hedge accounting (i.e., the entity no longer pursues that risk management objective); or
- The hedging instrument or instruments have been sold or terminated (regarding the entire volume that was part of the hedging relationship). It is not a termination or expiration if the hedging instrument is replaced or rolled over into another hedging instrument, if such replacement or roll-over is part of the entity's documented hedging strategy; or

- There is no longer an economic relationship between the hedged item and the hedging instrument or the effect of credit risk starts dominating the value changes that result from that economic relationship.
- The hedged item ceases to exist if either (i) the recognised hedged item matures, is sold or terminated, or (ii) the forecast transaction is no longer highly probable.

A part of a hedging relationship is discontinued (and hedge accounting continues for its remainder) when only a part of the hedging relationship ceases to meet the qualifying criteria. For example:

- On rebalancing of the hedging relationship, the hedge ratio might be adjusted by decreasing the volume of the hedged item that is part of the hedging relationship; hence, hedge accounting is discontinued only for the volume of the hedged item that is no longer part of the hedging relationship; or
- When the occurrence of some of the volume of the hedged item that is (or is a component of) a forecast transaction is no longer highly probable, hedge accounting is discontinued only for the volume of the hedged item whose occurrence is no longer highly probable. However, if an entity has a history of having designated hedges of forecast transactions and having subsequently determined that the forecast transactions are no longer expected to occur, the entity's ability to predict forecast transactions accurately is called into question when predicting similar future forecast transactions. This affects the assessment of whether similar forecast transactions are highly probable and hence whether they are eligible as hedged items.

An entity can designate a new hedging relationship that involves the hedging instrument or hedged item of a previous hedging relationship for which hedge accounting was (in part or in its entirety) discontinued. This does not constitute a continuation of a hedging relationship but is a restart. For example:

- A hedging instrument experiences such a severe credit deterioration that the entity replaces it with a new hedging instrument. This means that the original hedging relationship failed to achieve the risk management objective and is hence discontinued in its entirety. The new hedging instrument is designated as the hedge of the same exposure that was hedged previously and forms a new hedging relationship. Hence, the changes in the fair value or the cash flows of the hedged item are measured starting from, and by reference to, the date of designation of the new hedging relationship instead of the date on which the original hedging relationship was designated.
- Following rebalancing of a hedging relationship, the volume of the hedging instrument is reduced. The excess hedging instrument in that hedging relationship can be designated as the hedging instrument in another hedging relationship.

There are different accounting treatments depending upon the kind of hedge and the cause of discontinuance:

1) The hedging instrument of a cash flow hedge is terminated or sold. The hedging gains or losses that were previously recognised in equity remain in equity and are transferred to profit or loss when the hedged item is ultimately recognised in profit or loss.
2) The hedging instrument of a fair hedge is terminated or sold. There is no further fair valuing of the hedged item. Any previous adjustments to the carrying amount of the hedged item are amortised over the remaining maturity of the hedged item.

3) The fair value hedge fails the hedge effectiveness requirements. Adjustments to the carrying amount of the hedged item previously recorded as of the last assessment (which met the hedge effectiveness requirements) remain part of the hedged item's carrying value. If the entity can demonstrate exactly when the assessment failed, it can record the change in the fair value of the hedged item up to the last moment the hedge met the effectiveness requirements. From this moment there is no further fair valuing of the hedged item. The adjustments to the carrying value of the hedged item to date are amortised over the life of the hedged item. When the hedged item is carried at amortised cost, the amortisation is performed by recalculating its effective interest rate.

4) The firm commitment to a fair value hedge is no longer firm or the fair value hedged item no longer exists. Any amounts recorded on the statement of financial position (i.e., balance sheet) related to the change in fair value of the hedged item are reversed out to profit or loss.

5) A cash flow hedge fails the hedge effectiveness requirements, but the hedged forecast transaction is still expected to occur. The hedging gains or losses that were previously recorded in equity as of the last assessment (which met the hedge effectiveness requirements) remain deferred and are transferred from the cash flow hedge reserve to profit or loss when the forecast transaction is ultimately recognised in profit or loss. If the entity can demonstrate exactly when the cash flow hedge failed the effectiveness requirements, it can record the change in fair value on the hedging instrument up to the last moment the requirements were met.

6) The forecasted transaction of a cash flow hedge is either no longer highly probable or no longer expected to take place. Two different treatments are possible: (i) if the forecasted transaction is no longer highly probable but it is still expected to occur, the cumulative hedge gains or losses that were previously recorded in equity remain deferred in equity until the hedged cash flow is recognised in profit or loss; or (ii) if the forecasted transaction is no longer expected to take place, the cumulative hedge gains or losses that had been deferred up to that point in equity are immediately reclassified to profit or loss.

In any type of termination, if any derivatives from the terminated hedges are still outstanding, then any subsequent change in the fair value of these derivatives should be recorded in profit or loss, unless they are designated as the hedging instrument in a new cash flow hedge hedging relationship.

The following table summarises the accounting treatment for some of the hedging discontinuation events:

Discontinuation event	Fair value hedge	Cash flow hedge
Hedging instrument terminates or is sold	No further fair valuing of the hedged item. Any previous adjustments to the carrying amount of the hedged item are amortised over the remaining maturity of the hedged item	Deferred equity balance remains deferred in equity until forecast transaction impacts profit or loss
Hedged item terminates or is sold	Any amounts recorded on the statement of financial position related to the change in fair value of the hedged item are reversed out to profit or loss	Deferred equity balance is reclassified immediately to profit or loss

Discontinuation event	Fair value hedge	Cash flow hedge
Hedge fails the hedge effectiveness requirements	No further fair valuing of the hedged item. Any previous adjustments to the carrying amount of the hedged item are amortised over the remaining maturity of the hedged item	Deferred equity balance remains deferred in equity until forecast transaction impacts profit or loss
Forecast transaction still expected to occur, although not highly expected	Not applicable	Same as previous
Forecast transaction no longer expected to occur	Not applicable	Deferred equity balance is reclassified immediately to profit or loss

2.10 OPTIONS AND HEDGE ACCOUNTING

2.10.1 Intrinsic Value versus Time Value

The total value of an option before expiry is the sum of two components: its intrinsic value and its time value.

- The **intrinsic value** is the value that an option would have if it were exercised immediately. The intrinsic value of an option can be calculated using either the spot rate or the forward rate. In the case of equity and FX options, the intrinsic value is usually calculated using spot prices/rates. In the case of interest rate options, the intrinsic value is commonly calculated using forward rates.
- The **time value** is any value of the option other than its intrinsic value. As a result, options that have zero intrinsic value are comprised entirely of time value.

> Option total value = Intrinsic value + Time value

The intrinsic value of a call option on a stock is calculated as follows:

- When the stock price is above the strike price, the call option is said to have intrinsic value. This is because, were the call to expire at that moment, there would be a positive cash payout (ignoring the effect of dividends).
- When the stock price is below or at the strike price, the call option is said to have no intrinsic value. This is because, were the call to expire at that moment, there would be no cash payout.

> Call intrinsic value = Number of options × max[(Stock price – Strike price), 0]

The intrinsic value of a put option on a stock is calculated as follows:

- When the stock price is below the strike price, the put is said to have intrinsic value. This is because, were the put to expire at that moment, there would be a positive cash payout.

■ When the stock price is above or at the strike price, the put is said to have no intrinsic value. This is because, were the put to expire at that moment, there would be no cash payout (ignoring the effect of dividends).

Put intrinsic value = Number of options × max[(Strike price – Stock price), 0]

The time value of an option is the portion of the value of an option that is due to the fact that it has some time to expiration. The time value of an option represents the possibility that the option may finish in-the-money or further in-the-money. The time value will progressively erode as the option approaches its expiration date. At expiry there will be no time value. The time value component is calculated as the difference between the total value of an option and its intrinsic value:

Time value = Total value – Intrinsic value

Figure 2.14 illustrates the intrinsic value and time value components of a call option on 1 million IBM shares, a USD 180 strike and 6 months to expiration (note that the y axis has not been graphed using a linear scale to better highlight the concepts). The total value of the option has been calculated using an option pricing model. For example, assuming IBM's spot price at USD 210, the total value of the call option would be USD 37 million. The intrinsic value would be USD 30 million (= 1 million × (210 – 180)). Therefore, the option time value would be USD 7 million (= 37 million – 30 million). The following table summarises the intrinsic value and time value components for three stock price scenarios:

Spot price	USD 150	USD 180	USD 210
Intrinsic value	0	0	USD 30 million
Time value	USD 4 million	USD 13 million	USD 7 million
Total value	USD 4 million	USD 13 million	USD 37 million

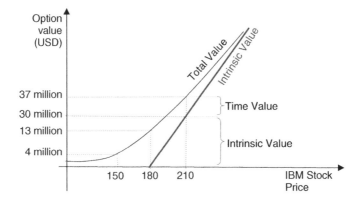

FIGURE 2.14   Call option on IBM stock – intrinsic and time values.

2.10.2 In-, At- or Out-of-the-Money

Options which have intrinsic value are described as being **in-the-money**. By the same reasoning, options which have no intrinsic value (e.g., in a call option, if the share price is below the strike price) are called **out-of-the-money**. If the option expires out-of-the-money, the holder will not exercise the option. An option is called **at-the-money** if the stock price (in the case of an equity option) is at the strike price.

Description	Call	Put	Intrinsic value
In-the-money	Stock price > Strike	Stock price < Strike	Yes
At-the-money	Stock price = Strike	Stock price = Strike	No
Out-of-the-money	Stock price < Strike	Stock price > Strike	No

Based on our previous call option on IBM with a strike price of USD 150:

Spot price	USD 150	USD 180	USD 210
Strike	USD 180	USD 180	USD 180
Moneyness	Out-of-the-money	At-the-money	In-the-money

At expiry, there will be no time value and there will be two different scenarios:

- the option expires in-the-money, resulting in a positive cash payout for the option buyer; or
- the option expires out-of-the-money, being worthless.

2.10.3 Accounting Treatment for the Time Value of Options

When an option is used in a hedging strategy and hedge accounting is applied, IFRS 9 gives entities two choices:

- To designate the option in its entirety as the hedging instrument. This is seldom chosen, unless the hedged item is an equity investment classified at FVOCI.
- To separate the option's intrinsic value and time value, and only designate the intrinsic value as the hedging instrument in the hedging relationship. The time value is, therefore, excluded from the hedging relationship. This is the alternative commonly chosen because it enhances hedge effectiveness as the option time value is not replicated in the hedged item.

Therefore, unless specifically stated, I will assume throughout this book that the second alternative is selected in hedging strategies involving options. The IFRS 9 accounting treatment of the time value of an option considers that the time value of an option at the start of a hedging relationship represents a premium for protection against risk (similar to paying a premium for insuring a risk).

The accounting of the time value *for instruments other than equity investments* can be viewed as a two-step process (relatively similar to the mechanics of cash flow hedge accounting, as shown in Figure 2.15).

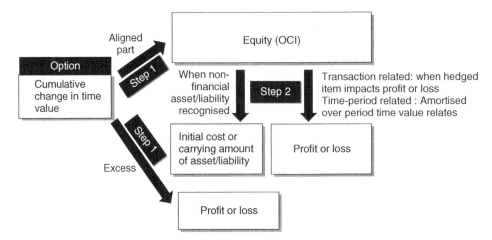

FIGURE 2.15 Accounting for the time value of options when excluded from a hedging relationship.

Step 1: Accumulation in OCI   The first step is to accumulate in OCI, over the term of the hedge, the cumulative change in fair value of the time value component of the option from the date of designation of the hedging instrument, to the extent that it relates to the hedged item.

The time value related to the hedged item is called the **aligned time value**. This time value represents the time value of an option that would have critical terms that perfectly match the hedged item. The method used to calculate of the amounts recognised in OCI is dependent on the comparison between the time value of the actual option (i.e., the option whose intrinsic value is the hedging instrument or, in other words, the option entered into by the entity) and the time value of the aligned option, at the inception of the hedging relationship.

Actual Time Value Greater than the Aligned Time Value
The entity determines the amount that is accumulated in OCI on the basis of the aligned time value. This means that the amount recognised in OCI is the change in aligned time value during the period (i.e., since the previous valuation). Any remainder, whether an excess or deficit, of the change in actual time value relative to the change in aligned time value is recognised in profit or loss.

Actual Time Value lower than the Aligned Time Value
The part of the cumulative fair value change of the option's time value element recognised in OCI is calculated as the lower of the following (in absolute terms):

- the cumulative fair value change of the actual time value; and
- the cumulative fair value change of the aligned time value.

Any excess of the cumulative change in the option's time value over that of the aligned time value is recognised in profit or loss.

Step 2: Recycling of Amounts Accumulated in OCI   The second step is to reclassify the amounts accumulated in OCI to profit or loss. The basis of this reclassification depends on the categorisation of the hedged item, which will be either:

- a **transaction related** hedged item (e.g., a forecast purchase of commodity); or
- a **time-period related** hedged item (e.g., an existing item, such as commodity inventory, hedged over a period of time).

The nature of the hedged item is that transaction costs in the former case, that of the cost for obtaining protection against a risk over a specific period of time in the latter case.

Transaction Related Time Values

A hedged item is transaction related if the nature of the hedged item is a transaction for which the time value (or the forward element in the case of forward contracts) has the character of costs of that transaction.

For transaction related hedged items the cumulative change in fair value deferred in OCI is recognised in profit or loss at the same time as the hedged item.

If the hedged item first gives rise to the recognition of a non-financial asset or a non-financial liability, or a firm commitment for a non-financial asset or a non-financial liability in a fair value hedging relationship, the amount in OCI is reclassified in the statement of financial position, being recorded as part of the initial cost or other carrying amount of the hedged item. Therefore, this amount is later recognised in profit or loss at the same time as the non-financial asset/liability affects profit or loss in accordance with the normal accounting for the hedged item. An example is an inventory purchase denominated in a foreign currency, whether it is a forecast transaction or a firm commitment, hedged against FX risk; the time value element in OCI would be added to the transaction costs in the initial measurement of the inventory.

If the hedged item is other than those covered in the previous paragraph, the amount in OCI is reclassified to profit or loss in the same period or periods during which the hedged expected future cash flows affect profit or loss. An example would be a sale of final goods denominated in a foreign currency hedged against FX risk, whether it is a forecast transaction or a firm commitment; the time value element in OCI would be included as part of the cost that is related to that sale (i.e., the time value element in OCI would be recognised in profit or loss in the same period as the revenue from the hedged sale).

However, if all or a portion of the amount accumulated in OCI is not expected to be recovered in one or more future periods, the amount that is not expected to be recovered shall be immediately reclassified to profit or loss.

Time-Period Related Time Values

A hedged item is time-period related if the nature of the hedged item is such that the time value element (or the forward element in a forward contract) has the character of a cost for obtaining protection against a risk over a particular period of time (but the hedged item does not result in a transaction that involves the notion of a transaction cost).

For time-period related hedged items the reclassification of amounts deferred in OCI is amortised to profit or loss (or within OCI for equity investments at FVOCI) on a systematic and rational basis over the period to which the time value element (or the forward element in a forward contract) relates. For example, if an option hedges the exposure to variability in 3-month interest rates for a 3-month period that starts in 6 months' time, the time value element is amortised during the period that spans months 7–9. Even though IFRS 9 does not prescribe a particular method, commonly the straight-line amortisation method is used.

An example would be a commodity inventory hedged against changes in fair value for 6 months using a commodity option (or a forward contract) with a corresponding life; the time value element (or forward element in the case of a forward contract) in OCI would be allocated to profit or loss over that 6-month period. Another example is a hedge of a net investment in a foreign operation that is hedged over 18 months using an FX option (or an FX forward contract), which would result in allocating the time value element (or the forward element in the case of a forward contract) over that 18-month period.

If a hedging relationship is discontinued, the remaining amount in OCI is immediately reclassified into profit or loss.

2.10.4 Example of Option Hedging a Transaction Related Item – Actual Time Value Exceeding Aligned Time Value

Imagine that on 1-Jan-X1 an entity bought a 3-year out-of-the-money option for an up-front premium of 14 million (i.e., the fair value of the option's time value component was 14 million). The option hedged a highly expected forecast purchase of natural gas expected to be received on 31-Dec-X3. The intrinsic value of the purchased option was designated as hedging instrument in a hedging relationship that started on 1-Jan-20X1. As a result, the option's time value was excluded from the hedging relationship. Suppose that at the start of the hedging relationship (hedge inception), the entity estimated that the time value of an option that replicated the main terms of the hedged item (i.e., the aligned time value) was 12 million. Suppose further that the time values at each relevant date were as portrayed in the following table:

Description	Initial (1-Jan-X1)	31-Dec-X1	31-Dec-X2	Expiry 31-Dec-X3
Actual time value	14 mn	12 mn	5 mn	0
Period change in actual time value	—	<2 mn>	<7 mn>	<5 mn>
Aligned time value	12 mn	9 mn	7 mn	0
Period change in aligned time value	—	<3 mn>	<2 mn>	<7 mn>

Because at hedge inception, the actual time value was higher than the aligned time value, the amount that was subsequently recognised in OCI was determined only on the basis of the aligned time value.

On 31-Dec-X1 the change in aligned time value since hedge inception was a 3 million loss (= 9 mn – 12 mn). Therefore, a 3 million loss was recognised in OCI. The change in actual time value since hedge inception was a loss of 2 million (=12 mn – 14 mn). The difference between both changes, a gain of 1 million (= <2 mn> – <3 mn>), was recognised in profit or loss.

On 31-Dec-X2 the change in aligned time value during the period was a 2 million loss (= 7 mn – 9 mn). Therefore, a 2 million loss was recognised in OCI. The change in actual time value during the period was a loss of 7 million (= 5 mn – 12 mn). The difference between both changes, a loss of 5 million (= <7 mn> – <2 mn>), was recognised in profit or loss.

On 31-Dec-X3 the change in aligned time value during the period was a 7 million loss (= 0 – 7 mn). Therefore, a 7 million loss was recognised in OCI. The change in actual time value during the period was a loss of 5 million (= 0 – 5 mn). The difference between both changes, a gain of 2 million (= <5 mn> – <7 mn>), was recognised in profit or loss.

Also on 31-Dec-X3 the natural gas was purchased and the amount accumulated in OCI, a negative 12 million (corresponding to the aligned time value at hedge inception) was reclassified, adjusting the initial carrying value of the natural gas. In other words, the value of the bought natural gas was increased by 12 million on the entity's statement of financial position.

The following table shows the amounts being recognised in OCI and in profit or loss at each relevant period and the carrying value of the options time value reserve of OCI:

Description	31-Dec-X1	31-Dec-X2	Expiry 31-Dec-X3	Recycling 31-Dec-X3
Period amount to OCI	<3 mn>	<2 mn>	<7 mn>	12 mn
Period amount to profit or loss	1 mn	<5 mn>	2 mn	—
Carrying value of OCI reserve	<3 mn>	<5 mn>	<12 mn>	-0-

Figure 2.16 depicts the effects in the entity's statement of financial position. The carrying amount of the natural gas purchased was increased by the amount of aligned time value at hedge inception (i.e., 12 million). This amount was recycled from the options time value reserve of OCI. Therefore, just prior to that reclassification, the carrying value of the options time value reserve of OCI was <12 million>, the aligned time value at hedge inception. The amount recognised in profit or loss since hedge inception was a 2 million loss, the difference, at hedge inception, between the aligned time value and the actual time value.

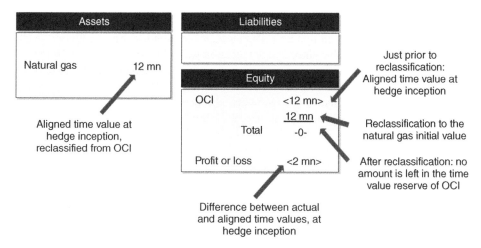

FIGURE 2.16   Effects on statement of financial position of time value recognition.

2.10.5 Example of Option Hedging a Transaction Related Item – Actual Time Value Lower Than Aligned Time Value

Imagine the situation described in the previous example, but with time values at each relevant date as portrayed in the following table:

Description	Initial (1-Jan-X1)	31-Dec-X1	31-Dec-X2	Expiry 31-Dec-X3
Actual time value (TV)	11 mn	10 mn	4 mn	0
Cumulative change in actual TV	—	<1 mn>	<7 mn>	<11 mn>
Aligned time value	12 mn	9 mn	7 mn	0
Cumulative change in actual TV	—	<3 mn>	<5 mn>	<12 mn>
Lower of cumulative changes in TV	—	<1 mn>	<5 mn>	<11 mn>
Change in actual TV (in period)	—	<1 mn>	<6 mn>	<4 mn>
Amount to OCI (in period)	—	<1 mn>	<4 mn>	<6 mn>
Amount to profit or loss (in period)	—	-0-	<2 mn>	2 mn
Carrying value of OCI reserve	—	<1 mn>	<5 mn>	<11 mn>

Because at hedge inception the actual time value was lower than the aligned time value, the amount that was subsequently recognised in OCI was determined by the lower of the cumulative change of the aligned time value and that of the actual time value. Any remainder of the change of the actual time value was recognised in profit or loss.

On 31-Dec-X1 the cumulative change in actual time value since hedge inception was a 1 million loss (= 10 mn – 11 mn). On that date, the cumulative change in aligned time value since hedge inception was a 3 million loss (= 9 mn – 12 mn). The lower of these amounts (ignoring their signs) was a 1 million loss. Therefore, a 1 million loss was recognised in OCI. The change in actual time value since hedge inception was a loss of 1 million (=10 mn – 11 mn), and since this amount would be fully recognised in OCI, no amount remained to be recognised in profit or loss.

On 31-Dec-X2 the cumulative change in actual time value since hedge inception was a 7 million loss (= 4 mn – 11 mn). On that date, the cumulative change in aligned time value since hedge inception was a 5 million loss (= 7 mn – 12 mn). The lower of these amounts (ignoring their signs) was a 5 million loss, to be recognised in OCI. As already a 1 million loss was recognised in OCI as of the previous reporting date, the amount to be recognised in OCI on 31-Dec-X2 was a 4 million loss. The change in actual time value during the period was a loss of 6 million (=4 mn – 10 mn), and since a 4 million loss would be recognised in OCI, a 2 million loss remained to be recognised in profit or loss.

On 31-Dec-X3 the cumulative change in actual time value since hedge inception was an 11 million loss (= 0 – 11 mn). On that date, the cumulative change in aligned time value since hedge inception was a 12 million loss (= 0 – 12 mn). The lower of these amounts (ignoring their signs) was an 11 million loss, to be recognised in OCI. As already a 5 million loss was recognised in OCI as of the previous reporting date, the amount to be recognised in OCI on 31-Dec-X3 was a 6 million loss. The change in actual time value during the period was a loss of 4 million (=0 – 4 mn), and since a 6 million loss would be recognised in OCI, a 2 million gain remained to be recognised in profit or loss.

Also on 31-Dec-X3 the natural gas was purchased and the amount accumulated in OCI, a negative 11 million was reclassified, adjusting the initial carrying value of the natural gas. In other words, the value of the bought natural gas was increased by 11 million on the entity's statement of financial position.

Figure 2.17 depicts the effects in the entity's statement of financial position. The carrying amount of the natural gas purchased was increased by the amount accumulated in OCI since hedge inception (i.e., 11 million). This amount was recycled from the options time value reserve of OCI. The amount recognised in profit or loss since hedge inception was nil, the difference between the actual time value at hedge inception (11 million) and the accumulated amount recognised in OCI (11 million as well). The fact that the amount accumulated in OCI coincided with the actual time value at hedge inception will not necessarily hold in all other instances. All that can be inferred is that the amount accumulated in OCI never exceeds the actual time value at hedge inception.

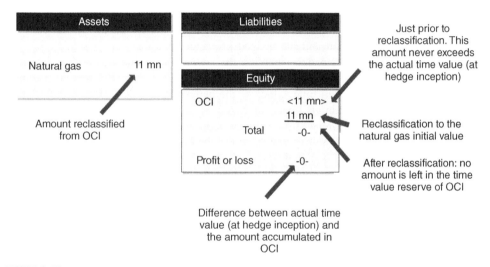

FIGURE 2.17   Effects on statement of financial position of time value recognition.

2.10.6   Example of Option Hedging a Time-Period Related Item – Actual Time Value Exceeding Aligned Time Value

Imagine that on 1-Jan-20X1 an entity bought a 3-year out-of-the-money option for an up-front premium of 14 million (i.e., the fair value of the option's time value component was 14 million). The option hedged the market value of a strategic quantity of natural gas stored by the entity with a view to selling it in 3 years' time (i.e., on 31-Dec-X3). The intrinsic value of the purchased option was designated as hedging instrument in a hedging relationship that started on 1-Jan-20X1. As a result, the option's time value was excluded from the hedging relationship. Suppose that at hedge inception the entity estimated that the time value of an option that replicated the main terms of the hedged item (i.e., the aligned time value) was 12 million. Suppose further that the time values at each relevant date were as portrayed in the following table:

Description	Initial (1-Jan-X1)	31-Dec-X1	31-Dec-X2	Expiry 31-Dec-X3
Actual time value (TV)	14 mn	12 mn	5 mn	0
Period change in actual time value	—	<2 mn>	<7 mn>	<5 mn>
Aligned time value	12 mn	9 mn	7 mn	0
Period change in aligned TV	—	<3 mn>	<2 mn>	<7 mn>
Aligned TV annual amortisation	—	<4 mn>	<4 mn>	<4 mn>
Amount to OCI (in period)	—	1 mn	2 mn	<3 mn>
Additional amount to profit or loss	—	1 mn	<5 mn>	2 mn

The hedged item in this example was a time-period item: it was already in the entity's statement of financial position and the hedged protected its value over a specific period of time (3 years). Because at hedge inception the actual time value was higher than the aligned time value, the amount that was subsequently recognised in OCI was determined only on the basis of the aligned time value. As the hedged item was a time-period related item, the amount recognised in OCI was amortised through profit or loss. In our example, a linear amortisation of the aligned time value at hedge inception (12 million), which was the amount that would be recognised in OCI, over the hedging relationship's 3-year term implied a 4 million (= 12 mn/3) annual amortisation.

On 31-Dec-X1 the change in aligned time value since hedge inception was a 3 million loss (= 9 mn – 12 mn), representing a 1 million (= <3 mn> – <4 mn>) deficit relative to the 4 million annual amortisation amount. As a result, a 1 million gain was recognised in OCI. The period change in actual time value was a 2 million loss (= 12 mn – 14 mn). The difference between (i) such change and (ii) the period change in aligned time value (i.e., 1 mn = <2 mn> – <3 mn>) was recognised in profit or loss, in addition to the amortisation amount. Therefore the total amount recognised in profit or loss on 31-Dec-X1 was a 3 million loss (= <4 mn> + 1 mn).

On 31-Dec-X2 the change in aligned time value during the period was a 2 million loss (= 7 mn – 9 mn), representing a 2 million (= <2 mn> – <4 mn>) deficit relative to the 4 million annual amortisation amount. Therefore, a 2 million gain was recognised in OCI. The change in actual time value during the period was a loss of 7 million (=5 mn – 12 mn). The difference between (i) such change and (ii) the period change in aligned time value (i.e., <5 mn> = <7 mn> – <2 mn>) was recognised in profit or loss, in addition to the amortisation amount. Therefore the total amount recognised in profit or loss on 31-Dec-X2 was a 9 million loss (= <4 mn> + <5 mn>).

On 31-Dec-X3 the change in aligned time value during the period was a 7 million loss (= 0 – 7 mn), representing a 3 million (= <7 mn> – <4 mn>) excess relative to the 4 million annual amortisation amount. Therefore, a 3 million loss was recognised in OCI. The change in actual time value during the period was a loss of 5 million (=0 – 5 mn). The difference between (i) such change and (ii) the period change in aligned time value (i.e., 2 mn = <5 mn> – <7 mn>) was recognised in profit or loss, in addition to the amortisation amount. Therefore the total amount recognised in profit or loss on 31-Dec-X3 was a 2 million loss (= <4 mn> + 2 mn).

Also on 31-Dec-X3, the natural gas was purchased. However, its carrying amount was not adjusted as a result of the option time value.

The following table shows the amounts being recognised in OCI and in profit or loss at each relevant period and the carrying value of the options time value reserve of OCI:

Description	Initial (1-Jan-X1)	31-Dec-X1	31-Dec-X2	Expiry 31-Dec-X3
Period amount to OCI	—	1 mn	2 mn	<3 mn>
Period amount to profit or loss	—	<3 mn>	<9 mn>	<2 mn>
Carrying value of OCI reserve	—	1 mn	3 mn	-0-

Figure 2.18 depicts the effects in the entity's statement of financial position. The option's time value had no effect on the carrying amount of the natural gas. The carrying amount of the time value reserve in OCI ended up being nil. The total amount recognised in profit or loss (14 million) corresponded to the actual time value at the start of the hedging relationship. In theory, through the amortisation such amount would have been gradually recorded in profit or loss over the 3 years. In practice, due to the significantly different behaviour of the actual time value relative to the aligned time value, the recognition in profit or loss notably differed from the targeted 4 million annual losses.

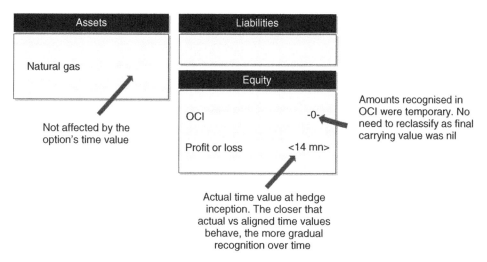

FIGURE 2.18   Effects on statement of financial position of time value recognition.

2.10.7 Example of Option Hedging a Time-Period Related Item – Actual Time Value Lower Than Aligned Time Value

Imagine the situation described in the previous example, but with time values at each relevant date as portrayed in the following table:

Description	Initial (1-Jan-X1)	31-Dec-X1	31-Dec-X2	Expiry 31-Dec-X3
Actual time value (TV)	11 mn	10 mn	4 mn	0
Cumulative change in actual TV	—	<1 mn>	<7 mn>	<11 mn>
Aligned time value	12 mn	9 mn	7 mn	0
Cumulative change in actual TV	—	<3 mn>	<5 mn>	<12 mn>
Lower of cumulative changes in TV	—	<1 mn>	<5 mn>	<11 mn>
Amortisation amount (in period)	—	<3.7 mn>	<3.7 mn>	<3.6 mn>
Cumulative amortisation	—	<3.7 mn>	<7.4 mn>	<11 mn>
Target cumulative amount in OCI	—	2.7 mn	2.4 mn	-0-
Amount already accumulated in OCI	—	-0-	2.7 mn	2.4 mn
Amount to OCI (in period)	—	2.7 mn	<0.3 mn>	<2.4 mn>
Period accounting entries:				
TV hedge reserve in OCI		2.7 mn	<0.3 mn>	<2.4 mn>
TV amortisation in profit or loss		<3.7 mn>	<3.7 mn>	<3.6 mn>
Other fin. gain/loss in profit or loss		-0-	<2.0 mn>	2 mn
Change in actual TV	—	**<1 mn>**	**<6.0 mn>**	**<4 mn>**
Carrying value of OCI reserve	—	2.7 mn	2.4 mn	-0-

Because at hedge inception the actual time value was lower than the aligned time value, the amount that was subsequently recognised in OCI was determined by the lower of the cumulative change of the aligned time value and that of the actual time value. As the hedged item was a time-period related item, the actual time value at the date of designation, to the extent that it related to the hedged item, was amortised through profit or loss. The amortisation was performed on a systematic and rational basis over the period during which the option's intrinsic value could affect profit or loss in accordance with hedge accounting (i.e., 3 years in our case). Any remainder of the change of the actual time value was recognised in profit or loss. The entity decided to amortise the 11 million actual time value at hedge inception on a linear basis over the 3-year hedge horizon, resulting in a 3.7 million annual amortisation amount (3.6 million for the third year).

On 31-Dec-X1 the cumulative change in actual time value since hedge inception was a 1 million loss (= 10 mn – 11 mn). On that date, the cumulative change in aligned time value since hedge inception was a 3 million loss (= 9 mn – 12 mn). The lower of these amounts (ignoring their signs) was a 1 million loss. A <3.7 million> amortisation amount was recognised in profit or loss. The 2.7 million difference between those amounts (<1 million> and <3.7 million>) was recognised in OCI. No additional amounts were recorded in profit or loss.

On 31-Dec-X2 the cumulative change in actual time value since hedge inception was a 7 million loss (= 4 mn – 11 mn). On that date, the cumulative change in aligned time value since hedge inception was a 5 million loss (= 7 mn – 12 mn). The lower of these amounts (ignoring their signs) was a 5 million loss. A <3.7 million> amortisation amount would be recognised in profit or loss on 31-Dec-X2, bringing the cumulative amortisation figure to <7.4 million>. The 2.4 million difference between those amounts (<5 million> and <7.4 million>) became the target amount in OCI (i.e., the carrying value of the time value reserve in OCI after record-ing all the accounting entries on 31-Dec-X2). As already a 2.7 million amount was recognised in OCI as of the previous reporting date, the amount to be recognised in OCI on 31-Dec-X2 was <0.3 million> (= 2.4 mn – 2.7 mn). The change in the actual time value during the period was <6 million>, of which <0.3 million> would be recognised in OCI and the remainder <5.7 million> would be recognised in profit or loss. The <5.7 million> amount in profit or loss was split between a <3.7 million> amortisation of the time value and an additional <2 million> representing the hedge's ineffective amount.

On 31-Dec-X3 the cumulative change in actual time value since hedge inception was an 11 million loss (= 0 – 11 mn). On that date, the cumulative change in aligned time value since hedge inception was a 12 million loss (= 0 – 12 mn). The lower of these amounts (ignoring their signs) was an 11 million loss. A <3.6 million> amortisation amount would be recognised in profit or loss on 31-Dec-X3, bringing the cumulative amortisation figure to <11 million>. The nil difference between those amounts (<11 million> and <11 million>) became the target amount in OCI (i.e., the carrying value of the time value reserve in OCI after recording all the accounting entries on 31-Dec-X3). As already 2.4 million was recognised in OCI as of the pre-vious reporting date, the amount to be recognised in OCI on 31-Dec-X3 was <2.4 million> (= 0 – 2.4 mn). The change in the actual time value during the period was <4 million>, of which <2.4 million> would be recognised in OCI and the remaining <1.6 million> would be recog-nised in profit or loss. The <1.6 million> amount in profit or loss was split between a <3.6 million> amortisation of the time value and an additional 2 million hedge ineffective amount.

2.10.8 Written Options

Whilst a written (i.e., sold) option on its own cannot be designated as hedging instrument in a hedging relationship, IFRS 9 permits a combination of purchased options and written options (e.g., in a tunnel or a collar) to be designated as a hedging instrument provided the following conditions are met:

- no net premium is received either at inception or over the life of the options; and
- it is designated as an offset to a purchased option, including one that is embedded in another financial instrument (e.g., a written call option used to hedge a callable liability).

The no net premium requirement may create illogical situations, as when an entity with a floating rate liability is interested in buying a collar (i.e., the combination of a cap and a floor). The entity initially buys only a cap and at a later date it sells a floor once floor options become more valuable. If at the start of the hedging relationship the premium of the floor was larger than the premium of the bought option, IFRS 9 forbids designating the collar as hedging instrument.

Another illogical situation is a collar (a combination of a purchased cap and a sold floor) that was part of a previous hedging relationship that has been discontinued, and that the entity wants to designate as hedging instrument in a new hedging relationship. The collar was zero cost when it was traded. If interest rates have declined since trade date, it is probable that on the date of designation of the new hedging relationship the floor sold would be worth more than the cap, resulting in a net written option, and thus invalidating the designation of the collar as a hedging instrument.

2.11 FORWARDS AND HEDGE ACCOUNTING

The fair value of a forward contract can be viewed as the combination of the fair value of its **spot component** (or **spot element**) and the fair value of its **forward component** (or **forward element**).

> Forward total value = Spot element value + Forward element value

Under IFRS 9, an entity may choose whether to designate as the hedging instrument a forward in its entirety or just its spot element (i.e., to exclude the forward element from a hedging relationship).

- If the forward element is **included** (i.e., the forward in its entirety is designated as the hedging instrument), the full fair value movement of the forward would be taken into account in the calculation of the effective part of the hedge.
- If the forward element is **excluded**, only the spot element is designated as the hedging instrument). In this case, only changes in the fair value of the spot element (i.e., changes in the fair value of the forward due to movements in the spot rate) would be taken into account in the calculation of the hedge effective part. The changes in the fair value of the forward element would be considered part of the ineffective part. An example of why an entity may only designate the spot element of a forward contract is when a forward contract is used to hedge an existing asset, such as inventory, which is not exposed to forward rate risk but instead is exposed to changes in spot prices.

The method chosen must be consistently applied for similar types of hedges.

Accounting for the Forward Element   When the forward element is excluded from a hedging relationship, the entity has the choice to either:

- recognise in profit or loss the change in the forward element fair value; or
- recognise changes in the forward element fair value in OCI to the extent that it relates to the hedged item, while amortising the initial forward element in profit or loss. The accounting treatment is similar to that for the time value element of options.

The accounting treatment under the second approach depends on whether the actual forward element exceeds the aligned time value and on whether the hedged item is a transaction related or a time-period related item. The accounting treatment is very similar to that of the value of options.

A key difference is that the accounting treatment for the forward element is, unlike the accounting for the time value of options, a choice rather than a requirement.

CHAPTER **3**

Fair Valuation – Credit and Debit Valuation Adjustments

This chapter covers the application of IFRS 13 *Fair Value Measurement* to the valuation of financial instruments and in particular credit and debit valuation adjustments (CVAs and DVAs).

3.1 FAIR VALUATION – OVERVIEW OF IFRS 13

IFRS 13 defines fair value, provides principles-based guidance on how to measure fair value, and requires information about those fair value measurements to be disclosed in the financial statements (see Figure 3.1). IFRS 13 applies when another IFRS requires or permits the measurement or disclosure of fair value (e.g., IFRS 9), or a measure that is based on fair value, except to the following standards:

- share-based payment transactions within the scope of IFRS 2 *Share-Based Payment*;
- leasing transactions within the scope of IAS 17 *Leases*; and
- measurements that have some similarities to fair value but are not fair value, such as net realisable value in IAS 2 *Inventories* or value in use in IAS 36 *Impairment of Assets*.

The disclosures required by this IFRS are not required for the following:

- plan assets measured at fair value in accordance with IAS 19 *Employee Benefits*;
- retirement benefit plan investments measured at fair value in accordance with IAS 26 *Accounting and Reporting by Retirement Benefit Plans*; and
- impaired assets measured at fair value less costs of disposal in accordance with IAS 36.

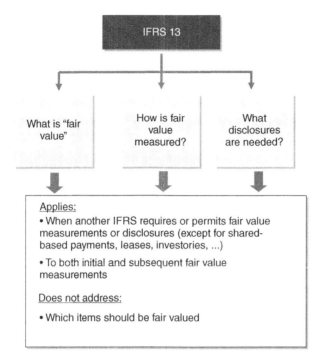

FIGURE 3.1   IFRS 13 summary.

3.1.1 Definition of Fair Value

IFRS 13 defines fair value (see Figure 3.2) as "the price that would be received to sell an asset or paid to transfer a liability in an orderly transaction between market participants at the measurement date". This definition of fair value emphasises that it is a market-based measurement, not an entity-specific measurement. When measuring fair value, an entity uses the assumptions that market participants would use when pricing the asset or liability under current market conditions, including assumptions about risk. As a result, an entity's intention to hold an asset or to settle or otherwise fulfil a liability is not relevant when measuring fair value.

Orderly Transaction   IFRS 13 defines an **orderly transaction** as a transaction that assumes exposure to the market for a period before the measurement date to allow for marketing activities that are usual and customary for transactions involving such assets or liabilities; it is not a forced transaction (e.g., a forced liquidation or a distressed sale). It is generally reasonable to assume that a transaction in which an asset or liability was exchanged between market participants is an orderly transaction. However, there will be circumstances in which an entity needs to assess whether a transaction is orderly, such as when the seller marketed the instrument to a single market participant or when the seller was forced to meet regulatory/legal requirements.

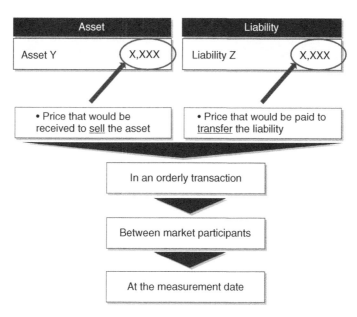

FIGURE 3.2   Fair value definition.

Principal Market versus Most Advantageous Market   Under IFRS 13, management determines fair value based on a hypothetical transaction that would take place in the principal market or, in its absence, the most advantageous market, for the asset or liability (see Figure 3.3). In most cases, these two markets would be the same. In evaluating principal or most advantageous markets, IFRS 13 restricts the eligible markets to those that the entity can access at the measurement date. Although an entity must be able to access the market, it does not need to be able to sell the particular asset or transfer the particular liability on the measurement date to be able to measure fair value on the basis of the price in that market.

The **principal market** is the market with the greatest volume and level of activity for the asset or liability, even if the prices in other markets are more advantageous. In the absence of evidence to the contrary, the market in which an entity normally transacts is presumed to be the principal market or the most advantageous market in the absence of a principal market.

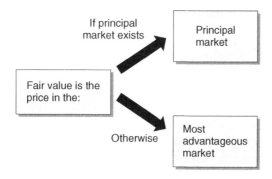

FIGURE 3.3   Market for fair value pricing.

The **most advantageous market** is the market that maximises the amount that would be received to sell the asset or minimises the amount that would be paid to transfer the liability, after taking into account transaction costs and transport costs.

Market Participants   Market participants are buyers and sellers in the principal (or most advantageous) market for the asset or liability that are:

- **Independent**. The transaction counterparties are not related parties as defined in IAS 24 *Related Party Disclosures*. However, this does not preclude related party transaction prices from being used as valuation inputs if there is evidence that the transactions were on market terms.
- **Knowledgeable**. Transaction counterparties have a reasonable understanding about the asset or liability, using all available information, including information that might be obtained through due diligence efforts that are usual and customary.
- **Able** to transact in the asset or liability.
- **Willing** to transact in the asset or liability. Transaction counterparties are motivated but not forced or otherwise compelled to transact.

IFRS 13 explains that a fair value measurement requires an entity to determine the following:

- The particular asset or liability being measured.
- For a non-financial asset, the highest and best use of the asset and whether the asset is used in combination with other assets or on a stand-alone basis.
- The market in which an orderly transaction would take place for the asset or liability.
- The appropriate valuation technique(s) to use when measuring fair value. The valuation technique(s) used should maximise the use of relevant observable inputs and minimise unobservable inputs. Those inputs should be consistent with the inputs a market participant would use when pricing the asset or liability.

3.1.2 Fair Value Hierarchy

To increase consistency and comparability in fair value measurements and related disclosures, IFRS establishes a fair value hierarchy. IFRS 13 carries over the three-level fair value hierarchy disclosures from IFRS 7, requiring an entity to distinguish between financial asset and financial liability fair values based on how observable the inputs to the fair value measurement are. The hierarchy categorises the inputs used in valuation techniques into three levels: level 1, level 2 and level 3. A fair value measurement is categorised within the hierarchy based on the lowest-level input that has a significant effect on the measure.

3.1.3 Level 1 Financial Instruments

If an entity holds a position in a single asset or liability and the asset or liability is traded in an **active** market for **identical** assets or liabilities that the entity can access at the measurement date, the fair value of the asset or liability is measured within **level 1**.

A quoted market price in an active market provides the most reliable evidence of fair value and is used without adjustment to measure fair value whenever available, with limited exceptions.

Level 1 financial instruments include high-liquidity government bonds and derivative, equity and cash products traded on high-liquidity exchanges.

The fair value is measured (see Figure 3.4) as the product of (i) the quoted price for the individual asset or liability and (ii) the quantity held by the entity, even if the market's normal daily trading volume is not sufficient to absorb the quantity held and placing orders to buy/sell the position in a single transaction might affect the quoted price.

FIGURE 3.4   Fair valuation of level 1 derivatives.

3.1.4 Level 2 Financial Instruments

Level 2 financial instruments are valued with valuation techniques where **all significant** inputs into the valuation are based on **observable market data**, or where the fair value can be determined by reference to similar instruments trading in active markets.

Level 2 inputs include:

- Quoted prices for similar assets or liabilities in active markets.
- Quoted prices for identical or similar assets or liabilities in markets that are not active. Instruments include, for example, poorly liquid equities.
- Inputs other than quoted prices that are observable for the asset or liability, for example interest rates and yield curves observable at commonly quoted intervals, implied volatilities and credit spreads. Instruments include most interest rate swaps, FX forwards, cross-currency swaps, FX and interest rate options, and market quoted credit default swaps (CDSs).

Level 2 and level 3 financial derivatives are valued using a valuation model. The output of a valuation model is always an estimate or approximation of a fair value that cannot be measured with complete certainty. As a result, valuations are adjusted (see Figure 3.5), where appropriate, to reflect close-out costs, credit exposure, model-driven valuation uncertainty, trading restrictions and other factors, when such factors would be considered by market participants in measuring fair value.

In the case of derivatives, entities typically start by calculating a mid-market fair valuation (i.e., a valuation using mid-market rate and/or price curves) that assumes no counterparty credit risk, and then the entity applies different adjustments to this valuation. In the case of a level 2 derivative recognised as an asset (see Figure 3.6) these adjustments reduce the mid-market fair value of the derivative by deducting other elements that would be taken into account by market participants were the entity to sell the derivative in the market (i.e., its exit price). These adjustments typically include:

FIGURE 3.5   Calculation of fair value of derivatives.

- mid-market to bid, or to offer, adjustment;
- non-performance adjustment (CVA or DVA); and
- funding value adjustment (FVA).

In the case of a level 2 liability derivative, the adjustment to the credit risk-free mid-market fair valuation would commonly include the elements shown in Figure 3.7. The non-performance adjustment is termed "debit valuation adjustment", and reduces the absolute value of the liability. Other adjustments would increase the value of the liability.

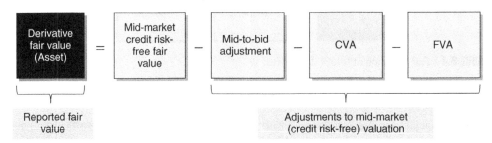

FIGURE 3.6   Fair valuation of level 2 (asset) derivatives.

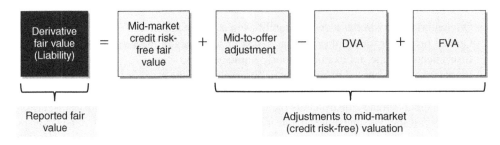

FIGURE 3.7   Fair valuation of level 2 (liability) derivatives.

3.1.5 Level 3 Financial Instruments

Financial instruments are classified as level 3 if their valuation incorporates significant inputs that are not based on observable market data (unobservable inputs). A valuation input is considered observable if it can be directly observed from transactions in an active market, or if there is compelling external evidence demonstrating an executable exit price. In other words, the fair valuation of the financial asset/liability requires the estimation of at least one input variable that has a **significant** impact on the valuation, because such variable price/rate is **unobservable** in the market. IFRS 13 does not specify when an input is deemed to be significant, but market practice assumes that an input variable is significant if it contributes more than 10% to the valuation of a financial instrument. An entity develops unobservable inputs using the best information available in the circumstances, which might include the entity's own data, taking into account all information about market participant assumptions that is reasonably available.

Level 3 financial instruments typically include correlation-based instruments (e.g., basket and spread options) for which the underlying correlation is unobservable, illiquid bonds and illiquid loans, and CDSs for which credit spreads are unobservable. Interest swaps, cross-currency swaps, inflation swaps, FX forwards and options with very long-dated maturities may also be level 3 financial instruments.

Similarly to level 2 derivatives, the fair value of a level 3 asset derivative is calculated by adjusting its credit risk-free mid-market fair valuation, but adding an additional adjusting element, as shown in Figure 3.8 for an asset derivative. This element addresses the inherent valuation uncertainty associated with the forecasting process, primarily uncertainty in estimating unobservable valuation input parameters and uncertainty in the output provided by the valuation model.

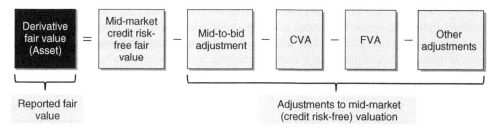

FIGURE 3.8   Fair valuation of level 3 (asset) derivatives.

3.1.6 Mid-to-Bid and Mid-to-Offer Adjustments

As a principle of IFRS 13, where an asset or a liability measured at fair value has a bid and an ask price, the entity must use the price within the bid–ask spread that is most representative of fair value. Mid-market pricing or other pricing conventions can be used as a practical expedient for fair value measurements within a bid–ask spread if these conventions do not contravene the principle.

Regarding level 2 and level 3 derivatives, the use of bid prices for long positions and ask prices for short positions is generally required because this is usually more representative of fair value than the practical expedient of using mid-market prices.

Any premium or discount applied must be consistent with the characteristics of the derivative asset or liability. However, no block discounts (i.e., a downward adjustment to a quoted price that would occur if a market participant were to sell a large holding of derivatives in one or a few transactions) are applied.

Instruments that are measured as part of a portfolio of combined long and short derivative positions are valued at mid-market levels to ensure consistent valuation of the long and short component risks. A valuation adjustment is then made to the overall net long or short exposure to move the fair value to bid or offer as appropriate, reflecting current levels of market liquidity. The bid–offer spreads used in the calculation of the valuation adjustment are obtained from market and broker sources.

An operational complexity of this approach is to allocate the adjustment to the individual derivative positions in the portfolio. IFRS 13 requires that an entity should allocate a portfolio-level adjustment to the individual financial assets and liabilities in the portfolio on a reasonable and consistent basis using a methodology appropriate in the circumstances.

3.1.7 Credit and Debit Valuation Adjustment

An important element of IFRS 9 is the requirement, when determining the fair value of a financial derivative, to include non-performance risk (i.e. the risk that the counterparty to the financial derivative or the entity will default before the maturity/expiration of the transaction and will be unable to meet all contractual payments, thereby resulting in a loss for the entity or the counterparty).

Suppose that an entity bought a 6-month option and paid an up-front premium. The option was, therefore, recognised as an asset. The entity was exposed to the credit risk of the counterparty to the option during the option's 6-month term. When fair valuing the option, the entity was required to adjust the option's fair value to incorporate the risk that the counterparty to the option could default before its expiration. This adjustment is referred to as **credit valuation adjustment**, and it is based on the rationale that a market participant would include it when determining the price it would pay to acquire the option. This valuation adjustment for credit reflects the estimated fair value of protection required to hedge the counterparty credit risk embedded in such instrument.

Conversely, let us assume that an entity sold a 6-month option and received an up-front premium. The option would be recognised as a liability. The counterparty to the option would be exposed to the credit risk of the entity during the next 6 months. When fair valuing the option, the entity would be required to adjust the option's fair value to incorporate the risk that the entity will default before its expiration. This adjustment is referred to as **debit valuation adjustment**.

IFRS 9 does not provide guidance on how CVA or DVA is to be calculated beyond requiring that the resulting fair value must reflect the credit quality of the instrument. Quantifying CVAs is a complex exercise due to the substantial number of assumptions involved and the interaction among these assumptions. There are a variety of ways to determine CVA, and judgement is required to assess the appropriateness of the method used.

3.1.8 Funding Valuation Adjustment

Imagine an uncollateralised swap between ABC (our entity) and Megabank in which the fair value (excluding FVA) was a EUR 10 million unrealised loss from ABC's perspective (i.e., the derivative was recognised in ABC's statement of financial position as a liability). As the derivatives agreement between ABC and Megabank was uncollateralised, ABC was not required to post any collateral to reduce Megabank's credit exposure to ABC. As a result, were ABC to become insolvent, Megabank would suffer a EUR 10 million loss.

Imagine further that, in turn, Megabank hedged its market risk exposure by entering into another derivative that mirrored the terms of our derivative with another bank (Hedgebank) with which a cash collateral agreement was in place (see Figure 3.9). As a result, Megabank had to post EUR 10 million in cash collateral to mitigate Hedgebank's exposure to Megabank, incurring a funding cost stemming from the financing of such cash collateral.

Alternatively, had the derivative between ABC and Megabank showed a EUR 10 million unrealised gain, Hedgebank would have posted EUR 10 million cash collateral with Megabank. Megabank would have placed that cash, earning a yield or reducing its funding needs.

Therefore, when Megabank quoted the derivative pricing to ABC on trade date, it should have taken into account the potential funding costs stemming from future potential favourable movements (from Megabank's perspective) in the derivative's fair value. Additionally, Megabank should have incorporated in the pricing the potential funding benefits stemming from future potential unfavourable movements in the derivative's fair value. The net adjustment is what is termed a **funding valuation adjustment**.

Thus, FVA incorporates the cost or benefit of unsecured funding into the fair valuation of a derivative to ensure an accurate exit price.

FIGURE 3.9   Derivative hedge process.

3.1.9 Model Uncertainty Adjustment

Uncertainties associated with the use of model-based valuations are incorporated into the measurement of fair value through the use of model reserves. These reserves reflect the amounts that an entity estimates should be deducted from valuations produced directly by models to incorporate uncertainties in the relevant modelling assumptions, in the model and market inputs used, or in the calibration of the model output to adjust for known model deficiencies. Model valuation adjustments are dependent on the size of portfolio, complexity of the model, whether the model is market standard and to what extent it incorporates all known risk factors. In arriving at these estimates, an entity considers a range of market practices, including how it believes market participants would assess these uncertainties. Model reserves should be reassessed periodically in light of information from market transactions, consensus pricing services and other relevant sources.

3.1.10 Day 1 Profit (or Loss)

For new transactions resulting in a financial derivative classified as level 2 or level 3, the financial instrument is initially recognised at the transaction price. Suppose that an option was bought from a client in exchange for the payment of an up-front premium of EUR 11 million. On the trading day the option was revalued using the entity's valuation model for options of that type. Suppose that the valuation indicated that the option was worth EUR 13 million. The EUR 2 million difference between the transaction price and the valuation price represented the transaction's initial profit. **Initial gains or losses** result from the difference between the model valuation and the initial transaction price. IFRS 9 permits gains or losses to be recognised at inception only when fair value is evidenced by observable market data (i.e., level 1 and level 2 instruments). Thus, entities are required to defer initial gains and losses for financial instruments with fair values that are based on significant unobservable inputs (i.e., level 3 instruments). In our example, the recognition of the transaction's initial profit was as follows (see Figure 3.9):

- For a derivative classified as a **level 1** or **level 2** instrument, the initial profit was recognised immediately in profit or loss. In this case, the entity recognised a EUR 2 million gain in profit or loss at the end of trade date and, in theory, the counterparty to the option recognised a EUR 2 million loss.
- For a derivative classified as a **level 3** instrument, the initial profit was *not* recognised, but rather deferred. The initial profit for level 3 derivatives is termed **day 1 profit**. The counterparty to the derivative would recognise a day 1 loss.

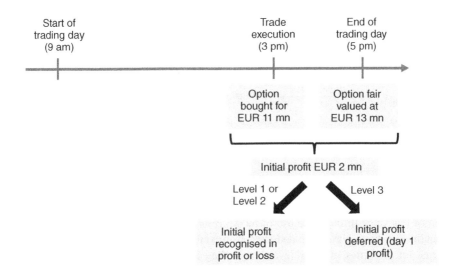

FIGURE 3.9   Derivative initial profit recognition.

In the case of assets, deferred day 1 profit is amortised (typically on a straight-line basis) over the term of the transaction and recognised as a liability. The amounts deferred may subsequently be recognised to the extent that factors change in such a way that the input is now observable to the market participants setting the price, or if the financial instrument in question is closed out.

3.2 CASE STUDY – CREDIT VALUATION ADJUSTMENT OF AN INTEREST RATE SWAP

In order to highlight the issues regarding the calculation of CVA/DVA, in this section the non-performance adjustment to fair value in an interest rate swap is calculated. Determining the CVA or DVA for a derivative, such as an interest rate swap, can be particularly challenging as on the same instrument there could be both future cash inflows and cash outflows, flows that may change during its life.

3.2.1 Simple One-Period Model of Default

A simple example of the calculation of CVAs is a cash flow – an "exposure at default" (EAD) – of 100 that is expected to be received in 1 year. Denote the probability that the counterparty will default over the next year by PD. If the counterparty does default, let us assume that it pays a recovery rate R, which is a fixed percentage of the cash flow amount. We further assume that this recovery is paid at the cash flow date. The expected cash flow amount can be estimated using a simple single-period binomial tree, as shown in Figure 3.10, where the credit adjusted value of the cash flow, CFAdjusted, is the expected payoff discounted off the risk-free curve. This gives:

$$CF_{Adjusted} = \underbrace{\frac{1}{1+r}}_{\substack{\text{Discount} \\ \text{factor}}} \times [\underbrace{PD \times 100 \times R}_{\substack{\text{Recovered} \\ \text{amount} \\ \text{upon default}}} + \underbrace{(1-PD) \times 100}_{\substack{\text{Amount if no} \\ \text{default}}}]$$

If the 1-year probability of default is 0.75%, the recovery rate R is assumed to be 60%, and the 1-year risk-free rate r is 5%, the CVA value of the cash flow is given by:

$$CFAdjusted = \frac{1}{1.05} \times [0.0075 \times 100 \times 0.60 + (1-0.0075) \times 100]$$

$$= 94.9524$$

Without the CVA, the present value of the cash flow would be:

$$CFUnadjusted = \frac{1}{1.05} \times 100 = 95.2381$$

Thus, the CVA is 0.2857 (= 95.2381 – 94.9524). This amount may alternatively be calculated as follows:

$$CVA\ Adjustment = Present\ value\ [EAD \times PD \times (1 \quad R)] = \frac{1}{1+5\%}[100 \times 0.0075\% \times 1 - 0.60\%] = 0.2857$$

The factor $1 - R$ is referred to as **loss given default** (LGD). Therefore, the CVA may be formulated as well as follows:

$$CVA\ Adjustment = Present\ value\ [EAD \times PD \times LGD] = \frac{1}{1+5\%}[100 \times 0.0075\% \times 0.40\%] = 0.2857$$

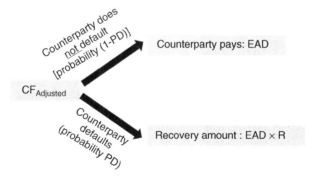

FIGURE 3.10   Simple one-period model of default.

3.2.2 Working Example of CVA in a Swap

Suppose that on 1 July 20X0 ABC issued a EUR 100 million 5-year floating rate debt linked to 6-month Euribor and, in order to fix the interest expense, entered into a 5-year swap with Megabank (on an uncollateralised basis) in which on a semiannual basis it paid a fixed rate of 3.20% and received 6-month Euribor on a EUR 100 million notional, as follows:

Interest rate swap terms	
Trade date	1 July 20X0
Counterparties	ABC and Megabank
Notional	EUR 100 million
Maturity	30 June 20X5
ABC pays	3.20%, semiannually, 30/360 basis
ABC receives	6-month Euribor, semiannually, actual/360 basis
Interest periods	Semiannually

On 1 July 20X3 (i.e., 2 years before maturity) ABC revalued the swap. On that date, the 2-year mid-market swap rate was 3.41% and ABC estimated based on market quotes that the bid-to-mid spread would be 1 basis point (i.e., 0.01%), resulting in a 2-year bid swap rate of 3.40%. The credit risk-free valuation, before CVA and FVA, was EUR 390,000, calculated as follows:

Settlement date	Euribor 6M rate	Swap fixed rate	Expected settlement amount	Discount factor	PV of expected settlement
31-Dec-X3	2%	3.20%	<589,000> *(1)*	0.9900 *(2)*	<583,000> *(3)*
30-Jun-X4	3%	3.20%	<75,000>	0.9751 *(4)*	<73,000>
31-Dec-X4	4%	3.20%	422,000	0.9558	403,000
30-Jun-X5	4.5%	3.20%	688,000	0.9344	643,000
				Total	**390,000**

Notes:

(1) <589,000> = 100 mn × (2% × 182 days/360 − 3.20% × 182 days/360)
(2) 0.9900 = 1/(1 + 2% × 182 days/360)
(3) <583,000> = <589,000> × 0.9900
(4) 0.9751 = 0.9900 × [1/(1 + 3% × 183 days/360)]

The expected first two negative settlement amounts (<589,000> and <75,000>) meant that ABC was expected to pay those amounts at their settlement date (31-Dec-X3 and 30-Jun-X4, respectively), and as a result, that Megabank would be exposed to ABC's credit risk (see Figure 3.11).

The positive expected last two settlement amounts (422,000 and 688,000) meant that ABC was supposed to receive those amounts at their settlement date (31-Dec-X4 and 30-Jun-X5, respectively), and as a result, that ABC would be exposed to Megabank's credit risk (see Figure 3.11).

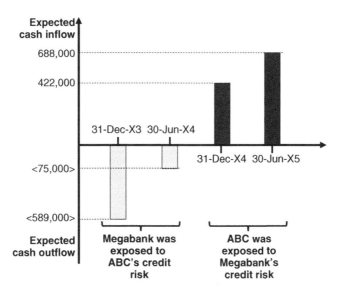

FIGURE 3.11   Swap expected settlement amounts.

The first step in calculating the DVA/CVA is to define a time grid (i.e., to divide into time buckets the period in which the derivative exposes either party to credit risk). In our example, the swap exposed either party until its maturity on 30 June 20X5. ABC decided to divide the term into four semiannual periods, coinciding with the swap interest periods (e.g., the first period from 1 July 20X3 to 31 December 20X3).

The second step encompassed calculating the present value (PV) of the EAD at each time bucket. The EAD represented the credit risk-free valuation of the swap at a certain point of time, or in other words, the exposure were one of the two counterparties to default at such moment. One "simple" way is to assume that rates will behave as expected by the market. In our case, the exposures during each time bucket had an upward sloping profile during the first three buckets (see Figure 3.12). The PV of the EAD for a bucket was calculated as the average of the bucket's start and end exposures, as shown in the following table:

Bucket	Start exposure	End exposure	PV EAD (average)
1	390,000	393,000	392,000
2	982,000	998,000	990,000
3	1,073,000	1,096,000	1,085,000
4	674,000	688,000	681,000

The start exposure at bucket 1 was the credit risk-free valuation as of 1 July 20X3, or 390,000. The end exposure corresponding to bucket 1 was the derivative's credit risk-free valuation as of 31 December 20X3 just prior to the <589,000> settlement amount:

Settlement date	Euribor 6M rate	Discount factor	Expected settlement amount	PV of expected settlement
31-Dec-X3		1	<589,000>	<589,000>
30-Jun-X4	3%	0.9850 *(1)*	<75,000>	<74,000> *(2)*
31-Dec-X4	4%	0.9655	422,000	407,000
30-Jun-X5	4.5%	0.9439	688,000	649,000
			Total	**393,000**

Notes:

        (1) 0.9850 = 1/(1 + 3% × 183 days/360)

        (2) <74,000> = <75,000> × 0.9850

The exposure at the start of bucket 2 was 982,000 (= 393,000 – (–589,000)) calculated as (i) the exposure at the end of bucket 1 minus (ii) <589,000>. The end exposure corresponding to bucket 2 was the credit risk-free valuation as of 31 December 20X4 just prior to the <75,000> settlement amount, as shown in the next table:

Settlement date	Euribor 6M rate	Discount factor	Expected settlement amount	PV of expected settlement
30-Jun-X4		1	<75,000>	<75,000>
31-Dec-X4	4%	0.9802 *(1)*	422,000	414,000 *(2)*
30-Jun-X5	4.5%	0.9583	688,000	659,000
			Total	**998,000**

Notes:

        (1) 0.9802 = 1/(1 + 4% × 182 days/360)

        (2) 414,000 = 422,000 × 0.9802

The exposures at buckets 3 and 4 were calculated similarly and have been omitted to avoid excessive repetition.

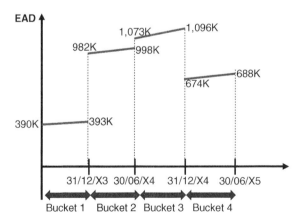

FIGURE 3.12 Exposures at default at each time bucket.

The third step encompassed calculating the probability of default. As illustrated in Figure 3.12, all the EADs were positive (i.e., ABC was exposed to Megabank's credit risk) and as a result each EAD was subject to the PD of Megabank.

Suppose that CDSs on Megabank were trading at 30, 40, 45 and 50 basis points for 6-, 12-, 18- and 24-month protection tenors, respectively. The probability of default from today until the settlement date can be approximated using the following expression:

$$\text{Cumulative PD} = 1 - \exp\left(\frac{-\text{CDS} \times \text{Maturity}}{\text{LGD}}\right)$$

where CDS is the credit default swap spread to obtain protection on the name that creates the credit exposure, Maturity is the time in years to the cash flow, and LGD is the loss given default. ABC assumed that Megabank's LGD was 40%.

The expression above provides the probability of default from today to the end date of the bucket (i.e., the cumulative PD). The PD for a specific time bucket (i.e., the probability of default from the start date to the end date of the bucket) is calculated as (i) the cumulative PD for the bucket minus (ii) the cumulative PD for the previous bucket, as follows:

Bucket	CDS	Maturity	LGD	Cumulative PD	PD
1	0.30%	0.5	40%	0.37%	0.37%
2	0.40%	1	40%	1.00%	0.63%
3	0.45%	1.5	40%	1.67% *(1)*	0.67% *(2)*
4	0.50%	2	40%	2.47%	0.80%

Notes:
> *(1)* 1.67% = 1 – exp(–0.45% × 1.5/40%)
> *(2)* 0.67% = 1.67% – 1.00%

Based on the method above, the CVA for a certain EAD can be calculated as the present value of the expected loss amount at the time of default:

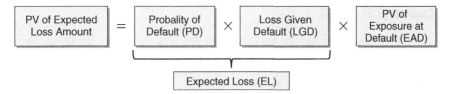

The expected loss amount is calculated by multiplying the probability of default, the loss given default and the present value of the exposure at default at the time of default:

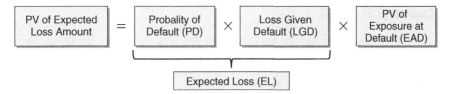

Bucket	PD	LGD	PV of EAD	PV of Expected Loss
1	0.37%	40%	392,000	1,000
2	0.63%	40%	990,000	2,000
3	0.67%	40%	1,085,000	3,000
4	0.80%	40%	681,000	2,000
			Total	8,000

Therefore the CVA was EUR 8,000, representing just 2% of the EUR 390,000 credit risk-free valuation.

3.2.3 Debit Valuation Adjustments

Similarly to derivatives on the asset side, when determining the fair value of a derivative on the liability side, IFRS 9 requires an adjustment to take into account the credit risk associated to the derivative. This adjustment is referred to as **debit valuation adjustment**. It represents the theoretical cost to counterparties of hedging, or the credit risk reserve that a counterparty could reasonably be expected to hold, against their credit risk exposure to the entity.

As noted above, the DVA reduces the value of a liability derivative (see Figure 3.13). The requisite of recognising a "lower loss" when an entity's own creditworthiness deteriorates is arguably somewhat fictitious, especially as it would be difficult to realise such a profit when closing out or transferring the derivative. Moreover, this requirement may lead to significant volatility in profit or loss in periods of credit market turmoil.

The mechanics of calculating DVAs are identical to those of CVAs, but incorporating the PD of the entity. The counterparty to the derivative would hold a financial asset and would be including a CVA that takes into account the credit risk of the entity.

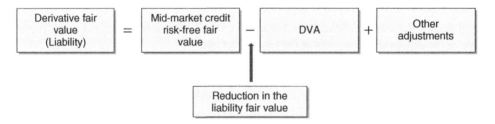

FIGURE 3.13   DVA effect on a liability derivative fair value.

3.2.4 Combining CVA and DVA

In our previous example, all EADs were positive, meaning that it was expected that, at all times during the life of the swap, ABC was exposed to Megabank's credit risk, while Megabank was not expected to be exposed to ABC's credit risk. There could be, however, situations in which positive EADs (subject to the PD of Megabank) and negative EADs (subject to the PD of ABC) are both present.

For example, let us imagine an EAD profile (as shown in Figure 3.14) in which the expected EADs (in present value terms) for buckets 1 and 2 were negative amounts

(<300,000> and <230,000>, respectively). The first time bucket amount meant that, were ABC to default during the period corresponding to such time bucket, Megabank would be exposed to 300,000 being owed by ABC. Megabank's expected loss would be calculated incorporating ABC's probability of defaulting during time bucket 1 and ABC's loss given default, as $300,000 \times PD_{ABC} \times LGD_{ABC}$. This amount would represent a DVA.

Conversely, imagine the expected EADs (in present value terms) for buckets 3 and 4 were positive amounts (150,000 and 220,000, respectively). The third time bucket amount meant that, were Megabank to default during the period corresponding to such time bucket, ABC would be exposed to 150,000 being owed by Megabank. ABC's expected loss would be calculated as $150,000 \times PD_{Megabank} \times LGD_{Megabank}$, $PD_{Megabank}$ being Megabank's PD during the period corresponding to time bucket 3 and $LGD_{Megabank}$ being Megabank's LGD in such a situation. This amount would represent a CVA.

Therefore, the CVA/DVA calculation of the fair value of the derivative would be the following sum (the DVAs are likely to exceed the CVAs):

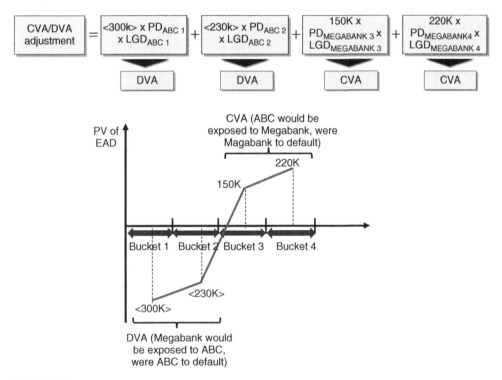

FIGURE 3.14   ABC's PV EAD profile.

3.2.5 Calculating CVA and DVA Using Monte Carlo Simulation

The previous example was relatively straightforward, as it assumed that:

- only one derivative was outstanding between ABC and Megabank;
- the derivative was uncollateralised;
- interest rates going forward will behave as expected by the market on valuation date; and
- both ABC and Megabank had observable CDS spreads.

Derivative Netting   In order to reduce the credit risk resulting from over-the-counter (OTC) derivative transactions, where OTC clearing is not available, entities may execute netting agreements. The aim of these agreements is that market gains and losses on derivative transactions entered into with a given counterparty are offset against one another. Thus, if either party defaults, the settlement figure is a single net amount, rather than a large number of positive and negative amounts relating to the individual transactions entered into with that counterparty.

The most common derivative netting agreement is the master agreement for derivatives published by the International Swaps and Derivatives Association (ISDA). A master agreement allows the netting of rights and obligations arising under derivative transactions that have been entered into under such a master agreement upon the entity's or the counterparty's default, resulting in a single net claim owed by or to the counterparty ("close-out netting").

The example provided above assumed that only one derivative existed between ABC and Megabank. It is relatively common that several derivatives are outstanding, formalised under a common ISDA agreement between the entity and the bank. In this situation, the calculation of the EAD at each time bucket has to incorporate all the derivatives that are subject to the same legal agreement.

Collateralisation   Entities often enter into collateral agreements with their banking counterparties in order to further reduce their derivatives position credit risk. Under a collateral agreement one party deposits certain financial instruments (the **collateral**) with the other party to secure, or reduce the counterparty credit risk arising from, portfolios of credit transactions between the two. The aim, as in netting, is to reduce counterparty risk by recovering all or part of the gains (the credit granted to the counterparty) generated by the transaction's mark-to-market at any given time. Depending on the direction of the flow of collateral, the agreement is either bilateral or unilateral. In a bilateral agreement, which is the most common, both parties can call for collateral. Alternatively, in a unilateral agreement only one of the two parties has the right to call. The collateral agreement must give the entity (and the counterparty in a bilateral agreement) the power to realise any collateral placed with it in the event of the failure of the counterparty.

Transactions subject to collateral agreements are marked to market periodically (usually daily) and the parameters agreed in the collateral agreement are applied, giving an amount of collateral (commonly cash) to be called from, returned to, or pledged to the counterparty.

The most common derivatives collateral agreement is the Credit Support Annex (CSA) to a master agreement for derivatives published by the ISDA. A CSA also provides for the right to terminate the related derivative transactions upon the counterparty's failure to honour a margin call, according to a standard procedure laid out in the CSA.

In our previous example there was no collateralisation of the swap. Were a CSA in place between ABC and Megabank, the overall EAD would be greatly reduced as collateral is posted to offset the swap's EAD.

Simulation of the EAD Profile – Monte Carlo Simulation Method   In our previous example, the EAD calculation for each time bucket assumed that interest rates during the life of the derivative will perform as expected on the valuation date. However, in practice it is unlikely that realised interest rates move exactly as expected.

Entities with significant resources may develop processes to calculate CVA/DVA in a more accurate manner. These entities are typically banks or corporates that either developed their own models or bought simulation packages from third party vendors. The process of calculating CVA/DVA can be divided into five steps (see Figure 3.15).

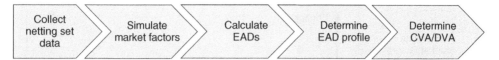

FIGURE 3.15 CVA/DVA calculation steps.

First Step: Collecting Netting Set Data

In a first step, the relevant data relating to a **netting set** is collected (see Figure 3.16). A netting set is a group of derivatives, and their related collateral, with a single counterparty to which the entity is credit exposed on a net basis from a legal perspective. In our previous example, all the outstanding derivatives and the collateral posted/received to secure these derivatives under the same ISDA agreement between ABC and Megabank constituted a netting set.

Also in this first step, all the market variables (commonly referred to as **market factors**) that affect the fair valuation of the derivatives in the netting set are identified. In our previous example, the swap was linked to the 6-month Euribor rate. In the netting set other market factors may be identified. Imagine that another swap in the netting set was linked to USD Libor 3-month rate. That second swap would bring two other market factors: the USD Libor 3-month rate and the EUR–USD FX rate.

Finally, the period from the valuation date until the maturity of the last derivative in the netting set is divided into time buckets (commonly referred to as the **time grid**). It is relatively common to divide the time period into quarterly time buckets.

FIGURE 3.16 CVA/DVA calculation: first step.

Second Step: Simulating Market Factors

In a second step, the market factors identified in the previous step are simulated: a large number of paths of future behaviour of the market factors are generated along the time grid. The simulation is often generated using a Monte Carlo simulation method which can simulate forward in time thousands of potential paths of movements of a market factor, based on a suitably chosen stochastic process for that market factor. This is the most complex part of the simulation process, especially when several market factors affect the netting set. The parameters of this process are calibrated based on historical market data (several years of history). The latest daily close of market values form the starting point of the simulation, and their volatilities and assumed correlations are added as inputs as well.

In our previous example, there was only a market factor (the Euribor 6-month rate). ABC would have also incorporated the term structure of volatilities of this interest rate using market cap and floor volatility information. The starting point of the Euribor 6-month rate would be its market level on valuation date (2% in our case). The result would be a large number of paths of future movement of the Euribor 6-month rate, as illustrated in Figure 3.17.

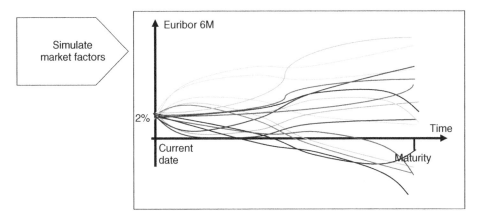

FIGURE 3.17 CVA/DVA calculation: second step.

Third Step: Calculating Exposure at Default Profile
In a third step, the netting set's exposure at default profile is determined. In a first task within the third step, the credit risk-free fair value – or mark-to-market (MtM) – of each derivative in the netting set is calculated for each time bucket across each path of market factors. Each MtM represents the claim owed by (a positive MtM) or to (a negative MtM) the counterparty, were one of the two parties to the derivative default. The MtM calculation takes into account credit mitigants such as collateral and break clauses. In our case, each path of Euribor 6-month rates generated a path of MtMs of the swap, each MtM path starting at EUR 390,000 and ending at nil (see Figure 3.18).

The next task within the third step is to divide the paths of MtMs into two groups: a first group of positive MtMs and a second group of negative MtMs (see Figure 3.19). A positive MtM means that the entity is exposed to the counterparty's credit risk. Conversely, a negative MtM means that the counterparty is exposed to the entity's credit risk.

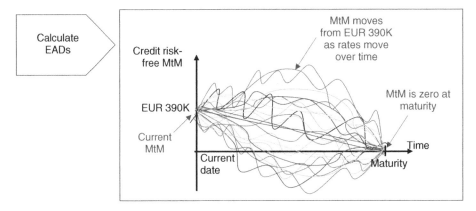

FIGURE 3.18 CVA/DVA calculation: third step, first task.

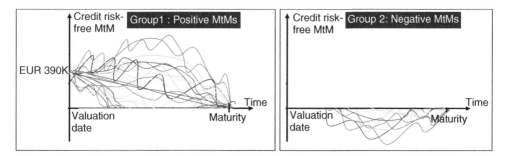

FIGURE 3.19 CVA/DVA calculation: third step, second task.

The third task within the third step is, for each group, to determine the EAD at each time bucket. A time bucket's EAD is calculated as the arithmetic average of the group's MtMs at such time bucket, as illustrated in Figure 3.20 for the group encompassing positive MtMs. The end outcome of the third step is the EAD profile for each group, as illustrated in Figure 3.21.

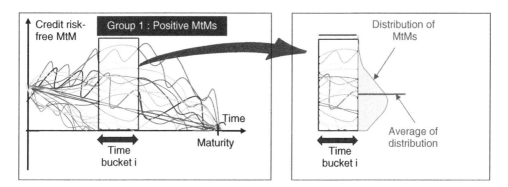

FIGURE 3.20 CVA/DVA calculation: third step, third task.

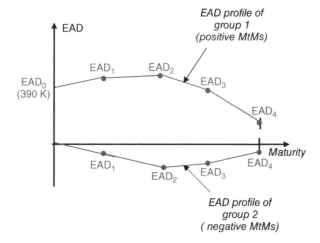

FIGURE 3.21 CVA/DVA calculation: third step, final outcome.

Fourth Step: Calculating the CVA/DVA

In a fourth step, the probability of default of the counterparty and the entity at each time bucket is calculated. The basis for the calculation of the PD is the CDS of the entity (or the counterparty's CDS as the case may be). If no CDS is trading in the market, PDs are calculated from other alternative sources. Figure 3.22 shows my own pecking order regarding the use of alternative sources when calculating the entity's (or the counterparty's) PDs:

- yields may be available for publicly traded bonds issued by the entity;
- CDSs may be available for competitors with a financial situation (i.e., rating) similar to that of the entity;
- CDSs may be available for an index of companies in the entity's industry, region and rating;
- PDs may be available for the entity's external ratings from the reports published by the rating agencies (e.g., Moody's); or
- the entity's banks may have rated the entity using an internal rating system for which an equivalent external rating may be inferred. The PD would be calculated using the method mentioned in Section 3.2.2.

Additionally, a loss given default is estimated for each time bucket for both the entity and the counterparty. Normally a constant LGD is assumed across all time buckets.

Next, the CVA/DVA is calculated as the sum of CVA and DVA. Because the amounts have opposite signs, there is a partial (or total) offset between them:

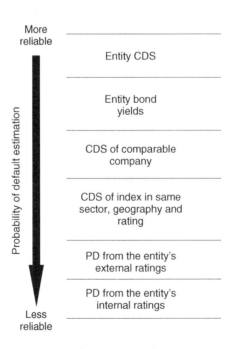

FIGURE 3.22   My own pecking order regarding PD calculation sources.

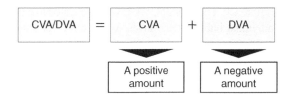

The CVA would be calculated as the sum of the expected loss at each time bucket of group 1. The expected loss corresponding to a time bucket would be determined by multiplying for each time bucket (i) the present value of the EAD, (ii) the counterparty's PD and (iii) the counterparty's LGD:

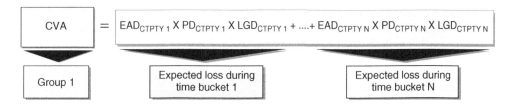

The DVA results in a negative amount, reducing the effect of the CVA. Similarly to the CVA calculation, the DVA would be calculated taking into account the present value of the EAD, the entity's PDs and LGDs:

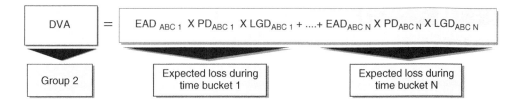

The overall CVA/DVA has been calculated for the portfolio of derivatives being part of the netting set. The final step in this process is to allocate the resulting CVA/DVA to the derivatives being part of the netting set.

When the derivative instruments are presented in a single line in the statement of financial position (e.g. because they are all assets or all liabilities or both but presented net) and they are not designated separately in a hedging relationship, disaggregating the single adjustment may not be necessary. However, in all other cases it will be necessary to allocate the net portfolio adjustment to the individual derivatives in the netting set. Whilst neither IFRS 13 nor IFRS 9 provides guidance on how to perform the allocation, IFRS 13 requires this allocation to be done on a reasonable and consistent basis. Two approaches are commonly used:

■ A relative fair value approach. The overall CVA/DVA is allocated to either the individual asset derivatives or the individual liability derivatives. When the CVA amount exceeds the DVA amount, resulting in a positive amount, the overall CVA/DVA is referred to as just CVA and it is allocated only to individual asset derivatives based on the relative credit risk-free fair value of each asset derivative. Thus, in that case, liability derivatives would not be allocated any CVA. Conversely, when the DVA amount exceeds the CVA amount, resulting in a negative amount, the overall CVA/DVA is referred to as just DVA and it is allocated only to individual liability derivatives based on the relative credit risk-free fair value of each liability derivative. Figure 3.23 illustrates how a 54,000 CVA (a positive overall CVA/DVA amount) is allocated among three asset derivatives in a netting set according to their credit risk-free valuation.

■ A relative credit adjustment approach. The overall CVA/DVA is allocated to each derivative (both assets and liabilities) based on their contribution to the CVA/DVA amount. This approach requires keeping track of the contribution of each derivative to the EAD profile. This method is theoretically sounder than the previous one, but in my opinion adds an operational complexity that is difficult to justify.

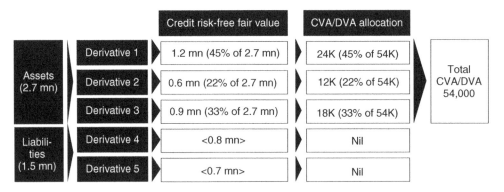

FIGURE 3.23   Example of CVA/DVA allocation using a relative fair value approach.

Other Effects of CVA/DVA   For a derivative designated as hedging instrument in a hedging relationship, changes in credit risk affecting the fair value of the derivative would typically be a source of hedge ineffectiveness because that change in value would not be replicated in the hedged item. In other words, CVA/DVA would affect the derivative but not the hedged item.

Where PD is estimated using unobservable inputs, the inclusion of CVA or DVA in the fair value of a derivative could in some cases cause the instrument to move from level 2 to level 3 if the credit adjustment is regarded as an unobservable input with a significant impact on the fair value of the derivative. A shift to level 3 of the hierarchy would prompt further disclosures to be made as IFRS 13 requires a reconciliation of beginning balances to ending balances for level 3 items, separately disclosing:

■ gains or losses recognised in profit or loss and where they are presented (with separate presentation of those relating to assets and liabilities held at the end of the reporting period);
■ gains or losses recognised in OCI;
■ purchases, sales issues and settlements (each separately); and
■ transfers into or out of level 3 (each separately) and the reasons for the transfer.

3.3 OVERNIGHT INDEX SWAP DISCOUNTING

When fair valuing derivative instruments, cash flows are discounted using discount factors which are derived from an interest rate curve. The data points in an interest rate curve are derived from a selection of liquid, benchmark instruments of different maturities that provide reliable prices, which can be observed in the particular marketplace.

At the time of writing there is no clear market consensus as to the most appropriate interest rate curve to apply in a valuation model. Entities have to ensure that their valuation results in a value for which a derivative asset could be exchanged, or a derivative liability settled, between market counterparties, which means that the discount rate should reflect only inputs that market participants would consider. In recent years there has been increased use of collateral in OTC derivative trading, and financial institutions have moved towards using multiple curves for collateralised and uncollateralised trades when fair valuing derivatives. Generally, the fair value of a collateralised derivative is different from the fair value of an otherwise identical but uncollateralised derivative since the posting of collateral mitigates risks associated with credit and funding costs. As a result, in liquid markets financial institutions use two benchmark interest rates:

- Libor interest rates, for uncollateralised trades;
- overnight index swap (OIS) rates for collateralised trades.

For collateralised transactions, entities generally view using OIS rates as appropriate for discounting purposes, since they reflect the rate payable on the overnight cash posted under their collateral agreements. The OIS curve in a currency is constructed from the overnight benchmark rate in such currency (e.g., the Euro Overnight Index Average).

CHAPTER **4**

An Introduction to Derivative Instruments

Before addressing the hedge accounting implications of the most common hedging strategies, it is helpful to examine the most common derivative instruments used in these strategies. The main characteristics of each derivative are described and, where relevant, its accounting implications under IFRS 9 are highlighted. A more detailed explanation of the accounting issues related to a specific derivative may be found in the numerous cases provided in this book.

4.1 FX FORWARDS

4.1.1 Product Description

An FX forward is the most common and simplest hedging instrument in the FX market. It is a contract to exchange a fixed amount of one currency for a fixed amount of another currency on a specific future date. Suppose that on 1 January 20X5 ABC, a European company, expects to purchase a USD 100 million machine from a US supplier. The purchase is expected to be paid in USD on 30 June 20X5. As a result, ABC is exposed, from the moment it places the order until it makes the payment, to an appreciation of the USD relative to the EUR. To hedge this exposure ABC may enter into an FX forward with the following terms:

FX forward terms	
Trade date	1 January 20X5
Counterparties	ABC and XYZ Bank
Maturity	30 June 20X5
ABC buys	USD 100 million
ABC sells	EUR 80 million
Forward Rate	1.2500
Settlement	Physical delivery

The FX forward locks in the exchange rate at which ABC will buy USD 100 million. In other words, ABC knows that (unless XYZ Bank defaults) on 30 June 20X5 it will receive USD 100 million in exchange for EUR 80 million (i.e., at an exchange rate of 1.2500), whatever the level of the EUR–USD exchange rate (i.e., the number of USD in exchange for 1 EUR) on that date (see Figures 4.1 and 4.2). ABC will use the received USD 100 million to pay the US supplier. The 1.2500 forward rate is, as of 1 January 20X5, the market expected EUR–USD rate for 30 June 20X5, so no premium is paid by either of the two parties to the forward at the beginning of the transaction.

Similarly, the hedge can be analysed by looking at the amount of EUR that ABC will need to sell in order to buy the USD 100 million at maturity, as a function of the EUR–USD exchange rate. Figure 4.3 shows that the FX forward locks in a EUR 80 million amount, whatever the EUR–USD rate at maturity.

Forward contracts may be settled by physical delivery or by cash settlement. The FX forward described previously will be settled by physical delivery. As a consequence, the parties will actually exchange currencies on 30 June 20X5: ABC agrees to buy USD 100 million and, simultaneously, to sell EUR 80 million. If the contract were to be settled by cash settlement, a final exchange rate would be set by observing an official fixing two business days prior to the maturity date, and then one counterparty will pay the other a settlement amount. For example, if two business days prior to maturity the official EUR–USD rate fixes at 1.3000, ABC would pay to XYZ Bank on 30 June 20X5 EUR 3,076,923.08 (= 100 million × (1/1.2500 − 1/1.3000)).

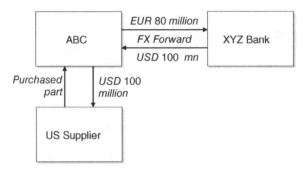

FIGURE 4.1   FX forward cash flows.

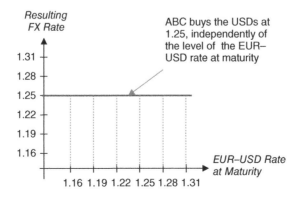

FIGURE 4.2   FX forward – resulting FX rate.

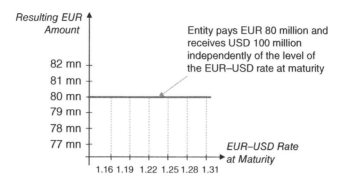

FIGURE 4.3 FX forward – EUR amount.

4.1.2 Forward Points

An FX forward is arguably the friendliest FX hedging instrument from the perspective of IFRS 9. The only particular point to note is the accounting treatment of the forward points. The forward points are the difference between the forward and spot prices. For example, if on 1 January 20X5 the spot EUR–USD rate was 1.2360 and the EUR–USD forward rate for 30 June 20X5 was 1.2500, then the forward points were 0.0140 (= 1.2500 – 1.2360). The forward points reflect the differential between USD and EUR interest rates from 1 January 20X5 to 30 June 20X5.

At maturity of the transaction the forward points become zero as spot and forward rates converge, as shown in Figure 4.4 (assuming that the EUR–USD spot rate on 30 June 20X5 trades at 1.3020).

The accounting treatment for forward contracts when hedge accounting is applied is covered in Chapter 2.

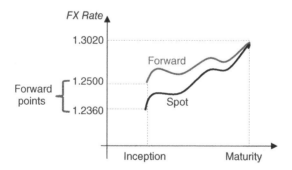

FIGURE 4.4 FX forward and spot rates convergence at maturity.

4.2 INTEREST RATE SWAPS

4.2.1 Product Description

An interest rate swap (often simply called a "swap") is the most commonly used instrument to hedge interest rate risk. In general, a swap is an exchange of interest payment flows in the same currency. Swaps are mostly used to change the interest rate risk profile of interest-bearing assets and/or liabilities.

Corporations and financial institutions usually enter into swaps to transform the interest rate basis of a debt instrument from a floating to fixed rate or vice versa. The two parties to a swap agree to exchange, at certain future dates, two sets of cash flows denominated in the same currency. The cash flows paid by one party reflect a fixed rate of interest while those of the other party reflect a floating rate of interest. The term "floating rate" or "variable rate" means that the interest rate used in an interest period is unknown until the commencement of such period. In the case of Euribor interest rates, the floating rate of a specific interest period is set two business days prior to the beginning of the interest period. All the stream of fixed rate payments is grouped together under the term **fixed leg**. Similarly, the **floating leg** groups all the floating rate payments. The swap is usually entered at market rates, and as a result there is no exchange of a premium at the inception of the swap.

The following example highlights the mechanics of swaps. On 15 January 20X0, ABC enters into a EUR 100 million notional, 3-year interest rate swap. Pursuant to the terms of the swap, ABC will pay semiannually a 5% fixed interest and receive annually a floating interest (Euribor 12-month rate), both calculated on the notional amount. The floating interest rate resets two business days prior to the commencement of each interest period (in accordance with the Euribor market convention). The terms of the swap are summarised below:

Interest rate swap terms	
Trade date	15 January 20X0
Parties	ABC and XYZ Bank
Maturity	3 years (15 January 20X3)
Notional	EUR 100 million
ABC pays	5.00% semiannually, 30/360 basis
ABC receives	Euribor 12-month annually, actual/360 basis Euribor 12-month is fixed two business days prior to the beginning of the annual interest period

The fixed leg of this swap has six interest periods, while the floating leg has three. Figure 4.5 shows the cash flow dates of the fixed and floating legs.

All the future fixed leg cash flows are known at the beginning of the swap. ABC will be paying EUR 2.5 million (= 100,000,000 × 5%/2) on 15 July and 15 January every year during the life of the swap, starting on 15 July 20X0.

Unlike the fixed leg cash flows, the future floating leg cash flows are unknown at the beginning of the swap (except the first one). The first floating cash flow will take place on 15 January 20X1 and its floating rate (i.e., 2.70%) is already known at the swap inception as it was fixed on 13 January 20X0 (i.e., two business days prior to the beginning of the first interest period). As a result, ABC expects to receive EUR 2,737,500 (=100,000,000 × 2.70% × 365/360) on 15 January 20X1, assuming 365 calendar days between 15 January 20X0 and 15 January 20X1. Each of the remaining floating leg cash flows will be determined two business days prior to the beginning of their corresponding interest period. For example, the cash flow to be received by ABC on 15 January 20X2 will be known on 13 January 20X1. There are several examples of swaps and their pricing mechanics in the cases covered in Chapter 7.

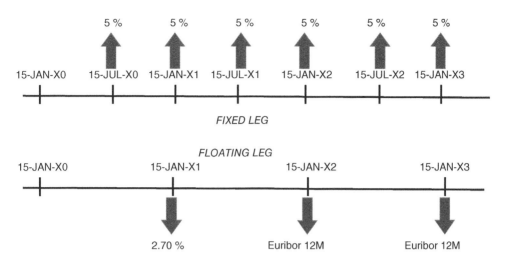

FIGURE 4.5 Interest rate swap flows.

4.2.2 IFRS 9 Accounting Implications

Interest rate swaps are the friendliest interest rate hedging instruments from the perspective of IFRS 9. There are two particular points that are covered in detail in Chapter 7 that I would like to highlight: firstly, the need to define hedging relationships involving swaps in such a way that eligibility for hedge accounting is maximised; and secondly, the need to exclude interest accrual amounts when calculating swap fair value changes.

In a hedge accounting context, a swap is often linked to a specific debt instrument (asset or liability). The market value of a swap and the debt instrument are usually determined using different yield curves. Typically, the market values a debt instrument using a yield curve that incorporates the issuer's credit spread, while swaps are valued by excluding credit spreads from the yield curve and subsequently credit/debit valuation adjusted to incorporate either the entity or the counterparty credit risk (see Chapter 3 for a more detailed explanation of CVAs and DVAs). As a result the interest rate sensitivities of a debt instrument and its related swap can be significantly different, endangering the eligibility for hedge accounting of a well-constructed hedge. When the debt instrument and the swap interest rate sensitivities are notably different, it is advisable to include in the hedging relationship only the interest rate risk (i.e., excluding other risks, such as the credit risk).

Often valuation dates fall within interest periods. When assessing whether a hedging relationship meets the effectiveness requirements, the inclusion or exclusion of accrued interest in the valuation of a swap may have a substantial impact. The solution to this problem is a simple one: interest accrual amounts need to be excluded when calculating a swap fair value. Excluding interest accrual amounts is especially relevant to making consistent fair value comparisons of debt instruments and swaps with unmatched interest periods. Additionally, excluding interest accrual amounts is also needed to avoid double counting interest income or expenses related to a swap, as the income or expenses associated with a cash flow is apportioned into the periods to which it relates. The calculation of accruals is quite straightforward, as shown in Chapter 7.

4.3 CROSS-CURRENCY SWAPS

4.3.1 Product Description

A **cross-currency swap** (CCS), or "currency swap" for short, is a contract to exchange interest payment flows in one currency for interest payment flows in another currency. CCSs are mostly used to change the interest rate risk and currency profile of interest-bearing assets and/or liabilities. They are also used to hedge investments in foreign subsidiaries.

Corporations and financial institutions usually enter into CCSs to transform the currency denomination of a debt obligation denominated in a foreign currency. The two parties to a CCS agree to exchange, at certain future dates, two set of cash flows denominated in different currencies. The cash flows paid by one party reflect a fixed (or a floating) rate of interest in one currency while those of the other party reflect a fixed (or floating) rate of interest in another currency.

In its simplest, and most common, form a CCS involves the following cash flows:

- An initial exchange of principal amounts. This initial exchange is sometimes not undertaken. The most common situation in which no initial exchange is needed is when the CCS is being undertaken to hedge already existing liabilities.
- A string of interim interest payments. Periodically, one party pays a fixed (or floating) interest on one of the principal amounts while the other party pays a fixed (or floating) interest on the other principal amounts. The payments are usually netted.
- A final re-exchange of principal amounts.

For example, suppose a borrower (ABC) is about to issue a GBP 70 million 5% fixed rate 5-year GBP-denominated bond. Because the borrower is only interested in raising variable rate EUR funds, it decides to transform the GBP fixed rate liability into a EUR floating rate liability by entering into a CCS. The terms of the bond and the swap are summarised in the following tables:

Bond terms	
Maturity	5 years
Notional	GBP 70 million
Coupon	5%, to be paid annually, 30/360 basis
Cross-currency swap terms	
Maturity date	5 years
Parties	ABC and Megabank
GBP nominal	GBP 70 million
EUR nominal	EUR 100 million
Initial exchange	On start date, ABC receives the EUR nominal and pays the GBP nominal
ABC pays	Euribor 12-month + 50 bps annually, actual/360 basis, on the EUR nominal
ABC receives	GBP 5% annually, on the GBP nominal
Final exchange	On maturity date, ABC receives the GBP nominal and pays the EUR nominal

Figure 4.6 shows the initial cash flows of the CCS and their interaction with the bond's initial flow. Through the CCS, the ABC delivers GBP 70 million (i.e., the issue proceeds) and receives EUR 100 million. As a result, ABC is in effect raising EUR funding.

Figure 4.7 depicts the periodic interest payments of the bond and the CCS. Through the CCS, ABC receives from Megabank an annual GBP 5% interest calculated on the GBP 70 million nominal, and pays annually to Megabank a EUR floating interest (Euribor 12-month plus 50 basis points) calculated on the EUR 100 million nominal. The borrower uses the CCS GBP receipts to meet the bond interest payments.

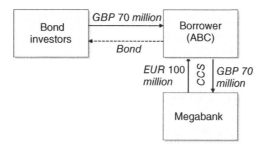

FIGURE 4.6   Bond and CCS: initial cash flows.

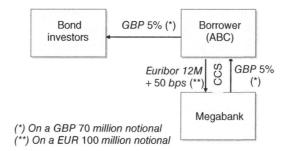

FIGURE 4.7   Bond and CCS: interim cash flows.

Figure 4.8 shows the CCS final cash flows and their interaction with the bond's redemption. On maturity date ABC re-exchanges the notionals, paying EUR 100 million and receiving GBP 70 million through the CCS. ABC then uses the received GBP 70 million to repay the GBP bond.

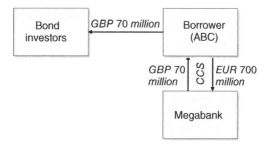

FIGURE 4.8   Bond and CCS: final cash flows.

Under the structure depicted, ABC effectively achieves EUR funding at Euribor plus 50 bps. Note that all the GBP cash flows have to be fully synchronised to eliminate the borrower's GBP exposure. Chapter 8 includes several examples of CCSs and their pricing mechanics.

4.3.2 IFRS 9 Accounting Implications

Cross-currency swaps are the most basic instruments to hedge foreign currency denominated liabilities. From an accounting perspective, as noted above for interest rate swaps, there are two particular points that are worth noting: firstly, there are several sources of ineffectiveness; and secondly, the need to exclude the interest accrual amounts when calculating CCS fair value changes.

In a hedge accounting context, a CCS is often linked to a specific foreign currency denominated liability. The fair value of a CCS contains several elements that may cause hedge ineffectiveness.

Firstly, a CCS fair value is adjusted to incorporate either the CCS counterparty's or the entity's non-performance (i.e., CVA/DVA). In a cash flow hedge, the fair valuation of the hedged cash flows does not incorporate the liability issuer's credit spread. As a result, in a cash flow hedge ineffectiveness may be caused by the CVAs/DVAs to the CCS, which can be substantial when the derivative (i.e., the CCS) is uncollateralised and long-term.

Secondly, a CCS market pricing incorporates a **basis** (referred to in IFRS 9 as "currency basis spread"), an adjustment to the theoretical CCS pricing that incorporates the appetite of the market for exchanging floating cash flows in the two currencies of the CCS. For example, imagine a floating-to-floating EUR–GBP CCS, in which a Euribor-linked EUR leg is exchanged for a Libor-linked GBP leg. Strong demand for receiving Euribor flows may lead to a Euribor-linked EUR leg being exchanged for a Libor-linked plus a spread GBP leg. This spread is commonly referred to as the basis. During the life of a CCS, the basis may fluctuate, affecting the CCS's fair value. Because the hedged liability (i.e., the hedged item) is not affected by the basis, fluctuations in the CCS basis may cause ineffectiveness. IFRS 9, similarly to the treatment of the forward element in forward contracts, allows the exclusion of the basis from the hedging relationship and temporary recognition of the change in the fair value of the basis element in OCI to the extent that it relates to the hedged item.

Thirdly, in a fair value hedge, the fair valuation of a CCS and its related liability may be determined using different yield curves. Commonly, when a CCS is collateralised (i.e., each party to the CCS posts/receives collateral to eliminate counterparty credit risk exposure) an OIS yield curve is used to fair value the CCS. The fair valuation of the hedged liability is performed using a non-OIS curve (typically a Euribor or Libor based yield curve). As a result the interest rate sensitivities of a liability and its related CCS can be significantly different, causing ineffectiveness even in a well-constructed hedge. When a liability and its CCS rate sensitivities are notably different, it is suggested that the hedging relationship is defined as the hedge of interest rate and FX risk only (i.e., excluding the liability's credit spread).

Often valuation dates fall within interest periods. The inclusion or exclusion of accrued interest in the valuation of a CCS can make a substantial difference. The solution to this problem is to exclude interest accrual amounts when calculating a CCS fair value. The exclusion is especially important in making consistent fair value comparisons of liabilities and CCS with different interest periods. The exclusion is also needed to avoid double counting the interest income or expenses related to a CCS, as the income or expenses associated with a cash flow is apportioned into the periods to which it relates. Chapter 8 includes detailed computations of the interest accruals of CCSs.

In addition to hedging foreign currency denominated liabilities, CCSs are used to hedge the FX exposure of net investments in foreign operations. For that type of hedge, IFRS 9 sets a special type of hedge accounting, called a "net investment hedge". When designated as hedging instruments of net investment hedges, some aspects of the accounting treatment of CCSs are unclear. This is particularly the case for CCSs in which the entity pays a fixed interest rate in the leg denominated in the group's functional currency leg. This accounting uncertainty is covered in more detail in Chapter 6.

4.4 STANDARD (VANILLA) OPTIONS

In this section the mechanics of standard options are described. Under IFRS 9, the accounting for an option's time value, when excluded from a hedging relationship, follows a particular treatment which was covered in detail in Chapter 2.

4.4.1 Product Description

In general there are two types of options: **standard** options and **exotic** options. Standard options, also called "vanilla options" or just "options", are the most basic option instruments. Unlike the terms of most exotic options, the terms of a standard option (nominal, strike, expiry date, etc.) are known at its inception. There are two types of standard options:

- **Call options**. A call gives the buyer the right, but not the obligation, to buy a specific amount of an underlying at a predetermined price on or before a specific future date.
- **Put options**. A put gives the buyer the right, but not the obligation, to sell a specific amount of an underlying at a predetermined price on or before a specific future date.

The buyer of the option has to pay a premium to the seller. Usually the premium is paid shortly after the option is agreed (e.g., two business days after trade date). The underlying can be any financial asset (e.g., a security, a currency, a commodity) or a financial index (e.g., a stock market index, an interest rate).

4.4.2 Standard Equity Options

Equity options are a means for their buyers to gain either long or short exposure to an equity underlying with a limited downside.

Call Options Equity call options allow an investor to take a bullish view on an underlying stock, a basket of stocks or a stock index.

- A physically settled European call option provides the buyer (the holder) the right, but not the obligation, to buy a specified number of shares of an equity underlying at a predetermined price (the strike price) at a future date (the expiration date). In return for this right, the buyer pays an up-front premium for the call.
- A cash-settled European call option provides the buyer the appreciation (i.e., the increase in value of the underlying shares relative to the strike price) of a specified number of shares of an equity underlying above a predetermined price (the strike price) at a future date (the expiration date). The buyer pays an up-front premium for the call.

At expiry, the holder of the call will exercise the option if the share price of the underlying stock is higher than the strike price. Thus, if the share price ends up lower than the strike price, the holder will not exercise the call. The holder has unlimited upside potential, while his/her loss is limited to the option premium paid.

As an example, suppose that on 3 June 20X1 ABC is looking to buy IBM stock in 6 months' time. ABC believes that IBM stock will significantly increase in value over the next 6 months and acquires from Gigabank a European call option on 1 million IBM shares. On 3 June 20X1, IBM stock is trading at USD 150. The physically settled call option has the following terms:

Physically settled call option – main terms	
Buyer	ABC Corp.
Seller	Gigabank
Option type	Call
Trade date	3-June-20X1
Expiration date	3-December-20X1
Option style	European
Shares	IBM
Number of options	1 million
Option entitlement	One share per option
Strike price	USD 180.00 (120% of the spot price)
Spot price	USD 150.00
Premium	2.66% of the notional amount USD 4 million (i.e., USD 4 per share)
Premium payment date	Two currency business days after the trade date (5-June-20X1)
Notional amount	Number of options × Spot price USD 150 million
Settlement method	Physical settlement
Settlement date	6-December-20X1 (three exchange business days after the Expiration date)

By buying the call option ABC has the right, but not the obligation, to buy on the settlement date 1 million shares of IBM at a strike price of USD 180 per share. Because upon exercise ABC would be buying the underlying stock, the call is a physically settled call. ABC pays Gigabank a premium of USD 4 million on 5 June 20X1. Because it is European-style, the option can only be exercised at expiry. On the expiration date, 3 December 20X1, ABC would be assessing whether to exercise the option, as follows:

- If IBM's stock price is greater than the USD 180 strike price, ABC would exercise the call. On the settlement date ABC would receive from Gigabank 1 million shares of IBM in exchange for USD 180 million. For example, if at expiry IBM stock is trading at USD 210, ABC would exercise the call option paying USD 180 per share for a stock worth USD 210 per share.

- If IBM's stock price is lower than or equal to the USD 180 strike price, ABC would not exercise the option.

In a similar example, suppose that ABC is not interested in having the right to buy 1 million shares of IBM but instead in receiving the appreciation of 1 million shares of IBM above USD 180. ABC then buys a cash-settled European call option on IBM stock with the following terms:

Cash-settled call option – main terms	
Buyer	ABC Corp
Seller	Gigabank
Option type	Call
Trade date	3-June-20X1
Expiration date	3-December-20X1
Option style	European
Shares	IBM
Number of options	1 million
Option entitlement	One share per option
Strike price	USD 180.00 (120% of the spot price)
Spot price	USD 150.00
Premium	2.66% of the notional amount USD 4 million (i.e., USD 4 per share)
Premium payment date	5-June-20X1 (two currency business days after the trade date)
Notional amount	Number of options × Spot price USD 150 million
Automatic exercise	Applicable
Settlement price	The closing price of the shares on the valuation date
Settlement method	Cash settlement
Cash settlement amount	The maximum of: (i) Number of options × (Settlement price – Strike price), and (ii) Zero
Cash settlement payment date	6-December-20X1 (three exchange business days after the expiration date)

ABC pays on 5 June 20X1 a USD 4 million premium. On the expiration date, ABC will exercise the call if IBM's stock price (the settlement price) is above the USD 180 strike price. What if ABC forgets to exercise the call? The contract includes a term, "automatic exercise", which prevents the buyer from forgetting to exercise an in-the-money option. In our option, the "automatic exercise" term is defined as "applicable", meaning that if the option is in-the-money on expiration date it would automatically be exercised. More precisely, on 6 December 20X1 ABC would receive the cash settlement amount. This amount is calculated as follows:

- If the settlement price is greater than the USD 180 strike price, the option would be exercised and ABC would receive an amount equivalent to Number of options × (Settlement price – Strike price) = 1 million × (Settlement price – 180). In other words, ABC receives from Gigabank the appreciation of the shares above USD 180. For example, if at expiry the IBM stock price has risen to USD 210, the call would be exercised and ABC would receive from Gigabank USD 30 million (= 1 million shares × (210 – 180)). Taking into account the USD 4 million initial premium paid, the overall payoff for ABC would be a profit of USD 26 million (=30 million – 4 million).
- If the settlement price is lower than or equal to the USD 180 strike price, the settlement would be zero. The option would not be exercised, and thus ABC would receive nothing. Taking into account the USD 4 million initial premium paid, the overall payoff for ABC would be a loss of USD 4 million.

Options strategies are often described using "payoff" graphs which show the value of an option (i.e., the cash settlement amount) on the expiration date after subtracting the up-front premium. Figure 4.9 shows the payoff for ABC under the IBM call. Note that in the graph the USD 4 million option premium has been taken into account, ignoring timing differences. In reality, the premium is paid up-front while the payout of the option is received shortly after the option expiration date.

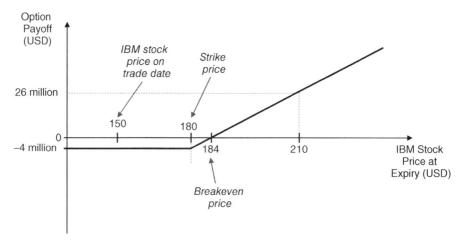

FIGURE 4.9 Payoff to the buyer of the call option.

Figure 4.9 shows that there is a positive payoff for ABC, the option buyer, when the stock price at expiration is greater than the USD 184 breakeven price. The breakeven price is calculated as the sum of the USD 4 per share call premium and the USD 180 strike. By the same reasoning, there is a negative payoff when the stock price at expiration is lower than the breakeven price. The graph also shows that for a buyer of a call the upside is unlimited, while the downside is limited to the initial premium paid.

Conversely, the seller of the IBM call (Gigabank in our example) has a positive payoff when the stock price at expiration is lower than the breakeven price (see Figure 4.10). Applying the same reasoning, there is a negative payoff for the seller of the option where the stock price at expiry is greater than the breakeven price. The graph also shows that for a seller of a call the upside is limited to the initial premium received, while there is an unlimited downside.

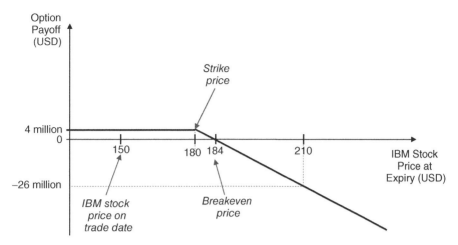

FIGURE 4.10   Payoff to the seller of the call option.

Put Options   Equity put options allows an investor to take bearish views on the underlying stock.

- A physically settled European put option provides the buyer (the holder) the right, but not the obligation, to sell a specified number of shares at a predetermined price (the strike price) at a future date (the expiration date). In return for this right, the buyer pays an up-front premium for the put.
- A cash-settled European put option provides the buyer the depreciation (i.e. the decrease in value of the underlying shares relative to the strike price) of a specified number of shares below a predetermined price (the strike price) at a future date (the expiration date). The buyer pays an up-front premium for the put.

As an example, suppose that on 3 June 20X1 ABC has a bearish view on IBM stock. ABC believes that IBM stock price will significantly fall over the next 6 months and acquires from Gigabank a European put option on 1 million IBM shares. On 3 June 20X1, IBM stock is trading at USD 150. Suppose further that ABC is not interested in having the right to sell 1 million shares of IBM but instead in having the right to receive the depreciation of IBM's stock below USD 120. The cash-settled put option has the following terms:

Cash-settled put option – main terms	
Buyer	ABC Corp
Seller	Gigabank
Option type	Put
Trade date	3-June-20X1
Expiration date	3-December-20X1
Option style	European
Shares	IBM

Cash-settled put option – main terms	
Number of options	1 million
Option entitlement	One share per option
Strike price	USD 120.00 (80% of the spot price)
Spot price	USD 150.00
Premium	1.33% of the notional amount USD 2 million (i.e., USD 2 per share)
Premium payment date	5-June-20X1 (two currency business days after the Trade date)
Notional amount	Number of options × Spot price USD 150 million
Settlement price	The closing price of the shares on the valuation date
Settlement method	Cash settlement
Cash settlement amount	The maximum of: (i) Number of options × (Strike price – Settlement price), and (ii) Zero
Cash settlement payment date	6-December-20X1 (three exchange business days after the expiration date)

ABC pays on 5 June 20X1 a USD 2 million premium. At expiry, the holder of the put (ABC) will exercise the option if IBM's stock price is lower than the USD 120 strike price. To put it more formally, on the cash settlement payment date (6 December 20X1) ABC would receive the cash settlement amount. This amount is calculated as follows:

- If the settlement price is lower than the USD 120 strike price, the option would be exercised and ABC would receive an amount equivalent to Number of options × (Strike price – Settlement price) = 1 million × (120 – Settlement price). In other words, ABC would receive from Gigabank the depreciation of the shares below USD 120. For example, if at expiry IBM stock price has fallen to USD 110, ABC would exercise the put receiving from Gigabank USD 10 million (= 1 million shares × (120 – 110)). Taking into account the USD 2 million initial premium paid, the overall payoff for ABC would be a profit of USD 8 million (=10 million – 2 million).
- If the settlement price is greater than or equal to the USD 120 strike price, the option would not be exercised and ABC would receive nothing as the cash settlement amount would be zero. Taking into account the USD 2 million initial premium paid, the overall payoff for ABC would be a loss of USD 2 million.

Figure 4.11 shows the payoff for ABC under the IBM put. The graph illustrates the value of the option (i.e., the cash settlement amount) on the expiration date after subtracting the USD 2 million up-front premium. Note that in the graph the option premium has been taken into account ignoring timing differences. In reality, the premium is paid up-front and the pay-out of the option is received shortly after the option expiration date.

The seller of the IBM put, Gigabank, has a positive payoff when the stock price at expiry is greater than the USD 118 breakeven price (see Figure 4.12). Applying the same reasoning, there is a negative payoff for the seller of the option when the stock price at expiry is lower than the USD 118 breakeven price. The graph also shows that the upside is limited to the initial premium paid, while there is a limited downside. The maximum downside for Gigabank is USD 118 million (= 120 million − 2 million), reached if IBM stock price trades at zero on the expiration date.

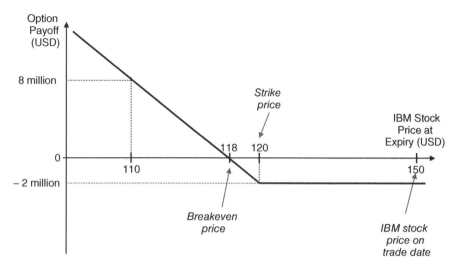

FIGURE 4.11   Payoff to the buyer of the put option.

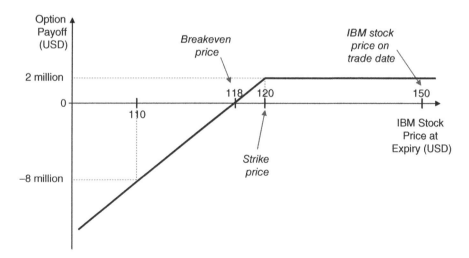

FIGURE 4.12   Payoff to the seller of the put option.

4.4.3 Standard Foreign Exchange Options

Most FX instruments involve two currencies: a specific amount of one currency is paid (or received) in exchange for receiving (or paying) a specific amount of another currency. An interesting aspect of FX options is that they are simultaneously a call and a put option. If the FX option is a call on one currency, it is necessarily a put option on another currency. Accordingly, when entering into an FX option, the term "call" (or "put") is accompanied by the currency for which the option is a call (or a put). For example, a EUR–USD option in which the option buyer benefits when the USD strengthens is simultaneously a USD call and a EUR put option. Likewise, a EUR–USD option in which the option buyer benefits when the USD weakens is simultaneously a USD put and a EUR call option.

As a first example, suppose that a European entity highly expects to sell a manufacturing plant to a US investor. The plant is expected to be sold for USD 100 million in 1 year. The entity is exposed to a declining USD relative to the EUR. Accordingly, the entity decides to hedge the FX risk arising from the highly expected sale by buying an option with the following characteristics:

EUR call/USD put terms	
Buyer	European entity
Option type	EUR call/USD put
Expiry	1 year
Notional	USD 100 million
Strike	1.16
Settlement	Cash settlement
Premium	EUR 1.8 million to be paid two business days after trade date

As this option is cash settled, the option will pay a EUR amount at expiry only when the option ends up being in-the-money (i.e., when the EUR–USD FX rate is greater than 1.16). The cash settlement amount (i.e., the option payoff) at expiry is calculated according to the following formula:

$$\text{EUR settlement amount} = \max\{\text{USD Notional} \times [1/1.16 - 1/(\text{FX rate at expiry})] , 0\}$$

Figure 4.13 shows the option's payoff (i.e., the settlement amount) as a function of the EUR USD spot rate at expiry, without taking into account the premium that the entity paid for the option.

On receipt of the USD 100 million, the entity will exchange the USD for EUR at the spot rate. The entity will also exercise the option at expiry when it ends up being in-the-money. The option payoff, if the option is exercised, will increase the EUR proceeds of the sale. Figure 4.14 shows the resulting EUR amount obtained through both transactions: the disposal of the plant and the option payoff. It can be observed that by purchasing the option the entity locked in a minimum EUR 86.2 million overall proceeds (excluding the option

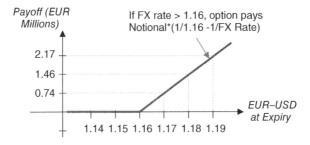

FIGURE 4.13 1.16 USD put/EUR call payoff at expiry (excluding premium).

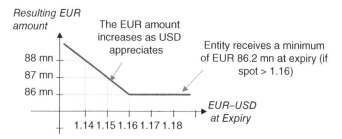

FIGURE 4.14 Option and plant disposal combined EUR amount (excluding premium).

premium), while potentially receiving higher proceeds were the USD to strengthen relative to the EUR below 1.16.

As a second example, suppose that a European entity highly expects to purchase a machine from a US supplier. The machine is expected to cost USD 100 million. The invoice will be paid in USD in 1 year. The entity is exposed to a rising USD relative to the EUR. Accordingly, the entity decides to hedge the FX risk arising from the highly expected purchase by buying a EUR put/USD call option, whose main terms are as follows:

EUR put/USD call terms	
Buyer	European entity
Option type	EUR put/USD call
Expiry	1 year
Notional	USD 100 million
Strike	1.16
Settlement	Cash settlement
Premium	EUR 1.6 million to be paid two business days after trade date

As this option is cash settled, the option will pay a EUR amount at expiry only when the option ends up being in-the-money (i.e., EUR–USD FX rate lower than 1.16). The cash settlement amount at expiry is calculated according to the following formula:

$$\text{EUR settlement amount} = \max\{\text{USD Notional} \times [1/(\text{FX rate at expiry}) - 1/1.16], 0\}$$

Figure 4.15 illustrates the option payoff (i.e., the settlement amount) as a function of the EUR–USD spot rate at expiry, excluding the premium that the entity paid for the option.

At maturity of the transaction and in order to meet the USD 100 million payment, the entity will receive USD 100 million in exchange for a EUR amount at the spot rate prevailing on such date. The entity will also exercise the option when it ends up being in-the-money, decreasing the total EUR cost of the purchase. Figure 4.16 shows the resulting EUR amount from both transactions (excluding the option premium). It can be observed that by purchasing the EUR put, the entity limits the maximum EUR amount to be paid for the machine to EUR 86.2 million, while benefiting from a lower total payment were the EUR to appreciate above 1.16.

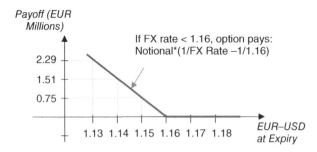

FIGURE 4.15 1.16 EUR put/USD call payoff at expiry (excluding premium).

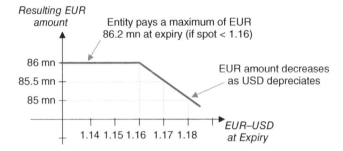

FIGURE 4.16 Option and machine purchase combined EUR amount (excluding premium).

Tunnel or Collar Combination In the two previous examples, the entity paid a premium for the protection gained. It is more common, though, to buy an option and simultaneously sell the opposite option to avoid paying a premium. Applying this strategy to our second example, the entity would have bought the 1.16 EUR put and simultaneously sold a 1.26 EUR call. If we assume that the EUR call premium was also EUR 1.6 million, the entity neither paid nor received a premium for the combination of the two options. This strategy, called a **zero-cost tunnel**, is the most popular FX option hedging strategy. In our example, the purchased EUR put limits the maximum EUR amount to be paid for the machine to EUR 86.2 million. At the same time, the sold EUR call limits the minimum EUR amount to be paid to EUR 79.4 million (= 100 million/1.26), as shown in Figure 4.17.

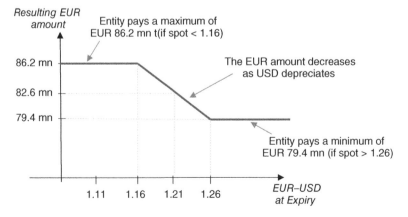

FIGURE 4.17 Option strategy and machine purchase combined EUR amount.

4.4.4 Interest Rate Options – Caps, Floors and Collars

When referring to interest rate options, the term **cap** is used instead of the term "call option". Similarly, the term **floor** is used instead of the term "put option". The reason for this is that a cap (floor) is in reality a string of call (put) options. For example, a borrower may prefer to pay a variable interest rate in a floating rate bond, but may require assurance that the interest payments do not exceed a maximum limit. An interest rate cap would achieve this objective by providing the issuer protection against rising interest rates. Usually, the borrower is not hedging only one interest payment but each interest payment on the bond. Therefore, a cap is in reality a string of options, each protecting a specific interest payment. Each option in a cap is called a **caplet**. Similarly, each option in a floor is called a **floorlet**.

Just as a borrower issuing a floating rate bond is concerned about rising interest rates, so an investor buying a floating rate bond is concerned about declining interest rates. An investor may prefer to receive a floating interest rate in a bond, but may require assurance that each interest receipt is not lower than a given minimum. An interest rate floor would achieve this objective by providing the issuer protection against low interest rates.

As an example, suppose that a borrower is about to issue a 5-year floating rate bond with an annual variable coupon of Euribor 12-month plus 50 basis points. The borrower expects interest rates to decline but wishes to be protected in case its view is wrong. As a result the borrower buys an interest rate cap. The cap provides protection when interest rates exceed 6%. The terms of the bond and the cap are summarised in the following tables:

Bond terms	
Maturity	5 years
Notional	EUR 100 million
Coupon	Euribor 12-month + 50 bps, to be paid annually
Interest rate cap terms	
Buyer	Borrower
Maturity	5 years
Notional	EUR 100 million
Cap rate	6%
Underlying	Euribor 12-month
Interest periods	Annual
Premium	EUR 2 million to be paid up-front

In each interest period that the Euribor 12-month fixes above the 6% cap rate, the borrower will receive from the seller of the cap an amount related to the difference between the Euribor 12-month rate and the 6% cap rate. In each interest period that the Euribor 12-month is fixed at or below the 6% cap rate, the borrower will receive nothing. Figure 4.18 shows a caplet payoff as a function of the Euribor 12-month rate, without taking into account the cap premium.

Figure 4.19 illustrates how the interest rate cap will operate in our example in conjunction with the bond. By entering into the cap, the borrower would achieve funding at a maximum rate of 6.50% (= 6% + 0.50%), without taking into account the cap premium.

- On any interest reset date that Euribor 12-month is fixed at a rate above 6%, the borrower will receive through the cap the difference between Euribor 12-month and 6%. Because the borrower pays Euribor 12-month plus 50 basis points to the bondholders, the borrower will effectively pay a total interest of 6.50% (= Euribor 12M + 0.50% – (Euribor 12M – 6%)).
- On any interest reset date that Euribor 12-month is fixed below or at the 6% cap rate, the borrower will receive nothing through the cap. Therefore, the borrower will effectively pay an interest of Euribor 12-month rate plus the 50 basis points bond spread. This interest will be lower than 6.50%.

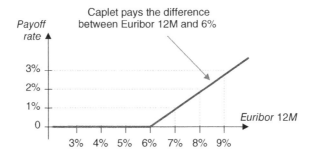

FIGURE 4.18   Caplet payoff (excluding premium).

Collar Strategy   Because the purchase of a cap requires the payment of an up-front premium, a cap is often transacted in conjunction with a floor to avoid making any up-front payments. The combination of a purchased cap and a sold floor is called a **collar**. In the case of a floating rate debt, a collar sets an upper and a lower limit on the interest a borrower would pay. If the premium of the cap is equal to the premium of the floor, the strategy is called a **zero-cost collar**, as no premium is exchanged at inception.

In our example, let us suppose that the borrower, in addition to buying the 6% cap, also sells a 4% floor. Through the floor, in each interest period that Euribor 12-month is fixed below 4%, the borrower will pay the floor buyer interest corresponding to the difference between the 4% and the Euribor 12-month rate (see Figure 4.20). In each interest period that Euribor 12-month is fixed at or above the 4% floor rate, the borrower will pay nothing.

Figure 4.21 illustrates how the collar will operate in our example in conjunction with the debt. Through the collar, the borrower will achieve funding at a maximum rate of 6.50% (= 6% + 0.50%) and at a minimum rate of 4.50% (= 4% + 0.50%).

- On any interest reset date that Euribor 12-month fixes above 6%, the cap will be exercised and the borrower will effectively pay 6.50% (6% plus the 50 basis points bond spread).

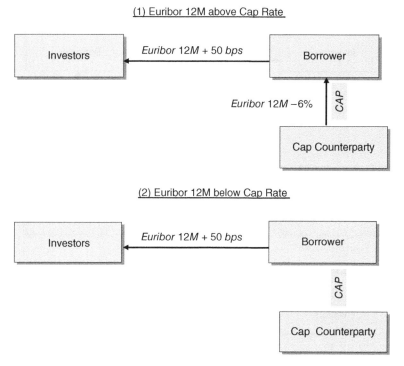

FIGURE 4.19 Floating rate bond and cap: combined interest cash flows (excluding premium).

- On any interest reset date that Euribor 12-month fixes between 4% and 6%, neither the cap nor the floor will be exercised. Thus, the borrower will pay the bond's Euribor 12-month rate plus 50 basis points spread coupon.
- On any interest reset date that Euribor 12-month fixes at a rate below 4%, the floor will be exercised. The borrower will pay the floor buyer the difference between 4% and Euribor 12-month. As a consequence, the borrower will effectively pay 4.50% (= Euribor 12M + 0.50% + 4% – Euribor 12M).

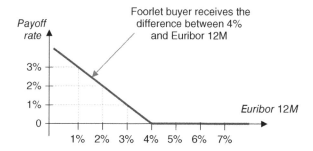

FIGURE 4.20 Floorlet payoff (excluding premium).

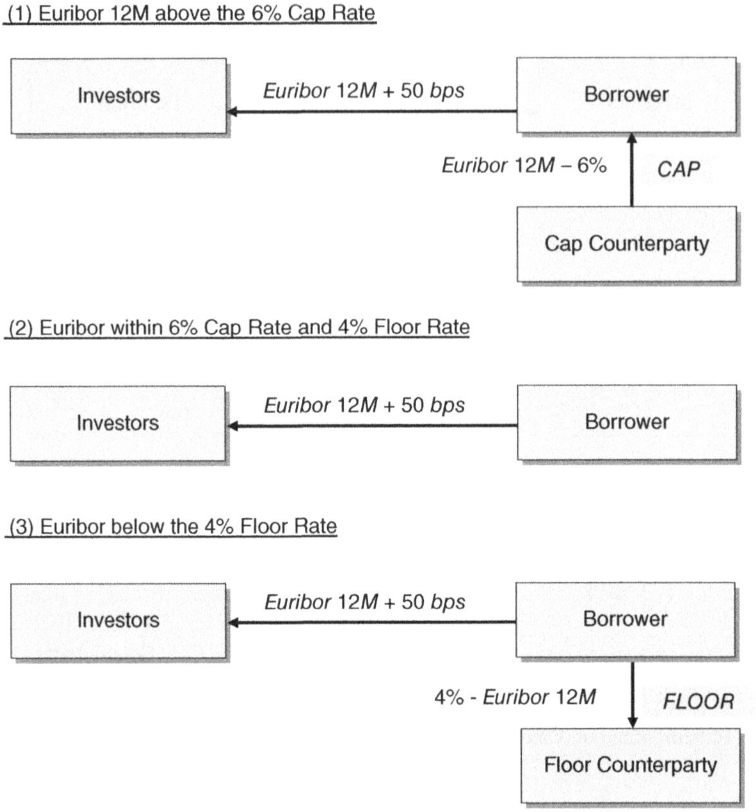
(1) Euribor 12M above the 6% Cap Rate
Investors
Euribor 12M + 50 bps
Borrower
Euribor 12M – 6%
CAP
Cap Counterparty
(2) Euribor within 6% Cap Rate and 4% Floor Rate
Investors
Euribor 12M + 50 bps
Borrower
(3) Euribor below the 4% Floor Rate
Investors
Euribor 12M + 50 bps
Borrower
4% - Euribor 12M
FLOOR
Floor Counterparty

FIGURE 4.21 Floating rate bond and zero-cost collar: combined interest cash flows.

4.5 EXOTIC OPTIONS

It was mentioned above that there are two types of options: vanilla (or standard or regular) and exotic options. Vanilla options have all their terms fixed and predetermined at their start. Exotic options are any other options that are not considered vanilla options. In general, exotic options have at least one term (e.g., the strike) whose final value depends on specific conditions being met during their life. The rationale behind most exotic options is to have a lower premium than their vanilla equivalents.

It is not easy to classify the exotic options into a small number of groups because their characteristics are very wide-ranging. Also, it would be unrealistic to try to provide all the different exotic options being developed, as financial markets continuously come up with new ones. However, one possible categorisation is as follows:

- **Path-dependent** options. The payoff of a path-dependent option depends on how the underlying price (or rate) has traded over the life of the option. The most popular path-dependent options are average rate options, barrier options, and range accrual options. An **average rate option**, also called an "Asian option", is an option whose payoff is determined by the average of its underlying price (or rate) during a pre-specified period of time before the option's expiry. **Barrier options** are the most popular exotic options, and I will cover them next. A **range accrual option** is an option whose payoff is determined by the number of days that the underlying stays within a specific range during a pre-specified period of time.

■ **Correlation** options. The payoff of a correlation option is affected by more than one underlying. The most popular correlation options are basket options, quanto options and spread options. A **basket option** is an option on a portfolio of underlyings. A **quanto option** is an option whose payoff denominated in one currency while its underlying is denominated in another currency. A **spread option** is an option whose payoff is determined by the difference of two prices (or indices or rates).

■ **Other types** of exotic options. This broad category groups all other options not included in the previous two categories. The most common options in this category are digital options. A **digital option** is an option whose payoff is either a fixed amount of cash (or other asset) or nothing.

4.6 BARRIER OPTIONS

The most popular type of exotic options are barrier options. Barrier options allow entities to tailor a hedging strategy to a very specific market view. The payoff of a barrier option depends on whether the price of the underlying crosses a given threshold, called the **barrier**, before maturity. Alternatively, in some barrier options the determination of whether the barrier has been crossed is determined only at maturity. I assume henceforth that the crossing of barrier is determined during the life of the option.

In general there are two types of barrier options: knock-in options and knock-out options:

■ **Knock-in options** do not exist when traded and come into existence only when the price of the underlying reaches the barrier at any time during the life of the option.
■ **Knock-out options** come out of existence when the price of the underlying reaches the barrier at any time during the life of the option.

The existence of the barrier lowers the probability of exercise, and therefore barrier options are cheaper than their vanilla counterparts. Thus, an entity that has a strong view about future movements on a specific FX rate can reduce its hedging costs by using barrier options, but it also needs to be prepared to assume the adverse consequences were its view wrong.

4.6.1 Knock-out Barrier Options – Product Description

A knock-out option at inception is a standard option. However, this option ceases to exist when its barrier is crossed. For example, imagine that a EUR-based USD exporter has the view that the EUR will strengthen against the USD over the next 6 months, while it expects the EUR not to appreciate beyond 1.28. The entity buys a 6-month EUR knock-out call with strike 1.16 and barrier 1.28. The premium of a knock-out option is lower than the premium of its equivalent standard option because the protection disappears when the 1.28 barrier is crossed.

■ If the EUR–USD never trades at or above 1.28 during the life of the option, the entity effectively has protection identical to a standard option with strike 1.16 (see Figure 4.22).
■ However, if at any time during the life of the option the 1.28 barrier is crossed, the option ceases to exist and the entity losses its protection (see Figure 4.23).

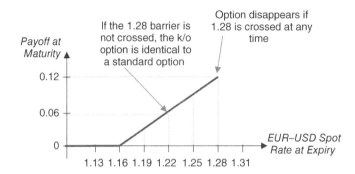

FIGURE 4.22   EUR knock-out call – barrier *not* hit: payoff at expiry (excluding premium).

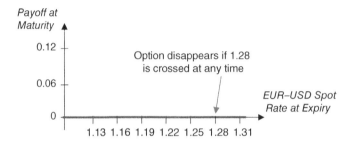

FIGURE 4.23   EUR knock-out call – barrier *was* hit: payoff at expiry (excluding premium).

4.6.2 Knock-in Barrier Options – Product Description

A knock-in option is an inactive option that automatically comes to life should the underlying rate trade at or beyond the barrier. For example, A EUR-based USD importer has the view that the EUR will weaken against the USD over the next 6 months, but expects the EUR to have a large movement beyond 1.05. The entity buys a 6-month EUR knock-in put with strike 1.15 and barrier 1.05. The premium of a knock-in option is lower than the premium of its equivalent standard option because there is protection only when the 1.05 barrier is crossed.

- If the EUR–USD exchange rate never trades at or below 1.05, the entity has no option – equivalent to the entity having no protection (see Figure 4.24).
- If the EUR–USD exchange rate trades at or below 1.05, the entity effectively has bought a standard option at substantial savings in option premium (see Figure 4.25).

The two barrier options just covered are the most common ones, involving a single barrier. More complex barrier options can be obtained with double barriers that activate or extinguish an option if, for example, the two barriers are crossed during the life of the option. Also, in our example, the exchange rate was monitored continuously to check if the barrier was crossed. Some barrier options observe the barrier only on specific dates. In summary, many different variations of barrier options are available in the financial markets.

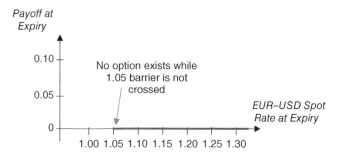

FIGURE 4.24   EUR knock-in put – barrier *not* hit: payoff at expiry (excluding premium).

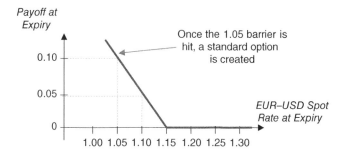

FIGURE 4.25   EUR knock-in put – barrier *was* hit: payoff at expiry (excluding premium).

4.7 RANGE ACCRUALS

A range accrual option is an option that accrues value for each day that a reference rate remains within a specified range (the accrual range) during the accrual observation period. For example, suppose that an investor buys an accrual option on the Euro Stoxx 50 index (the reference rate). The option has 6 months to expiration and pays EUR 10,000 for each day that the index closes in the range 3,000 to 3,200 (the accrual range). The investor pays a EUR 600,000 premium for the option. There are 130 trading days in the accrual observation period. Therefore, for the investor to break even, the reference rate must trade within the accrual range for 60 days (= 600,000/10,000), or 46% of the total trading days.

In the interest rates market, interesting alternatives to standard interest rate swaps are **range accrual swaps**. An example of a popular range accrual structure is the following. Suppose that a corporate wants to hedge its exposure to a 5-year EUR 100 million floating rate liability by paying a fixed rate of 4%, well below the market's 5% 5-year swap rate. Unlike a standard swap, the floating rate is conditional on how many days an observation rate (in our example the Euribor 12-month rate) is within a predefined range (e.g., 3.7–4.7%) in the interest period. The aim of the range accrual swap is to lower the fixed rate of the swap by assuming the risk that the Euribor 12-month rate fixes outside the accrual range. The interest flows are as follows (see Figure 4.26):

- The entity pays 4% annually, on EUR 100 million.
- The entity receives Euribor 12-month on the interest period's accrued nominal. The accrued nominal of an interest period is calculated using the formula

$$\text{Accrued nominal} = \frac{n}{N} \times \text{EUR } 100 \text{ million}$$

where n is number of fixings during the interest period that the Euribor 12-month is within the 3.70– 4.70% range, and N is the total number of fixings in the interest period.

FX range accrual forwards are an alternative to hedging with FX forwards. For each of the daily fixings up to maturity that the FX spot rate remains within a predetermined range, the forward nominal accrues a certain amount at a forward rate. The accrual forward rate is a better than market rate. For example, suppose that a EUR-based USD exporter wants to hedge a USD 40 million sale expected to take place in 3 months. The exporter expects the EUR–USD spot rate to trade within the 1.23–1.26 range during the next 2 months. The EUR–USD 3-month FX forward is 1.2500. Instead of entering into a standard forward at 1.2500, the exporter enters into a range accrual forward at 1.2400 with the following accruing terms:

- Every day the EUR–USD spot rate falls within the 1.23–1.26 range, the accrued notional increases by USD 1 million.
- Every day the EUR–USD spot rate falls outside the 1.23–1.26 range, there are no accruals.

The accrual observation period has 65 observation days. The exporter expects that a total of 40 observation days the EUR–USD will close within the accrual range.

Suppose further that on 50 days, the EUR–USD spot rate remained within the 1.23–1.26 range. As a consequence, the exporter ended up with a contract to sell USD 50 million (= 50 × 1 million) at a rate of 1.2400. The exporter then used the first USD 40 million of the range accrual forward to hedge the sale, but was left with a USD 10 million excess.

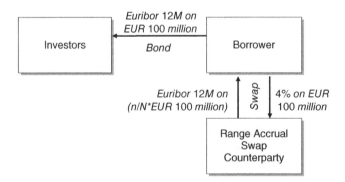

FIGURE 4.26   Range accrual – interest flows.

CHAPTER 5

Hedging Foreign Exchange Risk

Foreign exchange risk is the most common financial risk. Entities that have foreign currency transactions and operations are exposed to the risk that exchange rates can vary, causing unwanted fluctuations in earnings and in cash flows. Chapters 5, 6 and 8 deal with the accounting implications of FX hedges through the extensive use of cases. Chapter 5 covers the hedging of anticipated sales and purchases and their resulting receivables and payables. Chapter 6 examines the hedging of net investments in foreign entities. Chapter 8 covers the hedging of foreign currency denominated debt.

The accounting guidance on FX exposures and their hedging is included in two IFRS standards: IFRS 9 *Financial Instruments* and IAS 21 *The Effects of Changes in Foreign Exchange Rates*. A summary of IFRS 9 was given in Chapters 1 and 2. Some of the concepts of IAS 21 are outlined in this chapter and Chapter 6.

5.1 TYPES OF FOREIGN EXCHANGE EXPOSURE

An exposure to FX risk results mainly from the following transactions:

1) foreign currency forecasted sales and purchases, and receivables and payables resulting from such transactions;
2) interest and principal repayment on foreign currency denominated debt and deposits;
3) revaluation of foreign currency denominated equity investments;
4) receipt of dividends from foreign investments;
5) translation of profits of foreign operations;
6) translation of net assets of foreign operations;
7) competitive risk.

Competitive risk is the risk that an entity's future cash flows and earnings vary as a result of competitor's FX risk exposure. For example, a European car manufacturer is exposed to FX risk if a major Japanese competitor builds its cars in Japan, even if the European entity has all its manufacturing and sales denominated in EUR. In this case, unfavourable shifts in the EUR against the JPY can adversely affect the competitive position of the company.

5.2 INTRODUCTORY DEFINITIONS

5.2.1 Functional Currency and Presentation Currency

An entity's assets, liabilities and results are measured in a **functional currency**. IAS 21 defines the functional currency of an entity as "the currency of the primary economic environment in which the entity operates". Within a group, the functional currency of each entity must be determined individually based on its particular circumstances. IAS 21 ensures that the selection of the functional currency is a matter of fact rather than management choice. IAS 21 includes some primary indicators that must be given a priority in determining an entity's functional currency, and also some secondary indicators. The **primary indicators** are:

- The currency that mainly influences sales prices for its goods and services, and of the country whose competitive forces and regulations mainly determine the sale prices of its goods and services.
- The currency that mainly influences labour, material and other costs of providing goods or services.

If these primary indicators do not provide an obvious answer, then the entity would need to turn to the **secondary indicators**, as follows:

- The currency in which funds from financing activities (i.e., from issuing debt and equity instruments) are generated.
- The currency in which receipts from operating activities are usually retained.

IAS 21 also describes some other factors to consider in determining whether the functional currency of a foreign operation is the same as that of the parent company. For example, this would apply where a foreign subsidiary is used to market goods from the parent company and its cash is all remitted back to the parent.

In reality, most functional currencies used by each subsidiary throughout a group are generally the subsidiary's local currency (i.e., the currency of the country of its location). However, the group sometimes has a functional currency that differs from its local currency. This is often the case for oil companies and high-tech companies. For example, STMicroelectronics, despite being a Franco-Italian semiconductor company and incurring most of its labour costs in EUR, used the USD as its functional currency as "the reference currency for the semiconductor industry is the U.S. dollar, and product prices are mainly denominated in U.S. dollars".

The **presentation currency** is defined as the currency in which the financial statements are presented. Unlike the functional currency, the presentation currency can be any currency of choice. Presenting the financial statements in a currency other than the functional currency does not change the way in which the underlying items are measured. It merely expresses the underlying amounts, which are measured in the functional currency in a different currency.

Except where the functional currency is the currency of a hyperinflationary economy, an entity that translates financial statements from its functional currency into a presentation currency other than its functional currency uses the same method as for translating financial statements of a foreign operation.

5.2.2 Relevant Dates in an FX Transaction

Three different dates are relevant in a foreign currency transaction: the

- The **transaction date** – the date on which the transaction is initially recorded on the books.
- The **settlement date** – the date on which the payment or receipt is made.
- The **financial reporting dates** between the transaction date and the settlement date.

5.3 SUMMARY OF IAS 21 TRANSLATION RATES

All the items in the financial statements denominated in a currency different from the entity's functional currency are translated using specific exchange rates.

5.3.1 Monetary versus Non-monetary Items

In order to determine the appropriate translation exchange rate to use, IAS 21 groups assets and liabilities that are not part of the financial statements of a group's foreign operations into monetary accounts and non-monetary items. **Monetary items** are items that are settled in a fixed or determinable number of units of currency. All other assets and liabilities are non-monetary. Equity and income statement accounts are neither monetary nor non-monetary items. Examples of monetary and non-monetary items are:

Monetary items	
Assets	Liabilities
Accounts receivable	Accounts payable
Cash and cash equivalents	Long-term debt
Long-term receivables	Deferred income tax payables
Deferred income tax receivables	Intercompany payables
Intercompany receivables	Accrued liabilities
Investments in bonds	
Non-monetary items	
Assets	Liabilities
Inventory	Prepayments for goods
Property, plant and equipment	Provisions settled by delivery of a non-monetary asset
Investments in equities of another entity	

5.3.2 Translation Rates

Under IAS 21, the exchange rate to be used to translate the different FX denominated items is determined as follows:

1) Foreign currency transactions are translated at the exchange rate prevailing on the date of the transactions.
2) Monetary assets and liabilities are translated at the exchange rate prevailing at the reporting date. This FX rate is usually referred to as the "closing rate".
3) Non-monetary assets and liabilities that are not valued at fair value are translated at the exchange rate prevailing on the date of the transaction. In other words, there are no further retranslations.
4) Non-monetary items that are valued at fair value are translated at the exchange rate prevailing on the date when the latest fair value was determined.
5) Assets and liabilities of all the group foreign entities are translated at the closing rate.
6) Profit or loss statements of all the group foreign entities are translated at the average exchange rate for the period. Whilst it is also possible to use the exchange rate prevailing on each transaction date, in practice few entities adopt this alternative.

5.4 FOREIGN CURRENCY TRANSACTIONS

The type of foreign currency transaction covered in this chapter is a transaction that normally requires the payment (or receipt) of a fixed amount of foreign currency in exchange for the receipt (or delivery) of a fixed quantity of goods or services. Usually there is a span of time between when the transaction is initiated and when the foreign currency is to be paid or received, as shown in Figure 5.1.

First, the entity expects, without a high probability, the occurrence of the FX transaction. At a later stage, the entity expects the FX transaction to happen with a high probability. Next, the FX transaction is legally formalised, becoming a firm commitment. Then the goods/services are received or delivered, and a payable or receivable is recognised. Finally, the payable or receivable is settled, or in other words, payment/receipt is made.

An entity does not have to wait until the FX transaction is recorded in the statement of financial position (i.e., balance sheet) to apply hedge accounting. IFRS 9 allows highly probable transactions, firm commitments and payables/receivables to be designated as hedged items (see Figure 5.2).

5.4.1 Summary of Most Commonly Used FX Derivatives

The following table summarises the most frequently used FX hedging derivatives, and the implications of their use from an IFRS perspective:

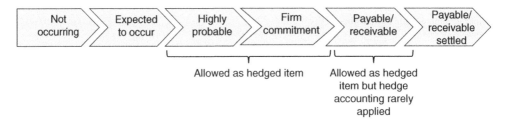

FIGURE 5.1 Chronology of an FX transaction.

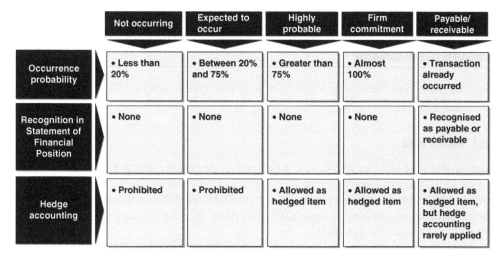

	Not occurring	Expected to occur	Highly probable	Firm commitment	Payable/receivable
Occurrence probability	• Less than 20%	• Between 20% and 75%	• Greater than 75%	• Almost 100%	• Transaction already occurred
Recognition in Statement of Financial Position	• None	• None	• None	• None	• Recognised as payable or receivable
Hedge accounting	• Prohibited	• Prohibited	• Allowed as hedged item	• Allowed as hedged item	• Allowed as hedged item, but hedge accounting rarely applied

FIGURE 5.2   Recognition of an FX transaction and application of hedge accounting.

Hedging FX derivative	Hedge accounting implications
FX forward	Most friendly FX instrument to qualify as hedging instrument. Effectiveness assessment can be based either on spot or on forward rates. If based on spot rates, changes in fair value due to forward points are recognised, at the entity's choice, in OCI (to the extent that they relate to the hedged item) or in profit or loss
FX option	Treated relatively favourably under IFRS 9. Time value commonly excluded from hedging relationship. In this case, time value changes are taken to OCI (to the extent that they relate to the hedged item), increasing volatility in OCI, and later recycled
FX tunnel	Written option subject to special conditions to qualify as hedging instrument. Time value commonly excluded from hedging relationship. In this case, time value changes are taken to OCI (to the extent that they relate to the hedged item), increasing volatility in OCI, and later recycled. Lower volatility in OCI than stand alone options due to potential offset between options' time value changes
Participating forward	Split between a forward and an option improves hedge accounting treatment
Knock-in forward	Split between a forward (eligible for hedge accounting) and a residual derivative (undesignated) may improve undesired effects in profit or loss. Hedge accounting treatment less challenging than KIKO or range accruals
KIKO forward	When knock-in barrier expected to be reached, suggested split between a forward (eligible for hedge accounting) and a residual derivative (undesignated). If knock-in barrier not expected to be reached, suggested split between an option (eligible for hedge accounting) and a residual derivative (undesignated). Accounting treatment can be specially challenging if knock-out barrier is likely to be crossed
Range accrual forward	Very challenging to meet requirements of hedge accounting, unless rebalancing is well designed. Rebalancing can be challenged by auditors and hedging relationship discontinuation may be required

5.5 CASE STUDY: HEDGING A FORECAST SALE AND SUBSEQUENT RECEIVABLE WITH AN FX FORWARD (FORWARD ELEMENT INCLUDED IN HEDGING RELATIONSHIP)

This case study illustrates the accounting treatment of highly expected FX transactions and their hedges through FX forwards.

5.5.1 Background

Suppose that on 1 October 20X4, ABC Corporation, an exporter whose functional currency was the EUR, was expecting to sell finished goods to a US client and the export to be denominated in USD. The sale was expected to occur on 31 March 20X5, and its related receivable was expected to be settled on 30 June 20X5. Sale proceeds were expected to amount to USD 100 million, to be received in USD.

The sale exposed the entity to a depreciating USD relative to the EUR until the future USD 100 million proceeds were exchanged into EUR. The following table summarises the effects on the resulting cash flow caused by fluctuations in the EUR–USD exchange rate:

EUR–USD exchange rate	Functional currency (EUR)	EUR value of USD sale proceeds
Goes up	Strengthens	Decrease in value
Goes down	Weakens	Increase in value

To hedge its exposure to the EUR–USD rate, on 1 October 20X4 ABC entered into an FX forward contract with the following terms:

FX forward terms	
Start date	1 October 20X4
Counterparties	ABC and XYZ Bank
Maturity	30 June 20X5
ABC sells	USD 100 million
ABC buys	EUR 80 million
Forward Rate	1.2500
Settlement	Physical delivery

The FX forward locked in the amount of EUR to be received in exchange for the USD 100 million sale, as shown in Figure 5.3.

5.5.2 Setting the Hedging Relationship Term

From an accounting perspective, the company was exposed to the EUR–USD exchange rate for three consecutive periods (see Figure 5.4):
  ▪ An initial period from the moment when the sale became highly expected to the moment when the goods were delivered. During this period, no FX remeasurement was required

from an accounting perspective. At the end of this period, the sale was recognised in the entity's profit and loss statement and its related USD receivable was recorded in the entity's statement of financial position. Both the sale and the receivable were translated into EUR at the EUR–USD spot rate prevailing on the day the sale was recognised.

- A second period that elapsed when the customer paid the receivable. During this period, the receivable was remeasured at each reporting date and changes in its fair value due to the EUR–USD exchange rate movements were recognised in profit or loss. At the end of this period, the USD payment was received and, as a result, the receivable was settled. Prior to its derecognition, the receivable was revalued using the EUR–USD rate prevailing on that date. The received USD cash was recognised in the entity's statement of financial position using the EUR–USD exchange rate used in the receivable's last revaluation.
- A final period that elapsed when the entity exchanged the USD cash into EUR cash. During this period, the USD cash was remeasured at each reporting date and changes in its fair value due to EUR–USD exchange rate movements were recognised in profit or loss. In our case, this third period did not exist as the exchange into EUR cash took place through the derivative at the same time as the receipt of the USD cash.

ABC designated the forward contract as the hedging instrument in a foreign currency cash flow hedge and the highly expected sale as the hedged item. When forwards are used, IFRS 9 permits an entity to choose whether or not to include the FX forward points (i.e., the **forward element**) in the hedging relationship. From a hedge accounting perspective, three alternatives are available:

- To designate the FX forward in its entirety as the hedging instrument. In other words, to include the forward element of the FX forward in the hedging relationship.
- To designate just the spot element of the FX forward as the hedging instrument (i.e., to exclude the forward element from the hedging relationship) and to temporarily recognise the change in the forward element in OCI to the extent that it relates to the hedged item.
- To designate just the spot element as the hedging instrument (i.e., to exclude the forward element from the hedging relationship) and to recognise the change in the forward element in profit or loss.

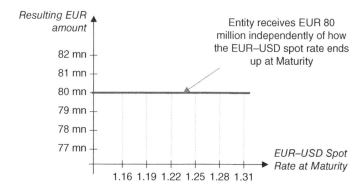

FIGURE 5.3 EUR proceeds from USD sale.

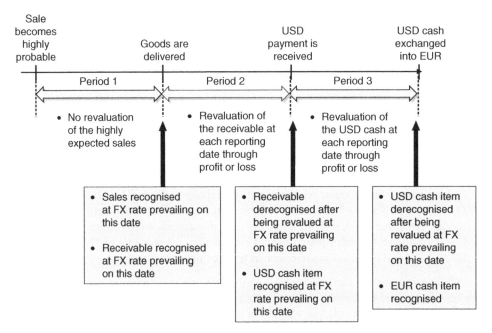

FIGURE 5.4 FX exposure of export transaction from an accounting perspective.

One important decision that ABC had to make was the term of the hedging relationship. ABC considered the following two approaches:

- To establish the term of the hedging relationship from 1 October 20X4 (i.e., when the forward was traded) to 30 June 20X5 (i.e., when the USD payment was received). Under this approach the hedged items were the forecast sale and its ensuing receivable. On 31 March 20X5, once the sales transaction was recognised, ABC decided either to maintain the hedging relationship or to discontinue it by changing the hedge objective. This section will cover the accounting mechanics under this alternative.
- To establish the term of the hedging relationship from 1 October 20X4 (i.e., when the forward was traded) to 31 March 20X5 (i.e., when the sale was recognised). Under this approach the hedged item was the forecast sale. Section 5.6 will cover the accounting mechanics under this alternative.

In the case covered in this section both the maturities of the hypothetical derivative and the hedging instrument coincided (30 June 20X5), enhancing hedge effectiveness. However, unless a discontinuation is provoked, it implied an extra operational burden as in the period from 31 March 20X5 to 30 June 20X5 an additional calculation/recognition of effective and ineffective parts and the subsequent reclassification of the effective part into profit or loss would be required.

An alternative to avoid such administrative complexity was to provoke on 31 March 20X5 the discontinuation of the hedging relationship by changing the hedge's risk management objective on that date, an approach that may be questioned by auditors. In this section I will cover this approach as well.

Figure 5.5 shows that the hedging relationship ended on 30 June 20X5, when the FX forward ended. As a result, the maturity of the hypothetical derivative and that of the hedging instrument (i.e., the forward) coincided.

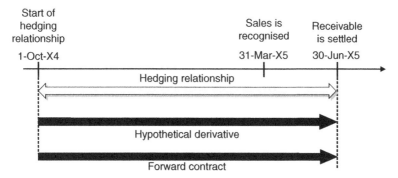

FIGURE 5.5   Transaction and hedging relationship timeframe.

5.5.3 Hedging Relationship Documentation

ABC designated the forward contract as the hedging instrument in a cash flow hedge. At the inception of the hedging relationship, ABC documented the hedging relationship as follows:

Hedging relationship documentation	
Risk management objective and strategy for undertaking the hedge	The objective of the hedge is to protect the EUR value of a USD 100 million cash flow stemming from a highly expected sale of finished goods, and its subsequent receivable. This hedging objective is consistent with the entity's overall FX risk management strategy of reducing the variability of its profit and loss statement caused by purchases and sales denominated in foreign currency. The designated risk being hedged is the risk of changes in the EUR fair value of the highly expected sale and its subsequent receivable due to unfavourable movements in the EUR–USD exchange rate
Type of hedge	Cash flow hedge
Hedged item	The hedged item is the cash flow stemming from a highly expected sale of USD 100 million of finished goods and its subsequent receivable, expected to be settled on 30 June 20X5. This sale is highly probable as the negotiations are at an advance stage and as similar transactions have occurred in the past with the potential buyer involving sales of similar size.
Hedging instrument	The forward contract with reference number 012545. The counterparty to the forward is XYZ Bank and the credit risk associated with this counterparty is considered to be very low. The forward contract has a 100 million USD notional, an 80 million EUR notional, a maturity on 30 June 20X5 and a physical settlement feature under which the entity will pay the USD notional in exchange for the EUR notional
Hedge effectiveness assessment	See below

5.5.4 Hedge Effectiveness Assessment – Hypothetical Derivative

Hedge effectiveness will be assessed by comparing changes in the fair value of the hedging instrument to changes in the fair value of a hypothetical derivative. The terms of the hypothetical derivative – a EUR–USD forward contract for maturity 30 June 20X5 with nil fair value at the start of the hedging relationship – reflected the terms of the hedged item. The terms of the hypothetical derivative were as follows:

Hypothetical derivative terms	
Start date	1 October 20X4
Counterparties	ABC and credit risk-free counterparty
Maturity	30 June 20X5
ABC sells	USD 100 million
ABC buys	EUR 79,872,000
Forward rate	1.2520 (*)
Initial fair value	Nil

(*) The forward rate of the hypothetical derivative (1.2520) was different from that of the hedging instrument (1.2500) due to the absence of CVA in the hypothetical derivative (the counterparty to the hypothetical derivative is assumed to be credit risk-free).

Changes in the fair value of the hedging instrument will be recognised as follows:

- The effective part of the gain or loss on the hedging instrument will be recognised in the cash flow hedge reserve of OCI. The accumulated amount in equity will be reclassified to profit or loss in the same period during which the hedged expected future cash flow affects profit or loss, adjusting the sales amount and thereafter the revaluation of the receivable.
- The ineffective part of the gain or loss on the hedging instrument will be recognised immediately in profit or loss.

Hedge effectiveness will be assessed prospectively at hedging relationship inception, on an ongoing basis at each reporting date and upon occurrence of a significant change in the circumstances affecting the hedge effectiveness requirements.

Hedge effectiveness assessment will be performed on a forward-forward basis. In other words, the forward element of both the hedging instrument and the expected cash flow will be included in the assessment.

The hedging relationship will qualify for hedge accounting only if all the following criteria are met:

1) The hedging relationship consists only of eligible hedge items and hedging instruments. The hedge item is eligible as it is a highly expected forecast transaction that exposes the entity's profit or loss to fair value risk and is reliably measurable. The hedging instrument is eligible as it is a derivative and it does not result in a net written option.
2) At hedge inception there is a formal designation and documentation of the hedging relationship and the entity's risk management objective and strategy for undertaking the hedge.
3) The hedging relationship is considered effective.

The hedging relationship will be considered effective if all the following requirements are met:

1) There is an economic relationship between the hedged item and the hedging instrument.
2) The effect of credit risk does not dominate the value changes that result from that economic relationship.
3) The hedge ratio of the hedging relationship is the same as that resulting from the quantity of hedged item that the entity actually hedges and the quantity of the hedging instrument that the entity actually uses to hedge that quantity of hedged item. The hedge ratio should not be intentionally weighted to create ineffectiveness.

Whether there is an economic relationship between the hedged item and the hedging instrument will be assessed on a qualitative basis. The assessment will be complemented by a quantitative assessment using the scenario analysis method for one scenario in which the EUR–USD FX rate at the end of the hedging relationship (30 June 20X5) will be calculated by shifting the EUR–USD spot rate prevailing on the assessment date by +10%, and the change in fair value of both the hypothetical derivative and the hedging instrument compared.

5.5.5 Hedge Effectiveness Assessment Performed at Hedge Inception

The hedging relationship was considered effective as all the following requirements were met:

1) There was an economic relationship between the hedged item and the hedging instrument. Based on the qualitative assessment performed, supported by a quantitative analysis, ABC concluded that the change in fair value of the hedged item was expected to be substantially offset by the change in fair value of the hedging instrument, corroborating that both elements had values that would generally move in opposite directions.
2) The effect of credit risk did not dominate the value changes resulting from that economic relationship as the credit ratings of both the entity and XYZ Bank were considered sufficiently strong.
3) The 1:1 hedge ratio of the hedging relationship was the same as that resulting from the quantity of hedged item that the entity actually hedged and the quantity of the hedging instrument that the entity actually used to hedge that quantity of hedged item. The hedge ratio was not intentionally weighted to create ineffectiveness.

Due to the fact that the main terms of the hedging instrument and those of the expected cash flow closely matched and the low credit risk exposure to the counterparty of the forward contract, it was concluded that the hedging instrument and the hedged item had values that would generally move in opposite directions. This conclusion was supported by a quantitative assessment, which consisted of one scenario analysis performed as follows. A EUR–USD spot rate at the end of the hedging relationship (1.3585) was simulated by shifting the EUR–USD spot rate prevailing on the assessment date (1.2350) by +10%. As shown in the table below, the change in fair value of the hedged item was expected to largely be offset by the change in fair value of the hedging instrument, corroborating that both elements had values that would generally move in opposite directions.

Scenario analysis assessment

	Hedging Instrument	Hypothetical Derivative
Nominal USD	100,000,000	100,000,000
Forward rate	1.2500	1.2520
Nominal EUR	80,000,000	79,872,000
Nominal USD	100,000,000	100,000,000
Market rate	1.3585 *(1)*	1.3585
Value in EUR	73,611,000 *(2)*	73,611,000
Difference	6,389,000 *(3)*	6,261,000
Discount factor	1.00	1.00
Fair value	6,389,000 *(4)*	6,261,000
	Degree of offset	**102.0% (5)**

Notes:
(1) Assumed spot rate on hedging relationship end date (30 June 20X5)
(2) 73,611,000 = 100,000,000/1.3585
(3) 6,389,000 = 80,000,000 – 73,611,000
(4) 6,389,000 = 6,389,000 × 1.00
(5) 102% = 6,389,000/6,261,000

The hedge ratio was established at 1:1, resulting from the USD 100 million of the hedged item that the entity actually hedged and the USD 100 million of the hedging instrument that the entity actually used to hedge that quantity of hedged item.

Another hedge assessment was performed on 31 December 20X4 (reporting date). That assessment was very similar to the one performed at inception and has been omitted to avoid unnecessary repetition. Similarly, the hedge ratio was assumed to be 1:1 on that assessment date.

5.5.6 Fair Valuation of Hedged Item and Hypothetical Derivative at the Relevant Dates

The spot and forward exchange rates prevailing at the relevant dates were as follows:

Date	Spot rate at indicated date	Forward rate for 30-Jun-20X5 *(*)*	Discount factor for 30-Jun-20X5
1-Oct-20X4	1.2350	1.2520	0.9804
31-Dec-20X4	1.2700	1.2800	0.9839
31-Mar-20X5	1.2950	1.3000	0.9901
30-Jun-20X5	1.3200	1.3200	1.0000

(*) Credit risk-free forward rate

The fair value calculation of the hedging instrument at each relevant date was as follows:

	1-Oct-20X4	31-Dec-20X4	31-Mar-20X5	30-Jun-20X5
Nominal EUR	80,000,000	80,000,000	80,000,000	80,000,000
Nominal USD	100,000,000	100,000,000	100,000,000	100,000,000
Forward rate for 30-Jun-20X5	/1.2520	/1.2800	/1.3000	/1.3200
Value in EUR	79,872,000	78,125,000	76,923,000 *(1)*	75,758,000
Difference	128,000	1,875,000	3,077,000 *(2)*	4,242,000
Discount factor	× 0.9804	× 0.9839	× 0.9901	× 1.0000
Credit risk-free fair value	125,000	1,845,000	3,047,000 *(3)*	4,242,000
CVA	<125,000> *(6)*	<3,000>	<1,000>	0
Fair value	0	1,842,000	3,046,000 *(4)*	4,242,000
Fair value change (period)	—	1,842,000	1,204,000 *(5)*	1,196,000

Notes:
>   *(1)* 76,923,000 = 100,000,000/1.3000
>   *(2)* 3,077,000 = 80,000,000 – 76,923,000
>   *(3)* 3,047,000 = 3,077,000 × 0.9901
>   *(4)* 3,046,000 =3,047,000+ <1,000>
>   *(5)* 1,204,000 = 3,046,000 – 1,842,000
>   *(6)* This figure includes a CVA as well as the bid/offer. The figure is relatively large due a substantial additional profit applied by XYZ Bank. ABC decided not to initially recognise any up-front loss on the trade

The fair value calculation of the hypothetical derivative at each relevant date was as follows:

	1-Oct-20X4	31-Dec-20X4	31-Mar-20X5	30-Jun-20X5
Nominal EUR	79,872,000	79,872,000	79,872,000	79,872,000
Nominal USD	100,000,000	100,000,000	100,000,000	100,000,000
Forward rate for 30-Jun-20X5	/1.2520	/1.2800	/1.3000	/1.3200
Value in EUR	79,872,000	78,125,000	76,923,000	75,758,000
Difference	0	1,747,000	2,949,000	4,114,000
Discount factor	× 0.9804	× 0.9839	× 0.9901	× 1.0000
Fair value	0	1,719,000	2,920,000	4,114,000
Fair value change (cumulative)	—	1,719,000	2,920,000	4,114,000

The calculation of the effective and ineffective parts of the change in fair value of the hedging instrument was performed as follows:

	31-Dec-20X4	31-Mar-20X5	30-Jun-20X5
Cumulative change in fair value of hedging instrument	1,842,000	3,046,000	4,242,000
Cumulative change in fair value of hypothetical derivative	1,719,000	2,920,000	4,114,000
Lower amount	1,719,000	2,920,000 (1)	4,114,000
Previous cumulative effective amount	Nil	1,719,000 (2)	2,920,000
Available amount	1,719,000	1,201,000 (3)	1,194,000
Period change in fair value of hedging instrument	1,842,000	1,204,000 (4)	1,196,000
Effective part	1,719,000	1,201,000 (5)	1,194,000
Ineffective part	123,000	3,000 (6)	2,000

Notes:
(1) Lower of 3,046,000 and 2,920,000
(2) Nil + 1,719,000, the sum of all prior effective amounts
(3) 2,920,000 – 1,719,000
(4) Change in the fair value of the hedging instrument since the last fair valuation
(5) Lower of 1,201,000 (available amount) and 1,204,000 (period change in fair value of hedging nstrument)
(6) 1,204,000 (period change in fair value of hedging instrument) – 1,201,000 (effective part)

5.5.7 Accounting Entries – Hedge Objective Unchanged: No Discontinuation

The required journal entries were as follows.

1) To record the forward contract trade on 1 October 20X4

No entries in the financial statements were required as the fair value of the forward contract was zero.

2) To record the closing of the accounting period on 31 December 20X4

The change in fair value of the forward since the last valuation was a EUR 1,842,000 gain, of which EUR 1,719,000 was effective and recorded in OCI, and EUR 123,000 was ineffective and recorded in profit or loss.

Forward contract (Asset)	1,842,000	
Cash flow hedge reserve (Equity)		1,719,000
Other financial income (Profit or loss)		123,000

3) Accounting entries on 31 March 20X5

The sale agreement was recorded at the EUR–USD spot rate prevailing on 31 March 20X5 (1.2950). Therefore, the sales EUR amount was EUR 77,220,000 (=100 million/1.2950). Because the sold machinery was not yet paid, a receivable was recognised. Suppose that the machinery was valued at EUR 68 million in ABC's statement of financial position, and that ABC recognised the delivery of the machinery.

Cost of goods sold (Profit or loss)	68,000,000	
Machinery (Asset)		68,000,000
Accounts receivable (Asset)	77,220,000	
Sales (Profit or loss)		77,220,000

The change in the fair value of the FX forward since the last valuation was a gain of EUR 1,204,000. The effective part was EUR 1,201,000 and recognised in OCI, while the ineffective part was EUR 3,000 and recorded in profit or loss.

Forward contract (Asset)	1,204,000	
Cash flow hedge reserve (Equity)		1,201,000
Other financial income (Profit or loss)		3,000

The recognition of the sales transaction in profit or loss caused the release to profit or loss of the deferred hedge results accumulated in OCI.

Cash flow hedge reserve (Equity)	2,920,000	
Sales (Profit or loss)		2,920,000

4) To record the settlement of the receivable and the forward on 30 June 20X5

The receivable was revalued at the spot rate prevailing on this date, showing a loss of EUR 1,463,000 (=100 million/1.3200 – 100 million/1.2950).

Other financial expenses (Profit or loss)	1,463,000	
Accounts receivable (Asset)		1,463,000

The change in the fair value of the forward contract since the last valuation was a gain of EUR 1,196,000. The effective part was EUR 1,194,000 and recognised in OCI, while the ineffective part was EUR 2,000 and recorded in profit or loss.

Forward contract (Asset)	1,196,000	
Cash flow hedge reserve (Equity)		1,194,000
Other financial income (Profit or loss)		2,000

The revaluation of the receivable in profit or loss caused the release to profit or loss of the deferred hedge results accumulated in OCI.

Cash flow hedge reserve (Equity)	1,194,000
Other financial income (Profit or loss)	1,194,000

The receipt of the USD 100 million cash payment from the customer was valued at the spot rate on 30 June 20X5 (1.32), or EUR 75,758,000 (=100 million/1.32).

USD Cash (Asset)	75,758,000
Accounts receivable (Asset)	75,758,000

The forward was settled: the USD 100 million cash was exchanged for EUR 80 million under the physical settlement provision of the forward.

EUR cash (Asset)	80,000,000
Forward contract (Asset)	4,242,000
USD cash (Asset)	75,758,000

The following table gives a summary of the accounting entries, excluding the entries related to the cost of goods sold. The table shows that the forward contract locked in a EUR 80 million overall income.

	Cash	Forward contract	Accounts receivable	Cash flow hedge reserve	Profit or loss
1-Oct-20X4					
Forward trade	0	0			
31 Dec-20X4					
Forward revaluation		1,842,000		1,719,000	123,000
31-Mar-20X5					
Forward revaluation		1,204,000		1,201,000	3,000
Reserve reclassification				<2,920,000>	2,920,000
Sale shipment			77,220,000		77,220,000

	Cash	Forward contract	Accounts receivable	Cash flow hedge reserve	Profit or loss
30-Jun-20X5					
Forward revaluation		1,196,000		1,194,000	2,000
Reserve reclassification				<1,194,000>	1,194,000
Forward settlement	80,000,000	<4,242,000>			
	<75,758,000>				
Receivable revaluation			<1,463,000>		<1,463,000>
Receivable settlement	75,758,000		<75,758,000>		
TOTAL	**80,000,000**	**-0-**	**-0-**	**-0-**	**80,000,000**

5.5.8 Accounting Entries – Hedge Risk Management Objective Changed: Discontinuation

In our previous approach, on 30 June 20X5 an additional calculation/recognition of effective and ineffective parts and the subsequent reclassification of the effective part into profit or loss was required. An alternative to avoid such administrative complexity was to discontinue the hedging relationship on 31 March 20X5 by changing the hedge's risk management objective on that date. Whilst under IFRS 9 voluntary discontinuation of a hedging relationship is not permitted, discontinuation is required when a hedging relationship does not meet its risk management objective. By changing the risk management objective an entity may provoke a mandatory discontinuation of the hedging relationship. In my view, this solution may be challenged by auditors, especially when a pattern of changing risk management objectives has been implemented solely to overcome the restrictions of IFRS 9. However, as happened with IAS 39 (the previous hedge accounting standard), over time the auditing community comes to accept practices that at the beginning of the implementation of a standard may seem questionable. I will cover this approach next.

The accounting entries up to, and including, 31 March 20X5 were identical to those of the previous example, so are omitted here.

On 31 March 20X5, following the recognition of the receivable, ABC updated the hedge documentation as follows: "The risk management of the EUR–USD foreign exchange risk stemming from the accounts receivable will no longer be managed under this hedging relationship, but instead in conjunction with the EUR–USD foreign exchange risk stemming from the FX forward as there is a natural offset in profit or loss of both risks. As a result of this change in the risk management objective, the hedging relationship is discontinued from 31 March 20X5".

The accounting entries made on 30 June 20X5 were as follows. The receivable was revalued at the spot rate prevailing on this date, showing a loss of EUR 1,463,000 (=100 million/1.3200 – 100 million/1.2950).

Other financial expenses (Profit or loss)	1,463,000	
Accounts receivable (Asset)		1,463,000

The change in the fair value of the forward contract since the last valuation was a gain of EUR 1,196,000, recognised in profit or loss, as the forward was undesignated.

Forward contract (Asset)	1,196,000	
Other financial income (Profit or loss)		1,196,000

The receipt of the USD 100 million cash payment from the customer was valued at the spot rate on 30 June 20X5, EUR 75,758,000 (=100 million/1.32).

USD Cash (Asset)	75,758,000	
Accounts receivable (Asset)		75,758,000

The forward was settled: the USD 100 million cash was exchanged for EUR 80 million under the physical settlement provision of the forward.

EUR cash (Asset)	80,000,000	
Forward contract (Asset)		4,242,000
USD cash (Asset)		75,758,000

The following table gives a summary of the accounting entries, excluding the entries related to the cost of goods sold:

	Cash	Forward contract	Accounts receivable	Cash flow hedge reserve	Profit or loss
1-Oct-20X4					
Forward trade	0	0			
31 Dec-20X4					
Forward revaluation		1,842,000		1,842,000	
31-Mar-20X5					
Forward revaluation		1,204,000		1,204,000	
Reserve reclassification				<3,046,000>	3,046,000
Sale recognition			77,220,000		77,220,000

	Cash	Forward contract	Accounts receivable	Cash flow hedge reserve	Profit or loss
30-Jun-20X5					
Forward revaluation		1,196,000			1,196,000
Forward settlement	80,000,000	<4,242,000>			
	<75,758,000>				
Receivable revaluation			<1,463,000>		<1,463,000>
Receivable settlement	75,758,000		<75,758,000>		
TOTAL	**80,000,000**	**-0-**	**-0-**	**-0-**	**80,000,000**

Note: Total figures may not match the sum of their corresponding components due to rounding.

5.6 CASE STUDY: HEDGING A FORECAST SALE WITH AN FX FORWARD

In the previous section a forecast sale and its subsequent receivable were hedged from an accounting perspective. As a result, the maturity of the hedging relationship was set on 30 June 20X5, the date on which the receivable was expected to be settled. This resulted in ABC either incurring an unnecessary administrative burden (stemming from the calculation of effective and ineffective parts and the recording of the resultant accounting entries) or provoking a discontinuation of the hedging relationship by changing its risk management objective.

In this section only the forecast sale will be hedged from an accounting perspective (i.e., its subsequent receivable will not be part of the hedging relationship). This approach overcomes some of the weaknesses inherent in the previous approach by establishing the end of the hedging relationship on 31 March 20X5, the date on which the sales transaction was recognised. Whilst this approach is simpler from an operational perspective, the ineffective part of the hedge is likely to be larger than that of the previous approach. Nonetheless, when the time lag between sale recognition and receivable settlement is not substantially long (as in our case) and when forwards are used, this approach works reasonably well. However, when a hedging strategy involves options, this approach may cause excessive ineffectiveness due to the potentially large differences between time value decay of the hedging instrument and the hypothetical derivative.

Additionally, in this section I will cover the different accounting alternatives that IFRS 9 allows when using forwards: (i) including the forward element in the hedging relationship, (ii) excluding the forward element from the hedging relationship and recognising its change in fair value in profit or loss and (iii) excluding the forward element from the hedging relationship and temporarily recognising its change in fair value in OCI to the extent that it related to the hedged item.

The background to the case covered is identical to that in Section 5.5. On 1 October 20X4, ABC Corporation, an exporter whose functional currency was the EUR, was expecting to sell finished goods to a US client and the export to be denominated in USD. The sale was expected to occur on 31 March 20X5, and its related receivable was expected to be settled on 30 June 20X5. Sale proceeds were expected to be USD 100 million, to be received in USD.

To hedge its exposure to the EUR–USD rate, on 1 October 20X4 ABC entered into an FX forward contract with the following terms:

FX forward terms	
Start date	1 October 20X4
Counterparties	ABC and XYZ Bank
Maturity	30 June 20X5
ABC sells	USD 100 million
ABC buys	EUR 80 million
Forward Rate	1.2500
Settlement	Physical delivery

The FX forward locked in the amount of EUR to be received (i.e., EUR 80 million) in exchange for the USD 100 million sale, as shown in Figure 5.3.

5.6.1 Setting the Hedging Relationship Term

As mentioned above, the hedging relationship would end on 31 March 20X5, when the sales transaction was recognised, before the FX forward matured (see Figure 5.6).

- Until 31 March 20X5, the effective part of the changes in fair value of the forward would be recorded in OCI.
- On 31 March 20X5, the hedged cash flow (i.e., the sale) would be recognised in ABC's profit or loss and, simultaneously, the amount previously recorded in equity would be reclassified to profit or loss. Also on 31 March 20X5 a receivable denominated in USD would be recognised in ABC's statement of financial position. The hedging relationship would end on that date.
- During the period from 31 March 20X5 until 30 June 20X5, the derivative would be undesignated. There would be an almost fully offset between FX gains and losses on the revaluation of the USD accounts receivable and revaluation gains and losses on the forward contract.

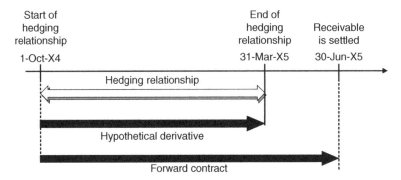

FIGURE 5.6   Transaction and hedging relationship timeframe.

5.6.2 Hedging Relationship Documentation

ABC designated the forward contract as the hedging instrument in a cash flow hedge of its USD-denominated highly expected sale. At the inception of the hedging relationship, ABC documented the hedging relationship as follows:

	Hedging relationship documentation
Risk management objective and strategy for undertaking the hedge	The objective of the hedge is to protect the EUR value of a USD 100 million cash flow stemming from a highly expected sale of finished goods. This hedging objective is consistent with the entity's overall FX risk management strategy of reducing the variability of its profit or loss statement caused by purchases and sales denominated in foreign currency. The designated risk being hedged is the risk of changes in the cash flow stemming from a highly expected sale due to unfavourable movements in the EUR–USD exchange rate
Type of hedge	Cash flow hedge
Hedged item	A USD 100 million sale of finished goods expected to take place on 31 March 20X5. This sale is highly probable as the negotiations are at an advanced stage and as similar transactions have occurred in the past with the potential buyer involving sales of similar size. For the avoidance of doubt, the ensuing receivable will not be part of the hedging relationship
Hedging instrument	The forward contract with reference number 012545. The counterparty to the forward is XYZ Bank and the credit risk associated with this counterparty is considered to be very low. The forward contract has a USD 100 million notional, EUR 80 million notional, maturity on 30 June 20X5 and a physical settlement feature under which the entity will pay the USD notional in exchange for the EUR notional
Hedge effectiveness assessment	See below

5.6.3 Hedge Effectiveness Assessment

Hedge effectiveness will be assessed by comparing changes in the fair value of the hedging instrument to changes in the fair value of a hypothetical derivative. The terms of the hypothetical derivative – a EUR–USD forward contract for maturity 31 March 20X5 with nil fair value at the start of the hedging relationship – reflected the terms of the hedged item. The terms of the hypothetical derivative were as follows:

Hypothetical derivative terms	
Start date	1 October 20X4
Counterparties	ABC and credit risk-free counterparty
Maturity	31 March 20X5
ABC sells	USD 100 million

(continued overleaf)

Hypothetical derivative terms	
ABC buys	EUR 80,257,000
Forward Rate	1.2460 (*)

(*) The forward rate of the hypothetical derivative (1.2460) was different from that of the hedging instrument (1.2500) due to their different maturity dates (31 March 20X5 and 30 June 20X5) and the absence of CVA in the hypothetical derivative (the counterparty to the hypothetical derivative is assumed to be credit risk-free).

Changes in the fair value of the hedging instrument will be recognised as follows:

- The effective part of the gain or loss on the hedging instrument will be recognised in the cash flow hedge reserve of OCI. The accumulated amount in equity will be reclassified to profit or loss in the same period during which the hedged expected future cash flow affects profit or loss, adjusting the sales amount.
- The ineffective part of the gain or loss on the hedging instrument will be recognised immediately in profit or loss.

Hedge effectiveness will be assessed prospectively at hedging relationship inception, on an ongoing basis at each reporting date and upon occurrence of a significant change in the circumstances affecting the hedge effectiveness requirements.

Hedge effectiveness assessment will be performed on a forward-forward basis. In other words, the forward element of both the hedging instrument and the expected cash flow will be included in the assessment.

The hedging relationship will qualify for hedge accounting only if all the following criteria are met:

1) The hedging relationship consists only of eligible hedge items and hedging instruments. The hedge item is eligible as it is a highly expected forecast transaction that exposes the entity's profit or loss statement to fair value risk, is reliably measurable and affects profit or loss. The hedging instrument is eligible as it is a derivative and does not result in a net written option.
2) At hedge inception there is a formal designation and documentation of the hedging relationship and the entity's risk management objective and strategy for undertaking the hedge.
3) The hedging relationship is considered effective.

The hedging relationship will be considered effective if all the following requirements are met:

1) There is an economic relationship between the hedged item and the hedging instrument.
2) The effect of credit risk does not dominate the value changes that result from that economic relationship.
3) The hedge ratio of the hedging relationship is the same as that resulting from the quantity of hedged item that the entity actually hedges and the quantity of the hedging instrument that the entity actually uses to hedge that quantity of hedged item. The hedge ratio should not be intentionally weighted to create ineffectiveness.

Whether there is an economic relationship between the hedged item and the hedging instrument will be assessed on a qualitative basis. The assessment will be complemented by a quantitative assessment using the scenario analysis method for one scenario in which the

EUR–USD FX rate at the end of the hedging relationship (31 March 20X5) will be calculated by shifting the EUR–USD spot rate prevailing on the assessment date by +10%, and the change in fair value of both the hypothetical derivative and the hedging instrument compared.

5.6.4 Hedge Effectiveness Assessment Performed at Hedge Inception

The hedging relationship was considered effective as all the following requirements were met:

1) There was an economic relationship between the hedged item and the hedging instrument. Based on the qualitative assessment performed supported by a quantitative analysis, ABC concluded that the change in fair value of the hedged item was expected to be substantially offset by the change in fair value of the hedging instrument, corroborating that both elements had values that would generally move in opposite directions.
2) The effect of credit risk did not dominate the value changes resulting from that economic relationship as the credit ratings of both the entity and XYZ Bank were considered sufficiently strong.
3) The 1:1 hedge ratio of the hedging relationship was the same as that resulting from the quantity of hedged item that the entity actually hedged and the quantity of the hedging instrument that the entity actually used to hedge that quantity of hedged item. The hedge ratio was not intentionally weighted to create ineffectiveness.

Due to the fact that the terms of the hedging instrument and those of the expected cash flow closely matched and the low credit risk exposure to the counterparty of the forward contract, it was concluded that the hedging instrument and the hedged item had values that would generally move in opposite directions. This conclusion was supported by a quantitative assessment, which consisted of one scenario analysis performed as follows. A EUR–USD spot rate at the end of the hedging relationship (1.3585) was simulated by shifting the EUR–USD spot rate prevailing on the assessment date (1.2350) by +10%. The fair value of the hedging instrument was calculated, assuming that the forward rate for 30 June 20X5 was 1.3625 and the discount factor from 31 March 20X5 to 30 June 20X5 was 0.99. As shown in the table below, the change in fair value of the hedged item was expected to largely be offset by the change in fair value of the hedging instrument, corroborating that both elements had values that would generally move in opposite directions.

| | Scenario analysis assessment | |
	Hedging instrument	**Hypothetical derivative**
Nominal USD	100,000,000	100,000,000
Forward rate	1.2500	1.2460
Nominal EUR	80,000,000	80,257,000
Nominal USD	100,000,000	100,000,000
Market rate	1.3625 *(1)*	1.3585 *(2)*
Value in EUR	73,394,000 *(3)*	73,611,000
Difference	6,606,000 *(4)*	6,646,000
Discount factor	0.99	1.00
Fair value (credit risk-free)	6,540,000 *(5)*	6,646,000

(continued overleaf)

	Scenario analysis assessment	
	Hedging instrument	**Hypothetical derivative**
CVA	<2,000>	
Fair value	6,538,000	6,646,000
	Degree of offset	**98% (6)**

Notes:
  (1) Forward rate to 30 June 20X5
  (2) Assumed spot rate on hedging relationship end date
  (3) 73,394,000 = 100,000,000/1.3625
  (4) 6,606,000 = 80,000,000 − 73,394,000
  (5) 6,540,000 = 6,606,000 × 0.99
  (6) 98% = 6,538,000/6,646,000

The hedge ratio was established at 1:1, resulting from the USD 100 million of hedged item that the entity actually hedged and the USD 100 million of the hedging instrument that the entity actually used to hedge that quantity of hedged item.

Another hedge assessment was performed on 31 December 20X4 (reporting date). That assessment was very similar to the one performed at inception and has been omitted to avoid unnecessary repetition. Additionally, the hedge ratio was assumed to be 1:1 on that assessment date.

5.6.5 Fair Valuation of Hedged Item and Hypothetical Derivative at the Relevant Dates

The spot and forward exchange rates prevailing at the relevant dates were as follows:

Date	Spot rate at indicated date	Forward rate for 30-Jun-20X5 (*)	Discount factor for 30-Jun-20X5	Forward rate for 31-Mar-20X5	Discount factor for 31-Mar-20X5
1-Oct-20X4	1.2350	1.2480	0.9804	1.2460	0.9842
31-Dec-20X4	1.2700	1.2800	0.9839	1.2770	0.9895
31-Mar-20X5	1.2950	1.3000	0.9901	1.2950	1.0000
30-Jun-20X5	1.3200	1.3200	1.0000	—	—

*) Credit risk-free forward rate

The fair value calculation of the hedging instrument at each relevant date was covered in Section 5.5.6, resulting in the following amounts:

	1-Oct-20X4	31-Dec-20X4	31-Mar-20X5	30-Jun-20X5
Fair value	0	1,842,000	3,046,000	4,242,000
Fair value change (period)	—	1,842,000	1,204,000	1,196,000

The fair value calculation of the hypothetical derivative at each relevant date was as follows:

	1-Oct-20X4	31-Dec-20X4	31-Mar-20X5
Nominal EUR	80,257,000	80,257,000	80,257,000
Nominal USD	100,000,000	100,000,000	100,000,000
Forward rate for 31-Mar-20X5	/1.2460	/1.2770	/1.2950
Value in EUR	80,257,000	78,309,000	77,220,000
Difference	0	1,948,000	3,037,000
Discount factor	× 0.9842	× 0.9895	× 1.0000
Fair value	0	1,928,000	3,037,000
Fair value change	—	1,928,000	1,109,000

The calculation of the effective and ineffective parts of the change in fair value of the hedging instrument was calculated as follows:

	31-Dec-20X4	31-Mar-20X5
Cumulative change in fair value of hedging instrument	1,842,000	3,046,000
Cumulative change in fair value of hypothetical derivative	1,928,000	3,037,000
Lower amount	1,842,000	3,037,000 *(1)*
Previous cumulative effective amount	Nil	1,842,000 *(2)*
Available amount	1,842,000	1,195,000 *(3)*
Period change in fair value of hedging instrument	1,842,000	1,204,000 *(4)*
Effective part	1,842,000	1,195,000 *(5)*
Ineffective part	Nil	9,000 *(6)*

Notes:
(1) 3,037,000 = lower of 3,046,000 and 3,037,000
(2) 1,842,000 = Nil + 1,842,000, the sum of all prior effective amounts
(3) 1,195,000 = 3,037,000 – 1,842,000
(4) Change in the fair value of the hedging instrument since the last fair valuation
(5) Lower of 1,195,000 (available amount) and 1,204,000 (period change in fair value of hedging instrument)
(6) 1,204,000 (period change in fair value of hedging instrument) – 1,195,000 (effective part)

5.6.6 Accounting Entries When the Forward Element is Included in the Hedging Relationship

The required journal entries were as follows.

1) To record the forward contract trade on 1 October 20X4

No entries in the financial statements were required as the fair value of the forward contract was zero.

2) To record the closing of the accounting period on 31 December 20X4

The change in fair value of the forward since the last valuation was a gain of EUR 1,842,000. As the hedge was fully effective, all that change in fair value was recorded in OCI and none in profit or loss.

Forward contract (Asset)	1,842,000	
Cash flow hedge reserve (Equity)		1,842,000

3) To record the sale agreement and the end of the hedging relationship on 31 March 20X5

The sale agreement was recorded at the EUR–USD spot rate prevailing on 31 March 20X5 (1.2950). Therefore, the sales EUR amount was EUR 77,220,000 (=100 million/1.2950). Because the sold machinery was not yet paid, a receivable was recognised. Suppose that the machinery was valued at EUR 68 million in ABC's statement of financial position, and that ABC recognised the delivery of the machinery.

Cost of goods sold (Profit or Loss)	68,000,000	
Machinery (Asset)		68,000,000
Accounts receivable (Asset)	77,220,000	
Sales (Profit or loss)		77,220,000

The change in the fair value of the FX forward since the last valuation was a gain of EUR 1,204,000. The effective part was EUR 1,195,000, recognised in OCI. The ineffective part was EUR 9,000, recognised in profit or loss.

Forward contract (Asset)	1,204,000	
Cash flow hedge reserve (Equity)		1,195,000
Other financial income (Profit or loss)		9,000

The recognition of the sales transaction in profit or loss caused the release to profit or loss of the deferred hedge results accumulated in OCI.

Cash flow hedge reserve (Equity)	3,037,000	
Sales (Profit or loss)		3,037,000

4) To record the settlement of the receivable and the forward on 30 June 20X5

The receivable was revalued at the spot rate prevailing on this date, showing a loss of EUR 1,463,000 (=100 million/1.3200 – 100 million/1.2950).

Other financial expenses (Profit or loss)	1,463,000	
Accounts receivable (Asset)		1,463,000

The change in the fair value of the forward contract since the last valuation was a gain of EUR 1,196,000. The gain was recognised in profit or loss as the derivative was no longer part of a hedging relationship (i.e., it was undesignated).

Forward contract (Asset)	1,196,000	
Other financial income (Profit or loss)		1,196,000

The receipt of the USD 100 million cash payment from the customer was valued at the spot rate on 30 June 20X5, EUR 75,758,000 (=100 million/1.32).

USD Cash (Asset)	75,758,000	
Accounts receivable (Asset)		75,758,000

The forward was settled: the USD 100 million cash was exchanged for EUR 80 million under the physical settlement provision of the forward.

EUR cash (Asset)	80,000,000	
Forward contract (Asset)		4,242,000
USD cash (Asset)		75,758,000

With the hedge, ABC locked in EUR 80 million proceeds from the USD sale. Including the EUR 68 million cost of goods sold, the hedge locked in EUR 12 million earnings before tax (EBT). The majority of the change in fair value of the forward contract during the hedging relationship (i.e., until 31 March 20X5) adjusted the sales amount. From that date, the entirety of change in fair value of the forward contract was recognised as "other financial income/expenses". The inclusion of the forward points in the hedging relationship caused the expected deterioration, during such relationship, of the exchange rate implied by the forward points to end up adjusting sales (i.e., within earnings before interest, taxes, depreciation and amortisation (EBITDA)), and not in the "other financial income/expenses" line. The effects of the hedge in ABC's profit or loss are shown in Figure 5.7. Without the hedge, the EBT and the proceeds from the sale would have been EUR 4,242,000 lower.

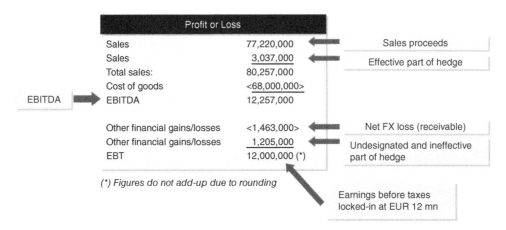

FIGURE 5.7 Effects of hedge in ABC's profit or loss statement (forward points included in hedging relationship).

The following table gives a summary of the accounting entries, excluding the entries related to the cost of goods sold. The table shows that the forward contract locked in a EUR 80 million overall income.

	Cash	Forward contract	Accounts receivable	Cash flow hedge reserve	Profit or loss
1-Oct-20X4					
Forward trade	0	0			
31 Dec-20X4					
Forward revaluation		1,842,000		1,842,000	
31-Mar-20X5					
Forward revaluation		1,204,000		1,195,000	9,000
Reserve reclassification				<3,037,000>	3,037,000
Sale recognition			77,220,000		77,220,000
30-Jun-20X5					
Forward revaluation		1,196,000			1,196,000
Forward settlement	80,000,000	<4,242,000>			
	<75,758,000>				
Receivable revaluation			<1,463,000>		<1,463,000>
Receivable settlement	75,758,000		<75,758,000>		
TOTAL	**80,000,000**	**-0-**	**-0-**	**-0-**	**80,000,000**

Note: Total figures may not match the sum of their corresponding components due to rounding.

5.6.7 Accounting Election When the Forward Element is Excluded from the Hedging Relationship

When an entity elects to exclude the forward element (i.e., the forward points) from a hedging relationship (i.e., only the spot element is part of such relationship), IFRS 9 allows entities to elect between:

- Recognising the changes in the forward element in profit or loss.
- Recognising the changes in the forward element temporarily in OCI to the extent that these changes relate to the hedged item. The amount accumulated in OCI is later reclassified to profit or loss – adjusting the sales figure – when the sale is recognised. In our example, it would mean that a substantial part of the forward points would adjust the sales figure.

It is likely that ABC would have selected the first alternative. Firstly, the forward element implied a loss because the forward rate (1.2500) was unfavourable relative to the spot rate (1.2350). As a result, under the first alternative the sales figure was likely to look better than under the second alternative. Secondly, the first alternative was much simpler than the second alternative from an operational perspective. However, the forward in its entirety (including both the spot and forward elements) could be thought of as "insurance" bought to guarantee that the proceeds from the sale were EUR 80 million, and probably the second alternative provided a more complete picture of the entity's activities by incorporating in the sales line the "insurance" related to such sale.

5.6.8 Accounting When the Forward Element is Excluded from the Hedging Relationship and Recognised in Profit or Loss

Suppose that in the previous hedge ABC decided to exclude the forward element from the hedging relationship and to recognise the change in the fair value of the forward element in profit or loss. Excluding the forward element from the hedging relationship implied that hedge effectiveness would assessed taking into only changes in fair value due to changes in the spot exchange rate (what is termed "spot-to-spot" assessment).

Forward Contract Fair Valuation The fair value of the forward component was calculated as the difference between the total fair value of the forward contract and the fair value of its spot component:

$$\boxed{\text{Fair Value of Forward Element}} = \boxed{\text{Total Fair Value}} - \boxed{\text{Fair Value of Spot Element}}$$

The changes in fair value of the spot and forward elements of the forward contract were calculated as follows (the total fair values of the forward contract were calculated in Section 5.6.5):

	1-Oct-20X4	31-Dec-20X4	31-Mar-20X5	30-Jun-20X5
Total fair value (FV)	0	1,842,000 *(1)*	3,046,000	4,242,000
Period FV change	—	1,842,000	1,204,000	1,196,000

(continued overleaf)

	1-Oct-20X4	31-Dec-20X4	31-Mar-20X5	30-Jun-20X5
Spot element fair valuations:				
Nominal in USD	100,000,000	100,000,000	100,000,000	
Initial spot rate	/1.2350	/1.2350	/1.2350	
Initial EUR amount	80,972,000	80,972,000	80,972,000	
Nominal in USD	100,000,000	100,000,000	100,000,000	
Spot rate	/1.2350	/1,2700	/1,2950	
Value in EUR	80,972,000	78,740,000	77,220,000	
Difference	-0-	2,232,000	3,752,000	
Discount factor	× 0.9804	× 0.9839	× 0.9901	
Fair value (spot element)	-0-	2,196,000	3,715,000	
Period FV change (spot element)	—	2,196,000	1,519,000	
Cumulative FV change (spot element)	—	2,196,000	3,715,000	
Forward element fair valuations:				
Fair value (forward element)	-0-	<354,000> *(2)*	<669,000>	
Period FV change (forward element)	—	<354,000>	<315,000>	
Cumulative FV change (forward element)	—	<354,000>	<669,000>	

Notes:

A split between the spot and forward components was not needed on 30-Jun-20X5, as the forward was undesignated from 31-Mar-20X5
From table in Section 5.6.5
1,842,000 (total fair value) – 2,196,000 (fair value of spot element)

The changes in the fair value of the spot and forward elements of the hypothetical derivative were calculated as follows (the total fair values of the hypothetical derivative were calculated in Section 5.6.5):

	1-Oct-20X4	31-Dec-20X4	31-Mar-20X5
Total fair value (FV)	-0-	1,928,000 *(1)*	3,037,000
Cumulative FV change	—	1,928,000	3,037,000
Spot element fair valuations:			
Nominal in USD	100,000,000	100,000,000	100,000,000
Initial spot rate	/1.2350	/1.2350	/1.2350
Initial nominal EUR	80,972,000	80,972,000	80,972,000
Nominal in USD	100,000,000	100,000,000	100,000,000
Spot rate	/1.2350	/1,2700	/1,2950
Value in EUR	80,972,000	78,740,000	77,220,000
Difference	-0-	2,232,000	3,752,000

	1-Oct-20X4	31-Dec-20X4	31-Mar-20X5
Discount factor	× 0.9842	× 0.9895	× 1.0000
Fair value (spot element)	-0-	2,209,000	3,752,000
Cumulative FV change (spot element)	—	2,209,000	3,752,000
Forward element fair valuations:			
Fair value (forward element)	-0-	<281,000> *(2)*	<715,000>
Cumulative FV change (forward element)	—	<281,000>	<715,000>

Notes:
      (1) From table in Section 5.6.5
      (2) 1,928,000 (total fair value) – 2,209,000 (fair value of spot element)

The effective and ineffective parts of the change in fair value of the hedging instrument (i.e., the spot component of the forward contract) were calculated as follows:

	31-Dec-20X4	31-Mar-20X5
Cumulative change in fair value of hedging instrument (spot element)	2,196,000	3,715,000
Cumulative change in fair value of hypothetical derivative (spot element)	2,209,000	3,752,000
Lower amount	2,196,000	3,715,000 (1)
Previous cumulative effective amount	Nil	2,196,000 (2)
Available amount	2,196,000	1,519,000 (3)
Period change in fair value of hedging instrument (spot element)	2,196,000	1,519,000 (4)
Effective part	2,196,000	1,519,000 (5)
Ineffective part	Nil	Nil (6)

Notes:
      (1) Lower of 3,715,000 and 3,752,000
      (2) Nil + 2,196,000, the sum of all prior effective amounts
      (3) 3,715,000 – 2,196,000
      (4) Change in the fair value of the hedging instrument (i.e., spot element) since the last fair valuation
      (5) Lower of 1,519,000 (available amount) and 1,519,000 (period change in fair value of hedging instrument – i.e., spot element)
      (6) 1,519,000 (period change in fair value of hedging instrument – i.e., spot element) – 1,519,000 (effective part)

Accounting Entries – Forward Element Changes through Profit or Loss   The accounting entries shown next assume that ABC elected to recognise the changes in the forward element in profit or loss. The required journal entries were as follows.

1) To record the forward contract trade on 1 October 20X4

No entries in the financial statements were required as the fair value of the forward contract was zero.

2) To record the closing of the accounting period on 31 December 20X4

The change in fair value of the spot element since the last valuation was a EUR 2,196,000 gain. That entire amount was considered effective and recorded in OCI, and as a result there was no ineffective amount. The change in fair value of the forward element resulted in a EUR 354,000 loss, recognised in profit or loss as it was excluded from the hedging relationship.

Forward contract (Asset)	1,842,000	
Financial expenses (Profit or loss)	354,000	
Cash flow hedge reserve (Equity)		2,196,000

3) To record the sale agreement and the end of the hedging relationship on 31 March 20X5

The sale agreement was recorded at the EUR–USD spot rate prevailing on the date the sales are recognised (1.2950). Therefore, the sales EUR amount was EUR 77,220,000 (=100 million/1.2950). Because the sold machinery was not yet paid, a receivable was recognised. Suppose that the machinery was valued at EUR 68 million in ABC's statement of financial position, and that ABC recognised the delivery of the machinery.

Accounts receivable (Asset)	77,220,000	
Sales (Profit or loss)		77,220,000
Cost of goods sold (Profit or loss)	68,000,000	
Machinery (Asset)		68,000,000

The change in fair value of the spot element since the last valuation was a EUR 1,519,000 gain. That entire amount was considered effective and recorded in OCI, and as a result there was no ineffective amount.
The change in fair value of the forward element resulted in a EUR 315,000 loss, recognised in profit or loss as it was excluded from the hedging relationship.

Forward contract (Asset)	1,204,000	
Financial expenses (Profit or loss)	315,000	
Cash flow hedge reserve (Equity)		1,519,000

The recognition of the sales transaction in profit or loss caused the release to profit or loss of the deferred hedge results accumulated in OCI.

Cash flow hedge reserve (Equity)	3,715,000	
Sales (Profit or loss)		3,715,000

4) To record the settlement of the receivable and the forward on 30 June 20X5

The receivable was revalued at the spot rate prevailing on this date, showing a EUR 1,463,000 (=100 million/1.3200 – 100 million/1.2950) loss.

Other financial expenses (Profit or loss)	1,463,000	
Accounts receivable (Asset)		1,463,000

The change in the fair value of the forward contract since the last valuation was a EUR 1,196,000 gain. Since the forward contract was no longer part of a hedging relationship, the gain was recognised in profit or loss.

Forward contract (Asset)	1,196,000	
Other financial income (Profit or loss)		1,196,000

The receipt of the USD 100 million cash payment from the customer was valued at the spot rate on 30 June 20X5, EUR 75,758,000 (=100 million/1.32).

USD Cash (Asset)	75,758,000	
Accounts receivable (Asset)		75,758,000

The forward was settled: the USD 100 million cash was exchanged for EUR 80 million under the physical settlement provision of the forward contract.

EUR cash (Asset)	80,000,000	
Forward contract (Asset)		4,242,000
USD cash (Asset)		75,758,000

The following table gives a summary of the accounting entries, excluding the entries related to the cost of goods sold. The table shows that the forward contract locked in a EUR 80 million overall income.

	Cash	Forward contract	Accounts receivable	Cash flow hedge reserve	Profit or loss
1-Oct-20X4					
Forward trade	0	0			
31 Dec-20X4					
Forward revaluation		1,842,000		2,196,000	<354,000>
31-Mar-20X5					
Forward revaluation		1,204,000		1,519,000	<315,000>
Reserve reclassification				<3,715,000>	3,715,000
Sale recognition			77,220,000		77,220,000
30-Jun-20X5					
Forward revaluation		1,196,000			1,196,000
Forward settlement	80,000,000	<4,242,000>			
	<75,758,000>				
Receivable revaluation			<1,463,000>		<1,463,000>
Receivable settlement	75,758,000		<75,758,000>		
TOTAL	**80,000,000**	**-0-**	**-0-**	**-0-**	**80,000,000**

Note: Total figures may not match the sum of their corresponding components due to rounding.

With the hedge ABC locked in EUR 80 million proceeds from the USD sale. Including the EUR 68 million cost of goods sold, the hedge locked in EUR 12 million in EBT. While all the change in fair value of the spot element (a EUR 3,715,000 gain) during the hedging relationship (i.e., until 31 March 20X5) adjusted the sales amount, the change in fair value of the forward element (a EUR 669,000 loss) was recognised in "financial expenses" of profit or loss and not within EBITDA, as shown in Figure 5.8. From that date, the entirety of the change in fair value of the forward contract was recognised as "other financial income/expenses". Without the hedge, the EBT and the proceeds from the sale would have been EUR 4,242,000 lower.

5.6.9 Accounting When the Forward Element is Excluded from the Hedging Relationship and Aligned Portion Temporarily Recognised in OCI

The accounting entries shown next assume that ABC elected to recognise the changes in the forward element temporarily in OCI to the extent that they related to the hedged item.

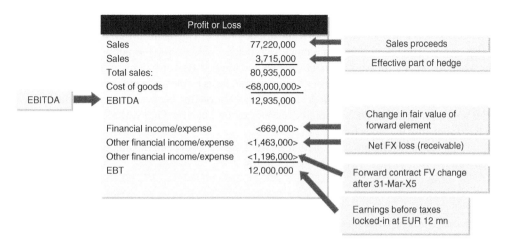

FIGURE 5.8 Effects of hedge in ABC's profit and loss statement (forward points excluded from hedging relationship and recognised through profit or loss).

The forward element of the forward contract entered into by ABC was called the **actual forward element**. That element was compared to the forward element of a theoretical forward that would have had critical terms that perfectly matched the hedged item – the **aligned forward element**.

The actual forward element valuations (see Section 5.6.8) at each relevant date were as follows:

	1-Oct-20X4	31-Dec-20X4	31-Mar-20X5
Actual forward element	-0-	<354,000>	<669,000>
Actual forward element (period change)	—	<354,000>	<315,000>
Actual forward element (cumulative change)	—	<354,000>	<669,000>

In our case, the aligned forward element corresponded to the forward element of the hypothetical derivative. Based on the hypothetical derivative's fair value and spot elements calculations in Section 5.6.8, the aligned forward element valuations at each relevant date were as follows:

	1-Oct-20X4	31-Dec-20X4	31-Mar-20X5
Fair value	-0-	1,928,000	3,037,000
Spot element	-0-	2,209,000	3,752,000
Aligned forward element	-0-	<281,000> *(1)*	<715,000>
Aligned forward element (period change)		<281,000>	<434,000> *(2)*

Notes:
   (1) 1,928,000 – 2,209,000
   (2) <715,000> – <281,000> (previous fair value of the aligned forward element)

At hedge inception, both the actual and the aligned forward elements were nil. Whilst IFRS 9 provides guidance when actual and aligned forward elements differ, it does not address a situation in which both forward elements coincide. ABC decided to apply the guidance set for when the actual forward element exceeds the aligned forward element: the amount to be recognised in OCI would be determined only on the basis of the aligned forward element. Any remainder would be recognised in profit or loss. Additionally, because in our case the hedged item was a transaction-related item, the amount accumulated in OCI was reclassified to profit or loss, adjusting the sales figure.

The split of the change in the actual forward element between the amounts recognised in OCI and in profit or loss was calculated as follows:

	31-Dec-20X4	31-Mar-20X5
Period change in actual forward element	<354,000>	<315,000>
Period change in aligned forward element	<281,000>	<434,000>
Amount in OCI	<281,000>	<434,000> *(1)*
Amount in profit or loss	<73,000>	119,000 *(2)*

Notes:
  (1) Equals the period change in aligned forward element
  (2) <315,000> – <434,000>

The required journal entries were as follows.

1) To record the forward contract trade on 1 October 20X4

No entries in the financial statements were required as the fair value of the forward contract was zero.

2) To record the closing of the accounting period on 31 December 20X4

The period change in the total fair value of the forward contract was a EUR 1,842,000 gain. The change in fair value of the spot element since the last valuation was a EUR 2,196,000 gain. That entire amount was considered effective and recorded in OCI, and as a result there was no ineffective amount. The change in fair value of the forward element resulted in a EUR 281,000 loss recognised in OCI and another EUR 73,000 loss recognised in profit or loss.

Forward contract (Asset)	1,842,000	
Forward element reserve (Equity)	281,000	
Other financial expenses (Profit or loss)	73,000	
Cash flow hedge reserve (Equity)		2,196,000

3) To record the sale agreement and the end of the hedging relationship on 31 March 20X5
The sale agreement was recorded at the EUR–USD spot rate prevailing on the date the sales are recognised (1.2950). Therefore, the sales EUR amount was EUR 77,220,000 (=100

million/1.2950). Because the sold machinery was not yet paid, a receivable was recognised. Suppose that the machinery was valued at EUR 68 million in ABC's statement of financial position, and that ABC recognised the delivery of the machinery.

Accounts receivable (Asset)	77,220,000	
Sales (Profit or loss)		77,220,000
Cost of goods sold (Profit or loss)	68,000,000	
Machinery (Asset)		68,000,000

The period change in the total fair value of the forward contract was a EUR 1,204,000 gain. The change in fair value of the spot element since the last valuation was a EUR 1,519,000 gain. That entire amount was considered effective and recorded in OCI, and as a result there was no ineffective amount.

The change in fair value of the forward element resulted in a EUR 315,000 loss, split between a EUR 434,000 loss recognised in OCI and a EUR 119,000 gain recognised in profit or loss.

Forward contract (Asset)	1,204,000	
Forward element reserve (Equity)	434,000	
Other financial income (Profit or loss)		119,000
Cash flow hedge reserve (Equity)		1,519,000

The recognition of the sales transaction in profit or loss caused the release to profit or loss of the EUR 3,715,000 deferred cash flow hedge results accumulated in OCI.

Cash flow hedge reserve (Equity)	3,715,000	
Sales (Profit or loss)		3,715,000

The recognition of the sales transaction in profit or loss caused the release to profit or loss of the EUR <715,000> forward element results accumulated in OCI.

Sales (Profit or loss)	715,000	
Forward element reserve (Equity)		715,000

4) To record the settlement of the receivable and the forward on 30 June 20X5

The receivable was revalued at the spot rate prevailing on this date, showing a loss of EUR 1,463,000 (=100 million/1.3200 – 100 million/1.2950).

Other financial expenses (Profit or loss)	1,463,000
Accounts receivable (Asset)	1,463,000

The change in the fair value of the forward contract since the last valuation was a gain of EUR 1,196,000. Since the forward contract was no longer part of a hedging relationship, the gain was recognised in profit or loss.

Forward contract (Asset)	1,196,000
Other financial income (Profit or loss)	1,196,000

The receipt of the USD 100 million cash payment from the customer was valued at the spot rate on 30 June 20X5, EUR 75,758,000 (=100 million/1.32).

USD Cash (Asset)	75,758,000
Accounts receivable (Asset)	75,758,000

The forward was settled: the USD 100 million cash was exchanged for EUR 80 million under the physical settlement provision of the forward.

EUR cash (Asset)	80,000,000
Forward contract (Asset)	4,242,000
USD cash (Asset)	75,758,000

The following table gives a summary of the accounting entries, excluding the entries related to the cost of goods sold. The table shows that the forward contract locked in EUR 80 million in overall income.

	Cash	Forward contract	Accounts receivable	Reserves in OCI	Profit or loss
1-Oct-20X4					
Forward trade	-0-	-0-			
31 Dec-20X4					
Forward revaluation		1,842,000		2,196,000	<73,000>
				<281,000>	
31-Mar-20X5					

	Cash	Forward contract	Accounts receivable	Reserves in OCI	Profit or loss
Forward revaluation		1,204,000		1,519,000 <434,000>	119,000
Cash flow hedge reserve reclassification				<3,715,000>	3,715,000
Forward element reserve reclassification				715,000	<715,000>
Sale recognition			77,220,000		77,220,000
30-Jun-20X5					
Forward revaluation		1,196,000			1,196,000
Forward settlement	80,000,000 <75,758,000>	<4,242,000>			
Receivable revaluation			<1,463,000>		<1,463,000>
Receivable settlement	75,758,000		<75,758,000>		
TOTAL	**80,000,000**	**-0-**	**-0-**	**-0-**	**80,000,000**

Note: Total figures may not match the sum of their corresponding components due to rounding.

This alternative increased the amount of the change in fair value of the forward temporarily recognised in OCI (see Figure 5.9), which helped reduce volatility in profit or loss. However, it was substantially more complex from an operational standpoint as the entity was required to keep track of the aligned time values. For such a short transaction, probably it was better just to recognise all the changes in the forward element in profit or loss.

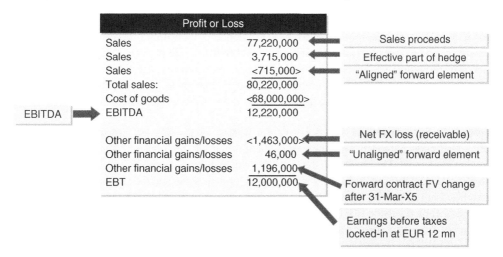

FIGURE 5.9 Effects of hedge in ABC's profit or loss statement (forward points excluded from hedging relationship and temporarily recognised through OCI).

5.6.10 Final Remarks: Inclusion versus Exclusion of the Forward Element

The forward element (i.e., the forward points) of an FX forward represents the expected depreciation of one currency relative to the other currency during a specific period. Forward points result from the interest rate differential between both currencies. Under IFRS 9, the measurement of the hedge effectiveness between the forecasted transaction and the FX forward may be based on either the spot element (i.e., excluding the forward element from the hedging relationship) or the forward contract in its entirety (i.e., including both the spot and the forward element in the hedging relationship). No method is best as both approaches have potential benefits and drawbacks. Whilst under both alternatives the EBT is the same, the effect on EBITDA is dependent on the chosen alternative.

I analyse next the impact of the three previous approaches on EBITDA. In our case, the forward points implied a depreciation of the USD relative to the EUR, a loss that necessarily arose during the life of the forward contract.

	Approach 1	Approach 2	Approach 3
Sales	80,257,000	80,935,000	80,220,000
Cost of goods sold	<68,000,000>	<68,000,000>	<68,000,000>
EBITDA	12,257,000	12,935,000	12,220,000
Financial income/expenses		<669,000>	
Other financial income/expenses	<257,000>	<267,000>	<220,000>
Earnings before tax	12,000,000	12,000,000	12,000,000

Note: Total figures may not match the sum of their corresponding components due to rounding.

Approach 1: Forward Element Included in the Hedging Relationship   Under this approach, the forward in its entirety was designated as the hedging instrument. When the forward element was included in the hedging relationship, the implied USD depreciation (to the extent that it related to the hedged item) was recorded within "sales" in EBITDA. As a result, the sales figure was reduced by the amount related to the USD depreciation implicit in the forward element amount, to the extent that the depreciation related to the hedge item (i.e., the hedge effective part). The amounts recognised in "other financial income and expenses" line outside EBITDA during the hedging relationship duration were those changes in the fair value of the forward element that were unrelated to the hedge item (i.e., the hedge ineffective part).

Approach 2: Forward Element Excluded from the Hedging Relationship and Recognised in Profit or Loss   Under this approach, only the spot element of the forward contract was designated as the hedging instrument. The changes in the forward element were recognised in profit or loss. Because the forward element was excluded from the hedging relationship and the changes in its fair value recognised in profit or loss, the implied USD depreciation during the hedging relationship duration was recorded outside EBITDA, in the "financial income and expenses" line of profit or loss.

In our case (an expected sale) the full exclusion of the forward element improved ABC's sales and EBITDA figures as the implied USD deterioration was kept outside EBITDA. Had the expected transaction been a purchase instead of a sale, the effect would have been the opposite: a lower EBITDA.

Approach 3: Forward Element Excluded from the Hedging Relationship and Temporarily Recognised in OCI When the forward element was excluded from the hedging relationship and the changes in its fair value temporarily recognised in OCI (to the extent that they related to the hedged item), the implied USD depreciation, to the extent that it related to the hedged item, was recorded, during the hedging relationship duration, within EBITDA and any remainder was recognised outside EBITDA (in the "other income and expenses" line of profit or loss). The result was relatively similar to that of the first approach. However, this approach required the computation of the aligned forward element, increasing the operational burden.

What I take from these three approaches is that when the hedging relationship is short, as in our case, approach 3 is unattractive due to its operational complexity. When the appreciation or depreciation of the foreign currency as implied by the forward element is substantial, an entity would need to carefully assess whether to include most of the appreciation/depreciation in the sales figure. This is the case when the currency pair has large interest rate differentials or when the hedging horizon is notably long.

5.7 CASE STUDY: HEDGING A FORECAST SALE AND SUBSEQUENT RECEIVABLE WITH A TUNNEL

This case covers the treatment of options under IFRS 9 when an option's time value is excluded from the hedging relationship. In this case the cash flow stemming from a highly expected forecast sale and its ensuing receivable denominated in a foreign currency is hedged from a hedge accounting perspective. The hedging contract is a tunnel – a combination of a call and a put.

Suppose that on 1 October 20X4 ABC Corporation, a company whose functional currency was the EUR, was expecting to export finished goods to a US client. The goods were expected to be shipped on 31 March 20X5, and a related sale receivable was expected to be settled on 30 June 20X5. Sale proceeds were expected to be USD 100 million to be billed in USD.

ABC had the view that the USD could appreciate against the EUR and wanted to benefit were its view right. At the same time, ABC wanted protection, in case its view was wrong. As a consequence, on 1 October 20X4 ABC entered into an FX tunnel with the following terms:

USD put/EUR call terms		USD call/EUR put terms	
Trade date	1 October 20X4	Trade date	1 October 20X4
Option buyer	ABC	Option buyer	XYZ Bank
Option seller	XYZ Bank	Option seller	ABC
USD notional	USD 100 million	USD notional	USD 100 million
Strike	1.2900	Strike	1.2120
EUR notional	EUR 77,519,000	EUR notional	EUR 82,508,000
Expiry date	30 June 20X5	Expiry date	30 June 20X5
Settlement	Physical delivery	Settlement	Physical delivery
Premium	EUR 1,400,000	Premium	EUR 1,400,000
Premium payment date	1 October 20X4	Premium payment date	1 October 20X4

In the FX options market, the term call (or put) is accompanied by the currency to which it is a call (or put), as discussed in Chapter 4. Additionally, a call on one of the two currencies is a put on the other currency. For example, when referring to a EUR–USD option, a call on the USD automatically implies a put on the EUR. In our case, ABC bought a USD put (or EUR call) with strike 1.2900. The USD put gave ABC the right, but not the obligation, to sell USD 100 million at a rate of 1.2900 on expiry date. This option protected ABC's sale from a depreciating USD above 1.2900. Consequently, ABC would only exercise the USD put if the EUR–USD exchange rate exceeded 1.2900 on expiry date, receiving EUR 77,519,000 in exchange for USD 100 million.

In order to avoid paying a premium, ABC also sold a USD call (or EUR put) with strike 1.2120. The USD call gave XYZ Bank the right to sell EUR 82,508,000 (=USD 100 million/1.2120) in exchange for USD 100 million. Thus, XYZ Bank would only exercise the USD call if the EUR–USD exchange rate was below 1.2120 at expiry.

The combination of both options is commonly referred to as a **tunnel** in the FX market. The same strategy in the interest rate market would be called a "collar". Because the premium to be paid for the purchased option equalled the premium to be received for the written (sold) option, this hedging strategy is called a **zero-cost tunnel**.

The zero-cost tunnel guaranteed ABC that the EUR proceeds stemming from the highly expected sale would be between EUR 77,519,000 and EUR 82,508,000. If the EUR–USD at maturity ended up between 1.2120 and 1.2900, neither option would be exercised and ABC would exchange the USD for EUR in the FX market at the prevailing EUR–USD FX spot rate. Figure 5.10 depicts the amount of EUR that ABC would get in exchange for USD 100 million as a function of the EUR–USD spot rate at expiry. Figure 5.11 shows the profile of the resulting exchange rate at which ABC would exchange USD 100 million, as a function of the EUR–USD spot rate at expiry.

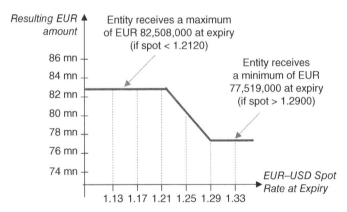

FIGURE 5.10   FX tunnel – resulting EUR amount.

When an option is used in a hedging strategy and hedge accounting is applied, IFRS 9 gives entities two choices:

- To designate the option in its entirety as the hedging instrument. This is seldom elected.
- To separate the option's intrinsic and time values, and to only designate the intrinsic value as the hedging instrument in the hedging relationship. The option's time value is, therefore, excluded from the hedging relationship. This is the alternative commonly used because it enhances hedge effectiveness as the option's time value is not replicated in the hedged item. In other words, from a hedge accounting perspective the hedged item is assumed to lack any time value.

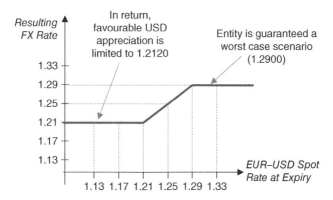

FIGURE 5.11   FX tunnel – resulting EUR–USD rate.

As a result, ABC designated the tunnel's intrinsic value (i.e., the intrinsic values of both the purchased and sold options) as the hedging instrument, and the highly expected sale and its subsequent receivable as the hedged item in a cash flow hedge of the foreign currency risk stemming from a highly expected forecast sale transaction. The option sold could be designated as part of the hedging instrument because:

- no net premium was received;
- the option sold was designated as an offset to the purchased option.

When options are involved, it is advisable, to the extent that it is feasible, to match both the end of the hedging relationship and the hedging instrument. Otherwise, important ineffectiveness may be present due to the mismatches between the actual and aligned time values. An **actual time value** is the time value of the option (or option combination) entered into. An **aligned time** value is the time value of an option (or option combination) that would replicate the hedged item.

Therefore, in our case, the hedging relationship would end on 30 June 20X5, when the FX tunnel expired (see Figure 5.12). Changes in actual time value of the tunnel, to the extent that they related to the hedged item, were recorded in the time value reserve of OCI.

On 31 March 20X5, the hedged cash flow (i.e., the sale) was recognised in ABC's profit or loss and, simultaneously, the amount previously recorded in OCI was reclassified to profit or loss. Also on 31 March 20X5 a receivable denominated in USD was recognised in ABC's statement of financial position.

During the period from 31 March 20X5 until 30 June 20X5, in theory there was no need to have a hedging relationship in place because there would be already an offset between FX gains and losses on the revaluation of the USD accounts receivable and revaluation gains and losses on the tunnel. During that period ABC could implement two approaches:

- To continue the hedging relationship. Changes in the actual option time value, to the extent that they related to the hedged item, would be recorded in OCI and simultaneously reclassified to profit or loss.
- To discontinue the hedging relationship by changing the hedge's risk management objective on 31 March 20X5. As mentioned in our previous case, whilst this is a simpler approach, an auditor may find it contrary to the prohibition under IFRS 9 of voluntary discontinuation of a hedging relationship.

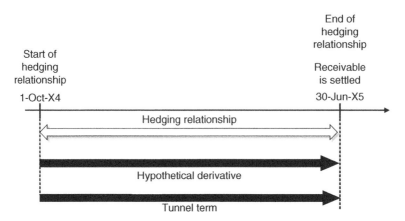

FIGURE 5.12   Transaction and hedging relationship timeframe.

5.7.1 Hedging Relationship Documentation

At inception of the hedging relationship, ABC documented the hedging relationship as follows:

Hedging relationship documentation	
Risk management objective and strategy for undertaking the hedge	The objective of the hedge is to protect the EUR value of the cash flow stemming from a USD 100 million highly expected sale of finished goods against unfavourable movements in the EUR–USD exchange rate beyond 1.2900
	In return for this protection, the EUR value of the cash flow related to the highly expected sale will not benefit from favourable movements in the EUR–USD exchange rate below 1.2120.
	This hedging objective is consistent with the entity's overall FX risk management strategy of reducing the variability of its profit or loss statement caused by purchases and sales denominated in foreign currency, using forwards and options.
	The designated risk being hedged is the risk of changes in the EUR fair value of the cash flows stemming from a highly expected sale
Type of hedge	Cash flow hedge
Hedged item	The cash flow stemming from a USD 100 million highly expected forecast sale of finished goods and its subsequent receivable, expected to be settled on 30 June 20X5. This sale is highly probable as (i) the negotiations are at an advanced stage and (ii) similar transactions have occurred in the past with the potential buyer, for sales of a similar size
Hedging instrument	The intrinsic value of the EUR–USD FX tunnel contract with reference numbers 017655 and 017656. The main terms of the tunnel are USD 100 million notional, expiry date on 30 June 20X5, a 1.2900 strike of the bought USD put and a 1.2120 strike of the sold USD call. The counterparty to the tunnel is XYZ Bank and the credit risk associated with this counterparty is considered to be very low.
	For the avoidance of doubt, the time value element of the tunnel contract is excluded from the hedging relationship
Hedge effectiveness assessment	See below

5.7.2 Hedge Effectiveness Assessment

Hedge effectiveness will be assessed by comparing changes in the fair value of the hedging instrument to changes in the fair value of a hypothetical derivative. Intrinsic values will be measured, comparing the spot exchange rate and the strike price. Effectiveness will be assessed only during those periods in which there is a change in intrinsic value.

The terms of the hypothetical derivative – a EUR–USD tunnel for maturity 30 June 20X5 with nil fair value at the start of the hedging relationship – reflected the terms of the hedged item. The terms of the hypothetical derivative were as follows:

Hypothetical derivative terms			
USD put/EUR call terms		**USD call/EUR put terms**	
Trade date	1 October 20X4	Trade date	1 October 20X4
Option buyer	ABC	Option buyer	Credit risk-free counterparty
Option seller	Credit risk-free counterparty	Option seller	ABC
USD notional	USD 100 million	USD notional	USD 100 million
Strike	1.2900	Strike	1.2150 (*)
EUR notional	EUR 77,519,000	EUR notional	EUR 82,305,000
Expiry date	30 June 20X5	Expiry date	30 June 20X5
Up-front premium	EUR 1,450,000	Up-front premium	EUR 1,450,000

(*) The USD call strike rate of the hypothetical derivative (1.2150) was different from that of the hedging instrument (1.2120) due to the absence of CVA in the hypothetical derivative (the counterparty to the hypothetical derivative is assumed to be credit risk-free).

Changes in the fair value of the hedging instrument (i.e., the tunnel's intrinsic value) will be recognised as follows:

- The effective part of the gain or loss on the hedging instrument will be recognised in the cash flow hedge reserve of OCI. The accumulated amount in equity will be reclassified to profit or loss in the same period during which the hedged expected future cash flow affects profit or loss. When the sale is recognised in profit or loss, the amount reclassified from OCI will adjust the sales amount. When the resulting receivable is remeasured though profit or loss, the amount reclassified from OCI will be recognised in the "other financial income/expenses" account of profit or loss.
- The ineffective part of the gain or loss on the hedging instrument will be recognised in profit or loss.

The change in time value of the tunnel (i.e., the "actual time value") will be excluded from the hedging relationship. Due to the absence of actual time value at the beginning and end of the hedging relationship, the changes in actual time value will be recognised temporarily in the time value reserve of OCI. No reclassification from OCI to profit or loss will be carried out during the term of the hedging relationship as the carrying value of the time value reserve in OCI is expected to be nil at the end of the hedging relationship.

Hedge effectiveness will be assessed prospectively at the hedging relationship inception, on an ongoing basis at each reporting date and upon occurrence of a significant change in the circumstances affecting the hedge effectiveness requirements.

The hedging relationship will qualify for hedge accounting only if all the following criteria are met:

1) The hedging relationship consists only of eligible hedge items and hedging instruments. The hedge item is eligible as it is a highly expected forecast transaction that exposes the entity to fair value risk, affects profit or loss and is reliably measurable. The hedging instrument is eligible as it is a derivative combination in which the written option represents an offset to the purchased option and does not result in a net written option.

2) At hedge inception there is a formal designation and documentation of the hedging relationship and the entity's risk management objective and strategy for undertaking the hedge.

3) The hedging relationship is considered effective.

The hedging relationship will be considered effective if the following three requirements are met:

1) There is an economic relationship between the hedged item and the hedging instrument.

2) The effect of credit risk does not dominate the value changes that result from that economic relationship.

3) The hedge ratio of the hedging relationship is the same as that resulting from the quantity of hedged item that the entity actually hedges and the quantity of the hedging instrument that the entity actually uses to hedge that quantity of hedged item. The hedge ratio should not be intentionally weighted to create ineffectiveness.

Whether there is an economic relationship between the hedged item and the hedging instrument will be assessed on a qualitative basis. The assessment will be complemented by a quantitative assessment using the scenario analysis method for two scenarios in which the EUR–USD FX rate at the end of the hedging relationship (30 June 20X5) will be simulated by shifting the EUR–USD spot rate prevailing on the assessment date by +10% and by –10%, and the change in fair value (i.e., the change in intrinsic values) of both the hypothetical derivative and the hedging instrument compared.

5.7.3 Hedge Effectiveness Assessment Performed at Hedge Inception

Hedge effectiveness was assessed on 1 October 20X4, at the start of the hedging relationship. The entity concluded that the hedging relationship was considered effective as the following three requirements were met:

1) There was an economic relationship between the hedged item and the hedging instrument. Based on the qualitative assessment performed, supported by a quantitative analysis, ABC concluded that the change in fair value of the hedged item was expected to be substantially offset by the change in fair value of the hedging instrument, corroborating that both elements had values that would generally move in opposite directions.

2) The effect of credit risk did not dominate the value changes resulting from that economic relationship as the credit ratings of both the entity and XYZ Bank were considered sufficiently strong.

3) The hedge ratio of the hedging relationship was the same as that resulting from the quantity of hedged item that the entity actually hedged and the quantity of the hedging instrument that the entity actually used to hedge that quantity of hedged item. The hedge ratio was not intentionally weighted to create ineffectiveness.

Economic Relationship Assessment Due to the fact that the terms of the hedging instrument and those of the expected cash flow closely matched and the low credit risk exposure to the counterparty to the tunnel, it was concluded that the hedging instrument and the hedged item had values that would generally move in opposite directions. This conclusion was supported by a quantitative assessment. This assessment consisted of two scenario analyses performed as follows.

Firstly, a (1.3585) EUR–USD spot rate at the end of the hedging relationship (i.e., 30 June 20X5) was assumed by shifting the EUR–USD spot rate prevailing on the assessment date (1.2350) by +10%. The fair value of the hedging instrument was calculated taking only the USD put intrinsic value (the USD call had no intrinsic value). As shown in the table below, the change in fair value of the hedged item was expected to largely be offset by the change in fair value of the hedging instrument, corroborating that both elements had values that would generally move in opposite directions.

	Scenario analysis assessment	
	Hedging instrument (USD put)	**Hypothetical derivative (USD put)**
Initial spot rate	1.2350	1.2350
Strike rate	1.2900	1.2900
Initial intrinsic value in EUR	Nil	Nil
Nominal USD	100,000,000	100,000,000
Final spot rate	1.3585 *(1)*	1.3585
Final intrinsic value	3,909,000 *(2)*	3,909,000
Change in intrinsic value	3,909,000 *(3)*	3,909,000
	Degree of offset	**100%**

Notes:

(1) Assumed spot rate on 30 June 20X5 (hedging relationship end date)

(2) 3,909,000 = max[100,000,000/1.2900 – 100,000,000/1.3585 , 0]

(3) 3,909,000 = Final intrinsic value – Initial intrinsic value = 3,909,000 – Nil

Secondly, a (1.1115) EUR–USD spot rate at the end of the hedging relationship (i.e., 30 June 20X5) was established by shifting the EUR–USD spot rate prevailing on the assessment date (1.2350) by –10%. The fair value of the hedging instrument was calculated taking only the USD call intrinsic value (the USD put had no intrinsic value). As shown in the table below, the change in fair value of the hedged item was expected to be largely offset by the change in fair value of the hedging instrument, corroborating that both elements had values that would generally move in opposite directions.

| | **Scenario analysis assessment** | |
	Hedging instrument (USD call)	**Hypothetical derivative (USD call)**
Initial spot rate	1.2350	1.2350
Strike rate	1.2120	1.2150
Initial intrinsic value in EUR	Nil	Nil
Nominal USD	100,000,000	100,000,000
Final spot rate	1.1115 *(1)*	1.1115
Final intrinsic value	<7,460,000> *(2)*	<7,664,000> *(3)*
Change in intrinsic value	<7,460,000> *(4)*	<7,664,000>
	Degree of offset	**97.3%** *(5)*

Notes:

(1) Assumed spot rate on 30 June 20X5 (hedging relationship end date)
(2) <7,460,000> = – max[100,000,000/1.1115 – 100,000,000/1.2120 , Zero]
(3) <7,664,000> = – max[100,000,000/1.1115 – 100,000,000/1.2150 , Zero]
(4) <7,460,000> = Final intrinsic value – Initial intrinsic value = <7,460,000> – Nil
(5) <7,460,000>/<7,664,000>

The hedge ratio was established at 1:1, resulting from the USD 100 million of hedged item that the entity actually hedged and the USD 100 million of the hedging instrument that the entity actually used to hedge that quantity of hedged item.

Another hedge assessment was performed on 31 December 20X4 (reporting date). This assessment was very similar to the one performed at inception and has been omitted to avoid unnecessary repetition. Additionally, the hedge ratio was assumed to be 1:1 on that assessment date.

5.7.4 Fair Valuation of Hedged Item and Hypothetical Derivative at the Relevant Dates

The actual spot exchange rates and discount factors prevailing at the relevant dates were as follows:

Date	Spot rate at indicated date	Discount factor for 30-Jun-20X5
1-Oct-20X4	1.2350	0.9804
31-Dec-20X4	1.2700	0.9839
31-Mar-20X5	1.2950	0.9901
30-Jun-20X5	1.3200	1.0000

The fair value of the tunnel was calculated using the Black–Scholes model and incorporating CVA/DVA. The intrinsic value was calculated using the spot rates. The time value of the tunnel was calculated as follows:

> **Tunnel time value = Tunnel total fair value – Tunnel intrinsic value**

The following table details the calculation of the changes in the tunnel intrinsic and time values. The time value of the instrument entered into is also referred to as the **actual time value**. It is worth noting that although the tunnel had no time value at the beginning and end of its life, its time value change showed a remarkable volatility.

	1-Oct-20X4	31-Dec-20X4	31-Mar-20X5	30-Jun-20X5
USD Put fair value	1,400,000	1,580,000	1,584,000	1,761,000 *(1)*
USD Call fair value	<1,400,000>	<490,000>	<89,000>	-0- *(2)*
Tunnel total fair value	**-0-**	**1,090,000**	**1,495,000**	**1,761,000** *(3)*
Expected cash flow in USD	100,000,000	100,000,000	100,000,000	100,000,000
USD put strike	/1.2900	/1.2900	/1.2900	/1.2900
EUR amount at USD put strike	77,519,000	77,519,000	77,519,000	77,519,000 *(4)*
Expected cash flow in USD	100,000,000	100,000,000	100,000,000	100,000,000
Spot rate	/1.2350	/1.2700	/1.2950	/1.3200
EUR amount at spot	80,972,000	78,740,000	77,220,000	75,758,000 *(5)*
USD put undisc. intrinsic value	-0-	-0-	299,000	1,761,000 *(6)*
Discount factor	× 0.9804	× 0.9839	× 0.9901	× 1.0000
USD put intrinsic value (credit risk-free)	-0-	-0-	296,000	1,761,000
CVA	—	-0-	<15,000>	-0-
USD put intrinsic value	**-0-**	**-0-**	**281,000**	**1,761,000** *(7)*
Expected cash flow in USD	100,000,000	100,000,000	100,000,000	100,000,000
USD call strike	/1.2120	/1.2120	/1.2120	/1.2120
EUR amount at USD call strike	82,508,000	82,508,000	82,508,000	82,508,000 *(8)*
Expected cash flow in USD	100,000,000	100,000,000	100,000,000	100,000,000
Spot rate	/1.2350	/1.2700	/1.2950	/1.3200
EUR amount at spot	80,972,000	78,740,000	77,220,000	75,758,000 *(9)*
USD call undisc. intrinsic value	-0-	-0-	-0-	-0- *(10)*
Discount factor	× 0.9804	× 0.9839	× 0.9901	× 1.0000
USD call intrinsic value (credit risk-free)	**-0-**	**-0-**	**-0-**	**-0-**
CVA	—	-0-	-0-	-0-
USD call intrinsic value	**-0-**	**-0-**	**-0-**	**-0-** *(11)*

(continued overleaf)

	1-Oct-20X4	31-Dec-20X4	31-Mar-20X5	30-Jun-20X5
Tunnel intrinsic value	-0-	-0-	281,000	1,761,000 *(12)*
Tunnel total fair value	-0-	1,090,000	1,495,000	1,761,000
Tunnel intrinsic value	-0-	-0-	281,000	1,761,000
Tunnel time value	-0-	1,090,000	1,214,000	-0-
Tunnel total fair value change	—	1,090,000	405, 000	**266,000** *(13)*
Tunnel intrinsic value change	—	-0-	281,000	**1,480,000** *(14)*
Tunnel time value change	—	1,090,000	124,000	**<1,214,000>** *(15)*

Notes:

(1) Calculated using the Black–Scholes model and incorporating CVA/DVA
(2) Calculated using the Black–Scholes model and incorporating CVA/DVA
(3) 1,761,000 = (1) + (2) = 1,761,000 + Nil
(4) 77,519,000 = 100,000,000/1.2900
(5) 75,758,000 = 100,000,000/1.3200
(6) 1,761,000 = max(77,519,000 – 75,758,000; 0)
(7) 1,761,000 = 1,761,000 × 1.0000+ Nil =(6) × Discount factor – CVA
(8) 82,508,000 = 100,000,000/1.2120
(9) 75,758,000 = 100,000,000/1.3200
(10) Nil = – max(75,758,000 – 82,508,000; 0)
(11) Nil = Nil × 1.0000 + Nil = (10) × Discount factor – CVA
(12) 1,761,000 = 1,761,000 + Nil = (7) + (11)
(13) 266,000 = 1,761,000 – 1,495,000
(14) 1,480,000 = 1,761,000 – 281,000
(15) <1,214,000> = Nil – 1,214,000

The following table shows the change in fair value of the hypothetical derivative. Remember that a hypothetical derivative has no time value, so only the change in its intrinsic value was needed to determine the hedge's effective and ineffective parts.

Hypothetical derivative fair valuation				
	1-Oct-20X4	31-Dec-20X4	31-Mar-20X5	30-Jun-20X5
Expected cash flow in USD	100,000,000	100,000,000	100,000,000	100,000,000
USD put strike	/1.2900	/1.2900	/1.2900	/1.2900
EUR amount at USD put strike	77,519,000	77,519,000	77,519,000	77,519,000
Expected cash flow in USD	100,000,000	100,000,000	100,000,000	100,000,000
Spot rate	/1.2350	/1.2700	/1.2950	/1.3200
EUR amount at spot	80,972,000	78,740,000	77,220,000	75,758,000
USD put undisc. intrinsic value	-0-	-0-	299,000	1,761,000

Hypothetical derivative fair valuation

	1-Oct-20X4	31-Dec-20X4	31-Mar-20X5	30-Jun-20X5
Discount factor	× 0.9804	× 0.9839	× 0.9901	× 1.0000
USD put intrinsic value	**-0-**	**-0-**	**296,000**	**1,761,000**
Expected cash flow in USD	100,000,000	100,000,000	100,000,000	100,000,000
USD call strike	/1.2120	/1.2120	/1.2120	/1.2120
EUR amount at USD call strike	82,508,000	82,508,000	82,508,000	82,508,000
Expected cash flow in USD	100,000,000	100,000,000	100,000,000	100,000,000
Spot rate	/1.2350	/1.2700	/1.2950	/1.3200
EUR amount at spot	80,972,000	78,740,000	77,220,000	75,758,000
USD call undisc. intrinsic value	-0-	-0-	-0-	-0-
Discount factor	× 0.9804	× 0.9839	× 0.9901	× 1.0000
USD call intrinsic value	**-0-**	**-0-**	**-0-**	**-0-**
Total intrinsic value	**-0-**	**-0-**	**296,000**	**1,761,000**
Hypothetical derivative (intrinsic) value change (cumulative)	**—**	**-0-**	**296,000**	**1,761,000**

5.7.5 Calculation of Effective and Ineffective Amounts

The effective and ineffective amounts of the change in fair value of the hedging instrument (i.e., the change in intrinsic value of the tunnel) were calculated, comparing such change with the change in fair value of the hypothetical derivative (remember that the hypothetical derivative had only intrinsic value) since hedge inception and taking into account the previously recorded effective amounts, as follows:

	31-Dec-20X4	31-Mar-20X5	30-Jun-20X5
Cumulative change in fair value of hedging instrument	-0-	281,000	1,761,000
Cumulative change in fair value of hypothetical derivative	-0-	296,000	1,761,000
Lower amount	-0-	281,000 (1)	1,761,000 (2)
Previous cumulative effective amount	-0-	-0-	281,000 *(3)*
Available amount	-0-	281,000	1,480,000 *(4)*
Period change in fair value of hedging instrument	-0-	281,000	1,480,000 *(5)*

(*continued overleaf*)

	31-Dec-20X4	31-Mar-20X5	30-Jun-20X5
Effective part	-0-	281,000	1,480,000 *(6)*
Ineffective part	-0-	-0-	-0- *(7)*

Notes:

(1) 281,000 = Lower of 281,000 and 296,000

(2) 1,761,000 = Lower of 1,761,000 and 1,761,000

(3) 281,000 = The sum of all prior effective amounts = Nil + 281,000

(4) 1,480,000 = 1,761,000 – 281,000 = (2) – (3)

(5) Change in the fair value of the hedging instrument (i.e., the tunnel's intrinsic value change) since the last fair valuation

(6) Lower of 1,480,000 (available amount) and 1,480,000 (period change in fair value of hedging instrument) = Lower of (4) and (5)

(7) Nil = 1,480,000 (period change in fair value of hedging instrument) – 1,480,000 (effective part)

Under IFRS 9 the cumulative change in fair value of the time value component of an option from the date of designation of the hedging instrument is temporarily accumulated in OCI to the extent that it relates to the hedged item.

In our case, due to the absence of actual time value at the beginning (1 October 20X4) and the end (30 June 20X5) of the hedging relationship, changes in actual time value were recognised temporarily in the time value reserve of OCI, as shown in the table below. No reclassification to profit or loss was carried out during the term of the hedging relationship as the carrying value of the time value reserve in OCI was expected to be nil at the end of the hedging relationship.

Amounts to be recognised in the time value reserve of OCI (in EUR)			
	1-Oct-20X4	31-Dec-20X4	31-Mar-20X5	30-Jun-20X5
New entry in reserve	—	1,090,000	124,000	<1,214,000>
Reserve carrying value	—	1,090,000	1,214,000	-0-

Of note is that the carrying value of the time value reserve when the sale was recognised in profit or loss (i.e., on 31 March 20X5) was not nil (i.e., EUR 1,214,000) as the tunnel was still alive. ABC decided that no reclassification to profit or loss was needed at that moment due to the reserve's expected convergence to nil at the end of the hedging relationship, a decision consistent with the fact that the entity paid no overall up-front premium for the protection.

An interesting situation may arise when a change in circumstances causes the hedging relationship to end prior to the maturity of the tunnel. Imagine for example that, after the tunnel was traded, the negotiations were accelerated and, as a result, the sale and the receivable were expected to occur sooner than initially anticipated. In this scenario, the hedging relationship would be shortened, causing the tunnel to last beyond the end of the hedging relationship. As a result, it is likely that the time value of the tunnel at the end of the hedging relationship would not be nil. Whilst IFRS 9 requires the changes in actual time value to be recorded in OCI to the extent that they relate to the hedged item, it does not provide guidance on how to proceed in such a particular situation. Furthermore, at the time of writing, the auditing community has not opined on how to treat such situations. In the meantime, it would be reasonable to maintain the original policy of recognising in OCI any changes in the actual time value and to reclassify to profit or loss any amount remaining in OCI at the end of the hedging relationship.

5.7.6 Accounting Entries

The required journal entries were as follows.

1) To record the tunnel trade on 1 October 20X4

No on-balance-sheet entries in the financial statements were required as the fair value of the tunnel was zero.

2) To record the closing of the accounting period on 31 December 20X4

The change in fair value of the tunnel since the last valuation was a gain of EUR 1,090,000. This gain was solely due to the tunnel's change in time value, which was recognised in OCI:

Tunnel contract (Asset)	1,090,000	
Time value reserve (Equity)		1,090,000

3) To record the sale agreement on 31 March 20X5

The sale agreement was recorded at the spot rate prevailing on that date (1.2950). Therefore, the EUR equivalent of the sale amount was EUR 77,220,000 (=100 million/1.2950). Because the machinery sold was not yet paid, a receivable was recognised. Suppose that the machinery was valued at EUR 68 million in ABC's statement of financial position.

Accounts receivable (Asset)	77,220,000	
Sales (Profit or loss)		77,220,000
Cost of goods sold (Profit or loss)	68,000,000	
Machinery (Asset)		68,000,000

The change in the fair value of the tunnel since the last valuation was a gain of EUR 405,000. Of this amount, a gain of EUR 281,000 was due to a change in the tunnel's intrinsic value, fully considered effective and recorded in equity (i.e., no ineffectiveness was present). The remainder, a gain of EUR 124,000, was due to a change in the tunnel's time value and taken to the time value reserve in OCI.

Tunnel contract (Asset)	405,000	
Cash flow hedge reserve (Equity)		281,000
Time value reserve (Equity)		124,000

The recognition of the sales transaction in profit or loss caused the release to profit or loss of the amounts accumulated in the cash flow hedge reserve of OCI (EUR 281,000).

| Cash flow hedge reserve (Equity) | 281,000 | |
| Sales (Profit or loss) | | 281,000 |

4) To record the settlement of the accounts receivable on 30 June 20X5

The receivable was revalued at the spot rate prevailing on this date, showing a loss of EUR 1,463,000 (=100 million/1.3200 – 100 million/1.2950).

| Other financial expenses (Profit or loss) | 1,463,000 | |
| Accounts receivable (Asset) | | 1,463,000 |

The change in the fair value of the tunnel since the last valuation was a gain of EUR 266,000. Of this amount, a gain of EUR 1,480,000 was due to a change in the tunnel's intrinsic value, fully considered effective and recorded in equity (i.e., no ineffectiveness was present). The remainder, a loss of EUR 1,214,000, was due to a change in the tunnel's time value, taken to the time value reserve in OCI.

Tunnel contract (Asset)	266,000	
Time value reserve (Equity)	1,214,000	
Cash flow hedge reserve (Equity)		1,480,000

Because the hedged item (the receivable) impacted profit or loss, the amounts accumulated in the cash flow hedge reserve were reclassified to profit or loss.

| Cash flow hedge reserve (Equity) | 1,480,000 | |
| Other financial income (Profit or loss) | | 1,480,000 |

ABC received USD 100 million from the client. Simultaneously, the tunnel expired and ABC exercised the USD put, exchanging the USD 100 million for EUR 77,519,000.

Cash (Asset)	77,519,000	
Tunnel contract (Asset)		1,761,000
Accounts receivable (Asset)		75,758,000

The following table gives a summary of the accounting entries, excluding the entries related to the cost of goods sold.

	Cash	Tunnel contract	Accounts receivable	Cash flow hedge reserve	Time value reserve	Profit or loss
1-Oct-20X4						
Tunnel trade	0	0				
31 Dec-20X4						
Tunnel revaluation		1,090,000			1,090,000	
31-Mar-20X5						
Sale recognition			77,220,000			77,220,000
Tunnel revaluation		405,000		281,000	124,000	
Reserve reclassification				<281,000>		281,000
30-Jun-20X5						
Tunnel revaluation		266,000		1,480,000	<1,214,000>	
Receivable revaluation			<1,463,000>			<1,463,000>
Reserve reclassification				<1,480,000>		1,480,000
Tunnel and receivable settlement	77,519,000	<1,761,000>	<75,758,000>			
TOTAL	**77,519,000**	**-0-**	**-0-**	**-0-**	**-0-**	**77,519,000**

Note: Total figures may not match the sum of their corresponding components due to rounding.

5.7.7 Accounting Entries – Discontinuation by Changing Risk Management Objective

In our previous approach, on 30 June 20X5 an additional calculation/recognition of effective and ineffective parts and the subsequent reclassification of the effective part into profit or loss were required, besides an additional calculation of the changes in actual time value. An alternative to avoid such administrative complexity was to discontinue the hedging relationship on 31 March 20X5 by changing the hedge's risk management objective on that date. Whilst under IFRS 9 voluntary discontinuation of a hedging relationship is not permitted, discontinuation is required when a hedging relationship does not meet its risk management objective. By changing the risk management objective an entity may provoke a mandatory discontinuation of the hedging relationship. In my view, this solution may be challenged by auditors, especially when a pattern of changing risk management objectives has been implemented solely to overcome the restrictions of IFRS 9. However, as happened with IAS 39 (the previous hedge accounting standard), over time the auditing community comes to accept practices that at the beginning of the implementation of a standard may seem questionable. I will cover this approach next.

On 31 March 20X5, following the recognition of the receivable, suppose that ABC updated the hedge documentation as follows: "The risk management of the EUR–USD foreign exchange risk stemming from the accounts receivable will no longer be managed under this hedging relationship, but instead in conjunction with the EUR–USD foreign exchange risk stemming from the FX tunnel as there is a natural offset in profit or loss of both risks when the tunnel is in-the-money. As a result of this change in the risk management objective, the hedging relationship is discontinued from 31 March 20X5."

The accounting entries up to, and including, 31 March 20X5 were identical to those of the previous example, and have therefore been omitted to avoid unnecessary repetition.

Additional Accounting Entries on 31 March 20X5 Originally, the hedging relationship was expected to last until 30 June 20X5 when the carrying value of such reserve was expected to be nil due to the absence of the tunnel's time value at its expiry on that date. The discontinuation of the hedging relationship on 31 March 20X5 caused an "unexpected" situation: a carrying value of the time value reserve amounting to EUR 1,214,000 at the end of the hedging relationship. To clear the situation, ABC decided to reclassify EUR 1,214,000 from the time value reserve into profit or loss.

Time value reserve (Equity)	1,214,000	
Other financial income (Profit or loss)		1,214,000

Accounting Entries on 30 June 20X5 The following accounting entries were made on 30 June 20X5. The receivable was revalued at the spot rate prevailing on this date, showing a loss of EUR 1,463,000 (=100 million/1.3200 – 100 million/1.2950):

Other financial expenses (Profit or loss)	1,463,000	
Accounts receivable (Asset)		1,463,000

The change in the fair value of the tunnel since the last valuation was a gain of EUR 266,000, recorded in profit or loss as the derivative was undesignated.

Tunnel contract (Asset)	266,000	
Other financial income (Profit or loss)		266,000

ABC received USD 100 million from the client. Simultaneously, the tunnel expired and ABC exercised the USD put, exchanging the USD 100 million for EUR 77,519,000.

Cash (Asset)	77,519,000	
Tunnel contract (Asset)		1,761,000
Accounts receivable (Asset)		75,758,000

The following table gives a summary of the accounting entries, excluding the entries related to the cost of goods sold:

	Cash	Tunnel contract	Accounts receivable	Cash flow hedge reserve	Time value reserve	Profit or loss
1-Oct-20X4						
Tunnel trade	0	0				
31 Dec-20X4						
Tunnel revaluation		1,090,000			1,090,000	
31-Mar-20X5						
Tunnel revaluation		405,000		281,000	124,000	
Reserve reclassification				<281,000>		281,000
Sale recognition			77,220,000			77,220,000
Reserve reclassification					<1,214,000>	1,214,000

(continued overleaf)

	Cash	Tunnel contract	Accounts receivable	Cash flow hedge reserve	Time value reserve	Profit or loss
30-Jun-20X5						
Tunnel revaluation		266,000				266,000
Receivable revaluation			<1,463,000>			<1,463,000>
Tunnel and receivable settlement	77,519,000	<1,761,000>	<75,758,000>			
TOTAL	**77,519,000**	**-0-**	**-0-**	**-0-**	**-0-**	**77,519,000**

Note: Total figures may not match the sum of their corresponding components due to rounding.

5.7.8 Final Remarks

The obligation to account for the time value of an option based on the aligned time value notably reduced the volatility in profit or loss, but operational complexity was significantly increased. In my view, IFRS 9 should allow entities to choose, when an option time value is excluded from the hedging relationship, between this approach and an alternative involving recognising all changes in an option time value in profit or loss. This choice is available in the case of forward elements of forward contracts and of basis elements of cross-currency swaps. Other approaches available to ABC would not work appropriately:

- To set 31 March 20X5 as the end of the hedging relationship. Under this approach, on 30 June 20X5 the change in fair value of the tunnel would be recognised in profit or loss, sparing ABC from performing the complex calculations of effective/ineffective parts and actual time values. However, due to the different maturities of the tunnel (30 June 20X5) and the hypothetical derivative (31 March 20X5), substantial volatility in profit or loss may be created due to potentially differing behaviours of the actual and aligned time values during the life of the hedging relationship.
- To designate the tunnel in its entirety as the hedging instrument. This would have reduced the operational complexity as it avoids calculating the time value component of the tunnel. However, substantial volatility may arise in profit or loss as the hypothetical derivative does not have time value. Additionally, there could be periods in which, due to time value changes in the tunnel, the change in fair value of the tunnel and that of the hypothetical derivative have opposite signs, potentially endangering the conclusion that there is an economic relationship between the hedged item and the hedging instrument.

5.8 CASE STUDY: HEDGING A FORECAST SALE AND SUBSEQUENT RECEIVABLE WITH A PARTICIPATING FORWARD

In this case, as in the previous cases, the cash flow stemming from a highly expected forecast sale and its ensuing receivable denominated in a foreign currency are hedged from a hedge accounting perspective. In this case, however, a participating forward is chosen to hedge the FX risk. The participating forward is one of the most basic and conservative hedges available.

As its name implies, this hedge provides guaranteed protection, while allowing the entity some degree of "participation" in favourable movements of the EUR–USD exchange rate.

Suppose that on 1 October 20X4, ABC Corporation, a company whose functional currency was the EUR, was expecting to sell finished goods to a US client. The sale was expected to occur on 31 March 20X5, and the sale receivable was expected to be settled on 30 June 20X5. Sale proceeds were expected to be USD 100 million, to be received in USD.

ABC had the view that the USD could appreciate against the EUR in the following months and wanted to benefit were its view right. At the same time, ABC wanted full protection in case its view was wrong. As a consequence, on 1 October 20X4, ABC entered into a participating forward with the following terms:

FX participating forward terms	
Start date	1 October 20X4
Counterparties	ABC and XYZ Bank
Maturity	30 June 20X5
ABC sells	USD 100 million
ABC buys	EUR 100 million/forward rate
Forward rate	1.2760, if final spot ≥ 1.2760
	1.2760 – (1.2760 – Final spot)/2, otherwise
Final spot	The EUR–USD spot rate at maturity
Premium	Zero
Settlement	Physical delivery

At maturity, ABC had the obligation to exchange USD 100 million for EUR at the forward rate. The forward rate was a function of the spot at maturity. The maximum forward rate was 1.2760. ABC participated in half of the USD appreciation below 1.2760. Figure 5.13 illustrates the resulting forward rate as a function of the EUR–USD spot rate at maturity. Figure 5.14 shows the EUR amount that ABC would receive in exchange for the USD 100 million, as a function of the EUR–USD spot rate at maturity.

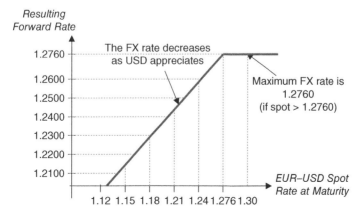

FIGURE 5.13 Participating forward resulting forward rate.

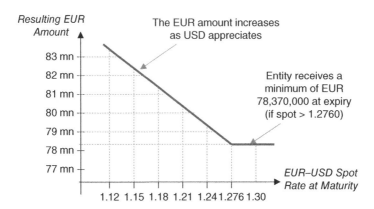

FIGURE 5.14 Participating forward resulting EUR amount.

5.8.1 Participating Forward Hedge Accounting Issues

One of the fundamental issues that ABC faced regarding the participating forward was how to formalise the instrument in order to minimise volatility in profit or loss (i.e., to maximise its eligibility for hedge accounting). ABC considered the following choices:

- **Alternative 1**. To divide the participating forward into the following two contracts (see Figure 5.15): (i) an FX forward at 1.2760 and a nominal of USD 50 million, and (ii) a purchase of a USD put with strike 1.2760 and a nominal of USD 50 million. Each contract would require a separate confirmation. This alternative should not encounter opposition from an external auditor as both the forward and the option are clearly eligible for designation as hedging instruments in a hedging relationship.
- **Alternative 2**. To designate the participating forward in its entirety as the hedging instrument. Whilst this alternative may bring some ineffectiveness, it is much simpler from an operational standpoint.
- **Alternative 3**. To divide the participating forward into the following two contracts: (i) a purchased USD put with strike 1.2760 and nominal 100 million, and (ii) a written USD call with strike 1.2760 and nominal 50 million. This alternative was discarded as it was likely to show a greater volatility in profit or loss than alternative 1 due to the recognition in profit or loss of the changes in the fair value of the written USD call.

In the following subsections I will cover the application of hedge accounting for alternatives 1 and 2.

5.8.2 Alternative 1: Participating Forward Split into a Forward and an Option

In this section the application of hedge accounting is covered step-by-step on a strategy in which our previous participating forward was split into two contracts (see Figure 5.15): (i) an FX forward contract at 1.2760 and a nominal of USD 50 million, and (ii) a purchase of a USD put contract with strike 1.2760 and a nominal of USD 50 million. Each contract required a separate confirmation to be considered as separate hedging instruments.

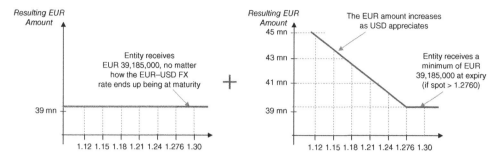

FIGURE 5.15 Participating forward – resulting EUR amount.

The terms of the two instruments were as follows:

Hedge 1: FX forward terms	
Start date	1 October 20X4
Counterparties	ABC and XYZ Bank
Maturity	30 June 20X5
ABC sells	USD 50 million
ABC sells	EUR 39,185,000
Forward rate	1.2760
Premium	ABC receives EUR 799,000 on the start date
Settlement	Physical delivery
Hedge 2: USD put/EUR call terms	
Start date	1 October 20X4
Option type	USD put/EUR call
Counterparties	ABC and XYZ Bank
Option buyer	ABC
Expiry	30 June 20X5
ABC buys	USD 50,000,000
ABC sells	EUR 39,185,000
Strike Rate	1.2760
Premium	ABC pays EUR 799,000 on the start date
Settlement	Physical delivery

In our case, there would be two hedging relationships. Each would end on 30 June 20X5, when the two contracts matured (see Figure 5.16). On 31 March 20X5, the hedged cash flow (i.e., the sale) would be recognised in ABC's profit or loss and, simultaneously, any amounts previously recorded in equity would be reclassified to profit or loss. Also on 31 March 20X5, a receivable denominated in USD would be recognised in ABC's statement of financial position.

During the period from 31 March 20X5 until 30 June 20X5, in theory it would not be necessary to have a hedging relationship in place because there would already be an off-set between FX gains and losses on the revaluation of the USD accounts receivable and revaluation gains and losses on the forward and the option. During that period ABC could implement two approaches:

- To continue the hedging relationship. Regarding the option, changes in the actual option time value, to the extent that they related to the hedged item, would be recorded in OCI and simultaneously reclassified to profit or loss.
- To discontinue the hedging relationship by changing the hedge's risk management objective on 31 March 20X5. As mentioned in our previous case, whilst this is a simpler approach, an auditor may find it contrary to the prohibition under IFRS 9 of voluntary discontinuation of a hedging relationship.

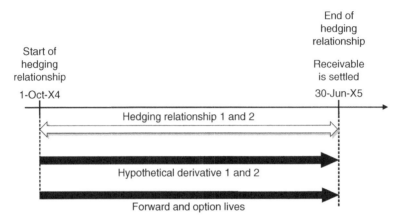

FIGURE 5.16   Hedge timeframe.

Hedging Relationship 1 – Documentation   At the inception of the first hedging relationship, ABC documented the relationship as follows:

Hedging relationship 1 – documentation	
Risk management objective and strategy for undertaking the hedge	The objective of the hedge is to protect the EUR value of the cash flow stemming from a USD 50 million highly expected sale of finished goods and its ensuing receivable against unfavourable movements in the EUR–USD exchange rate.
	This hedging objective is consistent with the entity's overall FX risk management strategy of reducing the variability of its profit or loss statement caused by purchases and sales denominated in foreign currency.
	The designated risk being hedged is the risk of changes in the EUR fair value of the highly expected sale
Type of hedge	Cash flow hedge
Hedged item	The cash flow stemming from a USD 50 million sale of finished goods expected to be shipped on 31 March 20X5 and its payment expected to be received on 30 June 20X5. This sale is highly probable as similar transactions have occurred in the past with the potential buyer, for sales of similar size, and the negotiations with the buyer are at an advanced stage

	Hedging relationship 1 – documentation
Hedging instrument	The forward contract with reference number 014565. The main terms of the forward are a USD 50 million notional, a 1.2760 forward rate, a 30 June 20X5 maturity and a physical settlement provision. The counterparty to the forward is XYZ Bank and the credit risk associated with this counterparty is considered to be very low
Hedge effectiveness assessment	See below

Hedge effectiveness will be assessed by comparing changes in the fair value of the hedging instrument in its entirety (i.e., both the forward and the spot elements are included in the hedging relationship) to changes in the fair value of a hypothetical derivative. The terms of the hypothetical derivative – a EUR–USD forward contract for maturity 30 June 20X5 with nil fair value at the start of the hedging relationship – reflected the terms of the hedged item. The terms of the hypothetical derivative are as follows:

Hypothetical derivative 1 – terms	
Start date	**1 October 20X4**
Counterparties	ABC and credit risk-free counterparty
Maturity	30 June 20X5
ABC sells	USD 50 million
ABC buys	EUR 39,936,000
Forward Rate	1.2520 *(*)*

(*) The forward rate of the hypothetical derivative (1.2520) was different from the forward rate of the hedging instrument (1.2760) – this was due to (i) their different initial fair values and (ii) the absence of CVA in the hypothetical derivative (the counterparty to the hypothetical derivative is assumed to be credit risk-free).

Changes in the fair value of the hedging instrument will be recognised as follows:

- The effective part of the gain or loss on the hedging instrument will be recognised in the cash flow hedge reserve of OCI. The accumulated amount in equity will be reclassified to profit or loss in the same period during which the hedged expected future cash flow affects profit or loss, initially adjusting the sale amount when the sale is recognised and thereafter adjusting the revaluation of the receivable.
- The ineffective part of the gain or loss on the hedging instrument will be recognised immediately in profit or loss.

Hedge effectiveness will be assessed prospectively at hedging relationship inception, on an ongoing basis at least upon each reporting date and upon occurrence of a significant change in the circumstances affecting the hedge effectiveness requirements.

Hedge effectiveness will be assessed, and effective/ineffective amounts will be calculated, on a forward-forward basis. In other words, the forward element of both the hedging instrument and the hypothetical derivative will be included in the hedging relationship.

The hedging relationship will qualify for hedge accounting only if all the following criteria are met:

1) The hedging relationship consists only of eligible hedge items and hedging instruments. The hedge item is eligible as it is a highly expected forecast transaction that exposes the entity to fair value risk, affects profit or loss and is reliably measurable. The hedging instrument is eligible as it is a derivative and it does not result in a net written option.
2) At hedge inception there is a formal designation and documentation of the hedging relationship and the entity's risk management objective and strategy for undertaking the hedge.
3) The hedging relationship is considered effective.

The hedging relationship will be considered effective if the following three requirements are met:

1) There is an economic relationship between the hedged item and the hedging instrument.
2) The effect of credit risk does not dominate the value changes that result from that economic relationship.
3) The hedge ratio of the hedging relationship is the same as that resulting from the quantity of hedged item that the entity actually hedges and the quantity of the hedging instrument that the entity actually uses to hedge that quantity of hedged item. The hedge ratio should not be intentionally weighted to create ineffectiveness.

Whether there is an economic relationship between the hedged item and the hedging instrument will be assessed on a qualitative basis. The assessment will be complemented by a quantitative assessment using the scenario analysis method for one scenario in which the EUR–USD FX rate at the end of the hedging relationship (30 June 20X5) will be calculated by shifting the EUR–USD spot rate prevailing on the assessment date by +10%, and the change in fair value of both the hypothetical derivative and the hedging instrument compared.

Hedging Relationship 2 – Documentation Additionally, at the inception of the second hedging relationship, ABC documented the relationship as follows:

Hedging relationship 2 – documentation	
Risk management objective and strategy for undertaking the hedge	The objective of the hedge is to protect the EUR value of the cash flow stemming from a USD 50 million highly expected sale of finished goods and its ensuing receivable against unfavourable movements in the EUR–USD exchange rate above 1.2760. This hedging objective is consistent with the entity's overall FX risk management strategy of reducing the variability of its profit or loss statement caused by purchases and sales denominated in foreign currency. The designated risk being hedged is the risk of changes in the EUR fair value of the highly expected sale
Type of hedge	Cash flow hedge
Hedged item	The cash flow stemming from a USD 50 million sale of finished goods expected to be shipped on 31 March 20X5 and its payment expected to be received on 30 June 20X5. This sale is highly probable as similar transactions have occurred in the past with the potential buyer, for sales of similar size, and the negotiations with the buyer are at an advanced stage

Hedging relationship 2 – documentation	
Hedging instrument	The intrinsic value of the purchased USD put/EUR call contract with reference number 014566. The main terms of the contract are a USD 50 million notional, a 1.2760 strike rate, a 30 June 20X5 maturity and a physical settlement provision. The counterparty to the option is XYZ Bank and the credit risk associated with this counterparty is considered to be very low
Hedge effectiveness assessment	See below

Hedge effectiveness will be assessed, and effective/ineffective amounts will be calculated, by comparing changes in the fair value of the hedging instrument to changes in the fair value of a hypothetical derivative. The terms of the hypothetical derivative – a USD put/EUR call contract for maturity 30 June 20X5 with strike price 1.2760 reflected the terms of the hedged item. The terms of the hypothetical derivative are as follows:

Hypothetical derivative 2 – terms	
Start date	**1 October 20X4**
Instrument	USD put/EUR call FX option
Counterparties	ABC and credit risk-free counterparty
Option buyer	ABC
Expiry	30 June 20X5
ABC buys	USD 50,000,000
ABC sells	EUR 39,185,000
Strike rate	1.2760
Initial aligned time value (premium)	EUR 820,000
Settlement	Physical delivery

Changes in the fair value of the hedging instrument (i.e., the option's intrinsic value) will be recognised as follows:

- The effective part of the gain or loss on the hedging instrument will be recognised in the cash flow hedge reserve of OCI. The accumulated amount in equity will be reclassified to profit or loss in the same period during which the hedged expected future cash flow affects profit or loss, initially adjusting the sales amount when the sale is recognised and thereafter adjusting the revaluation of the receivable.
- The ineffective part of the gain or loss on the hedging instrument will be recognised immediately in profit or loss.

The change in time value of the option will be excluded from the hedging relationship, and compared to the change in "aligned time" value. The aligned time value will be the time value of an option that has critical terms identical to those of the hedged item. Because, at the start of the hedging relationship, the aligned time value (EUR 820,000) exceeds the actual time value (EUR 799,000), the lower of their accumulated changes in fair value will be recognised temporarily in the time value reserve of OCI and reclassified to profit or loss when the hedged item impacts profit or loss. Any remainder will be recognised immediately in profit or loss.

Hedge effectiveness will be assessed prospectively at inception of the hedging relationship, on an ongoing basis at least upon each reporting date and upon occurrence of a significant change in the circumstances affecting the hedge effectiveness requirements.

The hedging relationship will qualify for hedge accounting only if all the following criteria are met:

1) The hedging relationship consists only of eligible hedge items and hedging instruments. The hedge item is eligible as it is a highly expected forecast transaction that exposes the entity to fair value risk, affects profit or loss and is reliably measurable. The hedging instrument is eligible as it is a bought financial option.
2) At hedge inception there is a formal designation and documentation of the hedging relationship and the entity's risk management objective and strategy for undertaking the hedge.
3) The hedging relationship is considered effective.

The hedging relationship will be considered effective if the following three requirements are met:

1) There is an economic relationship between the hedged item and the hedging instrument.
2) The effect of credit risk does not dominate the value changes that result from that economic relationship.
3) The hedge ratio of the hedging relationship is the same as that resulting from the quantity of hedged item that the entity actually hedges and the quantity of the hedging instrument that the entity actually uses to hedge that quantity of hedged item. The hedge ratio should not be intentionally weighted to create ineffectiveness.

Whether there is an economic relationship between the hedged item and the hedging instrument will be assessed on a qualitative basis. The assessment will be complemented by a quantitative assessment using the scenario analysis method for one scenario in which the EUR–USD FX rate at the end of the hedging relationship (30 June 20X5) will be established by shifting the EUR–USD spot rate prevailing on the assessment date by +10%, and the change in fair value (i.e., in time value) of both the hypothetical derivative and the hedging instrument compared.

Hedging Relationship 1 – Hedge Effectiveness Assessment Performed at Hedge Inception   The hedging relationship was considered effective as the following three requirements were met:

1) There was an economic relationship between the hedged item and the hedging instrument. Based on the qualitative assessment performed and supported by a quantitative analysis, ABC concluded that the change in fair value of the hedged item was expected to be substantially offset by the change in fair value of the hedging instrument, corroborating that both elements had values that would generally move in opposite directions.
2) The effect of credit risk did not dominate the value changes resulting from that economic relationship as the credit ratings of both the entity and XYZ Bank were considered sufficiently strong.
3) The hedge ratio of the hedging relationship was the same as that resulting from the quantity of hedged item that the entity actually hedged and the quantity of the hedging instrument that the entity actually used to hedge that quantity of hedged item. The hedge ratio was not intentionally weighted to create ineffectiveness.

Due to the fact that the main terms (USD notional, underlying and expiry date) of the hedging instrument and those of the expected cash flow closely matched (with the exception of the forward rate) and the low credit risk exposure to the counterparty of the forward contract, it was concluded that the hedging instrument and the hedged item had values that would generally move in opposite directions. This conclusion was supported by a quantitative assessment. This assessment consisted of one scenario analysis performed as follows. A EUR–USD spot rate at the end of the hedging relationship (1.3585) was assumed by shifting the EUR–USD spot rate prevailing on the assessment date (1.2350) by +10%. As shown in the table below, the change in fair value of the hedged item is expected to be substantially offset by the change in fair value of the hedging instrument, corroborating that both elements have values that will generally move in opposite directions.

Scenario analysis assessment		
	Hedging instrument	**Hypothetical derivative**
Nominal USD	50,000,000	50,000,000
Forward rate	1.2760	1.2520
Nominal EUR	39,185,000	39,936,000
Nominal USD	50,000,000	50,000,000
Final spot rate	1.3585 *(1)*	1.3585
Value in EUR	36,805,000 *(2)*	36,805,000
Final fair value EUR	2,380,000 *(3)*	3,131,000
Initial fair value EUR	<799,000>	Nil
Fair value change	3,179,000 *(4)*	3,131,000
	Degree of offset	**101.5%** *(5)*

Notes:
> *(1)* Assumed spot rate on hedging relationship end date
> *(2)* 50,000,000/1.3585
> *(3)* 39,185,000 − 36,805,000
> *(4)* 2,380,000 − (<799,000>)
> *(5)* 3,179,000/3,131,000

The hedge ratio was established at 1:1, resulting from the USD 50 million of hedged item that the entity actually hedged and the USD 50 million of the hedging instrument that the entity actually used to hedge that quantity of hedged item.

Another hedge assessment was performed on 31 December 20X4 (reporting date). This assessment was very similar to the one performed at inception and has been omitted to avoid unnecessary repetition. Additionally, the hedge ratio was assumed to be 1:1 on that assessment date.

Hedging Relationship 2 – Hedge Effectiveness Assessment Performed at Hedge Inception   The hedging relationship was considered effective as the following three requirements were met:

1) There was an economic relationship between the hedged item and the hedging instrument. Based on the qualitative assessment performed and supported by a quantitative analysis, ABC concluded that the change in fair value of the hedged item was expected to be substantially offset by the change in fair value of the hedging instrument, corroborating that both elements had values that would generally move in opposite directions.

2) The effect of credit risk did not dominate the value changes resulting from that economic relationship as the credit ratings of both the entity and XYZ Bank were considered sufficiently strong.
3) The hedge ratio of the hedging relationship was the same as that resulting from the quantity of hedged item that the entity actually hedged and the quantity of the hedging instrument that the entity actually used to hedge that quantity of hedged item. The hedge ratio was not intentionally weighted to create ineffectiveness.

Due to the fact that the terms (notionals, underlying, strike price and expiry date) of the hedging instrument and those of the expected cash flow closely matched and the low credit risk exposure to the counterparty to the option contract, it was concluded that the hedging instrument and the hedged item had values that would generally move in opposite directions. This conclusion was supported by a quantitative assessment. This assessment consisted of one scenario analysis performed as follows. A EUR–USD spot rate at the end of the hedging relationship (1.3585) was simulated by shifting the EUR–USD spot rate prevailing on the assessment date (1.2350) by +10%. The fair value of the hedging instrument was calculated taking only the option intrinsic value. As shown in the table below, the change in fair value of the hedged item was expected to largely be offset by the change in fair value of the hedging instrument, corroborating that both elements had values that would generally move in opposite directions.

Scenario analysis assessment		
	Hedging instrument	**Hypothetical derivative**
Initial spot rate	1.2350	1.2350
Strike rate	1.2760	1.2760
Initial intrinsic value in EUR	Nil	Nil
Nominal USD	50,000,000	50,000,000
Spot rate	1.3585 *(1)*	1.3585
Final intrinsic value in EUR	2,380,000 *(2)*	2,380,000
Change in intrinsic value	2,380,000 *(3)*	2,380,000
	Degree of offset	**100%** *(4)*

Notes:
   (1) Assumed spot rate on 30 June 20X5 (hedging relationship end date)
   (2) 2,380,000 = max[50,000,000/1.2760 – 50,000,000/1.3585, 0]
   (3) 2,380,000 = 2,380,000 – Nil
   (4) 100% = 2,380,000/2,380,000 = Change in fair value of hedging instrument/Change in fair value of hypothetical derivative. Remember that both fair values were only composed of intrinsic value.

The hedge ratio was established at 1:1, resulting from the USD 50 million of hedged item that the entity actually hedges and the USD 50 million of the hedging instrument that the entity actually uses to hedge that quantity of hedged item.

Another hedge assessment was performed on 31 December 20X4 (reporting date). This assessment was very similar to the one performed at inception and has been omitted to avoid unnecessary repetition. Additionally, the hedge ratio was assumed to be 1:1 on that assessment date.

Hedging Relationship 1 – Fair Valuations of Derivative Contracts and Hypothetical Derivative at the Relevant Dates
The actual spot and forward exchange rates prevailing at the relevant dates were as follows:

Date	Spot rate at indicated date	Forward rate for 30-Jun-20X5 (*)	Discount factor for 30-Jun-20X5
1-Oct-20X4	1.2350	1.2520	0.9804
31-Dec-20X4	1.2700	1.2800	0.9839
31-Mar-20X5	1.2950	1.3000	0.9901
30-Jun-20X5	1.3200	1.3200	1.0000

(*) Credit risk-free forward rate

The fair value calculation of hedging instrument 1 at each relevant date was as follows:

	1-Oct-20X4	31-Dec-20X4	31-Mar-20X5	30-Jun-20X5
Nominal EUR	39,185,000	39,185,000	39,185,000	39,185,000
Nominal USD	50,000,000	50,000,000	50,000,000	50,000,000
Forward rate for 30-Jun-20X5 (1)	/1.2520	/1.2800	/1.3000	/1.3200
Value in EUR	39,936,000	39,063,000	38,462,000 (2)	37,879,000
Difference	<751,000>	122,000	723,000 (3)	1,306,000
Discount factor	× 0.9804	× 0.9839	× 0.9901	× 1.0000
Credit risk-free fair value	<736,000>	120,000	716,000 (4)	1,306,000
CVA	<63,000>	<1,000>	<2,000>	-0-
Fair value	<799,000>	119,000	714,000 (5)	1,306,000
Fair value change (cumulative)	—	918,000	1,513,000 (6)	2,105,000
Fair value change (period)	—	918,000	595,000 (7)	592,000

Notes:
> (1) Credit risk-free forward rate
> (2) 38,462,000 = 50,000,000/1.3000
> (3) 723,000 = 39,185,000 – 38,462,000
> (4) 716,000 = 723,000 × 0.9901
> (5) 714,000 = 716,000 – 2,000
> (6) 1,513,000 = 714,000 – <799,000>
> (7) 595,000 = 714,000 – 119,000

The fair value calculation of hypothetical derivative 1 at each relevant date was as follows:

	1-Oct-20X4	31-Dec-20X4	31-Mar-20X5	30-Jun-20X5
Nominal EUR	39,936,000	39,936,000	39,936,000	39,936,000
Nominal USD	50,000,000	50,000,000	50,000,000	50,000,000
Forward rate for 30-Jun-20X5	/1.2520	/1.2800	/1.3000	/1.3200
Value in EUR	39,936,000	39,063,000	38,462,000	37,879,000
Difference	-0-	873,000	1,474,000	2,057,000
Discount factor	× 0.9804	× 0.9839	× 0.9901	× 1.0000
Fair value	-0-	859,000	1,459,000	2,057,000
Fair value change (Cumulative)	—	859,000	1,459,000	2,057,000

The calculation of the effective and ineffective amounts of the change in fair value of the hedging instrument 1 was as follows:

	31-Dec-20X4	31-Mar-20X5	30-Jun-20X5
Cumulative change in fair value of hedging instrument	918,000	1,513,000	2,105,000
Cumulative change in fair value of hypothetical derivative	859,000	1,459,000	2,057,000
Lower amount	859,000	1,459,000 *(1)*	2,057,000
Previous cumulative effective amount	Nil	859,000 *(2)*	1,454,000
Available amount	859,000	600,000 *(3)*	603,000
Period change in fair value of hedging instrument	918,000	595,000 *(4)*	592,000
Effective part	859,000	595,000 *(5)*	592,000
Ineffective part	59,000	Nil *(6)*	Nil

Notes:

(1) Lower of 1,513,000 and 1,459,000
(2) Nil +859,000, the sum of all prior effective amounts
(3) 1,459,000 – 859,000
(4) Change in the fair value of the hedging instrument since the last fair valuation
(5) Lower of 600,000 (available amount) and 595,000 (period change in fair value of hedging instrument)
(6) 595,000 (period change in fair value of hedging instrument) – 595,000 (effective part)

Hedging Relationship 2 – Fair Valuations of Hedged Item and Hypothetical Derivative at the Relevant Dates
Using the spot rates and discount factors from hedging relationship 1, the fair value of the option was calculated using the Black–Scholes model, and incorporating CVA/DVA. The intrinsic value was calculated using the spot rates. The time value of the option was calculated as follows:

> Option time value = Option total fair value – Option intrinsic value

The following table details the calculation of the changes in the option's intrinsic and time values from the option's total value. It is worth noting that although the option had no time value at the beginning and end of its life, its time value change showed a significant volatility.

	1-Oct-20X4	31-Dec-20X4	31-Mar-20X5	30-Jun-20X5
Option fair value	**799,000**	**941,000**	**1,017,000** *(1)*	**1,306,000**
Expected cash flow in USD	50,000,000	50,000,000	50,000,000	50,000,000
USD put strike	/1.2760	/1.2760	/1.2760	/1.2760
EUR amount at USD put strike	39,185,000	39,185,000	39,185,000 *(2)*	39,185,000
Expected cash flow in USD	50,000,000	50,000,000	50,000,000	50,000,000
Spot rate	/1.2350	/1.2700	/1.2950	/1.3200
EUR amount at spot	40,486,000	39,370,000	38,610,000 *(3)*	37,879,000
Undiscounted intrinsic value	-0-	-0-	575,000 *(4)*	1,306,000
Discount factor	× 0.9804	× 0.9839	× 0.9901	× 1.0000
Intrinsic value (credit risk-free)	-0-	-0-	569,000 *(5)*	1,306,000
CVA/DVA	-0-	-0-	<1,000>	-0-
Option intrinsic value	**-0-**	**-0-**	**568,000** *(6)*	**1,306,000**
Option total fair value	799,000	941,000	1,017,000	1,306,000
Option intrinsic value	-0-	-0-	568,000	1,306,000
Option time value	799,000	941,000	449,000	-0-
Period fair value change	—	**142,000**	**76,000** *(7)*	**289,000**

(continued overleaf)

	1-Oct-20X4	31-Dec-20X4	31-Mar-20X5	30-Jun-20X5
Period intrinsic value change	—	-0-	568,000 *(8)*	738,000
Period time value change	—	142,000	<492,000> *(9)*	<449,000>

Notes:
  (1) Calculated using Black–Scholes model
  (2) 39,185,000 = 50,000,000/1.2760
  (3) 38,610,000 = 50,000,000/1.2950
  (4) 575,000 = max(39,185,000 − 38,610,000; 0)
  (5) 569,000 = 575,000 × 0.9901
  (6) 568,000 = 569,000 + <1,000>
  (7) 76,000 = 1,017,000 − 941,000
  (8) 568,000 = 568,000 − Nil
  (9) <492,000> = 449,000 − 941,000

The following table shows the change in fair value of the hypothetical derivative. Remember that hypothetical derivatives have no time value, so only the change in its intrinsic value was calculated (it is noted below that the time value – the "aligned time value" – also needs to be calculated).

	Hypothetical derivative (i.e., intrinsic values)			
	1-Oct-20X4	31-Dec-20X4	31-Mar-20X5	30-Jun-20X5
Expected cash flow in USD	50,000,000	50,000,000	50,000,000	50,000,000
USD put strike	/1.2760	/1.2760	/1.2760	/1.2760
EUR amount at USD put strike	39,185,000	39,185,000	39,185,000	39,185,000
Expected cash flow in USD	50,000,000	50,000,000	50,000,000	50,000,000
Spot rate	/1.2350	/1.2700	/1.2950	/1.3200
EUR amount at spot	40,486,000	39,370,000	38,610,000	37,879,000
Undisc. intrinsic value	-0-	-0-	575,000	1,306,000
Discount factor	× 0.9804	× 0.9839	× 0.9901	× 1.0000
Intrinsic value	**-0-**	**-0-**	**568,000**	**1,306,000**
Intrinsic value change (cumulative)	**—**	**-0-**	**575,000**	**1,306,000**

The calculation of the effective and ineffective parts of the change in fair value of the hedging instrument (i.e., the change in intrinsic value of the option) was calculated as follows:

	31-Dec-20X4	31-Mar-20X5	30-Jun-20X5
Cumulative change in fair value of hedging instrument	-0-	568,000	1,306,000
Cumulative change in fair value of hypothetical derivative	-0-	575,000	1,306,000
Lower amount	-0-	568,000 *(1)*	1,306,000
Previous cumulative effective amount	-0-	-0- *(2)*	568,000
Available amount	-0-	568,000 *(3)*	738,000
Period change in fair value of hedging instrument	-0-	568,000 *(4)*	738,000
Effective part	-0-	568,000 *(5)*	738,000
Ineffective part	-0-	-0- *(6)*	-0-

Notes:
(1) 568,000 = Lower of 568,000 and 575,000
(2) Nil = Sum of all prior effective amounts
(3) 568,000 = 568,000 – Nil = (1) – (2)
(4) Change in the fair value of the hedging instrument since the last fair valuation
(5) Lower of 568,000 (available amount) and 568,000 (period change in fair value of hedging instrument) = Lower of (3) and (4)
(6) Nil = 568,000 (period change in fair value of hedging instrument) – 568,000 (effective part)

Under IFRS 9 the cumulative change in fair value of the time value component of an option from the date of designation of the hedging instrument, is accumulated in OCI to the extent that it relates to the hedged item.

The time value related to the hedged item is called the "aligned time value". This time value represents the time value of an option that would have critical terms perfectly matching those of the hedged item. In our case, the aligned time value corresponds to the time value of an option that has main terms identical to those of the hypothetical derivative (i.e., notional, strike rate, expiry date and underlying). Therefore, ABC had to compute the value changes in the hypothetical derivative, as if this derivative had time value (the "aligned option"). To do that, ABC had to compute first the fair value of the aligned option using Black–Scholes, and then the time value as follows:

Aligned option time value = Aligned option fair value – Aligned option intrinsic value

The following table shows the calculations of the cumulative change in the aligned time value. The intrinsic value was the hypothetical derivative's intrinsic value, taken from the previous table.

	Aligned time value			
	1-Oct-20X4	31-Dec-20X4	31-Mar-20X5	30-Jun-20X5
Total fair value	820,000	951,000	1,029,000	1,306,000
Total intrinsic value	-0-	-0-	575,000	1,306,000
Aligned time value	820,000	951,000	454,000	-0-
Cumulative change in aligned time value	—	131,000	<366,000>	<820,000>

Because at the start of the hedging relationship the actual time value (EUR 799,000) was lower than the aligned time value (EUR 820,000), the part of the cumulative fair value change of the actual time value recognised in OCI was calculated as the lower of the following (in absolute terms):

- the cumulative fair value change of the actual time value; and
- the cumulative fair value change of the aligned time value.

Any excess of the cumulative change in the option's time value over that of the aligned time value was recognised in profit or loss.

The comparison of the aligned amounts and the option's time value amounts was calculated as follows (the mechanics are similar to the previous calculation of effective and ineffective amounts related to the hedging instrument):

	31-Dec-20X4	31-Mar-20X5	30-Jun-X5
Cumulative actual time value change	142,000	<350,000>	<799,000>
Cumulative aligned time value change	131,000	<366,000>	<820,000>
Lower amount	131,000	<350,000>	<799,000>
Previous cumulative amount in OCI	-0-	131,000	<350,000>
Available amount	131,000	<481,000>	<449,000>
Period change in actual time value	142,000	<492,000>	<449,000>
Part in OCI	**131,000**	**<481,000>**	<449,000>
Part in profit or loss	**11,000**	**<11,000>**	-0-

Accounting Entries The required journal entries were as follows.

1) To record the forward and the option trades on 1 October, 20X4

At their inception, the fair values of the FX forward and the FX option were EUR <799,000> and 799,000 respectively.

Option contract (Asset)	799,000	
Cash (Asset)		799,000
Cash (Asset)	799,000	
Forward contract (Liability)		799,000

2) To record the closing of the accounting period on 31 December 20X4

The change in fair value of the forward since the last valuation was a EUR 918,000 gain, of which EUR 859,000 was considered to be effective and recorded in the cash flow hedge reserve of OCI, while EUR 59,000 was deemed to be ineffective and recorded in profit or loss.

Forward contract (Asset)	918,000	
Cash flow hedge reserve (Equity)		859,000
Other financial income (Profit or loss)		59,000

The change in fair value of the option since the last valuation was a gain of EUR 142,000, all due to a change in the option's time value. Of this amount 131,000 corresponded to an "aligned" time value change (recognised in the time value reserve of OCI) and the EUR 11,000 remainder was recognised in profit or loss.

Option contract (Asset)	142,000	
Time value reserve (Equity)		131,000
Other financial income (Profit or loss)		11,000

3) To record the sale agreement on 31 March 20X5

The sale agreement was recorded at the spot rate prevailing on that date (1.2950). Therefore, the sale EUR proceeds were EUR 77,220,000 (=100 million/1.2950). Because the machinery sold was not yet paid, a receivable was recognised. Suppose that the machinery was valued at EUR 68 million in ABC's statement of financial position.

Accounts receivable (Asset)	77,220,000	
Sales (Profit or loss)		77,220,000
Cost of goods sold (Profit or loss)	68,000,000	
Machinery (Asset)		68,000,000

The change in fair value of the forward since the last valuation was a gain of EUR 595,000, fully considered to be effective, and thus recorded in the cash flow hedge reserve of OCI. No ineffective amounts existed.

Forward contract (Asset)	595,000	
Cash flow hedge reserve (Equity)		595,000

The change in fair value of the option since the last valuation was a gain of EUR 76,000, split into a EUR 568,000 gain in the option's intrinsic value and a EUR 492,000 loss in the option's time value. All the change in the option's intrinsic value was considered to be effective and recorded in the cash flow hedge reserve of OCI. Regarding the change in time value, <481,000> corresponded to an "aligned" time value change (recognised in the time value reserve of OCI) and the EUR <11,000> remainder was recognised in profit or loss.

Option contract (Asset)	76,000	
Cash flow hedge reserve (Equity)		568,000
Time value reserve (Equity)	481,000	
Other financial expenses (Profit or loss)	11,000	

The recognition of the sales transaction in profit or loss caused the release to profit or loss of the deferred hedge results accumulated in equity: EUR 1,454,000 from the cash flow hedge reserve and EUR <350,000> from the time value reserve. The hedging relationship ended on this date.

Cash flow hedge reserve (Equity)	1,454,000	
Time value reserve (Equity)		350,000
Sales (Profit or loss)		1,104,000

4) To record the settlement of the receivable and the derivatives on 30 June 20X5

The receivable was revalued at the spot rate prevailing on this date, showing a loss of EUR 1,463,000 (=100 million/1.3200 – 100 million/1.2950):

Other financial expenses (Profit or loss)	1,463,000	
Accounts receivable (Asset)		1,463,000

The change in the fair value of the forward since the last valuation was a gain of EUR 592,000, fully deemed to be effective.

Forward contract (Asset)	592,000	
Cash flow hedge reserve (Equity)		592,000

The change in fair value of the option since the last valuation was a gain of EUR 289,000, split into a EUR 738,000 gain in the option's intrinsic value and a EUR 449,000 loss in the option's time value. All the change in the option's intrinsic value was considered to be effective and recorded in the cash flow hedge reserve of OCI. Regarding the change in time value, <449,000> corresponded to an "aligned" time value change (recognised in the time value reserve of OCI) and no amounts were recognised in profit or loss.

Option contract (Asset)	289,000	
Time value reserve (Equity)	449,000	
Cash flow hedge reserve (Equity)		738,000

The recognition of the revaluation of the accounts receivable in profit or loss caused the release to profit or loss of the deferred hedge results accumulated in equity: EUR 1,330,000 (=592,000 + 738,000) from the cash flow hedge reserve and EUR <449,000> from the time value reserve. The hedging relationship ended on this date.

Cash flow hedge reserve (Equity)	1,330,000	
Time value reserve (Equity)		449,000
Other financial income (Profit or loss)		881,000

On 30 June, 20X5 ABC received the USD 100 million from the client and eliminated the related account receivable. The USD 100 million receipt was valued at that date's exchange rate, EUR 75,758,000 (=100 mn/1.3200):

USD cash (Asset)	75,758,000	
Accounts receivable (Asset)		75,758,000

Simultaneously, both the forward and the option expired being exercised. Through the forward and the option, ABC sold USD 50 million, worth EUR 37,879,000, and received EUR 39,185,000. The fair value of the forward and the option just prior to settlement was EUR 1,306,000 (= 50 million × (1/1.2760 − 1/1.3200)).

EUR cash (Asset)	39,185,000	
Forward contract (Asset)		1,306,000
USD cash (Asset)		37,879,000
EUR cash (Asset)	39,185,000	
Option contract (Asset)		1,306,000
USD cash (Asset)		37,879,000

The following table gives a summary of the accounting entries, excluding the entries related to the cost of goods sold:

	Cash	Forward and option contracts	Accounts receivable	Cash flow hedge reserve	Time value reserve	Profit or loss
1-Oct-20X4						
Forward trade	799,000	<799,000>				
Option trade	<799,000>	799,000				
31 Dec-20X4						
Forward revaluation		918,000		859,000		59,000
Option revaluation		142,000			131,000	11,000
31-Mar-20X5						
Forward revaluation		595,000		595,000		
Option revaluation		76,000		568,000	<481,000>	<11,000>

	Cash	Forward and option contracts	Accounts receivable	Cash flow hedge reserve	Time value reserve	Profit or loss
Reserve reclassification				<2,022,000>	350,000	1,672,000
Sale shipment			77,220,000			77,220,000
30-Jun-20X5						
Forward revaluation		592,000		592,000		
Option revaluation		289,000		738,000	<449,000>	
Reserve reclassification				<1,330,000>	449,000	881,000
Forward settlement	1,306,000	<1,306,000>				
Option settlement	1,306,000	<1,306,000>				
Receivable revaluation			<1,463,000>			<1,463,000>
Receivable settlement	75,758,000		<75,758,000>			
TOTAL	**78,370,000**	**-0-**	**-0-**	**-0-**	**-0-**	**78,370,000**

Note: Total figures may not match the sum of their corresponding components due to rounding.

5.8.3 Alternative 2(a): Participating Forward in its Entirety

In this subsection I will cover an approach to apply hedge accounting when (i) a participating forward is involved and (ii) the entity does not want to split the instrument (see previous subsection) for hedge accounting purposes due to its operational complexity.

Under this approach the hedging instrument was the participating forward in its entirety. The hedged item was composed of two elements:

- The cash flow stemming from the first USD 50 million of the highly expected forecast sale. The risk management objective related to this first element was to mitigate its variability against movements in the EUR–USD FX rate.
- The cash flow stemming from the second USD 50 million of the highly expected forecast sale. The risk management objective related to this second element was to mitigate its variability against adverse movements in the EUR–USD FX rate above 1.2760.

Hedging Relationship Documentation   Consequently, the hedging relationship was documented as follows:

Hedging relationship documentation	
Risk management objective and strategy for undertaking the hedge	The objective of the hedge is twofold:
	Firstly, to mitigate the variability in EUR of the first USD 50 million cash flow stemming from a USD 100 million highly expected sale of finished goods and its ensuing receivable against unfavourable movements in the EUR–USD exchange rate.
	Secondly, to protect the EUR value of the second USD 50 million cash flow stemming from the above mentioned USD 100 million highly expected sale of finished goods and its ensuing receivable against unfavourable movements in the EUR–USD exchange rate above 1.2760.
	This hedging objective is consistent with the entity's overall FX risk management strategy of reducing the variability of its profit or loss statement caused by purchases and sales denominated in foreign currency.
	The designated risk being hedged is the risk of changes in the EUR value of the hedged cash flows due to movements in the EUR–USD exchange rate
Type of hedge	Cash flow hedge
Hedged item	The cash flow stemming from a USD 100 million sale of finished goods expected to be shipped on 31 March 20X5 and its payment expected to be received on 30 June 20X5. This sale is highly probable as similar transactions have occurred in the past with the potential buyer, for sales of similar size, and the negotiations with the buyer are at an advanced stage.
	Due to the two risk management objectives, for hedge assessment purposes, the hedged item was split into two highly expected cash flows of USD 50 million each, referred to as "hedged item 1" and "hedged item 2"
Hedging instrument	The participating forward contract with reference number 014569. The main terms of the participating forward are a USD 100 million notional, a forward rate that is a function of the EUR–USD spot rate at maturity (1.2760 – (1.2760 – final spot)/2), a 30 June 20X5 maturity and a physical settlement provision. The counterparty to the forward is XYZ Bank and the credit risk associated with this counterparty is considered to be very low
Hedge effectiveness assessment	See below

Hedge Effectiveness Assessment   Hedge effectiveness will be assessed by comparing changes in the fair value of the hedging instrument in its entirety to changes in the fair value of the hedged cash flows for the risks being hedged.

Changes in the fair value of the hedging instrument will be recognised as follows:

- The effective part of the gain or loss on the hedging instrument will be recognised in the cash flow hedge reserve of OCI. The accumulated amount in equity will be reclassified to profit or loss in the same period during which the hedged expected future cash flow affects profit or loss, initially adjusting the sales amount when the sale is recognised and thereafter adjusting the revaluation of the receivable.
- The ineffective part of the gain or loss on the hedging instrument will be recognised immediately in profit or loss.

Hedge effectiveness will be assessed prospectively at hedging relationship inception, on an ongoing basis at least upon each reporting date and upon occurrence of a significant change in the circumstances affecting the hedge effectiveness requirements.

The hedging relationship will qualify for hedge accounting only if all the following criteria are met:

1) The hedging relationship consists only of eligible hedge items and hedging instruments. The hedge item is eligible as it is a highly expected forecast transaction that exposes the entity to fair value risk, affects profit or loss and is reliably measurable. The hedging instrument is eligible as it is a derivative that does not result in a net written option.
2) At hedge inception there is a formal designation and documentation of the hedging relationship and the entity's risk management objective and strategy for undertaking the hedge.
3) The hedging relationship is considered effective.

The hedging relationship will be considered effective if the following three requirements are met:

1) There is an economic relationship between the hedged item and the hedging instrument.
2) The effect of credit risk does not dominate the value changes that result from that economic relationship.
3) The hedge ratio of the hedging relationship is the same as that resulting from the quantity of hedged item that the entity actually hedges and the quantity of the hedging instrument that the entity actually uses to hedge that quantity of hedged item. The hedge ratio should not be intentionally weighted to create ineffectiveness.

Whether there is an economic relationship between the hedged item and the hedging instrument will be assessed on a quantitative basis using the scenario analysis method for two scenarios in which the EUR–USD FX rate at the end of the hedging relationship (30 June 20X5) will be calculated by shifting the EUR–USD spot rate prevailing on the assessment date by ±10%, and the change in fair value of both the hedging instrument and the hedged item compared.

Hedge Effectiveness Assessment Performed at the Start of the Hedging Relationship The hedging relationship was considered effective as the following three requirements were met:

1) There was an economic relationship between the hedged item and the hedging instrument. Based on the quantitative assessment performed (see below), the entity concluded that the change in fair value of the hedged item was expected to be largely offset by the

change in fair value of the hedging instrument, corroborating that both elements had values that would generally move in opposite directions.

2) The effect of credit risk did not dominate the value changes resulting from that economic relationship as the credit ratings of both the entity and XYZ Bank were considered sufficiently strong.

3) The hedge ratio of the hedging relationship was the same as that resulting from the quantity of hedged item that the entity actually hedged and the quantity of the hedging instrument that the entity actually used to hedge that quantity of hedged item. The hedge ratio was not intentionally weighted to create ineffectiveness.

A quantitative assessment was performed using the scenario analysis method in which the performance of the hedging instrument and the hedged item was assessed under two scenarios.

In a first scenario, a EUR–USD spot rate at the end of the hedging relationship (1.3585) was assumed by shifting the EUR–USD spot rate prevailing on the assessment date (1.2350) by +10%. As shown in the table below, the change in fair value of the hedged item was expected to be largely offset by the change in fair value of the hedging instrument, corroborating that both elements have values that will generally move in opposite directions. Of note is that the hedged item was valued using forward rates (i.e., on a forward basis).

	First scenario analysis assessment			
	Hedging instrument	**Hedged item (1st element)**	**Hedged item (2nd element)**	**Hedged item (Total)**
Nominal USD	100,000,000	50,000,000	50,000,000	
Initial rate	1.2760 *(1)*	1.2520 *(2)*	1.2760 *(3)*	
Nominal EUR	78,370,000 *(4)*	39,936,000 *(5)*	39,185,000 *(6)*	
Nominal USD	100,000,000	50,000,000	50,000,000	
Final rate	1.3585 *(7)*	1.3585	1.3585	
Value in EUR	73,611,000 *(8)*	36,805,000 *(9)*	36,805,000 *(9)*	
Final fair value EUR	4,759,000 *(10)*	<3,131,000> *(11)*	<2,380,000> *(12)*	
Initial fair value EUR	Nil	Nil	Nil	
Fair value change	**4,759,000** *(13)*	<3,131,000>	<2,380,000>	**<5,511,000>**
			Degree of offset	**86.4%** *(14)*

Notes:

(1) Instrument forward rate when final FX rate was 1.3585

(2) According to its risk management objective, the 1st hedged item was fully protected (i.e., from 1.2520, the expected rate on 30-Jun-X5 as of the start of the hedging relationship)

(3) According to its risk management objective, the 2nd hedged item was protected from 1.2760

(4) 100,000,000/1.2760

(5) 50,000,000/1.2520

(6) 50,000,000/1.2760

(7) Spot rate at the end of the hedging relationship

(8) 100,000,000/1.3585

(9) 50,000,000/1.3585

(10) 78,370,000 – 73,611,000

(11) 36,805,000 – 39,936,000

(12) 36,805,000 – 39,185,000
(13) 4,759,000 – Nil
(14) 4,759,000/(– <5,511,000>)

In a second scenario, a EUR–USD spot rate at the end of the hedging relationship (1.1115) was assumed by shifting the EUR–USD spot rate prevailing on the assessment date (1.2350) by –10%. As shown in the table below, the change in fair value of the hedged item was expected to be largely offset by the change in fair value of the hedging instrument, corroborating that both elements have values that will generally move in opposite directions.

	Second scenario analysis assessment			
	Hedging instrument	**Hedged item (1st element)**	**Hedged item (2nd element)**	**Hedged item (Total)**
Nominal USD	100,000,000	50,000,000		
Initial rate	1.1938 *(1)*	1.2520 *(2)*		
Nominal EUR	83,766,000 *(3)*	39,936,000 *(4)*		
Nominal USD	100,000,000	50,000,000		
Final rate	1.1115 *(5)*	1.1115 *(5)*		
Value in EUR	89,969,000 *(6)*	44,984,000 *(7)*		
Final fair value EUR	<6,202,000> *(8)*	5,048,000 *(9)*	Nil *(10)*	
Initial fair value EUR	Nil	Nil	Nil	
Fair value change	**<6,202,000>** *(11)*	5,048,000	Nil	**5,048,000**
		Degree of offset		**122.9%** *(12)*

Notes:
(1) Instrument forward rate when final FX rate was 1.1115
(2) According to its risk management objective, the 1st hedged item was fully protected (i.e., from 1.2520, the expected rate on 30-Jun-X5 as of the start of the hedging relationship)
(3) 100,000,000/1.1938
(4) 50,000,000/1.2520
(5) Spot rate at the end of the hedging relationship
(6) 100,000,000/1.1115
(7) 50,000,000/1.1115
(8) 83,766,000 – 89,969,000
(9) 44,984,000 – 39,936,000
(10) According to its risk management objective, the 2nd hedged item was protected from 1.2760. Because the spot rate (1.1115) was below the spot rate at which the protection kicked in, the 2nd hedged item was not taken into account for this scenario analysis
(11) <6,202,000> – Nil
(12) <6,202,000>/(–5,048,000)

Under the two scenarios, the degree of offset was notably high. Under the second scenario, the degree of offset exceeded 100% because the hedging instrument benefited on just half of the appreciation of the USD relative to the EUR below 1.2760, while the hedged item benefited fully from such appreciation. In any case, the entity concluded that the degree of offset under the two scenarios were large enough to conclude that an economic relationship existed between the hedging instrument and the hedged item.

The hedge ratio was established at 1:1, resulting from the USD 100 million of hedged item that the entity actually hedged and the USD 100 million of the hedging instrument that the entity actually used to hedge that quantity of hedged item.

Another hedge assessment was performed on 31 December 20X4 (reporting date). This assessment was very similar to the one performed at inception and has been omitted to avoid unnecessary repetition. Additionally, the hedge ratio was assumed to be 1:1 on that assessment date.

Fair Valuations on 31 December 20X4 The fair valuations of the hedging instrument were calculated in the previous subsection. The fair value of the participating forward (EUR 1,060,000) was the sum of the fair values of the forward (EUR 119,000) and option (EUR 941,000) embedded contracts.

The fair valuation of the hedged item on 31 December 20X4 was performed on a forward basis based on a forward rate for 30 June 20X5 of 1.2800 and a 0.9839 discount factor as follows:

	Hedged item 1	Hedged item 2
Nominal EUR	39,936,000 *(1)*	39,185,000 *(2)*
Nominal USD	50,000,000	50,000,000
Rate for 30-Jun-20X5	/1.2800 *(3)*	/1.2800
Value in EUR	39,063,000 *(4)*	39,063,000 *(4)*
Difference	<873,000> *(5)*	<122,000>
Discount factor	× 0.9839	× 0.9839
Fair value	<859,000> *(6)*	<120,000>
Fair value change (Cumulative)	<859,000> *(7)*	<120,000>
Total fair value	**<979,000>** *(8)*	

Notes:
(1) 50,000,000/1.2520
(2) 50,000,000/1.2760
(3) Forward rate for 30 June 20X5 as of the valuation date
(4) 50,000,000/1.2800
(5) 39,063,000 – 39,936,000
(6) <873,000> × 0.9839
(7) <859,000> minus its initial fair value, which was nil
(8) <859,000> + <120,000>

The following table summarises the changes in values of both the hedging instrument and the hedged item:

	31-Dec-20X4
Participating forward fair value	1,060,000
Participating forward previous fair value	-0-
Change in participating forward fair value (period)	1,060,000

	31-Dec-20X4
Change in participating forward fair value (cumulative)	1,060,000
Hedged item fair value	<979,000>
Change in hedged item fair value (cumulative)	<979,000>

Fair Valuations on 31 March 20X5   The fair valuations of the hedging instrument were calculated in the previous subsection. The fair value of the participating forward (EUR 1,731,000) was the sum of the fair values of the forward (EUR 714,000) and the option (EUR 1,017,000) embedded contracts.

The fair valuation of the hedged item on 31 March 20X5 was performed on a forward basis based on a forward rate for 30 June 20X5 of 1.3000 and a 0.9901 discount factor as follows:

	Hedged item 1	**Hedged item 2**
Nominal EUR	39,936,000	39,185,000
Nominal USD	50,000,000	50,000,000
Rate for 30-Jun-20X5	/1.3000	/1.3000
Value in EUR	38,462,000	38,462,000
Difference	<1,474,000>	<723,000>
Discount factor	× 0.9901	× 0.9901
Fair value	<1,459,000>	<716,000>
Total fair value	**<2,175,000>**	

The following table summarises the changes in values of both the hedging instrument and the hedged item:

	31-March-20X5
Participating forward fair value	1,731,000
Participating forward previous fair value	1,060,000
Change in participating forward fair value (period)	671,000
Change in participating forward fair value (cumulative)	1,731,000
Hedged item fair value	<2,175,000>
Change in hedged item fair value (cumulative)	<2,175,000>

Fair Valuations on 30 June 20X5   The fair valuations of the hedging instrument were calculated in the previous subsection. The fair value of the participating forward (EUR 2,612,000) was the sum of the fair values of the forward (EUR 1,306,000) and the option (EUR 1,306,000) embedded contracts.

The fair valuation of the hedged item on 30 June 20X5 was performed based on a spot rate of 1.3200 and a 1.0000 discount factor as follows:

	Hedged Item 1	Hedged Item 2
Nominal EUR	39,936,000	39,185,000
Nominal USD	50,000,000	50,000,000
Rate for 30-Jun-20X5	/1.3200	/1.3200
Value in EUR	37,879,000	37,879,000
Difference	<2,057,000>	<1,306,000>
Discount factor	× 1.0000	× 1.0000
Fair value	<2,057,000>	<1,306,000>
Total fair value	<3,363,000>	

The following table summarises the changes in values of both the hedging instrument and the hedged item:

	30-Jun-20X5
Participating forward fair value	2,612,000
Participating forward previous fair value	1,731,000
Change in participating forward fair value (period)	881,000
Change in participating forward fair value (cumulative)	2,612,000
Hedged item fair value	<3,363,000>
Change in hedged item fair value (cumulative)	<3,363,000>

Calculation of Effective and Ineffective Amounts   The calculation of the effective and ineffective parts of the period change in fair value of the participating forward was performed as follows:

	31-Dec-20X4	31-Mar-20X5	30-Jun-20X5
Cumulative change in fair value of hedging instrument	1,060,000	1,731,000	2,612,000
Cumulative change in fair value of hedged item (opposite sign)	979,000	2,175,000	3,363,000
Lower amount	979,000	1,731,000	2,612,000
Previous cumulative effective amount	-0-	979,000	1,650,000
Available amount	979,000	752,000	962,000
Period change in fair value of hedging instrument	1,060,000	671,000	881,000
Effective part	979,000	671,000	881,000
Ineffective part	81,000	Nil	Nil

Accounting Entries   The required journal entries were as follows.

1) To record the forward and the option trades on 1 October, 20X4

At their inception, the fair value of the participating forward was zero. Consequently, no on-balance-sheet accounting entries were required.

2) To record the closing of the accounting period on 31 December 20X4

The change in fair value of the participating forward since the last valuation was a EUR 1,060,000 gain, of which EUR 979,000 was deemed to be effective and recorded in the cash flow hedge reserve of equity, while EUR 81,000 was deemed to be ineffective and recorded in profit or loss.

Participating forward (Asset)	1,060,000	
Cash flow hedge reserve (Equity)		979,000
Other financial income (Profit or loss)		81,000

3) To record the sale agreement on 31 March 20X5

The sale agreement was recorded at the spot rate prevailing on that date (1.2950). Therefore, the sale EUR proceeds were EUR 77,220,000 (=100 million/1.2950). Because the machinery sold was not yet paid, a receivable was recognised. Suppose that the machinery was valued at EUR 68 million in ABC's statement of financial position.

Accounts receivable (Asset)	77,220,000	
Sales (Profit or loss)		77,220,000
Cost of goods sold (Profit or loss)	68,000,000	
Machinery (Asset)		68,000,000

The change in fair value of the participating forward since the last valuation was a gain of EUR 671,000, fully considered to be effective and recorded in the cash flow hedge reserve of OCI.

Participating forward (Asset)	671,000	
Cash flow hedge reserve (Equity)		671,000

The recognition of the sales transaction in profit or loss caused the release to profit or loss of the EUR 1,650,000 deferred hedge results accumulated in the cash flow hedge reserve of equity.

Cash flow hedge reserve (Equity)	1,650,000	
Sales (Profit or loss)		1,650,000

4) To record the settlement of the receivable and the derivatives on 30 June 20X5

The receivable was revalued at the spot rate prevailing on this date, showing a loss of EUR 1,463,000 (=100 million/1.3200 – 100 million/1.2950):

Other financial expenses (Profit or loss)	1,463,000	
Accounts receivable (Asset)		1,463,000

The change in the fair value of the participating forward since the last valuation was a gain of EUR 881,000, fully deemed to be effective.

Participating forward (Asset)	881,000	
Cash flow hedge reserve (Equity)		881,000

The recognition of the revaluation of the accounts receivable in profit or loss caused the release to profit or loss of the EUR 881,000 deferred hedge results accumulated in the cash flow hedge reserve equity. The hedging relationship ended on this date.

Cash flow hedge reserve (Equity)	881,000	
Other financial income (Profit or loss)		881,000

On 30 June, 20X5, ABC received the USD 100 million from the client and eliminated the related account receivable. The USD 100 million receipt was valued at that date's exchange rate, EUR 75,758,000 (=100 mn/1.3200):

USD cash (Asset)	75,758,000	
Accounts receivable (Asset)		75,758,000

Simultaneously, the participating forward was settled: ABC sold USD 100 million, worth EUR 75,758,000, and received EUR 78,370,000. The fair value of the participating forward just prior to its settlement was EUR 2,612,000 (= 100 million × (1/1.2760 – 1/1.3200)).

EUR cash (Asset)	78,370,000	
Forward contract (Asset)		2,612,000
USD cash (Asset)		75,758,000

The following table gives a summary of the accounting entries, excluding the entries related to the cost of goods sold:

	Cash	Participating forward	Accounts receivable	Cash flow Hedge reserve	Profit or loss
1-Oct-20X4					
No entries					
31 Dec-20X4					
Partic. forward revaluation		1,060,000		979,000	81,000
31-Mar-20X5					
Partic. forward revaluation		671,000		671,000	
Reserve reclassification				<1,650,000>	1,650,000
Sale shipment			77,220,000		77,220,000
30-Jun-20X5					
Partic. forward revaluation		881,000		881,000	
Reserve reclassification				<881,000>	881,000
Partic. forward settlement	2,612,000	<2,612,000>			
Receivable revaluation			<1,463,000>		<1,463,000>
Receivable settlement	75,758,000		<75,758,000>		
TOTAL	**78,370,000**	**-0-**	**-0-**	**-0-**	**78,370,000**

Note: Total figures may not match the sum of their corresponding components due to rounding.

5.8.4 Alternative 2(b): Participating Forward in its Entirety – Readjusting the Hedge Ratio

Suppose that ABC decided to consider the whole participating forward as one instrument and, from an accounting perspective, tried to designate it as the hedging instrument in a hedging relationship. In this subsection I will cover an uncommon approach to the application of hedge accounting: the **rebalancing approach**. This approach rebalances the hedge ratio to changes in the circumstances surrounding a hedging relationship.

The rebalancing approach is an interesting alternative for the application of hedge accounting when exotic options are involved and either (i) it is not feasible a split of the derivative between a hedge accounting friendly part and an undesignated part or (ii) designating the derivative in its entirety results in economic assessments that are too dependent on the path followed by the underlying market variable. The rebalancing approach starts by estimating the quantity of hedged item that would be hedged with the quantity of derivative actually traded. Whilst this approach is notably less attractive than the two previous ones due to its complexity, I have included it is an interesting way to approach more structured hedges.

This approach is like starting to build a house from the roof down. It commences by calculating a **preliminary hedge ratio** at the inception of the hedging relationship, and subsequently adjusting it for changes in the EUR–USD FX rate. A hedge ratio provides the quantity of participating forward that on a "forward looking" basis provides the best hedge of the quantity of hedged item (i.e., the highly expected forecast sale denominated in USD).

$$\text{Hedge ratio} = \frac{\text{Notional of the hedged item}}{\text{National of the hedging instrument}}$$

I describe two alternative methods to estimate the preliminary hedge ratio: (i) using the implied delta and (ii) using historical market rates. My suggestion is to use the first method as it is the best estimate of the market expectations for the hedge ratio.

Preliminary Hedge Ratio Estimation Using Implied Delta It was shown earlier that our participating forward could be split into two contracts (see Figure 5.15): (i) an FX forward at 1.2760 and a nominal of USD 50 million, and (ii) a purchase of a USD put with strike 1.2760 and USD 50 million nominal. The quantity of participating forward was the sum of the quantities of the forward and the option:

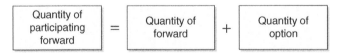

The quantity of forward to be used by ABC was USD 50 million as its probability of being exercised was 100% (i.e., there is no optionality in a forward as both parties will be obliged to exchange the notional amounts at maturity).

Whilst the quantity of forward was known, the quantity of option to be used by ABC depended on the EUR–USD spot rate at expiry. If the EUR–USD spot rate was above 1.2760, ABC would fully exercise the option, which may be interpreted as ABC using a USD 50 million quantity of the option. Alternatively, if the spot rate was at or below 1.2760 at expiry, ABC would not exercise the option, or in other words, ABC would not use any quantity of the option. Whilst ex ante ABC did not know whether the option would be exercised, the entity could estimate the option's probability of being exercised, which is approximated by the option's delta.

In order to calculate the appropriate hedge ratio, the quantity of hedged item should equal the quantity of participating forward. As noted above, the quantity of participating forward is unknown at the commencement of the hedging relationship and can be estimated according to the following expression:

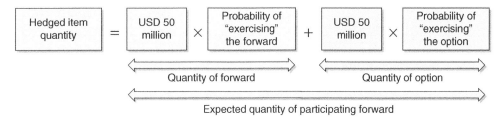

As mentioned previously, the quantity of forward was USD 50 million as the probability of "exercising" the forward was 100%. The probability of exercising an option can be approximated by using its delta. Therefore, the quantity of hedged item can be estimated as:

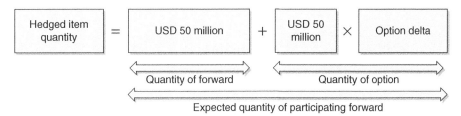

An option delta indicates the theoretical change in an option price with respect to changes in the price of the underlying price/rate. When the underlying price/rate changes by a small amount, the option price changes by the delta multiplied by that amount. The delta is commonly expressed as a percentage, measuring the change in an option price for a 1% change in the underlying price/rate.

The absolute value of the delta can be loosely interpreted as an approximate measure of the probability that an option will expire in-the-money (i.e., be exercised). If an option is very deep in-the-money, and therefore has a very high probability of being in-the-money at expiry, the absolute value of the delta will be close to 100%. If an option is very deep out-of-the-money, it has a low probability of being in-the-money at expiry, and therefore the absolute value of its delta will be close to zero. At-the-money options have a delta close to 50%, meaning roughly a 50% probability of being exercised at expiry. In our case, on 1 October 20X4 the delta of our option was 38%, using the Black–Scholes pricing model. The option delta as a function of the EUR–USD spot rate on that date had the profile depicted in Figure 5.17, showing that for example had the spot rate been 1.2028 the delta would have been 25%.

As a result, the hedge ratio was established at 0.69:1, and USD 69 million of the hedged item was hedged using USD 100 million of the participating forward.

Preliminary Hedge Ratio Estimation Using Historical Data   A second method to estimate a preliminary hedge ratio is to simulate the historical performance of the hedging relationship using actual EUR–USD spot rate past behaviour and calculating the quantity of participating forward that the entity would have used. The following table details a hedge ratio estimation using monthly observations during the previous 2 years. For example, on 1 May 20X2 the EUR–USD spot rate was 1.3197, a 6-month hedging relationship would have finished on 31

October 20X2 and the spot rate on this date was 1.2489, while the participating forward rate would have been 1.3607, resulting in a USD 50 million quantity being used as the option element would not have been exercised.

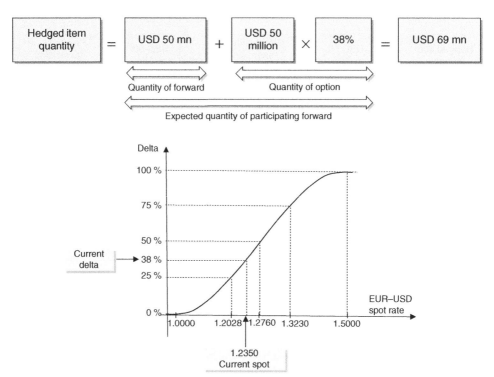

FIGURE 5.17   Option delta on 1 October 20X4.

According to the behaviour of the EUR–USD spot rate during the period from 1-May-X2 to 1-Apr-X4, the average quantity would have been USD 64,583,000, implying a 0.65:1 hedge ratio.

Date	Spot start hedging relationship	Spot end hedging relationship	Participating forward rate	Quantity used
1-May-X2	1.3197	1.2489	1.3607	50,000,000
1-Jun-X2	1.3175	1.2433	1.3585	50,000,000
1-Jul-X2	1.3016	1.2129	1.3426	50,000,000
1-Aug-X2	1.2783	1.2210	1.3193	50,000,000
1-Sep-X2	1.2501	1.1919	1.2911	50,000,000
1-Oct-X2	1.2869	1.1906	1.3279	50,000,000
1-Nov-X2	1.2489	1.2078	1.2899	50,000,000
1-Dec-X2	1.2433	1.1716	1.2843	50,000,000
1-Jan-X3	1.2129	1.1970	1.2539	50,000,000
1-Feb-X3	1.2210	1.2715	1.2620	100,000,000
1-Mar-X3	1.1919	1.2456	1.2329	100,000,000
1-Apr-X3	1.1906	1.2534	1.2316	100,000,000

Date	Spot start hedging relationship	Spot end hedging relationship	Participating forward rate	Quantity used
1-May-X3	1.2078	1.1897	1.2488	50,000,000
1-Jun-X3	1.1716	1.1875	1.2126	50,000,000
1-Jul-X3	1.1970	1.1716	1.2380	50,000,000
1-Aug-X3	1.2522	1.1483	1.2932	50,000,000
1-Sep-X3	1.2126	1.1201	1.2536	50,000,000
1-Oct-X3	1.2104	1.1569	1.2514	50,000,000
1-Nov-X3	1.1897	1.1271	1.2307	50,000,000
1-Dec-X3	1.1875	1.2110	1.2285	50,000,000
1-Jan-X4	1.1716	1.2250	1.2126	100,000,000
1-Feb-X4	1.1483	1.2233	1.1893	100,000,000
1-Mar-X4	1.1201	1.1985	1.1611	100,000,000
1-Apr-X4	1.1569	1.2123	1.1979	100,000,000

		Average quantity used:		USD 64,583,000

In order to avoid unnecessary repetition, I will cover next only the elements of the hedge that are particularly specific to this case. I will be using a preliminary hedge ratio of 0.69:1

Hedged Item Description in the Hedging Relationship Documentation   The hedged item was defined in the hedge documentation as follows: "USD 69 million sale of finished goods expected to take place on 31 March 20X5. This sale is highly probable as similar transactions have occurred in the past with the potential buyer, for sales of similar size, and the negotiations with the buyer are at an advanced stage. The amount of hedged item will be adjusted in accordance with the hedge ratio."

Hedging Instrument Description in the Hedging Relationship Documentation   The hedged item was defined in the hedge documentation as follows: "The participating forward contract with reference number 014565. The notional of the instrument is USD 100 million, its rate is 1.2760 and its maturity on 30 June 20X5. The counterparty to the instrument is XYZ Bank and the credit risk associated with this counterparty is considered to be very low."

Hypothetical Derivative   The initial terms of the hypothetical derivative were as follows:

Hypothetical derivative – terms	
Instrument	FX forward
Start date	1 October 20X4
Counterparties	ABC and credit risk-free counterparty
Maturity	30 June 20X5
ABC sells	USD 69 million
ABC buys	EUR 55,112,000
Forward rate	1.2520
Initial fair value	Zero

The notionals of the hypothetical derivative will be adjusted to reflect adjustments to the quantity of hedged item as a result of changes to the hedge ratio.

Fair Valuations at Inception and on 31 December 20X4   The fair valuations were calculated in the previous subsection. The fair value of the participating forward was the sum of the fair values of the embedded forward and option contracts.

	1-Oct-20X4	31-Dec-20X4
Participating forward fair value	-0-	1,060,000
Change in participating forward fair value	—	1,060,000
Hypothetical derivative fair value	-0-	1,185,000 (*)
Change in hypothetical derivative fair value	—	1,185,000

(*) 859,000 × 69 mn/50 mn, where EUR 859,000 was the fair value of "hedged item 1" on 31-Dec-20X4 (which had a USD 50 mn notional) from Section 5.8.3 (Fair Valuations on 31 December 20X4).

The calculation of the effective and ineffective parts of the period change in fair value of the participating forward was performed as follows:

	31-Dec-20X4
Cumulative change in fair value of hedging instrument	1,060,000
Cumulative change in fair value of hypothetical derivative	1,185,000
Lower amount	1,060,000
Previous cumulative effective amount	-0-
Available amount	1,060,000
Period change in fair value of hedging instrument	1,060,000
Effective part	1,060,000
Ineffective part	-0-

Re-estimation of the Hedge Ratio on 31 December 20X4   The hedge ratio was re-estimated on 31 December 20X4 using the implied delta of the participating forward. Remember that the quantity of the hedged item was estimated using the following expression:

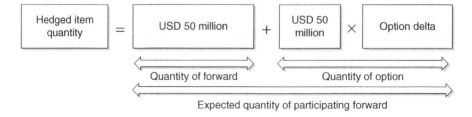

The embedded option's delta was 47% (see Figure 5.18), higher than at inception because the increase in the spot rate increased the option's probability of exercise. The estimate of the hedged item quantity was USD 74 million, calculated as follows:

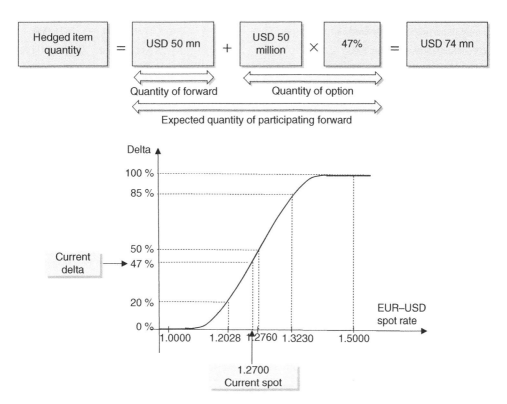

FIGURE 5.18 Option delta on 31 December 20X4.

The terms of the hypothetical derivative were adjusted, as shown below:

Hypothetical derivative – terms	
Instrument	FX forward
Start date	1 October 20X4
Counterparties	ABC and credit risk-free counterparty
Maturity	30 June 20X5
ABC sells	USD 74 million
ABC buys	EUR 59,105,000
Forward rate	1.2520
Initial fair value	Zero

218 ACCOUNTING FOR DERIVATIVES

Fair Valuations on 31 March 20X5

	31-Dec-20X4	31-Mar-20X5
Participating forward fair value	1,060,000	1,731,000
Change in participating forward fair value (period)	1,060,000	671,000
Hypothetical derivative fair value	Not needed	2,159,000 (*)
Change in hypoth. derivative fair value (cumulative since inception)	—	2,159,000

(*) 1,459,000 × 74 mn /50 mn, where EUR 1,459,000 was the fair value of "hedged item 1" on 31-Mar-20X5 (which had a USD 50 mn notional) from Section 5.8.3 (Fair Valuations on 31 March 20X5).

The calculation of the effective and ineffective parts of the period change in fair value of the participating forward was performed as follows:

	31-Mar-20X5
Cumulative change in fair value of hedging instrument	1,731,000
Cumulative change in fair value of hypothetical derivative	2,159,000
Lower amount	1,731,000
Previous cumulative effective amount	1,060,000
Available amount	671,000
Period change in fair value of hedging instrument	671,000
Effective part	671,000
Ineffective part	-0-

Re-estimation of the Hedge Ratio on 30 March 20X5   The hedge ratio was re-estimated on 30 March 20X5 using the implied delta of the participating forward. Remember that the quantity of the hedged item was estimated using the following expression:

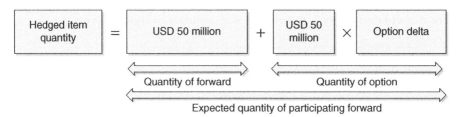

The embedded option's delta was 76% (see Figure 5.19), higher than at inception because the increase in the spot rate increased the option's probability of exercise. The estimate of the hedged item quantity was USD 88 million, calculated as follows:

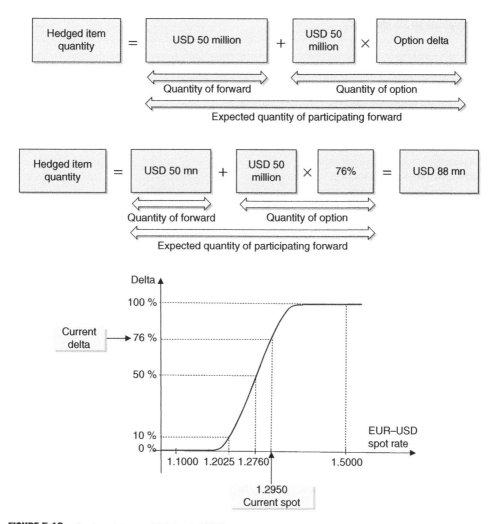

FIGURE 5.19 Option delta on 31 March 20X5.

The terms of the hypothetical derivative were adjusted, as shown below:

Hypothetical derivative – terms	
Instrument	FX forward
Start date	1 October 20X4
Counterparties	ABC and credit risk-free counterparty
Maturity	30 June 20X5
ABC sells	USD 88 million
ABC buys	EUR 70,288,000
Forward rate	1.2520
Initial fair value	Zero

Fair Valuations on 30 June 20X5

	31-Mar-20X5	30-Jun-20X5
Participating forward fair value	1,731,000	2,612,000
Change in participating forward fair value (period)	—	881,000
Hypothetical derivative fair value	Not needed	3,620,000 (*)
Change in hypoth. derivative fair value (cumulative since inception)	—	3,620,000

(*) 2,057,000 × 88 mn/50 mn, where EUR 2,057,000 was the fair value of "hedged item 1" on 30-Jun-20X5 (which had a USD 50 mn notional) from Section 5.8.3 (Fair Valuations on 30 June 20X5).

The calculation of the effective and ineffective parts of the period change in fair value of the participating forward was performed as follows:

	30-Jun-20X5
Cumulative change in fair value of hedging instrument	2,612,000
Cumulative change in fair value of hypothetical derivative	3,620,000
Lower amount	2,612,000
Previous cumulative effective amount	1,731,000
Available amount	881,000
Period change in fair value of hedging instrument	881,000
Effective part	881,000
Ineffective part	-0-

Accounting Entries   The required journal entries were as follows.

1) To record the participating forward contract trade on 1 October 20X4

No entries in the financial statements were required as the fair value of the participating forward contract was zero.

2) To record the closing of the accounting period on 31 December 20X4

The change in fair value of the participating forward since the last valuation was a gain of EUR 1,060,000. As the hedge was fully effective, all this change in fair value was recorded in OCI and none in profit or loss.

Participating forward contract (Asset)	1,060,000	
Cash flow hedge reserve (Equity)		1,060,000

3) To record the sale agreement and the end of the hedging relationship on 31 March 20X5

The sale agreement was recorded at the EUR–USD spot rate prevailing on the date the sales were recognised (1.2950). Therefore, the sales EUR amount was EUR 77,220,000 (=100 million/1.2950). Because the machinery sold was not yet paid, a receivable was recognised. Suppose that the machinery was valued at EUR 68 million in ABC's statement of financial position. The change in the fair value of the participating forward since the last valuation was a gain of EUR 671,000, fully effective and recognised in OCI. The recognition of the sales transaction in profit or loss caused the release to profit or loss of the EUR 1,731,000 deferred hedge results accumulated in OCI.

Cost of goods sold (Profit or loss)	68,000,000	
Machinery (Asset)		68,000,000
Accounts receivable (Asset)	77,220,000	
Sales (Profit or loss)		77,220,000
Participating forward contract (Asset)	671,000	
Cash flow hedge reserve (Equity)		671,000
Cash flow hedge reserve (Equity)	1,731,000	
Sales (Profit or loss)		1,731,000

4) To record the settlement of the receivable and the participating forward on 30 June 20X5

The receivable was revalued at the spot rate prevailing on this date, showing a loss of EUR 1,463,000 (=100 million/1.3200 – 100 million/1.2950).

The USD payment from the receivable was exchanged for EUR as soon as it was received. The spot rate on payment date was 1.32, so the USD 100 million payment was exchanged for EUR 75,758,000 (=100 million/1.32).

The change in the fair value of the participating forward since the last valuation was a gain of EUR 881,000, fully effective and recognised in OCI.

The revaluation of the receivable in profit or loss caused the release to profit or loss of the EUR 881,000 deferred hedge results accumulated in OCI.

The settlement of the FX participating forward resulted in the exchange of USD 100 million, worth EUR 75,758,000, for EUR 78,370,000. The fair value of the participating forward was EUR 2,612,000 (=100 million × (1/1.2760 – 1/1.32)).

Other financial expenses (Profit or loss)	1,463,000	
Accounts receivable (Asset)		1,463,000
USD cash (Asset)	75,758,000	
Accounts receivable (Asset)		75,758,000
Participating forward contract (Asset)	881,000	
Cash flow hedge reserve (Equity)		881,000
Cash flow hedge reserve (Equity)	881,000	
Other financial income (Profit or loss)		881,000

(continued overleaf)

EUR cash (Asset)	78,370,000
USD cash (Asset)	75,758,000
Participating forward contract (Asset)	2,612,000

The following table gives a summary of the accounting entries, excluding the entries related to the cost of goods sold:

	Cash	Forward and option contracts	Accounts receivable	Cash flow hedge reserve	Time value reserve	Profit or loss
1-Oct-20X4						
Part. fwd trade						
31 Dec-20X4						
Part. fwd revaluation		1,060,000		1,060,000		
31-Mar-20X5						
Part. fwd revaluation		671,000		671,000		
Reserve reclassification				<1,731,000>		1,731,000
Sale shipment			77,220,000			77,220,000
30-Jun-20X5						
Part. fwd revaluation		881,000		881,000		
Part. fwd settlement	2,612,000	<2,612,000>				
Receivable revaluation			<1,463,000>			<1,463,000>
Reserve reclassification				<881,000>		881,000
Receivable settlement	75,758,000		<75,758,000>			
TOTAL	**78,370,000**	**-0-**	**-0-**	**-0-**	**-0-**	**78,370,000**

Note: Total figures may not match the sum of their corresponding components due to rounding.

5.9 CASE STUDY: HEDGING A HIGHLY EXPECTED FOREIGN SALE WITH A KNOCK-IN FORWARD (INTRODUCTION)

In the previous cases, the hedging strategies were built using forward, standard options or a combination thereof ("standard derivatives"). The derivatives instrument in this case involves a knock-in forward, an instrument built with an exotic option.

Whilst the hedge accounting treatment of standard derivatives under IFRS 9 is relatively clear, the hedge accounting treatment of exotic options is notably less clear, and thus subject to multiple interpretations. A potential solution would be to split the exotic instrument into two parts: a first part that involves a group of standard derivatives for which the accounting treatment is clear, and a second part that includes the remainder. The first part would be eligible for hedge accounting and the second part would be treated as undesignated. This process of splitting the exotic instrument into the two parts is quite challenging as it generally results in multiple solutions. Therefore, readers seeking an optimal accounting solution etched in stone are bound to be disappointed. My objective is for readers to develop and exercise their own accounting judgement.

The risk being hedged in this case is the same as in the previous cases. On 1 October 20X4, ABC Corporation, a company whose functional currency was the EUR, was expecting to sell finished goods to a US client. The sale was expected to occur on 31 March 20X5, and the sale receivable was expected to be settled on 30 June 20X5. Sale proceeds were expected to be USD 100 million, to be received in USD.

ABC had the view that the USD would appreciate against the EUR during the following months and wanted to benefit were its view right. However, ABC thought that the USD appreciation would be relatively limited, not reaching 1.1620. At the same time, ABC wanted to be protected, were its view wrong. As a consequence, on 1 October 20X4 ABC entered into a knock-in forward with the following terms:

Knock-in forward – terms	
Instrument	FX knock-in forward
Start date	1 October 20X4
Counterparties	ABC and credit risk-free counterparty
Maturity	30 June 20X5
ABC sells	USD 100 million
ABC buys	EUR 79,365,000 (if barrier is reached prior to maturity)
Strike Rate	1.2600
Barrier	1.1620
Premium	Zero
Settlement	Physical delivery

The knock-in forward guaranteed an exchange rate slightly worse than that of a standard forward but, on the other hand, it allowed ABC a better exchange rate provided the spot rate did not reach 1.1620. On expiry, ABC had the right to exchange USD for EUR at a rate of 1.2600. In the event that the EUR–USD spot rate ever traded at or below 1.1620 during the instrument's life, ABC's right became a standard forward with forward rate 1.2600 (i.e., an obligation to exchange USD for EUR at a rate of 1.2600). ABC did not pay a premium to enter into the knock-in forward.

Figure 5.19 shows the EUR amount that ABC would get in exchange for the USD 100 million as a function of the EUR–USD spot rate at maturity, were the barrier *not hit* during the life of the instrument. It can be seen how ABC could benefit were the exchange rate at maturity below 1.2600, and that this benefit was limited by the 1.1620 barrier.

Figure 5.20 illustrates the EUR amount that ABC would get in exchange for the USD 100 million sale proceeds as a function of the EUR–USD spot rate at maturity, were the barrier *hit* during the life of the instrument. It shows that the instrument secured a worst-case rate of 1.2600, equivalent to a worst-case amount of EUR 79,365,000.

Figure 5.21 shows the resulting exchange rate at which ABC would exchange the proceeds from the USD sale as a function of the spot exchange rate at maturity, were the barrier *not* hit during the life of the knock-in forward. It can be seen that the knock-in forward allowed ABC to participate in a potential appreciation of the USD below 1.2600 provided that the EUR–USD spot rate did not reach the 1.1620 barrier level during the life of the instrument.

Figure 5.22 shows the resulting exchange rate at which ABC would exchange the proceeds from the USD sale, as a function of the exchange rate at maturity if the barrier *was* hit during the life of the instrument. It can be seen that once the 1.1620 level was reached, the resulting rate was 1.2600 (i.e., the knock-in forward became a standard forward).

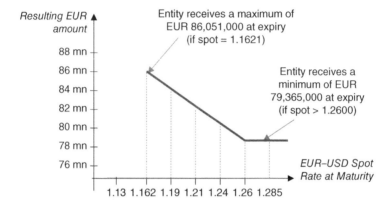

FIGURE 5.19 Knock-in resulting EUR amount – barrier *not* hit.

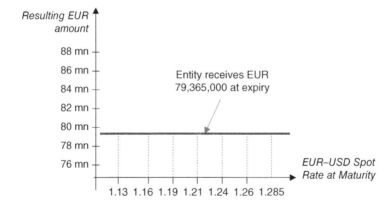

FIGURE 5.20 Knock-in resulting EUR amount – barrier *was* hit.

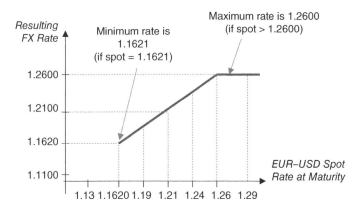

FIGURE 5.21 Knock-in resulting FX rate – barrier *not* hit.

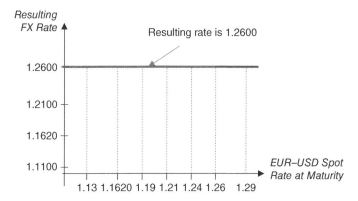

FIGURE 5.22 Knock-in resulting FX rate – barrier *was* hit.

5.9.1 Accounting Optimisation of the Knock-in Forward

One of the main issues that ABC faced regarding the knock-in forward was how to achieve the right balance between minimisation of volatility in profit or loss (i.e., maximisation of hedge accounting effectiveness) and minimisation of operational complexity. ABC considered the following choices:

1) Consider the whole knock-in forward as one instrument and, from an accounting perspective, try to designate it as the hedging instrument in a hedging relationship. If eligible for hedge accounting, the effective part of the change in fair value of the derivative would be temporarily accumulated in OCI, while the ineffective part would be recognised in profit or loss.
2) Divide the hedging instrument into two parts (see Figure 5.23): (i) an FX forward at 1.2600, and (ii) a purchased knock-out USD call with a 1.2600 strike and a 1.1620 barrier. The forward would be considered eligible for hedge accounting, and the knock-out option would be undesignated (i.e., considered as speculative). Therefore, all the changes in the fair value of the knock-out option would be recorded in profit or loss.

3) Divide the hedging instrument into two parts (see Figure 5.24): (i) a purchased standard USD put with strike 1.2600, and (ii) a written USD knock-in call with a 1.2620 strike and a 1.1620 barrier. Part (i) would be considered eligible for hedge accounting if the eligibility criteria are met. Part (ii) would be considered undesignated. In this choice, the changes in the fair value of the knock-in option would be recorded in profit or loss.

4) Consider the whole derivative as undesignated. As a consequence, all changes in fair value of the knock-in forward would be recorded in profit. This choice was the simplest, minimising operational complexity but, due to the potential negative effect on profit or loss volatility, it was discarded.

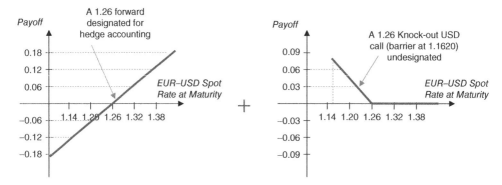

FIGURE 5.23 Knock-in forward approach 2: forward + knock-out option.

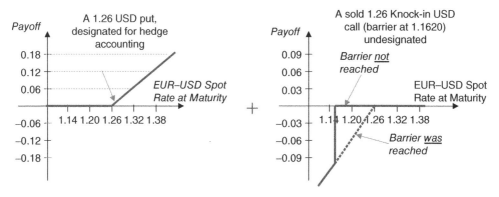

FIGURE 5.24 Knock-in forward approach 3: standard option + knock-in option.

5.10 CASE STUDY: HEDGING A FORECAST SALE AND SUBSEQUENT RECEIVABLE WITH A KNOCK-IN FORWARD (SPLITTING ALTERNATIVE)

In this section I assume that ABC discarded the possibility of designating the knock-in forward in its entirety as the hedging instrument, preferring to consider the other two choices, both of which divide the hedging instrument into two parts:

1) an FX forward at 1.2600, and a purchased knock-out USD call with a 1.2600 strike and a 1.1620 barrier (see Figure 5.23); and

2) a purchased standard USD put with strike 1.2600, and a written USD knock-in call with a 1.2620 strike and a 1.1620 barrier (see Figure 5.24).

In theory ABC could analyse which of these two choices would result in a lower profit or loss volatility by calculating the ineffective amounts under several scenarios. However, the first approach was selected due to its much simpler accounting treatment

5.10.1 Terms of the Split into a Forward and a Knock-out Option

As mentioned previously, ABC decided to adopt the first approach formalising the transaction through two different contracts: an FX forward and a knock-out USD call. The FX forward was designated as the hedging instrument in a hedging relationship of a highly expected cash flow. The terms of the forward contracts were as follows:

FX Forward Terms	
Instrument	FX forward
Trade date	1 October 20X4
Counterparties	ABC and XYZ Bank
Maturity	30 June 20X5
ABC sells	USD 100 million
ABC buys	EUR 79,365,000
Forward rate	1.2600
Settlement	Physical delivery
Initial fair value	ABC receives EUR 622,000 two business days following trade date

The knock-out USD call was considered undesignated (i.e., it was not part of any hedging relationship). Note that because the settlement of the FX forward was by physical delivery, the knock-out option settlement had to be in cash, so ABC did not deliver the USD 100 million twice. The terms of the knock-out USD call were as follows:

FX knock-out option terms	
Instrument	FX knock-out USD call
Trade date	1 October 20X4
Counterparties	ABC and XYZ Bank
Option buyer	ABC
Expiry	30 June 20X5
ABC sells	USD 100 million
ABC buys	EUR 79,365,000
Strike	1.2600
Barrier	1.1620

(*continued overleaf*)

FX knock-out option terms

Knock-out provision	The option will cease to exist if the EUR–USD spot rate reaches, or is below, the barrier level at any time until expiry
Settlement	Cash settlement
Initial fair value	ABC pays EUR 622,000 two business days following trade date

5.10.2 Hedging Relationship Documentation

ABC denominated the forward contract as the hedging instrument in a foreign currency cash flow hedge, and the highly expected forecast sale as the hedged item. The hedging relationship would end on 30 June 20X5 (see Figure 5.25).

On 31 March 20X5, the hedged cash flow (i.e., the sale) would be recognised in ABC's profit or loss and, simultaneously, any amounts previously recorded in equity would be reclassified to profit or loss. Also on 31 March 20X5 a receivable denominated in USD would be recognised in ABC's statement of financial position.

During the period from 31 March 20X5 until 30 June 20X5, in theory there was no need to have a hedging relationship in place because there would be already an offset between FX gains and losses on the revaluation of the USD accounts receivable and revaluation gains and losses on the forward. During that period ABC could implement two approaches:

- To continue the hedging relationship. Regarding the option, changes in the actual option time value, to the extent that they related to the hedged item, would be recorded in OCI and simultaneously reclassified to profit or loss. This is the approach covered in this section.
- To discontinue the hedging relationship by changing the hedge's risk management objective on 31 March 20X5. As mentioned in our previous case, whilst this is a simpler approach, an auditor may find it contrary to the prohibition under IFRS 9 of voluntary discontinuation of a hedging relationship. This approach was explained in Section 5.5.8.

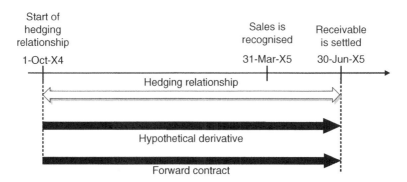

FIGURE 5.25   Hedge timeframe.

ABC decided to base its assessment of hedge effectiveness on variations in forward FX rates. In other words, the forward points (i.e., the forward element) of the FX forward were included in the hedging relationship. ABC documented the hedging relationship as follows:

Hedging relationship documentation	
Risk management objective and strategy for undertaking the hedge	The objective of the hedge is to protect the EUR value of the cash flow stemming from a USD 100 million highly expected sale of finished goods and its ensuing receivable against unfavourable movements in the EUR–USD exchange rate.
	This hedging objective is consistent with the entity's overall FX risk management strategy of reducing the variability of its profit or loss statement caused by purchases and sales denominated in foreign currency.
	The designated risk being hedged is the risk of changes in the EUR fair value of the highly expected cash flow
Type of hedge	Cash flow hedge
Hedged item	The cash flow stemming from a USD 100 million highly expected forecast sale of finished goods and its subsequent receivable, expected to be settled on 30 June 20X5. This sale is highly probable as similar transactions have occurred in the past with the potential buyer, for sales of similar size, and the negotiations with the buyer are at an advanced stage
Hedging instrument	The forward contract with reference number 014568. The main terms of the forward are a USD 100 million notional, a 1.2600 forward rate, a 30 June 20X5 maturity and a physical settlement provision. The counterparty to the forward is XYZ Bank and the credit risk associated with this counterparty is considered to be very low
Hedge effectiveness assessment	See below

5.10.3 Hedge Effectiveness Assessment

Hedge effectiveness will be assessed by comparing changes in the fair value of the hedging instrument in its entirety (i.e., both the forward and the spot elements are included in the hedging relationship) to changes in the fair value of a hypothetical derivative. The terms of the hypothetical derivative – a EUR–USD forward contract for maturity 30 June 20X5 with nil fair value at the start of the hedging relationship – reflected the terms of the hedged item. The terms of the hypothetical derivative are as follows:

Hypothetical Derivative -Terms	
Start date	1 October 20X4
Counterparties	ABC and credit risk-free counterparty
Maturity	30 June 20X5
ABC sells	USD 100 million

(continued overleaf)

ABC buys	EUR 79,872,000
Forward rate	1.2520 *(*)*
Initial fair value	Nil

(*) The forward rate of the hypothetical derivative (1.2520) was different from the forward rate of the hedging instrument (1.2600) – this was due to (i) their different initial fair values and (ii) the absence of CVA in the hypothetical derivative (the counterparty to the hypothetical derivative is assumed to be credit risk-free).

Changes in the fair value of the hedging instrument will be recognised as follows:

- The effective part of the gain or loss on the hedging instrument will be recognised in the cash flow hedge reserve of OCI. The accumulated amount in equity will be reclassified to profit or loss in the same period during which the hedged expected future cash flow affects profit or loss, initially adjusting the sales amount when the sale is recognised and thereafter adjusting the revaluation of the receivable.
- The ineffective part of the gain or loss on the hedging instrument will be recognised immediately in profit or loss.

Hedge effectiveness will be assessed prospectively at hedging relationship inception, on an ongoing basis at least upon each reporting date and upon occurrence of a significant change in the circumstances affecting the hedge effectiveness requirements.

Hedge effectiveness assessment will be performed, and effective/ineffective amounts will be calculated, on a forward-forward basis. In other words, the forward element of both the hedging instrument and the hypothetical derivative will be included in the hedging relationship.

The hedging relationship will qualify for hedge accounting only if all the following criteria are met:

1) The hedging relationship consists only of eligible hedge items and hedging instruments. The hedge item is eligible as it is a highly expected forecast transaction that exposes the entity to fair value risk, affects profit or loss and is reliably measurable. The hedging instrument is eligible as it is a derivative and it does not result in a net written option.
2) At hedge inception there is a formal designation and documentation of the hedging relationship and the entity's risk management objective and strategy for undertaking the hedge.
3) The hedging relationship is considered effective.

The hedging relationship will be considered effective if the following three requirements are met:

1) There is an economic relationship between the hedged item and the hedging instrument.
2) The effect of credit risk does not dominate the value changes that result from that economic relationship.
3) The hedge ratio of the hedging relationship is the same as that resulting from the quantity of hedged item that the entity actually hedges and the quantity of the hedging instrument that the entity actually uses to hedge that quantity of hedged item. The hedge ratio should not be intentionally weighted to create ineffectiveness.

Whether there is an economic relationship between the hedged item and the hedging instrument will be assessed on a quantitative basis using the scenario analysis method for two scenarios in which the EUR–USD FX rate at the end of the hedging relationship (30 June 20X5) will be calculated by shifting the EUR–USD spot rate prevailing on the assessment date by ±10%, and the change in fair value of both the hedging instrument and the hedged item compared.

5.10.4 Hedge Effectiveness Assessment Performed at Hedge Inception

The hedging relationship was considered effective as the following three requirements were met:

1) There was an economic relationship between the hedged item and the hedging instrument. Based on the quantitative assessment performed (see below), the entity concluded that the change in fair value of the hedged item was expected to be largely offset by the change in fair value of the hedging instrument, corroborating that both elements had values that would generally move in opposite directions.
2) The effect of credit risk did not dominate the value changes resulting from that economic relationship as the credit ratings of both the entity and XYZ Bank were considered sufficiently strong.
3) The hedge ratio of the hedging relationship was the same as that resulting from the quantity of hedged item that the entity actually hedged and the quantity of the hedging instrument that the entity actually used to hedge that quantity of hedged item. The hedge ratio was not intentionally weighted to create ineffectiveness.

A quantitative assessment was performed using the scenario analysis method in which the performance of the hedging instrument and the hedged item was assessed under two scenarios.

In a first scenario, a EUR–USD spot rate at the end of the hedging relationship (1.3585) was assumed by shifting the EUR–USD spot rate prevailing on the assessment date (1.2350) by +10%, as shown in the table below. Of note is that the hedged item was valued using forward rates (i.e., on a forward basis).

	Scenario analysis assessment	
	Hedging instrument	**Hypothetical derivative**
Nominal USD	100,000,000	100,000,000
Forward rate	1.2600	1.2520
Nominal EUR	79,365,000	79,872,000
Nominal USD	100,000,000	100,000,000
Final spot rate	1.3585 *(1)*	1.3585
Value in EUR	73,611,000 *(2)*	73,611,000
Difference	5,754,000 *(3)*	6,261,000
Discount factor	1.0000	1.0000
Final fair value	5,754,000 *(4)*	6,261,000

(continued overleaf)

Initial fair value	<622,000>	-0-
Fair value	6,376,000 *(5)*	6,261,000
Degree of offset		**101.8% *(6)***

Notes:

(1) Assumed spot rate on hedging relationship end date (30 June 20X5)
(2) 100,000,000/1.3585
(3) 79,365,000 – 73,611,000
(4) 5,754,000 × 1.0000
(5) 5,754,000 – <622,000>
(6) 6,376,000/6,734,000

In a second scenario, a EUR–USD spot rate at the end of the hedging relationship (1.1115) was assumed by shifting the EUR–USD spot rate prevailing on the assessment date (1.2350) by –10% as shown in the table below.

	Scenario analysis assessment	
	Hedging instrument	**Hypothetical derivative**
Nominal USD	100,000,000	100,000,000
Forward rate	1.2600	1.2520
Nominal EUR	79,365,000	79,872,000
Nominal USD	100,000,000	100,000,000
Market rate	1.1115	1.1115
Value in EUR	89,969,000	89,969,000
Difference	<10,604,000>	<10,097,000>
Discount factor	1.0000	1.0000
Final fair value	<10,604,000>	<10,097,000>
Initial fair value	<622,000>	-0-
Fair value change	<9,982,000>	<10,097,000>
Degree of offset		**98.9%**

Based on the results of the quantitative assessment, the change in fair value of the hedged item was expected to be largely offset by the change in fair value of the hedging instrument, corroborating that both elements have values that will generally move in opposite directions.

The hedge ratio was established at 1:1, resulting from the USD 100 million of hedged item that the entity actually hedged and the USD 100 million of the hedging instrument that the entity actually used to hedge that quantity of hedged item.

Another hedge assessment was performed on 31 December 20X4 (reporting date). That assessment was very similar to the one performed at inception and has been omitted to avoid unnecessary repetition. Similarly, the hedge ratio was assumed to be 1:1 on that assessment date.

5.10.5 Fair Valuations of Derivative Contracts and Hypothetical Derivative at the Relevant Dates

The actual spot and forward exchange rates prevailing at the relevant dates were as follows:

Date	Spot rate at indicated date	Forward rate for 30-Jun-20X5 (*)	Discount factor for 30-Jun-20X5
1-Oct-20X4	1.2350	1.2500	0.9804
31-Dec-20X4	1.2700	1.2800	0.9839
31-Mar-20X5	1.2950	1.3000	0.9901
30-Jun-20X5	1.3200	1.3200	1.0000

(*) Credit risk-free forward rate

Fair Valuation of the Hedging Instrument (Standard Forward Contract) The fair value calculation of the hedging instrument (i.e., the standard forward contract) at each relevant date was as follows (for the sake of simplicity I have included all CVAs/DVAs in the fair valuation of the undesignated part):

	1-Oct-20X4	31-Dec-20X4	31-Mar-20X5	30-Jun-20X5
Nominal EUR		79,365,000	79,365,000	79,365,000
Nominal USD		100,000,000	100,000,000	100,000,000
Forward rate for 30-Jun-20X5		/1.2800	/1.3000	/1.3200
Value in EUR		78,125,000	76,923,000 *(1)*	75,758,000
Difference		1,240,000	2,442,000 *(2)*	3,607,000
Discount factor		× 0.9839	× 0.9901	× 1.0000
Fair value	<622,000>	1,220,000	2,417,000 *(3)*	3,607,000
Fair value change (period)	—	1,842,000	1,197,000 *(4)*	1,190,000
Fair value change (cumulative)	—	1,842,000	3,039,000 *(5)*	4,229,000

Notes:
(1) 76,923,000 = 100,000,000/1.3000
(2) 2,442,000 = 79,365,000 − 76,923,000
(3) 2,417,000 = 2,442,000 × 0.9901
(4) 1,197,000 = 2,417,000 − 1,220,000
(5) 3,039,000 = 1,197,000 − <622,000>

Fair Valuation of the Hypothetical Derivative The fair value calculation of the hypothetical derivative at each relevant date was as follows:

	1-Oct-20X4	31-Dec-20X4	31-Mar-X5	30-Jun-X5
Fair value	-0-	1,719,000 *(1)*	2,920,000 *(2)*	4,114,000 *(3)*
Cumulative change	—	1,719,000	2,920,000	4,114,000

Notes:
> *(1)* (100 mn/1.2520 – 100 mn/1.2800) × 0.9839
> *(2)* (100 mn/1.2520 – 100 mn/1.3000) × 0.9901
> *(3)* (100 mn/1.2520 – 100 mn/1.3200) × 1.0000

Fair Valuation of the Knock-out Option The fair value of the knock-out option was computed using a closed-ended formula to value barrier options. Remember that all the change in the fair value of this option was recorded in profit or loss, as this option contract was undesignated. The fair value of the knock-out option at each relevant date was as follows:

	1-Oct-20X4	31-Dec-20X4	31-Mar-20X5	30-Jun-20X5
Fair value	622,000	690,000	360,000	-0-
Fair value change (period)	—	68,000	<330,000>	<360,000>

5.10.6 Calculation of Effective and Ineffective Amounts

The calculation of the effective and ineffective amounts of the change in fair value of the hedging instrument was as follows:

	31-Dec-20X4	31-Mar-20X5	30-Jun-20X5
Cumulative change in fair value of hedging instrument	1,842,000	3,039,000	4,229,000
Cumulative change in fair value of hypothetical derivative	1,719,000	2,920,000	4,114,000
Lower amount	1,719,000	2,920,000 *(1)*	4,114,000
Previous cumulative effective amount	Nil	1,719,000 *(2)*	2,916,000
Available amount	1,719,000	1,201,000 *(3)*	1,198,000
Period change in fair value of hedging instrument	1,842,000	1,197,000 *(4)*	1,190,000
Effective amount	1,719,000	1,197,000 *(5)*	1,190,000
Ineffective amount	123,000	Nil *(6)*	Nil

Notes:
> *(1)* Lower of 3,039,000 and 2,920,000
> *(2)* Nil + 1,719,000, the sum of all prior effective amounts
> *(3)* 2,920,000 – 1,719,000
> *(4)* Change in the fair value of the hedging instrument during the period (i.e., since the last fair valuation)
> *(5)* Lower of 1,201,000 (available amount) and 1,197,000 (period change in fair value of hedging instrument)
> *(6)* 1,197,000 (period change in fair value of hedging instrument) – 1,197,000 (effective part)

5.10.7 Accounting Entries

The required journal entries were as follows.

1) To record the standard forward and the knock-out option trades on 1 October, 20X4

At their inception, the fair values of the standard forward and the knock-out option were EUR <622,000> and 622,000, respectively.

Option contract (Asset)	622,000	
Cash (Asset)		622,000
Cash (Asset)	622,000	
Forward contract (Liability)		622,000

2) To record the closing of the accounting period on 31 December 20X4

The change in fair value of the standard forward since the last valuation was a gain of EUR 1,842,000, of which EUR 1,719,000 was deemed to be effective and recorded in the cash flow hedge reserve of equity, while EUR 123,000 was deemed to be effective and recorded in profit or loss.
The change in fair value of the knock-out option since the last valuation was a gain of EUR 68,000, recognised in profit or loss as it was undesignated.

Forward contract (Asset)	1,842,000	
Cash flow hedge reserve (Equity)		1,719,000
Other financial income (Profit or loss)		123,000
Option contract (Asset)	68,000	
Other financial income (Profit or loss)		68,000

3) To record the sale agreement on 31 March 20X5

The sale agreement was recorded at the spot rate prevailing on that date (1.2950). Therefore, the sale EUR proceeds were EUR 77,220,000 (=100 million/1.2950). Because the machinery sold was not yet paid, a receivable was recognised. Suppose that the machinery was valued at EUR 68 million in ABC's statement of financial position.
The change in fair value of the standard forward since the last valuation was a EUR 1,197,000 gain, fully deemed to be effective and recorded in the cash flow hedge reserve of OCI.
The change in fair value of the knock-out option since the last valuation was a EUR 330,000 loss, recognised in profit or loss as it was undesignated.
The recognition of the sales transaction in profit or loss caused the release to profit or loss of the EUR 2,916,000 deferred hedge results accumulated in OCI.

Accounts receivable (Asset)	77,220,000	
Sales (Profit or loss)		77,220,000
Cost of goods sold (Profit or loss)	68,000,000	
Machinery (Asset)		68,000,000
Forward contract (Asset)	1,197,000	
Cash flow hedge reserve (Equity)		1,197,000
Other financial expenses (Profit or loss)	330,000	
Option contract (Asset)		330,000
Cash flow hedge reserve (Equity)	2,916,000	
Sales (Profit or loss)		2,916,000

4) To record the settlement of the receivable, the standard forward and the knock-out option on 30 June 20X5

The receivable was revalued at the spot rate prevailing on this date, showing a loss of EUR 1,463,000 (=100 million/1.3200 – 100 million/1.2950).

The receivable was paid by the customer, and thus USD 100 million was received. The spot rate on payment date was 1.32, so the USD 100 million payment was valued at EUR 75,758,000 (=100 million/1.32).

The change in fair value of the standard forward since the last valuation was a gain of EUR 1,190,000, deemed to be fully effective and recorded in the cash flow hedge reserve of OCI.

The change in fair value of the knock-out option since the last valuation was a loss of EUR 360,000, recognised in profit or loss as it was undesignated.

The recognition of the receivable revaluation in profit or loss caused the recycling of the EUR 1,190,000 amount in the cash flow hedge reserve to profit or loss.

The settlement of the standard forward resulted in the payment of USD 100 million cash in exchange for EUR 79,365,000, representing an additional EUR 3,607,000 relative to the amount that settled the receivable.

The knock-out option expired worthless and as result was not exercised by ABC.

Other financial expenses (Profit or loss)	1,463,000	
Accounts receivable (Asset)		1,463,000
USD Cash (Asset)	75,758,000	
Accounts receivable (Asset)		75,758,000
Forward contract (Asset)	1,190,000	
Cash flow hedge reserve (Equity)		1,190,000
Other financial expenses (Profit or loss)	360,000	
Option contract (Asset)		360,000
Cash flow hedge reserve (Equity)	1,190,000	
Other financial income (Profit or loss)		1,190,000

EUR cash (Asset)	79,365,000
Forward contract (Asset)	3,607,000
USD cash (Asset)	75,758,000
Other financial expenses (Profit or loss)	360,000
Option contract (Asset)	360,000

The following table gives a summary of the accounting entries, excluding the entries related to the cost of goods sold:

	Cash	Forward and option contracts	Accounts receivable	Cash flow hedge reserve	Profit or loss
1-Oct-20X4					
Forward trade	622,000	<622,000>			
Option trade	<622,000>	622,000			
31 Dec-20X4					
Forward revaluation		1,842,000		1,719,000	123,000
Option revaluation		68,000			68,000
31-Mar-20X5					
Forward revaluation		1,197,000		1,197,000	
Option revaluation		<330,000>			<330,000>
Reserve reclassification				<2,916,000>	2,916,000
Sale shipment			77,220,000		77,220,000
30-Jun-20X5					
Forward revaluation		1,190,000		1,190,000	
Option revaluation		<360,000>			<360,000>
Forward settlement	3,607,000	<3,607,000>			
Option settlement					
Receivable revaluation			<1,463,000>		<1,463,000>
Reserve reclassification				<1,190,000>	1,190,000
Receivable settlement	75,758,000		<75,758,000>		
TOTAL	**79,365,000**	**-0-**	**-0-**	**-0-**	**79,365,000**

Note: Total figures may not match the sum of their corresponding components due to rounding.

5.11 CASE STUDY: HEDGING A FORECAST SALE AND SUBSEQUENT RECEIVABLE WITH A KNOCK-IN FORWARD (INSTRUMENT IN ITS ENTIRETY)

In this section I will cover an approach to apply hedge accounting when (i) a knock-in forward is involved and (ii) the entity does not want to split the instrument (see previous section) for hedge accounting purposes due to its operational complexity.

5.11.1 Hedging Relationship Documentation

Under the approach covered in this section the hedging instrument would be the knock-in forward in its entirety. The hedged item was the cash flow stemming from the USD 100 million of a highly expected forecast sale (see previous cases). The risk management objective was to mitigate its variability against movements in the EUR–USD FX rate. ABC documented the hedging relationship as follows:

Hedging relationship documentation	
Risk management objective and strategy for undertaking the hedge	The objective of the hedge is to protect the EUR value of the cash flow stemming from a USD 100 million highly expected sale of finished goods and its ensuing receivable against unfavourable movements in the EUR–USD exchange rate.
	This hedging objective is consistent with the entity's overall FX risk management strategy of reducing the variability of its profit or loss statement caused by purchases and sales denominated in foreign currency.
	The designated risk being hedged is the risk of changes in the EUR fair value of the highly expected cash flow
Type of hedge	Cash flow hedge
Hedged item	The cash flow stemming from a USD 100 million highly expected forecast sale of finished goods and its subsequent receivable, expected to be settled on 30 June 20X5. This sale is highly probable as similar transactions have occurred in the past with the potential buyer, for sales of similar size, and the negotiations with the buyer are at an advanced stage
Hedging instrument	The knock-in forward contract with reference number 014568. The main terms of the knock-in forward are a USD 100 million notional, a 1.2600 forward rate, a 1.1620 barrier, a 30 June 20X5 maturity and a physical settlement provision. The counterparty to the knock-in forward is XYZ Bank and the credit risk associated with this counterparty is considered to be very low
Hedge effectiveness assessment	See below

5.11.2 Hedge Effectiveness Assessment

Hedge effectiveness will be assessed by comparing changes in the fair value of the hedging instrument in its entirety to changes in the fair value of a hypothetical derivative. The terms of the hypothetical derivative – a EUR–USD forward contract for maturity 30 June 20X5 with nil fair value at the start of the hedging relationship – reflected the terms of the hedged item. The terms of the hypothetical derivative are as follows:

Hypothetical derivative – terms	
Start date	1 October 20X4
Counterparties	ABC and credit risk-free counterparty
Maturity	30 June 20X5
ABC sells	USD 100 million
ABC buys	EUR 79,872,000
Forward Rate	1.2520 *(*)*

(*) Market credit risk-free forward rate for 30 June 20X5

Changes in the fair value of the hedging instrument will be recognised as follows:

- The effective part of the gain or loss on the hedging instrument will be recognised in the cash flow hedge reserve of OCI. The accumulated amount in equity will be reclassified to profit or loss in the same period during which the hedged expected future cash flow affects profit or loss, initially adjusting the sales amount when the sale is recognised and thereafter adjusting the revaluation of the receivable.
- The ineffective part of the gain or loss on the hedging instrument will be recognised immediately in profit or loss.

Hedge effectiveness will be assessed prospectively at hedging relationship inception, on an ongoing basis at least upon each reporting date and upon occurrence of a significant change in the circumstances affecting the hedge effectiveness requirements.

Hedge effectiveness assessment will be performed, and effective/ineffective amounts will be calculated, on a forward-forward basis. In other words, the forward element of both the hedging instrument and the hypothetical derivative will be included in the hedging relationship.

The hedging relationship will qualify for hedge accounting only if all the following criteria are met:

1) The hedging relationship consists only of eligible hedge items and hedging instruments. The hedge item is eligible as it is a highly expected forecast transaction that exposes the entity to fair value risk, affects profit or loss and is reliably measurable. The hedging instrument is eligible as it is a derivative and it does not result in a net written option.
2) At hedge inception there is a formal designation and documentation of the hedging relationship and the entity's risk management objective and strategy for undertaking the hedge.
3) The hedging relationship is considered effective.

The hedging relationship will be considered effective if the following three requirements are met:

1) There is an economic relationship between the hedged item and the hedging instrument.
2) The effect of credit risk does not dominate the value changes that result from that economic relationship.
3) The hedge ratio of the hedging relationship is the same as that resulting from the quantity of hedged item that the entity actually hedges and the quantity of the hedging instrument that the entity actually uses to hedge that quantity of hedged item. The hedge ratio should not be intentionally weighted to create ineffectiveness.

Whether there is an economic relationship between the hedged item and the hedging instrument will be assessed on a quantitative basis using the scenario analysis method for two scenarios in which the EUR–USD FX rate at the end of the hedging relationship (30 June 20X5) will be calculated by shifting the EUR–USD spot rate prevailing on the assessment date by ±10%, and the change in fair value of both the hedging instrument and the hedged item compared.

5.11.3 Hedge Effectiveness Assessment Performed at Hedge Inception

The hedging relationship was considered effective as the following three requirements were met:

1) There was an economic relationship between the hedged item and the hedging instrument. Based on the quantitative assessment performed (see below), the entity concluded that the change in fair value of the hedged item was expected to be largely offset by the change in fair value of the hedging instrument, corroborating that both elements had values that would generally move in opposite directions.
2) The effect of credit risk did not dominate the value changes resulting from that economic relationship as the credit ratings of both the entity and XYZ Bank were considered sufficiently strong.
3) The hedge ratio of the hedging relationship was the same as that resulting from the quantity of hedged item that the entity actually hedged and the quantity of the hedging instrument that the entity actually used to hedge that quantity of hedged item. The hedge ratio was not intentionally weighted to create ineffectiveness.

A quantitative assessment was performed using the scenario analysis method in which the performance of the hedging instrument and the hedged item was assessed under two scenarios.

In a first scenario, a EUR–USD spot rate at the end of the hedging relationship (1.3585) was assumed by shifting the EUR–USD spot rate prevailing on the assessment date (1.2350) by +10%, as shown in the table below. Of note is that the hedged item was valued using forward rates (i.e., on a forward basis).

| | Scenario analysis assessment | |
	Hedging instrument	Hypothetical derivative
Nominal USD	100,000,000	100,000,000
Forward rate	1.2600	1.2520
Nominal EUR	79,365,000	79,872,000
Nominal USD	100,000,000	100,000,000

Final rate	1.3585 *(1)*	1.3585
Value in EUR	73,611,000 *(2)*	73,611,000
Difference	5,754,000 *(3)*	6,261,000
Discount factor	1.0000	1.0000
Final fair value	5,754,000 *(4)*	6,261,000
Initial fair value	-0-	-0-
Fair value	5,754,000 *(5)*	6,261,000
Degree of offset		**91.9% *(6)***

Notes:

    (1) Assumed spot rate on hedging relationship end date (30 June 20X5)
    (2) 100,000,000/1.3585
    (3) 79,365,000 − 73,611,000
    (4) 5,754,000 × 1.0000
    (5) 5,754,000 − Nil
    (6) 5,754,000/6,261,000

In a second scenario, a EUR–USD spot rate at the end of the hedging relationship (1.1115) was assumed by shifting the EUR–USD spot rate prevailing on the assessment date (1.2350) by −10% as shown in the table below. Under that scenario the 1.1620 barrier was reached and, as a result, the knock-in forward became a 1.2600 standard forward.

	Scenario analysis assessment	
	Hedging instrument	**Hypothetical derivative**
Nominal USD	100,000,000	100,000,000
Forward rate	1.2600	1.2520
Nominal EUR	79,365,000	79,872,000
Nominal USD	100,000,000	100,000,000
Market rate	1.1115	1.1115
Value in EUR	89,969,000	89,969,000
Difference	<10,604,000>	<10,097,000>
Discount factor	1.0000	1.0000
Final fair value	<10,604,000>	<10,097,000>
Initial fair value	-0-	-0-
Fair value change	<10,604,000>	<10,097,000>
Degree of offset		**98.9%**

Based on the results of the quantitative assessment, the change in fair value of the hedged item was expected to be largely offset by the change in fair value of the hedging instrument, corroborating that both elements have values that will generally move in opposite directions.

The hedge ratio was established at 1:1, resulting from the USD 100 million of hedged item that the entity actually hedged and the USD 100 million of the hedging instrument that the entity actually used to hedge that quantity of hedged item.

Another hedge assessment was performed on 31 December 20X4 (reporting date). That assessment was very similar to the one performed at inception and has been omitted to avoid unnecessary repetition. Similarly, the hedge ratio was assumed to be 1:1 on that assessment date.

Additional Comments Under the second scenario, the downward movement of the FX rate was sufficiently large to trigger the knock-in feature. Otherwise, the degree of offset would have been very different, potentially endangering the economic relationship requirement.

5.11.4 Fair Valuations of Hedging Instrument and Hypothetical Derivative at the Relevant Dates

The actual spot and forward exchange rates prevailing at the relevant dates were as follows:

Date	Spot rate at indicated date	Forward rate for 30-Jun-20X5 (*)	Discount factor for 30-Jun-20X5
1-Oct-20X4	1.2350	1.2500	0.9804
31-Dec-20X4	1.2700	1.2800	0.9839
31-Mar-20X5	1.2950	1.3000	0.9901
30-Jun-20X5	1.3200	1.3200	1.0000

(*) Credit risk-free forward rate

Fair Valuation of the Hedging Instrument (Knock-in Forward Contract in its Entirety) The fair value calculation of the hedging instrument (i.e., the standard forward contract) at each relevant date was as follows (adding the standard forward and knock-out options fair values from the previous section):

	1-Oct-20X4	31-Dec-20X4	31-Mar-20X5	30-Jun-20X5
Fair value	-0-	1,910,000	2,777,000	3,607,000
Fair value change (period)	—	1,910,000	867,000	830,000
Fair value change (cumulative)	—	1,910,000	2,777,000	3,607,000

Fair Valuation of the Hypothetical Derivative The fair value calculation of the hypothetical derivative at each relevant date was as follows:

	1-Oct-20X4	31-Dec-20X4	31-Mar-X5	30-Jun-X5
Fair value	-0-	1,719,000 *(1)*	2,920,000 *(2)*	4,114,000 *(3)*
Cumulative change	—	1,719,000	2,920,000	4,114,000

Notes:

    (1) (100 mn/1.2520 – 100 mn/1.2800) × 0.9839
    (2) (100 mn/1.2520 – 100 mn/1.3000) × 0.9901
    (3) (100 mn/1.2520 – 100 mn/1.3200) × 1.0000

5.11.5 Calculation of Effective and Ineffective Amounts

The calculation of the effective and ineffective amounts of the change in fair value of the hedging instrument was as follows:

	31-Dec-20X4	31-Mar-20X5	30-Jun-20X5
Cumulative change in fair value of hedging instrument	1,910,000	2,777,000	3,607,000
Cumulative change in fair value of hypothetical derivative	1,719,000	2,920,000	4,114,000
Lower amount	1,719,000	2,777,000 *(1)*	3,607,000
Previous cumulative effective amount	Nil	1,719,000 *(2)*	2,586,000
Available amount	1,719,000	1,058,000 *(3)*	1,021,000
Period change in fair value of hedging instrument	1,910,000	867,000 *(4)*	830,000
Effective amount	1,719,000	867,000 *(5)*	830,000
Ineffective amount	191,000	Nil *(6)*	Nil

Notes:

    (1) Lower of 2,777,000 and 2,920,000
    (2) 1,719,000, the sum of all prior effective amounts
    (3) 2,777,000 – 1,719,000
    (4) Change in the fair value of the hedging instrument during the period (i.e., since the last fair valuation)
    (5) Lower of 1,058,000 (available amount) and 867,000 (period change in fair value of hedging instrument)
    (6) 867,000 (period change in fair value of hedging instrument) – 867,000 (effective part)

5.11.6 Accounting Entries

The required journal entries were as follows.

1) To record the knock-in forward trade on 1 October, 20X4

No on-balance-sheet accounting entries were required as initial fair value of the knock-in forward was zero.

2) To record the closing of the accounting period on 31 December 20X4
The change in fair value of the knock-in forward since the last valuation was a EUR 1,910,000 gain, of which EUR 1,719,000 was deemed to be effective and recorded in the cash flow hedge reserve of equity, while EUR 191,000 was deemed to be effective and recorded in profit or loss.

Knock-in forward (Asset)	1,910,000	
Cash flow hedge reserve (Equity)		1,719,000
Other financial income (Profit or loss)		191,000

3) To record the sale agreement on 31 March 20X5

The sale agreement was recorded at the spot rate prevailing on that date (1.2950). Therefore, the sale EUR proceeds were EUR 77,220,000 (=100 million/1.2950). Because the machinery sold was not yet paid, a receivable was recognised. Suppose that the machinery was valued at EUR 68 million in ABC's statement of financial position.

The change in fair value of the knock-in forward since the last valuation was a gain of EUR 867,000, deemed to be fully effective and recorded in the cash flow hedge reserve of OCI.

The recognition of the sales transaction in profit or loss caused the release to profit or loss of the EUR 2,586,000 deferred hedge results accumulated in OCI.

Accounts receivable (Asset)	77,220,000	
Sales (Profit or loss)		77,220,000
Cost of goods sold (Profit or loss)	68,000,000	
Machinery (Asset)		68,000,000
Knock-in forward (Asset)	867,000	
Cash flow hedge reserve (Equity)		867,000
Cash flow hedge reserve (Equity)	2,586,000	
Sales (Profit or loss)		2,586,000

4) To record the settlement of the receivable, the knock-in forward on 30 June 20X5

The receivable was revalued at the spot rate prevailing on this date, showing a loss of EUR 1,463,000 (=100 million/1.3200 − 100 million/1.2950).

The receivable was paid by the customer, and thus USD 100 million was received. The spot rate on payment date was 1.32, so the USD 100 million payment was valued at EUR 75,758,000 (=100 million/1.32).

The change in fair value of the knock-in forward since the last valuation was a gain of EUR 830,000, fully deemed to be effective and recorded in the cash flow hedge reserve of OCI.

The recognition of the receivable revaluation in profit or loss caused the reclassification of the EUR 830,000 amount in the cash flow hedge reserve to profit or loss.

The settlement of the knock-in forward resulted in the payment of USD 100 million cash in exchange for EUR 79,365,000, representing an additional EUR 3,607,000 relative to the amount that settled the receivable.

Other financial expenses (Profit or loss)		1,463,000	
Accounts receivable (Asset)			1,463,000
USD Cash (Asset)		75,758,000	
Accounts receivable (Asset)			75,758,000
Knock-in forward (Asset)		830,000	
Cash flow hedge reserve (Equity)			830,000
Cash flow hedge reserve (Equity)		830,000	
Other financial income (Profit or loss)			830,000
EUR cash (Asset)		79,365,000	
Knock-in forward (Asset)			3,607,000
USD cash (Asset)			75,758,000

The following table gives a summary of the accounting entries, excluding the entries related to the cost of goods sold.

	Cash	Knock-in forward	Accounts receivable	Cash flow hedge reserve	Profit or loss
1-Oct-20X4					
Knock-in forward trade					
31 Dec-20X4					
Knock-in forward revaluation		1,910,000		1,719,000	191,000
31-Mar-20X5					
Knock-in forward revaluation		867,000		867,000	
Reserve reclassification				<2,586,000>	2,586,000
Sale shipment			77,220,000		77,220,000
30-Jun-20X5					
Knock-in forward revaluation		830,000		830,000	
Knock-in forward settlement	3,607,000	<3,607,000>			
Receivable revaluation			<1,463,000>		<1,463,000>
Reserve reclassification				<830,000>	830,000
Receivable settlement	75,758,000		<75,758,000>		
TOTAL	**79,365,000**	**-0-**	**-0-**	**-0-**	**79,365,000**

Note: Total figures may not match the sum of their corresponding components due to rounding.

5.12 CASE STUDY: HEDGING A FORECAST SALE AND SUBSEQUENT RECEIVABLE WITH A KNOCK-IN FORWARD (REBALANCING APPROACH)

Suppose that ABC decided to consider the whole knock-in forward as one instrument and, from an accounting perspective, tried to designate it as the hedging instrument in a hedging relationship. In this section I will cover the rebalancing approach to the application of hedge accounting. This approach rebalances the hedge ratio to changes in the circumstances surrounding a hedging relationship. This approach was covered in Section 5.8 for a participating forward.

5.12.1 Quantity of Hedged Item Estimation

The rebalancing approach is an interesting alternative for the application of hedge accounting when exotic options are involved and either (i) it is not feasible a split of the derivative between a hedge accounting friendly part and an undesignated part or (ii) designating the derivative in its entirety results in economic assessments that are too dependent on the path followed by the underlying market variable. The rebalancing approach starts by estimating the quantity of hedged item that would be hedged with the quantity of derivative actually traded.

Previously, it was mentioned that our knock-in forward could be split into two contracts (see Figure 5.23): (i) an FX forward at 1.2600, and (ii) a purchased knock-out USD call option with a 1.2600 strike and a 1.1620 barrier. Let us analyse two extreme scenarios:

■ The option was knocked out (i.e., the 1.1620 barrier was reached). The hedge would then consist of just a 1.2600 forward (i.e., a standard forward). The hedge ratio would be 1:1 as in order to hedge USD 100 million of the forecast sale ABC would use USD 100 million of the forward, because any change value of the sale would be almost fully offset by the change in the fair value of the resulting forward.

■ The option had a very high probability of being exercised (i.e., the option had a short time to expiry, was in-the-money and the probability of reaching the barrier was very low). In this scenario, it is as if the knock-in forward never existed as the changes in fair value of the forward would be almost fully offset by the changes in fair value of the option. The hedge ratio would be almost 0:1 (i.e., as if the forecast sale was unhedged).

The quantity of hedged item (i.e., the forecast sale) could be viewed as the difference between the quantity of forward and the quantity of (knock-out) option:

The quantity of forward to be used by ABC was USD 100 million as its probability of being exercised was 100% (i.e., there is no optionality in a forward, and both parties will exchange the notional amounts at maturity).

Whilst the quantity of forward was known, the quantity of option to be used by ABC depended on its probability of being exercised –whether the barrier would not be reached before the end of the hedging relationship and whether the option would be in-the-money (i.e., when a EUR–USD spot rate lower than 1.2600 results at expiry). If both the option exists and it is in-the-money at expiry, ABC would fully exercise the option, which can be interpreted as ABC using a USD 100 million quantity of the option. Alternatively, if either (i) the 1.1620 barrier was reached during the option's life or (ii) the spot rate was at or above 1.2600 at expiry, ABC would not exercise the option, or in other words, ABC would not use any quantity of the option. Whilst *ex ante* ABC did not know whether the option would be exercised, the entity could estimate the option's probability of being exercised.

In order to have the appropriate hedge ratio, the quantity of hedged item to be used should equal the quantity of knock-in forward. As noted above, the quantity of knock-in forward is unknown at the commencement of the hedging relationship and can be estimated according to the following expression:

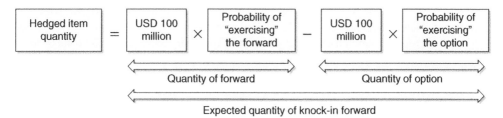

As mentioned previously, the quantity of forward was USD 100 million as the probability of "exercising" the forward was 100%. The probability of exercising an option can be approximated by its delta. Therefore, the quantity of hedged item can be estimated as:

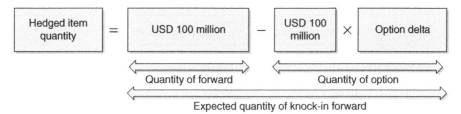

The absolute value of an option's delta can be loosely interpreted as an approximate measure of the probability that it will expire in-the-money. If a knock-out option is very deep in-the-money and has a very low probability of reaching its barrier (i.e., it has a very high probability of being in-the-money at expiry), the absolute value of its delta will be close to 100%. Conversely, if a knock-out option is very deep out-of-the-money or it is close to its barrier (i.e., it has a low probability of being in-the-money at expiry), the absolute value of its delta will be close to zero. In our case, on 1 October 20X4 the delta of our knock-out option was 29%. The knock-out option delta as a function of the EUR–USD spot rate on that date had the profile depicted in Figure 5.26, showing that, for example, had the spot rate been 1.2600 the delta would have been 35%.

As a result, the hedge ratio was established at 0.71:1, and USD 71 million of the hedged item was hedged using USD 100 million of the knock-in forward.

In our case, the hedging relationship would end on 30 June 20X5, when the knock-in forward contract matured (see Figure 5.27).

- Until 31 March 20X5, the effective parts of the changes in fair value of the knock-in forward would be recorded in OCI, while the ineffective parts would be recognised in profit or loss.
- On 31 March 20X5, the hedged cash flow (i.e., the sale) would be recognised in ABC's profit or loss and, simultaneously, cause the amounts previously recorded in equity (OCI) to be reclassified to profit or loss. Also on 31 March 20X5 a receivable denominated in USD would be recognised in ABC's statement of financial position.
- During the period from 31 March 20X5 until 30 June 20X5, the hedged item would be the USD accounts receivable resulting from the sale. This receivable would be revalued through profit or loss on 30 June 20X5.
- Also on 30 June 20X5, the effective part of the change in fair value of the knock-in forward would be recorded in OCI, while the ineffective part would be recognised in profit or loss. The amounts recognised in OCI would be reclassified to profit or loss, as the revaluation of the hedged item (i.e., the receivable) had impacted profit or loss. Therefore, there was no need to have a hedging relationship in place because already there would be an offset between the FX gains and losses on the revaluation of the USD accounts receivable and the revaluation gains and losses of the knock-in forward contract.

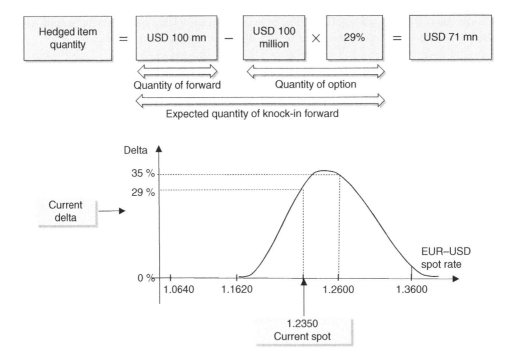

FIGURE 5.26 Option delta on 1 October 20X4.

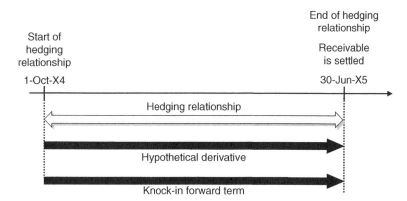

FIGURE 5.27   Hedge expected timeframe.

5.12.2 Hedging Relationship Documentation

At the inception of the hedging relationship, ABC documented the relationship as follows:

Hedging relationship documentation	
Risk management objective and strategy for undertaking the hedge	The objective of the hedge is to protect the EUR value of a USD denominated cash flow stemming from a highly expected sale of finished goods and its ensuing receivable against movements in the EUR–USD exchange rate. This hedging objective is consistent with the entity's overall FX risk management strategy of reducing the variability of its profit or loss statement caused by purchases and sales denominated in foreign currency. The designated risk being hedged is the exchange rate risk attributable to movements in the EUR–USD exchange rate
Type of hedge	Cash flow hedge
Hedged item	The cash flow stemming from a USD 71 million sale of finished goods and its subsequent receivable, expected to be settled on 30 June 20X5. This sale is highly probable as similar transactions have occurred in the past with the potential buyer, for sales of similar size, and the negotiations with the buyer are at an advanced stage. The quantity of hedged item will be adjusted to incorporate changes in the hedge ratio
Hedging instrument	The knock-in forward contract with reference number 014565. The contract has a notional of USD 100 million, a 30 June 20X5 maturity, a 1.2600 forward rate and a 1.1620 barrier. The counterparty to the knock-in forward is XYZ Bank and the credit risk associated with this counterparty is considered to be very low
Hedge effectiveness assessment	See below

5.12.3 Hedge Effectiveness Assessment

Hedge effectiveness will be assessed by comparing changes in the fair value of the hedging instrument to changes in the fair value of the hedged item.

The change in the fair value of the hedging instrument will be recognised as follows:

- The effective part of the gain or loss on the hedging instrument will be recognised in the cash flow hedge reserve of OCI. The accumulated amount in equity will be reclassified to profit or loss in the same period during which the hedged expected future cash flow affects profit or loss, adjusting the sales amount and thereafter the revaluation of the receivable.
- The ineffective part of the gain or loss on the hedging instrument will be recognised immediately in profit or loss.

Hedge effectiveness will be assessed prospectively at hedging relationship inception and on an ongoing basis at least upon each reporting date and upon occurrence of a significant change in the circumstances affecting the hedge effectiveness requirements.

The hedging relationship will qualify for hedge accounting only if all the following criteria are met:

1) The hedging relationship consists only of eligible hedge items and hedging instruments. The hedge item is eligible as it is a highly expected forecast transaction that exposes the entity to fair value risk, is reliably measurable and affects profit or loss. The hedging instrument is eligible as it is a derivative and it does not result in a net written option.
2) At hedge inception there is a formal designation and documentation of the hedging relationship and the entity's risk management objective and strategy for undertaking the hedge.
3) The hedging relationship is considered effective.

The hedging relationship will be considered effective if the following three requirements are met:

1) There is an economic relationship between the hedged item and the hedging instrument.
2) The effect of credit risk does not dominate the value changes that result from that economic relationship.
3) The hedge ratio of the hedging relationship is the same as that resulting from the quantity of hedged item that the entity actually hedges and the quantity of the hedging instrument that the entity actually uses to hedge that quantity of hedged item. The hedge ratio should not be intentionally weighted to create ineffectiveness.

Whether there is an economic relationship between the hedged item and the hedging instrument will be assessed on a quantitative basis using the scenario analysis method for four scenarios in which the EUR–USD FX rate at the end of the hedging relationship (30 June 20X5) will be calculated by shifting the EUR–USD spot rate prevailing on the assessment date by ±1 and ±0.5 standard deviations, and the changes in fair value of the hedging instrument with those of the hedging instrument compared.

5.12.4 Hedge Effectiveness Assessment Performed at Hedge Inception

The hedging relationship was considered effective as the following three requirements were met:

1) There was an economic relationship between the hedged item and the hedging instrument.
2) The effect of credit risk did not dominate the value changes resulting from that economic relationship as the credit ratings of both the entity and XYZ Bank were considered sufficiently strong.
3) The hedge ratio of the hedging relationship was the same as that resulting from the quantity of hedged item that the entity actually hedged and the quantity of the hedging instrument that the entity actually used to hedge that quantity of hedged item. The hedge ratio was not intentionally weighted to create ineffectiveness.

An assessment was performed at hedge inception using the scenario analysis method for four scenarios, as follows. The EUR–USD spot rates at the end of the hedging relationship (30 June 20X5) for each scenario (1.1325, 1.1827, 1.2897 and 1.3467) were simulated by shifting the EUR–USD spot rate prevailing on the assessment date (1.2350) by ±1 and ±0.5 standard deviations, assuming a 10% volatility. In the case of ±1 standard deviations, the expression used to calculate the FX rates was:

$$\text{Shifted spot} = \text{Current spot} \times e^{\pm 1 \times \sigma \times \sqrt{(Years)}}$$

$$\text{Shifted spot} = 1.2350 \times e^{\pm 1 \times 10\% \times \sqrt{0.75}}$$

As shown in the table below, the change in fair value of the hedged item was expected to be substantially offset by the change in fair value of the hedging instrument, corroborating that both elements had values that would generally move in opposite directions. The calculations related to the ±1 standard deviation shifts:

	−1 standard deviation		+1 standard deviation	
	Hedging instrument *(1)*	**Hedged item**	**Hedging instrument**	**Hedged item**
Nominal USD	100,000,000	71,000,000		71,000,000
Hedged rate	1.2600	1.2520 *(2)*		1.2520
Nominal EUR	79,365,000	56,709,000		56,709,000
Nominal USD	100,000,000	71,000,000		71,000,000
Final rate	1.1325	1.1325	1.3467	1.3467
Value in EUR	88,300,000	62,693,000		52,721,000
Difference	<8,935,000> *(3)*	5,984,000		<3,988,000> *(4)*
Change in fair value	<8,935,000>	5,984,000	5,109,000 *(5)*	<3,988,000>

Notes:

(1) The hedging instrument became a standard forward at 1.2600 as the embedded option was knocked out because the 1.1620 barrier was reached

(2) The credit risk-free forward rate for 30 June 20X5 prevailing at the start of the hedging relationship

(3) 79,365,000 − 88,300,000 = 100 mn/1.2600 − 100 mn/1.1325

(4) 52,721,000 − 56,891,000

(5) 100 mn/1.2600 − 100 mn/1.3467

The results of the quantitative assessments were as follows:

	Effectiveness assessment – scenario analysis results				
	−1 standard deviation	**−0.5 standard deviation**	**+0.5 standard deviation**	**+1 standard deviation**	**Total**
Final spot rate	1.1325	1.1827	1.2897	1.3467	
Change in fair value of hedging instrument	<8,935,000>	Nil *(1)*	1,828,000 *(2)*	5,109,000	<1,998,000>
Change in fair value of hedged item	5,802,000	3,141,000 *(3)*	<1,839,000> *(4)*	<4,170,000>	2,934,000
			Degree of offset		**68.1%**

Notes:

(1) The knock-in forward matured worthless as the EUR–USD spot rate ended up below 1.2600 and the barrier was assumed not to have been reached during the life of the instrument

(2) 100 mn/1.2600 – 100 mn/1.2897

(3) 71 mn/1.1827 – 71 mn/1.2480

(4) 71 mn/1.2897 – 71 mn/1.2480

The overall degree of offset was notably different from the expected 100%, being insufficient to conclude that the economic relationship criterion was met. Several factors contributed to such a difference:

■ The degree of offset was highly dependent on the EUR–USD spot rate path simulated. If instead of four scenarios, ABC had simulated a large number of risk-neutral scenarios (e.g., a thousand) using a Monte Carlo simulation method (see Figure 5.28), the average degree of offset would have been close to 100%.

■ The four scenarios used were not risk-neutral: the probability of a spot rate being shifted by, for example, +1 standard deviation is much lower than for a shift by +0.5 standard deviations. The degree of offsets should have been weighted by their probability of occurring.

Suppose that a more robust Monte Carlo analysis resulted in an overall degree of offset much closer to 100% and that, as a result, ABC concluded that the change in fair value of the hedged item was expected to largely be offset by the change in fair value of the hedging instrument, corroborating that both elements had values that would generally move in opposite directions.

As calculated previously, the hedge ratio was established at 0.71:1, resulting from the USD 71 million of hedged item that the entity actually hedged and the USD 100 million of the hedging instrument that the entity actually used to hedge that quantity of hedged item.

Another hedge assessment was performed on 31 December 20X4 (reporting date). This assessment was very similar to the one performed at inception and has been omitted to avoid unnecessary repetition. I assume that the hedge ratio was set at 0.76:1. As a result the quantity of hedged item changed to USD 76 million.

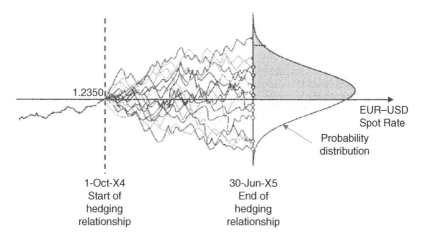

FIGURE 5.28 Spot rate simulation using Monte Carlo.

The hedge ratio was also estimated on 31 March 20X5, resulting in 0.95:1. As a result the quantity of hedged item changed to USD 95 million.

5.12.5 Fair Valuations at the Relevant Dates

The fair values of the knock-in forward (see Section 5.11) at each relevant date were as follows:

	1-Oct-20X4	31-Dec-20X4	31-Mar-X5	30-Jun-X5
Knock-in forward fair value	-0-	1,910,000	2.777,000	3,607,000
Cumulative change	-0-	1,910,000	2.777,000	3,607,000
Period change	—	1,910,000	867,000	830,000

The fair values of the hedged item at each relevant date were as follows:

	1-Oct-20X4	31-Dec-20X4	31-Mar-X5	30-Jun-X5
Hedged item quantity	71 mn	76 mn	95 mn	—
Hedged item fair value	-0-	<1,221,000> *(1)*	<2,219,000> *(2)*	<3,909,000> *(3)*
Cumulative change	—	<1,221,000>	<2,219,000>	<3,909,000>

Notes:
(1) (71 mn/1.2800 – 71 mn/1.2520) × 0.9839
(2) (76 mn/1.3000 – 76 mn/1.2520) × 0.9901
(3) (95 mn/1.3200 – 95 mn/1.2520) × 1.0000

5.12.6 Effective and Ineffective Amounts at the Relevant Dates

The calculation of the effective and ineffective amounts of the change in fair value of the hedging instrument was as follows:

	31-Dec-20X4	31-Mar-20X5	30-Jun-20X5
Cumulative change in fair value of hedging instrument	1,910,000	2,777,000	3,607,000
Cumulative change in fair value of hedged item (opposite sign)	1,221,000	2,219,000	3,909,000
Lower amount	1,221,000	2,219,000 *(1)*	3,607,000
Previous cumulative effective amount	Nil	1,221,000 *(2)*	2,088,000
Available amount	1,221,000	998,000 *(3)*	1,519,000
Period change in fair value of hedging instrument	1,910,000	867,000 *(4)*	830,000
Effective amount	1,221,000	867,000 *(5)*	830,000
Ineffective amount	689,000	Nil *(6)*	Nil

Notes:
> *(1)* Lower of 2,777,000 and 2,219,000
> *(2)* Nil + 1,221,000, the sum of all prior effective amounts
> *(3)* 2,219,000 – 1,221,000
> *(4)* Change in the fair value of the hedging instrument during the period (i.e., since the last fair valuation)
> *(5)* Lower of 998,000 (available amount) and 867,000 (period change in fair value of hedging instrument)
> *(6)* 867,000 (period change in fair value of hedging instrument) – 867,000 (effective part)

5.12.7 Accounting Entries

The required journal entries were as follows.

1) To record the knock-in forward contract trade on 1 October 20X4

No entries in the financial statements were required as the fair value of the knock-in forward contract was zero.

2) To record the closing of the accounting period on 31 December 20X4

The change in fair value of the knock-in forward since the last valuation was a EUR 1,910,000 gain, of which the effective part was EUR 1,221,000 and recorded in OCI, and the ineffective part was EUR 689,000 and recorded in profit or loss.

Knock-in forward contract (Asset)	1,910,000	
Cash flow hedge reserve (Equity)		1,221,000
Other financial income (Profit or loss)		689,000

3) To record the sale agreement and the end of the hedging relationship on 31 March 20X5

The sale agreement was recorded at the EUR–USD spot rate prevailing on the date the sales are recognised (1.2950). Therefore, the sales EUR amount was EUR 77,220,000

(=100 million/1.2950). Because the machinery sold was not paid, a receivable was recognised. Suppose that the machinery was valued at EUR 68 million in ABC's statement of financial position.

The change in the fair value of the knock-in forward since the last valuation was a gain of EUR 867,000, fully effective and recorded in OCI. No ineffectiveness was present.

The recognition of the sales transaction in profit or loss caused the release to profit or loss of the EUR 2,088,000 deferred hedge results accumulated in OCI.

Cost of goods sold (Profit or loss)	68,000,000	
Machinery (Asset)		68,000,000
Accounts receivable (Asset)	77,220,000	
Sales (Profit or loss)		77,220,000
Knock-in forward contract (Asset)	867,000	
Cash flow hedge reserve (Equity)		867,000
Cash flow hedge reserve (Equity)	2,088,000	
Sales (Profit or loss)		2,088,000

4) To record the settlement of the receivable and the knock-in forward on 30 June 20X5

The receivable was revalued at the spot rate prevailing on this date, showing a loss of EUR 1,463,000 (=100 million/1.3200 – 100 million/1.2950).

The receivable was paid by the customer, and thus USD 100 million was received. The spot rate on payment date was 1.32, so the USD 100 million payment was valued at EUR 75,758,000 (=100 million/1.32).

The change in fair value of the knock-in forward since the last valuation was a gain of EUR 830,000, fully deemed to be effective and recorded in the cash flow hedge reserve of OCI.

The recognition of the receivable revaluation in profit or loss caused the recycling of the EUR 830,000 amount in the cash flow hedge reserve to profit or loss.

The settlement of the knock-in forward resulted in the payment of USD 100 million cash in exchange for EUR 79,365,000, representing an additional EUR 3,607,000 relative to the amount that settled the receivable.

Other financial expenses (Profit or loss)	1,463,000	
Accounts receivable (Asset)		1,463,000
USD cash (Asset)	75,758,000	
Accounts receivable (Asset)		75,758,000
Knock-in forward (Asset)	830,000	
Cash flow hedge reserve (Equity)		830,000
Cash flow hedge reserve (Equity)	830,000	
Other financial income (Profit or loss)		830,000
EUR cash (Asset)	79,365,000	

(continued overleaf)

Knock-in forward (Asset)	3,607,000
USD cash (Asset)	75,758,000

The following table gives a summary of the accounting entries, excluding the entries related to the cost of goods sold:

	Cash	Knock-in forward	Accounts receivable	Cash flow hedge reserve	Profit or loss
1-Oct-20X4					
Knock-in forward trade					
31 Dec-20X4					
Knock-in forward revaluation		1,910,000		1,221,000	689,000
31-Mar-20X5					
Knock-in forward revaluation		867,000		867,000	
Reserve reclassification				<2,088,000>	2,088,000
Sale shipment			77,220,000		77,220,000
30-Jun-20X5					
Knock-in forward revaluation		830,000		830,000	
Knock-in forward settlement	3,607,000	<3,607,000>			
Receivable revaluation			<1,463,000>		<1,463,000>
Reserve reclassification				<830,000>	830,000
Receivable settlement	75,758,000		<75,758,000>		
TOTAL	**79,365,000**	**-0-**	**-0-**	**-0-**	**79,365,000**

Note: Total figures may not match the sum of their corresponding components due to rounding.

5.13   CASE STUDY: HEDGING A HIGHLY EXPECTED FOREIGN SALE WITH A KIKO FORWARD

In previous cases I have analysed a hedging strategy that involved a knock-in forward, an instrument built with a barrier option. I now turn to another popular instrument, a knock-in knock-out forward (**KIKO forward**), also built with barrier options: a knock-out option and a knock-in option with identical strikes. In this section I will cover how a KIKO could be split to make part of it eligible for hedge accounting, and how the split affects the accounting treatment of the hedge strategy.

The risk being hedged in this case is the same as in the previous cases. Suppose that on 1 October 20X4 ABC Corporation, a company whose functional currency was the EUR, was expecting to sell finished goods to a US client. The sale was expected to occur on 31 March 20X5, and its related sale receivable was expected to be settled on 30 June 20X5. Sale proceeds were expected to be USD 100 million, to be received in USD.

ABC was interested in entering into an FX forward, but wanted to improve the forward rate by incorporating its view regarding the EUR–USD exchange rate during the next 9 months. ABC forecasted that a potential USD appreciation was going to be quite limited, not reaching below 1.1000. At the same time, ABC had the view that a potential USD depreciation above 1.3500 was unlikely. As a consequence, on 1 October 20X4 ABC entered into a KIKO forward that was obtained by combining the purchase of a knock-out USD put and a written knock-in USD call with the following terms:

Knock-out USD put terms		Knock-in USD call terms	
Trade date	1 October 20X4	Trade date	1 October 20X4
Option buyer	ABC	Option buyer	XYZ Bank
Option seller	XYZ Bank	Option seller	ABC
USD notional	USD 100 million	USD notional	USD 100 million
Strike	1.2300	Strike	1.2300
Barrier	1.3500	Barrier	1.1000
EUR notional	EUR 81,301,000	EUR notional	EUR 81,301,000
Expiry date	30 June 20X5	Expiry date	30 June 20X5
Knock-out provision	Option ceases to exist if at any time until expiry date the EUR–USD spot exchange rate trades at, or above, the barrier	Knock-in provision	Option can only be exercised if at any time until expiry date the EUR–USD spot exchange rate trades at, or below, the barrier
Settlement	Physical delivery	Settlement	Physical delivery
Premium	EUR 850,000	Premium	EUR 850,000
Premium payment date	1 October 20X4	Premium payment date	1 October 20X4

There were four scenarios depending on the behaviour of the EUR–USD spot rate during the life of the KIKO forward:

1.10 barrier	1.35 barrier	Equivalent position	Comments
Not hit	Not hit	Purchased 1.2300 USD put	Best scenario. ABC had protection and participated in USD appreciation
Hit	Not hit	1.2300 forward	Good scenario. ABC ended up with a forward rate better than market forward (market forward would have been 1.2500)
Not hit	Hit	No derivative	Bad scenario. ABC ended up having no hedge in place
Hit	Hit	Written 1.2300 USD call	Worst scenario. ABC lost its protection and could not benefit from a USD appreciation

Graphically, the KIKO payoff at expiry in each of the four scenarios is shown in Figure 5.29. The combination of the hedging instrument payoff and the expected cash flow resulted in a EUR amount, to be received by ABC in exchange for the USD 100 million sale proceeds, that was dependent on the four potential scenarios, as shown in Figure 5.30.

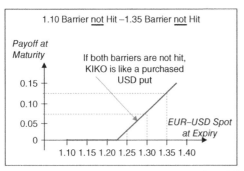

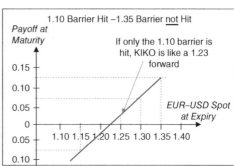

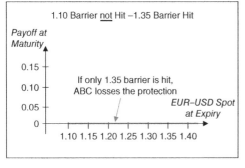

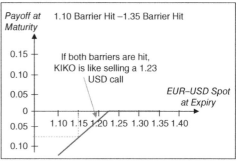

FIGURE 5.29 KIKO forward – scenarios.

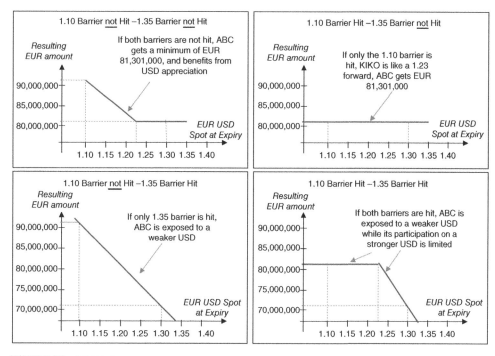

FIGURE 5.30 KIKO forward – resulting EUR amount.

5.13.1 Hedge Accounting Optimisation

One of the main issues that ABC faced regarding the KIKO forward was how to split the instrument into two parts, a first part eligible for hedge accounting and a second part treated as undesignated, to minimise the overall impact on profit or loss volatility. ABC considered the following choices:

1) Divide the KIKO into two contracts (see Figure 5.31): (i) a 1.2300 forward and (ii) a "residual" derivative.
2) Divide the KIKO into two contracts (see Figure 5.32): (i) a USD put option with a 1.2300 strike and (ii) a "residual" derivative.
3) Consider the KIKO in its entirety as eligible for hedge accounting, if the corresponding requirements were met.
4) Consider the whole KIKO as undesignated.

Approach 1: Split KIKO Forward into a Forward and a Residual Derivative Under this approach, ABC would divide the KIKO into two contracts (see Figure 5.31): (i) a 1.2300 forward and (ii) a "residual" derivative. The residual derivative would be a written knock-in USD put with a 1.2300 strike and a 1.3500 barrier, and a purchased knock-out USD call with a 1.2300 strike and a 1.1100 barrier. The forward would be considered eligible for hedge accounting while the residual derivative would be considered as undesignated (i.e., speculative). Therefore, all the changes in the fair value of the residual derivative would be recorded in profit or loss. This approach would be recommended were ABC to believe that the 1.1000 barrier was more likely to be crossed than the 1.3500 barrier. One of the strengths of this approach was that the hedge effective part was recognised in the "sales" line of profit or loss.

Approach 2: Split KIKO Forward into an Option and a Residual Derivative   Under this approach, ABC would divide the KIKO into two contracts (see Figure 5.32): (i) a standard USD put option with a 1.2300 strike and (ii) a "residual" derivative. The residual derivative would be the combination of (i) a written knock-in USD put with a 1.2300 strike and a 1.3500 barrier, and (ii) a written knock-in USD call with a 1.2300 strike and a 1.1100 barrier. The standard USD put option would be considered eligible for hedge accounting and the residual derivative would be considered as undesignated (i.e., speculative). Therefore, all the changes in the fair value of the residual derivative would be recorded in profit or loss. This approach would be recommended if ABC estimated that it was very unlikely that either the 1.1000 barrier or the 1.3500 barrier would be crossed. One of the strengths of this approach was that the hedge effective part was recognised in the "sales" line of profit or loss.

Approach 3: Designate the KIKO Forward in its Entirety as Hedging Instrument   Under this approach, ABC would designate the KIKO forward in its entirety as the hedging instrument in a hedging relationship. This approach is, in my view, quite challenging to apply. The hypothetical derivative would be a 1.2480 forward. It was observed in our previous case – a hedge with a knock-in forward – that, whilst it was a "genuine" hedge strategy because there was a hedge in place in any EUR–USD scenario, it was relatively complex to justify that there was an economic relationship between the hedged item and the derivative that gave rise to offset, due to a volatile hedge ratio. A KIKO forward is even more challenging to justify that an economic relationship between this instrument and the hedged item, especially when the EUR–USD spot rate is near the 1.35 barrier. Moreover, once the 1.35 barrier is reached, there will be no hedge in place triggering an early termination of the hedging relationship.

Approach 4: Do Not Apply Hedge Accounting   Under this approach, ABC would consider the whole KIKO as undesignated. In other words, hedge accounting would not be applied. As a consequence, all changes in fair value of the KIKO would be recorded in profit or loss. Whilst this approach was the simplest from an operational perspective, saving the operational effort in complying with hedge accounting, it could notably increase profit or loss volatility. This approach was discarded by ABC.

The following table summarises these four choices:

Approach	Hedging instrument	Hypothetical derivative	Comments
Split KIKO into standard forward and residual derivative	Standard forward	Standard forward	Recommended if probability of reaching the 1.10 barrier was notably greater than that of reaching the 1.35 barrier. Effective part of hedge recognised in "sales" line of profit or loss

Approach	Hedging instrument	Hypothetical derivative	Comments
Split KIKO into USD put and residual derivative	USD put	Standard forward	Recommended if it was unlikely that either the 1.10 barrier or 1.35 barrier would be crossed. Effective part of hedge and "aligned" time value recognised in "sales" line of profit or loss
Treat whole KIKO as designated	KIKO in its entirety	Standard forward	Challenging to prove economic relationship criterion. Hedging relationship would be terminated if 1.35 barrier is crossed
Treat whole KIKO as undesignated	N/A	N/A	Operationally, simplest approach, but two weaknesses: potential profit or loss volatility; and KIKO fair value changes not recognised in "sales" line of profit or loss

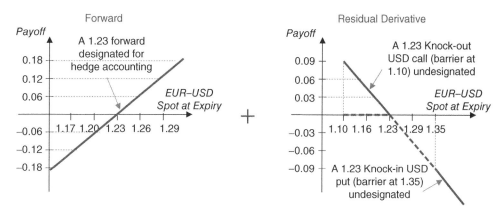

FIGURE 5.31 KIKO forward approach 1 – forward plus residual derivative.

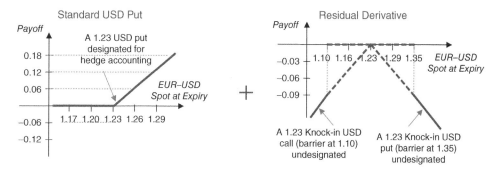

FIGURE 5.32 KIKO forward approach 2 – USD put option plus residual derivative.

5.13.2 Hedge Accounting Application for Approach 1 – Forward plus Residual Derivative

Suppose that ABC believed that the probability of crossing the 1.10 barrier was notably greater than that of crossing the 1.35 barrier. As a result, ABC selected the first approach, consisting of dividing the KIKO forward into two separate legal contracts: (i) a 1.2300 standard forward and (ii) a "residual" derivative.

The standard forward was designated as the hedging instrument in a cash flow hedging relationship. Hedge effectiveness was assessed by comparing the changes in fair value of the hedging instrument with the changes in fair value of a hypothetical derivative. The hypothetical derivative was a forward with zero initial fair value. The main terms of the actual forward (i.e., the hedging instrument) and the hypothetical derivative were as follows:

Forward terms		Hypothetical derivative terms	
Instrument	FX forward	Instrument	FX forward
Start date	1 October 20X4	Start date	1 October 20X4
Counterparties	ABC and XYZ Bank	Counterparties	ABC and credit risk-free counterparty
Maturity	30 June 20X5	Maturity	30 June 20X5
ABC sells	USD 100 million	ABC sells	USD 100 million
ABC buys	EUR 81,301,000	ABC buys	EUR 79,872,000
Forward rate	1.2300	Forward rate	1.2520
Initial fair value	EUR 850,000	Initial fair value	Zero

5.13.3 Hedging Relationship Documentation

The hedging relationship documentation was very similar to that in Section 5.10.2. The only differences are the terms of the hedging instrument, so we omit the documentation to avoid unnecessary repetition.

5.13.4 Hedge Effectiveness Assessment Performed at Hedge Inception

The hedging relationship was considered effective as the following three requirements were met:

1) There was an economic relationship between the hedged item and the hedging instrument.
2) The effect of credit risk did not dominate the value changes resulting from that economic relationship as the credit ratings of both the entity and XYZ Bank were considered sufficiently strong.
3) The hedge ratio of the hedging relationship was the same as that resulting from the quantity of hedged item that the entity actually hedged and the quantity of the hedging instrument that the entity actually used to hedge that quantity of hedged item. The hedge ratio was not intentionally weighted to create ineffectiveness.

Based on the results of the quantitative assessment performed, it was concluded that the hedging instrument and the hedged item had values that would generally move in opposite directions. The assessment consisted of two scenarios being analysed as follows.

A EUR–USD spot rate at the end of the hedging relationship (1.3585) was simulated by shifting the EUR–USD spot rate prevailing on the assessment date (1.2350) by +10%. As shown in the table below, the change in fair value of the hedged item was expected to be substantially offset by the change in fair value of the hedging instrument, corroborating that both elements had values that would generally move in opposite directions.

First scenario analysis assessment		
	Hedging instrument	**Hypothetical derivative**
Nominal USD	100,000,000	100,000,000
Forward rate	1.2300	1.2520
Nominal EUR	81,301,000	79,872,000
Nominal USD	100,000,000	100,000,000
Forward rate	1.3585 *(1)*	1.3585
Value in EUR	73,611,000 *(2)*	73,611,000
Final fair value	7,690,000 *(3)*	6,261,000
Initial fair value	850,000	-0-
Fair value change (cumulative)	6,840,000 *(4)*	6,261,000
	Degree of offset	**109.2% *(5)***

Notes:
(1) Assumed spot rate on hedging relationship end date
(2) 100,000,000/1.3585
(3) 81,301,000 – 73,611,000
(4) 7,690,000 – 850,000
(5) 6,840,000/6,261,000

In a second scenario, a EUR–USD spot rate at the end of the hedging relationship (1.1115) was assumed by shifting the EUR–USD spot rate prevailing on the assessment date (1.2350) by –10% as shown in the table below. Under that scenario I assume that the 1.1000 barrier was not reached.

Second scenario analysis assessment		
	Hedging instrument	**Hypothetical derivative**
Nominal USD	100,000,000	100,000,000
Forward rate	1.2300	1.2520
Nominal EUR	81,301,000	79,872,000
Nominal USD	100,000,000	100,000,000
Market rate	1.1115	1.1115
Value in EUR	89,969,000	89,969,000
Difference	<8,668,000>	<10,097,000>
Initial fair value	850,000	-0-
Fair value change	<9,518,000>	<10,097,000>
	Degree of offset	**94.3%**

The hedge ratio was established at 1:1, resulting from the USD 100 million of hedged item that the entity actually hedged and the USD 100 million of the hedging instrument that the entity actually used to hedge that quantity of hedged item.

Another hedge assessment was performed on 31 December 20X4 (reporting date). This assessment was very similar to the one performed at inception and has been omitted to avoid unnecessary repetition. Additionally, the hedge ratio was assumed to be 1:1 on that assessment date.

5.13.5 Fair Valuations of Derivative Contracts and Hypothetical Derivative at the Relevant Dates

The actual spot and forward exchange rates prevailing at the relevant dates were as follows (I assumed that on 15-Nov-20X4 the 1.1000 barrier was reached):

Date	Spot rate at indicated date	Forward rate for 30-Jun-20X5 (*)	Discount factor for 30-Jun-20X5
1-Oct-20X4	1.2350	1.2480	0.9804
15-Nov-X4	1.0900	1.1000 barrier was crossed	
31-Dec-20X4	1.2700	1.2800	0.9839
31-Mar-20X5	1.2950	1.3000	0.9901
30-Jun-20X5	1.3200	1.3200	1.0000

(*) Credit risk-free forward rate

Fair Valuation of the Hedging Instrument (Forward Contract)   The fair value calculation of the hedging instrument (i.e., the forward contract) at each relevant date was as follows:

	1-Oct-20X4	31-Dec-20X4	31-Mar-20X5	30-Jun-20X5
Nominal EUR	81,301,000	81,301,000	81,301,000	81,301,000
Nominal USD	100,000,000	100,000,000	100,000,000	100,000,000
Forward rate for 30-Jun-20X5	/1.2480	/1.2800	/1.3000	/1.3200
Value in EUR	80,128,000	78,125,000	76,923,000 (1)	75,758,000
Difference	1,173,000	3,176,000	4,378,000 (2)	5,543,000
Discount factor	× 0.9804	× 0.9839	× 0.9901	× 1.0000
Credit risk-free fair value	1,150,000	3,125,000	4,335,000 (3)	5,543,000
CVA/DVA	<300,000> (4)	<5,000>	<2,000>	-0-
Fair value	850,000	3,120,000	4,333,000 (5)	5,543,000
Fair value change (period)	—	2,270,000	1,213,000 (6)	1,210,000
Fair value change (cumulative)	—	2,270,000	3,483,000 (7)	4,693,000

Notes:

      (1) 100,000,000/1.3000

      (2) 81,301,000 – 76,923,000

      (3) 4,378,000 × 0.9901

      (4) This figure includes a CVA as well as the bid/offer. The figure is relatively large due a substantial additional profit applied by XYZ Bank. ABC decided not to initially recognise any up-front loss on the trade

      (5) 4,335,000 + <2,000>

      (6) 4,333,000 – 3,120,000

      (7) 4,333,000 – 850,000

Fair Valuation of the Hypothetical Derivative   The fair value calculation of the hypothetical derivative at each relevant date was as follows:

	1-Oct-20X4	31-Dec-20X4	31-Mar-X5	30-Jun-X5
Fair value	-0-	1,719,000 *(1)*	2,920,000 *(2)*	4,114,000 *(3)*
Cumulative change	—	1,719,000	2,920,000	4,114,000

Notes:

      (1) (100 mn/1.2520 – 100 mn/1.2800) × 0.9839

      (2) (100 mn/1.2520 – 100 mn/1.3000) × 0.9901

      (3) (100 mn/1.2520 – 100 mn/1.3200) × 1.0000

Fair Valuation of the Residual Derivative   The fair value of the knock-out option was computed using a closed-ended formula to value barrier options. Remember that all the change in the fair value of this option was recorded in profit or loss, as this option contract was undesignated.

On 15 November 20X4 the EUR–USD spot rate crossed the 1.1000 barrier. As a result, at that moment the knock-out USD call element of the residual derivative ceased to exist and the knock-in USD call of the KIKO became a standard USD call option from that date. The residual derivative fair value was calculated as follows:

Residual derivative fair value = KIKO forward fair value – Forward fair value

The fair value of the residual derivative at each relevant date was as follows:

	1-Oct-20X4	31-Dec-20X4	31-Mar-20X5	30-Jun-20X5
KIKO fair value (FV)	-0-	2,188,000	1,450,000	5,543,000
Forward fair value	850,000	3,120,000	4,333,000	5,543,000
Residual deriv. FV	<850,000>	<932,000>	<2,883,000>	-0-
Res. deriv. FV change	—	<82,000>	<1,951,000>	2,883,000

Calculation of Effective and Ineffective Parts   The calculation of the effective and ineffective parts of the change in fair value of the hedging instrument was as follows:

	31-Dec-20X4	31-Mar-20X5	30-Jun-20X5
Cumulative change in fair value of hedging instrument	2,270,000	3,483,000	4,693,000
Cumulative change in fair value of hypothetical derivative	1,719,000	2,920,000	4,114,000
Lower amount	1,719,000	2,920,000 *(1)*	4,114,000
Previous cumulative effective amount	Nil	1,719,000 *(2)*	2,920,000
Available amount	1,719,000	1,201,000 *(3)*	1,197,000
Period change in fair value of hedging instrument	2,270,000	1,213,000 *(4)*	1,210,000
Effective part	1,719,000	1,201,000 *(5)*	1,197,000
Ineffective part	551,000	12,000 *(6)*	13,000

Notes:

   (1) Lower of 3,483,000 and 2,920,000
   (2) Nil + 1,719,000, the sum of all prior effective amounts
   (3) 2,920 ,000 – 1,719,000
   (4) Change in the fair value of the hedging instrument since the last fair valuation
   (5) Lower of 1,201,000 (available amount) and 1,213,000 (period change in fair value of hedging instrument)
   (6) 1,213,000 (period change in fair value of hedging instrument) – 1,201,000 (effective part)

5.13.6 Accounting Entries

The required journal entries were as follows.

1) To record the forward and the residual derivative trades on 1 October, 20X4

At their inception, the fair values of the FX forward and the residual derivative were EUR 850,000 and <850,000>, respectively.

Forward contract (Asset)	850,000	
Cash (Asset)		850,000
Cash (Asset)	850,000	
Residual derivative contract (Liability)		850,000

2) To record the closing of the accounting period on 31 December 20X4

The change in fair value of the forward since the last valuation was a gain of EUR 2,270,000, of which EUR 1,719,000 was considered to be effective, and thus, recorded in the cash flow hedge reserve of OCI. The EUR 551,000 remainder represented the ineffective part, and was therefore recognised in profit or loss.
The change in fair value of the residual derivative since the last valuation was a EUR 82,000 loss, recognised in profit or loss as it was undesignated.

Forward contract (Asset)	2,270,000	
Cash flow hedge reserve (Equity)		1,719,000
Other financial income (Profit or loss)		551,000
Other financial expenses (Profit or loss)	82,000	
Residual derivative contract (Liability)		82,000

3) To record the sale agreement on 31 March 20X5

The sale agreement was recorded at the spot rate prevailing on that date (1.2950). Therefore, the sale EUR proceeds were EUR 77,220,000 (=100 million/1.2950). Because the machinery sold was not yet paid, a receivable was recognised. Suppose that the machinery was valued at EUR 68 million in ABC's statement of financial position.

The change in fair value of the forward since the last valuation was a gain of EUR 1,213,000, of which EUR 1,201,000 was considered to be effective and recorded in the cash flow hedge reserve of OCI, while EUR 12,000 was considered to be ineffective and recorded in profit or loss.

The change in fair value of the residual derivative since the last valuation was a EUR 1,951,000 loss, recognised in profit or loss as it was undesignated.

The recognition of the sales transaction in profit or loss caused the release to profit or loss of the EUR 2,920,000 deferred hedge results accumulated in OCI.

Accounts receivable (Asset)	77,220,000	
Sales (Profit or loss)		77,220,000
Cost of goods sold (Profit or loss)	68,000,000	
Machinery (Asset)		68,000,000
Forward contract (Asset)	1,213,000	
Cash flow hedge reserve (Equity)		1,201,000
Other financial income (Profit or loss)		12,000
Other financial expenses (Profit or loss)	1,951,000	
Residual derivative contract (Liability)		1,951,000
Cash flow hedge reserve (Equity)	2,920,000	
Sales (Profit or loss)		2,920,000

4) To record the settlement of the receivable and the forward on 30 June 20X5

The receivable was revalued at the spot rate prevailing on this date, showing a loss of EUR 1,463,000 (=100 million/1.3200 – 100 million/1.2950).

The receivable was paid by the customer, and thus USD 100 million was received. The spot rate on payment date was 1.32, so the USD 100 million payment was valued at EUR 75,758,000 (=100 million/1.32).

The change in the fair value of the forward since the last valuation was a gain of EUR 1,210,000, of which EUR 1,197,000 was considered to be effective and recorded in the cash flow hedge reserve of OCI, while EUR 13,000 was considered to be ineffective and recorded in profit or loss.

The settlement of the FX forward resulted in the payment of USD 100 million cash in exchange for EUR 81,301,000, representing an additional EUR 5,543,000 relative to the amount that settled the receivable.

The change in the fair value of the residual derivative since the last valuation was a gain of EUR 2,883,000. The residual derivative ended up worthless and, as a result, not exercised by either ABC or XYZ Bank.

The revaluation of the receivable in profit or loss caused the release to profit or loss of the EUR 1,197,000 deferred hedge results accumulated in OCI.

Other financial expenses (Profit or loss)	1,463,000	
Accounts receivable (Asset)		1,463,000
USD cash (Asset)	75,758,000	
Accounts receivable (Asset)		75,758,000
Forward contract (Asset)	1,210,000	
Cash flow hedge reserve (Equity)		1,197,000
Other financial income (Profit or loss)		13,000
EUR cash (Asset)	81,301,000	
USD cash (Asset)		75,758,000
Forward contract (Asset)		5,543,000
Residual derivative contract (Liability)	2,883,000	
Other financial income (Profit or loss)		2,883,000
Cash flow hedge reserve (Equity)	1,197,000	
Other financial income (Profit or loss)		1,197,000

The following table gives a summary of the accounting entries, excluding the entries related to the cost of goods sold:

	Cash	Forward and residual derivative contracts	Accounts receivable	Cash flow hedge reserve	Profit or loss
1-Oct-20X4					
Forward trade	<850,000>	850,000			
Res. der. trade	850,000	<850,000>			
31 Dec-20X4					

	Cash	Forward and residual derivative contracts	Accounts receivable	Cash flow hedge reserve	Profit or loss
Forward revaluation		2,270,000		1,719,000	551,000
Res. der. revaluation		<81,000>			<81,000>
31-Mar-20X5					
Forward revaluation		1,213,000		1,201,000	12,000
Res. der. revaluation		<1,951,000>			<1,951,000>
Reserve reclassification				<2,920,000>	2,920,000
Sale shipment			77,220,000		77,220,000
30-Jun-20X5					
Forward revaluation		1,210,000		1,197,000	13,000
Res. der. revaluation		2,883,000			2,883,000
Forward settlement	5,543,000	<5,543,000>			
Reserve reclassification settlement				<1,197,000>	1,197,000
Receivable revaluation			<1,463,000>		<1,463,000>
Receivable settlement	75,758,000		<75,758,000>		
TOTAL	**81,301,000**	**-0-**	**-0-**	**-0-**	**81,301,000**

Note: Total figures may not match the sum of their corresponding components due to rounding.

5.13.7 Additional Remarks

Figure 5.33 summarises the effects of the strategy on ABC's profit or loss. The strategy worked very well. The total proceeds from the strategy were EUR 81,300,000, equivalent to a EUR–USD rate of 1.2300. Sales were translated at a 1.2478 rate. The strategy was successful in hedging the FX exposure because the 1.35 barrier was not crossed.

Figure 5.34 illustrates the effects of the strategy on ABC's profit or loss, were the whole KIKO forward undesignated. All the change in fair value of the KIKO would have been recognised in profit or loss. The total proceeds from the strategy were EUR 81,300,000, equivalent to a EUR–USD rate of 1.2300. Sales were translated at a 1.2950 rate.

The story would have been dramatically different had the 1.35 barrier been reached during the instrument's life. Suppose that the 1.35 barrier was crossed before the maturity of the KIKO forward (remember that the 1.1000 barrier was already crossed in November 20X4). At that moment the knock-in USD put embedded in the residual derivative would have been triggered, becoming a standard USD put with strike 1.2300. As a result, under the combination of the 1.2300 forward and the short position in the 1.2300 standard USD put, ABC would have been exposed to a rising EUR–USD rate while not being able to benefit from a declining EUR–USD rate below 1.2300. The total proceeds from the whole strategy would have been EUR 75,757,000, equivalent to a 1.3200 exchange rate.

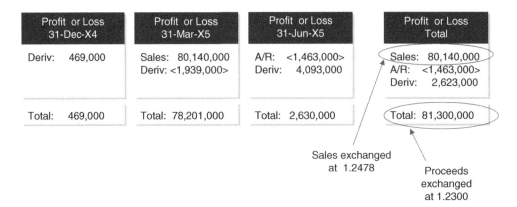

FIGURE 5.33   KIKO forward split into forward and residual derivative – effects on profit or loss.

FIGURE 5.34   KIKO forward undesignated – effects on profit or loss.

5.14 CASE STUDY: HEDGING A FORECAST SALE AND SUBSEQUENT RECEIVABLE WITH A RANGE ACCRUAL (PART 1)

In this case study, I will analyse another popular hedging strategy, a range accrual forward. The case will show that the eligibility of this instrument for hedge accounting can be complex to demonstrate and that the hedge ratio is likely to need rebalancing at each reporting date.

The risk being hedged in this case is the same as in the previous cases. Suppose that on 1 October 20X4 ABC Corporation, a company whose functional currency was the EUR, was expecting to sell finished goods to a US client. The sale was expected to occur on 31 March 20X5, and the sale receivable was expected to be settled on 30 June 20X5. Sale proceeds were expected to be USD 100 million to be received in USD.

ABC had the view that the EUR–USD spot rate would remain within a 1.22–1.25 range during the next several months and wanted to benefit from a more attractive hedge were its view right. As a consequence, on 1 October 20X4, ABC entered into a range accrual forward with the following terms:

FX range accrual terms	
Instrument	FX range accrual
Trade date	1 October 20X4
Counterparties	ABC and XYZ Bank
Maturity	30 June 20X5
ABC sells	USD nominal
ABC buys	EUR nominal, calculated as: USD nominal/Forward rate

USD nominal	USD 1,100,000 for each day that the reference rate fixes within the
	  accrual range during the accruing period. Maximum USD nominal:
	  USD 143 million

Accruing period	From, and including, 1 October 20X4 until, and including, 31 March 20X5 (a total of 130 fixings)
Accrual range	1.22–1.25
Reference rate	EUR–USD spot rate, European Central Bank fixing
Forward rate	1.2300
Settlement	Physical delivery
Initial fair value	Zero

On 30 June 20X5, ABC would exchange for EUR an amount of USD equal to the USD nominal, at 1.2300. This rate was notably better than the 1.2500 rate that XYZ Bank quoted to ABC for a standard forward contract. To obtain such an advantageous rate, ABC ran the risk of an uncertain USD nominal. On 31 March 20X5, the USD notional was determined by observing the number of business days in the accruing period that the EUR–USD rate fixed within the 1.22–1.25 range (see Figure 5.35). Each observation within the range added USD 1.1 million to the USD notional.

- ABC expected the number of days with fixings within the range to be 91, and thus the USD nominal to be USD 100,100,000 (=91 days × 1.1 million). In other words, ABC expected the EUR–USD spot rate to stay within the range for 70% (=91 days/130 days) of the total period.
- A proportion higher than 70% (more than 91 days) would imply an overhedged position. ABC would probably need to unwind the excess, becoming exposed to a declining EUR–USD spot rate in relation to the amount to be unwound.
- A proportion lower than 70% (less than 91 days) would imply an underhedged position, exposing ABC to a rising EUR–USD exchange rate in relation to the underhedged amount.

One of the main issues that ABC faced regarding the range accrual forward was whether to split the instrument to minimise the overall impact on profit or loss volatility without substantially increasing operational complexity. ABC considered the following choices:

1) to designate the range accrual in its entirety as the hedging instrument; and
2) to split the range accrual into a standard forward (designated as hedging instrument) and a remaining derivative (undesignated).

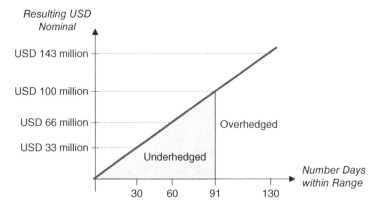

FIGURE 5.35   Range accrual forward: resulting USD nominal.

5.15 CASE STUDY: HEDGING A FORECAST SALE AND SUBSEQUENT RECEIVABLE WITH A RANGE ACCRUAL (DESIGNATION IN ITS ENTIRETY)

In this section I assume that ABC decided to designate the whole range accrual forward as the hedging instrument. The main challenge was to determine whether there was an economic relationship between the hedged item and the range accrual that gave rise to offset. This required judgement, relying on a complex regression analysis.

Even if it was concluded that the hedge was eligible for hedge accounting, an unexpectedly volatile EUR–USD rate might add substantial mismatches between the hedged item and the hedging instrument, jeopardising any future hedge accounting designation for other range accruals the entity may enter into.

However, a range accrual forward is a genuine economic hedge and, in my opinion, entities should not be reluctant to enter into value added economic hedges because of a potentially unfavourable accounting treatment, unless operationally too costly.

5.15.1 Hedging Relationship Documentation

ABC denominated the range accrual contract as the hedging instrument in a foreign currency cash flow hedge, and the highly expected forecast sale as the hedged item. The hedging relationship would end on 30 June 20X5, when the range accrual matured (see Figure 5.36).

ABC decided to base its assessment of hedge effectiveness on variations in forward FX rates. In other words, the forward points (i.e., the forward element) of the hypothetical derivative were included in the hedging relationship. ABC documented the hedging relationship as follows:

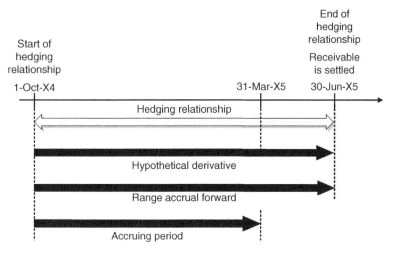

FIGURE 5.36 Hedging strategy timeframe.

Hedging relationship documentation	
Risk management objective and strategy for undertaking the hedge	The objective of the hedge is to protect the EUR value of a USD-denominated cash flow stemming from a highly expected sale of finished goods and its ensuing receivable against movements in the EUR–USD exchange rate. This hedging objective is consistent with the entity's overall FX risk management strategy of reducing the variability of its profit or loss statement caused by purchases and sales denominated in foreign currency. The designated risk being hedged is the exchange rate risk attributable to movements in the EUR–USD exchange rate
Type of hedge	Cash flow hedge
Hedged item	The cash flow stemming from a USD 100 million highly expected forecast sale of finished goods and its subsequent receivable, expected to be settled on 30 June 20X5. This sale is highly probable as similar transactions have occurred in the past with the potential buyer, for sales of similar size, and the negotiations with the buyer are at an advanced stage
Hedging instrument	The EUR–USD range accrual forward contract with reference number 014565. The counterparty to the contract is XYZ Bank and the credit risk associated with this counterparty is considered to be very low. The main terms are: a maturity on 30 June 20X5, a 1.2300 forward rate, a 1.22–1.25 accrual range observed up to the 31 March 20X5 and a USD 1.1 million notional for each business day that the spot EUR–USD is within the accrual range.
Hedge effectiveness assessment	See below

5.15.2 Hedge Effectiveness Assessment

Hedge effectiveness will be assessed by comparing changes in the fair value of the hedging instrument in its entirety to changes in the fair value of a hypothetical derivative. The fair valuation of the hypothetical derivative will include both the forward and the spot elements. The terms of the hypothetical derivative – a EUR–USD forward contract for maturity 30 June 20X5 with nil fair value at the start of the hedging relationship – reflected the terms of the hedged item. The terms of the hypothetical derivative are as follows:

Hypothetical derivative terms	
Instrument	FX forward
Start date	1 October 20X4
Counterparties	ABC and credit risk-free counterparty
Maturity	30 June 20X5
ABC sells	USD 100 million
ABC buys	EUR 79,872,000
Forward rate	1.2520
Initial fair value	Zero

Changes in the fair value of the hedging instrument will be recognised as follows:

- The effective part of the gain or loss on the hedging instrument will be recognised in the cash flow hedge reserve of OCI. The accumulated amount in equity will be reclassified to profit or loss in the same period during which the hedged expected future cash flow affects profit or loss, adjusting the sales amount or the revaluation of the receivable.
- The ineffective part of the gain or loss on the hedging instrument will be recognised immediately in profit or loss.

Hedge effectiveness will be assessed prospectively at hedging relationship inception and on an ongoing basis at least upon each reporting date and upon occurrence of a significant change in the circumstances affecting the hedge effectiveness requirements.

Hedge effectiveness assessment will be performed on a forward-forward basis. In other words, the forward element of the hypothetical derivative will be included in the assessment.

The hedging relationship will qualify for hedge accounting only if all the following criteria are met:

1) The hedging relationship consists only of eligible hedge items and hedging instruments. The hedge item is eligible as it is a highly expected forecast transaction that exposes the entity to fair value risk through profit or loss and is reliably measurable. The hedging instrument is eligible as it is a derivative and it does not result in a net written option.
2) At hedge inception there is a formal designation and documentation of the hedging relationship and the entity's risk management objective and strategy for undertaking the hedge.
3) The hedging relationship is considered effective.

The hedging relationship will be considered effective if the following three requirements are met:

1) There is an economic relationship between the hedged item and the hedging instrument.
2) The effect of credit risk does not dominate the value changes that result from that economic relationship.
3) The hedge ratio of the hedging relationship is the same as that resulting from the quantity of hedged item that the entity actually hedges and the quantity of the hedging instrument that the entity actually uses to hedge that quantity of hedged item. The hedge ratio should not be intentionally weighted to create ineffectiveness.

Whether there is an economic relationship between the hedged item and the hedging instrument will be assessed on a quantitative basis using a regression analysis method based on the EUR–USD FX rate during the previous 15 years and comparing the change in fair value of both the hypothetical derivative and the hedging instrument.

5.15.3 Hedge Effectiveness Assessment Performed at Hedge Inception

A regression analysis was performed on 1 October 20X4 to assess whether there is an economic relationship between the hedged item and the hedging instrument. The regression analysis was based on the EUR–USD FX rate actual performance during the previous 15 years and comparing the change in fair value of both the hypothetical derivative and the hedging instrument. The historical time horizon of 15 years was divided into 65 "simulation periods" of 9 months each. Each simulation period had an inception date and two subsequent balance sheet dates. In each simulation period, the behaviour of an equivalent hedging relationship using the historical data was simulated. Each observation pair (X, Y) was generated by computing the cumulative change in the fair value of a range accrual (variable X) and the cumulative change in fair value of a hypothetical derivative (observation Y), as shown in Figure 5.37. The terms of the range accrual and hypothetical derivative (accrual range and forward rates) were adjusted to conform to the market rates prevailing at the beginning of each simulation period. The results of the analysis were:

- A slope of 1.0. This was no coincidence as, prior to entering into the range accrual, its terms were designed to achieve such a slope.
- An R-squared of 82%.

The hedging relationship was considered effective as the following three requirements were met:

1) There was an economic relationship between the hedged item and the hedging instrument. Based on the quantitative analysis performed, the entity concluded that the change in fair value of the hedged item was expected to be substantially offset by the change in fair value of the hedging instrument, corroborating that both elements had values that would generally move in opposite directions.
2) The effect of credit risk did not dominate the value changes resulting from that economic relationship as the credit ratings of both the entity and XYZ Bank were considered sufficiently strong.
3) The hedge ratio of the hedging relationship was the same as that resulting from the quantity of hedged item that the entity actually hedged and the quantity of the hedging instrument that the entity actually used to hedge that quantity of hedged item. The hedge ratio was not intentionally weighted to create ineffectiveness.

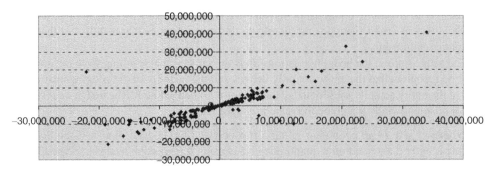

X axis: Cumulative change in fair value of hedging instrument
Y axis: Cumulative change in fair value of hypothetical derivative

FIGURE 5.37   Range accrual – regression analysis.

The hedge ratio was established at 1:1.43, based on the slope of the regression analysis. In other words, USD 100 million of hedged item was the quantity that the entity actually hedged and USD 143 million maximum USD notional was the quantity of the hedging instrument that the entity actually used to hedge that quantity of hedged item.

Another hedge assessment was performed on 31 December 20X4 (reporting date), when the EUR–USD spot rate was 1.2700. On that date, 66 days had already accrued within the accrual range, implying a minimum notional of USD 72.6 million. This assessment encompassed another regression in which each period already had 66 days accrued, 63 business days remaining to accrue and a relative position between the spot rate and the range accrual as shown in Figure 5.38. Suppose that after performing such regression its slope was 0.9, implying a 1:1.29 hedge ratio. In other words, USD 100 million of hedged item was the quantity that the entity actually hedged and USD 129 million maximum USD notional was the quantity of the hedging instrument that the entity actually used to hedge that quantity of hedged item. That hedge ratio meant that the hedging instrument represented 90% of the range accrual, while the 10% remainder was undesignated.

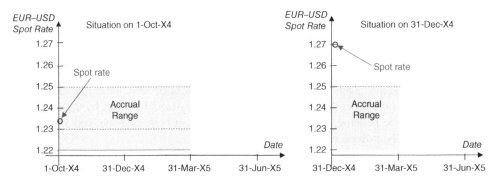

FIGURE 5.38   Range accrual – spot versus accrual range relative position.

5.15.4 Fair Valuations and Calculations of Effective/Ineffective Amounts

The behaviour of the EUR–USD spot rate during the life of the instrument is shown in Figure 5.39. The actual spot and forward exchange rates prevailing at the relevant dates were as follows:

Date	Spot rate at indicated date	Accumulated number of days within range	USD nominal	Forward rate for 30-June-20X5	Discount factor for 30-Jun-20X5
1-Oct-20X4	1.2350	—	-0-	1.2480	0.9804
31-Dec-20X4	1.2700	66	72,600,000	1.2800	0.9839
31-Mar-20X5	1.2950	100	110,000,000	1.3000	0.9901
30-Jun-20X5	1.3200	—	100,000,000 *(1)*	1.3200	1.0000

Note:

> *(1)* Assuming that an excess USD 10 million nominal was sold on 31-Mar-20X5 to eliminate the over-hedged situation

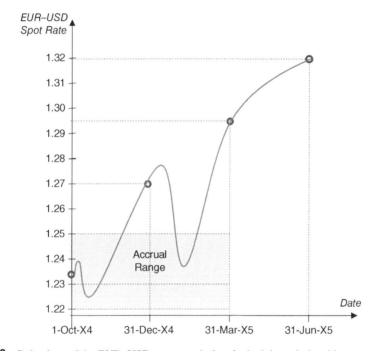

FIGURE 5.39 Behaviour of the EUR–USD spot rate during the hedging relationship term.

Fair Valuation of the Hedging Instrument and the Range Accrual Forward Contract The following table shows the fair values of the range accrual forward contract and the hedging instrument at each relevant date. The fair values of the range accrual were calculated using a Monte Carlo model. As a result of the hedged ratio, the hedging instrument represented 100% (up to 31-Dec-20X4), 90% (from 31-Dec-20X4 to 31-Mar-20X5) and 100% (from 31-Mar-20X5 to 30-Jun-20X5 after an excess USD 10 million of the range accrual was sold) of the range accrual.

	1-Oct-20X4	31-Dec-20X4	31-Mar-20X5	30-Jun-20X5
Range accrual fair value	-0-	2,611,000	4,768,000	5,543,000 *(1)*
Range accrual fair value change (period)	—	2,611,000	2,157,000 *(2)*	1,208,000 *(3)*
Hedging instrument fair value	-0-	2,611,000	4,291,000 *(4)*	5,543,000
Hedging instrument FV change (period)	—	2,611,000	1,941,000 *(5)*	1,208,000
Hedging instrument FV change (cumulative)	—	2,611,000	4,291,000	5,543,000
Undesignated part FV	—	—	477,000 *(6)*	—
Hedging instrument FV change (cumulative)	—	—	216,000 *(7)*	—

Notes:

(1) Taking into account that USD 10 million notional was sold on 31-Mar-20X5

(2) 4,768,000 – 2,611,000

(3) 5,543,000 – 4,335,000; relative to a valuation on 31-Mar-20X5 of EUR 4,335,000 (=4,768,000 – 433,000), to take into account the sale on that date

(4) 90% × 4,768,000 as after 31-Dec-X4 the hedging instrument was 90% of the range accrual

(5) 4,291,000 – 90% × 2,611,000

(6) 4,768,000 × 10%

(7) 477,000 – 10% × 2,611,000

On 31 March 20X5, ABC unwound the USD 10 million excess nominal in the market, receiving EUR 433,000.

Fair Valuation of the Hypothetical Derivative   The fair value calculation of the hypothetical derivative at each relevant date was as follows:

	1-Oct-20X4	31-Dec-20X4	31-Mar-X5	30-Jun-X5
Fair value	-0-	1,719,000 *(1)*	2,920,000 *(2)*	4,114,000 *(3)*
Cumulative change	—	1,719,000	2,920,000	4,114,000

Notes:

(1) (100 mn/1.2520 – 100 mn/1.2800) × 0.9839

(2) (100 mn/1.2520 – 100 mn/1.3000) × 0.9901

(3) (100 mn/1.2520 – 100 mn/1.3200) × 1.0000

Calculation of Effective and Ineffective Parts   The calculations of the effective and ineffective parts of the change in fair value of the hedging instrument were as follows:

	31-Dec-20X4	31-Mar-20X5	30-Jun-20X5
Cumulative change in fair value of hedging instrument	2,611,000	4,291,000	5,543,000
Cumulative change in fair value of hypothetical derivative	1,719,000	2,920,000	4,114,000
Lower amount	1,719,000	2,920,000 *(1)*	4,114,000
Previous cumulative effective amount	Nil	1,719,000 *(2)*	2,920,000
Available amount	1,719,000	1,201,000 *(3)*	1,194,000
Period change in fair value of hedging instrument	2,611,000	1,941,000 *(4)*	1,208,000
Effective part	1,719,000	1,201,000 *(5)*	1,194,000
Ineffective part	892,000	740,000 *(6)*	14,000

Notes:

(1) Lower of 4,291,000 and 2,920,000
(2) Nil + 1,719,000, the sum of all prior effective amounts
(3) 2,920,000 – 1,719,000
(4) Change in the fair value of the hedging instrument since the last fair valuation
(5) Lower of 1,201,000 (available amount) and 1,941,000 (period change in fair value of hedging instrument)
(6) 1,941,000 (period change in fair value of hedging instrument) – 1,201,000 (effective part)

5.15.5 Accounting Entries

The required journal entries were as follows.

1) To record the range acccrual trade on 1 October 20X4

There were no accounting entries as the range accrual forward had zero fair value at hedge inception.

2) To record the closing of the accounting period on 31 December 20X4

The change in fair value of the range accrual since the last valuation was a gain of EUR 2,611,000, of which EUR 1,719,000 was considered to be effective and recorded in the cash flow hedge reserve of OCI, and EUR 892,000 was considered to be ineffective and recorded in profit or loss.

Range accrual contract (Asset)	2,611,000	
Cash flow hedge reserve (Equity)		1,719,000
Other financial income (Profit or loss)		892,000

3) To record the sale agreement on 31 March 20X5

The sale agreement was recorded at the spot rate prevailing on that date (1.2950). Therefore, the sale EUR proceeds were EUR 77,220,000 (=100 million/1.2950). Because the machinery sold was not yet paid, a receivable was recognised. Suppose that the machinery was valued at EUR 68 million in ABC's statement of financial position.

The change in fair value of the range accrual since the last valuation was a gain of EUR 2,157,000, of which a EUR 1,941,000 gain corresponded to the hedging instrument (90% of the range accrual) and a EUR 216,000 gain corresponded to the undesignated part (10% of the range accrual). Regarding the EUR 1,941,000 gain related to the hedging instrument, EUR 1,201,000 was considered to be effective and recorded in the cash flow hedge reserve of OCI, while EUR 740,000 was considered to be ineffective and recorded in profit or loss. The EUR 216,000 gain related to the undesignated part was recognised in profit or loss.

The recognition of the sales transaction in profit or loss caused the release to profit or loss of the EUR 2,920,000 deferred hedge results accumulated in OCI.

The partial sale of the range accrual resulted in EUR 433,000 proceeds.

Accounts receivable (Asset)	77,220,000	
Sales (Profit or loss)		77,220,000
Cost of goods sold (Profit or loss)	68,000,000	
Machinery (Asset)		68,000,000
Range accrual contract (Asset)	2,157,000	
Cash flow hedge reserve (Equity)		1,201,000
Other financial income (Profit or loss)		740,000
Other financial income (Profit or loss)		216,000
Cash flow hedge reserve (Equity)	2,920,000	
Sales (Profit or loss)		2,920,000
Cash (Asset)	433,000	
Range accrual contract (Asset)		433,000

4) To record the settlement of the receivable and the range accrual on 30 June 20X5

The receivable was revalued at the spot rate prevailing on this date, showing a loss of EUR 1,463,000 (=100 million/1.3200 – 100 million/1.2950).

The receivable was paid by the customer, and thus USD 100 million was received. The spot rate on payment date was 1.32, so the USD 100 million payment was valued at EUR 75,758,000 (=100 million/1.32).

The change in the fair value of the range accrual since the last valuation was a gain of EUR 1,208,000, of which EUR 1,194,000 was considered to be effective and recorded in the cash flow hedge reserve of OCI, and EUR 14,000 was considered to be ineffective and recorded in profit or loss. Its settlement resulted in the payment of USD 100 million cash in exchange for EUR 81,301,000, representing an additional EUR 5,543,000 relative to the amount that settled the receivable.

The revaluation of the receivable in profit or loss caused the release to profit or loss of the EUR 1,194,000 deferred hedge results accumulated in OCI.

Other financial expenses (Profit or loss)	1,463,000	
Accounts receivable (Asset)		1,463,000
USD cash (Asset)	75,758,000	
Accounts receivable (Asset)		75,758,000
Range accrual contract (Asset)	1,208,000	
Cash flow hedge reserve (Equity)		1,194,000
Other financial income (Profit or loss)		14,000
EUR cash (Asset)	81,301,000	
Range accrual contract (Asset)		5,543,000
USD cash (Asset)		75,758,000
Cash flow hedge reserve (Equity)	1,194,000	
Other financial income (Profit or loss)		1,194,000

The following table gives a summary of the accounting entries, excluding the entries related to the cost of goods sold:

	Cash	Range accrual contract	Accounts receivable	Cash flow hedge reserve	Profit or loss
1-Oct-20X4					
Derivative trade					
31 Dec-20X4					
Derivative revaluation		2,611,000		1,719,000	892,000
31-Mar-20X5					
Derivative revaluation		2,157,000		1,201,000	956,000
Derivative partial sale	433,000	<433,000>			
Reserve reclassification				<2,920,000>	2,920,000
Sale shipment			77,220,000		77,220,000
30-Jun-20X5					
Derivative revaluation		1,208,000		1,194,000	14,000
Derivative settlement	5,543,000	<5,543,000>			
Receivable revaluation			<1,463,000>		<1,463,000>
Reserve reclassification				<1,194,000>	1,194,000
Receivable settlement	75,758,000		<75,758,000>		
TOTAL	**81,734,000**	**-0-**	**-0-**	**-0-**	**81,734,000**

Note: Total figures may not match the sum of their corresponding components due to rounding.

5.16 CASE STUDY: HEDGING FORECAST SALE AND SUBSEQUENT RECEIVABLE WITH A RANGE ACCRUAL (SPLITTING APPROACH)

In this section I have assumed that ABC decided to divide the range accrual into two separate legal contracts: a standard forward at 1.2300 and a "residual" derivative.

The standard forward was designated as the hedging instrument in a cash flow hedging relationship. Hedge effectiveness was assessed by comparing the changes in fair value of the hedging instrument with the changes in fair value of a hypothetical derivative. The hypothetical derivative was a forward with zero initial fair value.

The residual derivative was considered undesignated, and therefore not part of the hedging relationship.

The main terms of the hedging instrument and the hypothetical derivative were as follows:

Forward terms		Hypothetical derivative terms	
Instrument	FX forward	Instrument	FX forward
Start date	1 October 20X4	Start date	1 October 20X4
Counterparties	ABC and XYZ Bank	Counterparties	ABC and credit risk-free counterparty
Maturity	30 June 20X5	Maturity	30 June 20X5
ABC sells	USD 100 million	ABC sells	USD 100 million
ABC buys	EUR 81,301,000	ABC buys	EUR 79,872,000
Forward rate	1.2300	Forward rate	1.2520
Initial fair value	EUR 850,000	Initial fair value	Zero

This hedging relationship was identical to the one covered in Section 5.13.2 in which a KIKO forward was split into a 1.2300 standard forward and a residual derivative. Therefore, next I will directly focus on the information necessary to generate the accounting entries.

The residual derivative fair value was calculated as follows:

Residual derivative fair value = Range accrual fair value – Forward fair value

The fair value of the range accrual, the forward and the residual derivative at each relevant date was as follows:

	1-Oct-20X4	31-Dec-20X4	31-Mar-20X5	30-Jun-20X5
Range accrual fair value	-0-	2,611,000	4,768,000	5,543,000
Fair value change	—	2,611,000	2,157,000	1,208,000
Forward fair value	850,000	3,120,000	4,333,000	5,543,000

	1-Oct-20X4	31-Dec-20X4	31-Mar-20X5	30-Jun-20X5
Fair value change	—	2,270,000	1,213,000	1,210,000
Effective part	—	1,971,000	1,202,000	1,197,000
Ineffective part	—	299,000	11,000	13,000
Residual derivative fair value	<850,000>	<509,000>	435,000 *(1)*	— *(2)*
Fair value change	—	341,000	944,000	—

Notes:

    (1) The difference between 433,000 (see next note) and 435,000 (=4,768,000 – 4,333,000) was due to rounding errors

    (2) The residual derivative was sold on 31 March 20X5 and ABC received EUR 433,000.

5.16.1 Accounting Entries

The transaction's journal entries were as follows.

1) To record the forward and the residual derivative trades on 1 October, 20X4

At their inception, the fair values of the FX forward and the residual derivative were EUR 850,000 and <850,000> respectively.

Forward contract (Asset)	850,000	
Cash (Asset)		850,000
Cash (Asset)	850,000	
Residual derivative contract (Liability)		850,000

2) To record the closing of the accounting period on 31 December 20X4

The change in fair value of the forward since the last valuation was a gain of EUR 2,270,000, of which EUR 1,719,000 was considered to be effective, and thus recorded in the cash flow hedge reserve of OCI. The EUR 551,000 remainder represented the ineffective part, and was therefore recognised in profit or loss.

The change in fair value of the residual derivative since the last valuation was a EUR 341,000 gain, recognised in profit or loss as it was undesignated.

Forward contract (Asset)	2,270,000	
Cash flow hedge reserve (Equity)		1,719,000
Other financial income (Profit or loss)		551,000
Residual derivative contract (Liability)	341,000	
Other financial income (Profit or loss)		341,000

3) To record the sale agreement on 31 March 20X5

The sale agreement was recorded at the spot rate prevailing on that date (1.2950). Therefore, the sale EUR proceeds were EUR 77,220,000 (=100 million/1.2950). Because the machinery sold was not yet paid, a receivable was recognised. Suppose that the machinery was valued at EUR 68 million in ABC's statement of financial position.

The change in fair value of the forward since the last valuation was a gain of EUR 1,213,000, of which EUR 1,201,000 was considered to be effective and recorded in the cash flow hedge reserve of OCI, while EUR 12,000 was considered to be ineffective and recorded in profit or loss.

The change in fair value of the residual derivative since the last valuation was a EUR 944,000 gain, recognised in profit or loss as it was undesignated.

The recognition of the sales transaction in profit or loss caused the release to profit or loss of the EUR 2,290,000 deferred hedge results accumulated in OCI.

The residual derivative was sold, resulting in EUR 433,000 proceeds.

Accounts receivable (Asset)	77,220,000	
Sales (Profit or loss)		77,220,000
Cost of goods sold (Profit or loss)	68,000,000	
Machinery (Asset)		68,000,000
Forward contract (Asset)	1,213,000	
Cash flow hedge reserve (Equity)		1,201,000
Other financial income (Profit or loss)		12,000
Residual derivative contract (Asset)	944,000	
Other financial income (Profit or loss)		944,000
Cash flow hedge reserve (Equity)	2,290,000	
Sales (Profit or loss)		2,290,000
Other financial income (Profit or loss)	433,000	
Residual derivative contract (Asset)		433,000

4) To record the settlement of the receivable and the forward on 30 June 20X5

The receivable was revalued at the spot rate prevailing on this date, showing a loss of EUR 1,463,000 (=100 million/1.3200 – 100 million/1.2950).

The receivable was paid by the customer, and thus USD 100 million was received. The spot rate on payment date was 1.32, so the USD 100 million payment was valued at EUR 75,758,000 (=100 million/1.32).

The change in the fair value of the forward since the last valuation was a gain of EUR 1,210,000, of which EUR 1,197,000 was considered to be effective and recorded in the cash flow hedge reserve of OCI, while EUR 13,000 was considered to be ineffective and recorded in profit or loss.

The settlement of the FX forward resulted in the payment of USD 100 million cash in exchange for EUR 81,301,000, representing an additional EUR 5,543,000 relative to the amount that settled the receivable.

The revaluation of the receivable in profit or loss caused the release to profit or loss of the EUR 1,197,000 deferred hedge results accumulated in OCI.

Other financial expenses (Profit or loss)	1,463,000	
Accounts receivable (Asset)		1,463,000
USD cash (Asset)	75,758,000	
Accounts receivable (Asset)		75,758,000
Forward contract (Asset)	1,210,000	
Cash flow hedge reserve (Equity)		1,197,000
Other financial income (Profit or loss)		13,000
EUR cash (Asset)	81,301,000	
USD cash (Asset)		75,758,000
Forward contract (Asset)		5,543,000
Cash flow hedge reserve (Equity)	1,197,000	
Other financial income (Profit or loss)		1,197,000

The following table gives a summary of the accounting entries, excluding the entries related to the cost of goods sold:

	Cash	Forward and residual derivative contracts	Accounts receivable	Cash flow hedge reserve	Profit or loss
1-Oct-20X4					
Forward trade	<850,000>	850,000			
Res. der. trade	850,000	<850,000>			
31 Dec-20X4					
Forward revaluation		2,270,000		1,719,000	551,000
Res. der. revaluation		341,000			341,000
31-Mar-20X5					
Forward revaluation		1,213,000		1,201,000	12,000

(continued overleaf)

Res. der. revaluation	944,000				944,000
Reserve reclassification				<2,920,000>	2,920,000
Sale shipment			77,220,000		77,220,000
Sale residual derivative	433,000	<433,000>			
30-Jun-20X5					
Forward revaluation	1,210,000			1,197,000	13,000
Forward settlement	5,543,000	<5,543,000>			
Reserve reclassification settlement				<1,197,000>	1,197,000
Receivable revaluation			<1,463,000>		<1,463,000>
Receivable settlement	75,758,000		<75,758,000>		
TOTAL	**81,734,000**	**-0-**	**-0-**	**-0-**	**81,734,000**

Note: Total figures may not match the sum of their corresponding components due to rounding.

5.16.2 Final Remarks

This case highlighted the accounting challenge when hedging with range accrual forwards. Whilst the strategy worked very well from an economic point of view, it added volatility to the profit or loss statement (see Figure 5.40). The increase in profit or loss volatility was caused by the fair value volatility of the ineffective and undesignated parts. The objective of the hedging strategy – to notably reduce the FX exposure of the hedged cash flow – was achieved through the range accrual.

Two approaches were analysed: a first approach designating the whole range accrual as the hedging instrument, and a second approach splitting the range accrual into a standard forward and a residual derivative. Whilst both approaches resulted in an identical profit or loss structure, as shown in Figure 5.40, this outcome is not to be generalised because it is largely dependent on the behaviour of the EUR–USD spot rate during the life of the hedge.

ABC expected 70% of the EUR–USD fixings to fall within the accrual range. A large deviation from this percentage meant that ABC could be either overhedged or underhedged, adding undesired exposure to the EUR–USD rate. In our case, ABC was fortunate because while it ended up being overhedged, it unwound the excess hedge at favourable market rates. From an economic perspective, the range accrual performed very well. The USD 100 million sale proceeds were exchanged for EUR 81,735,000, implying a 1.2235 exchange rate, notably better than the 1.2500 original forward rate.

Approach 1: No split of range accrual

Approach 2: Split of range accrual into standard forward + residual derivative

FIGURE 5.40 Comparison of effects in profit or loss.

5.17 HEDGING ON A GROUP BASIS – THE TREASURY CENTRE CHALLENGE

Hedging activity using treasury centres may face particular accounting issues under IFRS 9, especially when internal hedges are involved. This section analyses the accounting implications when using a treasury centre to manage a whole group's foreign exchange risk.

It is a well-established practice in most large companies to centralise financial hedging activities into a group treasury centre. Treasury centres manage a broad range of functions for the group, including global cash and liquidity management, bank relationship management, funding of debt and equity, and risk management. Some companies have a single treasury centre that is based at corporate headquarters or a tax-efficient location, while others establish several centres, each strategically located to meet the needs of a specific region.

When hedging financial risk, the treasury centre of a group serves as an in-house bank netting off exposures arising across the group. Exposures are identified at the subsidiary level, and these subsidiaries then hedge using internal deals with the centre. The treasury centre then lays off the net risk position with external parties. This hedging approach is more efficient than having each subsidiary independently working with banks to hedge their local financial risk.

The following case study sheds some light on the accounting challenges faced by a centralised hedging policy. Suppose that a consolidated group has the structure shown in Figure 5.41. The group, whose presentation currency is the EUR, comprises a parent company, a treasury centre and three subsidiaries, A, B and C, whose functional currencies are the EUR, USD and JPY, respectively.

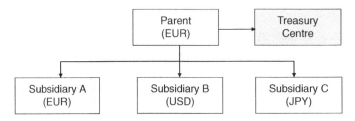

FIGURE 5.41   Group entities.

Subsidiary A's revenues were in EUR, GBP and JPY. It forecasted revenues of EUR 60, GBP 30 (i.e., the equivalent in GBP to EUR 30) and JPY 30. It forecasted sales costs related to those revenues of EUR 70 and JPY 30. For the sake of simplicity, suppose that all the flows were expected to take place on the same date. To hedge its exposure to GBP risk, Subsidiary A entered into an FX forward with the treasury centre at market rates, in which Subsidiary A agreed to sell GBP 30 and to buy EUR 30 on the date that the cash flows were expected to take place.

Subsidiary B's revenues were in USD, EUR and JPY. It forecasted revenues of USD 70 (i.e., the equivalent in USD to EUR 70), EUR 30 and JPY 30. It forecasted sales costs related to those revenues of USD 70 and JPY 30. For the sake of simplicity, suppose that all the flows were expected to take place on the same date. To hedge its exposure to EUR risk, Subsidiary B entered into an FX forward with the treasury centre at market rates, in which Subsidiary B agreed to sell EUR 30 and to buy USD 30 on the date that the cash flows were expected to take place.

Subsidiary C's revenues were in JPY and USD. It forecasted revenues of JPY 70 (i.e., the equivalent in JPY to EUR 70) and USD 30. It forecasted sales costs related to those revenues of JPY 70. For the sake of simplicity, suppose that all the flows were expected to take place on the same date. To hedge its exposure to USD risk, Subsidiary C entered into an FX forward with the treasury centre at market rates, under which Subsidiary C agreed to sell USD 30 and to buy JPY 30 on the date that the cash flows were expected to take place.

As a result, the treasury centre's net exposure with the subsidiaries was a long GBP 30 and a short JPY 30 (see Figure 5.42). In order to hedge that net exposure, the treasury centre entered into an FX forward with an external bank under which it agreed to sell GBP 30 and to buy JPY 30.

	EUR	GBP	JPY	USD
Subsidiary A	– 30	+ 30	+ 30 – 30	
Subsidiary B	+ 30		+ 30 – 30	– 30
Subsidiary C			- 30	+ 30
Total	-0-	+ 30	- 30	-0-

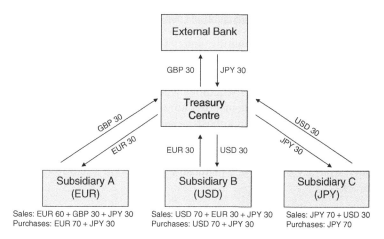

FIGURE 5.42   Group FX hedges.

5.17.1 Accounting Implications at Subsidiary Level

At a subsidiary level the hedges posed no particular accounting issues when preparing their entity-only financial statements. For example, in the case of Subsidiary A (see Figure 5.43), it could apply hedge accounting, assuming all other requirements were met, as the counterparty to the forward (the treasury centre) was an entity external to Subsidiary A and as the forecast transaction was highly probable and would be affecting profit or loss. Subsidiary A would designate the EUR–GBP forward as the hedging instrument in a cash flow hedge of its foreign currency denominated highly probable revenues of GBP 30 (the hedged item). Effective amounts of the changes in the fair value of the FX forward would be recorded in the cash flow hedge reserve of equity and reclassified to profit or loss when the hedged revenues ultimately affected profit or loss.

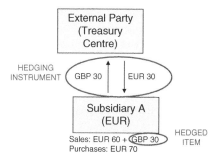

FIGURE 5.43   Subsidiary A's hedging position.

Whilst hedge accounting could not be applied (a derivative in itself cannot be a hedged item), from an accounting perspective the three internal hedges in conjunction with the external hedge did not pose a major challenge to the treasury centre. It measured all the FX forwards at fair value with changes in fair value recorded in profit or loss. As all the changes in these fair values were largely offset, the treasury centre had no volatility in profit or loss other than that caused by the CVAs/DVAs to the fair valuations of the forwards.

5.17.2 Accounting Implications at Consolidated Level

A key requirement of hedge accounting under IFRS 9 is that all hedging derivatives must involve a counterparty external to the entity (or group entities) being accounted for. Intragroup derivatives are not eligible for hedge accounting treatment in the consolidated accounts, causing significant difficulties where a group operates through a treasury centre. In these circumstances and in order to achieve hedge accounting it is usually necessary to identify, on a one-to-one basis, exposures in the group with external parties that may be designated as hedged items. In other words, the treasury centre would need to identify sufficient exposures in each of its various subsidiaries and designate, on a potentially arbitrary basis, some of those exposures on a one-to-one basis with its external contract.

Need to Split the JPY–GBP Forward?   The JPY–GBP forward hedged two separate risks: (i) a JPY–EUR exchange rate risk and (ii) a EUR–GBP exchange rate risk. The first the parent company needed to assess was whether it needed to split the JPY–GBP forward into two separate instruments: a JPY–EUR forward (selling EUR and buying JPY) and a EUR–GBP forward (selling GBP and buying EUR), as shown in Figure 5.44. This split, if needed, would undermine one of the main advantages of treasury centres: to lower the transaction costs of hedging.

Fortunately, IFRS 9 allows a single hedging instrument to be designated as a hedging instrument for more than one type of risk, provided that there is a specific designation of the hedging instrument and of the different risk positions as hedged items. In our case there was no need to split the external hedge into two separated contracts, or in other words, the single forward contract could be designated as hedging instrument in two separate hedging relationships:

- In a first hedging relationship, the risk being hedged was clearly identified as the exposure to variations in the JPY–EUR exchange rate. The hedged item was the cash flow stemming from highly expected purchases denominated in JPY, whose fair value could be reliably measured. The hedging instrument was the JPY receipt on the forward contract, whose fair value could be reliably measured.
- In a second hedging relationship, the risk being hedged was clearly identified as the exposure to variations in the EUR–GBP exchange rate. The hedged item was the cash flow stemming from highly expected sales denominated in GBP, whose fair value could be reliably measured. The hedging instrument was the GBP payment on the forward contract, whose fair value could be reliably measured.

JPY Risk: Hedge Item Candidate 1 Eligibility   The group could apply hedge accounting on consolidation in a cash flow hedging relationship in which the JPY leg of the JPY–GBP forward taken out by the treasury centre would be the hedging instrument and the cash flow stemming from Subsidiary A's highly expected forecast JPY purchase would be the hedged item, as shown in Figure 5.45, assuming all other requirements for hedge accounting were met.

This qualification was due to the *direct* future incorporation of Subsidiary A's JPY purchase in consolidated profit or loss, being converted into the group's EUR presentation currency. The exposure to movements in the JPY–EUR exchange rate constituted a cash flow risk, and therefore could be subject to cash flow hedge accounting.

JPY Risk: Hedge Item Candidate 2 Eligibility   The group could *not* apply hedge accounting on consolidation in a cash flow hedging relationship in which the JPY leg of the JPY–GBP forward taken out by the treasury centre would be the hedging instrument and the cash flow stemming from Subsidiary B's highly expected forecast JPY purchase would be the hedged item, as shown in Figure 5.45.

This non-qualification occurred because there was no JPY–EUR cash flow exposure that could affect consolidated profit or loss. Whilst Subsidiary B was exposed to movements in the JPY–USD exchange rate and Subsidiary B's USD profit or loss was translated into EUR upon consolidation (see Chapter 6), the exposure of the group to the JPY was an indirect exposure, constituting a translation risk rather than a cash flow exposure.

JPY Risk: Hedge Item Candidate 3 Eligibility   The group could *not* apply hedge accounting on consolidation in a cash flow hedging relationship in which the JPY leg of the JPY–GBP forward taken out by the treasury centre would be the hedging instrument and the cash flow stemming from Subsidiary C's highly expected forecast JPY purchase would be the hedged item, as shown in Figure 5.45.

This non-qualification occurred because there was no JPY–EUR cash flow exposure that could affect consolidated profit or loss. Subsidiary C was not exposed to movements in the JPY as its functional currency was the JPY. Whilst Subsidiary C's JPY profit or loss was translated into EUR upon consolidation, the exposure of the group to the JPY was an indirect exposure, constituting a translation risk rather than a cash flow exposure.

However, Subsidiary C's JPY profit or loss would become part of the net investment of the group in Subsidiary C, and consequently, changes in the JPY–EUR exchange rate would affect the cumulative translation adjustment upon consolidation (see Chapter 6). As a result, the group could apply net investment hedge accounting in a hedging relationship in which the hedging instrument would be the JPY leg of the JPY–GBP forward taken out by the treasury centre and the hedged item would be the JPY-denominated net assets of Subsidiary C.

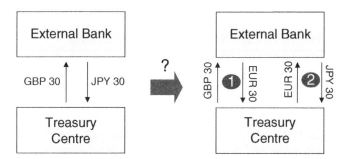

FIGURE 5.44   Treasury Centre's hedging position.

Conclusions   When a treasury centre is involved, the application of hedge accounting on the consolidated statements requires a process of arbitrary designation of the hedged item. At first sight it looks as if this process only involves an additional administrative burden. In reality the designation process is much more complicated than in our example.

First of all, bear in mind that the above example was much simplified as all the expected cash flows were expected to take place on the same date. In reality, there is often a time lag between timing of the external hedges and the timing of the identified hedged items. Timing differences may create significant hedge ineffectiveness.

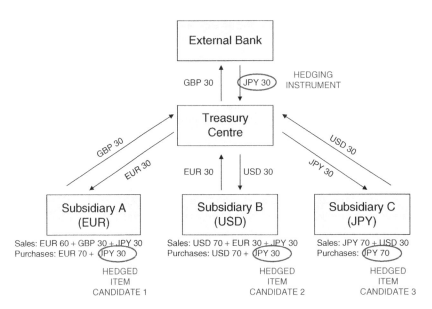

FIGURE 5.45 Hedge item candidates for the JPY exposure.

Secondly, it was assumed that the treasury centre netted out the group's exposure under the internal derivatives and the external derivatives. In reality, a treasury centre may decide to keep some residual risk or to hedge using a different currency pair, complicating matters further. For example, a foreign exchange exposure may be created by an illiquid currency and a treasury centre may prefer to take out a hedge on a different currency that is highly correlated to the illiquid one.

5.18 HEDGING FORECAST INTRAGROUP TRANSACTIONS

In its consolidated financial statements, a group may designate as the hedged item in a foreign currency cash flow hedge, a highly probable forecast transaction with an external party to the group, provided that the transaction is denominated in a currency other than the group's functional currency.

Whilst in general IFRS 9 does not permit an intragroup item to be a hedged item in the consolidated financial statements, there is an exception to this general rule:

1) When the intragroup monetary item results in an exposure to foreign exchange rate gains or losses that are not fully eliminated on consolidation in accordance with IAS 21 *The Effects of Changes in Foreign Exchange Rates*. In accordance with IAS 21, foreign exchange rate gains and losses on intragroup monetary items are not fully eliminated on consolidation when the intragroup monetary item is transacted between two group entities that have different functional currencies.

2) In the case of a highly probable forecast intragroup transaction, the transaction is denominated in a currency other than the functional currency of the entity entering into that transaction and the foreign currency risk will affect consolidated profit or loss.

The following are examples of forecast intragroup transactions that could result in the foreign exchange risk affecting consolidated profit or loss:

- Forecast sales and purchases of inventories between entities in a group with a subsequent sale of the inventory to a party external to the group. Any hedging gains or losses that are initially recognised in equity are reclassified to profit or loss in the same period that the foreign currency risk affects consolidated profit or loss. This would occur when the onward sale to the external party occurs (and not when intragroup sales occurs) because that is when the hedged transaction affects consolidated profit or loss.
- A forecast intragroup sale of equipment from a group entity that manufactured it to another group entity that uses the equipment. When the purchasing entity depreciates the equipment, the amount initially recognised in the consolidated financial statements for the equipment may change because the transaction is denominated in a currency other than the functional currency of the purchasing entity. In this example, a related external transaction does not exist and the item affects consolidated profit or loss.

Examples of forecast intragroup transactions unlikely to result in the foreign exchange risk affecting consolidated P&L are intragroup management fees, interest on intragroup loans or intragroup royalty payments.

IFRS 9 does not explicitly consider situations where the intragroup transaction is committed rather than forecast. In my view, committed transactions are also eligible for hedge accounting since they have a higher probability of occurrence.

5.18.1 Example of Hedge of Forecast Intragroup Transaction

ABC is a group that comprises operating subsidiaries A and B. The group has the EUR as its functional currency. Subsidiary A's functional currency is the GBP while Subsidiary B's functional currency is the USD.

Subsidiary A incurs most of its production costs in EUR. It sells most of its production to Subsidiary B, and these transactions are denominated in USD. In turn, Subsidiary B sells the product on to external customers, also in USD. Subsidiary A forecasts in March 20X6 that it will sell in June 20X6 USD 100 million of inventory to Subsidiary B. These sales are highly probable, and all the other IFRS 9 conditions for hedge accounting are met. Subsidiary B expects to sell this inventory to external customers in early September 20X6.

In January 20X6 Subsidiary A enters into a EUR–USD derivative to hedge its expected sale of USD 100 million to Subsidiary B in June 20X6.

The USD 100 million forecast intragroup sales can be designated in the consolidated financial statements as a hedged item in a foreign currency cash flow hedge (see Figure 5.46) as:

1) the sales are highly probable, and all other conditions for using hedge accounting are met;
2) the hedge is a cash flow hedge of foreign currency risk;
3) the sales are denominated in a currency (USD) other than Subsidiary A's functional currency (EUR); and
4) the existence of the expected onward sale of the inventory to third parties results in the hedged exposure affecting consolidated profit or loss.

Gains and losses on the EUR–USD derivative would be recognised in consolidated equity, to the extent that the hedge is effective. These amounts would be reclassified to consolidated profit or loss in September 20X6 when the external sales occur (i.e., when the hedged transaction affects consolidated profit or loss).

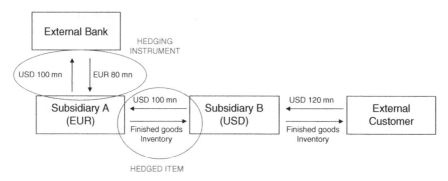

FIGURE 5.46   Hedging relationship.

CHAPTER 6

Hedging Foreign Subsidiaries

A group will often carry out activities through foreign operations. Foreign operations are those entities in a group's financial statements incorporated by consolidation, or the equity method, for which their functional currency is different from the currency in which the group's financial statements are reported (the presentation currency). A foreign operation's results and financial position are translated into the group's presentation currency, creating a foreign exchange exposure called **translation exposure**. For example, the revaluation differences resulting from the translation of net assets of a foreign operation into a group's presentation currency are included in the translation differences (or **exchange differences**) account, a component of consolidated shareholders' equity.

Many companies consider that the foreign exchange risk arising from foreign operations is only a translation risk – merely an accounting issue – with no impact on cash flows, and as a consequence there is no need to hedge it. This stance is flawed, especially in today's dynamic and competitive environment, as companies frequently buy and sell foreign operations. Disregarding translation exposures as "accounting exposures" and focusing solely on cash flows or transaction exposures could be risky. For example, adverse translation movements may result in a significant decrease of total consolidated equity and, in turn, a higher debt-to-equity ratio that could trigger covenants included in financing agreements (with severe implications for liquidity if debt needs to be repaid). Moreover, a large deficit in the translation differences account may distort future disposal decisions.

In this chapter, I explore the challenges faced by a consolidated group when hedging subsidiaries whose functional currency is different from the presentation currency of the consolidated group. Hedging a foreign subsidiary is often challenging (see Figure 6.1):

- It is a strategic decision. The size of a foreign operation's net assets is often very substantial relative to the equity of a group. Deciding whether or not to hedge a foreign operation can have a substantial effect on a group's capital, its related covenants and dividend policies. Also, a specific hedging strategy can affect future disposal decisions.
- It is technically complex. Hedging a foreign operation has to be assessed taking into account the group's other financial exposures. Moreover, a foreign operation's net assets will change during the hedging horizon and forecasting the amount to be hedged is not a straightforward exercise.

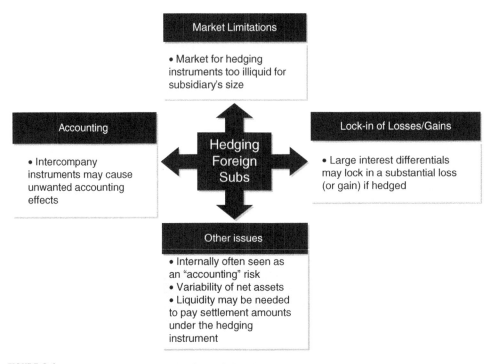

FIGURE 6.1   Challenges of hedging foreign subsidiaries.

- The selection of the adequate hedging instrument requires a careful analysis of its market and its accounting implications. For example, hedges may require using a proxy basket of currencies if the size of the foreign subsidiary's net assets is too large relative to the FX market for that foreign currency.
- It may create unwanted volatility. Hedge accounting may not be applied to some hedging strategies. Also some items of the foreign entity, such as profit and loss, may not be eligible as hedged items in a hedge accounting relationship.
- It may be costly. When interest rates in the foreign currency are substantially higher than those of the presentation currency, a hedge may imply locking in a loss over the life of the hedge.
- The effects of intragroup transactions (e.g., intragroup loans) have to be carefully assessed as they may create distortions when consolidated and/or affect a hedging strategy.
- It may result in large settlement amounts having to be paid by the entity under the hedging instrument, using precious cash resources.

This chapter deals with the measurement and hedging of foreign currency exposure caused by foreign operations. Through the cases provided in this chapter, five topics will be analysed in detail:

- Translation of a foreign operation's financial statements.
- Hedging of net investments in a foreign operation. A net investment means the entity's proportionate ownership interest in the net assets of the foreign operation.
- Measurement and hedging of dividends paid by a foreign operation to the parent company.

- Translation and hedging of a foreign operation's earnings.
- Interaction of dividends, earnings and net investments, and the hedging of the combined exposure.

These five topics are interdependent, and therefore their joint hedge needs to take into account the overall exposure.

6.1 STAND-ALONE VERSUS CONSOLIDATED FINANCIAL STATEMENTS

For simplicity, most cases in this chapter assume a group formed by two entities: (i) a parent company with the EUR as its functional and presentation currency and (ii) a controlled foreign operation (i.e., a subsidiary). When a subsidiary is not fully owned by the parent entity, adjustments related to minority interests are needed. The effect of minority interests is covered in Section 6.5 below. In this section, the three levels of financial statements – at the subsidiary, at the parent-only and at the consolidated level – are covered.

6.1.1 Subsidiary Financial Statements

The purpose of a subsidiary's stand-alone financial statements is to present the financial position of the subsidiary as if it were a single business enterprise. The parent company is considered merely as an outside investor. Normally, a subsidiary's financial statements are prepared according to the accounting principles of the country in which it operates. When local accounting principles are different from those of IFRS standards, the subsidiary's statements need to be restated to IFRS upon consolidation. In the cases provided, it is assumed that the subsidiary financial statements are prepared according to IFRS.

6.1.2 Parent-Only Financial Statements

The purpose of a parent's stand-alone financial statements is to present the financial position of the parent as if it were a single business enterprise. Its subsidiaries are treated purely as equity investments, ignoring the subsidiaries assets and liabilities.

Similarly to a subsidiary, a parent's stand-alone financial statements are prepared according to the local accounting standards prevailing in the parent's jurisdiction. The parent-only financial statements commonly use the cost method to account for their equity investments in subsidiaries. The general underlying concepts behind the cost method are the following (see Figure 6.2):

- The original cost of the investment is recognised in the parent-only financial statements in the "investment in subsidiary" account.
- No adjustments are made to reflect subsequent changes in the fair value of the investment unless there is serious doubt as to the realisation of the investment, in which case a permanent write-down is made.
- Undistributed earnings have no effect on the parent financial statements.
- When dividends are declared, dividend income is recognised. Neither the dividend declaration nor the actual dividend payments impact the carrying value of the investment in the parent-only financials.

Recognition of Investment in Subsidiary (Cost Method)

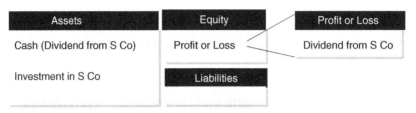

FIGURE 6.2   Parent-only financial statements.

Recognition of Investment in Subsidiary (Consolidation)

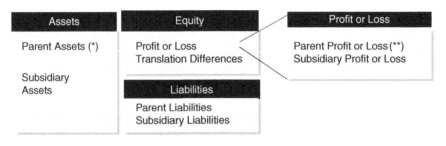

(*) Investment in subsidiary is eliminated
(**) Dividend from subsidiary is eliminated

FIGURE 6.3   Consolidated financial statements.

6.1.3 Consolidated Financial Statements

Because consolidated financial statements are prepared using IFRS guidelines, any subsidiary's financial statements not prepared according to IFRS rules need to be restated to IFRS. The purpose of the consolidated financial statements is to present, primarily for the benefit of the group's shareholders and creditors, the financial position of the parent company and all its subsidiaries as if the group were a single economic entity. All the assets and liabilities of each foreign subsidiary are taken into account as assets and liabilities of the group after being translated into the group's presentation currency. Similarly, each foreign subsidiary's profit or loss statement is also integrated in the group's profit and loss, after being translated into the group's presentation currency.

In consolidation, the parent's "investment in subsidiary" account is eliminated and the value of the translation differences is calculated as well. The carrying value of this account is a "plug" figure that balances all the translated assets and liabilities of each foreign subsidiary. Figure 6.3 summarises the consolidated balance sheet and profit or loss statements, assuming that there are no intragroup transactions.

6.2 THE TRANSLATION PROCESS

The rationale behind the translation of a foreign operation's financial statements is to preserve the item-to-item relationships (e.g., profitability ratios, liquidity ratios, specific asset to total assets percentages) that exist in the operation's foreign currency statements. The only way to maintain these relationships is to translate all the operation's assets and liabilities using a single exchange rate.

6.2.1 Basic Procedures prior to Translation

Certain fundamental procedures must be performed before the financial statements of foreign operations may be translated into EUR (i.e., the group's presentation currency).

- Restatement to IFRS. Operations conducted in a foreign entity must be accounted for using the accounting principles prevailing in its jurisdiction. When foreign currency financial statements use accounting principles that differ from IFRS, appropriate restatement adjustments must be made to those statements before translation so that they conform to IFRS. When a parent company has significant influence over a subsidiary, commonly a 20–50% interest, which must be accounted for under the equity method, the investee's foreign statements must also be adjusted to conform to IFRS principles before translation into EUR.
- Adjustments to the foreign operation's monetary items (e.g., receivables and payables). A foreign operation's monetary items in a currency other than the foreign operation's functional currency must be converted into the foreign operation's functional currency.
- Reconciliation of intragroup monetary items. For example, intragroup loans are commonly transferred between group entities with different functional currencies. Such transactions are usually recorded in separate intragroup accounts by each accounting entity. Such accounts must be reconciled with each other before translation to ensure that these accounts offset each other after translation.
- Elimination of the parent's investment in the foreign operation and the foreign operation's equity. In other words, the carrying amount of the parent investment in the foreign operation and the equity of the foreign operation corresponding to the parent ownership are eliminated.
- The accounting period translation gain or loss is computed and recognised in the "translation differences" account of equity. On disposal (or partial disposal or liquidation) of the foreign operation, the portion of the "translation differences" reserve that relates to the disposal (or liquidation) must be transferred to profit or loss in the reporting period in which the disposal is recognised.

6.2.2 Specific Translation Procedures

The individual accounts of a foreign operation are translated using the following procedures:

- All assets and liabilities are translated at the closing exchange rate. Assets and liabilities to be translated include any goodwill and fair value adjustments that arose on the acquisition of the foreign entity.
- Share capital and share premium are translated at historical exchange rates.
- Dividend payments, if any, are translated using the exchange rate in effect at the time of its declaration.
- Profit or loss accounts are translated at the average exchange rate for the accounting period. The exchange rate existing when each item was recognised in earnings can also be used, but in practice this alternative is rarely applied.
- The accounting period translation gain or loss resulting from the previous procedures is included in the "translation differences" account of equity.

6.2.3 Hyperinflationary Economies

The financial statements of a foreign operation in the currency of a hyperinflationary economy are first restated in accordance with IAS 29 *Financial Reporting in Hyperinflationary Economies*. All components are then translated into the presentation currency at the closing rate at the end of the reporting period. This prior adjustment is made to maintain the comparability of prior period information.

The reclassification of an economy as hyperinflationary may have substantial impact on the consolidated financial statements. Suppose that a group has a foreign subsidiary, and that due to the high level of inflation reached during the last year and the cumulative inflation rate over the last few years, the subsidiary's country is now considered a hyperinflationary economy. The main implications of this are as follows:

- Adjustment of the historical cost of non-monetary assets and liabilities and the various items of equity of the subsidiary from their date of acquisition or inclusion in the consolidated statement of financial position to the end of the accounting period for the changes in purchasing power of the currency caused by inflation. The cumulative impact of the accounting restatement to adjust for the effects of hyperinflation for years prior to the reclassification is shown in translation differences at the beginning of the reporting period.
- Adjustment of the income statement to reflect the financial loss caused by the impact of inflation in the reporting period on net monetary assets (loss of purchasing power).
- The various components in the profit or loss statement and statement of cash flows are adjusted for the inflation index since their generation, with a balancing entry in financial results and offsetting reconciling item in the statement of cash flows, respectively.
- All components of the financial statements of the foreign operation are translated at the closing exchange rate.

6.3 THE TRANSLATION DIFFERENCES ACCOUNT

Investments in foreign operations are exposed to exchange rate fluctuations. The "translation differences" account reports the accumulated translation gains and losses related to the translation of a foreign subsidiary's net asset position. This account is reported as a separate component of shareholders' equity. The "translation differences adjustment" for the accounting period is the difference between the "translation differences account" carrying values at the beginning and end of the period. The amount at the end of the period is calculated in such a way that the sum of all debits matches the sum of all credits in a foreign subsidiary's translated statement of financial position (i.e., balance sheet).

The balance of the translation differences account is removed from that account and reported in consolidated profit or loss on complete (or substantially complete) sale or liquidation of the foreign operation. On partial divestment of the foreign operation, the proportional part of the translation differences account relating to that foreign operation is recognised in profit or loss as part of the gain or loss on the partial divestment.

The translation differences account balance at the end of the accounting period is calculated as follows:

Calculation of the accounting period translation differences	
	translated assets (including goodwill and fair value adjustments)
less	translated liabilities (including fair value adjustments)
equals	**shareholders' equity**
less	translated shared capital
less	translated share premium
less	translated other comprehensive income
equals	**total retained earnings and translation differences**
less	beginning of accounting period retained earnings
less	translated net income
plus	translated dividends
equals	**end of accounting period translation differences**
less	beginning of accounting period translation differences
equals	**translation differences adjustment**

6.4 SPECIAL ITEMS THAT ARE PART OF A NET INVESTMENT

Not only is the equity investment in a foreign operation's assets and liabilities considered part of a net investment. Other items, such acquisition goodwill, fair value adjustments and some monetary items, may also be part of the net investment in a foreign subsidiary.

6.4.1 Goodwill and Fair Value Adjustments

When one company invests in another (either a subsidiary, associate or joint operation), all the assets and liabilities of the acquiree are fair valued. The fair value adjustments are the difference, at the time of acquisition, between the fair value and the book value of the acquiree's assets and liabilities. Goodwill is the difference between what the acquirer paid and the fair value of the acquiree's assets and liabilities. Under IAS 21, goodwill and fair value adjustments arising from the acquisition of a foreign operation are treated as assets and liabilities of the foreign operation and translated at the closing rate.

6.4.2 Long-Term Investments in a Foreign Subsidiary

Certain monetary items of the parent may be part of its net investment in a foreign operation. This situation occurs when, in addition to providing equity capital to a foreign operation, a parent company provides funds through, commonly, a loan that is similar to an equity investment. A loan is part of a parent's investment in a foreign operation when repayment is neither planned nor likely to occur in the foreseeable future. A history of repayments is likely to be indicative that a loan does not form part of the investment in a foreign operation. The impacts on the individual financial statements are as follows:

- When the loan is denominated in the functional currency of the foreign operation, exchange differences arising from the loan are recognised in profit or loss in the parent-only financial statements.
- When the loan is denominated in the functional currency of the parent, exchange differences arising from the loan are recognised in profit or loss in the foreign operation-only financial statements.
- When the loan is denominated in a currency that is not the functional currency of either the parent or the foreign operation, exchange differences are recognised in profit or loss in both the parent-only and foreign operation-only financial statements.

An entity may have other monetary items, such as a receivable from or payable to a foreign operation, for which settlement is neither planned nor likely to occur in the foreseeable future. These items are, in substance, part of the entity's net investment in that foreign operation. They do not include trade receivables or trade payables.

Example of Monetary Item Part of a Net Investment   Suppose that SubCo issues to ParentCo perpetual debt (i.e., debt without a legal maturity) denominated in USD with an annual interest rate of 4%. The perpetual debt has no issuer call option or holder put option. Thus, contractually it is just an infinite stream of interest payments in USD.

In the group's consolidated financial statements, the perpetual debt is considered a monetary item "for which settlement is neither planned nor likely to occur in the foreseeable future", and therefore, the perpetual debt can be considered part of ParentCo's net investment in SubCo. The interest payments are treated as interest receivable by ParentCo and interest payable by SubCo, not as repayment of the debt principal.

Foreseeable Future   IAS 21 does not specify a time period that might qualify as "foreseeable future". Therefore, the term "foreseeable future" is not meant to imply a specific time period, but is an intent-based indicator. An intragroup monetary item may qualify as part of the net investment in a foreign operation when:

- the parent does not intend to require repayment of the intragroup account (which cannot be represented if the debt has a maturity date that is not waived); and
- the parent's management views the intragroup account as part of its investment in the foreign operation.

EXAMPLE: Rolling Trade Receivables

IAS 21 specifically excludes trade receivables and trade payables as qualifying for an entity's net investment in a foreign operation. This exclusion also holds for trade receivables/payables that are consistently replaced with new ones, or trade receivables/payables for which a minimum balance is kept outstanding at all times. Intragroup transactions must be evaluated on an individual basis, not on an aggregate or net basis.

6.4.3 Disposal of a Foreign Operation

On disposal of a foreign operation, the cumulative amount of the exchange differences relating to that operation, recognised in other comprehensive income and accumulated in a separate component of equity, is reclassified from equity to profit or loss (as a reclassification adjustment) when the gain or loss on disposal is recognised.

In addition to the disposal of an entity's entire interest in a foreign operation, the following events, transactions or changes in circumstances are accounted for as disposals, even if the entity retains an interest in the former subsidiary, associate or joint operation:

* the loss of control over a subsidiary that includes a foreign operation;
* the loss of significant influence over an associate that includes a foreign operation; or
* the loss of joint control over a jointly controlled entity that includes a foreign operation.

Therefore, the loss of control, significant influence or joint control of an entity is accounted for as a disposal (not as a partial disposal) under IAS 21. Therefore, all of the exchange differences previously accumulated in equity are reclassified to profit or loss – none are attributed to the interest retained by the entity.

6.5 EFFECT OF MINORITY INTERESTS ON TRANSLATION DIFFERENCES

When minority interests relating to foreign entities exist, their share of the translation gains and losses should be added to the "minority interests" in the consolidated balance sheet, as described in the following example.

Suppose that ABC, a EUR based entity, had an 80% investment in a US subsidiary. The net assets of the foreign subsidiary were USD 1 billion. No activity took place during the period. The EUR–USD exchange rates were 1.0000 on 1 January and 1.2500 on 31 December. Thus, the translation adjustments loss was EUR 200 million (= 1 billion $\times$ (1/1.0000 – 1/1.2500)).

As ABC owned 80% of the subsidiary, a negative EUR 160 million was recorded in the translation differences account and the remaining EUR 40 million was subtracted from minority interests in the consolidated balance sheet.

6.6 HEDGING NET INVESTMENTS IN FOREIGN OPERATIONS

Under IFRS 9, for hedge accounting purposes the net investment is viewed as a single asset, as opposed to several individual assets and liabilities that comprise the balance sheet of a foreign operation. The accounting for hedges of net investments in foreign operations follows rules similar to those of cash flow hedges. That is, the effective portion of the change in fair value of the hedging instrument is temporarily recognised in equity, in the translation differences account.

The hedging of net investments in foreign operations is usually implemented by one of the group holding companies through the following instruments:

* non-derivatives, usually debt denominated in the subsidiary functional currency; and/or
* derivatives, usually FX forwards, FX options, or cross-currency swaps.

6.6.1 Net Investment Hedge Issuing Foreign Currency Debt

IFRS 9 allows the use of non-derivative financial instruments, such as foreign currency debt, to hedge a net investment. This is a common hedging alternative when an acquisition is financed with new debt. All the hedge accounting requirements of IFRS 9 must be met, including that an economic relationship must exist between gains and losses on the net investment and gains and losses on the debt.

6.6.2 Net Investment Hedge Using Derivatives

Sometimes the foreign operation's functional currency is non-convertible, making it impossible for a non-resident holding company to issue debt denominated in such foreign currency. It may also be that the debt market in the currency concerned is too illiquid to accommodate the placement of new debt. In these cases the group is basically left with derivatives to hedge the net investment.

A hedge of a net investment in a foreign subsidiary using derivatives is accounted for as follows (see Figure 6.4):

- The portion of the gain or loss on the hedging instrument that is determined to be an effective hedge is recognised directly in OCI of equity, in the translation differences reserve. Gains and losses previously recognised in this reserve are reclassified to profit or loss upon the disposal, or part disposal, of the foreign operation.
- The ineffective portion is reported in profit or loss.

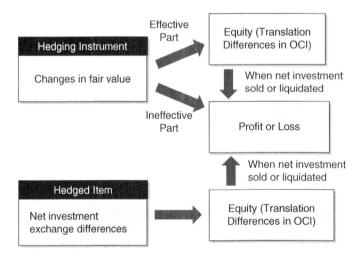

FIGURE 6.4   Net investment hedge using derivatives.

6.7 CASE STUDY: ACCOUNTING FOR NET INVESTMENTS IN FOREIGN OPERATIONS

Before addressing the hedge on net investments in foreign operations, it is important to understand the interaction of the different components behind the **translation differences** (or **exchange differences** or **cumulative translation**) account. A net investment in a foreign operation is the amount of a reporting entity's interest in the net assets of the operation. Any change in the translated value of the net assets of an operation into the group's presentation currency is included in the translation differences reserve of equity. The aim of a net investment hedge is therefore to minimise the variability of amounts in the translation differences account with respect to changes in foreign exchange rates. This case study describes the process of deriving translation differences.

Suppose that on 1 January 20X0 ParentCo (the parent company of a group whose presentation currency is the EUR) acquired 80% of SubCo (whose functional currency is the USD) for a USD 1.43 billion consideration (see Figure 6.5). The fair value of SubCo's identifiable net assets was USD 1.5 billion (USD 3.5 billion of assets and USD 2 billion of liabilities). The closing EUR–USD spot rate on 1 January 20X0 was 1.3000.

6.7.1 Elements of the Net Assets of a Foreign Subsidiary

It is important to note that the hedged item in a net investment hedge is a collection of the foreign operation's assets and liabilities. The net assets of a foreign operation change during the reporting period (see Figure 6.6). The change can be analysed by looking at the variation of the shareholders' equity of the foreign subsidiary during the accounting period:

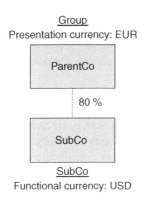

FIGURE 6.5 Group's structure post-acquisition.

- Profit or loss is generated in the foreign operation.
- Dividends are distributed to the foreign operation's shareholders.
- Capital investment is increased by the acquisition of the foreign operation's new or existing capital instruments.
- Capital investment is reduced by the sale or cancellation of the foreign operation's existing capital instruments.
- Additional other comprehensive income is generated or reduced in the foreign operation's financial position.
- Existing or new intragroup loans become part of the group's net investment as a result of it being considered that settlement is neither planned nor likely to occur in the foreseeable future.

▪ Existing goodwill is impaired or new goodwill is recognised as a result of an increase in ownership.

Goodwill and statement of financial position items are remeasured to fair value when a stake is acquired in a foreign operation (so it is consolidated by the group either as a subsidiary, joint operation or associate) are recognised as assets and liabilities of the investee and therefore translated at the closing exchange rate.

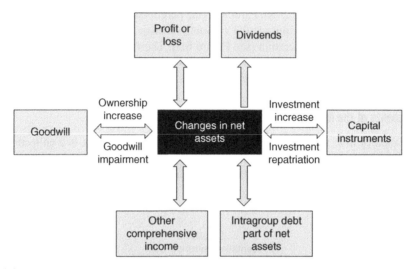

FIGURE 6.6 Elements of the net assets of a foreign subsidiary.

6.7.2 Translation Process on Acquisition Date

On 1 January 20X0, ParentCo acquired SubCo. Because SubCo's functional currency (USD) was not the currency of a hyperinflationary economy, SubCo's financial position was translated from its functional currency into the consolidated group's presentation currency (EUR) using the closing spot rate at the acquisition date, 1.3000.

SubCo's item	Fair value	EUR–USD rate	Translated EUR amount
Assets	USD 3,500 mn	1.3000	EUR 2,692 mn
Liabilities	USD 2,000 mn	1.3000	EUR 1,538 mn
Shareholders' equity	USD 1,500 mn	1.3000	EUR 1,154 mn

Each component of SubCo's shareholders' equity was also translated using the 1.3000 closing spot rate:

SubCo's equity item	Fair value	EUR–USD rate	Translated EUR amount
Share capital	USD 500 mn	1.3000	EUR 385 mn
Retained earnings	USD 800 mn	1.3000	EUR 615 mn
Other comprehensive income	USD 200 mn	1.3000	EUR 154 mn
Shareholders' equity	**USD 1,500 mn**	**1.3000**	**EUR 1,154 mn**

Goodwill   The group's consolidated statements included a goodwill item arising on the acquisition of SubCo. Goodwill was calculated as the difference between the consideration paid and the sum of the fair values of the underlying net assets. Goodwill was treated as an asset of SubCo, and therefore expressed in SubCo's functional currency (USD). The initial USD value of the goodwill was calculated as follows:

$$\text{Goodwill} = \text{USD } 1{,}430 \text{ mn} - 80\% \times 1{,}500 \text{ mn} = \text{USD } 230 \text{ million}$$

The EUR value of the goodwill on acquisition date was EUR 177 million (= USD 230 mn/1.3000).

Non-controlling Interest   The 20% of SubCo not owned by ParentCo was recognised as a non-controlling interest (i.e., a minority interest). The non-controlling interest was measured initially as a proportionate share of SubCo's net identifiable assets, as follows:

$$\text{NCI} = 20\% \times \text{USD } 1{,}500 \text{ mn} = \text{USD } 300 \text{ mn}$$

The EUR value of the non-controlling interest on acquisition date was EUR 231 mn (= USD 300 mn/1.3000).

On consolidation, the EUR 1.1 billion (= USD 1,430 mn/1.3000) carrying amount of the parent's investment in the subsidiary was replaced with the subsidiary's assets and liabilities and the non-controlling interest. Any goodwill arising on the acquisition of SubCo and any fair value adjustments to the carrying amounts of SubCo's assets and liabilities arising from the acquisition were treated as assets and liabilities of the foreign operation, and therefore expressed in the functional currency of the foreign operation.

Figures 6.7 and 6.8 show the stand-alone balance sheets of ParentCo's and SubCo, and Figure 6.9 shows the consolidated balance sheet, as of 1 January 20X0, the acquisition date (rounded to the nearest EUR million), and for simplicity assuming no intragroup transactions and no other entities in the group.

6.7.3 Translation Process on First Reporting Date

Let us examine the translation process carried out on the first reporting date following acquisition. To simplify our analysis, let us assume that the group reported its financial statements on an annual basis at year's end. Thus, the first reporting date following acquisition was 31 December 20X0. Figure 6.10 summarises SubCo's stand-alone balance sheet on that date.

ParentCo's Stand-alone Balance Sheet

Assets		Liabilities	
Investment in SubCo (USD 1,430 mn)	EUR 1,100 mn	ParentCo's liabilities	
ParentCo's other assets		**Equity**	
		ParentCo's equity	

FIGURE 6.7   ParentCo's stand-alone statement of financial position as of 1-Jan-20X0.

SubCo's Stand-alone Balance Sheet

Assets		Liabilities	
Assets	USD 3,500 mn	Liabilities	USD 2,000 mn
		Equity	
		Share capital	USD 500 mn
		Retained earnings	USD 800 mn
		Other comprehensive income	USD 200 mn

FIGURE 6.8   SubCo's stand-alone statement of financial position as of 1-Jan-20X0.

Group's Consolidated Balance Sheet

Assets		Liabilities	
Goodwill (USD 230 mn)	EUR 177 mn	ParentCo's liabilities	
ParentCo's other assets		SubCo's liabilities (USD 2,000 mn)	EUR 1,538 mn
SubCo's assets (USD 3,500 mn)	EUR 2,692 mn	**Equity**	
		ParentCo's equity	
		Non-controlling int. (USD 300 mn)	EUR 231 mn

FIGURE 6.9   Group's consolidated statement of financial position as of 1-Jan-20X0.

SubCo (Stand-alone Balance Sheet) as of 31-Dec-20X0

Assets		Liabilities	
Assets	USD 3,800 mn	Liabilities	USD 2,100 mn
		Equity	
		Share capital	USD 500 mn
		Opening retained earnings	USD 800 mn
		Profit or loss	USD 100 mn
		Dividends paid	<USD 40 mn>
		Other comprehensive income	USD 340 mn

FIGURE 6.10   SubCo's stand-alone balance sheet as of 31-Dec-20X0.

The calculation of the exchange differences can be split into the following steps (see Figure 6.11):

1) Take SubCo's statement of financial position (i.e., balance sheet) and translate each item, excluding goodwill.
2) Calculate the exchange differences (excluding goodwill) such that the translated assets equal the sum of (i) the translated liabilities and (ii) the translated shareholders' equity;
3) Allocate the exchange differences (excluding goodwill) between the group and the non-controlling interests, based on their share of the net assets.
4) Add the exchange differences due to the retranslation of goodwill to the group's exchange differences.

FIGURE 6.11 Process to calculate exchange differences.

Step 1: Translation of the Subsidiary's Statement of Financial Position The first step on 31 December 20X0 was to translate the subsidiary's balance sheet (excluding goodwill). Because SubCo's functional currency (USD) was not the currency of a hyperinflationary economy, SubCo's results and financial position were translated from its functional currency (USD) into the group's presentation currency (EUR) using the following procedures:

1) SubCo's assets and liabilities were translated at the EUR–USD closing rate on the reporting date (1.2000).
2) SubCo's profit or loss statement was translated using the average EUR–USD FX rate since the last reporting period (1.1500). Alternatively, IAS 21 permits the translation of income and expenses at the FX rates at the dates of the transactions, but this alternative is infrequently used as it is operationally more complex.
3) SubCo's distributed dividends were translated at the EUR–USD spot rate prevailing on the date that SubCo's shareholders meeting approved the payment of such dividend (it is assumed that it was 1.2500).
4) SubCo's remaining items were translated at their historical EUR–USD FX rates. IAS 21 does not state how these items should be translated, but in reality most entities use historical FX rates.
5) All resulting exchange rate differences were recognised in other comprehensive income.

Suppose that the EUR–USD closing spot rate on 31 December 20X0 and the 20X0 average EUR–USD rate were 1.2000 and 1.1500, respectively. Suppose also that the EUR–USD closing spot rate on the day the dividend was approved by SubCo's shareholders was 1.2500. The following table summarises the translation of SubCo's statement of financial position on 31 December 20X0.

SubCo's balance sheet item	Fair value	EUR–USD rate	Translated EUR amount
Assets (A)	USD 3,800 mn	1.2000 (closing)	EUR 3,167 mn
Liabilities (B)	USD 2,100 mn	1.2000 (closing)	EUR 1,750 mn

(continued overleaf)

SubCo's balance sheet item	Fair value	EUR–USD rate	Translated EUR amount
Share capital (C)	USD 500 mn	1.3000 (historical)	EUR 385 mn
Opening retained earnings (D)	USD 800 mn	1.3000 (historical)	EUR 615 mn
Profit or loss (E)	USD 100 mn	1.1500 (average)	EUR 87 mn
Dividends (F)	USD 40 mn	1.2500 (approval date)	EUR 32 mn
Opening OCI (G)	USD 200 mn	1.3000 (historical)	EUR 154 mn
Change in OCI during period (H)	USD 140 mn	1.2000 (closing)	EUR 117 mn
Exchange rate differences (A) – (B) – (C) – (D) – (E) + (F) – (G) – (H)			**EUR 91 mn**

The change in OCI was translated using the closing EUR–USD spot rate (1.3000). This translation assumes that all the change in OCI took place on the closing date. An alternative, probably more realistic, would be to use the average EUR–USD rate during the accounting period (i.e., 1.1500), similar to the conversion treatment of the profit or loss statement, assuming that the change in OCI took place gradually during that period.

Step 2: Calculation of Exchange Differences   In the second step, exchange differences, excluding goodwill, were calculated such that the translated assets equalled the sum of (i) the translated liabilities and (ii) the translated shareholders' equity. Figure 6.12 shows the translated balance sheet of SubCo and the carrying value of the exchange differences.

SubCo's Translated Balance Sheet as of 31-Dec-20X0

Assets		Liabilities	
Assets (USD 3,800 mn)	EUR 3,167 mn	Liabilities (USD 2,100 mn)	EUR 1,750 mn
		Equity	
		Share capital (USD 500 mn)	EUR 385 mn
		Opening ret. earnings (USD 800 mn)	EUR 615 mn
		Profit or loss (USD 100 mn)	EUR 87 mn
		Dividends paid (USD 40 mn)	<EUR 32 mn>
		Opening OCI (USD 200 mn)	EUR 154 mn
		New OCI (USD 140 mn)	EUR 117 mn
		Exchange differences (excl. goodwill)	EUR 91 mn

FIGURE 6.12   SubCo's translated statement of financial position as of 31-Dec-20X0.

Step 3: Allocation of Exchange Differences   In the third step, the EUR 91 mn exchange differences (excluding goodwill retranslation) were allocated to the group and to the non-controlling interests, based on their proportionate share of SubCo's net assets. In our case, ParentCo's share of SubCo's net assets was 80%. Therefore:

- Exchange differences attributable to the group, excluding goodwill retranslation, were EUR 73 mn (= EUR 91 mn × 80%).
- Exchange differences attributable to the non-controlling interests were EUR 18 mn (= EUR 91 mn × 20%).

Step 4: Exchange Differences due to Goodwill   Next, the exchange differences related to the good-will were calculated as follows:

- exchange differences attributable to the group, due to goodwill retranslation, were EUR 15 mn (= USD 230 mn/1.2000 − USD 230 mn/1.3000).

Finally, the exchange differences were calculated as follows:

- exchange differences attributable to the group EUR 88 mn (= EUR 73 mn + EUR 15 mn);
- exchange differences attributable to the non-controlling interests were EUR 18 mn.

6.8 CASE STUDY: NET INVESTMENT HEDGE WITH A FORWARD

The aim of this case study is to illustrate the hedge accounting mechanics when hedging a net investment in a foreign operation with an FX forward.

Suppose that ABC, a group whose presentation currency is the EUR, had a net investment in a US subsidiary (SubCo) whose functional currency was the USD. Suppose that ABC's net investment in the subsidiary was USD 500 million as of 1 January 20X1. On that date, ABC entered into an FX forward to hedge its net investment in the subsidiary, with the following terms:

FX forward terms	
Start date	1 January 20X1
Counterparties	ABC and XYZ Bank
Maturity	31 January 20X2
ABC buys	EUR 400 million
ABC sells	USD 500 million
Forward rate	1.2500
Settlement	Cash settlement

ABC designated the FX forward as the hedging instrument in a net investment hedge. The effectiveness of the hedge was assessed on a forward basis (i.e., the forward points of the FX forward were included in the assessment of hedge effectiveness).

6.8.1 Hedging Relationship Documentation

At its inception, ABC documented the hedging relationship as follows:

Hedging relationship documentation	
Risk manage-ment objective and strategy for undertaking the hedge	The objective of the hedge is to protect, in the group's consolidated financial statements, the value of the USD 500 million investment in the US subsidiary SubCo against unfavourable movements in the EUR–USD exchange rate. This hedging objective is consistent with ABC's overall FX risk management strategy of reducing the variability of its shareholders' equity as stated in the group's hedging policy using FX forwards, FX options and foreign currency debt. The risk being hedged is the risk of changes in the EUR–USD exchange rate that will result in changes in the value of the group's net investment in SubCo when translated into EUR. The risk is hedged from 1 January 20X0 to 31 January 20X2

(continued overleaf)

	Hedging relationship documentation
Type of hedge	Net investment hedge
Hedged item	The first USD 500 million of the net assets of SubCo
Hedging instrument	The FX forward contract with reference number 012345 entered into by the parent company ParentCo. The main terms of the contract are a USD 500 million notional, a 1.25000 forward rate and a maturity on 31 January 20X2. The counterparty to the forward is XYZ Bank and the credit risk associated with this counterparty is considered to be very low
Hedge effectiveness assessment	See below

6.8.2 Hedge Effectiveness Assessment

Hedge effectiveness will be assessed by comparing cumulative changes in the fair value of the hedging instrument to cumulative changes in the forward value of the net investment. For the avoidance of doubt, the forward element of the forward contract will be part of the hedging instrument.

Hedge effectiveness will be assessed prospectively at hedging relationship inception and on an ongoing basis at least upon each reporting date and upon occurrence of a significant change in the circumstances affecting the hedge effectiveness requirements.

The hedging relationship will qualify for hedge accounting only if all the following criteria are met:

1) The hedging relationship consists only of eligible hedge items and hedging instruments. The hedge item is eligible as it is a foreign operation that exposes the entity to currency retranslation risk and it is reliably measurable. The hedging instrument is eligible as it is a derivative and it does not result in a net written option.
2) At hedge inception there is a formal designation and documentation of the hedging relationship and the entity's risk management objective and strategy for undertaking the hedge.
3) The hedging relationship is considered effective.

The hedging relationship will be considered effective if the following three requirements are met:

1) There is an economic relationship between the hedged item and the hedging instrument.
2) The effect of credit risk does not dominate the fair value changes in the hedging relationship.
3) The weightings of the hedged item and the hedging instrument (i.e., hedge ratio) are designated based on the quantities of hedged item and hedging instrument that the entity actually uses to meet the risk management objective, unless doing so would deliberately create ineffectiveness.

Whether there is an economic relationship between the hedged item and the hedging instrument would be assessed on a qualitative basis by comparing the critical terms of the hedging instrument and the hedged item. The critical terms considered would be the notional amount, the term and the underlying. The assessment will be complemented by a quantitative assessment using the scenario analysis method for one scenario in which the EUR–USD FX rate at the end of the hedging relationship (31 January 20X2) will be calculated by shifting the EUR–USD spot rate prevailing on the assessment date by +10%, and the change in fair value of both the hypothetical derivative and the hedging instrument compared.

The effective and ineffective amounts of the change in fair value of the hedging instrument will be computed by comparing the cumulative change in fair value of the hedging instrument with that of the hedged item. The effective amount will be recognised in the "translation differences" reserve in OCI. Any part of the cumulative change in fair value of the hedging instrument that does not offset a corresponding cumulative change in the fair value of the hedged item will be treated as ineffectiveness and recorded in profit or loss.

6.8.3 Hedge Effectiveness Assessment Performed at Hedge Inception

An effectiveness assessment was performed at inception and at each reporting date. The assessment also included the relationship hedge ratio and an identification of the sources of potential ineffectiveness, as follows.

The hedge qualified for hedge accounting as it met the three effectiveness requirements:

1) Because the terms of the hedging instrument and those of the expected cash flow closely matched and due to the low credit risk exposure to the counterparty of the forward contract, it was concluded that the hedging instrument and the hedged item had values that would generally move in opposite directions, and hence that an economic relationship existed between the hedged item and the hedging instrument. This conclusion was supported by a quantitative assessment, which consisted of one scenario analysis performed as follows. A EUR–USD spot rate at the end of the hedging relationship (1.3530) was simulated by shifting the EUR–USD spot rate prevailing on the assessment date (1.2300) by +10%. As shown in the table below, the change in fair value of the hedged item was expected to be largely offset by the change in fair value of the hedging instrument, corroborating that both elements had values that would generally move in opposite directions.

Scenario analysis assessment *(1)*		
	Hedging instrument	**Hedged item**
Nominal USD	500,000,000	500,000,000 –
Forward rate	1.2500 *(2)*	1.2520 *(2)* –
Nominal EUR	400,000,000	399,361,000 –
Nominal USD	500,000,000	500,000,000 –
Final rate	1.3530	1.3530 –
Value in EUR	369,549,000	369,549,000 –
Difference	30,451,000	<29,812,000> –
Discount factor	1.00	1.00 –
Fair value	30,451,000	<29,812,000> –
Degree of offset	**102.1%**	

Notes:

    (1) See Section 5.5.5 for an explanation of the formulas

    (2) The forward rate of the hedging instrument and the hedged item differed due to the absence of CVA
       in the hedged item

2) Because the credit rating of the counterparty to the hedging instrument was relatively strong (rated A+ by Standard & Poor's) the effect of credit risk did not dominate the value changes resulting from that economic relationship.

3) The hedge ratio designated (1:1) was the one actually used for risk management and it did not attempt to avoid recognising ineffectiveness. Therefore, it was determined that a hedge ratio of 1:1 was appropriate.

There were two main sources of potential ineffectiveness: firstly, a significant credit deterioration of the counterparty to the hedging instrument (XYZ Bank); and secondly, a reduction of the net assets of the hedged foreign operation below the notional of the hedging instrument.

6.8.4 Fair Values and Calculation of Effective and Ineffective Amounts

In order to calculate the hedge's effective and ineffective amounts, ABC computed the fair value of the forward and the hypothetical derivative.

Fair Valuation of the Hedging Instrument   The spot and forward FX rates, and the fair values of the forward contract (i.e., the hedging instrument) on the relevant dates were as follows:

Date	EUR–USD spot	Credit risk-free forward EUR–USD	Discount factor	Forward fair value *(1)*
1-Jan-20X1	1.2300	1.2520	—	-0-
31-Dec-20X1	1.2850	1.2900	0.997	12,366,000
31-Jan-20X2	1.3300	1.3300	1.000	24,060,000

Note:
(1) Forward fair value = [(500 mn/1.25 – 500 mn/(Forward rate)] × Discount factor – CVA.

The CVA was considered to be immaterial on 31 December 20X1 due to the forward's short remaining life, and it was zero on 31 January 20X2. The immateriality conclusion on 31 December 20X1 was arrived at as follows. According to the above table, on 31 December 20X1 the fair value of the FX forward, prior to any CVAs/DVAs, was EUR 12,366,000. On 31 December 20X1 ABC assessed whether the adjustment for counterparty credit risk had a material impact on the forward's fair valuation. The EUR 12,366,000 fair value was the present value of the FX forward's expected payoff discounted at Euribor. The forward had 1 month to expiry (i.e., 31 days) and Euribor for such maturity was trading at 2.70%. Therefore, the expected payoff of the option was calculated as the future value of EUR 12,366,000:

$$\text{Expected payoff} = 12{,}366{,}000 \times (1 + 0.027 \times 31/360) = 12{,}395{,}000 \text{ (rounded)}$$

One-month EUR-denominated CDs issued by XYZ Bank were trading at 10 basis points (i.e., 0.10%) over 1-month Euribor. The credit adjusted fair value of the forward was calculated as the present value of the expected payoff using XYZ Bank's credit spread:

$$\text{Credit adjusted fair value} = 12{,}395{,}000/[1 + (0.027{+}0.001) \times 31/360] = 12{,}365{,}000$$
$$\text{(rounded)}$$

The difference between the credit adjusted and the unadjusted fair values was only EUR <1,000> (= 12,365,000 – 12,366,000), deemed to be immaterial.

Fair Valuation of the Hedged Item on a Forward Basis The fair values of the hedged item on a forward basis at each relevant date were as follows:

Date	EUR–USD credit risk-free forward	Discount factor	Cumulative change in hedge item valuation (*)
1-Jan-20X1	1.2520		—
31-Dec-20X1	1.2900	0.9970	<11,729,000>
31-Jan-20X2	1.3300	1.0000	<23,421,000>

(*) [500 mn/(Forward rate) – (500 mn/1.2520)] × Discount factor

Effective and Ineffective Amounts The calculation of the effective and ineffective parts of the change in fair value of the hedging instrument was as follows (see Section 5.5.6 for an explanation of the calculations):

	31-Dec-20X1	31-Jan-20X2
Cumulative change in fair value of hedging instrument	12,366,000	24,060,000
Cumulative change in fair value of hypothetical derivative	11,729,000	23,421,000
Lower amount	11,729,000	23,421,000
Previous cumulative effective amount	Nil	11,729,000
Available amount	11,729,000	11,692,000
Period change in fair value of hedging instrument	12,366,000	11,694,000
Effective part	11,729,000	11,692,000
Ineffective part	637,000	2,000

Net Investment Retranslation Gains/Losses The net investment translation into EUR at each relevant date was as follows:

Date	Spot EUR–USD	Net investment (USD)	Net investment (EUR) (*)	Period retranslation difference (EUR)
1-Jan-20X1	1.2300	500,000,000	406,504,000	—
31-Dec-20X1	1.2850	500,000,000	389,105,000	<17,399,000>
31-Jan-20X2	1.3300	500,000,000	375,940,000	<13,165,000>

(*) Net investment in EUR = 500 million/Spot rate

6.8.5 Accounting Entries – Forward Points Included in Hedging Relationship

Assuming that ABC reported annually at year's end, the accounting entries related to the hedge were as follows:

1) To record the forward contract trade on 1 January 20X1

No entries in the financial statements were required as the fair value of the forward contract was nil.

2) To record the closing of the accounting period on 31 December 20X1

The net investment lost EUR 17,399,000 in value over the period when translated into EUR.

Translation differences (Equity)	17,399,000	
Net investment in subsidiary (Asset)		17,399,000

The change in the fair value of the FX forward since the last valuation was a EUR 12,366,000 gain, of which a EUR 11,729,000 gain was deemed to be effective and recorded in the translation differences account, while a EUR 637,000 gain was considered to be ineffective and recorded in profit or loss.

FX forward (Asset)	12,366,000	
Translation differences (Equity)		11,729,000
Other financial income (Profit or loss)		637,000

3) Entries on 31 January 20X2

The net investment lost EUR 13,165,000 in value over the period when translated into EUR.

Translation differences (Equity)	13,165,000	
Net investment in subsidiary (Asset)		13,165,000

The change in the fair value of the FX forward since the last valuation was a EUR 11,694,000 (=24,060,000 – 12,366,000) gain, of which a EUR 11,692,000 gain was deemed to be effective and recorded in the translation differences account, while a EUR 2,000 gain was considered to be ineffective and recorded in profit or loss.

FX forward (Asset)	11,694,000	
Translation differences (Equity)		11,692,000
Other financial income (Profit or loss)		2,000

The settlement of the FX forward resulted in the receipt of EUR 24,060,000.

Cash (Asset)	24,060,000	
FX forward (Asset)		24,060,000

Let us analyse the hedge's accounting implications:

Translation differences:
Due to net investment translation		< 30,564,000 >
Due to effective part of hedge		23,421,000
	Total	< 7,143,000>

Profit or loss:
Due to ineffective part of hedge		639,000
	Total	<6,504,000>

Several conclusions can be inferred from the table above:

- Firstly, despite being fully hedged, the "translation differences" account showed a deficit. In other words, the net investment translation loss was not completely offset by the hedge. This deficit was exactly the change in fair value of the FX forward due to the forward points.
- Secondly, EUR 639,000 was recorded in profit or loss because the hedge experienced some ineffectiveness. The main source of ineffectiveness was the credit risk associated with the counterparty to the FX forward, which caused a difference between the terms of the forward and the hypothetical derivative.
- Finally, the hedge was also highly effective because the net assets of the foreign operation remained USD 500 million. Had the subsidiary experienced a large loss for the year ending in December 20X1, causing the net assets of SubCo to be less than the hedged amount, the change in fair value corresponding to the excess notional would have been recorded in profit or loss.

6.8.6 Accounting Entries – Forward Points Excluded from Hedging Relationship

IFRS 9 allows the forward points of a forward contract to be excluded from a hedging relationship. Forward points derive from the interest rate differential between the currencies specified in the FX forward. Let us see what the accounting treatment would have been had the forward points of the FX forward been excluded from the hedging relationship. The change in the FX forward fair value would have had two components: one component due to changes in the spot rate and a second component due to changes in the forward points. The following table shows the changes in fair value of the FX forward at each relevant date:

	1-Jan-20X1	31-Dec-20X1	31-Jan-20X2
Spot EUR–USD	1.2300	1.2850	1.3300
Discount factor	—	0.997	1.000
Forward total fair value *(1)*	-0-	12,366,000	24,060,000
Change in total fair value (period)	—	12,366,000	11,694,000
Change in fair value due to spot (period) *(2)*	—	17,399,000	13,165,000
Change in fair value due to spot (cumulative)	—	17,399,000	30,564,000
Change in fair value due to forward (period) *(3)*	—	<5,033,000>	<1,471,000>

Notes:
(1) Calculated in Section 6.8.4
(2) Change in fair value due to spot = [(500 million/1.23 – 500 million/(Spot rate)] × Discount factor, assuming no CVA on this component
(3) Change in fair value due to forward points = Change in total fair value – Change in fair value due to spot

Effective and Ineffective Amounts   The calculation of the effective and ineffective parts of the change in fair value of the hedging instrument was as follows (see Section 5.5.6 for an explanation of the calculations):

	31-Dec-20X1	31-Jan-20X2
Cumulative change in fair value of hedging instrument	17,399,000	30,564,000
Cumulative change in translation value of hedged item (opposite sign)	17,399,000	30,564,000
Lower amount	17,399,000	30,564,000
Previous cumulative effective amount	Nil	17,399,000
Available amount	17,399,000	13,165,000
Period change in fair value of hedging instrument	17,399,000	13,165,000
Effective part	17,399,000	13,165,000
Ineffective part	-0-	-0-

Net Investment Retranslation Gains/Losses   The net investment translation into EUR at each relevant date was as follows:

Date	Spot EUR–USD	Net investment (USD)	Net investment (EUR) (*)	Period retranslation difference (EUR)
1-Jan-20X1	1.2300	500,000,000	406,504,000	—
31-Dec-20X1	1.2850	500,000,000	389,105,000	<17,399,000>
31-Jan-20X2	1.3300	500,000,000	375,940,000	<13,165,000>

(*) Net investment in EUR = 500 million/Spot rate

The accounting entries were as follows, assuming that ABC closed its books annually at year's end:

1) To record the forward contract trade on 1 January, 20X1

No entries in the financial statements were required as the fair value of the forward contract was zero.

2) To record the closing of the accounting period on 31 December 20X1

The net investment lost 17,399,000 in value over the period when translated into EUR. In practice all the net assets of SubCo would have been translated. In our case, the retranslation of just USD 500 million of net assets was assumed and summarised in a "net investment in subsidiary" figurative account for illustrative purposes.

Translation differences (Equity)	17,399,000	
Net investment in subsidiary (Asset)		17,399,000

The change in the fair value of the FX forward since the last valuation was a EUR 12,366,000 gain. This change in fair value was affected by changes in the spot FX rate and by changes in the forward points. The change in this fair value due to movements in the FX spot was a EUR

17,399,000 gain. All the change due to spot rates was considered effective, as its accumulated change was equal to the accumulated change in translated value of the net investment since hedge inception. The effective part was recorded in the translation differences account. The rest of the change in the FX forward fair value was due to changes in the forward points, a EUR 5,033,000 loss, and was recorded in profit or loss as it was excluded from the hedging relationship.

FX forward (Asset)	12,366,000	
Other financial expenses (Profit or loss)	5,033,000	
Translation differences (Equity)		17,399,000

3) Accounting entries on 31 January 20X2

The net investment lost EUR 13,165,000 in value over the period when translated into EUR.

Translation differences (Equity)	13,165,000	
Net investment in subsidiary (Asset)		13,165,000

The change in the fair value of the FX forward since the last valuation was a gain of EUR 11,694,000 (=24,060,000 − 12,366,000). The change in this fair value due to movements in the FX spot rate was a EUR 13,165,000 gain. All the change due to spot rates was considered effective and recorded in the translation differences account. The rest of the change in the FX forward fair value, a EUR 1,471,000 loss, was due to changes in the forward points and recorded in profit or loss.

FX forward (Asset)	11,694,000	
Other financial expenses (Profit or loss)	1,471,000	
Translation differences (Equity)		13,165,000

The settlement of the FX forward resulted in the receipt of EUR 24,060,000 cash.

Cash (Asset)	24,060,000	
FX forward (Asset)		24,060,000

Let us analyse the hedge's accounting implications:

Translation differences:
Due to net investment translation	< 30,564,000 >
Due to effective part of hedge	30,564,000
Total	Nil

Profit or loss:
Due to ineffective part of hedge	-0-
Due to change in forward points	<6,504,000>
Total	<6,504,000>

As we can see, the net investment translation loss was fully offset by the hedge. This perfect offset was due to the assumed absence of CVA in the spot component of the forward (i.e., all CVA charges were assigned to the forward points component). All the change in fair value of the forward contract due to changes in the instrument's forward points was recorded in profit or loss.

6.8.7 Implications of the FX Forward Points

A decision on whether or not to include the forward points of the FX forward in the hedging relationship may have a strong effect in the financial statements.

In our case, on 1 January 20X1 the market expected a depreciation of the USD relative to the EUR because USD interest rates were higher than EUR interest rates. The expected depreciation was EUR 6,504,000 (= 500 mn/1.25 – 500 mn/1.23). In other words, at inception of the hedge the FX market expected the value of the investment to deteriorate by that amount during the period from 1 January 20X1 to 31 January 20X2. By entering into the FX forward, ABC locked in this EUR 6,504,000 deterioration. The effects of the decision on whether or not to include the forward points in the hedging relationship were the following:

1) If ABC decided to include the forward points in the hedging relationship, most of the value associated with the forward points would end up in the translation differences account and not in profit or loss. As a result, the translation differences account would show a large EUR 7,143,000 deficit because the effective amount on the FX forward (EUR 23,421,000) was notably lower than the loss on the net investment (EUR 30,564,000), as shown in Figure 6.13. That deficit was mostly due to the forward points. Conversely, had the interest rate differential implied an appreciation of the USD relative to the EUR the effect would have been the opposite: the translation differences account would have shown a large surplus.

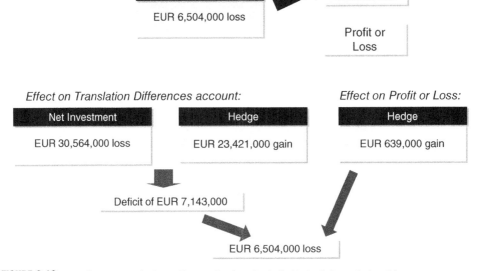

FIGURE 6.13   Net investment hedge – Forward points *included* in hedging relationship.

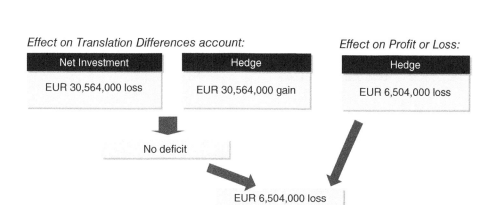

FIGURE 6.14   Net investment hedge – Forward points *excluded* from hedging relationship.

2) If ABC decided to exclude the forward points from the hedging relationship, all the value associated with the forward points (a EUR 6,504,000 loss) would end up in profit or loss, and not in the translation differences account. The translation differences account would show no deficit because all the loss on the net investment (EUR 30,564,000) was fully offset by the gain on the hedge, as shown in Figure 6.14.

In a situation like this case, in which the functional currency of the subsidiary is expected to depreciate relative to the presentation currency of the group, the inclusion of the forward points in a hedging relationship at first sight looks better because the deterioration in the value of the investment implied in the forward points will not show up in profit or loss. This, however, is a flawed conclusion. Remember that the amount deferred in the translation differences account will be recycled to profit or loss on disposal or liquidation of the subsidiary.

Let us imagine that ABC rolled the hedge over several years. Then the inclusion of the forward points in a hedging relationship could result in a large loss being deferred in equity. If one day ABC decided to sell the subsidiary, then the huge deficit would show up in profit or loss immediately. This reclassification could jeopardise an otherwise sound strategic decision to sell a subsidiary due to its negative accounting effects in profit or loss. Therefore, when the forward points imply a depreciation of the net investment value, the exclusion of the forward points from the hedging relationship is more conservative as there will be no significant deficit in the translation differences account. By excluding the forward points, the expected depreciation would be gradually recognised in profit or loss, as shown in Figure 6.15.

Other Remarks   On a consolidated basis the hedge worked notably well. Let us not forget that it was the parent company, ParentCo, that entered into the forward. In its stand-alone financial statements, unless ParentCo could apply hedge accounting, the forward would be fair valued

Forward points included in hedging relationship:

Profit or Loss	Translation Differences
No effect (until disposal of foreign operation)	Deficit of EUR 7,143,000

Forward points excluded from hedging relationship:

Profit or Loss	Translation Differences
Loss of EUR 6,504,000	No deficit

FIGURE 6.15   Net investment hedge – Summary of forward points impact.

with changes recognised through profit or loss, potentially causing volatility in ParentCo's profit or loss statement. An alternative for ParentCo was to designate its equity investment in SubCo as the hedged item in a fair value hedge of the exchange rate risk associated with the shares, provided that all of the conditions for hedge accounting were met.

6.9   CASE STUDY: NET INVESTMENT HEDGE USING FOREIGN CURRENCY DEBT

The aim of this case study is to illustrate the hedge of a foreign operation with a non-derivative financial instrument denominated in the functional currency of the foreign operation. This strategy is commonly used when the hedging horizon is long-term.

Suppose that ABC, a group whose presentation currency was the EUR, had a US subsidiary (SubCo) whose functional currency was the USD. Suppose further that ABC was looking to hedge a USD 500 million net investment in the US subsidiary for the next 3 years through the issuance of USD-denominated debt. Thus, on 1 January 20X0, ABC issued a 3-year fixed rate USD-denominated bond with the following terms:

USD-denominated bond terms	
Start date	1 January 20X0
Issuer	ABC
Maturity	31 December 20X2
Currency	USD
Notional	USD 500 million
Interest	5.20% annually, 30/360 basis

ABC designated the USD bond as the hedging instrument in a net investment hedge of its US subsidiary.

6.9.1   Hedging Relationship Documentation

At its inception, ABC documented the hedging relationship as follows:

Hedging relationship documentation

Risk management objective and strategy for undertaking the hedge	The objective of the hedge is to protect, in the group's consolidated financial statements, the value of the USD 500 million investment in the US subsidiary SubCo against unfavourable movements in the EUR–USD exchange rate. This hedging objective is consistent with ABC's overall FX risk management strategy of reducing the variability of its shareholders' equity as stated in the group's hedging policy using FX forwards, FX options and foreign currency debt. The risk being hedged is the risk of changes in the EUR–USD exchange rate that will result in changes in the value of the group's net investment in SubCo when translated into EUR. The risk is hedged from 1 January 20X0 to 31 December 20X2
Type of hedge	Net investment hedge
Hedged item	The first USD 500 million of the net assets of SubCo
Hedging instrument	The USD-denominated 3-year bond with reference number 016135. The bond has a USD 500 million notional and pays an annual 5.20% coupon
Hedge effectiveness assessment	See next

6.9.2 Hedge Effectiveness Assessment

Hedge effectiveness will be assessed by comparing the foreign currency gains and losses of the hedging instrument to the gains and losses on the translation amount of the net investment that are attributable to the hedged risk (i.e., changes in spot exchange rates). For the avoidance of doubt, hedge effectiveness assessment will be performed on a spot-spot basis. Accrued interest on the hedged item will be excluded from the hedging relationship.

Hedge effectiveness will be assessed prospectively at hedging relationship inception and on an ongoing basis at least upon each reporting date and upon occurrence of a significant change in the circumstances affecting the hedge effectiveness requirements.

The hedging relationship will qualify for hedge accounting only if all the following criteria are met:

1) The hedging relationship consists only of eligible hedge items and hedging instruments. The hedge item is eligible as it is a foreign operation that exposes the group to currency retranslation risk and it is reliably measurable. The hedging instrument is eligible as it is a non-derivative financial instrument.
2) At hedge inception there is a formal designation and documentation of the hedging relationship and the entity's risk management objective and strategy for undertaking the hedge.
3) The hedging relationship is considered effective.

The hedging relationship will be considered effective if the following three requirements are met:

1) There is an economic relationship between the hedged item and the hedging instrument.
2) The effect of credit risk does not dominate the fair value changes in the hedging relationship.
3) The weightings of the hedged item and the hedging instrument (i.e., hedge ratio) are designated based on the quantities of hedged item and hedging instrument that the entity actually uses to meet the risk management objective, unless doing so would deliberately create ineffectiveness.

Whether there is an economic relationship between the hedged item and the hedging instrument will be assessed on a qualitative basis by comparing the critical terms of the hedging instrument and the hedged item. The critical terms considered will be the notional amount, the term and the underlying. The qualitative assessment will be supplemented with a quantitative assessment using the scenario analysis method for one scenario in which a final spot rate will be calculated by shifting the EUR–USD spot rate prevailing on the assessment by +10%, and the variation in fair values of both the hedging instrument and the hedged item compared.

The effective and ineffective amounts of the change in fair value of the hedging instrument will be computed by comparing the cumulative change in fair value of the hedging instrument with that of the hedged item. The effective amount will be recognised in the "translation differences" reserve in OCI. Any part of the cumulative change in fair value of the hedging instrument that does not offset a corresponding cumulative change in the translation amount of the hedged item will be treated as ineffectiveness and recorded in profit or loss.

6.9.3 Hedge Effectiveness Assessment Performed at Hedge Inception

An effectiveness assessment was performed at inception and at each reporting date. The assessment also included the relationship hedge ratio and an identification of the sources of potential ineffectiveness, as follows:

The hedge qualified for hedge accounting as it met the three effectiveness requirements:

1) Because the critical terms (such as the nominal amount, maturity and underlying) of the hedging instrument and the hedged item matched, it was concluded that the hedging instrument and the hedged item had values that would generally move in the opposite directions, and hence that an economic relationship existed between the hedged item and the hedging instrument. This conclusion was supported by the quantitative assessment documented below.

2) Because the credit rating of counterparty to the hedging instrument was relatively strong (rated A+ by Standard & Poor's) the effect of credit risk did not dominate the value changes resulting from that economic relationship.

3) The hedge ratio designated (1:1) was the one actually used for risk management and it did not attempt to avoid recognising ineffectiveness. Therefore, it was determined that a hedge ratio of 1:1 was appropriate.

A test EUR–USD spot rate (1.3750) was simulated by shifting the EUR–USD spot rate prevailing on the assessment date (1.2500) by +10%. As shown in the table below, the change in fair value of the hedged item was expected to be largely offset by the change in fair value of the hedging instrument, corroborating that both elements had values that would generally move in opposite directions.

Scenario Analysis Assessment		
	Hedging Instrument	**Hedged Item**
Nominal USD	500,000,000	500,000,000
Initial spot rate	1.2500	1.2500
Initial EUR value	400,000,000	400,000,000
Nominal USD	500,000,000	500,000,000

	Scenario Analysis Assessment	
	Hedging Instrument	**Hedged Item**
Shifted spot rate	1.3750	1.3750
Final EUR value	363,636,000	363,636,000
Difference	36,364,000	<36,364,000>
Fair value change	36,364,000	<36,364,000>
	Degree of offset	**100.0%**

There were two are the main sources of potential ineffectiveness: firstly, a significant credit deterioration of the counterparty to the hedging instrument (XYZ Bank); and secondly, a reduction of the net assets of the hedged foreign operation below the hedging instrument notional.

6.9.4 Other Relevant Information

The net investment translation into EUR was calculated using the EUR–USD spot rate at each relevant date:

Date	Spot EUR–USD	Net Investment (USD)	Net Investment (EUR) (*)	Period Retranslation Difference (EUR)
1-Jan-20X0	1.2500	500,000,000	400,000,000	—
31-Dec-20X0	1.2700	500,000,000	393,701,000	<6,299,000>
31-Dec-20X1	1.3100	500,000,000	381,679,000	<12,022,000>
31-Dec-20X2	1.2900	500,000,000	387,597,000	5,918,000

(*) Net investment in EUR = 500 million/Spot rate

The fair value change of the foreign debt due to movements in the EUR–USD FX rate at each relevant date was as follows:

Date	EUR–USD spot rate	Bond carrying amount (USD)	Bond carrying amount (EUR) (*)	Period fair value change (EUR)
1-Jan-20X0	1.2500	500,000,000	400,000,000	—
31-Dec-20X0	1.2700	500,000,000	393,701,000	6,299,000
31-Dec-20X1	1.3100	500,000,000	381,679,000	12,022,000
31-Dec-20X2	1.2900	500,000,000	387,597,000	<5,918,000>

(*) Bond carrying amount (EUR) = Bond carrying amount (USD)/EUR–USD spot rate

The annual coupon flows that ABC paid during the life of the bond were USD 26 million (= USD 500 mn × 5.20%). The interest expense was translated at the average rate for the annual interest period as interest accrued over time. At each reporting date there was no accrued interest. The coupon payment was translated at the EUR–USD spot rate prevailing on payment date. Any difference between the translated amounts of interest expense and coupon payments were recognised in the "other financial income/expenses" line of profit or loss.

Date	Spot EUR–USD	Annual Average Spot EUR–USD	Coupon Payment (USD)	Coupon Payment (EUR)	Interest Expense (EUR)
31-Dec-20X0	1.2700	1.2650	26,000,000 (1)	20,472,000 (2)	20,553,000 (3)
31-Dec-20X1	1.3100	1.2840	26,000,000	19,847,000	20,249,000
31-Dec-20X2	1.2900	1.3020	26,000,000	20,155,000	19,969,000

Notes:
>   (1) Coupon payment USD = USD 500 mn × 5.20% = 26 mn
>   (2) Coupon payment EUR = USD coupon payment/Spot EUR–USD = 26 mn/1.2700
>   (3) Interest expense = Coupon payment/Annual Average spot = 26 mn/1.2650

6.9.5 Accounting Entries

In the case of a net investment hedge accounting using a bond (or a loan), only the changes in the bond's amortised cost and accrued interest arising from movements in the FX spot rate are reported in the same manner as the translation adjustment associated with the net investment. In this case, as the functional currency of the subsidiary and the currency denomination of the debt matched, and as the notional amount of the debt did not exceeded the net investment hedged amount, no hedge ineffectiveness was recognised in profit or loss.

Assuming that ABC closed its books annually at year's end, the accounting entries related to the hedge were as follows:

1) To record the bond issuance on 1 January 20X0

No transaction costs were incurred relating to the USD bond issuance. As a result, ABC proceeds from the bond issuance were USD 500 million. The debt was recognised as a financial liability at amortised costs. Assuming that ABC immediately converted the raised USD into EUR at the then prevailing EUR–USD spot rate (1.2500), the EUR proceeds from the bond were EUR 400 million (=500 million/1.25).

Cash (Asset)	400,000,000	
Financial debt (Liability)		400,000,000

2) To record the closing of the accounting period on 31 December 20X0

The net investment lost EUR 6,299,000 in value over the period when translated into EUR. In practice all the net assets of SubCo would have been translated. In our case, the retranslation of USD 500 million of net assets is assumed and summarised in a "net investment in subsidiary" figurative account for illustrative purposes.

Translation differences (Equity)	6,299,000	
Net investment in subsidiary (Asset)		6,299,000

The change in the bond's carrying amount due to the movement of the EUR–USD exchange rate was a gain of EUR 6,299,000. As the hedge had no ineffectiveness, all this change was recorded in the translation differences account:

Financial debt (Liability)	6,299,000	
Translation differences (Equity)		6,299,000

Under the bond, ABC paid on 31 December 20X0 a USD 26 million coupon after converting EUR 20,472,000 into USD on the FX spot market. The bond's USD interest expense was translated using the average EUR–USD rate for the annual interest period as interest accrued over time, resulting in EUR 20,553,000. The USD 26 million coupon payment was translated into EUR using the EUR–USD spot rate on the coupon payment date, resulting in EUR 20,472,000. The difference in translation rates gave rise to a EUR 81,000 gain.

Interest expense (Profit or loss)	20,553,000	
Other operating income (Profit or loss)		81,000
Cash (Asset)		20,472,000

3) To record the closing of the accounting period on 31 December 20X1

Following a similar approach to the accounting entries made on 31 December 20X0:

Translation differences (Equity)	12,022,000	
Net investment in subsidiary (Asset)		12,022,000
Financial debt (Liability)	12,022,000	
Translation differences (Equity)		12,022,000
Interest expense (Profit or loss)	20,249,000	
Other operating income (Profit or loss)		402,000
Cash (Asset)		19,847,000

4) To record the closing of the accounting period on 31 December 20X2

On 31 December 20X2, ABC repaid the USD 500 million bond principal. ABC exchanged the USD 500 million at the then prevailing EUR–USD spot rate (1.2900) for EUR 387,597,000 (=500 mn/1.29). Following a similar approach to the accounting entries made on 31 December 20X1, and adding the bond repayment:

Net investment in subsidiary (Asset)	5,918,000	
Translation differences (Equity)		5,918,000
Translation differences (Equity)	5,918,000	
Financial debt (Liability)		5,918,000

(continued overleaf)

Interest expense (Profit or loss)	19,969,000	
Other operating expenses (Profit or loss)	186,000	
Cash (Asset)		20,155,000
Financial debt (Liability)	387,597,000	
Cash (Asset)		387,597,000

6.9.6 Final Remarks

In our case the hedge performed very well, as the decline in value of the net investment due to the depreciation of the USD relative to the EUR was completely offset by the change in the carrying value of the USD debt (see Figure 6.16). However, two comments are worth noting:

- ABC's profit or loss statement was exposed to declines in the EUR–USD FX rate arising from the coupon payments.
- At bond maturity, ABC had to repay the USD 500 million notional. ABC had to exchange in the FX spot market an amount of EUR equivalent to USD 500 million. As a result, a severe decline in the EUR–USD FX rate could have had strong implications for the entity's cash resources.

FIGURE 6.16   Net investment hedge – Summary of impacts.

6.10 NET INVESTMENT HEDGING WITH CROSS-CURRENCY SWAPS

I now turn to the accounting treatment of net investment hedges using cross-currency swaps. CCSs are frequently used when the hedging horizon is long-term, as an alternative to issuing foreign debt.

Suppose that ABC, a group whose presentation currency was the EUR, had a net investment in a US subsidiary whose functional currency was the USD. Suppose further that ABC was looking to hedge its net investment in the US subsidiary for the next 3 years through a EUR–USD CCS. ABC had four choices (see Chapter 2 for a more detailed description of CCSs):

1) To enter into a pay floating/receive floating CCS. ABC would pay annually USD 12-month Libor on a USD nominal and receive annually 12-month Euribor on a EUR nominal.
2) To enter into a pay fixed/receive floating CCS. ABC would pay annually a fixed rate on a USD nominal and receive annually 12-month Euribor on a EUR nominal.

3) To enter into a pay floating/receive fixed CCS. ABC would pay annually USD 12-month Libor on a USD nominal and receive annually a fixed rate on a EUR nominal.

4) To enter into a pay fixed/receive fixed CCS. Under this choice, ABC would pay annually a fixed rate on a USD nominal and receive annually a fixed rate on a EUR nominal.

At maturity there would be a EUR cash payment or receipt calculated as the difference between the EUR nominal and the EUR value of the USD nominal. The fair value of a EUR–USD CCS is exposed to four different market risks: the movement in the EUR–USD spot rate, the movement of the USD interest rate curve, the movement of the EUR interest rate curve and the movement of the basis.

In a pay USD floating/receive EUR floating CCS, the fair value change due to interest rate movements is usually small relative to the fair value change due to the FX rate movement. As a consequence, the change in fair value of the CCS would primarily arise from changes in the EUR–USD spot rate. Because the value of the net investment being hedged is determined by translating the amount of the net investment into the group's presentation currency using the spot exchange rate, this hedge would be highly effective if well constructed.

In a pay USD fixed/receive EUR fixed CCS, the changes in its fair value due to movements in both interest rate curves can be substantial. This type of CCS equates to a string of FX forwards. Because effectiveness can be calculated using forward rates, this hedge would be highly effective if well constructed.

In a pay USD fixed/receive EUR floating CCS, the exposure to the USD interest rate curve can be important. Similarly, in a pay USD floating/receive EUR fixed CCS, the exposure to the EUR interest rate curve can be large. Because there could be significant differences between the change in fair value of these CCSs and the change in the net investment based in either spot rates or forward rates, substantial ineffectiveness may arise.

As a result, net investment hedges using floating-to-floating CCSs or fixed-to-fixed CCSs are expected to be highly effective. Substantial ineffectiveness may arise if either fixed-to-floating CCSs or floating-to-fixed CCSs are used as hedging instruments.

CCS	Expected ineffectiveness
Pay USD fixed/receive EUR fixed	Minimal (excluding basis)
Pay USD floating/receive EUR floating	Minimal (excluding basis)
Pay USD floating/receive EUR fixed	Potentially significant
Pay USD fixed/receive EUR floating	Potentially significant

Regarding the basis, IFRS 9 allows an entity to recognise changes in the basis element of a CCS temporarily in equity to the extent that these changes relate to the hedged item. This treatment is similar to the forward element of a forward contract.

6.11 CASE STUDY: NET INVESTMENT HEDGE WITH A FLOATING-TO-FLOATING CROSS-CURRENCY SWAP

The aim of this case study is to illustrate the hedge of a net investment in a foreign operation with a floating-to-floating CCS. ABC, a group with presentation currency the EUR, decided to enter into this type of CCS because the USD interest rate curve was markedly steep. When curves are very steep, short-term rates are notably lower than long-term rates, and entities paying a floating rate experience substantial savings relative to paying the fixed rate during the initial interest periods.

Suppose that ABC's objective was to hedge USD 500 million of its investment in its US subsidiary SubCo over the next 3 years. The terms of the CCS were as follows:

Cross-currency swap terms	
Start date	1 January 20X0
Counterparties	ABC and XYZ Bank
Maturity	31 December 20X2
EUR notional	EUR 400 million
USD notional	USD 500 million
Implied FX rate	1.2500
ABC pays	USD 12-month Libor + 10 bps annually, actual/360 basis, on the USD nominal
ABC receives	12-month Euribor annually, actual/360 basis, on the EUR nominal
Final exchange	On maturity date, there would be a EUR cash settlement amount based on the EUR–USD fixing prevailing on such date (i.e., there would be no notionals exchange)
	Settlement amount = 400 mn – 500 mn/EUR–USD fixing
	If the settlement amount were positive, ABC would receive the settlement amount
	If the settlement amount were negative, ABC would pay the absolute value of the settlement amount

It is important to note that the CCS did not have the usual exchange of principals at maturity. Instead the CCS had a "cash settlement" provision. The reason for this was that since ABC was not planning to sell the US subsidiary on the CCS maturity date, ABC was not interested on that date in selling USD 500 million and buying EUR 400 million. Instead ABC would receive (or pay) compensation equivalent to the depreciation (or appreciation) of its investment in the US subsidiary.

ABC designated the CCS as the hedging instrument in a net investment hedge.

6.11.1 Hedging Relationship Documentation

At its inception, ABC documented the hedging relationship as follows:

Hedging relationship documentation	
Risk management objective and strategy for undertaking the hedge	The objective of the hedge is to protect, in the group's consolidated financial statements, the value of the USD 500 million investment in the US subsidiary SubCo against unfavourable movements in the EUR–USD exchange rate.
	This hedging objective is consistent with ABC's overall FX risk management strategy of reducing the variability of its shareholders' equity as stated in the group's hedging policy using FX forwards, FX options and foreign currency debt.
	The risk being hedged is the risk of changes in the EUR–USD exchange rate that will result in changes in the value of the group's net investment in SubCo when translated into EUR. The risk is hedged from 1 January 20X0 to 31 December 20X2

Hedging relationship documentation	
Type of hedge	Net investment hedge
Hedged item	The first USD 500 million of the net assets of SubCo
Hedging instrument	The pay USD floating and receive EUR floating cross-currency swap with reference number 016795. The notionals are USD 500 million and EUR 400 million, the entity pays annually 12-month Euribor on the EUR leg and receives annually USD 12-month Libor on the USD leg, and the term is 3 years. The counterparty to the CCS is XYZ Bank and the credit risk associated with this counterparty is considered to be very low
Hedge effectiveness assessment	See below

6.11.2 Hedge Effectiveness Assessment

Hedge effectiveness will be assessed by comparing the change in fair value of the hedging instrument to the foreign currency gains and losses on the net investment that are attributable to the hedged risk (i.e., changes in spot exchange rates).

Hedge effectiveness will be assessed prospectively at hedging relationship inception and on an ongoing basis at least upon each reporting date and upon occurrence of a significant change in the circumstances affecting the hedge effectiveness requirements.

The hedging relationship will qualify for hedge accounting only if all the following criteria are met:

1) The hedging relationship consists only of eligible hedge items and hedging instruments. The hedge item is eligible as it is a foreign operation that exposes the group to currency retranslation risk and it is reliably measurable. The hedging instrument is eligible as it is a derivative instrument other than a written option.
2) At hedge inception there is a formal designation and documentation of the hedging relationship and the entity's risk management objective and strategy for undertaking the hedge.
3) The hedging relationship is considered effective.

The hedging relationship will be considered effective if the following three requirements are met:

1) There is an economic relationship between the hedged item and the hedging instrument.
2) The effect of credit risk does not dominate the fair value changes in the hedging relationship.
3) The weightings of the hedged item and the hedging instrument (i.e., hedge ratio) are designated based on the quantities of hedged item and hedging instrument that the entity actually uses to meet the risk management objective, unless doing so would deliberately create ineffectiveness.

Whether there is an economic relationship between the hedged item and the hedging instrument will be assessed on a qualitative basis by comparing the critical terms of the hedging instrument and the hedged item. The critical terms considered will be the notional amount, the term and the underlying.

The effective and ineffective amounts of the change in fair value of the hedging instrument will be computed by comparing the cumulative change in fair value of the hedging instrument with that of the hedged item. The effective amount will be recognised in the "translation differences" reserve in OCI. Any part of the cumulative change in fair value of the hedging instrument that does not offset a corresponding cumulative change in the fair value of the hedged item will be treated as ineffectiveness and recorded in profit or loss.

6.11.3 Hedge Effectiveness Assessment Performed at Hedge Inception

An effectiveness assessment was performed at inception and at each reporting date. The assessment also included the relationship hedge ratio and an identification of the sources of potential ineffectiveness.

The hedge qualified for hedge accounting as it met the three effectiveness requirements:

1) The critical terms (such as the nominal amount, maturity and underlying) of the hedging instrument and the hedged item matched. Although the CCS had interest payments/ receipts not present in the net investment, the change in fair value of the CCS was expected to be largely offset by the change in the translation amount of the net investment due to (i) the floating profile of both legs of the CCS and (ii) the concurrence of the dates on which the CCS's intermediate payments/receipts were made and the reporting dates. As a result it was concluded that the hedging instrument and the hedged item had values that would generally move in opposite directions, and hence that an economic relationship existed between the hedged item and the hedging instrument.
2) Because the credit rating of counterparty to the hedging instrument was relatively strong (rated A+ by Standard & Poor's) the effect of credit risk did not dominate the value changes resulting from that economic relationship.
3) The hedge ratio designated (1:1) was the one actually used for risk management and it did not attempt to avoid recognising ineffectiveness. Therefore, it was determined that a hedge ratio of 1:1 was appropriate.

There were three main sources of potential ineffectiveness: firstly, a significant credit deterioration of the counterparty to the hedging instrument (XYZ Bank); secondly, a reduction of the net assets of the hedged foreign operation below the hedging instrument notional; and finally, a substantial increase in the CCS basis.

6.11.4 Other Relevant Information

The net investment translation into EUR was calculated using the EUR–USD spot rate at each relevant date as follows:

Date	Spot EUR–USD	Net investment (USD)	Net investment (EUR) (*)	Period retranslation difference (EUR)
1-Jan-X0	1.2500	500,000,000	400,000,000	—
31-Dec-X0	1.2700	500,000,000	393,701,000	<6,299,000>
31-Dec-X1	1.3100	500,000,000	381,679,000	<12,022,000>
31-Dec-X2	1.2900	500,000,000	387,597,000	5,918,000

(*) Net investment in EUR = 500 million/Spot rate

The fair values of the CCS, including credit valuation adjustments and excluding accrued interest, at each reporting date were as follows:

Date	CCS fair value (EUR)	Period fair value change
31-Dec-X0	6,335,000	6,335,000
31-Dec-X1	18,502,000	12,167,000
31-Dec-X2	12,403,000	<6,099,000>

The effective and ineffective parts of the change in fair value of the CCS were the following (see Section 5.5.6 for an explanation of the calculations):

	31-Dec-X0	31-Dec-X1	31-Dec-X2
Cumulative change in fair value of hedging instrument	6,335,000	18,502,000	12,403,000
Cumulative change in translation value of hedged item (opposite sign)	6,299,000	18,321,000	12,403,000
Lower amount	6,299,000	18,321,000	12,403,000
Previous cumulative effective amount	Nil	6,299,000	18,321,000
Available amount	6,299,000	12,022,000	<5,918,000>
Period change in fair value of hedging instrument	6,335,000	12,167,000	<6,099,000>
Effective part	6,299,000	12,022,000	<5,918,00>
Ineffective part	36,000	145,000	<181,000>

The interest flows/expenses related to the USD leg of the CCS were as follows:

Date	Spot EUR–USD	Annual average EUR–USD	USD Libor rate	Interest payments (USD)	Interest expense (EUR)	Interest payment (EUR)
31-Dec-X0	1.2700	1.2650	5.20%	26,868,000 (1)	21,240,000 (2)	21,156,000 (3)
31-Dec-X1	1.3100	1.2840	5.50%	28,389,000	22,110,000	21,671,000
31-Dec-X2	1.2900	1.3020	5.70%	29,403,000	22,583,000	22,793,000

Notes:

(1) Interest payment (USD) = USD 500 million $\times$ (5.20%+0.10%) $\times$ 365/360
(2) Interest expense (EUR) = Interest payment (USD)/Annual average FX rate = 26,868,000/1.2650
(3) Interest payment (EUR) = Interest payment (USD)/Spot FX rate = 26,868,000/1.2700

The interest flows/expenses related to the EUR leg of the CCS were as follows:

Date	EUR Euribor Rate	Interest received/ income (EUR)
31-Dec-X0	4.00%	16,222,000 (*)
31-Dec-X1	4.20%	17,033,000
31-Dec-X2	4.40%	17,844,000

(*) Interest received = EUR 400 million $\times$ 4.00% $\times$ 365/360

6.11.5 Accounting Entries

Assuming that ABC closed its books annually at year's end, the accounting entries related to the hedge were as follows.

1) To record the CCS trade on 1 January 20X0

No entries in the financial statements were required as the fair value of the CCS was zero.

2) To record the closing of the accounting period on 31 December 20X0

The net investment lost EUR 6,299,000 in value over the period when translated into EUR. In practice all the net assets of SubCo would have been translated. In our case, the retranslation of just USD 500 million of net assets are assumed and summarised in a "net investment in subsidiary" figurative account for illustrative purposes.

Translation differences (Equity)	6,299,000	
Net investment in subsidiary (Asset)		6,299,000

The CCS fair value change, excluding accrued interest, was a gain of EUR 6,335,000. The effective part (EUR 6,299,000) was recognised in the translation differences account. The ineffective part (EUR 36,000) was recognised in profit or loss.

Cross-currency swap (Asset)	6,335,000	
Other financial income (Profit or loss)		36,000
Translation differences (Equity)		6,299,000

Under the USD leg of the CCS, ABC paid the equivalent of EUR 21,156,000 and recognised a EUR 21,240,000 interest expense. The EUR 84,000 difference between these amounts was recognised in profit or loss. Under the EUR leg of the CCS, ABC received EUR 16,222,000, recognised as interest income.

Financial expenses (Profit or loss)	21,240,000	
USD cash (Asset)		21,156,000
Other financial income (Profit or loss)		84,000
EUR cash (Asset)	16,222,000	
Financial income (Profit or loss)		16,222,000

3) To record the closing of the accounting period on 31 December 20X1

Translation differences (Equity)	12,022,000	
Net investment in subsidiary (Asset)		12,022,000

Cross-currency swap (Asset)	12,167,000	
Other financial income (Profit or loss)		145,000
Translation differences (Equity)		12,022,000
Financial expenses (Profit or loss)	22,110,000	
USD cash (Asset)		21,671,000
Other financial income (Profit or loss)		439,000
EUR cash (Asset)	17,033,000	
Financial income (Profit or loss)		17,033,000

4) To record the closing of the accounting period on 31 December 20X2

Net investment in subsidiary (Asset)	5,918,000	
Translation differences (Equity)		5,918,000
Translation differences (Equity)	5,918,000	
Other financial expenses (Profit or loss)	181,000	
Cross-currency swap (Asset)		6,099,000
Financial expenses (Profit or loss)	22,583,000	
Other financial expenses (Profit or loss)	210,000	
USD cash (Asset)		22,793,000
EUR cash (Asset)	17,844,000	
Financial income (Profit or loss)		17,844,000

Additionally on 31 December 20X2, a settlement amount was received under the CCS related to the notionals. The EUR–USD spot rate on that date was 1.2900. ABC received EUR 12,403,000 (= EUR 400 mn – USD 500 mn/1.2900):

EUR cash (Asset)	12,403,000	
Cross-currency swap (Asset)		12,403,000

6.11.6 Final Remarks

In our case the hedge performed very well, as the decline in value of the net investment due to the depreciation of the USD relative to the EUR was completely offset by the change in fair value of the CCS. Several comments are worth noting:

- The pay floating/receive floating CCS is an effective way to implement long-term hedges of net investments in foreign operations.
- ABC's profit or loss statement was *temporarily* exposed to the ineffective part of the hedge (i.e., to the excess of the CCS fair value change relative to the net investment

retranslation gain/loss). Ineffectiveness was due to changes in the CCS basis and to credit valuation adjustments. In our case, ABC's profit or loss was not exposed to changes in the fair value of the CCS due to movements in the USD and EUR interest rate curves because both legs were linked to floating interest rates and the absence of accrued interest. In reality, slight ineffectiveness may arise when the ends of the CCS interest periods do not coincide with the reporting dates.

■ In our case, the sum of all the ineffective parts during the life of the CCS was zero. In other words, the translation differences account showed no deficit because the changes in the net investment translation were perfectly offset by the fair value changes in the CCS.

■ IFRS 9 allows an entity to choose whether to exclude the basis component of a CCS from a hedging relationship and to recognise changes in this component in equity to the extent that they relate to hedged item.

■ At CCS maturity, ABC received EUR 12,403,000 in cash. In this case, the outcome was very favourable to ABC, but it could have been the other way around. In other words, a hedge of a large investment in a foreign operation through a CCS may have strong implications in an entity's cash resources.

■ The amount in the translation differences account will be reclassified from equity to profit or loss on disposal or liquidation of SubCo.

6.12 CASE STUDY: NET INVESTMENT HEDGE WITH A FIXED-TO-FIXED CROSS-CURRENCY SWAP

The aim of this case study is to illustrate the hedge of a net investment in a foreign operation with a fixed-to-fixed CCS. Assume that ABC's objective was to hedge USD 500 million of its investment in its US subsidiary SubCo over the next 3 years. The group's presentation currency was the EUR. SubCo's functional currency was the USD. The terms of the CCS were as follows:

Cross-currency swap terms	
Start date	1 January 20X0
Counterparties	ABC and XYZ Bank
Maturity	31 December 20X2
EUR notional	EUR 400 million
USD notional	USD 500 million
Implied FX rate	1.2500
ABC pays	6.10% annually, 30/360 basis, on the USD nominal
ABC receives	5% annually, 30/360 basis, on the EUR nominal
Final exchange	On maturity date, a EUR cash settlement amount (the "settlement amount") will be calculated based on the EUR–USD fixing (the "fixing") prevailing on such date (i.e., there would be no notional exchange). Settlement amount = EUR 400 mn – 500 mn/Fixing. If settlement amount is positive, ABC receives the settlement amount. If the settlement amount is negative, ABC pays the absolute value of the settlement amount.

As explained in the previous case, the CCS had a "cash settlement" provision to avoid exchanging principals at maturity. ABC designated the CCS as the hedging instrument in a net investment hedge.

An important element of the hedge is the definition of the amount of net assets being hedged. There are two alternative views within the accounting community on defining this amount, when hedged with fixed-to-fixed CCSs:

- the foreign currency notional of the CCS (in our case, USD 500 million);
- the sum of the undiscounted cash flows on the foreign currency leg of the CCS (in our case, USD 591.5 million ($= 500$ mn $+ 3 \times 6.10\% \times 500$ mn)).

In this case, I used the former alternative.

6.12.1 Hedging Relationship Documentation

ABC designated the CCS as the hedging instrument in a net investment hedge. At its inception, ABC documented the hedging relationship as follows:

Hedging relationship documentation	
Risk management objective and strategy for undertaking the hedge	The objective of the hedge is to protect, in the group's consolidated financial statements, the value of the USD 500 million investment in the US subsidiary SubCo against unfavourable movements in the EUR–USD exchange rate.
	This hedging objective is consistent with ABC's overall FX risk management strategy of reducing the variability of its shareholders' equity as stated in the group's hedging policy using FX forwards, FX options and foreign currency debt.
	The risk being hedged is the risk of changes in the EUR–USD exchange rate that will result in changes in the value of the group's net investment in SubCo when translated into EUR. The risk is hedged from 1 January 20X0 to 31 December 20X2
Type of hedge	Net investment hedge
Hedged item	The first USD 500 million of the net assets of SubCo
Hedging instrument	The pay USD fixed and receive EUR fixed cross-currency swap with reference number 016796. The notionals are USD 500 million and EUR 400 million, the interest payments are USD 6.10% and EUR 5.00%, and the term is 3 years. The counterparty to the CCS is XYZ Bank and the credit risk associated with this counterparty is considered to be very low
Hedge effectiveness assessment	See below

6.12.2 Hedge Effectiveness Assessment

Hedge effectiveness will be assessed by comparing changes in the fair value of the hedging instrument to changes in the fair value of a hypothetical derivative. In this hedging relationship, the terms of the hypothetical derivative mirror those of the hedging instrument except, due to the absence of CVA risk, the EUR leg fixed rate which is 4.99%.

Hedge effectiveness will be assessed prospectively at hedging relationship inception and on an ongoing basis at least upon each reporting date and upon occurrence of a significant change in the circumstances affecting the hedge effectiveness requirements.

The hedging relationship will qualify for hedge accounting only if all the following criteria are met:

1) The hedging relationship consists only of eligible hedge items and hedging instruments. The hedge item is eligible as it is a foreign operation that exposes the group to currency retranslation risk and it is reliably measurable. The hedging instrument is eligible as it is a derivative instrument other than a written option.
2) At hedge inception there is a formal designation and documentation of the hedging relationship and the entity's risk management objective and strategy for undertaking the hedge.
3) The hedging relationship is considered effective.

The hedging relationship will be considered effective if the following three requirements are met:

1) There is an economic relationship between the hedged item and the hedging instrument.
2) The effect of credit risk does not dominate the fair value changes in the hedging relationship.
3) The weightings of the hedged item and the hedging instrument (i.e., hedge ratio) are designated based on the quantities of hedged item and hedging instrument that the entity actually uses to meet the risk management objective, unless doing so would deliberately create ineffectiveness.

Whether there is an economic relationship between the hedged item and the hedging instrument will be assessed on a qualitative basis by comparing the critical terms of the hedging instrument and the hypothetical derivative. The critical terms considered will be the notional amounts, the interest periods and the fixed rates. The assessment will be complemented by a quantitative assessment using the scenario analysis method for one scenario in which a EUR–USD exchange rate will be simulated by shifting the spot price prevailing on the assessment date by +10%, and the change in fair value of the hedging instrument with that of the hypothetical derivative compared.

The effective and ineffective amounts of the change in fair value of the hedging instrument will be computed by comparing the cumulative change in fair value of the hedging instrument with that of the hypothetical derivative. The effective amount will be recognised in the "translation differences" reserve in OCI. Any part of the cumulative change in fair value of the hedging instrument that does not offset a corresponding cumulative change in the fair value of the hypothetical derivative will be treated as ineffectiveness and recorded in profit or loss.

6.12.3 Hedge Effectiveness Assessment Performed at Hedge Inception

An effectiveness assessment was performed at inception and at each reporting date. The assessment also included the relationship hedge ratio and an identification of the sources of potential ineffectiveness.

The hedge qualified for hedge accounting as it met the three effectiveness requirements:

1) Because the critical terms (such as notional amounts, interest periods and fixed rates) of the hedging instrument and the hypothetical derivative matched (or almost matched) it was concluded that the hedging instrument and the hedged item had values that would generally move in opposite directions, and hence that an economic relationship existed

between the hedged item and the hedging instrument. This conclusion was supported by the qualitative analysis documented below.

2) Because the credit rating of counterparty to the hedging instrument was relatively strong (rated A+ by Standard & Poor's) the effect of credit risk did not dominate the value changes that result from that economic relationship.

3) The hedge ratio designated (1:1) was the one actually used for risk management and it did not attempt to avoid recognising ineffectiveness. Therefore, it was determined that a hedge ratio of 1:1 was appropriate.

A test EUR–USD spot rate (1.3750) was simulated by shifting the EUR–USD spot rate prevailing on the assessment date (1.2500) by +10%. As shown in the table below, the change in fair value of the hedged item was expected to be largely offset by the change in fair value of the hedging instrument, corroborating that both elements had values that would generally move in opposite directions.

The fair value of the hypothetical derivative at inception of the hedging relationship, prior to the shift in the EUR–USD spot rate, was calculated as follows:

Hypothetical derivative fair valuation on 1-Jan-20X0				
	31-Dec-20X0	31-Dec-20X1	31-Dec-20X2	Total
USD leg:				
USD cash flow	<30,500,000>	<30,500,000>	<530,500,000>	
USD discount factor	0.9477	0.8930	0.8367	
PV USD cash flow	<28,905,000>	<27,237,000>	<443,859,000>	
EUR–USD spot rate	1.2500	1.2500	1.2500	
EUR translated amount	<23,124,000>	<21,790,000>	<355,086,000>	<400,000,000>
EUR leg:				
EUR cash flow	19,960,000	19,960,000	419,960,000	
EUR discount factor	0.9578	0.9121	0.8636	
PV EUR cash flow	19,118,000	18,206,000	362,676,000	400,000,000
			Total fair value	Nil

The fair value of the hypothetical derivative at inception of the hedging relationship, after the shift in the EUR–USD spot rate, was calculated as follows:

Hypothetical derivative fair valuation on 1-Jan-20X0				
	31-Dec-20X0	31-Dec-20X1	31-Dec-20X2	Total
USD leg:				
USD cash flow	<30,500,000>	<30,500,000>	<530,500,000>	
USD discount factor	0.9477	0.8930	0.8367	
PV USD cash flow	<28,905,000>	<27,237,000>	<443,859,000>	
EUR–USD spot rate	1.3750	1.3750	1.3750	
EUR translated amount	<21,022,000>	<19,809,000>	<322,807,000>	<363,638,000>

(continued overleaf)

Hypothetical derivative fair valuation on 1-Jan-20X0				
	31-Dec-20X0	31-Dec-20X1	31-Dec-20X2	Total
EUR leg:				
EUR cash flow	19,960,000	19,960,000	419,960,000	
EUR discount factor	0.9578	0.9121	0.8636	
PV EUR cash flow	19,118,000	18,206,000	362,676,000	400,000,000
			Total fair value	36,362,000

The change in fair value of the hedging instrument was calculated in a similar way, resulting in a EUR 36,347,000 gain. The difference between the fair value changes of the two instruments was mainly due to changes in CVA in the hedging instrument.

Scenario analysis assessment		
	Hedging instrument	**Hypothetical derivative**
Initial fair value	Nil	Nil
Final fair value	36,347,000	36,362,000
Fair value change	36,347,000	36,362,000
	Degree of offset	**100.0%**

The hedge ratio is established at 1:1.

There were three main sources of potential ineffectiveness: firstly, a significant credit deterioration of the counterparty to the hedging instrument (XYZ Bank); secondly, a reduction of the net assets of the hedged foreign operation below the hedging instrument notional; and finally, a substantial increase in the basis element of the CCS.

6.12.4 Other Relevant Information

The net investment translation into EUR was calculated using the EUR–USD spot rate at each relevant date as follows:

Date	Spot EUR–USD	Net investment (USD)	Net investment (EUR) (*)	Period retranslation difference (EUR)
1-Jan-20X0	1.2500	500,000,000	400,000,000	—
31-Dec-20X0	1.2700	500,000,000	393,701,000	<6,299,000>
31-Dec-20X1	1.3100	500,000,000	381,679,000	<12,022,000>
31-Dec-20X2	1.2900	500,000,000	387,597,000	5,918,000

(*) Net investment in EUR = 500 million/Spot rate

The fair values of the CCS and the hypothetical derivative, excluding accrued interest, at each reporting date are shown in the following table. Differences between both fair values arose primarily due to the CVA performed on the CCS.

Date	CCS Fair Value (EUR)	CCS Fair Value Change (EUR)	Hypothetical Deriv. Fair Value (EUR)	Hypothetical Der. Fair Value Change (EUR)	Effective Part of CCS Fair Value Change
31-Dec-20X0	7,559,000	7,559,000	7,594,000	7,594,000	7,559,000
31-Dec-20X1	21,985,000	14,426,000	21,996,000	14,402,000	14,426,000
31-Dec-20X2	12,403,000	<9,582,000 >	12,403,000	<9,593,000>	<9,582,000 >

The ineffective part of the change in fair value of the CCS was the excess of its cumulative change in fair value over that of the hypothetical derivative. In our case, no ineffectiveness was recognised. The effective and ineffective parts of the change in fair value of the CCS were the following (see Section 5.5.6 for an explanation of the calculations):

	31-Dec-20X0	31-Dec-20X1	31-Dec-20X2
Cumulative change in fair value of hedging instrument	7,559,000	21,985,000	12,403,000
Cumulative change in fair value of hypothetical derivative	7,594,000	21,996,000	12,403,000
Lower amount	7,559,000	21,985,000	12,403,000
Previous cumulative effective amount	Nil	7,559,000	21,985,000
Available amount	7,559,000	14,426,000	<9,582,000>
Period change in fair value of hedging instrument	7,559,000	14,426,000	<9,582,000>
Effective part	7,559,000	14,426,000	<9,582,000>
Ineffective part	Nil	Nil	Nil

The interest flows/expenses related to the USD leg of the CCS were as follows:

Date	Spot EUR–USD	Annual average EUR–USD	USD fixed rate	Interest payment (USD)	Interest expense (EUR)	Interest payment (EUR)
31-Dec-20X0	1.2700	1.2650	6.10%	30,500,000 (1)	24,111,000 (2)	24,016,000 (3)
31-Dec-20X1	1.3100	1.2840	6.10%	30,500,000	23,754,000	23,282,000
31-Dec-20X2	1.2900	1.3020	6.10%	30,500,000	23,425,000	23,643,000

Notes:
(1) Interest payment (USD) = USD 500 million × 6.10%
(2) Interest expense (EUR) = Interest payment (USD)/Annual average FX rate = 30,500,000/1.2650
(3) Interest payment (EUR) = Interest payment (USD)/Spot FX rate = 30,500,000/1.2700

The interest flows/expenses related to the EUR leg of the CCS were as follows:

Date	EUR fixed rate	Interest received/ income (EUR)
31-Dec-20X0	5.00%	20,000,000 (*)
31-Dec-20X1	5.00%	20,000,000
31-Dec-20X2	5.00%	20,000,000

(*) Interest received/income = EUR 400 million × 5.00%

6.12.5 Accounting Entries

Assuming that ABC closed its books annually at year's end, the accounting entries related to the hedge were as follows.

1) To record the CCS trade on 1 January 20X0

No entries in the financial statements were required as the fair value of the CCS was zero.

2) To record the closing of the accounting period on 31 December 20X0

The net investment lost EUR 6,299,000 in value over the period when translated into EUR. In practice all the net assets of SubCo would have been translated. In our case, the retranslation of just USD 500 million of net assets is assumed and summarised in a "net investment in subsidiary" figurative account for illustrative purposes.

Translation differences (Equity)	6,299,000	
Net investment in subsidiary (Asset)		6,299,000

The CCS fair value change, excluding accrued interest, was a gain of EUR 7,559,000. All this gain was effective and recognised in the translation differences account. There was no ineffective part, and therefore, no amount was recognised in profit or loss.

Cross-currency swap (Asset)	7,559,000	
Translation differences (Equity)		7,559,000

Under the USD leg of the CCS, ABC paid the equivalent of EUR 24,016,000 and recognised a EUR 21,111,000 interest expense. The EUR 95,000 difference between these amounts was recognised in profit or loss. Under the EUR leg of the CCS, ABC received EUR 20,000,000, recognised as interest income.

Financial expenses (Profit or loss)	21,111,000	
USD cash (Asset)		21,016,000
Other financial income (Profit or loss)		95,000
EUR cash (Asset)	20,000,000	
Financial income (Profit or loss)		20,000,000

3) To record the closing of the accounting period on 31 December 20X1

Translation differences (Equity)	12,022,000	
Net investment in subsidiary (Asset)		12,022,000
Cross-currency swap (Asset)	14,426,000	
Translation differences (Equity)		14,426,000
Financial expenses (Profit or loss)	23,754,000	
USD cash (Asset)		23,282,000
Other financial income (Profit or loss)		472,000
EUR cash (Asset)	20,000,000	
Financial income (Profit or loss)		20,000,000

4) To record the closing of the accounting period on 31 December 20X2

Net investment in subsidiary (Asset)	5,918,000	
Translation differences (Equity)		5,918,000
Translation differences (Equity)	9,582,000	
Cross-currency swap (Asset)		9,582,000
Financial expenses (Profit or loss)	23,425,000	
Other financial income (Profit or loss)	218,000	
USD cash (Asset)		23,643,000
EUR cash (Asset)	20,000,000	
Financial income (Profit or loss)		20,000,000

Additionally on 31 December 20X2, a settlement amount was received under the CCS representing a net amount related to the final exchange of notionals. The EUR–USD spot rate on this date was 1.2900. ABC received EUR 12,403,000 (= EUR 400 mn – USD 500 mn/1.2900):

Cash (Asset)	12,403,000	
Cross-currency swap (Asset)		12,403,000

6.13 CASE STUDY: HEDGING INTRAGROUP FOREIGN DIVIDENDS

Generally foreign subsidiaries distribute dividends to their shareholders. Because dividends are usually paid in the foreign subsidiary's functional currency, both the parent company and the group may be exposed to FX risk. In this section, I discuss the accounting impact of dividends at foreign subsidiary, parent and group levels, as well as the potential distortions that hedges may create. It is worth noting that hedging only dividends (i.e., without taking into account the earnings translation and net investment risk exposures) may end up creating undesirable effects in the consolidated financial statements.

6.13.1 Effects of Intercompany Foreign Dividends on Individual and Consolidated Statements

Suppose that ABC, a group whose presentation currency is the EUR, has a 100% owned US foreign subsidiary. The foreign subsidiary declared, and later paid, a dividend of USD 100 million to ABC. The exchange rates at the relevant dates were as follows:

Date	Spot EUR–USD	USD dividend	Dividend EUR value
Previous reporting date: 31-Dec-20X0	1.2000		
Declaration date: 1-Jan-20X1	1.2300	100 mn	81.3 mn
Reporting date: 31-Mar-20X1	1.2500	100 mn	80.0 mn
Dividend payment date: 30-Jun-20X1	1.2850	100 mn	77.8 mn

In order to analyse the FX exposure caused by the dividend, let us review the accounting of intragroup dividends from the subsidiary, parent and group perspectives.

Impact on the Subsidiary's Financial Statements   On declaration date (1 January 20X1), the subsidiary recorded a USD 100 million declared dividend as follows:

Retained earnings (Equity – Subsidiary)	USD 100,000,000	
Dividends payable (Liability – Subsidiary)		USD 100,000,000

On the first reporting date, 31 March 20X1, no accounting entries were required. On dividend payment date, 30 June 20X1, the subsidiary recorded the payment as follows:

Dividends payable (Liability – Subsidiary)	USD 100,000,000	
Cash (Asset – Subsidiary)		USD 100,000,000

As shown in the previous accounting entries, the subsidiary was not exposed to any FX risk because all the flows were denominated in its functional currency (USD).

Impact on the Parent's Stand-alone Financial Statements The required accounting entries on the parent financial statements were as follows:

1) Accounting entries on 1 January 20X1

Under the cost method, the parent recorded the foreign subsidiary's declared USD dividend as "dividend income" and as "dividend receivable". The exchange rate used to convert the USD amount into EUR was the exchange rate prevailing on the dividend declaration date (1.2300). As a result, on 1 January 20X1 the parent entity recorded a EUR 81,300,000 (= USD 100 mn/1.2300) dividend.

Dividends receivable (Asset – Parent)	EUR 81,300,000
Dividend income (Profit or loss – Parent)	EUR 81,300,000

2) Accounting entries on 31 March 20X1

In the parent's stand-alone financial statements, the dividend receivable constituted a monetary item denominated in a foreign currency (USD), and therefore it was revalued at each balance sheet date. Any changes in the exchange rate from the last revaluation resulted in an FX gain or loss that was recognised in profit or loss. Since 1 January 20X1, the USD 100 million dividend receivable lost EUR 1.3 million (=80,000,000 – 81,300,000) in value.

Other financial expenses (Profit or loss – Parent)	EUR 1,300,000
Dividends receivable (Asset – Parent)	EUR 1,300,000

3) Accounting entries on 30 June 20X1

On this date the USD dividend was received by the parent entity. The parent first had to revalue the dividend receivable, recognising a EUR 2,100,000 loss (=77,800,000 – 80,000,000):

Other financial expenses (Profit or loss – Parent)	EUR 2,100,000
Dividends receivable (Asset – Parent)	EUR 2,100,000

The receipt of the USD 100 million from the subsidiary was recorded as follows:

Cash (Asset – Parent)	EUR 77,800,000
Dividends receivable (Asset – Parent)	EUR 77,800,000

It can be seen that the parent entity was exposed to FX risk in its stand-alone statements. This exposure was caused by the revaluation of the USD-denominated monetary item resulting from the subsidiary's declared USD dividend.

Impact on the Group's Consolidated Financial Statements   ABC carried out the consolidation process at each reporting date.

1) Consolidation adjustments on 31 March 20X1

On this date, in the subsidiary's financial statements there was a USD dividend payable and in the parent's financial statements there was a USD dividend receivable. Upon consolidation, intragroup receivables and payables were eliminated and all its effects unwound.

Dividends payable (Liability – Subsidiary)	USD 100,000,000
Retained earnings (Equity – Subsidiary)	USD 100,000,000
Dividend income (Profit or Loss – Parent)	EUR 81,300,000
Dividends receivable (Asset – Parent)	EUR 81,300,000
Dividends receivable (Asset – Parent)	EUR 1,300,000
Other financial income (Profit or loss – Parent)	EUR 1,300,000

On this date also, ABC had to calculate the translation differences adjustment related to its net investment in the US subsidiary. I had only looked at the dividend portion of the net investment to isolate the dividend effect from the rest. As the dividend was still unpaid, the USD 100 million was still part of the net investment. The spot rate prevailing at the previous reporting date (31 December 20X0) was 1.2000. The spot rate prevailing at the current reporting date (31 March 20X1) was 1.2500. Accordingly, the change in the net investment was a EUR 3,333,000 (= 100 mn/1.25 – 100 mn/1.20) loss. The loss was recorded in the translation differences account of equity:

Translation differences (Equity – Consolidated)	EUR 3,333,000
USD cash (Asset – Consolidated)	EUR 3,333,000

2) Consolidation adjustments on 30 June 20X1

On this date and prior to the recognition of the dividend payment/receipt, the revaluation of the USD 100 million net investment showed a EUR 2,179,000 (= 100 mn/1.285 – 100 mn/1.25) loss that was recorded in the translation differences account of equity:

Translation differences (Equity – Consolidated)	EUR 2,179,000
USD cash (Asset – Consolidated)	EUR 2,179,000

Also on this date, the dividend was paid to the parent. As a result, the USD 100 million was now part of the parent's monetary assets and no longer part of the net investment in the subsidiary.

Upon consolidation, the revaluation of the parent monetary assets performed at the stand-alone parent level also remained at the consolidated level. The net investment exposure decreased as well, and thus the translation differences adjustment was computed on a smaller net assets base.

Summary of Impacts on the Financial Statements On dividend declaration date, 1 January 20X1, the accounting effects were the following (see Figure 6.17):

- In the subsidiary's financial statements, a dividend payable and a corresponding reduction in retained earnings were recognised.
- In the parent's financial statements, the declared dividend was valued at the then prevailing EUR–USD exchange rate and recognised as dividend income and dividend receivable. The recognition in profit or loss had a tax impact.
- In the consolidated financial statements, there was still no effect as no consolidation process took place.

On the first reporting date, 31 March 20X1, the accounting effects were the following:

- In the subsidiary's financial statements, there was no effect (see Figure 6.18).
- In the parent's financial statements, the declared dividend was revalued at the then prevailing EUR–USD exchange rate and recognised as FX gains or losses (a loss in our case) in profit or loss. The recognition in profit or loss had a tax impact. Figure 6.18 highlights these effects.
- In the consolidated financial statements, the declared dividend still remained part of the net investment, as it was still unpaid. Therefore, the FX gains and losses due to the net investment revaluation were recorded in the translation differences account in equity (see Figure 6.19). In our case, as the USD depreciated against the EUR, a translation loss was recorded.

Parent's Stand-alone Financial Statements (Cost Method)

Subsidiary's Stand-alone Financial Statements

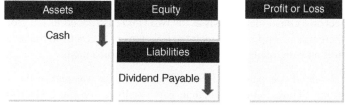

(*) Due to the revaluation of the USD Dividend Receivable

FIGURE 6.17 Dividend declaration (1-Jan-20X1) – effect on stand-alone financial statements.

Parent's Stand-alone Financial Statements (Cost Method)

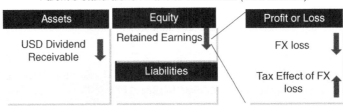

Subsidiary's Stand-alone Financial Statements

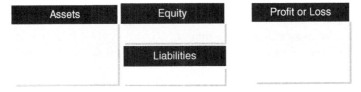

FIGURE 6.18 Reporting date (31-Mar-20X1) – effect on stand-alone financial statements.

Consolidated Financial Statements

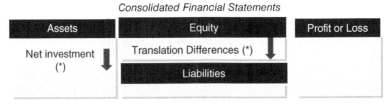

(*) Decline was due to a rise in EUR–USD exchange rate

FIGURE 6.19 Reporting date (31-Mar-20X1) – effect on consolidated financial statements.

On 30 June 20X1, the USD 100 million dividend was paid. This USD cash was transferred from the subsidiary's USD cash account to the parent's USD cash account. The accounting effects on the three different reported financial statements were the following:

- In the subsidiary's financial statements, the balance of the USD cash account showed a USD 100 million reduction and the dividend payable was cancelled (see Figure 6.20).
- In the parent's financial statements, there were several effects (see Figure 6.20). Firstly, there was an FX loss due to the revaluation of the dividend receivable. This loss was recognised in profit or loss, which also had a tax impact. Secondly, the balance of the USD cash account increased by USD 100 million and the dividend receivable was cancelled.
- In the consolidated financial statements, at first sight, the dividend payment seemed to have no effect on a consolidated basis as the two USD cash accounts are grouped together. However, there was an important effect: the FX gains or losses from the revaluation of the USD 100 million were recognised differently, as explained next.

Before the dividend was paid, the USD 100 million cash was part of the net investment in the US subsidiary. Thus, foreign exchange gains or losses on the USD 100 million cash remeasurement in EUR were recorded in the translation differences account in equity.

After the dividend was paid, the USD 100 million cash was part of the monetary items of a group entity (i.e., the parent) that had the same functional currency as the group.

Thus, foreign exchange gains or losses arising from the USD 100 million cash remeasurement impacted consolidated profit or loss.

Consequently, the effect of the dividend payment on a consolidated basis was a reduction in the net investment in the US subsidiary and an increase in the monetary items of the parent company (see Figure 6.21).

Parent's Stand-alone Financial Statements (Cost Method)

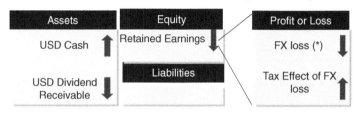

Subsidiary's Stand-alone Financial Statements

(*) Due to the revaluation of the USD Dividend Receivable

FIGURE 6.20   Divided payment date (30-Jun-20X1) – effect on stand-alone financial statements.

Consolidated Financial Statements

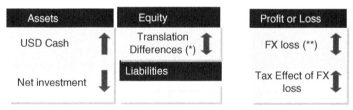

(*) The decline in net investment caused the translation differences account to be less exposed to the EUR–USD exchange rate
(**) The USD cash exposed the consolidated profit or loss to the EUR– USD exchange rate

FIGURE 6.21   Divided payment date (30-Jun-20X1) – effect on consolidated financial statements.

The FX risk would have been eliminated from 30 June 20X1 had the parent exchanged the USD 100 million for EUR in the FX spot market on that date.

6.13.2 Hedging Intercompany Foreign Dividends with an FX Forward

Many companies seek to hedge forecast foreign currency dividends distributed by their foreign subsidiaries. Next, the implications of hedging foreign intragroup dividends are discussed in detail.

Suppose that on 1 January 20X1 ABC (the parent company) hedged the declared dividend through an FX forward with the following terms:

FX forward terms	
Trade date	1 January 20X1
Nominal	USD 100,000,000
Maturity	30 June 20X1
Forward Rate	1.2320
Settlement	Cash settlement

Suppose further that the fair value of the FX forward at each relevant date was as follows:

Date	Forward to 30-Jun-20X1	Forward fair value
Declaration date: 1-Jan-20X1	1.2320	-0-
Reporting date: 31-Mar-20X1	1.2510	1,222,000
Dividend payment date: 30-Jun-20X1	1.2850	3,348,000

Subsidiary's Accounting Entries Relating to the FX Forward   No entries were required as the subsidiary was not a party to the FX forward.

Parent's Stand-alone Accounting Entries Relating to the FX Forward   The required accounting entries on the parent financial statements relating to the FX forward were as follows.

1) Entries on 1 January 20X1

No entries were required as the fair value of the forward was zero at its inception.

2) Entries on 31 March 20X1 (reporting date)

The change in fair value of the FX forward was a EUR 1,222,000 (=1,222,000 – 0) gain.

FX forward (Asset – Parent)	EUR 1,222,000	
FX gain (Profit or loss – Parent)		EUR 1,222,000

3) Entries on 30 June 20X1 (reporting and FX forward maturity dates)

On this date the FX forward matured. The change in fair value of the forward was a EUR 2,126,000 (=3,348,000 – 1,222,000) gain.

FX forward (Asset – Parent)	EUR 2,126,000	
FX gain (Profit or Loss – Parent)		EUR 2,126,000

Through the forward, ABC delivered the dividend proceeds (USD 100 million, having a market value of EUR 77,821,000) and received EUR 81,169,000:

EUR cash (Asset – Parent)	EUR 81,169,000
FX forward (Asset – Parent)	EUR 3,348,000
USD cash (Asset – Parent)	EUR 77,821,000

Consolidated Accounting Entries Relating to the FX Forward Whilst the USD 100 million dividend represented a forecast intragroup transaction, on a consolidated basis ABC was not be able to apply cash flow hedge accounting because the foreign risk did not affect consolidated profit or loss. As a result, the FX forward was undesignated. Therefore, no entries were required as no adjustments were necessary to the parent accounting entries.

Summary of Impacts of the Hedge on the Financial Statements On 31 March 20X1, the effects on the financial statements of the entities involved were the following:

- In the subsidiary's financial statements, there was no effect as the subsidiary was not a party to the FX forward.
- In the parent's profit or loss statement, the EUR 1,222,000 gain on the hedge largely offset the EUR 1,300,000 loss on the revaluation of the dividend receivable (see Figure 6.22). Therefore, the hedge performed well at the parent level.
- In the consolidated statements, the EUR 1,222,000 gain on the hedge showed up in profit or loss. This FX gain had no offsetting FX losses in profit or loss. The only FX loss showed up in the translation differences account, and as a result, the hedge largely eliminated the FX exposure (relating to the USD 100 million portion of the net investment in the subsidiary) of the consolidated equity. Therefore, while the FX forward offset the changes in the translation of USD 100 million of net assets, it exposed the consolidated profit or loss to movements in the EUR–USD exchange rate, as shown in Figure 6.23.

Parent's Stand-alone Financial Statements

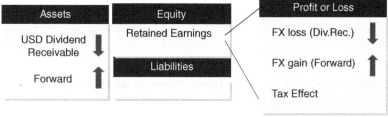

FIGURE 6.22 Reporting date (31-Mar-20X1) – effect on parent's stand-alone financial statements.

Consolidated Financial Statements

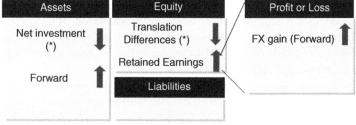

(*) Decrease was due to the rise in the EUR–USD exchange rate

FIGURE 6.23 Reporting date (31-Mar-20X1) – effect on consolidated financial statements.

On 30 June 20X1, the effects on the financial statements of the entities involved were the following:

- In the subsidiary's financial statements, there was no effect as the subsidiary was not a party to the FX forward.
- In the parent's profit or loss statement, the effect was similar to that on 31 March 20X1. The EUR 2,126,000 gain on the hedge largely offset the EUR 2,100,000 loss on the revaluation of the dividend receivable. Therefore, the hedge performed well at the parent level.
- In the consolidated statements, the effect was similar to that on 31 March 20X0. The FX forward showed a EUR 2,126,000 gain that was recognised in the consolidated profit or loss statement, while there was a EUR 2,179,000 gain in the translation differences account. Therefore, the consolidated profit or loss was exposed to movements in the EUR–USD exchange rate.

In summary, the hedge worked well at the individual financial statements, but created distortions in the consolidated profit or loss.

What ABC Could Have Done Better The distortion created by the hedge at the consolidated level could have been avoided if ABC had considered the FX forward as undesignated at the parent-only level. As a consequence, the changes in the FX forward fair value would have been recognised in profit or loss. ABC had already adopted this solution at the parent level. As discussed earlier, the hedge performed very well because the loss on the revaluation of the dividend receivable was almost completely offset by the gain in the FX forward (see Figure 6.22).

Alternatively, at the consolidated level, ABC could have designated the FX forward as the hedging instrument in a net investment hedge. The hedged item would have been USD 100 million of the net investment in the US subsidiary. As a consequence, the effective part of the change in the FX forward fair value would have been recognised in the translation differences account of equity. This way, there would have been a natural offset in the translation differences account between the effective part of the changes of the FX forward and the revaluation changes of the net investment. Section 6.8 includes a detailed explanation of the accounting mechanics of a net investment hedge with an FX forward.

Under this alternative, the parent's stand-alone accounting entries relating to the FX forward would have been identical to those covered previously. However, the consolidated accounting entries would have been different, as shown next.

Optimised Solution: Consolidated Accounting Entries Related to the FX Forward The accounting entries at the parent and consolidated levels resulting from the FX forward were as follows.

1) Entries on 1 January 20X1

None required.

2) Entries on 31 March 20X1 (reporting date)

The EUR 1,222,000 gain recognised at the parent level was reversed. At the consolidated level, the FX forward was designated as hedging instrument in a net investment hedge. Assuming that the hedge was completely effective, the changes in the fair value of the FX forward were recognised in the translation differences account.

FX gain (Profit or loss – Parent)	EUR 1,222,000
Translation differences (Equity- Consolidated)	EUR 1,222,000

3) Entries on 30 June 20X1

The EUR 2,126,000 gain on the forward was recorded similarly to the 31 March 20X0 adjustment.

FX gain (Profit or loss – Parent)	EUR 2,126,000
Translation differences (Equity- Consolidated)	EUR 2,126,000

Now the hedge performed very well at both the parent-only and consolidated levels, as shown in Figure 6.24.

(*) Decrease was related to the net investment, due to the rise in the EUR–USD exchange rate
(**) Increase was related to the FX forward, due to the rise in the EUR–USD exchange rate

FIGURE 6.24 Optimised solution – Effect on parent and consolidated financial statements.

6.14 CASE STUDY: HEDGING FOREIGN SUBSIDIARY EARNINGS

This case study illustrates a problem presently faced by many multinationals: the hedge of foreign earnings translation risk. Upon consolidation, most multinationals translate foreign subsidiaries' profit or loss at the average exchange rate for the accounting period. As a consequence, corporations are exposed to movements in that average exchange rate. The hedging problem arises because IFRS 9 at present does not allow the direct hedging of foreign earnings translation.

Suppose that ABC, a group whose presentation currency is the EUR, had a US subsidiary with a USD functional currency and that the subsidiary was expected to earn USD 400 million evenly during 20X0. Suppose further that ABC reported quarterly on a consolidated basis and that in order to hedge the quarterly translation exposure arising from the US subsidiary, ABC entered into the following four FX average rate forwards (AVRFs):

	AVRF 1	AVRF 2	AVRF 3	AVRF 4
Trade date	1-Jan-20X0	1-Jan-20X0	1-Jan-20X0	1-Jan-20X0
Nominal	USD 100 mn	USD 100 mn	USD 100 mn	USD 100 mn
Maturity	31-Mar-20X0	30-Jun-20X0	30-Sep-20X0	31-Dec-20X0
Forward rate	1.2500	1.2500	1.2500	1.2500
Final rate	The arithmetic average of the daily closing EUR–USD spot from 1-Jan-20X0 until 31-Mar-20X0	The arithmetic average of the daily closing EUR–USD spot from 1-Apr-20X0 until 30-Jun-20X0	The arithmetic average of the daily closing EUR–USD spot from 1-Jul-20X0 until 30-Sep-20X0	The arithmetic average of the daily closing EUR–USD spot from 1-Oct-20X0 until 31-Dec-20X0
Initial premium	EUR 475,000	EUR 150,000	<EUR 160,000>	<EUR 465,000>
Settlement	Cash settlement	Cash settlement	Cash settlement	Cash settlement

The payoff at maturity of each AVRF guaranteed an arithmetic average daily EUR–USD exchange rate during the quarter of 1.2500. For example, the EUR payoff of the first AVRF at maturity was:

$$\text{Payoff} = 100{,}000{,}000 \times (1/1.25 - 1/\text{Average})$$

where "Average" was the arithmetic average of the daily closing EUR–USD spot from 1-Jan-20X0 until 31-Mar-20X0.

The next thing that ABC had to decide was how to account for each AVRF. ABC had two alternatives:

- To treat each AVRF as undesignated, and therefore to recognise in profit or loss any changes in fair value of the AVRF. The potential increase in profit or loss volatility precluded ABC from adopting this alternative.
- To designate, in the consolidated statements, each AVRF as the hedging instrument in a hedge accounting relationship. The problem was that IFRS 9 did not allow the direct hedging of foreign earnings translation. One way to overcome this problem was to designate the AVRF as the hedging instrument in a cash flow hedge, as shown next.

The hedged item would be a highly expected forecast USD-denominated sales sufficient to equal the foreign subsidiary's forecast profit (USD 100 million) for each quarterly accounting period. ABC looked at all the entities within the group that had at least USD 100 million external sales denominated in USD. ABC found four entities that met such a requirement (see Figure 6.25).

- The parent entity. Because the functional currency of the parent entity was the EUR, the sales would be directly impacting consolidated profit or loss, constituting a transaction risk.

As a result, assuming that all other requirements for the application of hedge accounting were met, those highly expected forecast sales could be designated as the hedged item.

- Subsidiary A. Because the functional currency of this subsidiary was the EUR, its sales would be directly impacting consolidated profit or loss on consolidation, constituting a transaction risk. As a result, assuming that all other requirements for the application of hedge accounting were met, those highly expected forecast sales could be designated as the hedged item.
- Subsidiary B. Because the functional currency of this subsidiary was the USD, its USD-denominated sales would not expose this entity to FX risk. Although on consolidation those USD sales would be indirectly impacting consolidated profit or loss, as part of the translation of Subsidiary B's profit or loss, they could *not* be designated as a hedged item because their risk was a translation risk rather than a transaction risk.
- Subsidiary C. The functional currency of this subsidiary was the JPY. Although its highly forecast USD sales exposed, when occurring, Subsidiary C's profit or loss statement to FX risk, the incorporation of this risk into consolidated profit or loss would be as a translation risk rather than as a transaction risk. Consequently, those sales could *not* be designated as a hedged item.

ABC nominated four hedging relationships. In each hedging relationship, ABC designated the first USD 100 million of the parent entity's highly forecast USD-denominated sales as the hedged item in a cash flow hedge. The AVRF related to the quarterly period being hedged was designated as the hedging instrument. As a consequence, changes in the effective part of the AVRF fair value were initially recognised in equity, and reclassified to profit or loss once the hedged cash flow affected profit or loss.

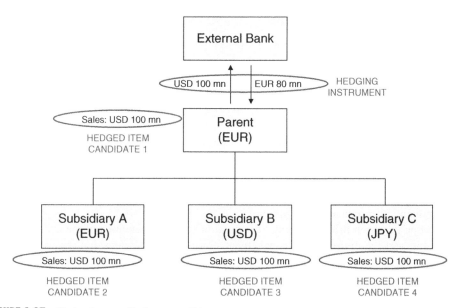

FIGURE 6.25 Hedge item preliminary candidates.

6.14.1 Hedging Relationship Documentation

The four hedging relationships, one for each quarter, were documented in a similar way. ABC documented the first quarter hedging relationship as follows:

Hedging relationship documentation	
Risk management objective and strategy for undertaking the hedge	The objective of the hedge is to protect the EUR value of the cash flow stemming from a USD 100 million highly expected forecast sales of finished goods against unfavourable movements in the EUR–USD exchange rate. This hedging objective is consistent with ABC's overall FX risk management strategy of reducing the variability of its profit or loss statement with FX forwards and options
Type of hedge	Cash flow hedge
Hedged item	The cash flows stemming from the first USD 100 million highly forecast sales of finished goods originated by the parent entity, expected to take place during the period from 1 January 20X0 to 30 March 20X0. The sales are highly expected to occur as the parent entity has a consistent history of generating sales denominated in USD well in excess of USD 100 million
Hedging instrument	The FX average rate forward contract with reference number 017812, notionals of USD 100 million and EUR 80 million, maturity 31-Mar-20X0, and FX rate 1.2500. The counterparty to the AVRF is XYZ Bank and the credit risk associated with this counterparty is considered to be very low
Hedge effectiveness assessment	See below

6.14.2 Hedge Effectiveness Assessment

Hedge effectiveness will be assessed by comparing, on a spot-spot basis, changes in the fair value of the hedging instrument to changes in the fair value of the highly expected cash flows.

Hedge effectiveness will be assessed prospectively at hedging relationship inception and on an ongoing basis at least upon each reporting date and upon occurrence of a significant change in the circumstances affecting the hedge effectiveness requirements.

The hedging relationship will qualify for hedge accounting only if all the following criteria are met:

1) The hedging relationship consists only of eligible hedge items and hedging instruments. The hedge item is eligible as it is a highly expected cash flow that exposes the entity to FX risk and it is reliably measurable. The hedging instrument is eligible as it is a derivative instrument other than a written option.
2) At hedge inception there is a formal designation and documentation of the hedging relationship and the entity's risk management objective and strategy for undertaking the hedge.
3) The hedging relationship is considered effective.

The hedging relationship will be considered effective if the following three requirements are met:

1) There is an economic relationship between the hedged item and the hedging instrument.
2) The effect of credit risk does not dominate the fair value changes in the hedging relationship.

3) The weightings of the hedged item and the hedging instrument (i.e., hedge ratio) are designated based on the quantities of hedged item and hedging instrument that the entity actually uses to meet the risk management objective, unless doing so would deliberately create ineffectiveness.

Whether there is an economic relationship between the hedged item and the hedging instrument will be assessed on a quantitative basis using a scenario analysis, comparing the cumulative change since hedge inception in the fair value of the expected cash flow arising from the forecast sale with the cumulative change since hedge inception in the fair value of the hedging instrument. The scenario to be analysed would be a 10% adverse move in the EUR–USD exchange rate.

The effective and ineffective amounts of the change in fair value of the hedging instrument will be computed by comparing the cumulative change in fair value of the hedging instrument with that of the hedged item. The effective amount will be recognised in the "cash flow hedge" reserve in equity. Any part of the cumulative change in fair value of the hedging instrument that does not offset a corresponding cumulative change in the fair value of the hedged item will be treated as ineffectiveness and recorded in profit or loss.

6.14.3 Hedge Effectiveness Assessment Performed at Hedge Inception

An effectiveness assessment was performed at inception and at each reporting date. The assessment also included the relationship hedge ratio and an identification of the sources of potential ineffectiveness. The conclusion that an economic relationship existed between the hedged item and the hedging instrument was justified by analysing one scenario in which the EUR–USD FX rate suffered a 10% unfavourable move during the quarter, as follows. The EUR–USD spot rate was 1.2392 at hedge inception (1 January 20X0). The hedged highly probable forecast sales for the first quarter were USD 100 million, split into three monthly forecast amounts of USD 33,333,000 for the months ending 31 January 20X0, 28 February 20X0 and 31 March 20X0. A 10% unfavourable move in the exchange rate implied a 1.3631 ($=1.2392 \times 1.10$) EUR–USD spot rate on 31 March 20X0. Assuming a gradual move in the FX spot rate during the quarter, it implied a 1.2805 spot rate ($= 1.2391 + 1/3 \times (1.3631 - 1.2392)$) on 31 January 20X0 and a 1.3218 spot rate ($= 1.2391 + 2/3 \times (1.3631 - 1.2392)$) on 28 February 20X0.

The expected cash flows hedged under the first hedging relationship were USD 33,333,000 at the end of each month within the quarter. The overall change in fair value of these cash flows was a EUR 4,993,000 loss as evidenced in the following table:

Date	Spot rate	Fair valued cash flow 1	Fair valued cash flow 2	Fair valued cash flow 3	Total fair value change
1-Jan-20X0	1.2392	26,899,000 (1)	26,899,000	26,899,000	
31-Jan-20X0	1.2805	26,031,000 (2)			
28-Feb-20X0	1.3218		25,218,000		
31-Mar-20X0	1.3631			24,455,000	
Change		<868,000> (3)	<1,681,000>	<2,444,000>	<4,993,000>

Notes:
(1) 33,333,000/1.2392 = 26,899,000
(2) 33,333,000/1.2805 = 26,031,000
(3) 26,031,000 − 26,899,000

The change in fair value of the hedging instrument was calculated as follows:

1) Fair value at inception: <475,000> (i.e., ABC received EUR 475,000 at the inception of AVRF 1).
2) Fair value at maturity: 4,346,000 (= 100 mn/1.25 − 100 mn/1.3218), where 1.3218 was the quarterly average rate (= (1.2805 + 1.3218 + 1.3631)/3)).
3) Hence, the change in fair value of the hedging instrument was a EUR 4,821,000 (= 4,346,000 + 475,000) gain.

The hedge qualified for hedge accounting as it met the three effectiveness requirements:

1) Because in the scenario analysed the change in fair value of the hedged item (a loss of EUR 4,993,000) and the change in fair value of the hedging instrument (a gain of EUR 4,891,000) moved in opposite directions, it was concluded that the hedging instrument and the hedged item had values that would generally move in opposite directions, and hence that an economic relationship existed between the hedged item and the hedging instrument.
2) Because the credit rating of counterparty to the hedging instrument was relatively strong (rated A+ by Standard & Poor's) the effect of credit risk did not dominate the value changes resulting from that economic relationship.
3) The hedge ratio designated (1:1) was the one actually used for risk management and it did not attempt to avoid recognising ineffectiveness. Therefore, it was determined that a hedge ratio of 1:1 was appropriate.

There were three main sources of potential ineffectiveness: firstly, a significant credit deterioration of the counterparty to the hedging instrument (XYZ Bank); secondly, a reduction of the net assets of the hedged foreign operation below the hedging instrument notional; and finally, a substantial increase in the CCS basis. The credit risk of the counterparty of the hedging instrument would be continuously monitored.

Similar assessments were performed for the other three hedging relationships with similar results. The group concluded that all four hedging relationships met the requirements for the application of hedge accounting. The assessments performed at each reporting date yielded similar conclusions.

6.14.4 Other Relevant Information

The spot EUR–USD exchange rates and the fair value of the AVRFs on the relevant dates were as follows:

Date	Spot rate	AVRF 1 fair value	AVRF 2 fair value	AVRF 3 fair value	AVRF 4 fair value
1-Jan-20X0	1.2392	<475,000>	<150,000>	160,000	465,000
31-Jan-20X0	1.2400				
28-Feb-20X0	1.2600				
31-Mar-20X0	1.2800	635,000	2,057,000	2,333,000	2,602,000
30-Apr-20X0	1.3000				
31-May-20X0	1.2900				
30-Jun-20X0	1.2700		2,280,000	1,451,000	1,738,000
31-Jul-20X0	1.2800				
31-Aug-20X0	1.2600				

Date	Spot rate	AVRF 1 fair value	AVRF 2 fair value	AVRF 3 fair value	AVRF 4 fair value
30-Sep-20X0	1.2500			844,000	211,000
31-Oct-20X0	1.2700				
30-Nov-20X0	1.2900				
31-Dec-20X0	1.3100				2,481,000

6.14.5 Accounting Entries

The required journal entries were as follows.

1) Entries on 1 January 20X0

The following entries were required as the fair value of the AVRFs at their inception were not zero.

Cash (Asset)	475,000	
FX derivative (AVRF 1) (Liability)		475,000
Cash (Asset)	150,000	
FX derivative (AVRF 2) (Liability)		150,000
FX derivative (AVRF 3) (Asset)	160,000	
Cash (Asset)		160,000
FX derivative (AVRF 4) (Asset)	465,000	
Cash (Asset)		465,000

2) To record the closing of the accounting period on 31 March 20X0

The change in fair value of the AVRFs since the last valuation were as follows:

AVRF 1, a gain of EUR 1,110,000 (=635,000+475,000);
AVRF 2, a gain of EUR 2,207,000 (=2,057,000+150,000);
AVRF 3, a gain of EUR 2,173,000 (=2,333,000-160,000);
AVRF 4, a gain of EUR 2,137,000 (=2,602,000-465,000).

For simplicity, all hedges were assumed to have been fully effective (in practice, a small ineffective part would have arisen due to the FX forward points), and hence, all the changes in the fair value of the AVRFs were recorded in equity:

FX derivative (AVRF 1) (Asset)	1,110,000	
Cash flow hedge reserve (Equity)		1,110,000

FX derivative (AVRF 2) (Asset)	2,207,000	
Cash flow hedge reserve (Equity)		2,207,000
FX derivative (AVRF 3) (Asset)	2,173,000	
Cash flow hedge reserve (Equity)		2,173,000
FX derivative (AVRF 4) (Asset)	2,137,000	
Cash flow hedge reserve (Equity)		2,137,000

USD 100 million sales of the parent entity, designated as the hedged item in the first hedging relationship, were recorded in the profit or loss statement of the parent and the group. As a consequence, the amounts related to AVRF 1 accumulated in equity (EUR 1,110,000) were reclassified to profit or loss:

Cash flow hedge reserve (Equity)	1,110,000	
Sales (Profit or loss)		1,110,000

Finally, AVRF 1 matured and ABC received EUR 635,000 ($=100$ mn $\times(1/1.25 - 1/\text{Average})$), where "Average" was the average of the spot rates at the end of each month during the first quarter ($= (1.24+1.26+1.28)/3$).

Cash (Asset)	635,000	
FX derivative (AVRF 1) (Asset)		635,000

3) To record the closing of the accounting period on 30 June 20X0

The change in fair value of the three remaining AVRFs since the last valuation was as follows:

AVRF 2, a gain of EUR 223,000 ($=2,280,000 - 2,057,000$);
AVRF 3, a loss of EUR 882,000 ($=1,451,000 - 2,333,000$);
AVRF 4, a loss of EUR 864,000 ($=1,738,000 - 2,602,000$).

As the hedges were assumed to be fully effective, all these changes in fair value were recorded in equity:

FX derivative (AVRF 2) (Asset)	223,000	
Cash flow hedge reserve (Equity)		223,000

Cash flow hedge reserve (Equity)	882,000	
FX derivative (AVRF 3) (Asset)		882,000
Cash flow hedge reserve (Equity)	864,000	
FX derivative (AVRF 4) (Asset)		864,000

USD 100 million sales of the parent entity, designated as the hedged item in the second hedging relationship, were recorded in the profit or loss statement of the parent and the group. As a consequence, the amounts related to AVRF 2 accumulated in equity (EUR 2,430,000 = 2,207,000 + 223,000) were recycled to profit or loss:

Cash flow hedge reserve (Equity)	2,430,000	
Sales (Profit or loss)		2,430,000

Finally, AVRF 2 matured and ABC received EUR 2,280,000 (=100 mn × (1/1.25 − 1/Average)), where "Average" was the average of the spot rates at the end of each month during the second quarter (= (1.30+1.29+1.27)/3).

Cash (Asset)	2,280,000	
FX derivative (AVRF 2) (Asset)		2,280,000

4) To record the closing of the accounting period on 30 September 20X0

The change in fair value of the two remaining AVRFs since the last valuation were as follows:

AVRF 3, a loss of EUR 607,000 (=844,000 − 1,451,000);
AVRF 4, a loss of EUR 1,527,000 (=211,000 − 1,738,000).

As the hedges were assumed to be fully effective, all these changes in fair value were recorded in equity:

Cash flow hedge reserve (Equity)	607,000	
FX derivative (AVRF 3) (Asset)		607,000
Cash flow hedge reserve (Equity)	1,527,000	
FX derivative (AVRF 4) (Asset)		1,527,000

USD 100 million sales of the parent entity, designated as the hedged item in the third hedging relationship, were recorded in the profit or loss statement of the parent and the group.

As a consequence, the amounts related to AVRF 3 accumulated in equity (EUR 684,000 = 2,173,000 – 882,000 – 607,000) were recycled to profit or loss:

Cash flow hedge reserve (Equity)	684,000	
Sales (Profit or loss)		684,000

Finally, AVRF 3 matured and ABC received EUR 844,000 (=100 mn × (1/1.25 – 1/Average)), where "Average" was the average of the spot rates at the end of each month during the third quarter (= (1.28+1.26+1.25)/3).

Cash (Asset)	844,000	
FX derivative (AVRF 3) (Asset)		844,000

5) To record the closing of the accounting period on 31 December 20X0

The change in fair value of AVRF 4 since the last valuation was a gain of EUR 2,270,000 (=2,481,000 –211,000). As the hedge was assumed to be completely effective, this change in fair value was recorded in equity:

FX derivative (AVRF 4) (Asset)	2,270,000	
Cash flow hedge reserve (Equity)		2,270,000

USD 100 million sales of the parent entity, designated as the hedged item in the fourth hedging relationship, were recorded in the profit or loss statement of the parent and the group. As a consequence, the amounts related to AVRF 4 accumulated in equity (EUR 2,016,000) were reclassified to profit or loss.

Cash flow hedge reserve (Equity)	2,016,000	
Sales (Profit or loss)		2,016,000

Finally, AVRF 4 matured and ABC received EUR 2,481,000 (=100 mn × (1/1.25 – 1/Average)), where "Average" was the average of the spot rates at the end of each month during the fourth quarter (= (1.27+1.29+1.31)/3).

Cash (Asset)	2,481,000	
FX derivative (AVRF 4) (Asset)		2,481,000

6.14.6 Final Remarks

The hedge worked well as the objective of protecting the EUR translation value of USD 400 million of the US subsidiary's profit or loss at an exchange rate of 1.2500, or EUR 320 million, was achieved on a pre-tax basis, as shown in Figure 6.26.

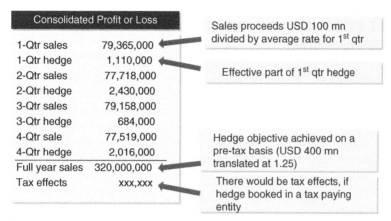

FIGURE 6.26   US subsidiary's earnings hedge – effect on consolidated profit or loss.

However, specific issues may arise as a result of implementing a hedging strategy like the one just covered. Five in particular are worth noting:

- Firstly, ABC needed to arbitrarily identify within the group external highly expected USD-denominated forecast sales and designate them as hedged items in the four hedging relationships. If the group were to hedge those identified forecast sales as well, they would be part of an additional hedging relationship and, therefore, not available to their designation as hedged items in our four hedging relationships.
- Secondly, when deciding the USD nominal of the AVRFs, ABC needed to forecast its foreign subsidiary earnings and inefficiencies may arise from inaccurate forecasts.
- Thirdly, there could be undesired tax effects in profit or loss. In our case both the hedging instruments and the hedged items were booked in the parent entity, allowing it to consider the application of hedge accounting in the parent's stand-alone financial statements. However, were the hedged items located in an entity different from the parent, the four AVRFs would have been classified as undesignated, and as a result, the change in fair value of the AVRFs would have been recorded in profit or loss, increasing the volatility of the parent's profit or loss statement. If this entity was a tax-paying entity, losses on the AVRFs would be tax deductible, while gains on the AVRFs would be taxed. These tax effects may affect the parent entity's ability to distribute dividends. In reality, most corporations execute consolidation-related hedges in a treasury centre, reducing undesired tax effects on their group hedges.
- Fourthly, the hedge may distort EBITDA figures if the hedging instrument gains/losses were not recorded, adjusting the sales line. This did not apply in our case, as the AVRF results adjusted the USD sales figures.
- Finally, the average EUR–USD exchange rate used to translate the subsidiary's profit or loss may differ from the average rate used in the AVRFs. Often, a subsidiary's profit

or loss is translated using the daily average rate during the accounting period ,while the group may decide to use monthly average rate in the AVRFs in order to reduce their administrative load. Average mismatches may create hedge ineffectiveness and result in undesired effects on profit or loss.

6.15 CASE STUDY: INTEGRAL HEDGING OF AN INVESTMENT IN A FOREIGN OPERATION

In my experience of advising multinationals on how to hedge their exposure to foreign subsidiaries, I have found an evolution (see Figure 6.27) in their hedging strategies over the years. Usually entities start hedging the exposure stemming from dividends received from their foreign subsidiaries. After a few years of hedging dividends, multinationals also address the exposure stemming from the translation of their subsidiaries' profit or loss statements. Finally, after gaining experience hedging earnings and dividends, multinationals also decide to hedge their net investment exposure.

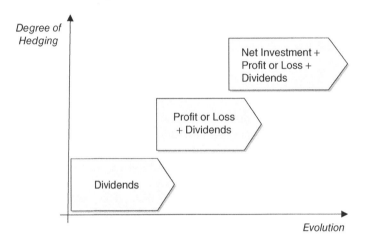

FIGURE 6.27 Foreign subsidiaries hedging – common evolution pattern.

If an entity hedges these three risks separately – dividends, income statement and net investment – it could experience severe hedging inefficiencies as the three risks are interrelated. A special analysis is then needed when trying to hedge the combined risk. The key to the analysis is to understand how the net assets of a subsidiary change during an accounting year and which exchange rates affect their translation into the group's consolidated financial statements.

Assuming yearly reporting, a net investment in a foreign subsidiary can be split into five different components (see Figure 6.28):

1) The net assets at the beginning of the year. The previous translation of this component was performed using the exchange rate prevailing at the closing of the previous year. As this component has to be revalued at the year-end exchange rate, the translation risk is caused by the change in the exchange rate from the end of the previous year to the end of the current year.

2) The investment in new equity issued by the subsidiary during the year. Investing in new capital increases the net investment in the subsidiary. A capital injection is initially recorded at the FX rate prevailing at the moment of the capital increase. As this component has to be revalued at the year-end exchange rate, the translation risk is caused by the change in the exchange rate from the capital injection date to the end of the current year.

3) The profit or loss generated by the subsidiary during the year. Positive earnings for the year increase the net investment in the subsidiary. Recall that a subsidiary's earnings are usually translated at the average exchange rate of the year. As this component has to be revalued at the year-end exchange rate, the translation risk is caused by the difference between the average exchange rate during the year and the exchange rate at the end of the current year.

4) The dividends distributed by the subsidiary during the year. Dividends decrease a net investment. On the consolidated statements, dividends effectively leave the net investment when they are paid. Once paid, dividends do not affect net investment risk (they become part of the parent's monetary assets). Thus, a translation risk is caused by the change in the exchange rate from the closing of the previous year to the exchange rate prevailing on dividend payment date.

5) The OCI generated by the subsidiary during the year. An increase in OCI for the year increases the net investment in the subsidiary. IAS 21 does not state the FX rate at which to translate changes in a subsidiary's OCI. The two most common alternatives are to translate them at the average exchange rate of the year or at the year-end exchange rate. In the former, the translation risk is caused by the difference between the average exchange rate during the year and the exchange rate at the end of the current year.

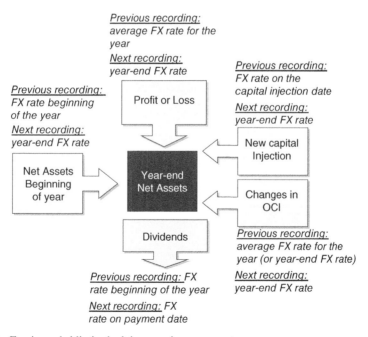

FIGURE 6.28 Foreign subsidiaries hedging – main components.

Let us consider a specific example. ABC, a group with the EUR as presentation currency, had a net investment in a US subsidiary whose functional currency was the USD. Suppose that at the beginning of 20X1 ABC was looking to fully hedge its net investment for the year ending 20X1. The expected changes to the net investment during the year 20X1 were as follows:

Net investment in US subsidiary Expected changes during year 20X1	
Net assets (including goodwill and fair value adjustments) at the beginning of the year (31-Dec-20X0)	USD 500 million
Expected subsidiary's net earnings	USD 120 million (USD 10 million per month)
Expected dividends (expected to be paid on 31-May-20X1)	USD 100 million
Expected changes in the subsidiary's OCI	No changes expected
Expected new capital injection (expected to be executed on 30-Sep-20X1)	USD 200 million

In order to get an idea of ABC's net investment exposure during 20X1, ABC produced the graph shown in Figure 6.29. During 20X1, the net investment was expected to increase by USD 10 million per month due to the subsidiary's net income. The net investment was expected to decline by USD 100 million due to subsidiary's expected dividend payment to the parent company on 31 May 20X1. Finally, the net investment was expected to increase by USD 200 million as a result of the parent's expected capital injection on 30 September 20X1.

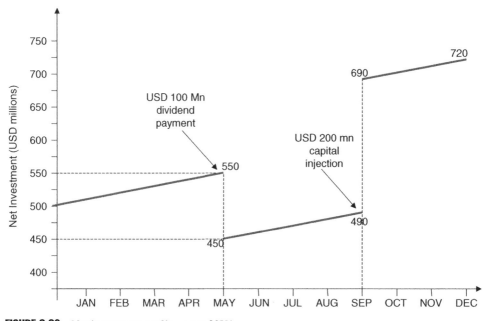

FIGURE 6.29   Net investment profile – year 20X1.

One way to perfectly hedge the profile shown in Figure 6.29 was to execute on 1 January 20X1 a series of FX forwards aimed at hedging the five building blocks shown in Figure 6.28: hedging the year-end net assets, hedging the subsidiary's expected net earnings, hedging the expected new capital to be invested in the subsidiary, and hedging the expected dividends to be paid by the subsidiary (see also Figure 6.30). There was no need to hedge the net assets at the beginning of the year, as its rate was already known (1.25).

Net Assets at Year-end	720 mn / (Year-end Rate)
Less Net Assets at Beginning-Year	500 mn / (1.25) ← *Beginning-of-year FX rate*
Less Translated Profit or Loss	120 mn / Average Rate
Less Capital Injection	200 mn / Injection Date Rate
Plus Dividend Paid	100 mn / Dividend Payment Date Rate
Equals Exchange Differences	

FIGURE 6.30 Exchange differences calculation – year 20X1.

Suppose that the market EUR–USD forward rates, as of 1 January 20X1, for the relevant dates were as follows:

Date	Forward rate (as of 1-Jan-20X1)
1 January 20X1	1.2500
31 May 20X1	1.2580
30 September 20X1	1.2650
31 December 20X1	1.2700
Average during 20X1	1.2600

Hedge 1: Hedging Year-end Net Assets The expected year-end net investment was USD 720 million, as shown in Figure 6.29. In order to hedge the year-end revaluation of the USD 720 million, ABC entered into a standard FX forward ("forward 1") with a nominal of USD 720 million and maturity 31 December 20X1. The forward rate for 31 December 20X1 was 1.2700. The forward payoff at maturity compensated ABC for any appreciation of the year-end rate:

Hedge 1: Forward 1 payoff = USD 720 million × (1/1.2700 − 1/(Year-end rate))

With this forward, ABC hedged the "net assets at year-end", as shown in Figure 6.31 (first line of the table).

	Hedge 1
Net Assets at Year-end	720 mn / (Year-end Rate)
Less Net Assets at Beginning-Year	500 mn / 1.25
Less Translated Profit or Loss	120 mn / Average Rate
Less Capital Injection	200 mn / Injection Date Rate
Plus Dividend Paid	100 mn / Dividend Payment Date Rate
Equals Exchange Differences	

FIGURE 6.31 Exchange differences calculation, hedge 1, year 20X1.

Hedge 2: Hedging the Subsidiary's Expected Net Earnings   The subsidiary's expected profit or loss was USD 120 million. This amount was to become part of the net investment at the average rate for 20X1 and was to be revalued at year's end. The revaluation at year's end was already included in hedge 1. Therefore, ABC needed to hedge the translation of the subsidiary's expected profit or loss at the average rate for the year 20X1. This hedge covered the third line of Figure 6.32.

Net Assets at Year-end	720 mn / (Year-end Rate)
Less Net Assets at Beginning-Year	500 mn / 1.25 *Hedge 2*
Less Translated Profit or Loss	120 mn / Average Rate
Less Capital Injection	200 mn / Injection Date Rate
Plus Dividend Paid	100 mn / Dividend Payment Date Rate

Equals Exchange Differences

FIGURE 6.32   Exchange differences calculation, hedge 2, year 20X1.

As seen in the case study in Section 6.14, the appropriate hedging instrument was an average rate forward (forward 2).

The average rate forward had a USD 120 million nominal amount and a 31 December 20X1 maturity. The market expected the average rate to be 1.26. Its payoff at maturity was:

Hedge 2: Forward 2 payoff = USD 120 million × (1/(Year average rate) – 1/1.2600)

Hedge 3: Hedging the Expected New Capital Injection into the Subsidiary   ABC's parent entity expected to add USD 200 million capital to its US subsidiary. From a "net investment" perspective, ABC was exposed to the year-end appreciation of the EUR–USD rate relative to the rate prevailing on the capital investment date (30 September 20X1). The first part (the year-end revaluation) was already hedged through hedge 1. ABC needed then to hedge ("hedge 3") the exposure to rate prevailing on the capital investment date, which was equivalent to hedge the fourth line of Figure 6.33.

Net Assets at Year-end	720 mn / (Year-end Rate)
Less Net Assets at Beginning-Year	500 mn / 1.25
Less Translated Profit or Loss	120 mn / Average Rate *Hedge 3*
Less Capital Injection	200 mn / Injection Date Rate
Plus Dividend Paid	100 mn / Dividend Payment Date Rate

Equals Exchange Differences

FIGURE 6.33   Exchange differences calculation, hedge 3, year 20X1.

The appropriate instrument was an FX forward ("forward 3") with a nominal of USD 200 million, maturity 30 September 20X1 and the following payoff at maturity:

Hedge 3: Forward 3 payoff = USD 200 million × (1/(30-Sept-20X1 rate) – 1/1.2650)

Hedge 4: Hedging the Expected Dividends Paid by the Subsidiary   ABC's parent entity expected to receive USD 100 million dividends from its US subsidiary on 31 May 20X1. As a result,

ABC's parent company was exposed to an appreciation of the EUR–USD FX rate prevailing on the dividend payment date (31 May 20X1).

The appropriate hedge was an FX forward ("forward 4") with a nominal of USD 100 million and maturity 31 May 20X1. This hedge covered the exposure outlined in the fifth line of Figure 6.34. The payoff of forward 4 at maturity compensated ABC from any appreciation of the 31 May 20X1 exchange rate:

Hedge 4: Forward 4 payoff = USD 100 million × (1/1.2580 – 1/(31-May-20X1 rate))

Net Assets at Year-end	720 mn / (Year-end Rate)
Less Net Assets at Beginning-Year	500 mn / 1.25
Less Translated Profit or Loss	120 mn / Average Rate
Less Capital Injection	200 mn / Injection Date Rate
Plus Dividend Paid	100 mn / Dividend Payment Date Rate
Equals Exchange Differences	

Hedge 4

FIGURE 6.34 Exchange differences calculation, hedge 4, year 20X1.

Expected Translation Differences Adjustment for the Year 20X1 As a result of these four hedges, ABC expected to recognise a translation differences deficit of EUR 6,921,000, as shown in Figure 6.35.

	Net Assets at Year-end	720 mn / 1.27 = EUR 566,929,000
Less	Net Assets at Beginning-Year	500 mn / 1.25 = EUR 400,000,000
Less	Translated Profit or Loss	120 mn / 1.26 = EUR 95,238,000
Less	Capital Injection	200 mn / 1.265 = EUR 158,103,000
Plus	Dividend Paid	100 mn / 1.258 = EUR 79,491,000
Equals	Exchange Differences	< EUR 6,921,000 >

FIGURE 6.35 Exchange differences calculation, integral hedge, year 20X1.

Hedge Performance Analysis Let us assess whether the integral hedge worked well in practice. Suppose that the market EUR–USD FX rates during 20X1 were as follows:

Date	Spot EUR–USD Rate
1 January 20X1	1.2500
31 May 20X1	1.3000
30 September 20X1	1.2000
31 December 20X1	1.3500
Average during 20X1	1.2800

The following table shows the translation exchange differences for the year 20X1, excluding the hedge. It highlights that without the hedge, the translation differences account would have shown a deficit of EUR 50,161,000.

	Component	Calculation	EUR amount
	Net assets at year's end	720 Mn/1.35	533,333,000
less	Net assets at beginning-of-year	500 Mn/1.25	<400,000,000>
less	Translated profit or loss	120 Mn/1.28	<93,750,000>
less	Capital injection	200 Mn/1.20	<166,667,000>
plus	Dividend	100 Mn/1.30	76,923,000
equals	Translation exchange differences		<50,161,000>

Fortunately, ABC had a hedge in place. The hedge was implemented through four instruments, each designed to eliminate the exposure to the EUR–USD rate of each component of the net investment in the US subsidiary. The following table details the payoffs of each instrument:

	Payoff calculation	EUR amount
Hedge 1	720 mn × (1/1.27 – 1/1.35)	33,596,000
Hedge 2	120 mn × (1/1.28 – 1/1.26)	<1,488,000>
Hedge 3	200 mn × (1/1.20 – 1/1.265)	8,564,000
Hedge 4	100 mn × (1/1.258 – 1/1.30)	2,568,000
	Total hedge payoff	43,240,000

Through the integral hedge, ABC received EUR 43,240,000. Therefore, the translation differences account showed "only" an adjustment of a EUR 6,921,000 deficit (see the following table). The hedge worked very well, as this amount was exactly the amount that ABC expected (see Figure 6.35).

	EUR amount
Translation differences adjustment without hedge	<50,161,000>
Hedge payoff	43,240,000
Total translation differences adjustment	<6,921,000>

Additional Remarks   A couple of particular issues are worth noting:

- Firstly, hedge 2 was aimed at eliminating the exposure of the translation differences account from a depreciation of the EUR–USD average rate over 20X1. This hedge was exactly the opposite of the profit or loss translation hedge that was discussed in the case study in Section 6.14. Therefore, as both hedges cancelled out, there was no need to implement both hedges simultaneously.
- Secondly, hedge 4 was aimed at eliminating the exposure of the translation differences account from an appreciation of the 31 May 20X1 EUR–USD rate. This hedge was exactly the same as the dividend hedge that was discussed in Section 6.13. Therefore, if ABC implemented the net investment integral hedge, there would be no need to implement the dividend hedge mentioned in that section.

CHAPTER 7

Hedging Interest Rate Risk

This chapter focuses on one of the most common financial risks that an entity may hedge: interest rate risk. This risk arises from entities holding interest-bearing financial assets and/ or liabilities, or from forecasted or committed future transactions including an interest-bearing element. An entity's ability to manage interest rate exposure can enhance financial exposure, mitigate losses, and reduce funding costs.

The most common interest rate exposures stem from the following situations:

1) An already recognised financial liability (or asset) that pays (or receives) a fixed interest rate. In this case, the interest rate risk relates to the fair value change in the financial liability (or asset) due to movements in interest rates.
2) An already recognised financial liability (or asset) that pays (or receives) a floating interest rate (i.e., future interest payments are linked to a benchmark interest index). In this case, the interest rate risk relates to variations in future cash flows.
3) Highly probable anticipated future issuance of an interest-bearing financial liability (or asset). In this case, the interest rate risk relates to variations in future cash flows.

The objective of this chapter is *not* to identify the appropriate hedging strategy to mitigate exposure to changes in interest rates. Instead, its objective is to provide practical insight into the accounting implications of a chosen interest rate hedging strategy. In order to emphasise the practical angle of interest rate hedge accounting, several cases are analysed in detail.

7.1 COMMON INTEREST RATE HEDGING STRATEGIES

The following table summarises the most common hedging strategies applied by corporations:

Hedged item	Risk	Type of hedge	Common hedging strategies
Existing fixed rate debt	Exposure to variability in fair value	Fair value hedge of a recognised liability (or asset)	1) Convert the interest paid (or received) into floating by entering into an interest rate swap

(continued overleaf)

Hedged item	Risk	Type of hedge	Common hedging strategies
			2) If an asset, lock in a minimum value by buying a put option to sell the asset at a specified price (or buying a payer swaption) 3) If a liability, lock in a maximum value by buying a call option to repurchase the liability at a specified price (or buying a receiver swaption)
Existing floating rate debt	Exposure to variability in interest rate payments (or receipts)	Cash flow hedge of a recognised liability (or asset)	1) Convert the interest paid (or received) to fixed by entering into an interest rate swap 2) Limit the maximum interest paid (or received) by buying a cap (or floor)
Highly expected issuance of, or firm commitment to issue, fixed rate debt	Exposure to variability in interest rate payments due to changes in interest rates to date of issuance	Cash flow hedge of a highly expected issue or of a firm commitment	1) Lock in the future interest to be paid by entering into a forward starting pay-fixed receive-floating interest rate swap 2) Limit the future interest to be paid by buying a cap or by entering into a forward starting collar 3) Participate in declines in interest rates by buying a payer swaption 4) Participate in declines in interest rates by buying a put option on a similar bond
Highly expected issuance of, or firm commitment to issue, floating rate debt	Exposure to variability in interest rate payments due to changes in interest rates to date of payment	Cash flow hedge of a highly expected issue or of a firm commitment	1) Lock in future interest payments by entering into a forward starting pay-fixed receive-floating interest rate swap 2) Limit future interest payments by buying a forward starting cap collar 3) Participate in declines in interest rates by buying a payer swaption 4) Participate in declines in interest rates by buying a put option on a similar bond

7.2 SEPARATION OF EMBEDDED DERIVATIVES IN STRUCTURED DEBT INSTRUMENTS

In the fixed income market it is not unusual to find bonds that pay interest that differs considerably from the interest that otherwise would be paid by the issuer, or received by the investor, on a standard bond. A yield different from a market yield is usually achieved by adding a derivative in the financial instrument –an "embedded derivative" – to a debt-like "host contract". The accounting for hybrid instruments was covered discussed in Section 1.6.

When the host contract is a financial asset within the scope of IFRS 9, the hybrid financial instrument is *not* bifurcated; instead it is assessed in its entirety for classification under the standard.

A financial asset containing an embedded derivative is not considered a hybrid financial instrument if the economic characteristics and risks of the embedded derivative are clearly and closely related to those of the host contract.

When the host contract is a financial liability within the scope of IFRS 9, a hybrid financial instrument *is* bifurcated. Separation means that the embedded derivative is accounted for as a stand-alone derivative.

A financial liability does not require the separation of the embedded derivative from the rest of the liability (the "host contract") if:

1) the combined instrument is already measured at fair value through profit or loss; or
2) the economic characteristics and risks of the embedded derivative are clearly and closely related to those of the host contract.

An embedded derivative is assumed to be **closely related** to the host contract if it satisfies the following three requirements:

1) The embedded derivative could not potentially result in the investor failing to recover substantially all of its initially recorded investment.
2) The embedded derivative could potentially result in the issuer having to pay a leveraged rate of return. Usually the accounting community interprets this requirement as met when the debt holder could not receive twice, or more than twice, its initial yield on the instrument.
3) The embedded derivative does not extend the maturity date of fixed rate debt, except when interest rates are reset to market rates. In other words, the exercise price of the embedded option – whether a put, call or other prepayment option – is not approximately equal to the amortised cost of the host debt instrument.

The following are examples of structured bonds and whether or not, in my view, the closely-related condition is met. They assume that the yield of an equivalent fixed rate bond would be 6%:

- A collared floater that pays a floating rate bond with a maximum and a minimum. The embedded cap and floor are not in-the-money at inception.
- An inverse floater, a bond that pays a coupon that varies inversely with changes in the interest rate.
- A constant maturity swap, a bond that pays a coupon that is a percentage of a medium-term or long-term interest rate.

▪ A range floater, a bond that pays a coupon that depends on the number of days that an underlying reference interest rate stays within a pre-established range.
▪ A ratchet floater, a bond that pays a floating interest rate whose increase or decrease each period is limited relative to the previous coupon.
▪ A callable bond, a bond that pays an initial above market interest rate and that can be cancelled by the issuer on a specific date (or dates).
▪ An inflation-linked bond (see Section 12.2), a bond that pays a fixed interest on a principal amount that is indexed to the inflation rate.

Coupon	Investor may *not* recover initial investment?	Issuer may pay more than twice the market rate?	Option to extend fixed rate debt at non-market rates?	Need to separate embedded derivative?
Collared floater: Euribor 12M + 1%, with a maximum of 8% and a minimum of 4%	No	No	No	No
Inverse floater: 10% – Euribor 12M, with a minimum of 0%	No	No	No	No
Inverse floater: 14% – 2 × Euribor 12M, with a minimum of 2%	No	Yes	No	Yes
Inverse floater: 10% – 2 × Euribor 12M, without a minimum	Yes	No	No	Yes
Constant maturity swap: 75% × (10-year swap rate) + 1%	No	No	No	No
Constant maturity swap: 200% × (10-year swap rate)	No	Yes	No	Yes
Range accrual: 6% × (Number days within range)/ (Total days in period) Range is 3–4%	No	No	No	No
Ratchet floater: Euribor 12M + 60 bps Coupon cannot increase more than 35 bps relative to previous coupon	No	No	No	No

Coupon	Investor may *not* recover initial investment?	Issuer may pay more than twice the market rate?	Option to extend fixed rate debt at non-market rates?	Need to separate embedded derivative?
Callable bond: 6% annually. Bond can be cancelled after year 3	No	No	Yes	Yes
Inflation-linked bond: 4% on principal. Principal is adjusted to inflation. Inflation is related to the economic environment of the currency of issuance	No	No	No	No
Inflation-linked bond: 4% on principal. Principal is adjusted to inflation. Inflation is not related to the economic environment of the currency of issuance	No	No	No	Yes

7.3 INTEREST ACCRUALS

When fair valuing the hedging instrument and its related debt, settlement/interest accruals on each instrument have to be excluded. Otherwise double counting may occur in the profit or loss statement, causing unnecessary accounting headaches. The case study in Section 7.7 illustrates the effects of not excluding settlement/interest accruals from fair valuations.

In the case of an interest rate swap in which the entity pays a floating amount linked to a floating rate (the floating leg) and receives a fixed amount (the fixed leg), the appropriate fair valuation of a swap is as follows:

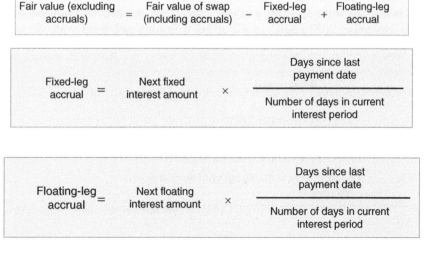

where

7.4 MOST COMMON INTEREST RATE DERIVATIVE INSTRUMENTS

The following table lists the most common interest rate derivative instruments:

Hedging instrument	Comments
Interest rate swap	Most friendly interest rate instrument to qualify for hedge accounting. Substitution of hedged asset/liability with hypothetical derivative recommended in cash flow hedges
Purchased cap (or floor)	Relatively friendly application of hedge accounting. Time value commonly excluded from hedging relationship. Recognised temporarily in equity to the extent that it relates to the hedged item. Substitution of hedged asset/liability with hypothetical derivative in cash flow hedges
Collar	Same as previous above
Swap in arrears	Fair value hedge requires robust assessment of economic relationship between debt instrument and swap. Substantial ineffectiveness may arise during the last few interest periods
KIKO collar	Challenging application of hedge accounting unless instrument is split between hedge accounting friendly derivative and undesignated residual derivative

7.5 CASE STUDY: HEDGING A FLOATING RATE LIABILITY WITH AN INTEREST RATE SWAP

This case study covers the hedge with an interest rate swap of the variability in interest payments pertaining to a floating rate debt due to changes in interest rates. When hedging interest rate risk, swaps are the friendliest instruments from an IFRS 9 perspective. A particular point addressed in this case is the application of the "critical terms method" to assess effectiveness.

On 31 December 20X0, ABC issued at par a floating rate bond with the following characteristics:

Bond terms	
Issue date	31 December 20X0
Maturity	5 years (31 December 20X5)
Notional	EUR 100 million
Coupon	Euribor 12M + 1.50% annually, actual/360 basis
Euribor fixing	Euribor is fixed at the beginning of the annual interest period

ABC decided to mitigate its exposure to movements in the Euribor 12-month interest rate by, simultaneously with the issuance of the bond, entering into an interest rate swap with the following terms:

Interest rate swap terms	
Trade date	31 December 20X0
Counterparties	ABC and XYZ Bank
Notional	EUR 100 million
Maturity	5 years (31 December 20X5)
ABC pays	3.86% annually, actual/360 basis
ABC receives	Euribor 12M annually, actual/360 basis
Euribor fixing	Euribor is fixed at the beginning of the annual interest period
Initial fair value	Nil

The interest rate swap was designated as the hedging instrument in a cash flow hedge of the coupon payments on the bond. The credit spread associated with the bond (150 basis points) was excluded from the hedging relationship. The combination of the bond and the swap resulted in an overall interest expense of 5.36% (= 3.86% plus the 150 bps spread).

7.5.1 Hedging Relationship Documentation

ABC documented the hedging relationship as follows:

Hedging relationship documentation	
Risk management objective and strategy for undertaking the hedge	The objective of the hedge is to mitigate the variability of the cash flows stemming from the floating rate coupon payments related to a debt instrument issued by the entity against unfavourable movements in the Euribor 12-month rate.
	This hedging objective is consistent with the entity's overall interest rate risk management strategy of achieving a target mix between fixed and floating rate liabilities with interest rate swaps and collars.
	Interest rate risk. The designated risk being hedged is the risk of changes in the EUR value of the hedged cash flows due to movements in the Euribor 12-month interest rate
Type of hedge	Cash flow hedge
Hedged item	The cash flows stemming from the coupons of the bond with reference number 08754 issued on 31 December 20X0 with a 5-year maturity, a EUR 100 million notional, and a Euribor 12-month plus 1.50% annual coupon. The coupons are highly expected to occur as the bond has already been issued.
	The 1.50% credit spread is excluded from the hedging relationship

(continued overleaf)

Hedging relationship documentation	
Hedging instrument	The interest rate swap with reference number 014569. The main terms of the swap are a EUR 100 million notional, a 5-year maturity, a 3.86% fixed rate to be paid by the entity and a Euribor 12-month rate to be received by the entity. The counterparty to the swap is XYZ Bank and the credit risk associated with this counterparty is considered to be very low
Hedge effectiveness assessment	See below

7.5.2 Hedge Effectiveness Assessment

Hedge effectiveness will be assessed by comparing changes in the fair value of the hedging instrument to changes in the fair value of a hypothetical derivative. The terms of the hypothetical derivative are such that its fair value changes exactly offset the changes in fair value of the hedged item for the risk being hedged. The hypothetical derivative is a theoretical interest rate swap with no counterparty credit risk and with zero initial fair value, whose main terms are as follows:

Hypothetical derivative terms	
Start date	31 December 20X0
Counterparties	ABC and credit risk-free counterparty
Notional	EUR 100 million
Maturity	5 years (31 December 20X5)
ABC pays	3.87% annually, actual/360 basis
ABC receives	Euribor 12M annually, actual/360 basis
Euribor fixing	Euribor is fixed at the beginning of the annual interest period
Initial fair value	Nil

The fixed rate of the hypothetical derivative is higher than that of the hedging instrument due to the absence of CVA in the former.

Changes in the fair value of the hedging instrument will be recognised as follows:

- The effective part of the gain or loss on the hedging instrument will be recognised in the cash flow hedge reserve of OCI in equity. The accumulated amount in equity will be reclassified to profit or loss in the same period during which the hedged expected future cash flow affects profit or loss, adjusting interest expense.
- The ineffective part of the gain or loss on the hedging instrument will be recognised immediately in profit or loss.

Hedge effectiveness will be assessed prospectively at hedging relationship inception, on an ongoing basis at least upon each reporting date and upon occurrence of a significant change in the circumstances affecting the hedge effectiveness requirements.

The hedging relationship will qualify for hedge accounting only if all the following criteria are met:

1) The hedging relationship consists only of eligible hedge items and hedging instruments. The hedge item is eligible as it is a group of highly expected forecast cash flows that exposes the entity to fair value risk, affects profit or loss and is reliably measurable. The hedging instrument is eligible as it is a derivative that does not result in a net written option.

2) At hedge inception there is a formal designation and documentation of the hedging relationship and the entity's risk management objective and strategy for undertaking the hedge.

3) The hedging relationship is considered effective.

The hedging relationship will be considered effective if the following three requirements are met:

1) There is an economic relationship between the hedged item and the hedging instrument.

2) The effect of credit risk does not dominate the value changes that result from that economic relationship.

3) The hedge ratio of the hedging relationship is the same as that resulting from the quantity of hedged item that the entity actually hedges and the quantity of the hedging instrument that the entity actually uses to hedge that quantity of hedged item. The hedge ratio should not be intentionally weighted to create ineffectiveness.

Whether there is an economic relationship between the hedged item and the hedging instrument will be assessed on a qualitative basis comparing the critical terms (notional, interest periods, underlying and fixed rates) of the hypothetical derivative and the hedging instrument. The assessment will be complemented by a quantitative assessment using the scenario analysis method for one scenario in which Euribor interest rates will be shifted upwards by 2% and the changes in fair value of the hypothetical derivative and the hedging instrument compared.

7.5.3 Hedge Effectiveness Assessment Performed at the Start of the Hedging Relationship

The hedging relationship was considered effective as the following three requirements were met:

1) There was an economic relationship between the hedged item and the hedging instrument. Based on the qualitative assessment performed supported by a quantitative analysis, ABC concluded that the change in fair value of the hedged item was expected to be substantially offset by the change in fair value of the hedging instrument, corroborating that both elements had values that would generally move in opposite directions.

2) The effect of credit risk did not dominate the value changes resulting from that economic relationship as the credit ratings of both the entity and XYZ Bank were considered sufficiently strong.

3) The hedge ratio of the hedging relationship was the same as that resulting from the quantity of hedged item that the entity actually hedged and the quantity of the hedging instrument that the entity actually used to hedge that quantity of hedged item. The hedge ratio was not intentionally weighted to create ineffectiveness.

Due to the fact that the terms of the hedging instrument and those of the expected cash flow closely matched and the low credit risk exposure to the counterparty of the swap contract, it was concluded that the hedging instrument and the hedged item had values that would generally move in opposite directions. This conclusion was supported by a quantitative assessment, which consisted of one scenario analysis performed as follows. A parallel shift of +2% occurring on the assessment date was simulated. The fair values of the hedging instrument and the hypothetical derivatives were calculated and compared to their initial fair values. As shown in the table below, the high degree of offset implied that the change in fair value of the hedged item was expected to largely be offset by the change in fair value of the hedging instrument, corroborating that both elements had values that would generally move in opposite directions.

Scenario analysis assessment		
	Hedging instrument	**Hypothetical derivative**
Initial fair value	Nil	Nil
Final fair value	8,860,000	8,911,000
Cumulative fair value change	8,860,000	8,911,000
	Degree of offset	**99.4%**

The degree of offset would have been slightly larger than 100%, had the hedging instrument had no CVA. In this case, the large positive amount and the 5-year remaining term resulted in a substantial CVA.

The following potential sources of ineffectiveness were identified:

- a substantial deterioration in credit risk of either the entity or the counterparty to the hedging instrument; and
- a change in the timing or amounts of the hedged highly expected cash flows.

The hedge ratio was set at 1:1.

ABC also performed assessments on each reporting date, yielding the same conclusions. These assessments have been omitted to avoid unnecessary repetition.

7.5.4 Fair Valuations, Effective/Ineffective Amounts and Cash Flow Calculations

Fair Valuations of Hedging Instrument and Hypothetical Derivative As an example, the following table details the fair valuation of the hedging instrument on 31 December 20X1:

Date	Euribor 12M *(1)*	Discount factor	Expected floating leg cash flow *(2)*	Fixed leg cash flow *(3)*	Expected settlement amount *(4)*	Present value *(5)*
31-Dec-20X2	4.21%	0.9591	4,268,000	<3,914,000>	354,000	340,000
31-Dec-20X3	4.80%	0.9146	4,867,000	<3,914,000>	953,000	872,000
31-Dec-20X4	5.00%	0.8705	5,069,000	<3,914,000>	1,155,000	1,005,000
31-Dec-20X5	5.12%	0.8275	5,191,000	<3,914,000>	1,277,000	1,057,000
CVA/DVA						<31,000>
Total						3,243,000

Notes:

    (1) The expected Euribor 12-month rate, as of 31 December 20X1, to be fixed two business days prior to the commencement of the interest period

    (2) Expected floating leg cash flow = 100 mn × Euribor 12M × 365/360, assuming 365 calendar days in the interest period

    (3) Fixed leg cash flow = 100 mn × 3.86% × 365/360, assuming 365 calendar days in the interest period

    (4) Expected settlement amount = Expected floating leg cash flow – Absolute value[Fixed leg cash flow]

    (5) Present value = Expected settlement amount × Discount factor

Similarly, the following table details the fair valuation of the hypothetical derivative on 31 December 20X1:

Date	Euribor 12M	Discount factor	Expected floating leg cash flow	Fixed leg cash flow (*)	Expected settlement amount	Present value
31-Dec-20X2	4.21%	0.9591	4,268,000	<3,924,000>	344,000	330,000
31-Dec-20X3	4.80%	0.9146	4,867,000	<3,924,000>	943,000	862,000
31-Dec-20X4	5.00%	0.8705	5,069,000	<3,924,000>	1,145,000	997,000
31-Dec-20X5	5.12%	0.8275	5,191,000	<3,924,000>	1,267,000	1,048,000
CVA/DVA						Nil
Total						3,237,000

(*) Fixed leg cash flow = 100 mn × 3.87% × 365/360, assuming 365 calendar days in the interest period

The fair values of the hedging instrument and the hypothetical derivative at each relevant date were as follows:

Date	Hedging instrument fair value	Period change	Cumulative change	Hypothetical derivative fair value	Cumulative change
31-Dec-20X1	3,243,000	3,243,000	3,243,000	3,237,000	3,237,000
31-Dec-20X2	850,000	<2,393,000>	850,000	832,000	832,000
31-Dec-20X3	276,000	<574,000>	276,000	263,000	263,000
31-Dec-20X4	<87,000>	<363,000>	<87,000>	<78,000>	<78,000>
31-Dec-20X5	Nil	87,000	Nil	Nil	Nil

Effective and Ineffective Amounts   The ineffective part of the change in fair value of the swap was the excess of its cumulative change in fair value over that of the hypothetical derivative. The effective and ineffective parts of the change in fair value of the swap were the following (see Section 5.5.6 for an explanation of the calculations):

	31-Dec-X1	31-Dec-X2	31-Dec-X3	31-Dec-X4	31-Dec-X5
Cumulative change in fair value of hedging instrument	3,243,000	850,000	276,000	<87,000>	Nil
Cumulative change in fair value of hypothetical derivative	3,237,000	832,000	263,000	<78,000>	Nil
Lower amount	3,237,000	832,000	263,000	<78,000>	Nil
Previous cumulative effective amount	—	3,237,000	844,000	270,000	<78,000>
Available amount	3,237,000	<2,405,000>	<581,000>	<348,000>	78,000
Period change in fair value of hedging instrument	3,243,000	<2,393,000>	<574,000>	<363,000>	87,000
Effective part	3,237,000	<2,393,000>	<574,000>	<348,000>	78,000
Ineffective part	6,000	Nil	Nil	<15,000>	9,000

Bond Coupon Payments and Swap Settlement Amounts   The bond coupon payments and swap settlement amounts at each relevant date were as follows:

Date	Period Euribor 12M	Bond interest *(1)*	Swap settlement amount *(2)*
31-Dec-20X1	3.21%	<4,775,000>	<659.000>
31-Dec-20X2	4.21%	<5,789,000>	354.000
31-Dec-20X3	3.71%	<5,282,000>	<152.000>
31-Dec-20X4	3.80%	<5,374,000>	<61.000>
31-Dec-20X5	3.95%	<5,526,000>	91.000

Notes:

(1) <100 mn> × (Euribor 12M + 1.50%) × 365/360, assuming 365 calendar days in the interest period
(2) 100 mn × (Euribor 12M) × 365/360 − 100 mn × 3.86% × 365/360, assuming 365 calendar days in the interest period

7.5.5 Accounting Entries

The required journal entries were the following.

1) Entries on 31 December 20X0

To record the issuance of the bond:

Cash (Asset)	100,000,000	
Financial debt (Liability)		100,000,000

No journal entries were required to record the swap since its fair value was zero at inception.

2) Entries on 31 December 20X1

The bond paid a EUR 4,775,000 coupon.

Interest expense (Profit or loss)	4,775,000	
Cash (Asset)		4,775,000

The change in fair value of the swap since the last valuation was a EUR 3,243,000 gain, of which EUR 3,237,000 was deemed to be effective and recorded in the cash flow hedge reserve of equity, while EUR 6,000 was deemed to be ineffective and recorded in profit or loss.

Derivative contract (Asset)	3,243,000	
Cash flow hedge reserve (Equity)		3,237,000
Other financial income (Profit or loss)		6,000

Under the swap the entity paid a EUR 659,000 settlement amount.

Interest expense (Profit or loss)	659,000	
Cash (Asset)		659,000

3) Entries on 31 December 20X2

The bond paid a EUR 5,789,000 coupon. The change in fair value of the swap since the last valuation was a EUR 2,393,000 loss, fully effective and recorded in the cash flow hedge reserve of equity. Under the swap the entity received a EUR 354,000 settlement amount.

Interest expense (Profit or loss)	5,789,000	
Cash (Asset)		5,789,000
Cash flow hedge reserve (Equity)	2,393,000	
Derivative contract (Asset)		2,393,000
Cash (Asset)	354,000	
Interest income (Profit or loss)		354,000

4) Entries on 31 December 20X3

The bond paid a EUR 5,282,000 coupon. The change in fair value of the swap since the last valuation was a EUR 574,000 loss, fully effective and recorded in the cash flow hedge reserve of equity. Under the swap the entity paid a EUR 152,000 settlement amount.

Interest expense (Profit or loss)	5,282,000	
Cash (Asset)		5,282,000
Cash flow hedge reserve (Equity)	574,000	
Derivative contract (Asset)		574,000
Interest expense (Profit or loss)	152,000	
Cash (Asset)		152,000

5) Entries on 31 December 20X4

The bond paid a EUR 5,374,000 coupon. The change in fair value of the swap since the last valuation was a EUR 363,000 loss, of which EUR 348,000 was deemed to be effective and recorded in the cash flow hedge reserve of equity, while EUR 15,000 was deemed to be ineffective and recorded in profit or loss. Under the swap the entity paid a EUR 61,000 settlement amount.

Interest expense (Profit or loss)	5,374,000	
Cash (Asset)		5,374,000
Cash flow hedge reserve (Equity)	348,000	
Other financial expenses (Profit or loss)	15,000	
Derivative contract (Asset)		363,000
Interest expense (Profit or loss)	61,000	
Cash (Asset)		61,000

6) Entries on 31 December 20X5

The bond paid a EUR 5,526,000 coupon and repaid the EUR 100 million principal. The change in fair value of the swap since the last valuation was a EUR 87,000 gain, of which EUR 78,000 was deemed to be effective and recorded in the cash flow hedge reserve of equity, while EUR 9,000 was deemed to be ineffective and recorded in profit or loss. Under the swap the entity received a EUR 91,000 settlement amount.

Interest expense (Profit or loss)	5,526,000	
Financial debt (Liability)	100,000,000	
Cash (Asset)		105,526,000
Derivative contract (Asset)	87,000	
Cash flow hedge reserve (Equity)		78,000
Other financial income (Profit or loss)		9,000
Cash (Asset)	91,000	
Interest income (Profit or loss)		91,000

7.5.5 Final Remarks

The total interest expense/income recognised during the interest period ending 31 December 20X1 was EUR 5,434,000 (= 4,775,000 + 659,000). The objective of entering into the hedge was to fix the overall interest rate at 5.36%, which represented a EUR 5,434,000 (= 100 mn × (3.86% + 1.50%) × 365/360) interest expense. Therefore, the objective was fully met during that interest period. This was true for all interest periods in which the swap fair value change was fully effective. In periods during which ineffectiveness was present, the difference between the actual and the target interest expenses was notably small.

The end date of the interest periods coincided with the reporting dates. This resulted in no accrual amounts to be recorded. When there are accrual amounts, the fair valuation of the swap should exclude these amounts, or otherwise a double counting in profit or loss would occur.

7.6 CASE STUDY: HEDGING A FLOATING RATE LIABILITY WITH A ZERO-COST COLLAR

This section covers the hedge with a zero-cost collar of the variability in interest payments pertaining to a floating rate debt due to changes in interest rates. The hedge accounting treatment of caps and collars is relatively clear from an IFRS 9 perspective. The hedged liability is identical to that in the previous case:

Bond terms	
Issue date	31 December 20X0
Maturity	5 years (31 December 20X5)
Notional	EUR 100 million
Coupon	Euribor 12M + 1.50% annually, actual/360 basis
Euribor fixing	Euribor is fixed at the beginning of the annual interest period

ABC decided to protect its exposure to adverse movements in the Euribor 12-month interest rate by, alongside the issuance of the bond, buying a cap which set a maximum interest to be paid each interest period. Simultaneously, to avoid paying an up-front premium, ABC sold an interest rate floor which set a minimum interest to be paid each interest period. Recall that the combination of a cap and a floor is called a collar. In our case, ABC entered into a collar with the following terms:

Interest rate cap terms	
Trade date	31 December 20X0
Buyer	ABC
Seller	XYZ Bank
Notional	EUR 100 million
Maturity	5 years (31 December 20X5)
Cap rate	4.85% annually, actual/360 basis
Underlying	Euribor is fixed at the beginning of the annual interest period
Up-front premium	EUR 950,000
Interest rate floor terms	
Trade date	31 December 20X0
Buyer	XYZ Bank
Seller	ABC
Notional	EUR 100 million
Maturity	5 years (31 December 20X5)
Floor rate	3.18% annually, actual/360 basis
Underlying	Euribor is fixed at the beginning of the annual interest period
Up-front premium	EUR 950,000

When an option is used in a hedging strategy and hedge accounting is applied, IFRS 9 gives entities two choices:

- To designate the option in its entirety as the hedging instrument. This is seldom chosen.
- To separate the option's intrinsic and time values, and to designate only the intrinsic value as the hedging instrument in the hedging relationship. The option's time value is, therefore, excluded from the hedging relationship. This is the alternative commonly used because it enhances hedge effectiveness as the option's time value is not replicated in the hedged item. In other words, from a hedge accounting perspective the hedged item is assumed to lack any time value.

As a result, ABC designated the collar's intrinsic value (i.e., the intrinsic values of both the purchased and sold options) as the hedging instrument, and the highly expected variable coupons of the bond as the hedged item in a cash flow hedge of interest rate risk. The sold floor could be designated as part of the hedging instrument because:

1) no net premium was received;

2) the sold floor was designated as an offset to the purchased cap.

The credit spread associated with the bond (150 basis points) was excluded from the hedging relationship. The combination of the bond and the collar resulted in an overall interest rate between 4.68% (= 3.18% floor rate plus the 150 basis points spread) and 6.35% (= 4.85% cap rate plus the 150 basis points spread).

7.6.1 Hedging Relationship Documentation

ABC documented the hedging relationship as follows:

	Hedging relationship documentation
Risk management objective and strategy for undertaking the hedge	The objective of the hedge is to protect the variability of the cash flows stemming from the floating rate coupon payments related to a debt instrument issued by the entity against unfavourable movements in the Euribor 12-month rate above 4.85%. To achieve this objective while not paying an up-front premium for the hedge, the entity does not benefit from favourable movements in the Euribor 12M below 3.18%. This hedging objective is consistent with ABC's overall risk management strategy of managing the exposure to interest rate risk through the proportion of fixed and floating rate net debt in its total debt portfolio, using swaps and interest rate options. Interest rate risk. The designated risk being hedged is the risk of changes in the EUR value of the hedged cash flows due to movements in the Euribor 12-month interest rate
Type of hedge	Cash flow hedge
Hedged item	The cash flows stemming from the coupons of the bond with reference number 08754 issued on 31 December 20X0 with a 5-year maturity, a EUR 100 million notional, and a Euribor 12-month plus 1.50% annual coupon. The coupons are highly expected to occur as the bond has already been issued. The 1.50% credit spread is excluded from the hedging relationship
Hedging instrument	The intrinsic value of a zero-cost collar (the combination of a purchased cap and a sold floor) with reference number 014571. The main terms of the collar are a EUR 100 million notional, a 5-year maturity, a 4.85% cap rate, a 3.18% floor rate and a Euribor 12-month interest rate underlying. The counterparty to the collar is XYZ Bank and the credit risk associated with this counterparty is considered to be very low. For the avoidance of doubt, the collar's time value is excluded from the hedging relationship
Hedge effectiveness assessment	See below

7.6.2 Hedge Effectiveness Assessment

Hedge effectiveness will be assessed by comparing changes in the fair value of the hedging instrument to changes in the fair value of a hypothetical derivative. Effectiveness will be assessed only during those periods in which there is a change in intrinsic value.

The terms of the hypothetical derivative are such that its fair value changes exactly offset the changes in fair value of the hedged item for the risk being hedged. As the risk being hedged was the cash flow exposure to adverse movements in the Euribor 12-month rate above 4.85% while paying no up-front premium, the hypothetical derivative is a theoretical interest rate collar with no counterparty credit risk, with zero fair value at the start of the hedging relationship, a cap rate of 4.85% and a floor rate such that the collar results in a zero-cost option combination. The main terms of the hypothetical derivative were as follows:

Hypothetical derivative terms			
Cap terms		**Floor terms**	
Start date	31 December 20X0	Trade date	31 December 20X0
Buyer	ABC	Buyer	Credit risk-free counterparty
Seller	Credit risk-free counterparty	Seller	ABC
Notional	EUR 100 million	Notional	EUR 100 million
Maturity	5 years (31 December 20X5)	Maturity	5 years (31 December 20X5)
Cap rate	4.85%, actual/360 basis	Floor rate	3.20%, actual/360 basis (*)
Underlying	Euribor 12-month, fixed at the beginning of the annual interest period	Underlying	Euribor 12-month, fixed at the beginning of the annual interest period

(*) The floor rate of the hypothetical derivative (3.20%) was different from that of the hedging instrument (3.18%) due to the absence of CVA in the hypothetical derivative (the counterparty to the hypothetical derivative is assumed to be credit risk-free).

Changes in the fair value of the hedging instrument (i.e., the collar's intrinsic value) will be recognised as follows:

- The effective part of the gain or loss on the hedging instrument will be recognised in the cash flow hedge reserve of OCI in equity. The accumulated amount in equity will be reclassified to profit or loss in the same period during which the hedged expected future cash flow affects profit or loss, adjusting interest expense.
- The ineffective part of the gain or loss on the hedging instrument will be recognised immediately in profit or loss.

The change in time value of the collar (the "actual time value") will be excluded from the hedging relationship. Due to the absence of actual time value at the beginning and end of the hedging relationship, the changes in actual time value will be recognised temporarily in the time value reserve of OCI. No reclassification from OCI to profit or loss will be carried out during the term of the hedging relationship as the carrying value of the time value reserve in OCI is expected to be nil at the end of the hedging relationship.

Hedge effectiveness will be assessed prospectively at hedging relationship inception, on an ongoing basis at least upon each reporting date and upon occurrence of a significant change in the circumstances affecting the hedge effectiveness requirements.

The hedging relationship will qualify for hedge accounting only if all the following criteria are met:

1) The hedging relationship consists only of eligible hedge items and hedging instruments. The hedge item is eligible as it is a group of highly expected forecast cash flows that exposes the entity to fair value risk, affects profit or loss and is reliably measurable. The hedging instrument is eligible as it is a derivative combination that does not result in a net written option and the option sold is designated as an offset to the purchased option.
2) At hedge inception there is a formal designation and documentation of the hedging relationship and the entity's risk management objective and strategy for undertaking the hedge.
3) The hedging relationship is considered effective.

The hedging relationship will be considered effective if the following three requirements are met:

1) There is an economic relationship between the hedged item and the hedging instrument.
2) The effect of credit risk does not dominate the value changes that result from that economic relationship.
3) The hedge ratio of the hedging relationship is the same as that resulting from the quantity of hedged item that the entity actually hedges and the quantity of the hedging instrument that the entity actually uses to hedge that quantity of hedged item. The hedge ratio should not be intentionally weighted to create ineffectiveness.

Whether there is an economic relationship between the hedged item and the hedging instrument will be assessed on a quantitative basis using the scenario analysis method for two scenarios in which Euribor interest rates will be shifted upwards and downwards by 2% and the changes in fair value of the hypothetical derivative and the hedging instrument compared.

7.6.3 Hedge Effectiveness Assessment Performed at the Start of the Hedging Relationship

The hedging relationship was considered effective as the following three requirements were met:

1) There was an economic relationship between the hedged item and the hedging instrument. Based on the quantitative assessment performed, the entity concluded that the change in fair value of the hedged item was expected to be substantially offset by the change in fair value of the hedging instrument, corroborating that both elements had values that would generally move in opposite directions.
2) The effect of credit risk did not dominate the value changes resulting from that economic relationship as the credit ratings of both the entity and XYZ Bank were considered sufficiently strong.
3) The hedge ratio of the hedging relationship was the same as that resulting from the quantity of hedged item that the entity actually hedged and the quantity of the hedging instrument that the entity actually used to hedge that quantity of hedged item. The hedge ratio was not intentionally weighted to create ineffectiveness.

A quantitative assessment was performed to support the conclusion that the hedging instrument and the hedged item had values that would generally move in opposite directions. The quantitative assessment consisted of two scenario analyses performed as follows.

A parallel shift of +2% occurring on the assessment date was simulated. The fair values of the hedging instrument and the hypothetical derivatives were calculated and compared to their initial fair values. As shown in the table below, the assessment resulted in a high degree of offset, corroborating that both elements had values that would generally move in opposite directions.

Scenario 1 analysis assessment		
	Hedging instrument	**Hypothetical derivative**
Initial fair value	-0-	-0-
Final fair value	4,456,000	4,521,000
Cumulative fair value change	4,456,000	4,521,000
	Degree of offset	**98.6%**

Similarly, a parallel shift of –2% occurring on the assessment date was also simulated. As shown in the table below, the assessment resulted in a high degree of offset, again corroborating that both elements had values that would generally move in opposite directions.

Scenario 2 analysis assessment		
	Hedging instrument	**Hypothetical derivative**
Initial fair value	-0-	-0-
Final fair value	<6,261,000>	<6,358,000>
Cumulative fair value change	<6,261,000>	<6,358,000>
	Degree of offset	**98.5%**

The following potential sources of ineffectiveness were identified:

▪ a substantial deterioration in credit risk of either the entity or the counterparty to the hedging instrument; and
▪ a change in the timing or amounts of the hedged highly expected cash flows.

The hedge ratio was set at 1:1.

ABC also performed assessments on each reporting date, yielding the same conclusions. These assessments have been omitted to avoid unnecessary repetition.

7.6.4 Fair Valuations, Effective/Ineffective Amounts and Cash Flow Calculations

Fair Valuations of Hedging Instrument   As an example, the following tables detail the split between the intrinsic value and the time value of the collar on 31 December 20X0 and 31 December 20X1. The fair value of the collar was calculated using the Black–Scholes model and incorporating CVA/DVA.

IFRS 9 does not specify how to calculate the intrinsic value of cap (or a collar). The most accurate way is to calculate for each caplet/floorlet the present value of an undiscounted intrinsic amount by comparing the implied forward interest rate with the cap/floor rate. The sum of the discounted values yields the intrinsic value of the cap/floor. The time value of the collar was calculated as follows:

Collar time value = Collar total fair value – Collar intrinsic value

Collar fair valuation on 31 December 20X0

Date	Euribor 12M	Discount factor	Cap intrinsic value (undiscounted) *(1)*	Floor intrinsic value (undiscounted) *(2)*	Total intrinsic value (present value) *(3)*
31-Dec-20X1	3.21%	0.9685	-0-	-0-	-0-
31-Dec-20X2	3.40%	0.9667	-0-	-0-	-0-
31-Dec-20X3	3.90%	0.9299	-0-	-0-	-0-
31-Dec-20X4	4.37%	0.8904	-0-	-0-	-0-
31-Dec-20X5	4.60%	0.8507	-0-	-0-	-0-
CVA/DVA					-0-
Total intrinsic value					
Time value *(4)*					**-0-**
Fair value *(5)*					**-0-**

Notes:

(1) 100 mn × max(Euribor 12M – 4.85%; 0) × 365/360, assuming 365 calendar days in the interest period

(2) <100 mn> × max(3.18% – Euribor 12M; 0) × 365/360, assuming 365 calendar days in the interest period

(3) (Undiscounted cap intrinsic value + Undiscounted floor intrinsic value) × Discount factor

(4) Fair value – Intrinsic value

(5) Initial fair value was nil, calculated using the Black–Scholes model

Collar fair valuation on 31 December 20X1

Date	Euribor 12M	Discount factor	Cap intrinsic value (undiscounted)	Floor intrinsic value (undiscounted)	Total intrinsic value (present value)
31-Dec-20X2	4.21%	0.9591			-0-
31-Dec-20X3	4.80%	0.9146			-0-
31-Dec-20X4	5.00%	0.8705	152,000		132,000
31-Dec-20X5	5.12%	0.8275	274,000		227,000
CVA/DVA					<4,000>
Total intrinsic value					**355,000**
Time value					**217,000**
Fair value					**572,000**

The following table summarises the split between the collar's intrinsic and time value at each reporting date:

Date	Collar intrinsic value	Collar time value	Collar total fair value	Period change in intrinsic value	Period change in time value	Period change in total fair value
31-Dec-20X0	-0-	-0-	-0-	—	—	—
31-Dec-20X1	355,000	217,000	572,000	355,000	217,000	572,000
31-Dec-20X2	130,000	300,000	430,000	<225,000>	83,000	<142,000>
31-Dec-20X3	-0-	170,000	170,000	<130,000>	<130,000>	<260,000>
31-Dec-20X4	-0-	20,000	20,000	-0-	<150,000>	<150,000>
31-Dec-20X5	-0-	-0-	-0-	-0-	<20,000>	<20,000>

Effective and Ineffective Amounts   The following table summarises the fair value cumulative changes of the hedging instrument (i.e., the collar's intrinsic value) and the hypothetical derivative (which had intrinsic value only):

Date	Hedging instrument fair value	Cumulative change	Hypothetical derivative fair value	Cumulative change
31-Dec-20X0	-0-	—	-0-	—
31-Dec-20X1	355,000	355,000	345,000	345,000
31-Dec-20X2	130,000	130,000	128,000	128,000
31-Dec-20X3	-0-	-0-	-0-	-0-
31-Dec-20X4	-0-	-0-	-0-	-0-
31-Dec-20X5	-0-	-0-	-0-	-0-

The ineffective part of the change in fair value of the hedging instrument was the excess of its cumulative change in fair value over that of the hypothetical derivative. The effective and ineffective parts of the change in fair value of the swap were the following (see Section 5.5.6 for an explanation of the calculations):

	31-Dec-X1	31-Dec-X2	31-Dec-X3	31-Dec-X4	31-Dec-X5
Cumulative change in fair value of hedging instrument	355,000	130,000	-0-	-0-	-0-
Cumulative change in fair value of hypothetical derivative	345,000	128,000	-0-	-0-	-0-
Lower amount	345,000	128,000	-0-	-0-	-0-
Previous cumulative effective amount	—	345,000	128,000	-0-	-0-

	31-Dec-X1	31-Dec-X2	31-Dec-X3	31-Dec-X4	31-Dec-X5
Available amount	345,000	<217,000>	<128,000>	-0-	-0-
Period change in fair value of hedging instrument	355,000	<225,000>	<130,000>	-0-	-0-
Effective part	345,000	<217,000>	<128,000>	-0-	-0-
Ineffective part	10,000	<8,000>	<2,000>	-0-	-0-

Time Value Reserve Amounts   Under IFRS 9, when the time value component of an option is excluded from the hedging relationship, its cumulative change in fair value from the date of designation of the hedging instrument is temporarily accumulated in OCI to the extent that it relates to the hedged item.

In our case, due to the absence of actual time value at the beginning (31 December 20X0) and end (31 December 20X5) of the hedging relationship, changes in actual time value were recognised temporarily in the time value reserve of OCI, as shown in the table below. No reclassification to profit or loss was carried out during the term of the hedging relationship as the carrying value of the time value reserve in OCI was expected to be nil at the end of the hedging relationship.

Amounts to be recognised in the time value reserve of OCI (in EUR)					
	31-Dec-X1	31-Dec-X2	31-Dec-X3	31-Dec-X4	31-Dec-X4
New entry in reserve	217,000	83,000	<130,000>	<150,000>	<20,000>
Reserve carrying value	217,000	300,000	170,000	20,000	-0-

Bond Coupon Payments and Swap Settlement Amounts   The bond coupon payments and swap settlement amounts at each relevant date were as follows:

Date	Period Euribor 12M	Bond interest *(1)*	Collar settlement amount *(2)*
31-Dec-20X1	3.21%	<4,775,000>	-0-
31-Dec-20X2	4.21%	<5,789,000>	-0-
31-Dec-20X3	3.71%	<5,282,000>	-0-
31-Dec-20X4	3.80%	<5,374,000>	-0-
31-Dec-20X5	3.95%	<5,526,000>	-0-

Notes:
(1) <100 mn> × (Euribor 12M + 1.50%) × 365/360, assuming 365 calendar days in the interest period
(2) 100 mn × max[Euribor 12M − 4.85%, 0] × 365/360 − 100 mn × max[3.18% − Euribor 12M, 0] × 365/360, assuming 365 calendar days in the interest period

7.6.5 Accounting Entries

The required journal entries were as follows.

1) Entries on 31 December 20X0

To record the issuance of the bond:

Cash (Asset)	100,000,000	
Financial debt (Liability)		100,000,000

No journal entries were required to record the collar since its fair value was zero at inception.

2) Entries on 31 December 20X1

The bond paid a EUR 4,775,000 coupon.

Interest expense (Profit or loss)	4,775,000	
Cash (Asset)		4,775,000

The change in the fair value of the collar since the last valuation was a gain of EUR 572,000. Of this amount, a gain of EUR 355,000 was due to a change in the collar's intrinsic value, split between a 345,000 effective amount recorded in equity, and a EUR 10,000 ineffective amount recorded in profit or loss. The remainder, a gain of EUR 217,000, was due to a change in the collar's time value and taken to the time value reserve in OCI.

Derivative contract (Asset)	572,000	
Cash flow hedge reserve (Equity)		345,000
Other financial income (Profit or loss)		10,000
Time value reserve (Equity)		217,000

No settlement amounts were paid or received under the collar.

3) Entries on 31 December 20X2

The bond paid a EUR 5,789,000 coupon. The change in the fair value of the collar since the last valuation was a EUR 142,000 loss. Of this amount, a EUR 225,000 loss was due to a change in the collar's intrinsic value, split between a EUR <217,000> effective amount recorded in equity, and a EUR <8,000> ineffective amount recorded in profit or loss. The remainder, a EUR 83,000 gain, was due to a change in the collar's time value and taken to the time value reserve in OCI. No settlement amounts were paid or received under the collar.

Interest expense (Profit or loss)	5,789,000	
Cash (Asset)		5,789,000
Cash flow hedge reserve (Equity)	217,000	
Other financial expenses (Profit or loss)	8,000	
Derivative contract (Asset)		142,000
Time value reserve (Equity)		83,000

4) Entries on 31 December 20X3

The bond paid a EUR 5,282,000 coupon. The change in the fair value of the collar since the last valuation was a EUR 260,000 loss. Of this amount, a EUR 130,000 loss was due to a change in the collar's intrinsic value, split between a EUR <128,000> effective amount recorded in equity, and a EUR <2,000> ineffective amount recorded in profit or loss. The remainder, a EUR 130,000 loss, was due to a change in the collar's time value and taken to the time value reserve in OCI. No settlement amounts were paid or received under the collar.

Interest expense (Profit or loss)	5,282,000	
Cash (Asset)		5,282,000
Cash flow hedge reserve (Equity)	128,000	
Other financial expenses (Profit or loss)	2,000	
Time value reserve (Equity)	130,000	
Derivative contract (Asset)		260,000

5) Entries on 31 December 20X4

The bond paid a EUR 5,374,000 coupon. The change in fair value of the collar since the last valuation was a EUR 150,000 loss, all of which was due to a change in the collar's time value and recorded in the time value reserve of equity. No settlement amounts were paid or received under the collar.

Interest expense (Profit or loss)	5,374,000	
Cash (Asset)		5,374,000
Time value reserve (Equity)	150,000	
Derivative contract (Asset)		150,000

6) Entries on 31 December 20X5

The bond paid a EUR 5,526,000 coupon and repaid the EUR 100 million principal. The change in fair value of the collar since the last valuation was a EUR 20,000 loss, all of which was due to a change in the collar's time value and recorded in the time value reserve of equity. No settlement amounts were paid or received under the collar.

Interest expense (Profit or loss)	5,526,000	
Financial debt (Liability)	100,000,000	
Cash (Asset)		105,526,000
Time value reserve (Equity)	20,000	
Derivative contract (Asset)		20,000

7.6.6 Final Remarks

In the case just covered, the collar had no intrinsic value at the start of the hedging relationship because both the cap rate (4.85%) and the floor rate (3.18%) were well "away" from the 3.86% swap rate. The accounting for the time value component of a collar that has a zero time value both at the start and end of the hedging relationship is relatively simple, as all the changes in time value are recognised in the time value reserve of OCI and no reclassification is needed.

Imagine instead a zero-cost collar in which the cap and floor rates were 4.50% and 3.52%, respectively. Ignoring CVAs/DVAs, this floor would have had a EUR <336,000> intrinsic value at the start of the hedging relationship. Because the collar had an initial zero fair value at the start of the hedging relationship, it would have had a EUR 336,000 time value at that moment, as shown in the following table:

Collar fair valuation on 31 December 20X0					
Date	Euribor 12M	Discount factor	Cap intrinsic value (undiscounted)	Floor intrinsic value (undiscounted)	Total intrinsic value (present value)
31-Dec-20X1	3.21%	0.9685	-0-	<314,000>	<304,000>
31-Dec-20X2	3.40%	0.9667	-0-	<122,000>	<118,000>
31-Dec-20X3	3.90%	0.9299	-0-	-0-	-0-
31-Dec-20X4	4.37%	0.8904	-0-	-0-	-0-
31-Dec-20X5	4.60%	0.8507	101,000	-0-	86,000
Total intrinsic value (excl. CVA/DVA)					<336,000>
Time value					336,000
Fair value					-0-

Implications of a Non-zero Initial Intrinsic Value   A non-zero intrinsic value at the start of a hedging relationship has important operational implications.

Firstly, the entity would need to keep track of the intrinsic and time values of each caplet /floorlet combination and to compare them with the intrinsic and time values to the corresponding caplet/floorlet combination of the hypothetical/aligned derivative. As a result, effective /ineffective amounts have to be separately calculated for each caplet/floorlet combination, a notably complex exercise.

Secondly, substantial differences between the cap/floor rates of the hedging instrument and the hypothetical derivative may occur if an excessively strict auditor requires the hypothetical derivative's cap/floor rates to be out-of-the-money, or in other words, to have no intrinsic value at the start of the hedging relationship. In our example, in which the actual collar rates were 3.52–4.50%, the hypothetical derivative rates would have been 3.21–4.60%. Fortunately, the accounting community commonly requires the hypothetical derivative cap and the floor rates to be above and below the swap rate respectively, accepting a non-zero intrinsic value at the commencement of the hedging relationship. In our example, a hypothetical derivative with strikes 3.54–4.50% would have been acceptable as the hypothetical swap rate (3.87%) was between both strikes.

In Section 7.13 an example of a collar with a non-zero initial intrinsic and time values is covered.

Implications of a Non-zero Initial Time Value   Besides the need to keep track of the time value of each caplet/floorlet separately, a non-zero time value at start of a hedging relationship requires a different accounting treatment for the time value component (the "actual" time value), as explained in Section 2.10. The actual time value is compared at the start of the hedging relationship with a theoretical time value (the "aligned" time value).

- If the actual time value is greater than the aligned time value, then the amount that is subsequently recognised in OCI is determined only on the basis of the aligned time value. Any remainder of the change in the actual time value is recognised in profit or loss.
- If the actual time value is lower than the aligned time value, then the amount that is subsequently recognised in OCI is the lower of the cumulative change of the actual and aligned time values. Any remainder of the change in the actual time value is recognised in profit or loss.

7.7   IMPLICATIONS OF INTEREST ACCRUALS AND CREDIT SPREADS

In this section I cover the implications, when calculating fair values of financial instruments, of interest or settlement amounts accruals. The main conclusion is that interest accrual amounts should be excluded when computing fair values of derivatives. Inclusion of accruals may cause important errors in the financial statements. This case is based in a fair value hedge of a two-year bond to show how to properly take into account interest accruals.

7.7.1   Background Information

On 31 March 20X0, ABC issued at par a EUR 100 million, 2-year fixed rate bond with a 3.78% annual coupon. ABC's hedging policy was to swap all new issues to floating and at a later stage decide, on a portfolio basis, the proportion of fixed versus floating exposure.

Accordingly, on the date on which the bond was issued ABC considered entering into an interest rate swap in which it would receive 3.78% annually and would pay Euribor 12-month annually. However, because the yield curve on 31 March 20X0 was very steep, ABC preferred instead to enter into a swap in which it would receive 3.78% annually and pay Euribor 3-month quarterly. The main terms of the bond and the swap were as follows:

Bond terms	
Issue date	31 March 20X0
Maturity	2 years (31 March 20X2)
Notional	EUR 100 million
Coupon	4.78% annually, 30/360 basis

Interest rate swap terms	
Trade date	31 March 20X0
Counterparties	ABC and XYZ Bank
Maturity	2 years (31 March 20X2)
Notional	EUR 100 million
Initial fair value	Zero
ABC pays	Euribor 3M quarterly, actual/360 basis
ABC receives	3.78% annually, 30/360 basis
Euribor fixing	Euribor is fixed at the beginning of the annual interest period

Figure 7.1 shows the cash flows of the two legs of the swap. Under the floating leg, ABC had to pay Euribor 3-month each quarter. Under the fixed leg, ABC had to receive 3.78% each year.

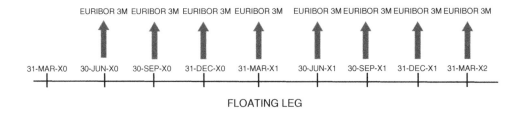

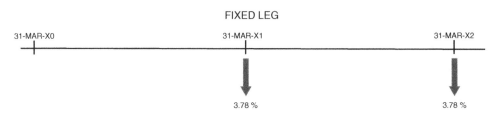

FIGURE 7.1   Swap interest cash flows.

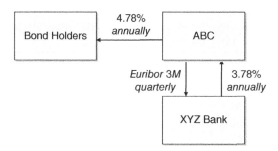

FIGURE 7.2 Hedging strategy interest flows.

Figure 7.2 depicts the strategy's interest flows. Through the swap ABC paid quarterly Euribor 3-month and received 3.78% annually. ABC used the 3.78% cash flows it received under the swap to partially pay the bond interest. As a result, ABC obtained synthetically a EUR floating liability in which it paid Euribor plus 100 basis points.

7.7.2 Credit Spread and Hedge Accounting

ABC designated the swap as the hedging instrument in a fair value hedge of the bond. Hedge effectiveness was assessed by comparing changes in the fair value of the hedging instrument to changes in the fair value of the hedged item. One decision ABC had to make was whether to include the credit spread in the hedging relationship. In other words, when defining in the hedge documentation the risk being hedged, to choose between:

- Hedging all the risks (i.e., credit and interest rate risks in our case). The hedged item would be fair valued in its entirety.
- Hedging only interest rate risk and, as a result, excluding credit risk from the hedging relationship. The hedged item would be defined as the bond cash flows representing a 3.78% interest rate (i.e., the first EUR 3.87 million). The hedged item would be fair valued for changes in interest rates only.

Because the swap only hedged interest rate risk, the latter was chosen. Therefore, the hedged item was the cash flows corresponding to the first EUR 3.87 million of each coupon payment.

7.7.3 Interest Accruals and Fair Valuations

A key element, when derivatives with several settlement dates are involved, is the interaction between interest accruals and fair valuations. Suppose that ABC reported its financial statements on an annual basis every 31 December. Therefore, the first reporting date after hedge inception was 31 December 20X0. By that date and regarding the floating leg of the hedging instrument, four quarterly Euribor 3-month fixings had already been set and interest for three quarters had already being paid, as shown in the following table:

Hedging instrument floating leg (31 December 20X0)			
Cash flow date	Euribor 3M fixing date	Euribor 3M	Paid floating amount
30-Jun-X0	29-Mar-X0	2.00%	506,000
30-Sep-X0	28-Jun-X0	2.50%	632,000

(continued overleaf)

Hedging instrument floating leg (31 December 20X0)			
Cash flow date	Euribor 3M fixing date	Euribor 3M	Paid floating amount
31-Dec-X0	28-Sep-X0	3.00%	758,000
31-Mar-X1	29-Dec-X0	3.50%	Not yet paid
30-Jun-X1	29-Mar-X1	Not yet fixed (implied 3.69%)	Not yet paid
30-Sep-X1	28-Jun-X1	Not yet fixed (implied 3.75%)	Not yet paid
31-Dec-X1	28-Sep-X1	Not yet fixed (implied 3.81%)	Not yet paid
31-Mar-X2	29-Dec-X1	Not yet fixed (implied 3.85%)	Not yet paid

Regarding the fixed leg of the hedging instrument, the rates were already known but no interest was paid by 31 December 20X0:

Cash flow date	Fixed rate	Received fixed amount
31-Mar-X1	3.78%	Not yet received
31-Mar-X2	3.78%	Not yet received

The fair value of the swap on 31 December 20X0 was the following, ignoring CVAs/DVAs:

Date	Euribor 3M	Discount factor	Expected floating leg cash flow	Fixed leg cash flow	Net amount	Present value
31-Mar-X1	3.50%	0.9913	<875,000>	3,780,000	2,905,000	2,880,000
30-Jun-X1	3.69%	0.9908	<933,000>		<933,000>	<924,000>
30-Sep-X1	3.75%	0.9815	<948,000>		<948,000>	<930,000>
31-Dec-X1	3.81%	0.9721	<963,000>		<963,000>	<936,000>
31-Mar-X2	3.85%	0.9627	<973,000>	3,780,000	2,807,000	2,702,000
Fair value						**2,792,000**

If no further adjustments are applied, the profit or loss statement on 31-December-20X0 was as follows:

	Amount
Floating leg income on 30-Jun-X0	<506,000>
Floating leg income on 30-Sep-X0	<632,000>
Floating leg income on 31-Dec-X0	<758,000>
Accrual of fixed leg to be received on 31-Mar-X1	2,848,000 (*)
Change in fair value of swap	2,782,000
Total	3,734,000

(*) 3,780,000 × (275 days from 31-Mar-X0 to 31-Dec-X0)/(365 days from 31-Mar-X0 to 31-Mar-X1)

A profit of EUR 3,734,000 is great news for ABC. The bad news is that this profit or loss statement is wrong as it is double counting the accrual of the amounts to be received on 31-Mar-X1. ABC is recognising the accrual corresponding to the swap's fixed leg (EUR 2,848,000) to be settled on 31 March 20X1. Simultaneously, ABC is including that amount when fair valuing the swap: a EUR 3,780,000 cash flow corresponding to 31 March 20X1 (see "fixed leg cash flow" amount in the first line of the swap fair valuation).

ABC should have fair valued the swap excluding any accruals amounts, as shown in the following table:

Date	Euribor 3M	Discount factor	Expected floating leg cash flow	Fixed leg cash flow	Net amount	Present value
31-Mar-X1	3.50%	0.9913	<875,000>	932,000 (*)	57,000	56,000
30-Jun-X1	3.69%	0.9908	<933,000>		<933,000>	<924,000>
30-Sep-X1	3.75%	0.9815	<948,000>		<948,000>	<930,000>
31-Dec-X1	3.81%	0.9721	<963,000>		<963,000>	<936,000>
31-Mar-X2	3.85%	0.9627	<973,000>	3,780,000	2,807,000	2,702,000
Fair value						32,000

(*) 3,780,000 × 90/365

ABC's profit or loss statement on 31-December-20X0 was as follows:

	Amount
Floating leg income on 30-Jun-X0	<506,000>
Floating leg income on 30-Sep-X0	<632,000>
Floating leg income on 31-Dec-X0	<758,000>
Accrual of fixed leg to be received on 31-Mar-X1	2,848,000 (*)
Change in fair value of swap	32,000
Total	984,000

(*) 3,780,000 × (275 days from 31-Mar-X0 to 31-Dec-X0)/(365 days from 31-Mar-X0 to 31-Mar-X1)

ABC reported a EUR 984,000, mostly stemming from the differential between the 2.75% average interest rate paid during the period (2.75% = (2.00% + 2.50% + 3.00% + 3.50%)/4) and the 3.78% interest rate received. An additional EUR 32,000 was due to the change in fair value of the swap, excluding accrual amounts.

Regarding the hedged item, the conclusion is identical: interest accruals have to be excluded from the fair valuation of the hedged item. Otherwise, a double counting in profit or loss would occur.

7.8 CASE STUDY: HEDGING A FIXED RATE LIABILITY WITH AN INTEREST RATE SWAP

This section covers the hedge with an interest rate swap of a fixed rate liability, applying a fair value hedge. Because the issued debt paid a fixed rate coupon, the entity was not exposed to the variability in interest payments due to changes in interest rates, so why was the entity interested in changing its interest rate risk profile? Usually an entity's funding department raises and secure funds to attain the entity's funding needs. The funding department has specific funding targets for new issuance of debt. The funding targets are set, for each maturity, as a spread to the corresponding floating rate (e.g., a 50 bpd spread for 1-year debt, a 160 bps points spread for 5-year debt, etc.). Generally, the funding department is not interested in issuing fixed rate debt, while investors often require a fixed rate instrument. Accordingly, the funding department may issue a fixed rate bond and simultaneously transform the bond coupons into floating rate interest through a pay-floating/receive-fixed interest rate swap, effectively funding itself at Libor plus a spread. At a later stage, the entity may decide to convert back to fixed with a pay-fixed/receive-floating interest rate swap to achieve on a portfolio basis a certain mix of floating versus fixed liabilities.

7.8.1 Background Information

On 31 July 20X0, ABC issued at par a fixed rate bond with the following characteristics:

Bond terms	
Issue date	31 July 20X0
Issuer	ABC
Issue proceeds	EUR 100 million (100% of notional)
Maturity	3 years (31 July 20X3)
Notional	EUR 100 million
Coupon	4.94% annually, 30/360 basis

ABC's policy was to immediately swap to floating all new debt issues and later, as part of its overall hedging policy, decide what fixed-floating mix was the most appropriate for the whole corporation. Accordingly, simultaneously with the issuance of the bond, ABC entered into a receive-fixed pay-floating interest rate swap with XYZ Bank with the following terms:

Interest rate swap terms	
Trade date	31 July 20X0
Counterparties	ABC and XYZ Bank
Maturity	3 years (31 July 20X3)
Notional	EUR 100 million
Initial fair value	Zero
ABC pays	Euribor 12M annually, actual/360 basis
ABC receives	4.34% annually, 30/360 basis
Euribor fixing	Euribor is fixed 2 days prior to the commencement of the annual interest period

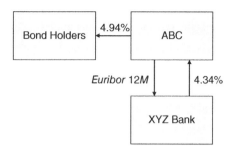

FIGURE 7.3 Hedging strategy interest flows.

Under the swap, ABC paid annually Euribor 12-month and received annually 4.34%. ABC then used the 4.34% received and added 0.60% to pay the 4.94% bond interest. The combination of the bond and the swap resulted in ABC paying an interest of Euribor 12-month plus 60 bps, as shown in Figure 7.3. The 60 bps credit spread was the difference between the bond's coupon rate (4.94%) and the swap's fixed rate (4.34%).

The swap was designated as the hedging instrument in a fair value hedge of the bond.

7.8.2 Hedging Relationship Documentation

ABC documented the hedging relationship as follows:

	Hedging relationship documentation
Risk management objective and strategy for undertaking the hedge	The objective of the hedge is to reduce the variability of the fair value of a fixed rate bond issued by the entity.
	This hedging objective is consistent with the group's overall interest rate risk management strategy of transforming all new issued debt into floating rate, and thereafter managing the exposure to interest rate risk through the proportion of fixed and floating rate net debt in its total debt portfolio.
	Interest rate risk. The designated risk being hedged is the risk of changes in the EUR fair value of the hedged item attributable to changes in the Euribor interest rates.
	Fair value changes attributable to credit or other risks are not hedged in this relationship. Accordingly, the 60 bps credit spread is excluded from the hedging relationship
Type of hedge	Fair value hedge
Hedged item	The coupons and principal of the three-year 4.94% fixed rate bond with reference number 678902. As the bond credit spread (60 bps) is excluded from the hedging relationship, only the cash flows related to the interest rate component of the coupons will be part of the hedging relationship (i.e., those corresponding to a 4.34% rate or EUR 4.34 million). The EUR 100 million principal is included in the hedging relationship in its entirety.

(continued overleaf)

Hedging relationship documentation	
Hedging instrument	The interest rate swap with reference number 014569. The main terms of the swap are a EUR 100 million notional, a 3-year maturity, a 4.34% fixed rate to be received by the entity and a Euribor 12-month rate to be paid by the entity. The counterparty to the swap is XYZ Bank and the credit risk associated with this counterparty is considered to be very low
Hedge effective- ness assessment	See below

7.8.3 Hedge Effectiveness Assessment

Hedge effectiveness will be assessed by comparing changes in the fair value of the hedging instrument to changes in the fair value of the hedged item. Changes in the fair value of the hedging instrument (i.e., the swap) will be recognised as follows:

- The effective part of the gain or loss on the hedging instrument will be recognised in profit or loss, adjusting interest income/expenses.
- The ineffective part of the gain or loss on the hedging instrument will be recognised in profit or loss, as other financial income/expenses.

Hedge effectiveness will be assessed prospectively at hedging relationship inception, on an ongoing basis at least upon each reporting date and upon occurrence of a significant change in the circumstances affecting the hedge effectiveness requirements.

The hedging relationship will qualify for hedge accounting only if all the following criteria are met:

1) The hedging relationship consists only of eligible hedge items and hedging instruments. The hedge item is eligible as it is an already recognised liability that exposes the entity to fair value risk, affects profit or loss and is reliably measurable. The hedging instrument is eligible as it is a derivative that does not result in a net written option.
2) At hedge inception there is a formal designation and documentation of the hedging relationship and the entity's risk management objective and strategy for undertaking the hedge.
3) The hedging relationship is considered effective.

The hedging relationship will be considered effective if the following three requirements are met:

1) There is an economic relationship between the hedged item and the hedging instrument.
2) The effect of credit risk does not dominate the value changes that result from that economic relationship.
3) The hedge ratio of the hedging relationship is the same as that resulting from the quantity of hedged item that the entity actually hedges and the quantity of the hedging instrument that the entity actually uses to hedge that quantity of hedged item. The hedge ratio should not be intentionally weighted to create ineffectiveness.

Whether there is an economic relationship between the hedged item and the hedging instrument will be assessed on a quantitative basis using the scenario analysis method for two scenarios in which Euribor interest rates will be shifted upwards and downwards by 2% and the changes in fair value of the hedged item and the hedging instrument compared.

7.8.4 Hedge Effectiveness Assessment Performed at the Start of the Hedging Relationship

On 31 July 20X0 ABC performed a hedge effectiveness assessment which was documented as described next.

The hedging relationship was considered effective as the following three requirements were met:

1) There was an economic relationship between the hedged item and the hedging instrument. Based on the quantitative assessment performed, the entity concluded that the change in fair value of the hedged item was expected to be substantially offset by the change in fair value of the hedging instrument, corroborating that both elements had values that would generally move in opposite directions.
2) The effect of credit risk did not dominate the value changes resulting from that economic relationship as the credit ratings of both the entity and XYZ Bank were considered sufficiently strong.
3) The hedge ratio of the hedging relationship was the same as that resulting from the quantity of hedged item that the entity actually hedged and the quantity of the hedging instrument that the entity actually used to hedge that quantity of hedged item. The hedge ratio was not intentionally weighted to create ineffectiveness.

A quantitative assessment was performed to support the conclusion that the hedging instrument and the hedged item had values that would generally move in opposite directions. The quantitative assessment consisted of two scenario analyses performed as follows.

A parallel shift of +2% occurring on the assessment date was simulated. The fair values of the hedging instrument and the hedged item were calculated and compared to their initial fair values. As shown in the table below, the assessment resulted in a high degree of offset, corroborating that both elements had values that would generally move in opposite directions.

Scenario 1 analysis assessment: +2% parallel shift		
	Hedging instrument	**Hedged item**
Initial fair value	-0-	100,000,000
Final fair value	<5,302,000>	94,629,000
Cumulative fair value change	<5,302,000>	5,371,000
	Degree of offset	**98.7%**

Similarly, a parallel shift of –2% occurring on the assessment date was also simulated. As shown in the table below, the assessment resulted in a high degree of offset, corroborating that both elements had values that would generally move in opposite directions.

Scenario 2 analysis assessment: –2% parallel shift		
	Hedging instrument	**Hedged item**
Initial fair value	-0-	100,000,000
Final fair value	5,746,000	105,822,000
Cumulative fair value change	5,746,000	<5,822,000>
	Degree of offset	**98.7%**

The following potential sources of ineffectiveness were identified:

- a substantial deterioration in credit risk of either the entity or the counterparty to the hedging instrument; and
- a change in the timing or amounts of the hedged highly expected cash flows.

The hedge ratio was set at 1:1.

ABC also performed assessments at each reporting date, yielding similar conclusions. These assessments have been omitted to avoid unnecessary repetition.

7.8.5 Fair Valuations, Effective/Ineffective Amounts and Cash Flow Calculations

Fair Valuations of the Hedging Instrument The Euribor 12-month rate fixings at the relevant dates were as follows:

Euribor 12M fixings	
29-Jul-X0	3.70%
29-Jul-X1	3.85%
29-Jul-X2	4.05%

The fair value of the swap was computed by summing the present value of each expected future net settlement, and adjusting for CVA/DVA. The fair value of the swap on 31 December 20X0 was calculated using the market yield curve on that date as follows:

Date	Implied Euribor	Discount factor	Expected floating leg cash flow	Fixed leg cash flow	Net amount	Present value
31-Jul-X1	3.80%	0.9781	<2,179,000> *(1)*	2,521,000 *(2)*	342,000 *(3)*	335,000 *(4)*
31-Jul-X2	4.40%	0.9363	<4,461,000> *(5)*	4,340,000 *(6)*	<121,000>	<113,000>
31-Jul-X3	4.90%	0.8920	<4,968,000>	4,340,000	<628,000>	<560,000>
CVA/DVA						4,000
Fair value						**<334,000>**

Notes:

(1) 100 mn × 3.70% × 212/360, where 3.70% was the Euribor 12M rate fixed two business days prior to 31-Jul-X0 (i.e., two business days prior to the commencement of the interest period) and 212 is the number of calendar days from 31-Dec-X0 to 31-Jul-X1)

(2) 100 mn × 4.34% × 212/365, where 4.34% was the swap fixed rate and 212 is the number of calendar days from 31-Dec-X0 to 31-Jul-X1

(3) <2,179,000> + 2,521,000

(4) 342,000 × 0.9781

(5) 100 mn × 4.40% × 365/360, where 4.40% was the implied Euribor 12M rate for 29-Jul-X1 (i.e., two business days prior to 31-Jul-X1) and 365 is the number of calendar days in the interest period (i.e., from 31-Jul-X1 to 31-Jul-X2)

(6) 100 mn × 4.34% × 365/360, where 4.34% was the swap fixed rate and 365 is the number of calendar days in the interest period (i.e., from 31-Jul-X1 to 31-Jul-X2)

The fair value of the swap on 31 December 20X1 was calculated using the market yield curve on that date as follows:

Date	Implied Euribor	Discount factor	Expected floating leg cash flow	Fixed leg cash flow	Net amount	Present value
31-Jul-X2	3.95%	0.9773	<2,267,000> (1)	2,521,000 (2)	254,000	248,000
31-Jul-X3	4.15%	0.9378	<4,208,000>	4,340,000	132,000	124,000
CVA/DVA						<4,000>
Fair value						**368,000**

Notes:

(1) 100 mn × 3.85% × 212/360, where 3.85% was the Euribor 12M rate fixed two business days prior to 31-Jul-X1 (i.e., two business days prior to the commencement of the interest period) and 212 is the number of calendar days from 31-Dec-X1 to 31-Jul-X2)

(2) 100 mn × 4.34% × 212/365, where 4.34% was the swap fixed rate and 212 is the number of calendar days from 31-Dec-X1 to 31-Jul-X2

The fair value of the swap on 31 December 20X2 was calculated using the market yield curve on that date as follows:

Date	Implied Euribor	Discount factor	Expected floating leg cash flow	Fixed leg cash flow	Net amount	Present value
31-Jul-X3	4.20%	0.9759	<2,385,000>	2,521,000	136,000	133,000
CVA/DVA						<1,000>
Fair value						**132,000**

Fair Valuations of the Hedged Item　　The fair value of the hedged item was computed by summing up the present value of each future EUR 4.34 million fixed cash flow. Remember that the risk being hedged was interest rate risk only. Therefore, changes in the fair value of the bond due to changes in ABC's credit spread were not part of the hedged item fair valuations. The cash flows being hedged were the first EUR 4,340,000 of each annual coupon, a portion of the EUR 4,940,000 annual coupon.

The fair value of the bond on 31 December 20X0 was calculated using the market yield curve on that date as follows:

Date	Discount factor	Expected cash flow	Present value
31-Jul-X1	0.9781	<2,521,000> *(1)*	<2,466,000> *(2)*
31-Jul-X2	0.9363	<4,340,000> *(3)*	<4,064,000>
31-Jul-X3	0.8920	<104,340,000>	<93,071,000>
Fair value			**<99,601,000>**

Notes:

(1) 4,340,000 × 212/365, where 4,340,000 was the hedged cash flow of the bond coupon and 212 is the number of calendar days from 31-Dec-X0 to 31-Jul-X1

(2) 2,521,000 × 0.9781

(3) The hedged cash flow expected to occur on 31-Jul-X2

The fair value of the bond on 31 December 20X1 was calculated using the market yield curve on that date as follows:

Date	Discount factor	Expected cash flow	Present value
31-Jul-X2	0.9773	<2,521,000>	<2,464,000>
31-Jul-X3	0.9378	<104,340,000>	<97,850,000>
Fair value			**<100,314,000>**

The fair value of the bond on 31 December 20X2 was calculated using the market yield curve on that date as follows:

Date	Discount factor	Expected cash flow	Present value
31-Jul-X3	0.9759	<102,521,000>	<100,050,000>
Fair value			**<100,050,000>**

Calculations of Effective and Ineffective Amounts   The period changes in fair value of the hedging instrument and the hedged item were as follows:

Date	Hedging instrument fair value	Period change	Hedged item fair value	Period change
31-Jul-X0	-0-	—	<100,000,000>	—
31-Dec-X0	<334,000>	<334,000>	<99,601,000>	399,000
31-Dec-X1	368,000	702,000	<100,314,000>	<713,000>
31-Dec-X2	132,000	<236,000>	<100,050,000>	264,000
31-Jul-X3	-0-	<132,000>	<100,000,000>	50,000

The ineffective part of the change in fair value of the hedging instrument was the excess of its period change in fair value over that of the hedged item. The effective and ineffective parts of the period change in fair value of the swap were as follows:

	31-Dec-X0	31-Dec-X1	31-Dec-X2	31-Jul-X3
Period change in fair value of hedging instrument	<334,000>	702,000	<236,000>	<132,000>
Period change in fair value of hedged item (opposite sign)	<399,000>	713,000	<264,000>	<50,000>
Lower amount	<334,000>	702,000	<236,000>	<50,000>
Effective part	<334,000>	702,000	<236,000>	<50,000>
Ineffective part	-0-	-0-	-0-	<82,000>

The effective part of the change in fair value of the hedged item was the effective part of the change in fair value of the hedging instrument (see previous table). Any remainder was considered to be ineffective. The effective and ineffective parts of the period change in fair value of the hedged item were as follows:

	31-Dec-X0	31-Dec-X1	31-Dec-X2	31-Jul-X3
Period change in fair value of hedged item	399,000	<713,000>	264,000	50,000
Effective part of change in fair value of hedging instrument (opposite sign)	334,000	<702,000>	236,000	50,000
Ineffective part (excess)	65,000	<11,000>	28,000	-0-

Calculations of Accrual Amounts

	Bond coupon accrual	Swap settlement amount accrual
31-Dec-X0	<2,071,000> *(1)*	247,000 *(2)*
31-Jul-X1	<2,869,000> *(3)*	342,000 *(4)*
31-Dec-X1	<2,071,000>	183,000
31-Jul-X2	<2,869,000>	254,000
31-Dec-X2	<2,071,000>	98,000
31-Jul-X3	<2,869,000>	136,000

Notes:

(1) 100 mn × 4.94% × 153/365, where 4.94% was the bond's interest rate corresponding to the cash flows being hedged (i.e., the hedged item) and 153 is the number of calendar days from 31-Jul-X0 to 31-Dec-X0)

(2) 100 mn × 3.70% × 153/360 – 100 mn × 4.34% × 153/365, where 3.70% was the Euribor 12-month
    rate fixed two business days prior to 31-Jul-X0 (i.e., the commencement of the interest period), 153 is
    the number of calendar days from 31-Jul-X0 to 31-Dec-X0) and 4.34% was the swap's fixed rate
(3) 100 mn × 4.94% × 212 /365, where 4.94% was the bond's interest rate corresponding to the cash
    flows being hedged (i.e., the hedged item) and 212 is the number of calendar days from 31-Dec-X0
    to 31-Jul-X1)
(4) 100 mn × 3.70% × 212/360 – 100 mn × 4.34% × 212/365, where 3.70% was the Euribor 12-month
    rate fixed two business days prior to 31-Jul-X0 (i.e., the commencement of the interest period), 212
    is the number of calendar days from 31-Dec-X0 to 31-Jul-X1) and 4.34% was the swap's fixed rate

7.8.6 Accounting Entries

The required journal entries were the following.

1) Entries on 31 July 20X0

To record the issuance of the bond:

Cash (Asset)	100,000,000	
Financial debt (Liability)		100,000,000

No journal entries were required to record the swap since its fair value was zero at inception.

2) Entries on 31 December 20X0

To record the EUR 2,071,000 accrual of the bond coupon:

Interest expense (Profit or loss)	2,071,000	
Interest payable (Liability)		2,071,000

To record the EUR 247,000 accrual of the settlement amount of the swap:

Interest receivable (Asset)	247,000	
Interest income (Profit or loss)		247,000

The change in fair value of the swap since the last valuation was a EUR 334,000 loss, fully
effective and recorded as interest expense in profit or loss.

Interest expense (Profit or loss)	334,000	
Derivative contract (Liability)		334,000

The change in fair value of the bond, for the risk being hedged, since the last valuation was a EUR 399,000 gain, of which a EUR 334,000 gain was considered to be effective and recorded as interest income in profit or loss. The excess EUR 65,000 gain was considered to be ineffective and recorded as other financial income in profit or loss.

Financial debt (Liability)	399,000	
Interest income (Profit or loss)		334,000
Other financial income (Profit or loss)		65,000

3) Entries on 31 July 20X1

To record the EUR 2,869,000 accrual of the bond coupon:

Interest expense (Profit or loss)	2,869,000	
Interest payable (Liability)		2,869,000

To record the EUR 342,000 accrual of the settlement amount of the swap:

Interest receivable (Asset)	342,000	
Interest income (Profit or loss)		342,000

ABC paid the EUR 4,940,000 bond coupon.

Interest payable (Liability)	4,940,000	
Cash (Asset)		4,940,000

ABC received the EUR 589,000 settlement amount under the swap.

Cash (Asset)	589,000	
Interest receivable (Asset)		589,000

4) Entries on 31 December 20X1

These recognised the EUR 2,071,000 accrual of the bond coupon and the EUR 183,000 accrual of the settlement amount of the swap. The change in fair value of the swap since the last valuation was a EUR 702,000 gain, fully considered to be effective and recorded as interest income in profit or loss. The change in fair value of the bond, for the risk being hedged, since the last valuation was a EUR 713,000 loss, split between a EUR 702,000 loss considered to be effective and recorded as interest expense in profit or loss, and a EUR 11,000 loss considered to be ineffective and recorded as other financial expenses in profit or loss.

Interest expense (Profit or loss)	2,071,000	
Interest payable (Liability)		2,071,000
Interest receivable (Asset)	183,000	
Interest income (Profit or loss)		183,000
Derivative contract (Asset)	702,000	
Interest income (Profit or loss)		702,000
Interest expense (Profit or loss)	702,000	
Other financial expenses (Profit or loss)	11,000	
Financial debt (Liability)		713,000

5) Entries on 31 July 20X2

These recognised the EUR 2,869,000 accrual of the bond coupon, the EUR 254,000 accrual of the settlement amount of the swap, the payment of the EUR 4,940,000 bond coupon, and the payment of the EUR 437,000 settlement amount under the swap.

Interest expense (Profit or loss)	2,869,000	
Interest payable (Liability)		2,860,000
Interest receivable (Asset)	254,000	
Interest income (Profit or loss)		254,000
Interest payable (Liability)	4,940,000	
Cash (Asset)		4,940,000
Cash (Asset)	437,000	
Interest receivable (Asset)		437,000

6) Entries on 31 December 20X2

These recognised the EUR 2,071,000 accrual of the bond coupon and the EUR 98,000 accrual of the settlement amount of the swap. The change in fair value of the swap since the last valuation was a EUR 236,000 loss, fully considered to be effective and recorded as interest expense in profit or loss. The change in fair value of the bond, for the risk being hedged, since the last valuation was a EUR 264,000 gain, split between a EUR 236,000 gain considered to be effective and recorded as interest income in profit or loss, and a EUR 28,000 gain considered to be ineffective and recorded as other financial income in profit or loss.

Interest expense (Profit or loss)	2,071,000	
Interest payable (Liability)		2,071,000
Interest receivable (Asset)	98,000	
Interest income (Profit or loss)		98,000
Interest expense (Profit or loss)	236,000	
Derivative contract (Asset)		236,000
Financial debt (Liability)	264,000	
Interest income (Profit or loss)		236,000
Other financial income (Profit or loss)		28,000

7) Entries on 31 July 20X3

These recognised the EUR 2,869,000 accrual of the bond coupon, the EUR 136,000 accrual of the settlement amount of the swap, the payment of the EUR 104,940,000 bond coupon and principal, and the payment of the EUR 234,000 settlement amount under the swap. The change in fair value of the swap since the last valuation was a EUR 132,000 loss, split between a EUR <50,000> effective amount recorded as interest expense in profit or loss and a EUR <82,000> ineffective amount recorded as other financial expenses in profit or loss. The change in fair value of the hedged item since the last valuation was a EUR 50,000 gain, fully deemed to be effective and recorded as interest income in profit or loss

Interest expense (Profit or loss)	2,869,000	
Interest payable (Liability)		2,860,000
Interest receivable (Asset)	136,000	
Interest income (Profit or loss)		136,000
Interest payable (Liability)	4,940,000	
Financial debt (Liability)	100,000,000	
Cash (Asset)		104,940,000
Cash (Asset)	234,000	

Interest receivable (Asset)		234,000
Interest expense (Profit or loss)	50,000	
Other financial expenses (Profit or loss)	82,000	
Derivative contract (Asset)		132,000
Financial debt (Liability)	50,000	
Interest income (Profit or loss)		50,000

The following table gives a summary of the accounting entries.

	Cash	Interest receivable	Derivative contract	Financial debt	Interest payable	Profit or loss
31-Jul-20X0						
Bond issuance	100,000,000			100,000,000		
Derivative trade			—			
31 Dec-20X0						
Bond coupon accrual					2,071,000	<2,071,000>
Swap settlement amount accrual		247,000				247,000
Swap fair valuation			<334,000>			<334,000>
Hedged item fair valuation				<399,000>		399,000
31-Jul-20X1						
Bond coupon accrual					2,869,000	<2,869,000>
Swap settlement amount accrual		342,000				342,000
Bond coupon payment	<4,940,000>				<4,940,000>	
Swap settlement amount receipt	589,000	<589,000>				
31-Dec-20X1						
Bond coupon accrual					2,071,000	<2,071,000>
Swap settlement amount accrual		183,000				183,000

Swap fair valuation			702,000			702,000
Hedged item fair valuation				713,000		<713,000>
31-Jul-20X2						
Bond coupon accrual					2,869,000	<2,869,000>
Swap settlement amount accrual		254,000				254,000
Bond coupon payment	<4,940,000>			<4,940,000>		
Swap settlement amount receipt	437,000	<437,000>				
31-Dec-20X2						
Bond coupon accrual					2,071,000	<2,071,000>
Swap settlement amount accrual		98,000				98,000
Swap fair valuation			<236,000>			<236,000>
Hedged item fair valuation				<264,000>		264,000
31-Jul-20X3						
Bond coupon accrual					2,869,000	<2,869,000>
Swap settlement amount accrual		136,000				136,000
Bond coupon and principal payment	<104,940,000>			<100,000,000>	<4,940,000>	
Swap settlement amount receipt	234,000	<234,000>				
Swap fair valuation			<132,000>			<132,000>
Hedged item fair valuation				<50,000>		50,000
TOTAL	-0-	-0-	-0-	-0-	-0-	-0-

Note: Total figures may not match the sum of their corresponding components due to rounding.

7.8.7 Concluding Remarks

By excluding the credit risk from the hedging relationship, ABC did not need to calculate the change in fair value of the bond due to all risks, but rather just due to interest rate risk.

In order to assess whether ABC achieved its objective of funding itself at Euribor 12-month plus 60 bps, let us take a look at ABC's profit or loss statement during the first interest period (from 31 July 20X0 to 31 July 20X1):

Profit and loss Interest income/expense From 31-Jul-X0 to 31-Jul-X1	
Entries on 31-Dec-X0:	
Bond coupon accrual	<2,071,000>
Swap settlement accrual	247,000
Change in swap fair value	<334,000>
Change in hedged item fair value	334,000
Entries on 31-Jul-X1:	
Bond coupon accrual	<2,869,000>
Swap settlement accrual	342,000
Total	**<4,351,000>**

The total interest expense for the period was EUR 4,351,000. This expense implied an interest rate of 4.29% on an actual/360 basis. ABC's objective was to fund itself at Euribor 12-month (set at 3.70% for the interest period) plus the 0.60% spread, or incurring an overall interest expense of EUR 4,360,000 (= 100 mn × (3.70% + 0.60%) × 365/360). Therefore, ABC incurred an interest expense remarkably close to its funding objective. Additionally, ABC's profit or loss during the period recognised other financial income of EUR 65,000 due to hedge ineffectiveness.

7.9 CASE STUDY: HEDGING A FUTURE FIXED RATE ISSUANCE WITH AN INTEREST RATE SWAP

The aim of this case study is to illustrate the accounting treatment of hedges of highly expected future issuance of fixed rate debt with a forward starting interest rate swap. A forward starting swap is just a swap that starts sometime in the future. With this type of hedge the entity takes advantage of low interest rates prior to issuing the debt and/or does not want to take the risk of higher rates at issuance date.

7.9.1 Background Information

On 1 January 20X0, ABC (an entity with the EUR as functional currency) expected to issue a fixed rate bond on 15 July 20X0 with the following characteristics:

Bond terms	
Expected issue date	15 July 20X0
Issuer	ABC
Issue proceeds	EUR 100 million (100% of notional)
Expected maturity	3 years (15 July 20X3)
Notional	EUR 100 million
Coupon	Fixed, to be paid annually (30/360 basis)
	The coupon is expected to be set on the issue date at the EUR 3-year swap rate plus a 100 bps credit spread

ABC was exposed to upward movements in the 3-year swap rate and to a widening of its own credit spread. ABC wanted to protect itself against potential increases in the 3-year interest rate until issuance date, by locking in the future coupon payment at 5.61% (assuming a spread of 100 basis points). Accordingly, on 1 January 20X0 ABC entered into a forward starting receive-fixed pay-floating interest rate swap with XYZ Bank with the following terms:

Interest rate swap terms	
Trade date	1 January 20X0
Start date	15 July 20X0
Counterparties	ABC and XYZ Bank
Maturity	3 years (15 July 20X3)
Notional	EUR 100 million
ABC pays	Euribor 12M annually (actual/360 basis)
ABC receives	4.61% annually (30/360 basis)
Euribor fixing	Euribor is fixed 2 days prior to the commencement of the annual interest period
Initial fair value	Zero

ABC planned to cancel the swap on the bond issue date (15 July 20X0). ABC designated the swap as the hedging instrument in a cash flow hedge of the highly expected issuance of the fixed rate bond. The effective amounts of the change in fair value of the swap until cancellation date would be recognised in equity. Following the bond issuance, the amounts accumulated in equity would be subsequently gradually recycled to profit or loss when the bond coupons impacted profit or loss. If the hedge was well constructed, the effective interest rate of the new bond would be close to the sum of the swap fixed rate and the credit spread, or 5.61% (= 4.61% + 1%).

7.9.2 Hedging Relationship Documentation

ABC documented the hedging relationship as follows:

Hedging relationship documentation	
Risk management objective and strategy for undertaking the hedge	The objective of the hedge is to eliminate the variability of the highly expected future cash outflows stemming from a planned issuance of a fixed rate bond by the entity. This hedging objective is consistent with the group's overall interest rate risk management strategy of managing the exposure to interest rate risk through the proportion of fixed and floating rate net debt in its total debt portfolio with interest rate swaps, caps and collars. Interest rate risk. The designated risk being hedged is the risk of changes in the EUR value of the hedged item attributable to changes in the Euribor interest rate. Fair value changes attributable to credit or other risks are not hedged in this relationship. Accordingly, the expected 100 basis points credit spread is excluded from the hedging relationship
Type of hedge	Cash flow hedge
Hedged item	The coupon cash flows of a 3-year fixed rate bond highly expected to be issued on 15 July 20X0 The issuance is highly expected to occur as it has been approved by the Board of Directors and a group of banks have been mandated
Hedging instrument	The interest rate swap with reference number 014569. The main terms of the swap are a EUR 100 million notional, a forward starting date on 15 July 20X0, a 3-year maturity, a 4.61% fixed rate to be received by the entity and a Euribor 12-month rate to be paid by the entity. The counterparty to the swap is XYZ Bank and the credit risk associated with this counterparty is considered to be very low. The interest rate swap is expected to be unwound on its forward starting date, which is expected to coincide with the bond's issue date
Hedge effectiveness assessment	See below

7.9.3 Hedge Effectiveness Assessment

Hedge effectiveness will be assessed by comparing changes in the fair value of the hedging instrument to changes in the fair value of a hypothetical derivative. The terms of the hypothetical derivative are such that its fair value changes exactly offset the changes in fair value of the hedged item for the risk being hedged. The hypothetical derivative is a theoretical interest rate swap with no counterparty credit risk and with zero initial fair value, whose main terms are as follows:

Hypothetical derivative terms	
Trade date	1 January 20X0
Start date	15 July 20X0
Counterparties	ABC and credit risk-free counterparty
Maturity	3 years (15 July 20X3)
Notional	EUR 100 million
ABC pays	Euribor 12M annually, actual/360 basis
ABC receives	4.615% annually, 30/360 basis
Euribor fixing	Euribor is fixed 2 days prior to the commencement of the annual interest period
Initial fair value	Zero

The fixed rate of the hypothetical derivative is higher than that of the hedging instrument due to the absence of CVA in the former.

Changes in the fair value of the hedging instrument (i.e., the swap) will be recognised as follows:

- The effective part of the gain or loss on the hedging instrument will be recognised in the cash flow hedge reserve of equity. Following the bond issuance, the amounts accumulated in equity will be reclassified to profit or loss, on a linear basis, in the same period during which the hedged expected future cash flows affect profit or loss, adjusting interest expense.
- The ineffective part of the gain or loss on the hedging instrument will be recognised in profit or loss, as other financial income/expenses.

Hedge effectiveness will be assessed prospectively at hedging relationship inception, on an ongoing basis at least upon each reporting date and upon occurrence of a significant change in the circumstances affecting the hedge effectiveness requirements.

The hedging relationship will qualify for hedge accounting only if all the following criteria are met:

1) The hedging relationship consists only of eligible hedge items and hedging instruments. The hedge item is eligible as it is a group of highly expected cash flows that will expose the entity to fair value risk, will affect profit or loss and is reliably measurable. The hedging instrument is eligible as it is a derivative that does not result in a net written option.
2) At hedge inception there is a formal designation and documentation of the hedging relationship and the entity's risk management objective and strategy for undertaking the hedge.
3) The hedging relationship is considered effective.

The hedging relationship will be considered effective if the following three requirements are met:

1) There is an economic relationship between the hedged item and the hedging instrument.
2) The effect of credit risk does not dominate the value changes that result from that economic relationship.
3) The hedge ratio of the hedging relationship is the same as that resulting from the quantity of hedged item that the entity actually hedges and the quantity of the hedging instrument

that the entity actually uses to hedge that quantity of hedged item. The hedge ratio should not be intentionally weighted to create ineffectiveness.

Whether there is an economic relationship between the hedged item and the hedging instrument will be assessed on a qualitative basis by comparing the critical terms (notional, interest periods, underlying and fixed rates) of the hypothetical derivative and the hedging instrument. The assessment will be complemented by a quantitative assessment using the scenario analysis method for one scenario in which Euribor interest rates will be shifted upwards by 2% and the changes in fair value of the hypothetical derivative and the hedging instrument compared.

7.9.4 Hedge Effectiveness Assessment Performed at the Start of the Hedging Relationship

On 1 January 20X0 ABC performed a hedge effectiveness assessment which was documented as described next.

The hedging relationship was considered effective as the following three requirements were met:

1) There was an economic relationship between the hedged item and the hedging instrument. Based on the qualitative assessment performed, supported by a quantitative analysis, the entity concluded that the change in fair value of the hedged item was expected to be substantially offset by the change in fair value of the hedging instrument, corroborating that both elements had values that would generally move in opposite directions.
2) The effect of credit risk did not dominate the value changes resulting from that economic relationship as the credit ratings of both the entity and XYZ Bank were considered sufficiently strong.
3) The hedge ratio of the hedging relationship was the same as that resulting from the quantity of hedged item that the entity actually hedged and the quantity of the hedging instrument that the entity actually used to hedge that quantity of hedged item. The hedge ratio was not intentionally weighted to create ineffectiveness.

Due to the fact that the terms of the hedging instrument and those of the expected cash flow closely matched and the low credit risk exposure to the counterparty of the swap contract, it was concluded that the hedging instrument and the hedged item had values that would generally move in opposite directions. This conclusion was supported by a quantitative assessment, which consisted of one scenario analysis performed as follows.

A parallel shift of +2% occurring on the assessment date was simulated. The fair values of the hedging instrument and the hypothetical derivative were calculated and compared to their initial fair values. As shown in the table below, the high degree of offset implied that the change in fair value of the hedged item was expected to largely be offset by the change in fair value of the hedging instrument, corroborating that both elements had values that would generally move in opposite directions.

Scenario analysis assessment		
	Hedging instrument	**Hypothetical derivative**
Initial fair value	Nil	Nil
Final fair value	5,290,000	5,358,000
Cumulative fair value change	5,290,000	5,358,000
	Degree of offset	**98.7%**

The following potential sources of ineffectiveness were identified:

■ a substantial deterioration in credit risk of either the entity or the counterparty to the hedging instrument; and
■ a change in the timing or amounts of the hedged highly expected cash flows.

The hedge ratio was set at 1:1.

ABC also performed assessments at each reporting date, yielding similar conclusions. These assessments have been omitted to avoid unnecessary repetition.

7.9.5 Fair Valuations, Effective/Ineffective Amounts and Cash Flow Calculations

Suppose that ABC reported its financial statements on a quarterly basis at the end of each March, June, September and December.

Fair Valuations of Hedging Instrument and Hypothetical Derivative   As an example, the following table details the fair valuation of the hedging instrument on 31 March 20X0:

Date	Euribor 12M *(1)*	Discount factor	Expected floating leg cash flow *(2)*	Fixed leg cash flow *(3)*	Expected settlement amount *(4)*	Present value *(5)*
15-Jul-X1	4.25%	0.9477	4,309,000	<4.610.000>	<301,000>	<285,000>
15-Jul-X2	4.70%	0.9046	4,765,000	<4.610.000>	155,000	140,000
15-Jul-X3	5.12%	0.8600	5,191,000	<4.610.000>	581,000	500,000
CVA/DVA						<5,000>
Total						350,000

Notes:

(1) The expected Euribor 12-month rate, as of 31 March 20X0, to be fixed on 13 July 20X0 (i.e., two business days prior to the commencement of the interest period)

(2) Expected floating leg cash flow = 100 mn × Euribor 12M × 365/360, assuming 365 calendar days in the interest period

(3) Fixed leg cash flow = 100 mn × 4.61%

(4) Expected settlement amount = Expected floating leg cash flow + Fixed leg cash flow

(5) Present value = Expected settlement amount × Discount factor

Similarly, the following table details the fair valuation of the hypothetical derivative on 31 March 20X0:

Date	Euribor 12M	Discount factor	Expected floating leg cash flow	Fixed leg cash flow *(*)*	Expected settlement amount	Present value
15-Jul-X1	4.25%	0.9477	4,309,000	<4.615.000>	<301,000>	<285,000>
15-Jul-X2	4.70%	0.9046	4,765,000	<4.615.000>	155,000	140,000
15-Jul-X3	5.12%	0.8600	5,191,000	<4.615.000>	581,000	500,000
CVA/DVA						-0-
Total						341,000

(*) Fixed leg cash flow = 100 mn × 4.615%

The fair values of the hedging instrument and the hypothetical derivative at each relevant date were as follows:

Date	Hedging instrument fair value	Period change	Cumulative change	Hypothetical derivative fair value	Cumulative change
1-Jan-X0	Nil	—	—	Nil	—
31-Mar-X0	350,000	350,000	350,000	341,000	341,000
30-Jun-X0	136,000	<214,000>	136,000	124,000	124,000
15-Jul-X0	468,000	332,000	468,000	461,000	461,000

Effective and Ineffective Amounts   The ineffective part of the change in fair value of the swap was the excess of its cumulative change in fair value over that of the hypothetical derivative. The effective and ineffective parts of the change in fair value of the swap were the following (see Section 5.5.6 for an explanation of the calculations):

	31-Mar-X0	30-Jun-X0	15-Jul-X0
Cumulative change in fair value of hedging instrument	350,000	136,000	468,000
Cumulative change in fair value of hypothetical derivative	341,000	124,000	461,000
Lower amount	341,000	124,000	461,000
Previous cumulative effective amount	—	341,000	127,000
Available amount	341,000	<217,000>	334,000
Period change in fair value of hedging instrument	350,000	<214,000>	332,000
Effective part	341,000	<214,000>	332,000
Ineffective part	9,000	Nil	Nil

7.9.6 Accounting Entries

Suppose that ABC reported its financial statements on a quarterly basis at the end of each March, June, September and December. The required journal entries were as follows.

1) Entries on 1 January 20X0

No journal entries were required to record the swap since its fair value was zero at inception.

2) Entries on 31 March 20X0

The change in fair value of the swap since the last valuation was a EUR 350,000 gain, split between a EUR 341,000 effective amount recorded in the cash flow hedge reserve of OCI and a EUR 9,000 ineffective amount recorded as other financial income in profit or loss.

Derivative contract (Asset)	350,000	
Cash flow hedge reserve (Equity)		341,000
Other financial income (Profit or loss)		9,000

3) Entries on 30 June 20X0

The change in fair value of the swap since the last valuation was a EUR 214,000 loss, fully deemed to be effective and recorded in the cash flow hedge reserve of OCI.

Cash flow hedge reserve (Equity)	214,000	
Derivative contract (Asset)		214,000

4) Entries on 15 July 20X0

The change in fair value of the swap since the last valuation was a EUR 332,000 gain, fully deemed to be effective and recorded in the cash flow hedge reserve of OCI.

Derivative contract (Asset)	332,000	
Cash flow hedge reserve (Equity)		332,000

The swap was cancelled. ABC received EUR 468,000.

Cash (Asset)	468,000	
Derivative contract (Asset)		468,000

The bond was issued. The coupon rate (5.78%) was the 3-year swap rate prevailing on 15 July 20X0 (4.78%) plus a credit spread of 100 basis points, implying a EUR 5,780,000 annual coupon.

5) Entries on each 30 September (20X0, 20X1 and 20X3)

The number of days between 15 July 20X0 and 30 September 20X0 was 77. The accrued interest of the bond was EUR 1,219,000 (= 5,780,000 × 77/365).

Interest expense (Profit or loss)	1,219,000	
Interest payable (Liability)		1,219,000

On this date, the carrying amount of the cash flow hedge reserve was EUR 468,000. ABC decided to allocate this amount on a linear basis to the bond coupons. Therefore each coupon was assigned EUR 156,000 (=468,000/3). The accrued amount of the cash flow reserve assigned to the interest period was EUR 33,000 (= 156,000 × 77/365).

Cash flow hedge reserve (Equity)	33,000	
Interest expense (Profit or loss)		33,000

6) Entries on the last day of each December, March and June during the term of the bond

Assuming 91 calendar days in the interest period, the accrued interest of the bond was EUR 1,441,000 (= 5,780,000 × 91/365).

Interest expense (Profit or loss)	1,441,000	
Interest payable (Liability)		1,441,000

The accrued amount of the cash flow reserve assigned to the interest period was EUR 39,000 (= 156,000 × 91/365), where EUR 156,000 was the annual reclassification of the amounts in the cash flow hedge reserve.

Cash flow hedge reserve (Equity)	39,000	
Interest expense (Profit or loss)		39,000

7) Entries on each 15 July during the term of the bond

The number of days between 30 June and 15 July was 15. The accrued interest of the bond was EUR 238,000 (= 5,780,000 × 15/365).

Interest expense (Profit or loss)	238,000	
Interest payable (Liability)		238,000

The accrued amount of the cash flow reserve assigned to the interest period was EUR 6,000 (= 156,000 × 15/365), where EUR 156,000 was the annual reclassification of the amounts in the cash flow hedge reserve.

Cash flow hedge reserve (Equity)	6,000	
Interest income (Profit or loss)		6,000

The coupon and principal of the bond were paid.

Interest payable (Liability)	5,780,000	
Cash (Asset)		5,780,000

Additionally, on 15 July 20X3 the principal of the bond was repaid.

Financial debt (Liability)	100,000,000	
Cash (Asset)		100,000,000

7.9.7 Concluding Remarks

In order to assess whether ABC achieved its objective of funding itself at 5.61%, let us take a look at ABC's profit or loss statement during the first yearly period (from 15 July 20X0 to 15 July 20X1):

Profit or Loss **Interest Income/Expense** **From 15-Jul-X0 to 15-Jul-X1**	
Entries on 30-Sep-X0:	
Bond coupon accrual	<1,219,000>
Cash flow hedge reserve	33,000
Entries on 31-Dec-X0:	
Bond coupon accrual	<1,441,000>
Cash flow hedge reserve	39,000
Entries on 31-Mar-X1:	
Bond coupon accrual	<1,441,000>
Cash flow hedge reserve	39,000
Entries on 30-Jun-X1:	
Bond coupon accrual	<1,441,000>
Cash flow hedge reserve	39,000
Entries on 15-Jul-X1:	
Bond coupon accrual	<238,000>
Swap settlement accrual	6,000
Total	<5,624,000>

The total interest expense for the period was EUR 5,624,000. This expense implied an interest rate of 5.624% in 30/360 basis. ABC's objective was to fund itself at 5.61% (4.61% swap rate plus 1.00% credit spread), or incurring an overall interest expense of EUR 5,610,000 (= 100 mn × 5.61%). Therefore, ABC incurred an interest expense remarkably close to its funding objective. Additionally, ABC's profit or loss during the period recognised other financial income of EUR 9,000 due to hedge ineffectiveness.

7.10 CASE STUDY: HEDGING A FUTURE FLOATING RATE ISSUANCE WITH AN INTEREST RATE SWAP

The aim of this case study is to illustrate the accounting treatment of hedges of highly expected future issuance of floating rate debt with a forward starting interest rate swap (i.e., a swap that starts sometime in the future). With this type of hedge the entity takes advantage of low interest rates prior to issuing the debt, and/or does not want to take the risk of higher swap rates at issuance date.

7.10.1 Background Information

On 1 January 20X0, ABC (an entity whose functional currency was the EUR) expected to issue a floating rate bond on 15 July 20X0 with the following characteristics:

Bond terms	
Expected issue date	15 July 20X0
Issuer	ABC
Issue proceeds	EUR 100 million (100% of notional)
Expected maturity	3 years (15 July 20X3)
Notional	EUR 100 million
Coupon	Euribor 12-month plus a credit spread, to be paid annually, actual/360 basis. The expected credit spread was 100 bps

ABC was exposed to upward movements in the 12-month Euribor rate and to a widening of its own credit spread. ABC planned to mitigate its exposure to interest rates by synthetically converting the floating rate bond coupons into fixed with a 3-year pay-fixed receive-floating interest rate swap. ABC considered the following alternatives:

1) To wait until the bond was issued to enter into a pay-fixed receive-floating swap. Under this alternative the entity would be exposed to a rising 3-year swap rate until the bond's issue date, but would benefit were this swap rate to decline.
2) To lock in the current interest rates by entering into a swap that would start on the planned issue date (a forward starting swap). Under this alternative, the entity would eliminate its exposure to a rising 3-year swap rate, but would not benefit were this swap rate to decline.

ABC chose the second alternative – to enter into a forward starting swap – to protect itself against potential increases in the 3-year swap rate. Accordingly, on 1 January 20X0 ABC entered into a forward starting pay-fixed receive-floating interest rate swap with XYZ Bank with the following terms:

Interest rate swap terms	
Trade date	1 January 20X0
Start date	15 July 20X0
Counterparties	ABC and XYZ Bank
Maturity	3 years (15 July 20X3)
Notional	EUR 100 million
ABC pays	4.61% annually, 30/360 basis
ABC receives	Euribor 12M annually, actual/360 basis
Euribor fixing	Euribor is fixed 2 days prior to the commencement of the annual interest period
Initial fair value	Zero

ABC designated the swap as the hedging instrument in a cash flow hedge of the highly expected cash flows stemming from the floating rate bond. The effective amounts of the change in fair value of the swap would be recognised in equity. Following the bond issuance, the amounts accumulated in equity would be subsequently recycled to profit or loss when the bond coupons impacted profit or loss. If the hedge was well constructed, the effective interest rate of the new bond would be close to the sum of the swap fixed rate and the credit spread, or 5.61% (= 4.61% + 1%), as shown in Figure 7.4.

7.10.2 Hedging Relationship Documentation

ABC documented the hedging relationship as follows:

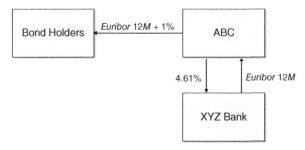

FIGURE 7.4 Hedging strategy interest flows.

Hedging relationship documentation	
Risk management objective and strategy for undertaking the hedge	The objective of the hedge is to eliminate the variability of the highly expected future cash outflows stemming from a planned issuance of a floating rate bond by the entity.
	This hedging objective is consistent with the group's overall interest rate risk management strategy of managing the exposure to interest rate risk through the proportion of fixed and floating rate net debt in its total debt portfolio with interest rate swaps, caps and collars.
	Interest rate risk. The designated risk being hedged is the risk of changes in the EUR value of the hedged item attributable to changes in the Euribor interest rates.
	Fair value changes attributable to credit or other risks are not hedged in this relationship. Accordingly, the expected 100 basis points credit spread is excluded from the hedging relationship
Type of hedge	Cash flow hedge
Hedged item	The coupon cash flows of a 3-year floating rate bond highly expected to be issued on 15 July 20X0.
	The issuance is highly expected to occur as it has been approved by the Board of Directors and a group of banks have been mandated
Hedging instrument	The interest rate swap with reference number 014569. The main terms of the swap are a EUR 100 million notional, a forward starting date on 15 July 20X0, a 3-year maturity, a 4.61% fixed rate to be received by the entity and a Euribor 12-month rate to be paid by the entity. The counterparty to the swap is XYZ Bank and the credit risk associated with this counterparty is considered to be very low
Hedge effectiveness assessment	See below

7.10.3 Hedge Effectiveness Assessment

Hedge effectiveness will be assessed by comparing changes in the fair value of the hedging instrument to changes in the fair value of a hypothetical derivative. The terms of the hypothetical derivative are such that its fair value changes exactly offset the changes in fair value of the hedged item for the risk being hedged. The hypothetical derivative is a theoretical interest rate swap with no counterparty credit risk and with zero initial fair value, whose main terms are as follows:

Hypothetical derivative terms	
Trade date	1 January 20X0
Start date	15 July 20X0
Counterparties	ABC and credit risk-free counterparty
Maturity	3 years (15 July 20X3)
Notional	EUR 100 million
ABC pays	Euribor 12M annually, actual/360 basis
ABC receives	4.615% annually, 30/360 basis

Euribor fixing	Euribor is fixed 2 days prior to the commencement of the annual interest period
Initial fair value	Zero

The fixed rate of the hypothetical derivative is higher than that of the hedging instrument due to the absence of CVA in the former.

Changes in the fair value of the hedging instrument (i.e., the swap) will be recognised as follows:

- The effective part of the gain or loss on the hedging instrument will be recognised in the cash flow hedge reserve of equity. Following the bond issuance, the amounts accumulated in equity will be reclassified to profit or loss in the same period during which the hedged expected future cash flows affect profit or loss, adjusting interest expense.
- The ineffective part of the gain or loss on the hedging instrument will be recognised in profit or loss, as other financial income/expenses.

Hedge effectiveness will be assessed prospectively at hedging relationship inception, on an ongoing basis at least upon each reporting date and upon occurrence of a significant change in the circumstances affecting the hedge effectiveness requirements.

The hedging relationship will qualify for hedge accounting only if all the following criteria are met:

1) The hedging relationship consists only of an eligible hedge item and hedging instrument. The hedge item is eligible as it is a group of highly expected cash flows that will expose the entity to fair value risk, will affect profit or loss and is reliably measurable. The hedging instrument is eligible as it is a derivative that does not result in a net written option.
2) At hedge inception there is a formal designation and documentation of the hedging relationship and the entity's risk management objective and strategy for undertaking the hedge.
3) The hedging relationship is considered effective.

The hedging relationship will be considered effective if the following three requirements are met:

1) There is an economic relationship between the hedged item and the hedging instrument.
2) The effect of credit risk does not dominate the value changes that result from that economic relationship.
3) The hedge ratio of the hedging relationship is the same as that resulting from the quantity of hedged item that the entity actually hedges and the quantity of the hedging instrument that the entity actually uses to hedge that quantity of hedged item. The hedge ratio should not be intentionally weighted to create ineffectiveness.

Whether there is an economic relationship between the hedged item and the hedging instrument will be assessed on a qualitative basis by comparing the critical terms (notional, interest periods, underlying and fixed rates) of the hypothetical derivative and the hedging instrument. The assessment will be complemented by a quantitative assessment using the scenario analysis method for one scenario in which Euribor interest rates will be shifted upwards by 2% and the changes in fair value of the hypothetical derivative and the hedging instrument compared.

7.10.4 Hedge Effectiveness Assessment Performed at the Start of the Hedging Relationship

On 1 January 20X0 and at each reporting date ABC performed a hedge effectiveness assessment. The documentation related to the assessment performed on 1 January 20X0 was described in Section 7.9.4.

The following potential sources of ineffectiveness were identified:

- a substantial deterioration in credit risk of either the entity or the counterparty to the hedging instrument; and
- a change in the timing or amounts of the hedged highly expected cash flows.

The hedge ratio was set at 1:1.

7.10.5 Fair Valuations, Effective/Ineffective Amounts and Cash Flow Calculations

Suppose that ABC reported its financial statements on an annual basis on 31 December.

Fair Valuations of Hedging Instrument and Hypothetical Derivative   As an example, the following table details the fair valuation of the hedging instrument on 31 December 20X0:

Cash flow date	Euribor	Discount factor	Expected floating leg cash flow	Fixed leg cash flow	Expected settlement amount *(1)*	Present value *(2)*
15-Jul-X1	4.30% *(3)*	0.9771	2,287,000 *(4)*	<2,476,000> *(5)*	<189,000>	<185,000>
15-Jul-X2	4.70% *(6)*	0.9327	4,765,000 *(7)*	<4,610,000> *(8)*	155,000	145,000
15-Jul-X3	5.12%	0.8867	5,191,000	<4,610,000>	581,000	515,000
CVA/DVA						<7,000>
Total						468,000

Notes:

(1) Expected settlement amount = Expected floating leg cash flow + Fixed leg cash flow

(2) Present value = Expected settlement amount × Discount factor

(3) 4.30% was the Euribor rate, on an actual/360 basis, from 31-Dec-20X0 to 15-Jul-20X1, used to calculate the discount factor

(4) 100 mn × 4.20% × 196/360, where 4.20% was the Euribor 12M fixed on 13-Jul-20X0 and 196 is the number of calendar days from 31-Dec-20X0 to 15-Jul-20X1

(5) 100 mn × 4.61% × 196/365, where 4.61% was the swap's fixed rate and 196 is the number of calendar days from 31-Dec-20X0 to 15-Jul-20X1. Although the fixed rate basis was 30/360, it was approximated with an actual/365 basis to keep it simpler

(6) The expected Euribor 12-month rate, as of 31 December 20X0, to be fixed on 13 July 20X1 (i.e., two business days prior to the commencement of the interest period)

(7) 100 mn × 4.70% × 365 /360, where 4.70% was the expected Euribor 12M to be fixed on 13-Jul-20X1 and 365 is the number of calendar days from 15-Jul-20X1 to 15-Jul-20X2

(8) 100 mn × 4.61%, where 4.61% was the swap's fixed rate

Similarly, the following table details the fair valuation of the hypothetical derivative on 31 March 20X0:

Date	Euribor 12M	Discount factor	Expected floating leg cash flow	Fixed leg cash flow (*)	Expected settlement amount	Present value
15-Jul-X1	4.30%	0.9771	2,287,000	<2,478,000>	<191,000>	<187,000>
15-Jul-X2	4.70%	0.9327	4,765,000	<4,615,000>	150,000	140,000
15-Jul-X3	5.12%	0.8867	5,191,000	<4,615,000>	576,000	511,000
CVA/DVA						-0-
Total						464,000

(*) Fixed leg cash flow = 100 mn × 4.615%

The fair values of the hedging instrument and the hypothetical derivative at each relevant date were as follows:

Date	Hedging instrument fair value	Period change	Cumulative change	Hypothetical derivative fair value	Cumulative change
1-Jan-X0	-0-	—	—	-0-	—
31-Dec-X0	468,000	468,000	468,000	464,000	464,000
31-Dec-X1	779,000	311,000	779,000	781,000	781,000
31-Dec-X2	264,000	<515,000>	264,000	264,000	264,000
15-Jul-X3	-0-	<264,000>	-0-	-0-	-0-

Effective and Ineffective Amounts The ineffective part of the change in fair value of the swap was the excess of its cumulative change in fair value over that of the hypothetical derivative. The effective and ineffective parts of the change in fair value of the swap were the following (see Section 5.5.6 for an explanation of the calculations):

	31-Dec-X0	31-Dec-X1	31-Dec-X2	15-Jul-X3
Cumulative change in fair value of hedging instrument	468,000	779,000	264,000	-0-
Cumulative change in fair value of hypothetical derivative	464,000	781,000	264,000	-0-
Lower amount	464,000	779,000	264,000	-0-
Previous cumulative effective amount	—	464,000	775,000	264,000
Available amount	464,000	315,000	<511,000>	<264,000>
Period change in fair value of hedging instrument	468,000	311,000	<515,000>	<264,000>
Effective part	464,000	311,000	<511,000>	<264,000>
Ineffective part	4,000	Nil	<4,000>	Nil

Bond and Swap Accrual Amounts

	Euribor 12M (1)	Days (2)	Swap settlement amount accrual (3)	Bond coupon accrual (4)
31-Dec-X0	4.20%	169	<163,000>	<2,441,000>
15-Jul-X1	4.20%	196	<189,000>	<2,831,000>
31-Dec-X1	4.70%	169	72,000	<2,676,000>
15-Jul-X2	4.70%	196	83,000	<3,103,000>
31-Dec-X2	5.05%	169	236,000	<2,840,000>
15-Jul-X3	5.05%	196	274,000	<3,294,000>

Notes:

(1) Euribor 12-month fixed on the prior 13 July (i.e., 2 days prior to the interest period)

(2) Calendar days from the previous date (i.e., either from the previous 15 July or 31 December, as appropriate)

(3) 100 mn × Euribor 12M × Days/360 – 100 mn × 4.61% × Days/365

(4) 100 mn × (Euribor 12M + 1%) × Days/360

7.10.6 Accounting Entries

Suppose that ABC reported its financial statements on an annual basis on 31 December. The required journal entries were the following.

1) Entries on 1 January 20X0

No journal entries were required to record the swap since its fair value was zero at inception.

2) Entries on 15 July 20X0

The bond was issued at par.

Cash (Asset)	100,000,000	
Financial debt (Liability)		100,000,000

3) Entries on 31 December 20X0

The bond's accrued coupon was EUR 2,441,000.

Interest expense (Profit or loss)	2,441,000	
Interest payable (Liability)		2,441,000

The swap's accrued settlement amount was EUR <163,000>.

Interest expense (Profit or loss)	163,000	
Interest payable (Liability)		163,000

The change in fair value of the swap since the last valuation was a EUR 468,000 gain, split between a EUR 464,000 effective amount recorded in the cash flow hedge reserve of OCI and a EUR 4,000 ineffective amount recorded as other financial income in profit or loss.

Derivative contract (Asset)	468,000	
Cash flow hedge reserve (Equity)		464,000
Other financial income (Profit or loss)		4,000

4) Entries on 15 July 20X1

The bond's accrued coupon was EUR 2,831,000. The EUR 5,272,000 coupon was paid.

Interest expense (Profit or loss)	2,441,000	
Interest payable (Liability)		2,441,000
Interest payable (Liability)	5,272,000	
Cash (asset)		5,272,000

The swap's accrued settlement amount was EUR <189,000>. The EUR <352,000> settlement amount was paid.

Interest expense (Profit or loss)	189,000	
Interest payable (Liability)		189,000
Interest payable (Liability)	352,000	
Cash (asset)		352,000

5) Entries on 31 December 20X1

The bond's accrued coupon was EUR 2,676,000. The swap's accrued settlement amount was EUR 72,000. The change in fair value of the swap since the last valuation was a EUR 311,000 gain, fully deemed to be effective and recorded in the cash flow hedge reserve of OCI.

Interest expense (Profit or loss)	2,676,000	
Interest payable (Liability)		2,676,000

Interest receivable (Asset)	72,000	
Interest income (Profit or loss)		72,000
Derivative contract (Asset)	311,000	
Cash flow hedge reserve (Equity)		311,000

6) Entries on 15 July 20X2

The bond's accrued coupon was EUR 3,103,000. The EUR 5,779,000 coupon was paid. The swap's accrued settlement amount was EUR 83,000. The EUR 155,000 settlement amount was received.

Interest expense (Profit or loss)	3,103,000	
Interest payable (Liability)		3,103,000
Interest payable (Liability)	5,779,000	
Cash (asset)		5,779,000
Interest receivable (Asset)	83,000	
Interest income (Profit or loss)		83,000
Cash (Asset)	155,000	
Interest receivable (Asset)		155,000

7) Entries on 31 December 20X2

The bond's accrued coupon was EUR 2,840,000. The swap's accrued settlement amount was EUR 236,000. The change in fair value of the swap since the last valuation was a EUR 515,000 loss, split between a EUR <511,000> effective amount recorded in the cash flow hedge reserve of OCI and a EUR <4,000> ineffective amount recorded as other financial expenses in profit or loss.

Interest expense (Profit or loss)	2,840,000	
Interest payable (Liability)		2,840,000
Interest receivable (Asset)	236,000	

Interest income (Profit or loss)		236,000
Cash flow hedge reserve (Equity)	511,000	
Other financial expenses (Profit or loss)	4,000	
Derivative contract (Asset)		515,000

8) Entries on 15 July 20X3

The bond's accrued coupon was EUR 3,294,000. Both the EUR 6,134,000 coupon and the EUR 100 million principal were paid. The swap's accrued settlement amount was EUR 274,000. The EUR 510,000 settlement amount was received. The change in fair value of the swap since the last valuation was a EUR 264,000 loss, fully deemed to be effective and recorded in the cash flow hedge reserve of OCI.

Interest expense (Profit or loss)	3,294,000	
Interest payable (Liability)		3,294,000
Interest payable (Liability)	6,134,000	
Financial debt (Liability)	100,000,000	
Cash (asset)		106,134,000
Interest receivable (Asset)	274,000	
Interest income (Profit or loss)		274,000
Cash (Asset)	510,000	
Interest receivable (Asset)		510,000
Cash flow hedge reserve (Equity)	264,000	
Derivative contract (Asset)		264,000

7.10.7 Concluding Remarks

In order to assess whether ABC achieved its objective of funding itself at 5.61%, let us take a look at ABC's profit or loss statement during the first yearly period (from 15 July 20X0 to 15 July 20X1):

Profit or Loss Interest Income/Expense From 15-Jul-X0 to 15-Jul-X1	
Entries on 30-Dec-X0:	
Bond coupon accrual	<2,441,000>
Swap settlement amount accrual	<163,000>
Entries on 15-Jul-X1:	
Bond coupon accrual	<2,831,000>
Swap settlement accrual	<189,000>
Total	<5,624,000>

The total interest expense for the period was EUR 5,624,000. This expense implied an interest rate of 5.624% on a 30/360 basis. ABC's objective was to fund itself at 5.61% (4.61% swap rate plus 1.00% credit spread), or incurring an overall interest expense of EUR 5,610,000 (= 100 mn × 5.61%). Therefore, ABC incurred an interest expense remarkably close to its funding objective. Additionally, ABC's profit or loss during the period recognised other financial income of EUR 4,000 due to hedge ineffectiveness.

7.11 CASE STUDY: HEDGING A FIXED RATE LIABILITY WITH A SWAP IN ARREARS

This case study illustrates the accounting treatment of a hedge of a fixed rate liability with a swap in arrears. This hedging strategy takes advantage of an unusually steep yield curve. The fixed legs of a swap in arrears and a standard swap are identical. The difference between them lies in the fixing of the floating leg:

- In a standard swap, the Euribor rate is set at the beginning of the interest period (specifically, two business days prior to the commencement of the period).
- In a swap in arrears, the Euribor rate is set at the end of the interest period (specifically, two business days prior to the end of the period).

The payment of the floating-leg interest is made at the end of the interest period. For example, suppose that the interest period of the floating leg starts on 15 July 20X0 and ends on 15 July 20X1, and that the underlying variable is the Euribor 12-month rate. Under a standard swap, the Euribor 12-month rate will be fixed on 13 July 20X0 and the floating leg interest will be paid on 15 July 20X1 (see Figure 7.5). Under a swap in arrears, the Euribor 12-month rate will be fixed on 13 July 20X1 and the floating leg interest will be paid on 15 July 20X1 (see Figure 7.5).

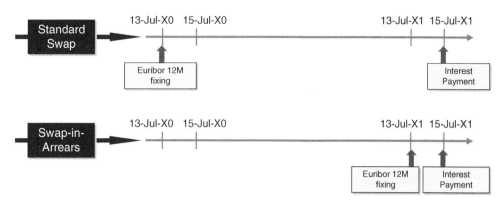

FIGURE 7.5 Floating leg interest period – standard swap versus swap in arrears.

7.11.1 Background Information

On 1 January 20X0, ABC issued at par a fixed rate bond with the following characteristics:

Bond terms	
Issue date	1 January 20X0
Issuer	ABC
Issue proceeds	EUR 100 million (100% of notional)
Expected maturity	3 years (31 December 20X2)
Notional	EUR 100 million
Coupon	6.12% annually, 30/360 basis

ABC's interest rate risk management strategy was to immediately swap to floating all new debt issues and later, as part of its overall hedging policy, decide which fixed-floating mix was appropriate for the whole corporation. First, ABC considered entering into a standard swap in which ABC would pay Euribor 12-month and receive 5.12%. Through the standard swap, ABC would be effectively funding itself at Euribor 12M plus 100 bps (= 6.12% − 5.12%). Because the EUR yield curve was unusually steep, ABC preferred instead to enter into a swap in arrears with the following terms:

Interest rate swap-in-arrears terms	
Trade date	1 January 20X0
Start date	1 January 20X0
Counterparties	ABC and XYZ Bank

Maturity	3 years (31 December 20X2)
Notional	EUR 100 million
ABC receives	5.70% annually, 30/360 basis
ABC pays	Euribor 12M annually, actual/360 basis
Euribor fixing	Euribor is fixed 2 days prior to the end of the annual interest period
Initial fair value	Zero

Under the swap in arrears, ABC paid annually Euribor 12-month in arrears and received annually 5.70%. ABC then used the 5.70% received and added 0.42% to pay the 6.12% bond interest. The combination of the bond and the swap resulted in ABC paying an interest of Euribor 12M in arrears plus 42 bps, as shown in Figure 7.6. The 42 bps spread was the difference between the bond coupon (6.12%) and the swap fixed rate (5.70%).

The swap in arrears was designated as the hedging instrument in a fair value hedge of the bond.

7.11.2 Hedging Relationship Documentation

ABC documented the hedging relationship as follows:

Hedging relationship documentation	
Risk management objective and strategy for undertaking the hedge	The objective of the hedge is to reduce the variability of the fair value of a fixed rate bond issued by the entity. This hedging objective is consistent with the group's overall interest rate risk management strategy of transforming all new issued debt into floating rate, and thereafter managing the exposure to interest rate risk through the proportion of fixed and floating rate net debt in its total debt portfolio. Interest rate risk. The designated risk being hedged is the risk of changes in the EUR fair value of the hedged item attributable to changes in the Euribor interest rate. Fair value changes attributable to credit or other risks are not hedged in this relationship. Accordingly, the 60 basis points credit spread is excluded from the hedging relationship
Type of hedge	Fair value hedge
Hedged item	The coupons and principal of the 3-year 6.12% fixed rate bond with reference number 678908. As the bond credit spread (100 basis points) is excluded from the hedging relationship, only the cash flows related to the interest rate component of the coupons will be part of the hedging relationship (i.e., those corresponding to a 5.12% rate or EUR 5.12 million). The EUR 100 million principal is included in the hedging relationship in its entirety

Hedging instrument	The interest rate swap in arrears with reference number 014573. The main terms of the swap are a EUR 100 million notional, a 3-year maturity, a 5.70% fixed rate to be received by the entity and a Euribor 12-month rate to be paid by the entity. The Euribor 12-month rate is fixed two business days prior to the end of the interest period. The counterparty to the swap is XYZ Bank and the credit risk associated with this counterparty is considered to be very low
Hedge effectiveness assessment	See next below

7.11.3 Hedge Effectiveness Assessment

Hedge effectiveness will be assessed by comparing changes in the fair value of the hedging instrument to changes in the fair value of the hedged item. Changes in the fair value of the hedging instrument (i.e., the swap) will be recognised as follows:

- The effective part of the gain or loss on the hedging instrument will be recognised in profit or loss, adjusting interest income/expense.
- The ineffective part of the gain or loss on the hedging instrument will be recognised in profit or loss, as other financial income/expenses.

Hedge effectiveness will be assessed prospectively at hedging relationship inception, on an ongoing basis at least upon each reporting date and upon occurrence of a significant change in the circumstances affecting the hedge effectiveness requirements.

The hedging relationship will qualify for hedge accounting only if all the following criteria are met:

1) The hedging relationship consists only of eligible hedge items and hedging instruments. The hedge item is eligible as it is an already recognised liability that exposes the entity to fair value risk, affects profit or loss and is reliably measurable. The hedging instrument is eligible as it is a derivative that does not result in a net written option.
2) At hedge inception there is a formal designation and documentation of the hedging relationship and the entity's risk management objective and strategy for undertaking the hedge.
3) The hedging relationship is considered effective.

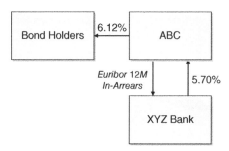

FIGURE 7.6 Hedging strategy interest flows.

The hedging relationship will be considered effective if the following three requirements are met:

1) There is an economic relationship between the hedged item and the hedging instrument,
2) The effect of credit risk does not dominate the value changes that result from that economic relationship,
3) The hedge ratio of the hedging relationship is the same as that resulting from the quantity of hedged item that the entity actually hedges and the quantity of the hedging instrument that the entity actually uses to hedge that quantity of hedged item. The hedge ratio should not be intentionally weighted to create ineffectiveness.

Whether there is an economic relationship between the hedged item and the hedging instrument will be assessed on a quantitative basis using the regression analysis method, comparing the changes in fair value of the hedged item and the hedging instrument.

7.11.4 Hedge Effectiveness Assessment Performed at the Start of the Hedging Relationship

On 1 January 20X0 ABC performed a hedge effectiveness assessment which was documented as described next.

The hedging relationship was considered effective as the following three requirements were met:

1) There was an economic relationship between the hedged item and the hedging instrument.
2) The effect of credit risk did not dominate the value changes resulting from that economic relationship as the credit ratings of both the entity and XYZ Bank were considered sufficiently strong.
3) The hedge ratio of the hedging relationship was the same as that resulting from the quantity of hedged item that the entity actually hedged and the quantity of the hedging instrument that the entity actually used to hedge that quantity of hedged item. The hedge ratio was not intentionally weighted to create ineffectiveness.

A quantitative assessment was performed to support the conclusion that the hedging instrument and the hedged item had values that would generally move in opposite directions. The quantitative assessment consisted of a regression analysis performed as shown in Figure 7.7.

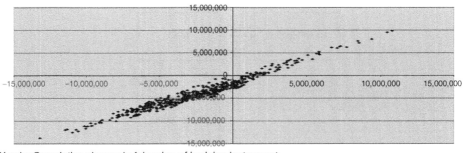

X axis: Cumulative change in fair value of hedging instrument
Y axis: Cumulative change in fair value of hedged item

FIGURE 7.7   Swap in arrears – regression analysis.

A regression analysis assesses the level of correlation between changes in the clean (i.e., excluding accruals) fair value of the hedging instrument and the changes in the clean fair value of the hedged item, using historical interest rate information. If a high correlation exists, then movements in the fair value of the bond can be reasonably expected to trigger similar offsetting movements in the fair value of the swap. The analysis was based on historical EUR interest rates over the previous 15 years (the "historical time horizon"). The historical time horizon was divided into 156 "simulation periods" of 3 years each, as shown in Figure 7.8.

Each simulation period had an inception date and three subsequent annual balance sheet dates. During each simulation period, the behaviour of an equivalent hedging relationship using the historical data was simulated. At the beginning of the simulation period, the terms of the hedging instrument and hedged item were determined as if the hedge were entered into on that date. The terms were such that the simulated hedge terms were equivalent to the actual terms but taking into account the market rates prevailing at the beginning of the simulation period. Each observation pair (X, Y) was generated by computing the cumulative change in the fair value of the simulation hedging instrument (variable X) and the cumulative change in fair value of the simulation hypothetical derivative (observation Y). Figure 7.9 highlights the process for the first simulation, which started 15 years prior to 1 January 20X0.

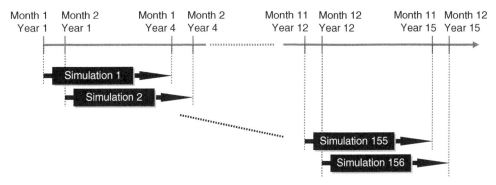

FIGURE 7.8 Regression analysis – simulation periods.

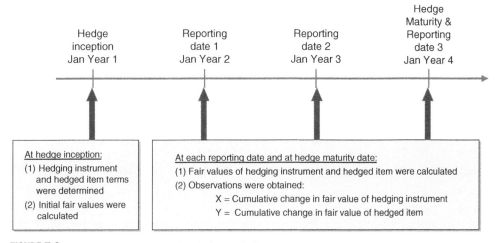

FIGURE 7.9 Regression analysis – simulation periods.

The results of the regression analysis showed an *R*-squared of 90.2%, a slope of the regression line of 1.00, and the *F*-statistic indicated statistical significance at the 95% confidence level. Based on these results, the entity concluded that the change in fair value of the hedged item was expected to be substantially offset by the change in fair value of the hedging instrument, corroborating that both elements had values that would generally move in opposite directions.

The following potential sources of ineffectiveness were identified:

- a substantial deterioration in credit risk of either the entity or the counterparty to the hedging instrument; and
- a change in the timing or amounts of the hedged highly expected cash flows.

The hedge ratio was set at 1:1.

ABC also performed assessments at each reporting date, yielding similar conclusions. These assessments have been omitted to avoid unnecessary repetition. The credit risk of the entity and the counterparty to the hedging instrument were continuously monitored and throughout the hedge life both credit risks were considered to be very low.

7.11.5 Fair Valuations, Effective/Ineffective Amounts and Cash Flow Calculations

Fair Valuations of the Hedging Instrument   The Euribor 12-month rate fixings at the relevant dates were as follows:

Euribor 12M fixings	
29-Dec-W9	4.44%
29-Dec-X0	4.94%
29-Dec-X1	5.64%
29-Dec-X2	6.00%

The fair value of the swap was computed by summing the present value of each expected future net settlement, and adjusting for CVA/DVA. The fair value of the swap on 1 January 20X0 was zero.

The fair value of the swap on 31 December 20X0 was calculated using the market yield curve on that date as follows:

Cash flow date	Discount factor	Expected Euribor 12M	Expected floating leg cash flow	Fixed leg cash flow	Net amount	Present value
31-Dec-X1	0.9523	5.70%	<5,779,000> *(1)*	5,700,000 *(2)*	<79,000> *(3)*	<75,000> *(4)*
31-Dec-X2	0.9003	6.10%	<6,185,000>	5,700,000	<485,000>	<437,000>
CVA/DVA						8,000
Fair value						<504,000>

Notes:

    (1) 100 mn × 5.70% × 365/360, where 5.70% was the expected Euribor 12M rate to be fixed on 29-Dec-X1 (i.e., two business days prior to the end date of the interest period) and 365 is the number of calendar days from 31-Dec-X0 to 31-Dec-X1)

    (2) 100 mn × 5.70%, where 5.70% was the swap fixed rate

    (3) <5,779,000> + 5,700,000

    (4) <79,000> × 0.9523

The fair value of the swap on 31 December 20X1 was calculated using the market yield curve on that date as follows:

Date	Discount factor	Expected Euribor 12M	Expected floating leg cash flow	Fixed leg cash flow	Net amount	Present value
31-Dec-X2	0.9459	6.14%	<6,225,000> *(1)*	5,700,000 *(2)*	<525,000> *(3)*	<497,000> *(4)*
CVA/DVA						5,000
Fair value						<492,000>

Notes:

    (1) 100 mn × 6.14% × 365/360, where 6.14% was the expected Euribor 12-month rate to be fixed on 29-Dec-X2 (i.e., two business days prior to the end date of the interest period) and 365 is the number of calendar days from 31-Dec-X1 to 31-Dec-X2)

    (2) 100 mn × 5.70%, where 5.70% was the swap fixed rate

    (3) <6,225,000> + 5,700,000

    (4) <525,000> × 0.9459

The fair value of the swap on 31 December 20X2 was zero.

Fair Valuations of the Hedged Item   The fair value of the hedged item was computed by summing up the present value of each future EUR 5.12 million fixed cash flow. Remember that the risk being hedged was interest rate risk only. Therefore, changes in the fair value of the bond due to changes in ABC's credit spread were not part of the hedged item fair valuations. The cash flows being hedged were the first EUR 5,120,000 of each annual coupon, a portion of the EUR 6,120,000 annual coupon.

The fair value of the hedged item on 1 January 20X0 was EUR <100 million>.

The fair value of the bond on 31 December 20X0 was calculated using the market yield curve on that date as follows:

Date	Discount factor	Expected cash flow	Present value
31-Dec-X1	0.9523	<5,120,000> *(1)*	<4,876,000>
31-Dec-X3	0.9003	<105,120,000>	<94,640,000>
Fair value			<99,516,000>

Notes:

    (1) The hedged cash flow of the bond coupon

    (2) 5,120,000 × 0.9523

The fair value of the bond on 31 December 20X1 was calculated using the market yield curve on that date as follows:

Date	Discount factor	Expected cash flow	Present value
31-Jul-X3	0.9459	<105,120,000>	<99,433,000>
Fair value			<99,433,000>

The fair value of the bond on 31 December 20X2 was EUR <100 million>.

Calculations of Effective and Ineffective Amounts   The period changes in fair value of the hedging instrument and the hedged item were as follows:

Date	Hedging instrument fair value	Period change	Hedged item fair value	Period change
31-Jul-X0	-0-	—	<100,000,000>	—
31-Dec-X0	<504,000>	<504,000>	<99,516,000>	484,000
31-Dec-X1	<492,000>	12,000	<99,433,000>	83,000
31-Dec-X2	-0-	492,000	<100,000,000>	<567,000>

The ineffective part of the change in fair value of the hedging instrument was the excess of its period change in fair value over that of the hedged item. The effective and ineffective parts of the period change in fair value of the swap were as follows:

	31-Dec-X0	31-Dec-X1	31-Dec-X2
Period change in fair value of hedging instrument	<504,000>	12,000	492,000
Period change in fair value of hedged item (opposite sign)	<484,000>	<83,000>	567,000
Lower amount	<484,000>	-0- (*)	492,000
Effective part	<484,000>	-0-	492,000
Ineffective part	<20,000>	12,000	-0-

(*) There was no offset between the period change in fair values of the hedging instrument and the hedged item

The effective part of the change in fair value of the hedged item was the effective part of the change in fair value of the hedging instrument (see previous table). Any remainder was considered to be ineffective. The effective and ineffective parts of the period change in fair value of the hedged item were as follows:

	31-Dec-X0	31-Dec-X1	31-Dec-X2
Period change in fair value of hedged item	484,000	83,000	<567,000>
Effective part of change in fair value of hedging instrument (opposite sign)	484,000	-0-	<492,000>
Ineffective part (excess)	-0-	83,000	<75,000>

Calculations of Bond Coupon and Swap Settlement Amounts

Cash flow date	Bond coupon	Euribor fixing (in arrears)	Swap settlement amount
31-Dec-X0	<6,120,000> *(1)*	4.94%	691,000 *(2)*
31-Dec-X1	<6,120,000>	5.64%	<18,000>
31-Dec-X2	<6,120,000>	6.00%	<383,000>

Notes:

    (1) 100 mn × 6.12%

    (2) 100 mn × 5.70% − 100 mn × 4.94% × 365/360, where 5.70% was the swap's fixed rate, 4.94% was the Euribor 12M rate fixed two business days prior to 31-Dec-X0 (i.e., 29-Dec-X0) and 365 is the number of calendar days from 1-Jan-X0 to 31-Dec-X0)

7.11.6 Accounting Entries

Suppose that ABC reported its financial statements on an annual basis on 31 December. The required journal entries were the following.

1) Entries on 1 January 20X0

The bond was issued at par.

Cash (Asset)	100,000,000	
Financial debt (Liability)		100,000,000

    No journal entries were required to record the swap in arrears since its fair value was zero at inception.

2) Entries on 31 December 20X0

The EUR 6,120,000 (=100 million × 6.12%) bond coupon was paid.

Interest expense (Profit or loss)	6,120,000	
Cash (Asset)		6,120,000

The EUR 691,000 swap settlement amount was received.

Cash (Asset)	691,000	
Interest income (Profit or loss)		691,000

The change in fair value of the swap since the last valuation was a EUR 504,000 loss, of which EUR <484,000> was deemed to be effective and recorded as interest expense in profit or loss, while EUR <20,000> was deemed to be ineffective and recorded as other financial expenses in profit or loss.

Interest expense (Profit or loss)	484,000	
Other financial expenses (Profit or loss)	20,000	
Derivative contract (Asset)		504,000

The change in fair value of the hedged item since the last valuation was a EUR 484,000 gain, fully deemed to be effective and recorded as interest income in profit or loss.

Financial debt (Liability)	484,000	
Interest income (Profit or loss)		484,000

3) Entries on 31 December 20X1

The EUR 6,120,000 (= 100 million × 6.12%) bond coupon was paid. The EUR <18,000> swap settlement amount was paid. The change in fair value of the swap since the last valuation was a EUR 12,000 gain, fully deemed to be ineffective and recorded as other financial income in profit or loss. The change in fair value of the hedged item since the last valuation was a EUR 83,000 gain, fully deemed to be ineffective and recorded as other financial income in profit or loss.

Interest expense (Profit or loss)	6,120,000	
Cash (Asset)		6,120,000
Interest expense (Profit or loss)	18,000	
Cash (Asset)		18,000
Derivative contract (Asset)	12,000	
Other financial income (Profit or loss)		12,000
Financial debt (Liability)	83,000	
Other financial income (Profit or loss)		83,000

4) Entries on 31 December 20X2

The EUR 6,120,000 (= 100 million × 6.12%) bond coupon was paid. The bond's EUR 100 million principal was repaid. The EUR <383,000> swap settlement amount was paid. The change in fair value of the swap since the last valuation was a EUR 492,000 gain, fully deemed to be effective and recorded as interest income in profit or loss. The change in fair value of the hedged item since the last valuation was a EUR 567,000 loss of which EUR <492,000> was deemed to be effective and recorded as interest expense in profit or loss, while EUR <75,000> was deemed to be ineffective and recorded as other financial expenses in profit or loss.

Interest expense (Profit or loss)	6,120,000	
Financial debt (Liability)	100,000,000	
Cash (Asset)		106,120,000
Interest expense (Profit or loss)	383,000	
Cash (Asset)		383,000
Derivative contract (Asset)	492,000	
Other financial income (Profit or loss)		492,000
Interest expense (Profit or loss)	492,000	
Other financial expenses (Profit or loss)	75,000	
Financial debt (Liability)		567,000

The following table gives a summary of the accounting entries:

	Cash	Derivative contract	Financial debt	Profit or loss
1-Jan-20X0				
Bond issuance	100,000,000		100,000,000	
Derivative trade		—		
31 Dec-20X0				
Bond coupon	<6,120,000>			<6,120,000>
Swap settlement amount	691,000			691,000
Swap fair valuation		<504,000>		<504,000>
Hedged item fair valuation			<484,000>	484,000
31-Dec-20X1				
Bond coupon	<6,120,000>			<6,120,000>
Swap settlement amount	<18,000>			<18,000>
Swap fair valuation		12,000		12,000
Hedged item fair valuation			<83,000>	83,000

	Cash	Derivative contract	Financial debt	Profit or loss
31-Dec-20X2				
Bond coupon	<6,120,000>			<6,120,000>
Bond principal	<100,000,000>		<100,000,000>	
Swap settlement amount	<383,000>			<383,000>
Swap fair valuation		492,000		492,000
Hedged item fair valuation			567,000	<567,000>
TOTAL	**<18,070,000>**	**-0-**	**-0-**	**<18,070,000>**

Note: Total figures may not match the sum of their corresponding components due to rounding.

7.11.7 Concluding Remarks

ABC tried to synthetically convert the 6.12% bond coupon into a floating interest rate. Rather than targeting the cost of funding of Euribor 12-month plus 100 basis points with a standard swap, ABC tried to achieve a slightly better cost of funding by entering into a swap in arrears. The table below summarises the annual cost of funding achieved ("actual funding") and how it compared to a Euribor 12-month plus 1% funding ("target funding"). By implementing the in-arrears strategy, ABC saved EUR 201,000 in financial costs. Therefore, ABC's view that the interest rate curve on 1 January 20X0 was too steep (i.e., was discounting too high future Euribor 12-month rates) was right.

	Euribor 12M *(1)*	Target funding *(2)*	Actual funding	Savings
Period from 1-Jan-X0 to 31-Dec-X0	4.44%	<5,516,000>	<5,449,000>	67,000
Period from 31-Dec-X0 to 31-Dec-X1	4.94%	<6,023,000>	<6,043,000>	<20,000>
Period from 31-Dec-X0 to 31-Dec-X1	5.64%	<6,732,000>	<6,578,000>	154,000
Total				**201,000**

Notes:
    (1) Euribor 12-month fixed 2 days prior to the commencement of the interest period
    (2) 100 mn × (Euribor 12M + 1%) × 365/360

From an accounting perspective, there is a risk of substantial ineffectiveness during the last few reporting dates prior to the end of the hedging relationship.

7.12 CASE STUDY: HEDGING A FLOATING RATE LIABILITY WITH A KIKO COLLAR

This case study illustrates the accounting treatment of a hedge of a floating rate liability with a European KIKO collar. Section 5.13 covered the hedge of a highly expected foreign sale with an FX KIKO forward in which the barriers were continuously observed (an "American" KIKO). The KIKO covered in this section is a "European" KIKO because the barriers were only observed at expiry of the options. Therefore, it was irrelevant whether a barrier was crossed prior to option expiry. In other words, ABC only had to worry about whether the barrier was crossed at expiry. The hedged liability is the same as in Sections 7.5 and 7.6.

This case study also covers a collar whose initial intrinsic and time values were other than zero, showing the substantial operational complexity of having to calculate effective and ineffective amounts, and amounts recognised in the time value reserve, for each separate caplet/floorlet.

7.12.1 Background Information

On 31 December 20X0, ABC issued at par a floating rate bond with the following characteristics:

Bond terms	
Issue date	31 December 20X0
Maturity	5 years (31 December 20X5)
Notional	EUR 100 million
Coupon	Euribor 12M + 1.50% annually, actual/360 basis
Euribor fixing	Euribor is fixed at the beginning of the annual interest period

ABC had the view that the curve was too steep and that the Euribor 12-month rate was unlikely, during the next 5 years, either to rise above 5.25% or fall below 2.90%. To incorporate this view, ABC hedged its exposure under the bond to Euribor 12-month rate increases by entering into a European KIKO collar. The KIKO collar comprised a knock-out cap and a knock-in floor. The terms of the knock-out cap were as follows:

Knock-out cap terms	
Start date	31 December 20X0
Counterparties	ABC and XYZ Bank
Cap buyer	ABC
Maturity	5 years (31 December 20X5)
Notional amount	EUR 100 million
Premium	EUR 890,000
Strike	3.75% annually, actual/360 basis
Underlying	Euribor 12-month rate. Euribor is fixed at the beginning of the annual interest period
Barrier	5.25%
Knock-out event	Caplet ceases to exist if the Euribor 12-month rate is set at or above the barrier for the interest period ending on the expiry date

Each caplet could only be exercised if the Euribor 12-month rate was set below 5.25% for the interest period ending on the expiry date. Thus, if at the beginning of an interest period the Euribor 12-month was at or above 5.25%, ABC had no protection for that period. Nonetheless, the remaining caplets remained active. Figure 7.10 depicts the payoff of each caplet.

The main terms of the knock-in floor were as follows:

Knock-in floor terms	
Start date	31 December 20X0
Counterparties	ABC and XYZ Bank
Floor buyer	XYZ Bank
Maturity	5 years (31 December 20X5)
Notional amount	EUR 100 million
Premium	EUR 890,000
Strike	3.52% annually, actual/360 basis
Underlying	Euribor 12-month rate Euribor is fixed at the beginning of the annual interest period
Barrier	2.90%
Knock-in event	Floorlet can only be exercised if the Euribor 12-month rate is set at or below the barrier for the interest period ending on the expiry date

Each floorlet could only be exercised if the Euribor 12-month rate was set at or below 2.90% for the interest period ending on the expiry date. In other words, if at the beginning of an interest period Euribor 12-month was above 2.90%, the corresponding floorlet would not be exercised and, consequently, ABC would not need to make any payment under the floorlet. Nonetheless, any remaining floorlets could be activated at their corresponding expiry, were the Euribor 12-month rate at the commencement of their interest period to be below 2.90%. Figure 7.11 depicts the payoff of each floorlet.

There were four scenarios depending on the behaviour of the Euribor 12-month rate at each expiry date.

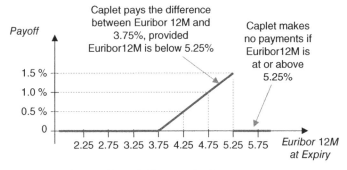

FIGURE 7.10 Knock-out caplet payoff (excluding premium).

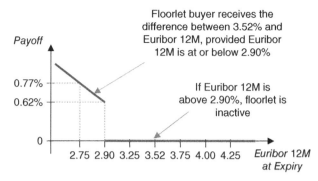

FIGURE 7.11 Knock-in floorlet payoff (excluding premium).

2.90% barrier	5.25% barrier	Equivalent position	Comments
Not hit	Not hit	Purchased 3.75% cap	Best scenario. ABC had protection and participated in Euribor 12M rate declines
Hit	Not hit	3.75%–3.52% collar	Good scenario, ABC ended up with a collar at much better terms than a market swap (swap would have been 3.86%)
Not Hit	Hit	No derivative	Bad scenario, ABC ended up having no hedge in place
Hit	Hit	Sold 2.90% floor	Worst scenario, ABC lost its protection and could not benefit from declining Euribor 12M rates below 3.52%

7.12.2 Split between Hedge Accounting Compliant Derivative and Residual Derivative

From an accounting perspective, IFRS 9 does not provide particular guidance about the application of hedge accounting for exotic hedging strategies such as the KIKO collar. Even if an entity applies hedge accounting, a decision that an auditor may well challenge, substantial ineffectiveness may arise. Nonetheless, IFRS 9 provides a relatively clear guidance on hedging strategies involving swaps, caps and collars. From an accounting perspective, a sound strategy would be to *contractually* split the KIKO collar into two parts, a first part eligible for hedge accounting and a second part treated as undesignated, reducing the potential impact on profit or loss volatility. ABC considered the following choices:

1) Divide the KIKO into two contracts: (i) a standard collar and (ii) a "residual" derivative. The standard collar would be the combination of a bought 3.75% cap and a sold 2.90% floor. The residual derivative would be the rest of the KIKO collar payoff not included in the standard collar.

2) Divide the KIKO into two contracts: (i) a standard collar and (ii) a "residual" derivative. The standard collar would be the combination of a bought 3.75% cap and a sold 3.52% floor. The residual derivative would be the rest of the KIKO collar payoff not included in the standard collar.

3) Divide the KIKO into two contracts: (i) a combination of two standard collars, and (ii) a "residual" derivative. One standard collar would be the combination of a bought 3.75% cap and a sold 2.90% floor. The other standard collar would be a bought very out-of-the money floor (e.g., with a 0.50% floor rate) and a sold 5.25% cap. The residual derivative would be the rest of the KIKO collar payoff not included in the combination of standard collars. This alternative was valid under IFRS 9 as the sold floors were entered into in combination with purchased caps and the combination did not result in a net premium to be received by the entity. ABC discarded this choice as it was too complex.

4) Consider the KIKO in its entirety as eligible for hedge accounting, if the corresponding requirements were met. Under this approach, ABC would designate the KIKO collar in its entirety as the hedging instrument in a hedging relationship. This approach would have been, in my view, quite challenging to apply. Effectiveness would be assessed comparing the changes in the fair value of the KIKO forward against those of a hypothetical derivative – a swap with an initial zero fair value and no counterparty credit risk. Due to their very different payoffs, the economic relationship requirement is likely not to be met for scenarios in which Euribor 12-month reaches 5.25% (when the protection is lost). As a result, ABC discarded this choice.

5) Consider the whole KIKO as undesignated. Whilst this was the simplest choice, ABC discarded this choice due to its potential adverse impact on profit or loss volatility.

ABC was thus left with only the first two choices. The first choice was better if Euribor 12-month rates traded well above 2.90%. Otherwise the second choice was preferable. Because it expected the Euribor 12-month to trade, during the next 5 years, well above 2.90%, ABC selected the first choice:

▪ The standard collar combined a purchased 3.75% cap and a sold 2.90% floor (see Figure 7.12). The effective changes in the intrinsic value of the collar would be recorded in equity (in the cash flow hedge reserve) and subsequently reclassified to profit or loss when the hedged cash flows impacted profit or loss. Changes in the time value of the collar would be recorded in equity to the extent that they related to the hedged item.

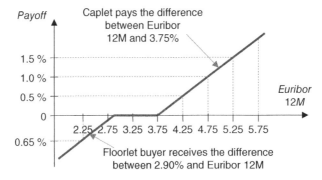

FIGURE 7.12   Hedging instrument payoff (bought 3.75% cap, sold 2.90% floor).

▪ The residual derivative would have terms such that when combined with the standard collar terms, the KIKO collar terms were obtained. Changes in fair value of the residual derivative would be recorded in profit or loss as it was classified as undesignated.

Remember that the two parts had to be formalised in separate contracts. The main terms of the standard collar were as follows:

Standard collar terms			
Cap terms		**Floor terms**	
Start date	31 December 20X0	Start date	31 December 20X0
Counterparties	ABC and XYZ Bank	Counterparties	ABC and XYZ Bank
Cap buyer	ABC	Floor seller	ABC
Maturity	5 years (31- Dec-X5)	Maturity	5 years (31-Dec-X5)
Notional amount	EUR 100 million	Notional amount	EUR 100 million
Premium	EUR 2,237,000	Premium	EUR 280,000
Strike	3.75% annually, actual/360 basis	Strike	2.90% annually, actual/360 basis
Underlying	Euribor 12M rate set at the beginning of the interest period ending on the expiry date	Underlying	Euribor 12M rate set at the beginning of the interest period ending on the expiry date

The residual derivative comprised the following two options:

▪ a sold knock-in cap with a 3.75% strike and a 5.25% barrier; and
▪ a sold digital floor with strike 2.90% and 0.62% payoff (=3.52% − 2.90%).

7.12.3 Hedging Relationship Documentation

ABC documented the hedging relationship as follows:

Hedging relationship documentation	
Risk management objective and strategy for undertaking the hedge	The objective of the hedge is to protect the variability of the cash flows stemming from the floating rate coupon payments related to a debt instrument issued by the entity against unfavourable movements in the Euribor 12-month rate above 3.75%. To achieve this objective and to reduce the hedge overall cost, the entity does not benefit from favourable movements in the Euribor 12M below 2.90%.
	This hedging objective is consistent with ABC's overall risk management strategy of managing the exposure to interest rate risk through the proportion of fixed and floating rate net debt in its total debt portfolio, using swaps and interest rate options.
	Interest rate risk. The designated risk being hedged is the risk of changes in the EUR value of the hedged cash flows due to movements in the Euribor 12-month interest rate

Hedging relationship documentation	
Type of hedge	Cash flow hedge
Hedged item	The cash flows stemming from the coupons of the bond with reference number 08759 issued on 31 December 20X0 with a 5-year maturity, a EUR 100 million notional, and a Euribor 12-month plus 1.50% annual coupon. The coupons are highly expected to occur as the bond has already been issued.
	The 1.50% credit spread is excluded from the hedging relationship
Hedging instrument	The intrinsic value of a collar (the combination of a purchased cap and a sold floor) with reference number 014577. The main terms of the collar are a EUR 100 million notional, a 5-year maturity, a 3.75% cap rate, a 2.90% floor rate, a Euribor 12-month interest rate underlying and a EUR 1,957,000 up-front cost. The counterparty to the collar is XYZ Bank and the credit risk associated with this counterparty is considered to be very low.
	For the avoidance of doubt, the collar's time value is excluded from the hedging relationship
Hedge effectiveness assessment	See below

7.12.4 Hedge Effectiveness Assessment

Hedge effectiveness will be assessed by comparing changes in the fair value of the hedging instrument to changes in the fair value of a hypothetical derivative. Effectiveness will be assessed only during those periods in which there is a change in intrinsic value.

The next two paragraphs were not included in the hedge documentation, having been added to explain how I selected the terms of the hypothetical derivative.

The hypothetical derivative is a derivative whose changes in fair value perfectly offset the changes in fair value of the hedged item for variations in the risk being hedged. In the case of "one-sided risks" IFRS states that "the hypothetical derivative would represent the intrinsic value of a hypothetical option that at the time of designation of the hedging relationship is at the money if the hedged price level is the current market level, or out of the money if the hedged price level is above (or, for a hedge of a long position, below) the current market level". IFRS 9 does not provide particular guidance on how the terms of the hypothetical derivative are determined when a combination of options is used. At the time of writing, the accounting community has not reached a consensus on how to set the level of the hypothetical derivative, especially regarding the level of the sold option.

As the risk being hedged was the cash flow exposure to adverse movements in the Euribor 12-month rate above 3.75% while not benefiting from favourable movements in the Euribor 12-month rate below 2.90%, the preliminary levels of the hypothetical derivative were a theoretical interest rate collar with no counterparty credit risk, a 3.75% cap rate and a 2.90% floor rate. The 3.75% cap rate was in-the-money at the start of the hedging relationship because the swap rate was 3.86% (see the case study in Section 7.5). Because the strike rate in a hypothetical derivative has to be either at-the-money or out-of-the-money, the lowest eligible cap rate in our case was 3.86%, the at-the-money level. The floor rate (2.90%) was lower than the swap rate, therefore being out-of-the-money, an eligible level for the hypothetical derivative.

The main terms of the hypothetical derivative were the following:

Hypothetical derivative terms			
Cap terms		**Floor terms**	
Start date	31 December 20X0	Trade date	31 December 20X0
Buyer	ABC	Buyer	Credit risk-free counterparty
Seller	Credit risk-free counterparty	Seller	ABC
Notional	EUR 100 million	Notional	EUR 100 million
Maturity	5 years (31 December 20X5)	Maturity	5 years (31 December 20X5)
Cap rate	3.86%, actual/360 basis	Floor rate	2.90%, actual/360 basis
Underlying	Euribor 12-month, fixed at the beginning of the annual interest period ending on the expiry date	Underlying	Euribor 12-month, fixed at the beginning of the annual interest period ending on the expiry date

Changes in the fair value of the hedging instrument (i.e., the collar's intrinsic value) will be recognised as follows:

- The effective part of the gain or loss on the hedging instrument will be recognised in the cash flow hedge reserve of OCI in equity. The accumulated amount in equity will be reclassified to profit or loss in the same period during which the hedged expected future cash flow affects profit or loss, adjusting interest expense.
- The ineffective part of the gain or loss on the hedging instrument will be recognised immediately in profit or loss.

The change in time value of the collar (the "actual time value") will be excluded from the hedging relationship. The changes in actual time value will be recognised temporarily in the time value reserve of equity to the extent that they relate to the hedged item.

Hedge effectiveness will be assessed prospectively at hedging relationship inception, on an ongoing basis at least upon each reporting date and upon occurrence of a significant change in the circumstances affecting the hedge effectiveness requirements.

The hedging relationship will qualify for hedge accounting only if all the following criteria are met:

1) The hedging relationship consists only of eligible hedge items and hedging instruments. The hedge item is eligible as it is a group of highly expected forecast cash flows that exposes the entity to fair value risk, affects profit or loss and is reliably measurable. The hedging instrument is eligible as it is a string of derivative combinations that does not result in a net written option and the sold options are designated as an offset to the purchased options.
2) At hedge inception there is a formal designation and documentation of the hedging relationship and the entity's risk management objective and strategy for undertaking the hedge.
3) The hedging relationship is considered effective.

The hedging relationship will be considered effective if the following three requirements are met:

1) There is an economic relationship between the hedged item and the hedging instrument.
2) The effect of credit risk does not dominate the value changes that result from that economic relationship.
3) The hedge ratio of the hedging relationship is the same as that resulting from the quantity of hedged item that the entity actually hedges and the quantity of the hedging instrument that the entity actually uses to hedge that quantity of hedged item. The hedge ratio should not be intentionally weighted to create ineffectiveness.

Whether there is an economic relationship between the hedged item and the hedging instrument will be assessed on a quantitative basis using the scenario analysis method for two scenarios in which Euribor interest rates will be shifted upwards and downwards by 2% and the changes in fair value of the hypothetical derivative and the hedging instrument compared.

7.12.5 Hedge Effectiveness Assessment Performed at the Start of the Hedging Relationship

The hedging relationship was considered effective as the following three requirements were met:

1) There was an economic relationship between the hedged item and the hedging instrument. Based on the quantitative assessment performed, the entity concluded that the change in fair value of the hedged item was expected to be substantially offset by the change in fair value of the hedging instrument, corroborating that both elements had values that would generally move in opposite directions.
2) The effect of credit risk did not dominate the value changes resulting from that economic relationship as the credit ratings of both the entity and XYZ Bank were considered sufficiently strong.
3) The hedge ratio of the hedging relationship was the same as that resulting from the quantity of hedged item that the entity actually hedged and the quantity of the hedging instrument that the entity actually used to hedge that quantity of hedged item. The hedge ratio was not intentionally weighted to create ineffectiveness.

A quantitative assessment was performed to support the conclusion that the hedging instrument and the hedged item had values that would generally move in opposite directions. The quantitative assessment consisted of two scenario analyses performed as follows:

A parallel shift of +2% occurring on the assessment date was simulated. The fair values of the hedging instrument and the hypothetical derivatives were calculated and compared to their initial fair values. As shown in the table below, the assessment resulted in a high degree of offset, corroborating that both elements had values that would generally move in opposite directions.

Scenario 1 analysis assessment		
	Hedging instrument	**Hypothetical derivative**
Initial fair value	1,410,000 *(1)*	1,136,000
Final fair value	9,308,000	8,957,000
Cumulative fair value change	7,898,000	7,821,000
	Degree of offset	**101.0%** *(2)*

Notes:

(1) Only the intrinsic value of the collar was part of the hedging relationship

(2) The degree of offset was not 100% due to the differing cap rates and CVAs/DVAs

Similarly, a parallel shift of –2% occurring on the assessment date was also simulated. As shown in the table below, the assessment resulted in a high degree of offset, corroborating that both elements had values that would generally move in opposite directions.

Scenario 2 analysis assessment		
	Hedging instrument	**Hypothetical derivative**
Initial fair value	1,410,000	1,136,000
Final fair value	<4,886,000>	<4,985,000>
Cumulative fair value change	<6,296,000>	<6,121,000>
	Degree of offset	**102.9%**

The following potential sources of ineffectiveness were identified:

- a substantial deterioration in credit risk of either the entity or the counterparty to the hedging instrument; and
- a change in the timing or amounts of the hedged highly expected cash flows.

The hedge ratio was set at 1:1.

ABC also performed assessments on each reporting date, yielding the same conclusions. These assessments have been omitted to avoid unnecessary repetition.

7.12.6 Fair Valuations, Effective/Ineffective Amounts and Cash Flow Calculations

Fair Valuations of the Collar and Residual Derivative The following table summarises the split between the collar's intrinsic and time values, and the fair value of the residual derivative at each reporting date:

Date	Collar intrinsic value	Collar time value	Collar total fair value	Residual derivative fair value	KIKO collar fair value (*)
31-Dec-20X0	1,410,000	547,000	1,957,000	<1,957,000>	0
31-Dec-20X1	3,618,000	297,000	3,915,000	<2,775,000>	1,140,000
31-Dec-20X2	1,120,000	187,000	1,307,000	<974,000>	333,000
31-Dec-20X3	646,000	105,000	751,000	<523,000>	228,000
31-Dec-20X4	192,000	-0-	192,000	-0-	192,000
31-Dec-20X5	-0-	-0-	-0-	-0-	-0-

(*) The sum of (i) the collar total fair value and (ii) the residual derivative fair value. While not needed for the accounting entries, they are included for illustration purposes only

Effective and Ineffective Amounts The change in fair value of the hedging instrument (i.e., the change in intrinsic value of the collar) was split between an effective and an ineffective part. The effective amounts were based on the lower of (in absolute terms):

- the cumulative change in the fair value of the hedging instrument; and
- the cumulative change in the fair value of the hypothetical derivative.

In our case, both the hedging instrument and the hypothetical derivative comprised five "collarlets" (i.e., caplet–floorlet combinations), expiring on the last day of each year X1–X5.

The effective and ineffective amounts were calculated for each collarlet separately. The following table summarises the fair values of each collarlet in the hedging instrument (i.e., the intrinsic values of each collarlet in the collar):

	Hedging instrument fair values				
	Collarlet 1	Collarlet 2	Collarlet 3	Collarlet 4	Collarlet 5
31-Dec-X0	-0-	-0-	139,000	551,000	720,000
31-Dec-X1	-0-	440,000	959,000	1,086,000	1,133,000
31-Dec-X2		-0-	-0-	369,000	751,000
31-Dec-X3			-0-	48,000	598,000
31-Dec-X4				-0-	192,000
31-Dec-X5					-0-

The following table summarises the fair values of each collarlet in the hypothetical derivative:

	Hypothetical derivative fair values				
	Collarlet 1	Collarlet 2	Collarlet 3	Collarlet 4	Collarlet 5
31-Dec-X0	-0-	-0-	38,000	460,000	638,000
31-Dec-X1	-0-	340,000	872,000	1,006,000	1,057,000
31-Dec-X2			-0-	272,000	663,000
31-Dec-X3			-0-	-0-	505,000
31-Dec-X4				-0-	88,000
31-Dec-X5					-0-

The ineffective part was the excess of the period change in fair value over the effective part. As an example, the effective and ineffective parts of the change in fair value of floorlet 4 were calculated as follows (see Section 5.5.6 for an explanation of the calculations) at each reporting date:

	31-Dec-X1	31-Dec-X2	31-Dec-X3	31-Dec-X4
Cumulative change in fair value of hedging instrument	535,000	<182.000>	<503.000>	<551.000>
Cumulative change in fair value of hypothetical derivative	546,000	<188.000>	<460.000>	<460.000>

Lower amount	535,000	<182.000>	<460.000>	<460.000>
Previous cumulative effective amount	-0-	535.000	<182.000>	<460.000>
Available amount	535,000	<717.000>	<278.000>	-0-
Period change in fair value of hedging instrument	535,000	<717.000>	<321.000>	<48.000>
Effective part	**535,000**	**<717.000>**	**<278.000>**	**-0-**
Ineffective part	**-0-**	**0**	**<43.000>**	**<48.000>**

The following table summarises the effective and ineffective amounts corresponding to each collarlet:

	31-Dec-X1	31-Dec-X2	31-Dec-X3	31-Dec-X4	31-Dec-X5
Collarlet 1:					
Period change in fair value	-0-				
Effective amounts	-0-				
Ineffective amounts	-0-				
Amounts reclassified adjusting interest expense					
Collarlet 2:					
Period change in fair value	440,000	<440,000>			
Effective amounts	340,000	<340,000>			
Ineffective amounts	100,000	<100,000>			
Amounts reclassified adjusting interest expense					
Collarlet 3:					
Period change in fair value	820,000	<959,000>	-0-		
Effective amounts	820,000	<872,000>	-0-		
Ineffective amounts	-0-	<87,000>	-0-		
Amounts reclassified adjusting interest expense			<52,000>		
Collarlet 4:					
Period change in fair value	535,000	<717,000>	<321,000>	<48,000>	
Effective amounts	535,000	<717,000>	<278,000>	-0-	
Ineffective amounts	-0-	-0-	<43,000>	<48,000>	
Amounts reclassified adjusting interest expense				<460,000>	

(*continued overleaf*)

	31-Dec-X1	31-Dec-X2	31-Dec-X3	31-Dec-X4	31-Dec-X5
Collarlet 5:					
Period change in fair value	413,000	<382,000>	<153,000>	<406,000>	<192,000>
Effective amounts	413,000	<382,000>	<153,000>	<406,000>	<110,000>
Ineffective amounts	-0-	-0-	-0-	-0-	<82,000>
Amounts reclassified adjusting interest expense					<638,000>
Totals:					
Effective amounts	**2,108,000**	**<2,311,000>**	**<431,000>**	**<406,000>**	**<110,000>**
Ineffective amounts	**100,000**	**<187,000>**	**<43,000>**	**<48,000>**	**<82,000>**
Amounts reclassified adjusting interest expense	**-0-**	**-0-**	**<52,000>**	**<460,000>**	**<638,000>**

Time Value Reserve Amounts   Under IFRS 9, when the time value component of an option is excluded from a hedging relationship, its cumulative change in fair value from the date of designation of the hedging instrument is temporarily accumulated in the time value reserve of OCI to the extent that it relates to the hedged item.

In our case, due to the collar having time value at the beginning of the hedging relationship (31 December 20X0), the temporary recognition in the time value reserve depended on whether (i) the time value (the "actual" time value) of each caplet/floorlet of the traded collar (the "actual" collar) related to (ii) the time value (the "aligned" time value) of a corresponding caplet/floorlet that had critical terms that perfectly matched those of the hedged item. In our case the aligned time value corresponded to a collar (the "aligned" collar) whose terms matched those of the hypothetical derivative (i.e., notional, strike rate, interest periods and underlying).

In our case, both the actual and the aligned collars comprised five "collarlets" as already described. The actual and aligned time values of each collarlet were calculated from the collarlet fair value which was calculated using Black–Scholes, as follows:

Collarlet time value = Collarlet fair value – Collarlet intrinsic value

The following table summarises the actual time values of each collarlet:

	Actual time values				
	Collarlet 1	**Collarlet 2**	**Collarlet 3**	**Collarlet 4**	**Collarlet 5**
31-Dec-X0	-0-	55,000	109,000	164,000	219,000
31-Dec-X1	-0-	-0-	50,000	99,000	148,000
31-Dec-X2		-0-	-0-	62,000	125,000
31-Dec-X3			-0-	-0-	105,000

31-Dec-X4	-0-	-0-
31-Dec-X5		-0-

The following table summarises the aligned time values of each collarlet:

	Collarlet 1	Collarlet 2	Collarlet 3	Collarlet 4	Collarlet 5
		Aligned time values			
31-Dec-X0	-0-	60,000	120,000	181,000	241,000
31-Dec-X1	-0-	-0-	56,000	111,000	166,000
31-Dec-X2		-0-	-0-	63,000	125,000
31-Dec-X3			-0-	-0-	110,000
31-Dec-X4				-0-	-0-
31-Dec-X5					-0-

Because the collarlets' actual time value exceeded their aligned time value at the start of the hedging relationship, the amounts recognised in the time value reserve of OCI were based on the lower of (in absolute terms):

- the cumulative change in actual time value; and
- the cumulative change in aligned time value.

Any excess of the change in actual time value over the amount recognised in the time value reserve was recognised in profit or loss. As an example, the calculations performed for collarlet 4 are detailed in the following table (the mechanics were similar to those of the calculation of effective and ineffective amounts performed previously for the hedging instrument):

Collarlet 4 – split between time value reserve and profit or loss amounts				
	31-Dec-X1	**31-Dec-X2**	**31-Dec-X3**	**31-Dec-X4**
Cumulative actual time value change	<65,000>	<102,000>	<164,000>	<164,000>
Cumulative aligned time value change	<70,000>	<118,000>	<181,000>	<181,000>
Lower amount	<65,000>	<102,000>	<164,000>	<164,000>
Previous amounts in time value reserve	-0-	<65,000>	<102,000>	<164,000>
Available amount	<65,000>	<37,000>	<62,000>	-0-
Period change in actual time value	<65,000>	<37,000>	<62,000>	-0-
Part to time value reserve	**<65,000>**	**<37,000>**	**<62,000>**	**-0-**
Part to profit or loss	**-0-**	**-0-**	**-0-**	**-0-**

The following table summarises the amounts recognised in the time value reserve and in profit or loss corresponding to the actual time value of each collarlet:

	31-Dec-X1	31-Dec-X2	31-Dec-X3	31-Dec-X4	31-Dec-X5
Collarlet 1:					
Period change in actual time value	-0-				
Amounts to time value reserve	-0-				
Amounts to profit or loss	-0-				
Collarlet 2:					
Period change in actual time value	<55,000>	-0-			
Amounts to time value reserve	<55,000>	-0-			
Amounts to profit or loss	-0-	-0-			
Amounts reclassified adjusting interest expense		<55,000>			
Collarlet 3:					
Period change in actual time value	<59,000>	<50,000>	-0-		
Amounts to time value reserve	<59,000>	<50,000>	-0-		
Amounts to profit or loss	-0-	-0-	-0-		
Amounts reclassified adjusting interest expense			<109,000>		
Collarlet 4:					
Period change in actual time value	<65,000>	<37,000>	<62,000>	-0-	
Amounts to time value reserve	<65,000>	<37,000>	<62,000>	-0-	
Amounts to profit or loss	-0-	-0-	-0-	-0-	
Amounts reclassified adjusting interest expense				<164,000>	
Collarlet 5:					
Period change in actual time value	<71,000>	<23,000>	<20,000>	<105,000>	-0-
Amounts to time value reserve	<71,000>	<23,000>	<20,000>	<105,000>	-0-

Amounts to profit or loss	-0-	-0-	-0-	-0-	-0-
Amounts reclassified adjust-ing interest expense					<219,000>
Totals:					
Amounts to time value reserve	**<250,000>**	**<110,000>**	**<82,000>**	**<105,000>**	**-0-**
Amounts to profit or loss	**-0-**	**-0-**	**-0-**	**-0-**	**-0-**
Amounts reclassified adjusting interest expense	**-0-**	**<55,000>**	**<109,000>**	**<164,000>**	**<219,000>**

Bond Coupon Payments, Collar and Residual Derivative Settlement Amounts The bond coupon payments, collar and residual derivative settlement amounts at each relevant date were as follows:

Date	Period Euribor 12M	Bond interest *(1)*	Collar settlement amount *(2)*	Residual derivative settlement amount *(3)*
31-Dec-20X1	3.21%	<4,775,000>	-0-	-0-
31-Dec-20X2	4.21%	<5,789,000>	466,000	-0-
31-Dec-20X3	3.71%	<5,282,000>	-0-	-0-
31-Dec-20X4	3.80%	<5,374,000>	51,000	-0-
31-Dec-20X5	3.95%	<5,526,000>	203,000	-0-

Notes:
(1) <100 mn> × (Euribor 12M + 1.50%) × 365/360, assuming 365 calendar days in the interest period
(2) 100 mn × max[Euribor 12M – 3.75%, 0] × 365/360 – 100 mn × max[2.90% – Euribor 12M, 0] × 365/360, assuming 365 calendar days in the interest period
(3) This is given by one of the following:
    (i) if Euribor 12M ≥ 5.25%, <100 mn> × max[Euribor 12M – 3.75%, 0] × 365/360;
    (ii) if Euribor 12M ≤ 2.90%, <100 mn> × 0.62% × 365/360; or
    (iii) if 5.25% >Euribor 12M > 2.90%, zero

7.12.7 Accounting Entries

The required journal entries were as follows.

1) Entries on 31 December 20X0.

The bond was issued.

Cash (Asset)	100,000,000	
Financial debt (Liability)		100,000,000

The collar and the residual derivative were traded simultaneously.

Collar contract (Asset)	1,957,000	
Cash (Asset)		1,957,000
Cash (Asset)	1,957,000	
Residual derivative (Liability)		1,957,000

2) Entries on 31 December 20X1

The bond paid a EUR 4,775,000 coupon.

| Interest expense (Profit or loss) | 4,775,000 | |
| Cash (Asset) | | 4,775,000 |

The change in fair value of the collar was a EUR 1,958,000 gain. The change in fair value of the hedging instrument (i.e., the collar's intrinsic value) since the last valuation was a EUR 2,208,000 gain, of which EUR 2,108,000 was deemed to be effective and recorded in the cash flow hedge reserve of equity, and EUR 100,000 was deemed to be ineffective and recorded in profit or loss. The change in actual time value since the last valuation was a EUR 250,000 loss, fully recognised in the time value reserve of OCI.

Collar contract (Asset)	1,958,000	
Cash flow hedge reserve (Equity)		2,108,000
Other financial income (Profit or loss)		100,000
Time value reserve (Equity)	250,000	

There was no settlement amount related to the collar. The change in fair value of the residual derivative was a EUR 818,000 loss. There was no settlement amount related to the residual derivative. No amounts were reclassified from the cash flow hedge reserve. No amounts were reclassified from the time value reserve.

| Other financial expenses (Profit or loss) | 818,000 | |
| Residual derivative (Liability) | | 818,000 |

3) Entries on 31 December 20X2

The bond paid a EUR 5,789,000 coupon. The change in fair value of the collar was a EUR 2,608,000 loss. The change in fair value of the hedging instrument (i.e., the collar's intrinsic value) since the last valuation was a EUR 2,498,000 loss, of which EUR <2,311,000>

was deemed to be effective and recorded in the cash flow hedge reserve of equity, and EUR <187,000> was deemed to be ineffective and recorded in profit or loss. The change in actual time value since the last valuation was a EUR 110,000 loss, fully recognised in the time value reserve of OCI. The entity received a EUR 466,000 settlement amount related to the collar. The change in fair value of the residual derivative was a EUR 1,801,000 gain. There was no settlement amount related to the residual derivative. No amounts were reclassified from the cash flow hedge reserve. EUR <55,000> was reclassified from the time value reserve.

Interest expense (Profit or loss)	5,789,000	
Cash (Asset)		5,789,000
Cash flow hedge reserve (Equity)	2,311,000	
Other financial expenses (Profit or loss)	187,000	
Time value reserve (Equity)	110,000	
Collar contract (Asset)		2,608,000
Cash (Asset)	466,000	
Interest income (Profit or loss)		466,000
Residual derivative (Liability)	1,801,000	
Other financial income (Profit or loss)		1,801,000
Interest expense (Profit or loss)	55,000	
Time value reserve (Equity)		55,000

4) Entries on 31 December 20X3

The bond paid a EUR 5,282,000 coupon. The change in fair value of the collar was a EUR 556,000 loss. The change in fair value of the hedging instrument (i.e., the collar's intrinsic value) since the last valuation was a EUR 474,000 loss, of which EUR <431,000> was deemed to be effective and recorded in the cash flow hedge reserve of equity, and EUR <43,000> was deemed to be ineffective and recorded in profit or loss. The change in actual time value since the last valuation was a EUR 82,000 loss, fully recognised in the time value reserve of OCI. There was no settlement amount related to the collar. The change in fair value of the residual derivative was a EUR 451,000 gain. There was no settlement amount related to the residual derivative. EUR <52,000> was reclassified from the cash flow hedge reserve. EUR <109,000> was reclassified from the time value reserve.

Interest expense (Profit or loss)	5,282,000	
Cash (Asset)		5,282,000
Cash flow hedge reserve (Equity)	431,000	
Other financial expenses (Profit or loss)	43,000	
Time value reserve (Equity)	82,000	

Collar contract (Asset)		556,000
Residual derivative (Liability)	451,000	
Other financial income (Profit or loss)		451,000
Interest expense (Profit or loss)	52,000	
Cash flow hedge reserve (Equity)		52,000
Interest expense (Profit or loss)	109,000	
Time value reserve (Equity)		109,000

5) Entries on 31 December 20X4

The bond paid a EUR 5,374,000 coupon. The change in fair value of the collar was a EUR 559,000 loss. The change in fair value of the hedging instrument (i.e., the collar's intrinsic value) since the last valuation was a EUR 454,000 loss, of which EUR <406,000> was deemed to be effective and recorded in the cash flow hedge reserve of equity, and EUR <48,000> was deemed to be ineffective and recorded in profit or loss. The change in actual time value since the last valuation was a EUR 105,000 loss, fully recognised in the time value reserve of OCI. The entity received a EUR 51,000 settlement amount related to the collar. The change in fair value of the residual derivative was a EUR 523,000 gain. There was no settlement amount related to the residual derivative. EUR <460,000> was reclassified from the cash flow hedge reserve. EUR <164,000> was reclassified from the time value reserve.

Interest expense (Profit or loss)	5,374,000	
Cash (Asset)		5,374,000
Cash flow hedge reserve (Equity)	406,000	
Other financial expenses (Profit or loss)	48,000	
Time value reserve (Equity)	105,000	
Collar contract (Asset)		559,000
Cash (Asset)	51,000	
Interest income (Profit or loss)		51,000
Residual derivative (Liability)	523,000	
Other financial income (Profit or loss)		523,000
Interest expense (Profit or loss)	460,000	
Cash flow hedge reserve (Equity)		460,000
Interest expense (Profit or loss)	164,000	
Time value reserve (Equity)		164,000

6) Entries on 31 December 20X5

The bond paid a EUR 5,526,000 coupon and repaid the EUR 100 million principal. The change in fair value of the collar was a EUR 192,000 loss. The change in fair value of the hedging instrument (i.e., the collar's intrinsic value) since the last valuation was a EUR 192,000 loss, of which EUR <110,000> was deemed to be effective and recorded in the cash flow hedge reserve of equity, and EUR <82,000> was deemed to be ineffective and recorded in profit or loss. There was no change in actual time value since the last valuation. The entity received a EUR 203,000 settlement amount related to the collar. The collar matured. There was no change in fair value of the residual derivative. There was no settlement amount related to the residual derivative. The residual derivative matured. EUR <638,000> was reclassified from the cash flow hedge reserve. EUR <219,000> was reclassified from the time value reserve.

Interest expense (Profit or loss)	5,282,000	
Financial debt (Liability)	100,000,000	
Cash (Asset)		105,282,000
Cash flow hedge reserve (Equity)	110,000	
Other financial expenses (Profit or loss)	82,000	
Collar contract (Asset)		192,000
Cash (Asset)	203,000	
Interest income (Profit or loss)		203,000
Interest expense (Profit or loss)	638,000	
Cash flow hedge reserve (Equity)		638,000
Interest expense (Profit or loss)	219,000	
Time value reserve (Equity)		219,000

7.12.8 Concluding Remarks

The objective of entering into the KIKO was to protect the entity from a rising Euribor 12-month rate and to achieve a cost of funding better than a hedged involving a swap. The 5-year swap rate was 3.86%, implying an annual cost of funding (the "benchmark cost of funding") of EUR 5,434,000 (= 100 mn × (3.86% + 1.50%) × 365/360) when the 1.50% credit margin was included.

The table below compares the actual and the benchmark annual cost of funding during each annual interest period. Whilst the funding savings totalled EUR 1,388,000, a remarkably favourable outcome, the revaluation of the residual derivative and the ineffective parts of the hedging instrument generated substantial volatility in the entity's profit or loss statement.

Finally, fortunately the entity's interest rate view was right and neither barrier was reached. Otherwise, the outcome would have been rather different.

	Actual annual cost of funding and savings achieved				
	31-Dec-X1	**31-Dec-X2**	**31-Dec-X3**	**31-Dec-X4**	**31-Dec-X5**
Interest expense	<4,775,000>	<5,378,000>	<5,443,000>	<5,947,000>	<5,936,000>
Other financial income/expenses	<718,000>	1.614.000	408.000	475.000	<82.000>
Total actual	**<5,493,000>**	**<3,764,000>**	**<5,035,000>**	**<5,472,000>**	**<6,018,000>**
Benchmark cost of funding	<5,434,000>	<5,434,000>	<5,434,000>	<5,434,000>	<5,434,000>
Savings	**<59,000>**	**1,670,000**	**399,000**	**<38,000>**	**<584,000>**
Total savings: EUR 1,388,000					

CHAPTER 8

Hedging Foreign Currency Liabilities

The global nature of the capital markets allows many entities to fund in the lowest cost market available to them. Frequently, entities capture lower costs of funds and greater market liquidity by raising capital in currencies other than their functional currency. Because a foreign currency liability is a monetary item, IAS 21 requires the liability to be translated into the entity's functional currency using the exchange rate prevailing at the reporting date, as covered in Chapter 6. The translation gains or losses on the debt are recorded in profit or loss. Thus, absence of an FX hedging strategy may result in significant volatility in profit or loss. This chapter deals with the hedge accounting treatment of foreign currency borrowings swapped back into the issuer's functional currency.

The most common technique to hedge foreign debt is through cross-currency swaps (CCS) that convert the debt's foreign cash flows back into the entity's functional currency. Assuming the EUR as the issuer's functional currency and a USD-denominated debt, there are four potential hedging situations (which are covered in the four case studies in this chapter):

USD liability	CCS characteristics	Resulting EUR liability	Type of hedge
Floating	Receive USD floating – pay EUR floating	Floating	Fair value
Fixed	Receive USD fixed – pay EUR floating	Floating	Fair value
Floating	Receive USD floating – pay EUR fixed	Fixed	Cash flow
Fixed	Receive USD fixed – pay EUR fixed	Fixed	Cash flow

8.1 CASE STUDY: HEDGING A FLOATING RATE FOREIGN CURRENCY LIABILITY WITH A RECEIVE-FLOATING PAY-FLOATING CROSS-CURRENCY SWAP

This case study illustrates the accounting treatment of a hedge of a floating rate foreign currency liability with a pay-floating receive-floating CCS. Because this case is very complex, it is necessary to discuss in detail some of the challenging aspects of the case, especially the selection of the most suitable hedging instrument, the interaction between the translation of the foreign currency liability and the hedge item fair value adjustments, and the calculation of accruals.

8.1.1 Background Information

On 15 July 20X0, ABC issued a USD-denominated floating rate bond. ABC's functional currency was the EUR. The bond had the following main terms:

Bond terms	
Issue date	15 July 20X0
Maturity	3 years (15 July 20X3)
Notional	USD 100 million
Coupon	USD Libor 12M + 0.50% annually, actual/360 basis
USD Libor fixing	Libor is fixed 2 days prior to the beginning of each annual interest period

Since ABC's objective was to raise EUR floating funding, on the issue date ABC entered into a CCS. Through the CCS, the entity agreed to receive a floating rate equal to the bond coupon and pay a Euribor floating rate plus a spread. The CCS had the following terms:

Cross-currency swap terms	
Trade date	15 July 20X0
Start date	15 July 20X0
Counterparties	ABC and XYZ Bank
Maturity	3 years (15 July 20X3)
USD nominal	USD 100 million
EUR nominal	EUR 80 million
Initial exchange	On start date, ABC receives the EUR nominal and pays the USD nominal
ABC pays	Euribor 12M + 49 bps annually, actual/360 basis, on the EUR nominal Euribor is fixed two business days prior to the beginning of each annual interest period
ABC receives	USD Libor 12M + 0.50 bps annually, actual/360 basis. Libor is fixed 2 days prior to the beginning of each annual interest period
Final exchange	On maturity date, ABC receives the USD nominal and pays the EUR nominal

The mechanics of the CCS are described next. It can be seen that through the combination of the USD bond and the CCS, ABC synthetically obtained a EUR floating liability.

On the issue date at the start of the CCS, there was an initial exchange of nominal amounts through the CCS: ABC delivered the USD 100 million debt issuance proceeds and received EUR 80 million. The resulting EUR–USD exchange rate was 1.2500. The combination of the bond and CCS had the same effect as if ABC had issued a EUR-denominated bond, as shown in Figure 8.1.

An exchange of interest payments took place annually. ABC received USD Libor-linked interest on the USD nominal and paid Euribor-linked interest on the EUR nominal. ABC used the USD Libor cash flows it received under the CCS to pay the bond interest. Figure 8.2 shows the strategy's intermediate cash flows.

At maturity of the CCS and the debt, ABC re-exchanged the CCS nominals, using the USD 100 million it received through the CCS to redeem the bond issue, and delivering EUR 80 million to the CCS counterparty. Note that this final exchange was made at exactly the same rate used in the initial exchange (1.2500). Figure 8.3 shows the strategy's cash flows at maturity.

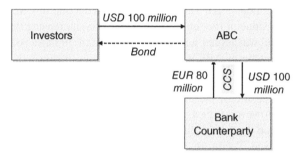

FIGURE 8.1 Bond and CCS combination – initial cash flows.

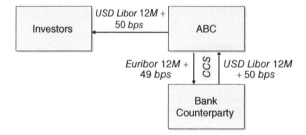

FIGURE 8.2 Bond and CCS combination – intermediate cash flows.

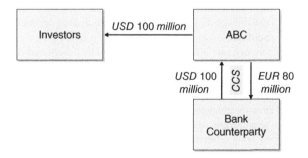

FIGURE 8.3 Bond and CCS combination – final cash flows.

8.1.2 Determining Risk Components to Include in the Hedging Relationship

The aim of the CCS was to hedge the changes in fair value of the bond. There were three risks affecting the bond's fair value:

- Exchange rate risk. An appreciation of the USD relative to the EUR would increase the EUR value of the bond's USD cash outflows, increasing the bond's fair value. Conversely, a depreciation of the USD relative to the EUR would decrease the EUR value of the bond's USD flows to be paid by ABC, decreasing the bond's fair value.
- Interest rate risk. The bond coupons were linked to the USD Libor 12-month rate. An increase in USD Libor rates would decrease the present value of the future USD cash flows, decreasing the bond's fair value. Conversely, a decline in USD Libor rates would increase the present value of the future USD cash flows, increasing the bond's fair value.
- Credit risk. The bond was issued with a credit margin of 50 basis points. During the life of the bond, a narrowing of ABC's credit margin would increase the bond's fair value. Conversely, a widening of the credit margin would decrease the bond's fair value.

The CCS hedged the exposure of the bond's fair value to the first two risks (exchange risk and interest rate risk). However, to hedge the third element (credit risk) would have implied ABC buying protection on its own credit risk, which no counterparty would provide unless a proxy credit name was used. Therefore, the bond's credit risk was excluded from the hedging relationship. Fair valuations of the hedged item would assume that the initial 50 bps credit margin remained unchanged during the term of the hedge.

When assessing effectiveness and calculating effective and ineffective amounts, the helpful simplification of a hypothetical derivative could not be used for fair value hedges. Therefore ABC needed to fair value the hedged item.

8.1.3 Hedging Relationship Documentation

ABC documented the hedging relationship as follows:

Hedging relationship documentation	
Risk management objective and strategy for undertaking the hedge	The objective of the hedge is to reduce the variability of the fair value of a foreign currency denominated floating rate bond issued by the entity.
	This hedging objective is consistent with the group's overall interest rate risk management strategy of transforming all new issued foreign-denominated debt into floating rate, and thereafter managing the exposure to interest rate risk through the proportion of fixed and floating rate net debt in its total debt portfolio.
	Exchange rate and interest rate risk. The designated risk being hedged is the risk of changes in the EUR fair value of the hedged item attributable to changes in the EUR–USD exchange rate and USD Libor interest rate.
	Fair value changes attributable to credit or other risks are not hedged in this relationship. Accordingly, the 50 bps credit spread is excluded from the hedging relationship
Type of hedge	Fair value hedge

Hedged item	The coupons and principal of the 3-year USD floating rate bond with reference number 678902. The main terms of the bond are a USD 100 million principal, an annual coupon of USD Libor plus 0.50% calculated on the principal
Hedging instrument	The cross-currency swap with reference number 014569. The main terms of the CCS are a USD 100 million nominal, a EUR 80 million nominal, a 3-year maturity, a USD annual interest of USD Libor 12-month rate plus 0.50% on the USD nominal to be received by the entity and a EUR annual interest of Euribor 12-month rate plus 0.49% on the EUR nominal to be paid by the entity. The counterparty to the CCS is XYZ Bank and the credit risk associated with this counterparty is considered to be very low
Hedge effectiveness assessment	See below

8.1.4 Hedge Effectiveness Assessment

Hedge effectiveness will be assessed by comparing changes in the fair value of the hedging instrument to changes in the fair value of the hedged item. Changes in the fair value of the hedging instrument (i.e., the CCS) will be recognised as follows:

- The effective part of the gain or loss on the hedging instrument will be recognised in profit or loss, adjusting interest income/expense.
- The ineffective part of the gain or loss on the hedging instrument will be recognised in profit or loss, as other financial income/expenses.

Hedge effectiveness will be assessed prospectively at hedging relationship inception, on an ongoing basis at least upon each reporting date and upon occurrence of a significant change in the circumstances affecting the hedge effectiveness requirements.

The hedging relationship will qualify for hedge accounting only if all the following criteria are met:

1) The hedging relationship consists only of eligible hedge items and hedging instruments. The hedge item is eligible as it is an already recognised liability that exposes the entity to fair value risk, affects profit or loss and is reliably measurable. The hedging instrument is eligible as it is a derivative that does not result in a net written option.
2) At hedge inception there is a formal designation and documentation of the hedging relationship and the entity's risk management objective and strategy for undertaking the hedge.
3) The hedging relationship is considered effective.

The hedging relationship will be considered effective if the following three requirements are met:

1) There is an economic relationship between the hedged item and the hedging instrument.
2) The effect of credit risk does not dominate the value changes that result from that economic relationship.
3) The hedge ratio of the hedging relationship is the same as that resulting from the quantity of hedged item that the entity actually hedges and the quantity of the hedging instrument that the entity actually uses to hedge that quantity of hedged item. The hedge ratio should not be intentionally weighted to create ineffectiveness.

Whether there is an economic relationship between the hedged item and the hedging instrument will be assessed on a quantitative basis using the scenario analysis method for two scenarios:

- In a first scenario, USD Libor interest rates will be shifted upwards by 2%, the EUR–USD exchange rate increased by 10%, and the changes in fair value of the hedged item and the hedging instrument compared.
- In a second scenario, USD Libor interest rates will be shifted downwards by 2%, the EUR–USD exchange rate reduced by 10%, and the changes in fair value of the hedged item and the hedging instrument compared.

8.1.5 Hedge Effectiveness Assessment Performed at the Start of the Hedging Relationship

On 15 July 20X0 ABC performed a hedge effectiveness assessment which was documented as described next.

The hedging relationship was considered effective as the following three requirements were met:

1) There was an economic relationship between the hedged item and the hedging instrument. Based on the quantitative assessment performed, the entity concluded that the change in fair value of the hedged item was expected to be substantially offset by the change in fair value of the hedging instrument, corroborating that both elements had values that would generally move in opposite directions.
2) The effect of credit risk did not dominate the value changes resulting from that economic relationship as the credit ratings of both the entity and XYZ Bank were considered sufficiently strong.
3) The hedge ratio of the hedging relationship was the same as that resulting from the quantity of hedged item that the entity actually hedged and the quantity of the hedging instrument that the entity actually used to hedge that quantity of hedged item. The hedge ratio was not intentionally weighted to create ineffectiveness.

A quantitative assessment was performed to support the conclusion that the hedging instrument and the hedged item had values that would generally move in opposite directions. The quantitative assessment consisted of two scenario analyses as follows:

A parallel shift of +2% in the USD Libor interest rate and +10% in the EUR–USD spot rate, occurring simultaneously on the assessment date, was simulated. The fair values of the hedging instrument and the hedged item were calculated and compared to their initial fair values. As shown in the table below, the assessment resulted in a high degree of offset, corroborating that both elements had values that would generally move in opposite directions.

Scenario 1 analysis assessment		
	Hedging instrument	**Hedged item**
Initial fair value	-0-	<81,094,000>
Final fair value	<7,353,000>	<73,692,000>
Cumulative fair value change	<7,353,000>	7,402,000
	Degree of offset	**99.3%**

Similarly, a parallel shift of –2% in the USD Libor interest rate and –10% in the EUR–USD spot rate, occurring simultaneously on the assessment date was simulated. As shown in the table below, the assessment resulted in a high degree of offset, corroborating that both elements had values that would generally move in opposite directions.

Scenario 2 analysis assessment		
	Hedging instrument	**Hedged item**
Initial fair value	-0-	<81,094,000>
Final fair value	9,023,000	<90,157,000>
Cumulative fair value change	9,023,000	<9,063,000>
	Degree of offset	**99.6%**

The following potential sources of ineffectiveness were identified:

- a substantial deterioration in credit risk of either the entity or the counterparty to the hedging instrument; and
- a change in the timing or amounts of the hedged highly expected cash flows.

The hedge ratio was set at 1:1.

ABC also performed assessments at each reporting date, yielding similar conclusions. These assessments have been omitted to avoid unnecessary repetition.

8.1.6 Fair Valuations, Effective/Ineffective Amounts and Cash Flow Calculations

Fair Valuations of the Hedged Item When calculating the fair value of the hedged item it is important to remember that credit risk was excluded from the hedging relationship. As a result, the expected cash flows were discounted using the USD Libor curve flat (i.e., without any credit spread). Otherwise, large inefficiencies may arise. The fair value of the hedged item on 15 July 20X0 was calculated as follows:

Hedged item fair valuation on 15-Jul-X0					
Cash flow date	**Implied USD Libor** *(1)*	**Discount factor** *(2)*	**Spread** *(3)*	**Expected cash flow** *(4)*	**Present value** *(5)*
15-Jul-X1	5.40%	0.9481	0.50%	<5,982,000>	<5,672,000>
15-Jul-X2	5.60%	0.8972	0.50%	<6,185,000>	<5,549,000>
15-Jul-X3	5.78%	0.8475	0.50%	<106,367,000>	<90,146,000>
		USD fair value			**<101,367,000>**
		EUR–USD spot			**1.2500 (6)**
		EUR fair value			**<81,094,000>**

Notes:

(1) The implied USD Libor rate. For example, 5.40% was the USD Libor 12M rate set on 13-Jul-X0, and 5.60% and 5.78% were the USD Libor 12M rates expected to be set on 13-Jul-X1 and 13-Jul-X2 respectively

*(2) The discount factor from the cash flow date to the valuation date. For example, 0.9481 was calcu-
lated as 1/(5.40% × 365/360), 365 being the number of calendar days from the valuation date to
15-Jul-X1*

(3) The bond's credit margin over USD Libor 12M

*(4) The expected cash flow to be paid on such date. For example, <5,982,000> was calculated as: <100
mn> × (5.40% + 0.50%) × 365/360, 365 being the number of calendar days in the interest period*

(5) Expected cash flow × Discount factor

(6) EUR–USD spot rate on valuation date

Just to clarify, the fair value calculated differed from the initial carrying amount of
the bond, which was EUR 80 million (USD 100 million proceeds divided by the 1.2500
spot rate). Had the discount factors been based on the USD Libor curve plus 0.50% (i.e.,
credit risk included), the valuation would have been EUR 80 million, as detailed in the
following table:

Bond fair valuation on 15-Jul-X0					
Cash flow date	Implied USD Libor	Discount factor	Spread	Expected cash flow	Present value
15-Jul-X1	5.40%	0.9436 (*)	0.50%	<5,982,000>	<5,645,000>
15-Jul-X2	5.60%	0.8886	0.50%	<6,185,000>	<5,496,000>
15-Jul-X3	5.78%	0.8354	0.50%	<106,367,000>	<88,859,000>
			USD fair value		**<100,000,000>**
			EUR–USD spot		**1.2500**
			EUR fair value		**<80,000,000>**

(*) 1/[(5.40%+0.50%) × 365/360], 365 being the number of calendar days from the valuation date to 15-Jul-X1

Therefore, the carrying amount of the USD bond did not represent its full fair value but a mix
between amortised cost and an element corresponding to the fair valuation due to interest rate
movements since the start of the hedging relationship.

The fair value of the hedged item on 31 December 20X0 was calculated as follows:

Hedged item fair valuation on 31-Dec-X0					
Cash flow date	Implied USD Libor	Discount factor	Spread	Expected cash flow	Present value
15-Jul-X1	5.50% (1)	0.9709 (2)	0.50%	<3,212,000> (3)	<3,119,000>
15-Jul-X2	5.75%	0.9174	0.50%	<6,337,000>	<5,814,000>
15-Jul-X3	5.85%	0.8660	0.50%	<106,438,000>	<92,175,000>
			USD fair value		**<101,108,000>**
			EUR–USD spot		**1.2800**
			EUR fair value		**<78,991,000>**

Notes:

(1) The implied USD Libor rate from 31-Dec-X0 to 15-Jul-X1

(2) 1/(5.50% × 196/360), 196 being the number of calendar days from the valuation date (31-Dec-X0) to 15-Jul-X1

(3) <100 mn> × (5.40% + 0.50%) × 196/360, where 5.40% was the USD Libor 12M rate fixed on 13-Jul-X0 and 196 is the number of calendar days from the valuation date (31-Dec-X0) to 15-Jul-X1

The fair value of the hedged item on 31 December 20X1 was calculated as follows:

Hedged item fair valuation on 31-Dec-X1					
Cash flow date	Implied USD Libor	Discount factor	Spread	Expected cash flow	Present value
15-Jul-X2	5.65%	0.9702	0.50%	<3,294,000>	<3,196,000>
15-Jul-X3	5.90%	0.9154	0.50%	<106,489,000>	<97,480,000>
			USD fair value		**<100,676,000>**
			EUR–USD spot		**1.2200**
			EUR fair value		**<82,521,000>**

The fair value of the hedged item on 31 December 20X2 was calculated as follows:

Hedged item fair valuation on 31-Dec-X2					
Cash flow date	Implied USD Libor	Discount factor	Spread	Expected cash flow	Present value
15-Jul-X3	5.90%	0.9689	0.50%	<103,348,000>	<100,134,000>
			USD fair value		**<100,134,000>**
			EUR–USD spot		**1.1500**
			EUR fair value		**<87,073,000>**

The fair value of the hedged item on 15 July 20X3 was calculated as follows:

Hedged item fair valuation on 15-Jul-X3					
Cash flow date	Implied USD Libor	Discount factor	Spread	Expected cash flow	Present value
15-Jul-X3	—	1.0000	—	<100,000,000>	<100,000,000>
			USD fair value		**<100,000,000>**
			EUR–USD spot		**1.1100**
			EUR fair value		**<90,909,000>**

Fair Valuations of the Hedging Instrument   The fair value of the hedging instrument on 15 July 20X0 was calculated as follows:

Cash flow date	Implied interest rate	Discount factor	Spread	Expected cash flow	Present value
Hedging instrument fair valuation on 15-Jul-X0					
Cash flows of USD leg:					
31-Jul-X1	5.40%	0.9481	0.50%	5,982,000	5,672,000
31-Jul-X2	5.60%	0.8972	0.50%	6,185,000	5,549,000
31-Jul-X3	5.78%	0.8475	0.50%	106,367,000	90,146,000
				Total USD	**101,367,000**
				Total EUR (1.2500)	**81,094,000**
Cash flows of EUR leg:					
31-Jul-X1	4.50%	0.9564	0.49%	<4,047,000>	<3,871,000>
31-Jul-X2	4.71%	0.9128	0.49%	<4,218,000>	<3,850,000>
31-Jul-X3	4.89%	0.8697	0.49%	<84,364,000>	<73,371,000>
				Total EUR	<81,092,000>
				Fair value (before adjustments)	2,000
				Adjustments (CVA/DVA and basis)	<2,000>
				Fair value (including adjustments)	-0-

It can be observed that the valuations of the USD leg of the CCS and of the hedged item were of opposite sign. The expected cash flow of the EUR leg was calculated as EUR 80 mn × (Euribor 12M + 0.49%) × Days/360, where Days was the number of days in the interest period.

The fair value of the hedging instrument on 31 December 20X0 was calculated as follows:

Cash flow date	Implied interest rate	Discount factor	Spread	Expected cash flow	Present value
Hedging instrument fair valuation on 31-Dec-X0					
Cash flows of USD leg:					
31-Jul-X1	5.50%	0.9709	0.50%	3,212,000	3,119,000
31-Jul-X2	5.75%	0.9174	0.50%	6,337,000	5,814,000
31-Jul-X3	5.85%	0.8660	0.50%	106,438,000	92,175,000
				Total USD	**101,108,000**
				Total EUR (1.2800)	**78,991,000**
Cash flows of EUR leg:					
31-Jul-X1	4.60%	0.9756	0.49%	<2,173,000>	<2,120,000>
31-Jul-X2	4.80%	0.9303	0.49%	<4,291,000>	<3,992,000>

31-Jul-X3	4.95%	0.8858	0.49%	<84,412,000>	<74,772,000>
			Total EUR		<80,884,000>

Fair value (before adjustments)	<1,893,000>
Adjustments (CVA/DVA and basis)	57,000>
Fair value (including adjustments)	<1,836,000>

The fair value of the hedging instrument on 31 December 20X1 was calculated as follows:

		Hedging instrument fair valuation on 31-Dec-X1			
Cash flow date	**Implied interest rate**	**Discount factor**	**Spread**	**Expected cash flow**	**Present value**
Cash flows of USD leg:					
31-Jul-X2	5.65%	0.9702	0.50%	3,294,000	3,196,000
31-Jul-X3	5.90%	0.9154	0.50%	106,489,000	97,480,000
			Total USD		**100,676,000**
			Total EUR (1.2200)		**82,521,000**
Cash flows of EUR leg:					
31-Jul-X2	4.80%	0.9745	0.49%	<2,282,000>	<2,224,000>
31-Jul-X3	4.95%	0.9279	0.49%	<84,412,000>	<78,326,000>
			Total EUR		<80,550,000>
		Fair value (before adjustments)			1,971,000
		Adjustments (CVA/DVA and basis)			<49,000>
		Fair value (including adjustments)			1,922,000

The fair value of the hedging instrument on 31 December 20X2 was calculated as follows:

		Hedging instrument fair valuation on 31-Dec-X2			
Cash flow date	**Implied interest rate**	**Discount factor**	**Spread**	**Expected cash flow**	**Present value**
Cash flows of USD leg:					
31-Jul-X3	5.90%	0.9689	0.50%	103,348,000	100,134,000
			Total USD		**100,134,000**
			Total EUR (1.1500)		**87,073,000**
Cash flows of EUR leg:					
31-Jul-X3	4.95%	0.9738	0.49%	<82,369,000>	<80,211,000>
			Total EUR		<80,211,000>
		Fair value (before adjustments)			6,862,000
		Adjustments (CVA/DVA and basis)			<69,000>
		Fair value (including adjustments)			6,793,000

The fair value of the hedging instrument on 15 July 20X3 was calculated as follows:

Hedging instrument fair valuation on 15-Jul-X3					
Cash flow date	Implied interest rate	Discount factor	Spread	Expected cash flow	Present value
Cash flows of USD leg:					
31-Jul-X3	—	1.0000	—	100,000,000	100,000,000
			Total USD		**100,000,000**
			Total EUR (1.1100)		**90,909,000**
Cash flows of EUR leg:					
31-Jul-X3	—	1.0000	—	<80,000,000>	<80,000,000>
			Total EUR		<80,000,000>
		Fair value (before adjustments)			10,909,000
		Adjustments (CVA/DVA and basis)			-0-
		Fair value (including adjustments)			10,909,000

Effective and Ineffective Amounts   The following table summarises the period changes in the fair value of the hedged item and the hedging instrument:

	Hedging instrument		Hedged item	
	Fair value	Period change	Fair value	Period change
15-Jul-X0	-0-	—	<81,094,000>	—
31-Dec-X0	<1,836,000>	<1,836,000>	<78,991,000>	2,103,000
31-Dec-X1	1,922,000	3,758,000	<82,521,000>	<3,530,000>
31-Dec-X2	6,793,000	4,871,000	<87,073,000>	<4,552,000>
15-Jul-X3	10,909,000	4,116,000	<90,909,000>	<3,836,000>

On each valuation date, the effective part was the lower of the two period fair value changes (taking into account their opposing signs) and the ineffective part was any remainder:

	Hedging instrument			Hedged item		
	Period change	Effective part	Ineffective part	Period change	Effective part	Ineffective part
31-Dec-X0	<1,836,000>	<1,836,000>	-0-	2,103,000	1,836,000	267,000
31-Dec-X1	3,758,000	3,530,000	228,000	<3,530,000>	<3,530,000>	-0-
31-Dec-X2	4,871,000	4,552,000	319,000	<4,552,000>	<4,552,000>	-0-
15-Jul-X3	4,116,000	3,836,000	280,000	<3,836,000>	<3,836,000>	-0-

Accruals and Payable/Receivable Amounts   The following table summarises the accruals and payables related to the bond:

Bond accruals and payables						
	USD Libor 12M	Average EUR–USD	Spot EUR–USD	EUR coupon accrual *(1)*	EUR payable amount *(2)*	Retranslation payable *(3)*
31-Dec-X0	5.40%	1.2630	1.2800	<2,193,000>	<2,164,000>	
15-Jul-X1	5.40%	1.2680	1.2400	<2,533,000>	<2,590,000>	<70,000>
31-Dec-X1	5.55%	1.2320	1.2200	<2,305,000>	<2,328,000>	
15-Jul-X2	5.55%	1.2170	1.2100	<2,707,000>	<2,722,000>	<19,000>
31-Dec-X2	5.65%	1.1680	1.1500	<2,472,000>	<2,510,000>	
15-Jul-X3	5.65%	1.1240	1.1000	<2,979,000>	<3,044,000>	<114,000>

Notes:

   (1) USD 100 mn × (USD Libor 12M + 0.50%) × (Days/360)/Average EUR–USD, where Days was the number of calendar days in the accrual period (i.e., 169 for accrual periods ending on 31 December and 196 for accrual periods ending on 15 July)
   (2) USD 100 mn × (USD Libor 12M + 0.50%) × (Days/360)/Spot EUR–USD
   (3) USD payable amount × (1/previous Spot EUR–USD – 1/current Spot EUR–USD), where USD payable amount was the USD 100 mn × (USD Libor 12M + 0.50%) × Days/360 corresponding to the previous accrual period

There was no need to retranslate into EUR the USD carrying amount of the bond, as it was already included in the fair valuation of the hedged item. Otherwise a double counting will occur.

   The accruals and payables related to the USD leg of the CCS were identical to those of the bond, but of opposite sign. The following table summarises the accruals and payables related to the EUR leg of the CCS:

CCS EUR leg accruals and payables				
	Euribor 12M	Days	EUR leg accrual *(*)*	Payable amount
31-Dec-X0	4.50%	169	1,874,000	1,874,000
15-Jul-X1	4.50%	196	2,173,000	2,173,000
31-Dec-X1	4.75%	169	1,968,000	1,968,000
15-Jul-X2	4.75%	196	2,282,000	2,282,000
31-Dec-X2	4.95%	169	2,043,000	2,043,000
15-Jul-X3	4.95%	196	2,369,000	2,369,000

(*) 100 mn × (Euribor 12M + 0.49%) × Days/360, where Days was the number of calendar days in the accruing period

Note on Fair Value Adjustments and Translation   The USD bond was recognised at amortised cost. Without the hedge, being a floating rate bond and being issued at par, the effective interest rate in each interest period was the USD Libor 12-month plus 50 bps corresponding to such period. Also, the carrying amount of the bond was a constant USD 100 million. The translation of the carrying amount into EUR was relatively straightforward, calculated by dividing USD 100 million by the EUR–USD spot rate prevailing on the reporting date.

When fair value hedge accounting is applied to a hedge of a debt instrument, the carrying value of the debt is adjusted for movements in the hedged risk. IFRS 9 requires the fair value adjustment to be amortised to profit or loss as early as when the adjustment is made and no later than when the hedged item ceases to be fair value adjusted. This amortisation is included as part of the revised effective interest rate. Therefore:

- If ABC chose to amortise the fair value adjustment as soon as the adjustment was made, then because the fair value adjustment changed for each reporting period during the hedging relationship term, a revised effective interest rate needed to be determined at the start of each reporting period. Accordingly, the bond's effective interest rate had to take into account the fair value adjustments to the carrying amount of the USD bond, being different from the USD Libor 12M plus 50 bps corresponding to such period.
- Alternatively, if ABC chose to start amortising the adjustment when hedge accounting ceased it only needed to recalculate the effective interest rate at that point. Accordingly, the bond's effective interest rate was the USD Libor 12M plus 50 bps corresponding to the prevailing interest period, during the hedging relationship term. ABC adopted this alternative due to its much lower operational burden.

Regarding the translation of the fair value adjustments, the fair valuations of the hedged item for the risk being hedged were performed in EUR. Therefore, these fair valuations already included the translation into EUR of the fair value adjustments.

8.1.7 Accounting Entries

The required journal entries were as follows.

1) Journal entries on 15 July 20X0

The bond was issued.

Cash (Asset)	80,000,000	
Financial debt (Liability)		80,000,000

No entries were required to record the CCS as its initial fair value was zero.

2) Journal entries on 31 December 20X0

The accrued interest of the bond was EUR <2,193,000>. The payable related to this accrued interest was EUR <2,164,000>.

Interest expense (Profit or loss)	2,193,000	
Interest payable (Liability)		2,164,000
Other financial income (Profit or loss)		29,000

The change in fair value of the hedged item for the risk being hedged produced a EUR 2,103,000 gain, of which EUR 1,836,000 was deemed to be effective and EUR 267,000 ineffective.

Financial debt (Liability)	2,103,000	
Interest income (Profit or loss)		1,836,000
Other financial income (Profit or loss)		267,000

The accrual of the USD leg of the CCS was EUR 2,193,000. The receivable related to this accrued interest was EUR 2,164,000.

Interest receivable (Asset)	2,164,000	
Other financial expenses (Profit or loss)	29,000	
Interest income (Profit or loss)		2,193,000

The accrual of the EUR leg of the CCS was EUR <1,874,000>.

Interest expense (Profit or loss)	1,874,000	
Interest payable (Liability)		1,874,000

The change in fair value of the CCS produced a EUR 1,836,000 loss, fully deemed to be effective.

Interest expense (Profit or loss)	1,836,000	
Derivative contract (Liability)		1,836,000

3) Journal entries on 15 July 20X1

The accrued interest of the bond was EUR <2,533,000>. The payable related to this accrued interest was EUR <2,590,000>.

Interest expense (Profit or loss)	2,533,000	
Other financial expenses (Profit or loss)	57,000	
Interest payable (Liability)		2,590,000

The interest payable corresponding to the bond's previous accrued interest was retranslated, producing a EUR 70,000 loss.

Other financial expenses (Profit or loss)	70,000	
Interest payable (Liability)		70,000

The bond coupon was paid using the amount received under the USD leg of the CCS.

Interest payable (Liability)	4,824,000	
Cash (Asset)		4,824,000

The accrued interest of the USD leg was EUR 2,533,000. The receivable related to this accrued interest was EUR 2,590,000.

Interest receivable (Asset)	2,590,000	
Interest income (Profit or loss)		2,533,000
Other financial income (Profit or loss)		57,000

The interest receivable corresponding to the USD leg's previous accrued interest was retranslated, producing a EUR 70,000 gain.

Interest receivable (Asset)	70,000	
Other financial income (Profit or loss)		70,000

The interest receivable corresponding to the USD leg was received.

Cash (Asset)	4,824,000	
Interest receivable (Asset)		4,824,000

The accrual of the EUR leg was EUR <2,173,000>.

Interest expense (Profit or loss)	2,173,000	
Interest payable (Liability)		2,173,000

The interest payable corresponding to the EUR leg was paid.

Interest payable (Liability)	4,047,000	
Cash (Asset)		4,047,000

4) Journal entries on 31 December 20X1

The accrued interest of the bond was EUR <2,305,000>. The payable related to this accrued interest was EUR <2,328,000>.

Interest expense (Profit or loss)	2,305,000	
Other financial expenses (Profit or loss)	23,000	
Interest payable (Liability)		2,328,000

The change in fair value of the hedged item for the risk being hedged produced a EUR 3,530,000 loss, fully deemed to be effective.

Interest expense (Profit or loss)	3,530,000	
Financial debt (Liability)		3,530,000

The accrual of the USD leg of the CCS was EUR 2,305,000. The receivable related to this accrued interest was EUR 2,328,000.

Interest receivable (Asset)	2,328,000	
Interest income (Profit or loss)		2,305,000
Other financial income (Profit or loss)		23,000

The accrual of the EUR leg was EUR <1,968,000>.

Interest expense (Profit or loss)	1,968,000	
Interest payable (Liability)		1,968,000

The change in fair value of the CCS produced a EUR 3,758,000 gain, of which EUR 3,530,000 was deemed to be effective and EUR 228,000 ineffective.

Derivative contract (Asset)	3,758,000	
Interest income (Profit or loss)		3,530,000
Other financial income (Profit or loss)		228,000

5) Journal entries on 15 July 20X2

The accrued interest of the bond was EUR <2,707,000>. The payable related to this accrued interest was EUR <2,722,000>.

Interest expense (Profit or loss)	2,707,000	
Other financial expenses (Profit or loss)	15,000	
Interest payable (Liability)		2,722,000

The interest payable corresponding to the bond's previous accrued interest was retranslated, producing a EUR 19,000 loss.

Other financial expenses (Profit or loss)	19,000	
Interest payable (Liability)		19,000

The bond coupon was paid using the USD amounts received under the USD leg of the CCS.

Interest payable (Liability)	5,069,000	
Cash (Asset)		5,069,000

The accrued interest of the USD leg was EUR 2,707,000. The receivable related to this accrued interest was EUR 2,722,000.

Interest receivable (Asset)	2,722,000	
Interest income (Profit or loss)		2,722,000
Other financial income (Profit or loss)		15,000

The interest receivable corresponding to the USD leg's previous accrued interest was retranslated, producing a EUR 19,000 gain.

Interest receivable (Asset)	19,000	
Other financial income (Profit or loss)		19,000

The interest receivable corresponding to the USD leg was received.

Cash (Asset)	5,069,000	
Interest receivable (Asset)		5,069,000

The accrual of the EUR leg was EUR <2,282,000>.

Interest expense (Profit or loss)	2,282,000	
Interest payable (Liability)		2,282,000

The interest payable corresponding to the EUR leg was paid.

Interest payable (Liability)	4,250,000	
Cash (Asset)		4,250,000

6) Journal entries on 31 December 20X2
The accrued interest of the bond was EUR <2,472,000>. The payable related to this accrued interest was EUR <2,510,000>.

Interest expense (Profit or loss)	2,472,000	
Other financial expenses (Profit or loss)	38,000	
Interest payable (Liability)		2,510,000

The change in fair value of the hedged item for the risk being hedged produced a EUR 4,552,000 loss, fully deemed to be effective.

Interest expense (Profit or loss)	4,552,000	
Financial debt (Liability)		4,552,000

The accrual of the USD leg of the CCS was EUR 2,472,000. The receivable related to this accrued interest was EUR 2,510,000.

Interest receivable (Asset)	2,510,000	
Interest income (Profit or loss)		2,472,000
Other financial income (Profit or loss)		38,000

The accrual of the EUR leg was EUR <2,043,000>.

Interest expense (Profit or loss)	2,043,000	
Interest payable (Liability)		2,043,000

The change in fair value of the CCS produced a EUR 4,871,000 gain, of which EUR 4,552,000 was deemed to be effective and EUR 319,000 ineffective.

Derivative contract (Asset)	4,871,000	
Interest income (Profit or loss)		4,552,000
Other financial income (Profit or loss)		319,000

7) Journal entries on 15 July 20X3

The accrued interest of the bond was EUR <2,979,000>. The payable related to this accrued interest was EUR <3,044,000>.

Interest expense (Profit or loss)	2,979,000	
Other financial expenses (Profit or loss)	65,000	
Interest payable (Liability)		3,044,000

The interest payable corresponding to the bond's previous accrued interest was retranslated, producing a EUR 114,000 loss.

Other financial expenses (Profit or loss)	114,000	
Interest payable (Liability)		114,000

The bond coupon and principal were paid/repaid by using the amounts received under the USD leg of the CCS. The bond principal represented EUR 90,909,000 (= USD 100 mn/1.1000).

Interest payable (Liability)	5,668,000	
Financial debt (Liability)	90,909,000	
Cash (Asset)		96,577,000

The accrued interest of the USD leg was EUR 2,979,000. The receivable related to this accrued interest was EUR 3,044,000.

Interest receivable (Asset)	3,044,000	
Interest income (Profit or loss)		2,979,000
Other financial income (Profit or loss)		65,000

The interest receivable corresponding to the USD leg's previous accrued interest was retranslated, producing a EUR 114,000 gain.

Interest receivable (Asset)	114,000	
Other financial income (Profit or loss)		114,000

The interest receivable corresponding to the USD leg was received.

Cash (Asset)	5,668,000	
Interest receivable (Asset)		5,668,000

The accrual of the EUR leg was EUR <2,369,000>.

Interest expense (Profit or loss)	2,369,000	
Interest payable (Liability)		2,369,000

The interest payable corresponding to the EUR leg was paid.

Interest payable (Liability)	4,412,000	
Cash (Asset)		4,412,000

The change in fair value of the hedged item for the risk being hedged produced a EUR 3,836,000 loss, fully deemed to be effective.

Interest expense (Profit or loss)	3,836,000	
Financial debt (Liability)		3,836,000

The change in fair value of the CCS produced a EUR 4,116,000 gain, of which EUR 3,836,000 was deemed to be effective and EUR 280,000 ineffective.

Derivative contract (Asset)	4,116,000	
Interest income (Profit or loss)		3,836,000
Other financial income (Profit or loss)		280,000

The CCS notionals were exchanged. ABC paid EUR 80 million and received USD 100 million (worth EUR 90,909,000). The difference was worth EUR 10,909,000 (= 90,909,000 – 80,000,000).

Cash (Asset)	10,909,000	
Derivative contract (Asset)		10,909,000

The remaining EUR 1,094,000 fair value adjustments related to the bond were amortised to profit or loss.

Other financial expenses (Profit or loss)	1,094,000	
Financial debt (Liability)		1,094,000

The following table gives a summary of the accounting entries:

	Cash	Interest receivable	Derivative contract	Financial debt	Interest payable	Profit or loss
15-Jul-X0						
Bond issuance	80,000,000			80,000,000		
31-Dec-X0						
Bond accrued coupon					2,164,000	<2,164,000>
Hedged item revaluation				<2,103,000>		2,103,000
CCS accrual USD leg		2,164,000				2,164,000
CCS accrual EUR leg					1,874,000	<1,874,000>
CCS revaluation			<1,836,000>			<1,836,000>
15-Jul-X1						
Bond accrued coupon					2,590,000	<2,590,000>

	Cash	Interest receivable	Derivative contract	Financial debt	Interest payable	Profit or loss
Bond accrual retranslation					70,000	<70,000>
Bond coupon payment	<4,824,000>				<4,824,000>	
CCS accrual USD leg		2,590,000				2,590,000
CCS interest receivable retranslation		70,000				70,000
CCS USD leg receipt	4,824,000	<4,824,000>				
CCS accrual EUR leg					2,173,000	<2,173,000>
CCS EUR leg payment	<4,047,000>				<4,047,000>	
31-Dec-X1						
Bond accrued coupon					2,328,000	<2,328,000>
Hedged item revaluation				3,530,000		<3,530,000>
CCS accrual USD leg		2,328,000				2,328,000
CCS accrual EUR leg					1,968,000	<1,968,000>
CCS revaluation			3,758,000			3,758,000
15-Jul-X2						
Bond accrued coupon					2,722,000	<2,722,000>
Bond accrual retranslation					19,000	<19,000>
Bond coupon payment	<5,069,000>				<5,069,000>	
CCS accrual USD leg		2,722,000				2,722,000
CCS interest receivable retranslation		19,000				19,000
CCS USD leg receipt	5,069,000	<5,069,000>				
CCS accrual EUR leg					2,282,000	<2,282,000>
CCS EUR leg payment	<4,250,000>				<4,250,000>	

(continued overleaf)

	Cash	Interest receivable	Derivative contract	Financial debt	Interest payable	Profit or loss
31-Dec-X2						
Bond accrued coupon					2,510,000	<2,510,000>
Hedged item revaluation				4,552,000		<4,552,000>
CCS accrual USD leg		2,510,000				2,510,000
CCS accrual EUR leg					2,043,000	<2,043,000>
CCS revaluation			4,871,000			4,871,000
15-Jul-X3						
Bond accrued coupon					3,044,000	<3,044,000>
Bond accrual retranslation					114,000	<114,000>
Bond coupon payment	<96,577,000>			<90,909,000>	<5,668,000>	
CCS accrual USD leg		3,044,000				3,044,000
CCS interest receivable retranslation		114,000				114,000
CCS USD leg receipt	5,668,000	<5,668,000>				
CCS accrual EUR leg					2,369,000	<2,369,000>
CCS EUR leg payment	<4,412,000>				<4,412,000>	
Hedged item revaluation				3,836,000		<3,836,000>
CCS revaluation			4,116,000			4,116,000
CCS exchange	10,909,000		<10,909,000>			
Fair value amortisation				1,094,000		<1,094,000>
	<12,709,000>	-0-	-0-	-0-	-0-	<12,709,000>

8.1.8 Concluding Remarks

ABC's objective when entering into the combination of the bond and the CCS was to incur an expense representing Euribor 12-month plus 0.49%.

During the first year of the term of the bond (and of the hedging relationship) the overall impact of the strategy on profit or loss was a EUR 3,780,000 expense. The target expense during the first year was EUR 4,047,000 (= 80 mn × (4.50% + 0.49%) × 365/360), corresponding to a 4.50% Euribor 12-month rate. The difference was due to the EUR 267,000 ineffective part of the change in fair value of the hedged item. Nonetheless, the net cash outflow was exactly EUR 4,047,000.

During the second year the overall impact of the strategy on profit or loss was a EUR 4,022,000 expense. The target expense during the second year was EUR 4,250,000 (= 80 mn × (4.75% + 0.49%) × 365/360), corresponding to a 4.75% Euribor 12-month rate. The difference was due to the EUR 228,000 ineffective part of the change in fair value of the CCS. However, the net cash outflow was exactly EUR 4,250,000.

During the third year the overall impact of the strategy on profit or loss was a EUR 4,907,000 expense. The target expense during the third year was EUR 4,412,000 (= 80 mn × (4.95% + 0.49%) × 365/360), corresponding to a 4.95% Euribor 12-month rate. The EUR 495,000 (= 1,094,000 – 599,000) difference was due to the EUR 599,000 ineffective part of the change in fair value of the CCS and the EUR 1,094,000 amortisation of the fair value. Nonetheless, the net cash outflow was exactly EUR 4,412,000.

The sum of the interest expense over the three years equalled the sum of the three expense targets. Therefore over the three years, both from a cash and expense perspective, ABC achieved its objective of funding itself at Euribor 12-month plus 0.49%.

Finally, note that in our case the basis of the CCS was included in the hedging relationship. The full fair value movement of the CCS, including the basis component, was taken into account in the calculation of the effective part of the hedge. As a consequence, a volatile behaviour of the basis could have created substantial ineffectiveness. Similarly to the treatment of forward components of forward contracts, when the basis component of a CCS is excluded from a hedging relationship, IFRS 9 allows the choice between:

- recognising in profit or loss the change in the basis element fair value; and
- recognising changes in the basis element fair value in OCI to the extent that it relates to the hedged item, while amortising the initial basis element in profit or loss.

8.2 CASE STUDY: HEDGING A FIXED RATE FOREIGN CURRENCY LIABILITY WITH A RECEIVE-FIXED PAY-FLOATING CROSS-CURRENCY SWAP

This case study illustrates the accounting treatment of a fair value hedge of a fixed rate foreign currency financing with a pay-floating receive-fixed CCS.

8.2.1 Background Information

On 15 July 20X0, ABC issued a USD-denominated floating rate bond. ABC's functional currency was the EUR. The bond had the following main terms:

Bond terms	
Issue date	15 July 20X0
Maturity	3 years (15 July 20X3)
Notional	USD 100 million
Coupon	6.09% annually, actual/360 basis

Since ABC's objective was to raise EUR floating funding, on the issue date ABC entered into a CCS. Through the CCS, the entity agreed to receive a USD fixed rate equal to the bond coupon and pay a Euribor floating rate plus a spread. The CCS had the following terms:

Cross-currency swap terms	
Trade date	15 July 20X0
Start date	15 July 20X0
Counterparties	ABC and XYZ Bank
Maturity	3 years (15 July 20X3)
USD nominal	USD 100 million
EUR nominal	EUR 80 million
Initial exchange	On start date, ABC receives the EUR nominal and pays the USD nominal
ABC pays	Euribor 12M + 49 bps annually, actual/360 basis, on the EUR nominal. Euribor is fixed two business days prior to the beginning of each annual interest period
ABC receives	6.09% annually, actual/360 basis
Final exchange	On maturity date, ABC receives the USD nominal and pays the EUR nominal

The mechanics of the CCS are described next. It can be seen that through the combination of the USD bond and the CCS, ABC synthetically obtained a EUR floating liability.

On the issue date at the start of the CCS, there was an initial exchange of nominal amounts through the CCS: ABC delivered the USD 100 million debt issuance proceeds and received EUR 80 million. The resulting EUR–USD exchange rate was 1.2500. The combination of the bond and CCS had the same effect as if ABC had issued a EUR-denominated bond, as shown in Figure 8.4.

An exchange of interest payments took place annually. ABC received USD 6.09% interest on the USD nominal and paid Euribor-linked interest on the EUR nominal. ABC used the USD fixed cash flows it received under the CCS to pay the bond interest. Figure 8.5 shows the strategy's intermediate cash flows.

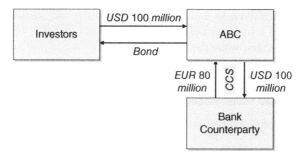

FIGURE 8.4   Bond and CCS combination – initial cash flows.

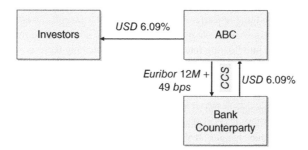

FIGURE 8.5   Bond and CCS combination – intermediate cash flows.

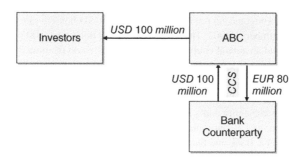

FIGURE 8.6   Bond and CCS combination – final cash flows.

On maturity of the CCS and the debt, ABC re-exchanged the CCS nominals, using the USD 100 million it received through the CCS to redeem the bond issue, and delivering EUR 80 million to the CCS counterparty. Note that this final exchange was made at exactly the same rate used in the initial exchange (1.2500). Figure 8.6 shows the strategy's cash flows at maturity.

ABC designated the CCS as the hedging instrument in a fair value hedge of the exchange rate and interest rate risks (see Section 8.1.2 for a discussion of the risk components of the bond). Credit risk was excluded from the hedging relationship. Therefore, fair valuations of the hedged item would assume that the initial credit margin of 50 basis points remained unchanged during the term of the hedge.

When assessing effectiveness and calculating effective and ineffective amounts, the helpful simplification of a hypothetical derivative could not be used for fair value hedges. Therefore ABC needed to fair value the hedged item.

8.2.2 Hedging Relationship Documentation

ABC documented the hedging relationship as follows:

Hedging relationship documentation	
Risk management objective and strategy for undertaking the hedge	The objective of the hedge is to reduce the variability of the fair value of a foreign currency denominated fixed rate bond issued by the entity.
	This hedging objective is consistent with the group's overall interest rate risk management strategy of transforming all new issued foreign-denominated debt into floating rate, and thereafter managing the exposure to interest rate risk through the proportion of fixed and floating rate net debt in its total debt portfolio.
	Exchange rate and interest rate risk. The designated risk being hedged is the risk of changes in the EUR fair value of the hedged item attributable to changes in the EUR–USD exchange rate and USD Libor interest rates.
	Fair value changes attributable to credit or other risks are not hedged in this relationship. Accordingly, the 50 bps credit spread is excluded from the hedging relationship
Type of hedge	Fair value hedge
Hedged item	The coupons and principal of the 3-year USD floating rate bond with reference number 678902. The main terms of the bond are a USD 100 million principal and an annual coupon of 6.09% calculated on the principal
Hedging instrument	The cross-currency swap with reference number 014569. The main terms of the CCS are a USD 100 million nominal, a EUR 80 million nominal, a 3-year maturity, a USD annual interest of 6.09% on the USD nominal to be received by the entity and a EUR annual interest of Euribor 12-month rate plus 0.49% on the EUR nominal to be paid by the entity. The counterparty to the CCS is XYZ Bank and the credit risk associated with this counterparty is considered to be very low
Hedge effectiveness assessment	See below

8.2.3 Hedge Effectiveness Assessment

Hedge effectiveness will be assessed by comparing changes in the fair value of the hedging instrument to changes in the fair value of the hedged item. Changes in the fair value of the hedging instrument (i.e., the CCS) will be recognised as follows:

- The effective part of the gain or loss on the hedging instrument will be recognised in profit or loss, adjusting interest income/expense.
- The ineffective part of the gain or loss on the hedging instrument will be recognised in profit or loss, as other financial income/expenses.

Hedge effectiveness will be assessed prospectively at hedging relationship inception, on an ongoing basis at least upon each reporting date and upon occurrence of a significant change in the circumstances affecting the hedge effectiveness requirements.

The hedging relationship will qualify for hedge accounting only if all the following criteria are met:

1) The hedging relationship consists only of eligible hedge items and hedging instruments. The hedge item is eligible as it is an already recognised liability that exposes the entity to fair value risk, affects profit or loss and is reliably measurable. The hedging instrument is eligible as it is a derivative that does not result in a net written option.
2) At hedge inception there is a formal designation and documentation of the hedging relationship and the entity's risk management objective and strategy for undertaking the hedge.
3) The hedging relationship is considered effective.

The hedging relationship will be considered effective if the following three requirements are met:

1) There is an economic relationship between the hedged item and the hedging instrument.
2) The effect of credit risk does not dominate the value changes that result from that economic relationship.
3) The hedge ratio of the hedging relationship is the same as that resulting from the quantity of hedged item that the entity actually hedges and the quantity of the hedging instrument that the entity actually uses to hedge that quantity of hedged item. The hedge ratio should not be intentionally weighted to create ineffectiveness.

Whether there is an economic relationship between the hedged item and the hedging instrument will be assessed on a quantitative basis using the scenario analysis method for two scenarios:

- In a first scenario, USD Libor interest rates will be shifted upwards by 2%, the EUR–USD exchange rate increased by 10%, and the changes in fair value of the hedged item and the hedging instrument compared.
- In a second scenario, USD Libor interest rates will be shifted downwards by 2%, the EUR–USD exchange rate reduced by 10%, and the changes in fair value of the hedged item and the hedging instrument compared.

8.2.4 Hedge Effectiveness Assessment Performed at the Start of the Hedging Relationship

On 15 July 20X0 ABC performed a hedge effectiveness assessment which was documented as described next.

The hedging relationship was considered effective as the following three requirements were met:

1) There was an economic relationship between the hedged item and the hedging instrument. Based on the quantitative assessment performed, the entity concluded that the change in fair value of the hedged item was expected to be substantially offset by the change in fair value of the hedging instrument, corroborating that both elements had values that would generally move in opposite directions.

2) The effect of credit risk did not dominate the value changes resulting from that economic relationship as the credit ratings of both the entity and XYZ Bank were considered sufficiently strong.

3) The hedge ratio of the hedging relationship was the same as that resulting from the quantity of hedged item that the entity actually hedged and the quantity of the hedging instrument that the entity actually used to hedge that quantity of hedged item. The hedge ratio was not intentionally weighted to create ineffectiveness.

A quantitative assessment was performed to support the conclusion that the hedging instrument and the hedged item had values that would generally move in opposite directions. The quantitative assessment consisted of two scenario analyses performed as follows.

A parallel shift of +2% in the USD Libor interest rate and +10% in the EUR–USD spot rate, occurring simultaneously on the assessment date, was simulated. The fair values of the hedging instrument and the hedged item were calculated and compared to their initial fair values. As shown in the table below, the assessment resulted in a high degree of offset, corroborating that both elements had values that would generally move in opposite directions.

Scenario 1 analysis assessment		
	Hedging instrument	**Hedged item**
Initial fair value	-0-	<81,102,000>
Final fair value	<11,168,000>	<69,877,000>
Cumulative fair value change	<11,168,000>	11,225,000
	Degree of offset	**99.5%**

Similarly, a parallel shift of –2% the USD Libor interest rate and –10% in the EUR–USD spot rate, occurring simultaneously on the assessment date, was simulated. As shown in the table below, the assessment resulted in a high degree of offset, corroborating that both elements had values that would generally move in opposite directions.

Scenario 2 analysis assessment		
	Hedging instrument	**Hedged item**
Initial fair value	-0-	<81,102,000>
Final fair value	14,070,000	<95,104,000>
Cumulative fair value change	14,070,000	<14,102,000>
	Degree of offset	**99.8%**

The following potential sources of ineffectiveness were identified:

▪ a substantial deterioration in credit risk of either the entity or the counterparty to the hedging instrument; and
▪ a change in the timing or amounts of the hedged highly expected cash flows.

The hedge ratio was set at 1:1.

ABC also performed assessments at each reporting date, yielding similar conclusions. These assessments have been omitted to avoid unnecessary repetition.

8.2.5 Fair Valuations, Effective/Ineffective Amounts and Cash Flow Calculations

Fair Valuations of the Hedged Item When calculating the fair value of the hedged item it is important to remember that credit risk was excluded from the hedging relationship. As a result, the expected cash flows were discounted using the USD Libor curve flat (i.e., without any credit spread). Otherwise, large inefficiencies may arise. The fair value of the hedged item on 15 July 20X0 was calculated as follows:

Hedged item fair valuation on 15-Jul-X0

Cash flow date	Implied USD Libor *(1)*	Discount factor *(2)*	Expected cash flow *(3)*	Present value *(4)*
15-Jul-X1	5.40%	0.9481	<6,175,000>	<5,855,000>
15-Jul-X2	5.60%	0.8972	<6,175,000>	<5,540,000>
15-Jul-X3	5.78%	0.8475	<106,175,000>	<89,983,000>
			USD fair value	**<101,378,000>**
			EUR–USD spot	**1.2500 *(5)***
			EUR fair value	**<81,102,000>**

Notes:

(1) The implied USD Libor rate. For example, 5.40% was the USD Libor 12M rate set on 13-Jul-X0, and 5.60% and 5.78% were the USD Libor 12M rate expected to be set on 13-Jul-X1 and 13-Jul-X2 respectively

(2) The discount factor from the cash flow date to the valuation date. For example, 0.9481 was calculated as 1/(5.40% × 365/360), 365 being the number of calendar days from the valuation date to 15-Jul-X1

(3) The expected cash flow to be paid on such date. For example, <6,175,000> was calculated as <100 mn> × 6.09% × 365/360, 365 being the number of calendar days in the interest period

(4) Expected cash flow × Discount factor

(5) EUR–USD spot rate on valuation date

The fair value of the hedged item on 31 December 20X0 was calculated as follows:

Hedged item fair valuation on 31-Dec-X0

Cash flow date	Implied USD Libor	Discount factor	Expected cash flow	Present value
15-Jul-X1	5.50% (1)	0.9709 (2)	<3,316,000> (3)	<3,220,000>
15-Jul-X2	5.75%	0.9174	<6,175,000>	<5,665,000>
15-Jul-X3	5.85%	0.8660	<106,175,000>	<91,948,000>
			USD fair value	**<100,833,000>**
			EUR–USD spot	**1.2800**
			EUR fair value	**<78,776,000>**

Notes:

(1) The implied USD Libor rate from 31-Dec-X0 to 15-Jul-X1

(2) 1/(5.50% × 196/360), 196 being the number of calendar days from the valuation date (31-Dec-X0) to 15-Jul-X1

(3) <100 mn> × 6.09% × 196/360, where 6.09% was bond's the fixed rate and 196 was the number of calendar days from the valuation date (31-Dec-X0) to 15-Jul-X1

The fair value of the hedged item on 31 December 20X1 was calculated as follows:

Hedged item fair valuation on 31-Dec-X1				
Cash flow date	Implied USD Libor	Discount factor	Expected cash flow	Present value
15-Jul-X2	5.65%	0.9702	<3,316,000>	<3,217,000>
15-Jul-X3	5.90%	0.9154	<106,175,000>	<97,193,000>
			USD fair value	<100,410,000>
			EUR–USD spot	1.2200
			EUR fair value	<82,303,000>

The fair value of the hedged item on 31 December 20X2 was calculated as follows:

Hedged item fair valuation on 31-Dec-X2				
Cash flow date	Implied USD Libor	Discount factor	Expected cash flow	Present value
15-Jul-X3	5.90%	0.9689	<103,316,000>	<100,103,000>
			USD fair value	<100,103,000>
			EUR–USD spot	1.1500
			EUR fair value	<87,046,000>

The fair value of the hedged item on 15 July 20X3 was calculated as follows:

Hedged item fair valuation on 15-Jul-X3				
Cash flow date	Implied USD Libor	Discount factor	Expected cash flow	Present value
15-Jul-X3	—	1.0000	<100,000,000>	<100,000,000>
			USD fair value	<100,000,000>
			EUR–USD spot	1.1100
			EUR fair value	<90,909,000>

Fair Valuations of the Hedging Instrument   The fair value of the hedging instrument on 15 July 20X0 was calculated as follows:

Hedging instrument fair valuation on 15-Jul-X0					
Cash flow date	Implied interest rate	Discount factor	Spread	Expected cash flow	Present value
Cash flows of USD leg:					
31-Jul-X1	5.40%	0.9481		6,175,000	5,855,000
31-Jul-X2	5.60%	0.8972		6,175,000	5,540,000
31-Jul-X3	5.78%	0.8475		106,175,000	89,983,000
			Total USD		**101,378,000**
			Total EUR (1.2500)		**81,102,000**
Cash flows of EUR leg:					
31-Jul-X1	4.50%	0.9564	0.49%	<4,047,000>	<3,871,000>
31-Jul-X2	4.71%	0.9128	0.49%	<4,218,000>	<3,850,000>
31-Jul-X3	4.89%	0.8697	0.49%	<84,364,000>	<73,371,000>
			Total EUR		**<81,092,000>**
			Fair value (before adjustments)		**10,000**
			Adjustments (CVA/DVA and basis)		**<10,000>**
			Fair value (including adjustments)		**-0-**

It can be observed that the valuations of the USD leg of the CCS and of the hedged item were of opposite sign. The expected cash flow of the EUR leg was calculated as EUR 80 mn × (Euribor 12M + 0.49%) × Days/360, where Days was the number of days in the interest period.

The fair value of the hedging instrument on 31 December 20X0 was calculated as follows:

Hedging instrument fair valuation on 31-Dec-X0					
Cash flow date	Implied interest rate	Discount factor	Spread	Expected cash flow	Present value
Cash flows of USD leg:					
31-Jul-X1	5.50%	0.9709		3,316,000	3,220,000
31-Jul-X2	5.75%	0.9174		6,175,000	5,665,000
31-Jul-X3	5.85%	0.8660		106,175,000	91,948,000
			Total USD		**100,833,000**
			Total EUR (1.2800)		**78,776,000**
Cash flows of EUR leg:					
31-Jul-X1	4.60%	0.9756	0.49%	<2,173,000>	<2,120,000>
31-Jul-X2	4.80%	0.9303	0.49%	<4,291,000>	<3,992,000>
31-Jul-X3	4.95%	0.8858	0.49%	<84,412,000>	<74,772,000>
			Total EUR		**<80,884,000>**
			Fair value (before adjustments)		**<2,108,000>**
			Adjustments (CVA/DVA and basis)		**63,000>**
			Fair value (including adjustments)		**<2,045,000>**

The fair value of the hedging instrument on 31 December 20X1 was calculated as follows:

Hedging instrument fair valuation on 31-Dec-X1					
Cash flow date	Implied interest rate	Discount factor	Spread	Expected cash flow	Present value
Cash flows of USD leg:					
31-Jul-X2	5.65%	0.9702		3,316,000	3,217,000
31-Jul-X3	5.90%	0.9154		106,175,000	97,193,000
			Total USD		100,410,000
			Total EUR (1.2200)		82,303,000
Cash flows of EUR leg:					
31-Jul-X2	4.80%	0.9745	0.49%	<2,282,000>	<2,224,000>
31-Jul-X3	4.95%	0.9279	0.49%	<84,412,000>	<78,326,000>
			Total EUR		<80,550,000>
			Fair value (before adjustments)		1,753,000
			Adjustments (CVA/DVA and basis)		<44,000>
			Fair value (including adjustments)		1,709,000

The fair value of the hedging instrument on 31 December 20X2 was calculated as follows:

Hedging instrument fair valuation on 31-Dec-X2					
Cash flow date	Implied interest rate	Discount factor	Spread	Expected cash flow	Present value
Cash flows of USD leg:					
31-Jul-X3	5.90%	0.9689		103,316,000	100,103,000
			Total USD		100,103,000
			Total EUR (1.1500)		87,046,000
Cash flows of EUR leg:					
31-Jul-X3	4.95%	0.9738	0.49%	<82,369,000>	<80,211,000>
			Total EUR		<80,211,000>
			Fair value (before adjustments)		6,835,000
			Adjustments (CVA/DVA and basis)		<68,000>
			Fair value (including adjustments)		6,767,000

The fair value of the hedging instrument on 15 July 20X3 was calculated as follows:

Hedging instrument fair valuation on 15-Jul-X3					
Cash flow date	Implied interest rate	Discount factor	Spread	Expected cash flow	Present value
Cash flows of USD leg:					
31-Jul-X3	—	1.0000		100,000,000	100,000,000
			Total USD		**100,000,000**
			Total EUR (1.1100)		**90,909,000**
Cash flows of EUR leg:					
31-Jul-X3	—	1.0000		<80,000,000>	<80,000,000>
			Total EUR		**<80,000,000>**
		Fair value (before adjustments)			**10,909,000**
		Adjustments (CVA/DVA and basis)			**-0-**
		Fair value (including adjustments)			**10,909,000**

Effective and Ineffective Amounts   The following table summarises the period changes in the fair value of the hedged item and the hedging instrument:

	Hedging instrument		Hedged item	
	Fair value	Period change	Fair value	Period change
15-Jul-X0	-0-	—	<81,102,000>	—
31-Dec-X0	<2,045,000>	<2,045,000>	<78,776,000>	2,326,000
31-Dec-X1	1,709,000	3,754,000	<82,303,000>	<3,527,000>
31-Dec-X2	6,767,000	5,058,000	<87,046 ,000>	<4,743,000>
15-Jul-X3	10,909,000	4,142,000	<90,909,000>	<3,863,000>

On each valuation date, the effective part was the lower of the two period fair value changes (taking into account their opposing signs) and the ineffective part was any remainder.

	Hedging instrument			Hedged item		
	Period change	Effective part	Ineffective part	Period change	Effective part	Ineffective part
31-Dec-X0	<2,045,000>	<2,045,000>	-0-	2,326,000	2,045,000	281,000
31-Dec-X1	3,754,000	3,527,000	227,000	<3,527,000>	<3,527,000>	-0-
31-Dec-X2	5,058,000	4,743,000	315,000	<4,743,000>	<4,743,000>	-0-
15-Jul-X3	4,142,000	3,863,000	279,000	<3,863,000>	<3,863,000>	-0-

Accruals and Payable/Receivable Amounts   The following table summarises the accruals and payables related to the bond:

	Average EUR–USD	Spot EUR–USD	EUR coupon accrual *(1)*	EUR payable amount *(2)*	Retranslation payable *(3)*
31-Dec-X0	1.2630	1.2800	<2,264,000>	<2,234,000>	
15-Jul-X1	1.2680	1.2400	<2,615,000>	<2,674,000>	<72,000>
31-Dec-X1	1.2320	1.2200	<2,321,000>	<2,343,000>	
15-Jul-X2	1.2170	1.2100	<2,725,000>	<2,740,000>	<19,000>
31-Dec-X2	1.1680	1.1500	<2,448,000>	<2,486,000>	
15-Jul-X3	1.1240	1.1000	<2,950,000>	<3,015,000>	<113,000>

Notes:

  (1) USD 100 mn × 6.09% × (Days/360)/Average EUR–USD, where Days was the number of calendar days in the accrual period (i.e., 169 for accrual periods ending on 31 December and 196 for accrual periods ending on 15 July)

  (2) USD 100 mn × 6.09% × (Days/360)/Spot EUR–USD

  (3) USD payable amount × (1/previous Spot EUR–USD – 1/current Spot EUR–USD), where USD payable amount was the USD 100 mn × 6.09% × Days/360 corresponding to the previous accrual period

There was no need to retranslate into EUR the USD carrying amount of the bond, as it was already included in the fair valuation of the hedged item. Otherwise a double counting would occur.

The accruals and payables related to the USD leg of the CCS were identical to those of the bond, but with opposite sign. The following table summarises the accruals and payables related to the EUR leg of the CCS:

CCS EUR leg accruals and payables				
	Euribor 12M	Days	EUR leg accrual (*)	Payable amount
31-Dec-X0	4.50%	169	1,874,000	1,874,000
15-Jul-X1	4.50%	196	2,173,000	2,173,000
31-Dec-X1	4.75%	169	1,968,000	1,968,000
15-Jul-X2	4.75%	196	2,282,000	2,282,000
31-Dec-X2	4.95%	169	2,043,000	2,043,000
15-Jul-X3	4.95%	196	2,369,000	2,369,000

(*) 100 mn × (Euribor 12M + 0.49%) × Days/360, where Days was the number of calendar days in the accruing period

Note on Fair Value Adjustments and Translation   The bond was recognised at amortised cost. As the bond was issued at par, the initial effective interest rate was 6.09%. ABC chose to start amortising fair value adjustments when hedge accounting ceased, avoiding having to recalculate the effective interest rate each time a fair value adjustment was performed. Accordingly, the bond's effective interest rate remained 6.09% during the hedging relationship term. See comments in Section 8.1.6.

Regarding the translation of the carrying amount and the fair value adjustments, the fair valuations of the hedged item for the risk being hedged were performed in EUR. Therefore, these fair valuations already included the translation into EUR of both the amortised cost amount and the fair value adjustments.

8.2.6 Accounting Entries

The required journal entries were as follows.

1) Journal entries on 15 July 20X0
The bond was issued.

Cash (Asset)	80,000,000	
Financial debt (Liability)		80,000,000

No entries were required to record the CCS as its initial fair value was zero.
2) Journal entries on 31 December 20X0
The accrued interest of the bond was EUR <2,264,000>. The payable related to this accrued interest was EUR <2,234,000>.

Interest expense (Profit or loss)	2,264,000	
Interest payable (Liability)		2,234,000
Other financial income (Profit or loss)		30,000

The change in fair value of the hedged item for the risk being hedged produced a EUR 2,326,000 gain, of which EUR 2,045,000 was deemed to be effective and EUR 281,000 ineffective.

Financial debt (Liability)	2,326,000	
Interest income (Profit or loss)		2,045,000
Other financial income (Profit or loss)		281,000

The accrual of the USD leg of the CCS was EUR 2,264,000. The receivable related to this accrued interest was EUR 2,234,000.

Interest receivable (Asset)	2,234,000	
Other financial expenses (Profit or loss)	30,000	
Interest income (Profit or loss)		2,264,000

The accrual of the EUR leg of the CCS was EUR <1,874,000>.

Interest expense (Profit or loss)	1,874,000	
Interest payable (Liability)		1,874,000

The change in fair value of the CCS produced a EUR 2,045,000 loss, fully deemed to be effective.

Interest expense (Profit or loss)	2,045,000	
Derivative contract (Liability)		2,045,000

3) Journal entries on 15 July 20X1

The accrued interest of the bond was EUR <2,615,000>. The payable related to this accrued interest was EUR <2,674,000>.

Interest expense (Profit or loss)	2,615,000	
Other financial expenses (Profit or loss)	59,000	
Interest payable (Liability)		2,674,000

The interest payable corresponding to the bond's previous accrued interest was retranslated, producing a EUR 72,000 loss.

Other financial expenses (Profit or loss)	72,000	
Interest payable (Liability)		72,000

The bond coupon was paid using the amount received under the USD leg of the CCS.

Interest payable (Liability)	4,980,000	
Cash (Asset)		4,980,000

The accrued interest of the USD leg was EUR 2,615,000. The receivable related to this accrued interest was EUR 2,674,000.

Interest receivable (Asset)	2,674,000	
Interest income (Profit or loss)		2,615,000
Other financial income (Profit or loss)		59,000

The interest receivable corresponding to the USD leg's previous accrued interest was retranslated, producing a EUR 72,000 gain.

Interest receivable (Asset)	72,000	
Other financial income (Profit or loss)		72,000

The interest receivable corresponding to the USD leg was received.

Cash (Asset)	4,980,000	
Interest receivable (Asset)		4,980,000

The accrual of the EUR leg was EUR <2,173,000>.

Interest expense (Profit or loss)	2,173,000	
Interest payable (Liability)		2,173,000

The interest payable corresponding to the EUR leg was paid.

Interest payable (Liability)	4,047,000	
Cash (Asset)		4,047,000

4) Journal entries on 31 December 20X1

The accrued interest of the bond was EUR <2,321,000>. The payable related to this accrued interest was EUR <2,343,000>.

Interest expense (Profit or loss)	2,321,000	
Other financial expenses (Profit or loss)	22,000	
Interest payable (Liability)		2,343,000

The change in fair value of the hedged item for the risk being hedged produced a EUR 3,527,000 loss, fully deemed to be effective.

Interest expense (Profit or loss)	3,527,000	
Financial debt (Liability)		3,527,000

The accrual of the USD leg of the CCS was EUR 2,321,000. The receivable related to this accrued interest was EUR 2,343,000.

Interest receivable (Asset)	2,343,000	
Interest income (Profit or loss)		2,321,000
Other financial income (Profit or loss)		22,000

The accrual of the EUR leg of the CCS was EUR <1,968,000>.

Interest expense (Profit or loss)	1,968,000	
Interest payable (Liability)		1,968,000

The change in fair value of the CCS produced a EUR 3,754,000 gain, of which EUR 3,527,000 was deemed to be effective and EUR 227,000 ineffective.

Derivative contract (Asset)	3,754,000	
Interest income (Profit or loss)		3,527,000
Other financial income (Profit or loss)		227,000

5) Journal entries on 15 July 20X2
The accrued interest of the bond was EUR <2,725,000>. The payable related to this accrued interest was EUR <2,740,000>.

Interest expense (Profit or loss)	2,725,000	
Other financial expenses (Profit or loss)	15,000	
Interest payable (Liability)		2,740,000

The interest payable corresponding to the bond's previous accrued interest was retranslated, producing a EUR 19,000 loss.

Other financial expenses (Profit or loss)	19,000	
Interest payable (Liability)		19,000

The bond coupon was paid using the USD amounts received under the USD leg of the CCS.

Interest payable (Liability)	5,102,000	
Cash (Asset)		5,102,000

The accrued interest of the USD leg was EUR 2,725,000. The receivable related to this accrued interest was EUR 2,740,000.

Interest receivable (Asset)	2,740,000	
Interest income (Profit or loss)		2,725,000
Other financial income (Profit or loss)		15,000

The interest receivable corresponding to the USD leg's previous accrued interest was retranslated, producing a EUR 19,000 gain.

Interest receivable (Asset)	19,000	
Other financial income (Profit or loss)		19,000

The interest receivable corresponding to the USD leg was received.

Cash (Asset)	5,102,000	
Interest receivable (Asset)		5,102,000

The accrual of the EUR leg was EUR <2,282,000>.

Interest expense (Profit or loss)	2,282,000	
Interest payable (Liability)		2,282,000

The interest payable corresponding to the EUR leg was paid.

Interest payable (Liability)	4,250,000	
Cash (Asset)		4,250,000

6) Journal entries on 31 December 20X2

The accrued interest of the bond was EUR <2,448,000>. The payable related to this accrued interest was EUR <2,486,000>.

Interest expense (Profit or loss)	2,448,000	
Other financial expenses (Profit or loss)	38,000	
Interest payable (Liability)		2,486,000

The change in fair value of the hedged item for the risk being hedged produced a EUR 4,743,000 loss, fully deemed to be effective.

Interest expense (Profit or loss)	4,743,000	
Financial debt (Liability)		4,743,000

The accrual of the USD leg of the CCS was EUR 2,448,000. The receivable related to this accrued interest was EUR 2,486,000.

Interest receivable (Asset)	2,486,000	
Interest income (Profit or loss)		2,448,000
Other financial income (Profit or loss)		38,000

The accrual of the EUR leg was EUR <2,043,000>.

Interest expense (Profit or loss)	2,043,000	
Interest payable (Liability)		2,043,000

The change in fair value of the CCS produced a EUR 5,058,000 gain, of which EUR 4,743,000 was deemed to be effective and EUR 315,000 ineffective.

Derivative contract (Asset)	5,058,000	
Interest income (Profit or loss)		4,743,000
Other financial income (Profit or loss)		315,000

7) Journal entries on 15 July 20X3

The accrued interest of the bond was EUR <2,950,000>. The payable related to this accrued interest was EUR <3,015,000>.

Interest expense (Profit or loss)	2,950,000	
Other financial expenses (Profit or loss)	65,000	
Interest payable (Liability)		3,015,000

The interest payable corresponding to the bond's previous accrued interest was retranslated, producing a EUR 113,000 loss.

Other financial expenses (Profit or loss)	113,000	
Interest payable (Liability)		113,000

The bond coupon and principal were paid/repaid using the amounts received under the USD leg of the CCS. The bond principal represented EUR 90,909,000 (= USD 100 mn/1.1000).

Interest payable (Liability)	5,614,000	
Financial debt (Liability)	90,909,000	
Cash (Asset)		96,523,000

The accrued interest of the USD leg was EUR 2,950,000. The receivable related to this accrued interest was EUR 3,015,000.

Interest receivable (Asset)	3,015,000	
Interest income (Profit or loss)		2,950,000
Other financial income (Profit or loss)		65,000

The interest receivable corresponding to the USD leg's previous accrued interest was retranslated, producing a EUR 113,000 gain.

Interest receivable (Asset)	113,000	
Other financial income (Profit or loss)		113,000

The interest receivable corresponding to the USD leg was received.

Cash (Asset)	5,614,000	
Interest receivable (Asset)		5,614,000

The accrual of the EUR leg was EUR <2,369,000>.

Interest expense (Profit or loss)	2,369,000	
Interest payable (Liability)		2,369,000

The interest payable corresponding to the EUR leg was paid.

Interest payable (Liability)	4,412,000	
Cash (Asset)		4,412,000

The change in fair value of the hedged item for the risk being hedged produced a EUR 3,863,000 loss, fully deemed to be effective.

Interest expense (Profit or loss)	3,863,000	
Financial debt (Liability)		3,863,000

The change in fair value of the CCS produced a EUR 4,142,000 gain, of which EUR 3,863,000 was deemed to be effective and EUR 279,000 ineffective.

Derivative contract (Asset)	4,142,000	
Interest income (Profit or loss)		3,863,000
Other financial income (Profit or loss)		279,000

The CCS notionals were exchanged. ABC paid EUR 80 million and received USD 100 million (worth EUR 90,909,000). The difference was worth EUR 10,909,000 (= 90,909,000 – 80 mn).

Cash (Asset)	10,909,000	
Derivative contract (Asset)		10,909,000

The remaining EUR 1,102,000 fair value adjustments related to the bond were amortised to profit or loss.

Other financial expenses (Profit or loss)	1,102,000
Financial debt (Liability)	1,102,000

The following table gives a summary of the accounting entries:

	Cash	Interest receivable	Derivative contract	Financial debt	Interest payable	Profit or loss
15-Jul-X0						
Bond issuance	80,000,000			80,000,000		
31-Dec-X0						
Bond accrued coupon					2,234,000	<2,234,000>
Hedged item revaluation				<2,326,000>		2,326,000
CCS accrual USD leg		2,234,000				2,234,000
CCS accrual EUR leg					1,874,000	<1,874,000>
CCS revaluation			<2,045,000>			<2,045,000>
15-Jul-X1						
Bond accrued coupon					2,674,000	<2,674,000>
Bond accrual retranslation					72,000	<72,000>
Bond coupon payment	<4,980,000>				<4,980,000>	
CCS accrual USD leg		2,674,000				2,674,000
CCS interest receivable retranslation		72,000				72,000
CCS USD leg receipt	4,980,000	<4,980,000>				
CCS accrual EUR leg					2,173,000	<2,173,000>
CCS EUR leg payment	<4,047,000>				<4,047,000>	
31-Dec-X1						
Bond accrued coupon					2,343,000	<2,343,000>
Hedged item revaluation				3,527,000		<3,527,000>
CCS accrual USD leg		2,343,000				2,343,000
CCS accrual EUR leg					1,968,000	<1,968,000>
CCS revaluation			3,754,000			3,754,000

(continued overleaf)

15-Jul-X2

Bond accrued coupon					2,740,000	<2,740,000>
Bond accrual retranslation					19,000	<19,000>
Bond coupon payment	<5,102,000>				<5,102,000>	
CCS accrual USD leg		2,740,000				2,740,000
CCS interest receivable retranslation		19,000				19,000
CCS USD leg receipt	5,102,000	<5,102,000>				
CCS accrual EUR leg					2,282,000	<2,282,000>
CCS EUR leg payment	<4,250,000>				<4,250,000>	

31-Dec-X2

Bond accrued coupon					2,486,000	<2,486,000>
Hedged item revaluation				4,743,000		<4,743,000>
CCS accrual USD leg		2,486,000				2,486,000
CCS accrual EUR leg					2,043,000	<2,043,000>
CCS revaluation			5,058,000			5,058,000

15-Jul-X3

Bond accrued coupon					3,015,000	<3,015,000>
Bond accrual retranslation					113,000	<113,000>
Bond coupon payment	<96,523,000>			<90,909,000>	<5,614,000>	
CCS accrual USD leg		3,015,000				3,015,000
CCS interest receivable retranslation		113,000				113,000
CCS USD leg receipt	5,614,000	<5,614,000>				
CCS accrual EUR leg					2,369,000	<2,369,000>
CCS EUR leg payment	<4,412,000>				<4,412,000>	
Hedged item revaluation				3,863,000		<3,863,000>
CCS revaluation			4,142,000			4,142,000
CCS exchange	10,909,000		<10,909,000>			
Fair value amortisation				1,102,000		<1,102,000>
	<12,709,000>	-0-	-0-	-0-	-0-	<12,709,000>

8.2.7 Concluding Remarks

ABC's objective when entering into the combination of the bond and the CCS was to incur an expense representing Euribor 12-month plus 0.49%.

During the first year of the term of the bond (and of the hedging relationship) the overall impact of the strategy on profit or loss was a EUR 3,766,000 expense. The target expense during the first year was EUR 4,047,000 (= 80 mn × (4.50% + 0.49%) × 365/360), corresponding to a 4.50% Euribor 12-month rate. The difference was due to the EUR 281,000 ineffective part of the change in fair value of the hedged item. Nonetheless, the net cash outflow was exactly EUR 4,047,000.

During the second year the overall impact of the strategy on profit or loss was a EUR 4,023,000 expense. The target expense during the second year was EUR 4,250,000 (= 80 mn × (4.75% + 0.49%) × 365/360), corresponding to a 4.75% Euribor 12-month rate. The difference was due to the EUR 227,000 ineffective part of the change in fair value of the CCS. However, the net cash outflow was exactly EUR 4,250,000.

During the third year the overall impact of the strategy on profit or loss was a EUR 4,920,000 expense. The target expense during the third year was EUR 4,412,000 (= 80 mn × (4.95% + 0.49%) × 365/360), corresponding to a 4.95% Euribor 12-month rate. The EUR 508,000 (= 1,102,000 − 594,000) difference was due to the EUR 594,000 ineffective part of the change in fair value of the CCS and the EUR 1,102,000 amortisation of the fair value. Again, the net cash outflow was exactly EUR 4,412,000.

The sum of the interest expense over the three years equalled the sum of the three expense targets. Therefore over the three years, both from a cash and expense perspective, ABC achieved its objective of funding itself at Euribor 12-month plus 0.49%.

Finally, note that in our case the CCS basis was included in the hedging relationship. The full fair value movement of the CCS, including the basis component, was taken into account in the calculation of the effective part of the hedge. As a consequence, a volatile behaviour of the basis could have created substantial ineffectiveness. Similarly to the treatment of forward components of forward contracts, when the basis component of a CCS is excluded from a hedging relationship, IFRS 9 allows the choice between:

- recognising in profit or loss the change in the basis element fair value; and
- recognising changes in the basis element fair value in OCI to the extent that it relates to the hedged item, while amortising the initial basis element in profit or loss.

8.3 CASE STUDY: HEDGING A FLOATING RATE FOREIGN CURRENCY LIABILITY WITH A RECEIVE-FLOATING PAY-FIXED CROSS-CURRENCY SWAP

This case study illustrates the accounting treatment of a cash flow hedge of a floating rate foreign currency liability with a pay-fixed receive-floating CCS.

8.3.1 Background Information

On 15 July 20X0, ABC issued a USD-denominated floating rate bond. ABC's functional currency was the EUR. The bond had the following main terms:

Bond terms	
Issue date	15 July 20X0
Maturity	3 years (15 July 20X3)
Notional	USD 100 million
Coupon	USD Libor 12M + 0.50% annually, actual/360 basis
USD Libor fixing	Libor is fixed 2 days prior to the beginning of each annual interest period

Since ABC's objective was to raise EUR fixed funding, on the issue date ABC entered into a CCS. Through the CCS, the entity agreed to receive a floating rate equal to the bond coupon and pay a EUR fixed amount. The CCS had the following terms:

Cross-currency swap terms	
Trade date	15 July 20X0
Start date	15 July 20X0
Counterparties	ABC and XYZ Bank
Maturity	3 years (15 July 20X3)
USD nominal	USD 100 million
EUR nominal	EUR 80 million
Initial exchange	On start date, ABC receives the EUR nominal and pays the USD nominal
ABC pays	5.19% annually, actual/360 basis, on the EUR nominal
ABC receives	USD Libor 12M + 0.50 bps annually, actual/360 basis. Libor is fixed 2 days prior to the beginning of each annual interest period
Final exchange	On maturity date, ABC receives the USD nominal and pays the EUR nominal

The mechanics of the CCS are described next. It can be seen that through the combination of the USD bond and the CCS, ABC synthetically obtained a EUR fixed liability.

On the issue date at the start of the CCS, there was an initial exchange of nominal amounts through the CCS: ABC delivered the USD 100 million debt issuance proceeds and received EUR 80 million. The resulting EUR–USD exchange rate was 1.2500. The combination of the bond and CCS had the same effect as if ABC had issued a EUR-denominated bond, as shown in Figure 8.7.

An exchange of interest payments took place annually. ABC received USD Libor-linked interest on the USD nominal and paid 5.19% interest on the EUR nominal. ABC used the USD Libor cash flows it received under the CCS to pay the bond interest. Figure 8.8 shows the strategy's intermediate cash flows.

On maturity of the CCS and the debt, ABC re-exchanged the CCS nominals, using the USD 100 million it received through the CCS to redeem the bond issue, and delivering EUR

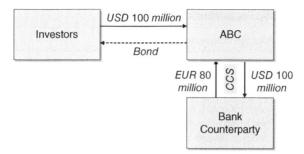

FIGURE 8.7   Bond and CCS combination – initial cash flows.

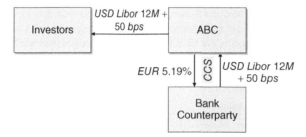

FIGURE 8.8   Bond and CCS combination – intermediate cash flows.

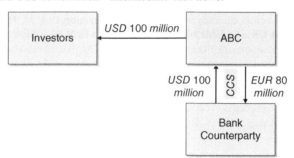

FIGURE 8.9   Bond and CCS combination – final cash flows.

80 million to the CCS counterparty. Note that this final exchange was made at exactly the same rate used in the initial exchange (1.2500). Figure 8.9 shows the strategy's cash flows at maturity.

Because the aim of the CCS was to eliminate the EUR variability of the cash flows stemming from the floating rate bond, ABC designated the CCS as the hedging instrument in a cash flow hedge. The exposures being hedged were the bond's interest rate and exchange rate risks. As explained in Section 8.1.2, the bond's credit risk was excluded from the hedging relationship.

ABC used a hypothetical derivative when assessing effectiveness and calculating effective and ineffective amounts, a tool that could be applied for cash flow hedges. Therefore, ABC did not need to fair value the hedged item, fair valuing instead a hypothetical derivative. In my view, in our case it was simpler to fair value the hedged item than to fair value the hypothetical derivative, but I have used the hypothetical derivative approach because it is the approach commonly used by the accounting community for cash flow hedges.

8.3.2 Hedging Relationship Documentation

ABC documented the hedging relationship as follows:

Hedging relationship documentation

Risk management objective and strategy for undertaking the hedge	The objective of the hedge is to eliminate variability of the cash flows stemming from the floating rate coupon payments related to a USD-denominated debt instrument issued by the entity, against unfavourable movements in the USD Libor 12-month rate and the EUR–USD exchange rate.
	This hedging objective is consistent with the group's overall interest rate risk management strategy of transforming with cross-currency swaps all new issued foreign-denominated debt into EUR (either into floating or fixed rate), and thereafter managing the exposure to interest rate risk through the proportion of fixed and floating rate net debt in its total debt portfolio.
	Exchange rate and interest rate risk. The designated risk being hedged is the risk of changes in the EUR fair value of the hedged item attributable to changes in the EUR–USD exchange rate and USD Libor interest rates.
	Fair value changes attributable to credit or other risks are not hedged in this relationship
Type of hedge	Cash flow hedge
Hedged item	The coupons and principal of the 3-year USD floating rate bond with reference number 678902. The main terms of the bond are a USD 100 million principal, an annual coupon of USD Libor plus 0.50% calculated on the principal
Hedging instrument	The cross-currency swap with reference number 014577. The main terms of the CCS are a USD 100 million nominal, a EUR 80 million nominal, a 3-year maturity, a USD annual interest of USD Libor 12-month rate plus 0.50% on the USD nominal to be received by the entity and a EUR annual interest of 5.19% on the EUR nominal to be paid by the entity. The counterparty to the CCS is XYZ Bank and the credit risk associated with this counterparty is considered to be very low
Hedge effectiveness assessment	See below

8.3.3 Hedge Effectiveness Assessment

Hedge effectiveness will be assessed by comparing changes in the fair value of the hedging instrument to changes in the fair value of a hypothetical derivative. The terms of the hypothetical derivative are such that its fair value changes exactly offset the changes in fair value of the hedged item for the risk being hedged. The hypothetical derivative is a theoretical cross-currency swap with no counterparty credit risk and with zero initial fair value, whose main terms are as follows:

Hypothetical derivative terms	
Trade date	15 July 20X0
Start date	15 July 20X0
Counterparties	ABC and credit risk-free counterparty
Maturity	3 years (15 July 20X3)
USD nominal	USD 100 million

EUR nominal	EUR 80 million
Initial exchange	On start date, ABC receives the EUR nominal and pays the USD nominal
ABC pays	5.20% annually, actual/360 basis, on the EUR nominal
ABC receives	USD Libor 12M + 0.50 bps annually, actual/360 basis, on the USD nominal. Libor is fixed 2 days prior to the beginning of each annual interest period
Final exchange	On maturity date, ABC receives the USD nominal and pays the EUR nominal

The EUR leg fixed rate of the hypothetical derivative is higher than that of the hedging instrument due to the absence of CVA in the former.

Changes in the fair value of the hedging instrument will be recognised as follows:

- The effective part of the gain or loss on the hedging instrument will be recognised in the cash flow hedge reserve of OCI in equity, after taking into account the bond's retranslation gains/losses. The accumulated amount in equity will be reclassified to profit or loss in the same period during which the hedged expected future cash flow affects profit or loss, adjusting interest expense.
- The ineffective part of the gain or loss on the hedging instrument will be recognised immediately in profit or loss.

Hedge effectiveness will be assessed prospectively at hedging relationship inception, on an ongoing basis at least upon each reporting date and upon occurrence of a significant change in the circumstances affecting the hedge effectiveness requirements.

The hedging relationship will qualify for hedge accounting only if all the following criteria are met:

1) The hedging relationship consists only of eligible hedge items and hedging instruments. The hedge item is eligible as it is a group of highly expected forecast cash flows that exposes the entity to fair value risk, affects profit or loss and is reliably measurable. The hedging instrument is eligible as it is a derivative that does not result in a net written option.
2) At hedge inception there is a formal designation and documentation of the hedging relationship and the entity's risk management objective and strategy for undertaking the hedge.
3) The hedging relationship is considered effective.

The hedging relationship will be considered effective if the following three requirements are met:

1) There is an economic relationship between the hedged item and the hedging instrument.
2) The effect of credit risk does not dominate the value changes that result from that economic relationship.
3) The hedge ratio of the hedging relationship is the same as that resulting from the quantity of hedged item that the entity actually hedges and the quantity of the hedging instrument that the entity actually uses to hedge that quantity of hedged item. The hedge ratio should not be intentionally weighted to create ineffectiveness.

Whether there is an economic relationship between the hedged item and the hedging instrument will be assessed on a qualitative basis by comparing the critical terms (notional, interest periods, underlying and fixed rates) of the hypothetical derivative and the hedging instrument. The assessment will be complemented by a quantitative assessment using the scenario analysis method for one scenario in which USD Libor and Euribor interest rates will be shifted upwards by 2%, the EUR–USD spot rate increased by 10%, and the changes in fair value of the hypothetical derivative and the hedging instrument compared.

8.3.4 Hedge Effectiveness Assessment Performed at the Start of the Hedging Relationship

The hedging relationship was considered effective as the following three requirements were met:

1) There was an economic relationship between the hedged item and the hedging instrument. Based on the qualitative assessment performed supported by a quantitative analysis, the entity concluded that the change in fair value of the hedged item was expected to be substantially offset by the change in fair value of the hedging instrument, corroborating that both elements had values that would generally move in opposite directions.
2) The effect of credit risk did not dominate the value changes resulting from that economic relationship as the credit ratings of both the entity and XYZ Bank were considered sufficiently strong.
3) The hedge ratio of the hedging relationship was the same as that resulting from the quantity of hedged item that the entity actually hedged and the quantity of the hedging instrument that the entity actually used to hedge that quantity of hedged item. The hedge ratio was not intentionally weighted to create ineffectiveness.

Due to the fact that the terms of the hedging instrument and those of the expected cash flow closely matched and the low credit risk exposure to the counterparty of the cross-currency swap contract, it was concluded that the hedging instrument and the hedged item had values that would generally move in opposite directions. This conclusion was supported by a quantitative assessment, which consisted of one scenario analysis performed as follows. A parallel shift of +2% in the USD Libor and Euribor interest rates and +10% in the EUR–USD spot rate, occurring on the assessment date, was simulated. The fair values of the hedging instrument and the hypothetical derivatives were calculated and compared to their initial fair values. As shown in the table below, the high degree of offset implied that the change in fair value of the hedged item was expected to be largely offset by the change in fair value of the hedging instrument, corroborating that both elements had values that would generally move in opposite directions.

Scenario analysis assessment		
	Hedging instrument	**Hypothetical derivative**
Initial fair value	-0-	-0-
Final fair value	<2,999,000>	<3,097,000>
Cumulative fair value change	<2,999,000>	<3,097,000>
	Degree of offset	**96.8%**

The following potential sources of ineffectiveness were identified:

▪ a substantial deterioration in credit risk of either the entity or the counterparty to the hedging instrument; and
▪ a change in the timing or amounts of the hedged highly expected cash flows.

The hedge ratio was set at 1:1.

ABC also performed assessments on each reporting date, yielding the same conclusions. These assessments have been omitted to avoid unnecessary repetition.

8.3.5 Fair Valuations, Effective/Ineffective Amounts and Cash Flow Calculations

Fair Valuations of the Hedging Instrument   The fair value of the hedging instrument on 15 July 20X0 was calculated as follows:

Cash flow date	Implied interest rate	Discount factor	Spread/fixed rate	Expected cash flow	Present value
Hedging instrument fair valuation on 15-Jul-X0					
Cash flows of USD leg:					
31-Jul-X1	5.40%	0.9481	0.50%	5,982,000	5,672,000
31-Jul-X2	5.60%	0.8972	0.50%	6,185,000	5,549,000
31-Jul-X3	5.78%	0.8475	0.50%	106,367,000	90,146,000
			Total USD		**101,367,000**
			Total EUR (1.2500)		**81,094,000**
Cash flows of EUR leg:					
31-Jul-X1	4.50%	0.9564	5.19%	<4,210,000>	<4,026,000>
31-Jul-X2	4.71%	0.9128	5.19%	<4,210,000>	<3,843,000>
31-Jul-X3	4.89%	0.8697	5.19%	<84,210,000>	<73,237,000>
			Total EUR		**<81,106,000>**
			Fair value (before adjustments)		**<12,000>**
			Adjustments (CVA/DVA and basis)		**12,000**
			Fair value (including adjustments)		**-0-**

The expected cash flow of the EUR leg was calculated as EUR 80 mn × 5.19% × Days/360, where Days was the number of days in the interest period, and in respect of the 31 July 20X3 cash flow, the EUR 80 million nominal was also added.

The fair value of the hedging instrument on 31 December 20X0 was calculated as follows:

Cash flow date	Implied interest rate	Discount factor	Spread/ fixed rate	Expected cash flow	Present value
Hedging instrument fair valuation on 31-Dec-X0					
Cash flows of USD leg:					
31-Jul-X1	5.50%	0.9709	0.50%	3,212,000	3,119,000
31-Jul-X2	5.75%	0.9174	0.50%	6,337,000	5,814,000
31-Jul-X3	5.85%	0.8660	0.50%	106,438,000	92,175,000
			Total USD		**101,108,000**
			Total EUR (1.2800)		**78,991,000**

(continued overleaf)

Cash flows of EUR leg:

31-Jul-X1	4.60%	0.9756	5.19%	<2,261,000>	<2,206,000>
31-Jul-X2	4.80%	0.9303	5.19%	<4,210,000>	<3,917,000>
31-Jul-X3	4.95%	0.8858	5.19%	<84,210,000>	<74,593,000>
			Total EUR		<80,716,000>
			Fair value (before adjustments)		<1,725,000>
			Adjustments (CVA/DVA and basis)		52,000>
			Fair value (including adjustments)		<1,673,000>

The fair value of the hedging instrument on 31 December 20X1 was calculated as follows:

	Hedging instrument fair valuation on 31-Dec-X1				
Cash flow date	Implied interest rate	Discount factor	Spread/ fixed rate	Expected cash flow	Present value
Cash flows of USD leg:					
31-Jul-X2	5.65%	0.9702	0.50%	3,294,000	3,196,000
31-Jul-X3	5.90%	0.9154	0.50%	106,489,000	97,480,000
			Total USD		**100,676,000**
			Total EUR (1.2200)		**82,521,000**
Cash flows of EUR leg:					
31-Jul-X2	4.80%	0.9745	5.19%	<2,261,000>	<2,203,000>
31-Jul-X3	4.95%	0.9279	5.19%	<84,210,000>	<78,138,000>
			Total EUR		<80,341,000>
			Fair value (before adjustments)		2,180,000
			Adjustments (CVA/DVA and basis)		<55,000>
			Fair value (including adjustments)		2,125,000

The fair value of the hedging instrument on 31 December 20X2 was calculated as follows:

	Hedging instrument fair valuation on 31-Dec-X2				
Cash flow date	Implied interest rate	Discount factor	Spread/ fixed rate	Expected cash flow	Present value
Cash flows of USD leg:					
31-Jul-X3	5.90%	0.9689	0.50%	103,348,000	100,134,000
			Total USD		**100,134,000**
			Total EUR (1.1500)		**87,073,000**
Cash flows of EUR leg:					
31-Jul-X3	4.95%	0.9738	5.19%	<82,261,000>	<80,106,000>
			Total EUR		<80,106,000>

Fair value (before adjustments)	6,967,000
Adjustments (CVA/DVA and basis)	<70,000>
Fair value (including adjustments)	6,897,000

The fair value of the hedging instrument on 15 July 20X3 was calculated as follows:

Hedging instrument fair valuation on 15-Jul-X3

Cash flow date	Implied interest rate	Discount factor	Spread/ fixed rate	Expected cash flow	Present value
Cash flows of USD leg:					
31-Jul-X3	—	1.0000	—	100,000,000	100,000,000
			Total USD		**100,000,000**
			Total EUR (1.1100)		**90,909,000**
Cash flows of EUR leg:					
31-Jul-X3	—	1.0000	—	<80,000,000>	<80,000,000>
			Total EUR		<80,000,000>
		Fair value (before adjustments)			10,909,000
		Adjustments (CVA/DVA and basis)			-0-
		Fair value (including adjustments)			10,909,000

Fair Valuations of the Hypothetical Derivative   The fair value of the hypothetical derivative on 15 July 20X0 was calculated as follows:

Hypothetical derivative fair valuation on 15-Jul-X0

Cash flow date	Implied interest rate	Discount factor	Spread/Fixed rate	Expected cash flow	Present value
Cash flows of USD leg:					
31-Jul-X1	5.40%	0.9481	0.50%	5,982,000	5,672,000
31-Jul-X2	5.60%	0.8972	0.50%	6,185,000	5,549,000
31-Jul-X3	5.78%	0.8475	0.50%	106,367,000	90,146,000
			Total USD		**101,367,000**
			Total EUR (1.2500)		**81,094,000**
Cash flows of EUR leg:					
31-Jul-X1	4.50%	0.9564	5.20%	<4,218,000>	<4,034,000>
31-Jul-X2	4.71%	0.9128	5.20%	<4,218,000>	<3,850,000>
31-Jul-X3	4.89%	0.8697	5.20%	<84,218,000>	<73,244,000>
			Total EUR		<81,128,000>
		Fair value (before adjustments)			<34,000>
		Adjustments (CVA/DVA and basis)			34,000
		Fair value (including adjustments)			-0-

The expected cash flow of the EUR leg was calculated as EUR 80 mn × 5.20% × Days/360, where Days was the number of days in the interest period, and in respect of the 31 July 20X3 cash flow, the EUR 80 million nominal was also added.

The fair value of the hypothetical derivative on 31 December 20X0 was calculated as follows:

Hypothetical derivative fair valuation on 31-Dec-X0					
Cash flow date	Implied interest rate	Discount factor	Spread/ fixed rate	Expected cash flow	Present value
Cash flows of USD leg:					
31-Jul-X1	5.50%	0.9709	0.50%	3,212,000	3,119,000
31-Jul-X2	5.75%	0.9174	0.50%	6,337,000	5,814,000
31-Jul-X3	5.85%	0.8660	0.50%	106,438,000	92,175,000
			Total USD		**101,108,000**
			Total EUR (1.2800)		**78,991,000**
Cash flows of EUR leg:					
31-Jul-X1	4.60%	0.9756	5.20%	<2,265,000>	<2,210,000>
31-Jul-X2	4.80%	0.9303	5.20%	<4,218,000>	<3,924,000>
31-Jul-X3	4.95%	0.8858	5.20%	<84,218,000>	<74,600,000>
			Total EUR		<80,734,000>
			Fair value (before adjustments)		<1,743,000>
			Adjustments (CVA/DVA and basis)		17,000>
			Fair value (including adjustments)		<1,726,000>

The fair value of the hypothetical derivative on 31 December 20X1 was calculated as follows:

Hypothetical derivative fair valuation on 31-Dec-X1					
Cash flow date	Implied interest rate	Discount factor	Spread/ fixed rate	Expected cash flow	Present value
Cash flows of USD leg:					
31-Jul-X2	5.65%	0.9702	0.50%	3,294,000	3,196,000
31-Jul-X3	5.90%	0.9154	0.50%	106,489,000	97,480,000
			Total USD		**100,676,000**
			Total EUR (1.2200)		**82,521,000**
Cash flows of EUR leg:					
31-Jul-X2	4.80%	0.9745	5.20%	<2,265,000>	<2,207,000>
31-Jul-X3	4.95%	0.9279	5.20%	<84,218,000>	<78,146,000>
			Total EUR		<80,353,000>
			Fair value (before adjustments)		2,168,000
			Adjustments (CVA/DVA and basis)		<11,000>
			Fair value (including adjustments)		2,157,000

The fair value of the hypothetical derivative on 31 December 20X2 was calculated as follows:

Hypothetical derivative fair valuation on 31-Dec-X2					
Cash flow date	Implied interest rate	Discount factor	Spread/ fixed rate	Expected cash flow	Present value
Cash flows of USD leg:					
31-Jul-X3	5.90%	0.9689	0.50%	103,348,000	100,134,000
			Total USD		**100,134,000**
			Total EUR (1.1500)		**87,073,000**
Cash flows of EUR leg:					
31-Jul-X3	4.95%	0.9738	5.20%	<82,265,000>	<80,110,000>
			Total EUR		**<80,110,000>**
			Fair value (before adjustments)		**6,963,000**
			Adjustments (CVA/DVA and basis)		**<21,000>**
			Fair value (including adjustments)		**6,942,000**

The fair value of the hypothetical derivative on 15 July 20X3 was calculated as follows:

Hypothetical derivative fair valuation on 15-Jul-X3					
Cash flow date	Implied interest rate	Discount factor	Spread/ fixed rate	Expected cash flow	Present value
Cash flows of USD leg:					
31-Jul-X3	—	1.0000	—	100,000,000	100,000,000
			Total USD		**100,000,000**
			Total EUR (1.1100)		**90,909,000**
Cash flows of EUR leg:					
31-Jul-X3	—	1.0000	—	<80,000,000>	<80,000,000>
			Total EUR		**<80,000,000>**
			Fair value (before adjustments)		**10,909,000**
			Adjustments (CVA/DVA and basis)		**-0-**
			Fair value (including adjustments)		**10,909,000**

Calculation of Effective and Ineffective Amounts The ineffective part of the change in fair value of the hedging instrument was the excess of its cumulative change in fair value over that of the hypothetical derivative. The fair values of the hedging instrument and the hypothetical derivative at each relevant date were as follows:

Date	Hedging instrument fair value	Period change	Cumulative change	Hypothetical derivative fair value	Cumulative change
15-Jul-X0	-0-	—	—	-0-	—
31-Dec-X0	<1,673,000>	<1,673,000>	<1,673,000>	<1,726,000>	<1,726,000>
31-Dec-X1	2,125,000	<3,798,000>	2,125,000	2,157,000	2,157,000
31-Dec-X2	6,897,000	<4,772,000>	6,897,000	6,942,000	6,942,000
15-Jul-X3	10,909,000	<4,012,000>	10,909,000	10,909,000	10,909,000

The effective and ineffective parts of the change in fair value of the hedging instrument were the following (see Section 5.5.6 for an explanation of the calculations):

	Effective and ineffective amounts			
	31-Dec-X0	**31-Dec-X1**	**31-Dec-X2**	**15-Jul-X3**
Cumulative change in fair value of hedging instrument	<1,673,000>	2,125,000	6,897,000	10,909,000
Cumulative change in fair value of hypothetical derivative	<1,726,000>	2,157,000	6,942,000	10,909,000
Lower amount	<1,673,000>	2,125,000	6,897,000	10,909,000
Previous cumulative effective amount	-0-	<1,673,000>	2,125,000	6,897,000
Available amount	<1,673,000>	3,798,000	4,772,000	4,012,000
Period change in fair value of hedging instrument	<1,673,000>	3,798,000	4,772,000	4,012,000
Effective part	<1,673,000>	3,798,000	4,772,000	4,012,000
Ineffective part	-0-	-0-	-0-	-0-

Fair value hedges of foreign currency debt were covered in the previous two case studies (see Sections 8.1 and 8.2). Fair value hedges require a fair valuation of the bond (i.e., the hedged item) for the risk(s) being hedged. There was no need to retranslate into EUR the USD carrying amount of the bond, as it was already included in the fair valuation of the hedged item. Otherwise a double counting would occur.

In a cash flow hedge, the recognition of the hedged item is not affected by the application of hedge accounting. Since the foreign currency bond is a monetary item, IAS 21 requires its carrying amount to be retranslated at each reporting date using the spot rate prevailing on such date. The adjustments to the cash flow hedge reserve of equity have to take into account the hedged item retranslation gains or losses. In other words, the effective parts of the hedge are recognised in the cash flow hedge reserve of equity after the hedged item's retranslation gains/losses. The following table summarises the amounts of retranslation gains/losses and the amounts recognised in the cash flow hedge reserve:

Retranslation gains/losses and amounts in cash flow hedge reserve				
	31-Dec-X0	31-Dec-X1	31-Dec-X2	15-Jul-X3
Bond USD carrying amount	100,000,000	100,000,000	100,000,000	100,000,000
EUR–USD spot rate	1.28	1.22	1.15	1.10
EUR translated amount	78,125,000	81,967,000	86,957,000	90.909.000
Retranslation gain/loss	1,875,000	<3,842,000>	<4,990,000>	<3,952,000>
Effective part	<1,673,000>	3,798,000	4,772,000	4,012,000
Difference	202,000	<44,000>	<218,000>	60,000
Amount to be recognised in cash flow hedge reserve	202,000	<44,000>	<218,000>	60,000
Cumulative amounts in cash flow hedge reserve	202,000	158,000	<60,000>	-0-

For the sake of clarity, let us look at the 31 December 20X0 figures. The effective part indicated that, in theory, EUR <1,673,000> would be added to the cash flow hedge reserve. However, EUR <1,875,000> was reclassified from this reserve to profit or loss to offset the bond's EUR 1,875,000 retranslation gain. As a result, EUR 202,000 was added to the cash flow hedge reserve on that date.

Accruals and Payable/Receivable Amounts The following table summarises the accruals and payables related to the bond:

Bond accruals and payables						
	USD Libor 12M	Average EUR–USD	Spot EUR–USD	EUR coupon accrual *(1)*	EUR payable amount *(2)*	Retranslation payable *(3)*
31-Dec-X0	5.40%	1.2630	1.2800	<2,193,000>	<2,164,000>	
15-Jul-X1	5.40%	1.2680	1.2400	<2,533,000>	<2,590,000>	<70,000>
31-Dec-X1	5.55%	1.2320	1.2200	<2,305,000>	<2,328,000>	
15-Jul-X2	5.55%	1.2170	1.2100	<2,707,000>	<2,722,000>	<19,000>
31-Dec-X2	5.65%	1.1680	1.1500	<2,472,000>	<2,510,000>	
15-Jul-X3	5.65%	1.1240	1.1000	<2,979,000>	<3,044,000>	<114,000>

Notes:
(1) USD 100 mn × (USD Libor 12M + 0.50%) × (Days/360)/Average EUR–USD, where Days was the number of calendar days in the accrual period (i.e., 169 for accrual periods ending on 31 December and 196 for accrual periods ending on 15 July)
(2) USD 100 mn × (USD Libor 12M + 0.50%) × (Days/360)/Spot EUR–USD
(3) USD payable amount × (1/previous Spot EUR–USD – 1/current Spot EUR–USD), where USD payable amount was the USD 100 mn × (USD Libor 12M + 0.50%) × Days/360 corresponding to the previous accrual period

The accruals and payables related to the USD leg of the CCS were identical to those of the bond, but with opposite sign. The following table summarises the accruals and payables related to the EUR leg of the CCS:

CCS EUR leg accruals and payables				
	Fixed rate	**Days**	**EUR Leg accrual** (*)	**Payable amount**
31-Dec-X0	5.19%	169	1,949,000	1,949,000
15-Jul-X1	5.19%	196	2,261,000	2,261,000
31-Dec-X1	5.19%	169	1,949,000	1,949,000
15-Jul-X2	5.19%	196	2,261,000	2,261,000
31-Dec-X2	5.19%	169	1,949,000	1,949,000
15-Jul-X3	5.19%	196	2,261,000	2,261,000

(*) 100 mn × 5.19% × Days/360, where Days was the number of calendar days in the accruing period

8.3.6 Accounting Entries

The required journal entries were as follows.

1) Journal entries on 15 July 20X0
The bond was issued.

Cash (Asset)	80,000,000	
Financial debt (Liability)		80,000,000

No entries were required to record the CCS as its initial fair value was zero.
2) Journal entries on 31 December 20X0
The accrued interest of the bond was EUR <2,193,000>. The payable related to this accrued interest was EUR <2,164,000>.

Interest expense (Profit or loss)	2,193,000	
Interest payable (Liability)		2,164,000
Other financial income (Profit or loss)		29,000

The accrual of the USD leg of the CCS was EUR 2,193,000. The receivable related to this accrued interest was EUR 2,164,000.

Interest receivable (Asset)	2,164,000	
Other financial expenses (Profit or loss)	29,000	
Interest income (Profit or loss)		2,193,000

The accrual of the EUR leg was EUR <1,949,000>.

Interest expense (Profit or loss)	1,949,000	
Interest payable (Liability)		1,949,000

The retranslation of the bond's carrying amount into EUR resulted in a EUR 1,875,000 gain. The change in fair value of the CCS produced a EUR 1,673,000 loss, fully deemed to be effective. The difference between these two amounts was recognised in the cash flow hedge reserve of equity.

Financial debt (Liability)	1,875,000	
Other financial income (Profit or loss)		1,875,000
Other financial expenses (Profit or loss)	1,875,000	
Derivative contract (Liability)		1,673,000
Cash flow hedge reserve (Equity)		202,000

3) Journal entries on 15 July 20X1

The accrued interest of the bond was EUR <2,533,000>. The payable related to this accrued interest was EUR <2,590,000>.

Interest expense (Profit or loss)	2,533,000	
Other financial expenses (Profit or loss)	57,000	
Interest payable (Liability)		2,590,000

The interest payable corresponding to the bond's previous accrued interest was retranslated, producing a EUR 70,000 loss.

Other financial expenses (Profit or loss)	70,000	
Interest payable (Liability)		70,000

The bond coupon was paid using the amount received under the USD leg of the CCS.

Interest payable (Liability)	4,824,000	
Cash (Asset)		4,824,000

The accrued interest of the USD leg was EUR 2,533,000. The receivable related to this accrued interest was EUR 2,590,000.

Interest receivable (Asset)	2,590,000	
Interest income (Profit or loss)		2,533,000
Other financial income (Profit or loss)		57,000

The interest receivable corresponding to the USD leg's previous accrued interest was retranslated, producing a EUR 70,000 gain.

Interest receivable (Asset)	70,000	
Other financial income (Profit or loss)		70,000

The interest receivable corresponding to the USD leg was received.

Cash (Asset)	4,824,000	
Interest receivable (Asset)		4,824,000

The accrual of the EUR leg was EUR <2,261,000>.

Interest expense (Profit or loss)	2,261,000	
Interest payable (Liability)		2,261,000

The interest payable corresponding to the EUR leg was paid.

Interest payable (Liability)	4,210,000	
Cash (Asset)		4,210,000

4) Journal entries on 31 December 20X1
The accrued interest of the bond was EUR <2,305,000>. The payable related to this accrued interest was EUR <2,328,000>.

Interest expense (Profit or loss)	2,305,000	
Other financial expenses (Profit or loss)	23,000	
Interest payable (Liability)		2,328,000

The accrual of the USD leg of the CCS was EUR 2,305,000. The receivable related to this accrued interest was EUR 2,328,000.

Interest receivable (Asset)	2,328,000	
Interest income (Profit or loss)		2,305,000
Other financial income (Profit or loss)		23,000

The accrual of the EUR leg was EUR <1,949,000>.

Interest expense (Profit or loss)	1,949,000	
Interest payable (Liability)		1,949,000

The retranslation of the bond's carrying amount into EUR resulted in a EUR 3,842,000 loss. The change in fair value of the CCS produced a EUR 3,798,000 gain, fully deemed to be effective. The difference between these two amounts was recognised in the cash flow hedge reserve of equity.

Other financial expenses (Profit or loss)	3,842,000	
Financial debt (Liability)		3,842,000
Derivative contract (Liability)	3,798,000	
Cash flow hedge reserve (Equity)	44,000	
Other financial income (Profit or loss)		3,842,000

5) Journal entries on 15 July 20X2

The accrued interest of the bond was EUR <2,707,000>. The payable related to this accrued interest was EUR <2,722,000>.

Interest expense (Profit or loss)	2,707,000	
Other financial expenses (Profit or loss)	15,000	
Interest payable (Liability)		2,722,000

The interest payable corresponding to the bond's previous accrued interest was retranslated, producing a EUR 19,000 loss.

Other financial expenses (Profit or loss)	19,000	
Interest payable (Liability)		19,000

The bond coupon was paid using the USD amounts received under the USD leg of the CCS.

Interest payable (Liability)	5,069,000	
Cash (Asset)		5,069,000

The accrued interest of the USD leg was EUR 2,707,000. The receivable related to this accrued interest was EUR 2,722,000.

Interest receivable (Asset)	2,722,000	
Interest income (Profit or loss)		2,707,000
Other financial income (Profit or loss)		15,000

The interest receivable corresponding to the USD leg's previous accrued interest was retranslated, producing a EUR 19,000 gain.

Interest receivable (Asset)	19,000	
Other financial income (Profit or loss)		19,000

The interest receivable corresponding to the USD leg was received.

Cash (Asset)	5,069,000	
Interest receivable (Asset)		5,069,000

The accrual of the EUR leg was EUR <2,261,000>.

Interest expense (Profit or loss)	2,261,000	
Interest payable (Liability)		2,261,000

The interest payable corresponding to the EUR leg was paid.

Interest payable (Liability)	4,210,000	
Cash (Asset)		4,210,000

6) Journal entries on 31 December 20X2

The accrued interest of the bond was EUR <2,472,000>. The payable related to this accrued interest was EUR <2,510,000>.

Interest expense (Profit or loss)	2,472,000	
Other financial expenses (Profit or loss)	38,000	
Interest payable (Liability)		2,510,000

The accrual of the USD leg of the CCS was EUR 2,472,000. The receivable related to this accrued interest was EUR 2,510,000.

Interest receivable (Asset)	2,510,000	
Interest income (Profit or loss)		2,472,000
Other financial income (Profit or loss)		38,000

The accrual of the EUR leg was EUR <1,949,000>.

Interest expense (Profit or loss)	1,949,000	
Interest payable (Liability)		1,949,000

The retranslation of the bond's carrying amount into EUR resulted in a EUR 4,990,000 loss. The change in fair value of the CCS produced a EUR 4,772,000 gain, fully deemed to be effective. The difference between these two amounts was recognised in the cash flow hedge reserve of equity.

Other financial expenses (Profit or loss)	4,990,000	
Financial debt (Liability)		4,990,000
Derivative contract (Liability)	4,772,000	
Cash flow hedge reserve (Equity)	218,000	
Other financial income (Profit or loss)		4,990,000

7) Journal entries on 15 July 20X3

The accrued interest of the bond was EUR <2,979,000>. The payable related to this accrued interest was EUR <3,044,000>.

Interest expense (Profit or loss)	2,979,000	
Other financial expenses (Profit or loss)	65,000	
Interest payable (Liability)		3,044,000

The interest payable corresponding to the bond's previous accrued interest was retranslated, producing a EUR 114,000 loss.

Other financial expenses (Profit or loss)	114,000	
Interest payable (Liability)		114,000

The bond coupon and principal were paid/repaid using the USD leg amounts. The bond principal represented EUR 90,909,000 (= USD 100 mn/1.1000).

Interest payable (Liability)	5,668,000	
Financial debt (Liability)	90,909,000	
Cash (Asset)		96,577,000

The accrued interest of the USD leg was EUR 2,979,000. The receivable related to this accrued interest was EUR 3,044,000.

Interest receivable (Asset)	3,044,000	
Interest income (Profit or loss)		2,979,000
Other financial income (Profit or loss)		65,000

The interest receivable corresponding to the USD leg's previous accrued interest was retranslated, producing a EUR 114,000 gain.

Interest receivable (Asset)	114,000	
Other financial income (Profit or loss)		114,000

The interest receivable corresponding to the USD leg was received.

Cash (Asset)	5,668,000	
Interest receivable (Asset)		5,668,000

The accrual of the EUR leg was EUR <2,261,000>.

Interest expense (Profit or loss)	2,261,000	
Interest payable (Liability)		2,261,000

The interest payable corresponding to the EUR leg was paid.

Interest payable (Liability)	4,210,000	
Cash (Asset)		4,210,000

The retranslation of the bond's carrying amount into EUR resulted in a EUR 3,952,000 loss. The change in fair value of the CCS produced a EUR 4,012,000 gain, fully deemed to be effective. The difference between these two amounts was recognised in the cash flow hedge reserve of equity.

Other financial expenses (Profit or loss)	3,952,000	
Financial debt (Liability)		3,952,000
Derivative contract (Liability)	4,012,000	
Cash flow hedge reserve (Equity)		60,000
Other financial income (Profit or loss)		3,952,000

The CCS notionals were exchanged. ABC paid EUR 80 million and received USD 100 million (worth EUR 90,909,000). The difference was worth EUR 10,909,000 (= 90,909,000 – 80 mn).

Cash (Asset)	10,909,000	
Derivative contract (Asset)		10,909,000

The following table gives a summary of the accounting entries:

	Cash	Interest receivable	Derivative contract	Financial debt	Interest payable	Cash flow hedge reserve	Profit or loss
15-Jul-X0							
Bond issuance	80,000,000			80,000,000			
31-Dec-X0							
Bond accrued coupon					2,164,000		<2,164,000>
CCS accrual USD leg		2,164,000					2,164,000
CCS accrual EUR leg					1,949,000		<1,949,000>
Bond retranslation				<1,875,000>			1,875,000
CCS revaluation			<1,673,000>			202,000	<1,875,000>
15-Jul-X1							
Bond accrued coupon					2,590,000		<2,590,000>
Bond accrual retranslation					70,000		<70,000>
Bond coupon payment	<4,824,000>				<4,824,000>		
CCS accrual USD leg		2,590,000					2,590,000
CCS interest receivable retranslation		70,000					70,000
CCS USD leg receipt	4,824,000	<4,824,000>					
CCS accrual EUR leg					2,261,000		<2,261,000>
CCS EUR leg payment	<4,210,000>				<4,210,000>		
31-Dec-X1							
Bond accrued coupon					2,328,000		<2,328,000>
CCS accrual USD leg		2,328,000					2,328,000
CCS accrual EUR leg					1,949,000		<1,949,000>
Bond retranslation				3,842,000			<3,842,000>
CCS revaluation			3,798,000			<44,000>	3,842,000

	(1)	(2)	(3)	(4)
15-Jul-X2				
Bond accrued coupon			2,722,000	<2,722,000>
Bond accrual retranslation			19,000	<19,000>
Bond coupon payment	<5,069,000>		<5,069,000>	
CCS accrual USD leg			2,722,000	2,722,000
CCS interest receivable retranslation			19,000	19,000
CCS USD leg receipt	5,069,000			<5,069,000>
CCS accrual EUR leg			2,261,000	<2,261,000>
CCS EUR leg payment	<4,210,000>			<4,210,000>
31-Dec-X2				
Bond accrued coupon			2,510,000	<2,510,000>
CCS accrual USD leg			2,510,000	2,510,000
CCS accrual EUR leg			1,949,000	<1,949,000>
Bond retranslation		4,990,000		<4,990,000>
CCS revaluation		4,772,000	<218,000>	4,990,000
15-Jul-X3				
Bond accrued coupon			3,044,000	<3,044,000>
Bond accrual retranslation			114,000	<114,000>
Bond coupon payment	<96,577,000>	<90,909,000>	<5,668,000>	
CCS accrual USD leg			3,044,000	3,044,000
CCS interest receivable retranslation			114,000	114,000
CCS USD leg receipt	5,668,000			<5,668,000>
CCS accrual EUR leg			2,261,000	<2,261,000>
CCS EUR leg payment	<4,210,000>			<4,210,000>
Bond retranslation		3,952,000		<3,952,000>
CCS revaluation		4,012,000	60,000	3,952,000
CCS exchange	10,909,000	<10,909,000>		<12,630,000>
	<12,630,000>	-0-	-0-	-0-

8.3.7 Concluding Remarks

ABC's objective when entering into the combination of the bond and the CCS was to incur an annual expense representing 5.19%, or EUR 4,210,000 (= 80 mn × 5.19% × 365/360).

During the first, second and third years of the term of the bond (and of the hedging relationship) the overall impact of the strategy on profit or loss was an annual expense of EUR 4,210,000. The annual net cash outflow was exactly EUR 4,210,000 as well. Therefore, ABC's objective was fully achieved.

This outcome occurred because there were no ineffective amounts. Otherwise, the target still would have been achieved from an annual net cash flow perspective, but not from an annual expense perspective. Even in the presence of inefficiencies, the overall 3-year expense would have been EUR 12,630,000 (=4,210,000 × 3).

As mentioned in the previous case studies, the basis component of the CCS was part of the hedging instrument. A notably volatile behaviour of the basis could have created significant inefficiencies. When the basis component of a CCS is excluded from the hedging instrument, IFRS 9 allows an entity to recognise changes in the fair value of this component either in profit or loss or temporarily in OCI to the extent that those changes relate to the hedged item.

8.4 CASE STUDY: HEDGING A FIXED RATE FOREIGN CURRENCY LIABILITY WITH A RECEIVE-FIXED PAY-FIXED CROSS-CURRENCY SWAP

This case study illustrates the accounting treatment of a cash flow hedge of a fixed rate foreign currency financing with a pay-fixed receive-fixed CCS.

8.4.1 Background Information

On 15 July 20X0, ABC issued a USD-denominated fixed rate bond. ABC's functional currency was the EUR. The bond had the following main terms:

Bond terms	
Issue date	15 July 20X0
Maturity	3 years (15 July 20X3)
Notional	USD 100 million
Coupon	6.09% annually, actual/360 basis

Since ABC's objective was to raise EUR fixed funding, on the issue date ABC entered into a CCS. Through the CCS, the entity agreed to receive a fixed rate equal to the bond coupon and pay a EUR fixed amount. The CCS had the following terms:

Cross-currency swap terms	
Trade date	15 July 20X0
Start date	15 July 20X0
Counterparties	ABC and XYZ Bank
Maturity	3 years (15 July 20X3)

USD nominal	USD 100 million
EUR nominal	EUR 80 million
Initial exchange	On start date, ABC receives the EUR nominal and pays the USD nominal
ABC pays	5.19% annually, actual/360 basis, on the EUR nominal
ABC receives	6.09% annually, actual/360 basis
Final exchange	On maturity date, ABC receives the USD nominal and pays the EUR nominal

The mechanics of the CCS are described next. It can be seen that through the combination of the USD bond and the CCS, ABC synthetically obtained a EUR fixed liability.

On the issue date at the start of the CCS, there was an initial exchange of nominal amounts through the CCS: ABC delivered the USD 100 million debt issuance proceeds and received EUR 80 million. The resulting EUR–USD exchange rate was 1.2500. The combination of the bond and CCS had the same effect as if ABC had issued a EUR-denominated bond, as shown in Figure 8.10.

An exchange of interest payments took place annually. ABC received 6.09% interest on the USD nominal and paid 5.19% interest on the EUR nominal. ABC used the USD cash flows it received under the CCS to pay the bond interest. Figure 8.11 shows the strategy's intermediate cash flows.

On maturity of the CCS and the debt, ABC re-exchanged the CCS nominals, using the USD 100 million it received through the CCS to redeem the bond issue, and delivering EUR 80

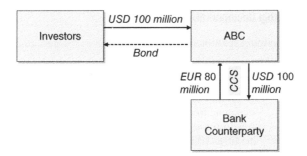

FIGURE 8.10 Bond and CCS combination – initial cash flows.

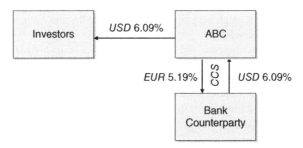

FIGURE 8.11 Bond and CCS combination – intermediate cash flows.

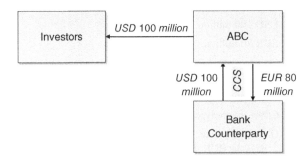

FIGURE 8.12 Bond and CCS combination – final cash flows.

million to the CCS counterparty. Note that this final exchange was made at exactly the same rate used in the initial exchange (1.2500). Figure 8.12 shows the strategy's cash flows at maturity.

Because the aim of the CCS was to eliminate the EUR variability of the cash flows stemming from the foreign currency fixed rate bond, ABC designated the CCS as the hedging instrument in a cash flow hedge. The exposure being hedged was the bond's exchange rate risks. As explained in Section 8.1.2, the bond's credit risk was excluded from the hedging relationship. Also, because of its fixed rate coupons, the bond did not expose ABC to interest rate risk.

ABC used a hypothetical derivative when assessing effectiveness and calculating effective and ineffective amounts, a tool that could be applied for cash flow hedges. Therefore, ABC did not need to fair value the hedged item, fair valuing instead a hypothetical derivative.

8.4.2 Hedging Relationship Documentation

ABC documented the hedging relationship as follows:

Hedging relationship documentation	
Risk management objective and strategy for undertaking the hedge	The objective of the hedge is to eliminate variability of the cash flows stemming from the coupon payments related to a USD-denominated debt instrument issued by the entity, against unfavourable movements in the EUR–USD exchange rate.
	This hedging objective is consistent with the group's overall interest rate risk management strategy of transforming with cross-currency swaps all new issued foreign-denominated debt into EUR (either into fixed or floating rate), and thereafter managing the exposure to interest rate risk through the proportion of fixed and floating rate net debt in its total debt portfolio.
	Exchange rate risk. The designated risk being hedged is the risk of changes in the EUR value of the cash flows related to the hedged item attributable to changes in the EUR–USD exchange rate.
	Fair value changes attributable to credit or other risks are not hedged in this relationship
Type of hedge	Cash flow hedge
Hedged item	The coupons and principal of the 3-year USD floating rate bond with reference number 678902. The main terms of the bond are a USD 100 million principal, an annual coupon of 6.09% calculated on the principal

| Hedging instrument | The cross-currency swap with reference number 014579. The main terms of the CCS are a USD 100 million nominal, a EUR 80 million nominal, a 3-year maturity, a USD annual interest of 6.09% on the USD nominal to be received by the entity and a EUR annual interest of 5.19% on the EUR nominal to be paid by the entity. The counterparty to the CCS is XYZ Bank and the credit risk associated with this counterparty is considered to be very low |
| Hedge effectiveness assessment | See below |

8.4.3 Hedge Effectiveness Assessment

Hedge effectiveness will be assessed by comparing changes in the fair value of the hedging instrument to changes in the fair value of a hypothetical derivative. The terms of the hypothetical derivative are such that its fair value changes exactly offset the changes in fair value of the hedged item for the risk being hedged. The hypothetical derivative is a theoretical cross-currency swap with no counterparty credit risk and with zero initial fair value, whose main terms are as follows:

Hypothetical derivative terms	
Trade date	15 July 20X0
Start date	15 July 20X0
Counterparties	ABC and credit risk-free counterparty
Maturity	3 years (15 July 20X3)
USD nominal	USD 100 million
EUR nominal	EUR 80 million
Initial exchange	On start date, ABC receives the EUR nominal and pays the USD nominal
ABC pays	5.20% annually, actual/360 basis, on the EUR nominal
ABC receives	6.09% annually, actual/360 basis, on the USD nominal
Final exchange	On maturity date, ABC receives the USD nominal and pays the EUR nominal

The EUR leg fixed rate of the hypothetical derivative is higher than that of the hedging instrument due to the absence of CVA in the former.

Changes in the fair value of the hedging instrument will be recognised as follows:

- The effective part of the gain or loss on the hedging instrument will be recognised in the cash flow hedge reserve of OCI in equity, after taking into account the bond's retranslation gains/losses. The accumulated amount in equity will be reclassified to profit or loss in the same period during which the hedged expected future cash flow affects profit or loss, adjusting interest expense.
- The ineffective part of the gain or loss on the hedging instrument will be recognised immediately in profit or loss.

Hedge effectiveness will be assessed prospectively at hedging relationship inception, on an ongoing basis at least upon each reporting date and upon occurrence of a significant change in the circumstances affecting the hedge effectiveness requirements.

The hedging relationship will qualify for hedge accounting only if all the following criteria are met:

1) The hedging relationship consists only of eligible hedge items and hedging instruments. The hedge item is eligible as it is a group of highly expected forecast cash flows that exposes the entity to fair value risk, affects profit or loss and is reliably measurable. The hedging instrument is eligible as it is a derivative that does not result in a net written option.
2) At hedge inception there is a formal designation and documentation of the hedging relationship and the entity's risk management objective and strategy for undertaking the hedge.
3) The hedging relationship is considered effective.

The hedging relationship will be considered effective if the following three requirements are met:

1) There is an economic relationship between the hedged item and the hedging instrument.
2) The effect of credit risk does not dominate the value changes that result from that economic relationship.
3) The hedge ratio of the hedging relationship is the same as that resulting from the quantity of hedged item that the entity actually hedges and the quantity of the hedging instrument that the entity actually uses to hedge that quantity of hedged item. The hedge ratio should not be intentionally weighted to create ineffectiveness.

Whether there is an economic relationship between the hedged item and the hedging instrument will be assessed on a qualitative basis by comparing the critical terms (notional, interest periods, underlying and fixed rates) of the hypothetical derivative and the hedging instrument. The assessment will be complemented by a quantitative assessment using the scenario analysis method for one scenario in which the EUR–USD spot rate will be increased by 10%, and the changes in fair value of the hypothetical derivative and the hedging instrument compared.

8.4.4 Hedge Effectiveness Assessment Performed at the Start of the Hedging Relationship

The hedging relationship was considered effective as the following three requirements were met:

1) There was an economic relationship between the hedged item and the hedging instrument. Based on the qualitative assessment performed supported by a quantitative analysis, the entity concluded that the change in fair value of the hedged item was expected to be substantially offset by the change in fair value of the hedging instrument, corroborating that both elements had values that would generally move in opposite directions.
2) The effect of credit risk did not dominate the value changes resulting from that economic relationship as the credit ratings of both the entity and XYZ Bank were considered sufficiently strong.

3) The hedge ratio of the hedging relationship was the same as that resulting from the quantity of hedged item that the entity actually hedged and the quantity of the hedging instrument that the entity actually used to hedge that quantity of hedged item. The hedge ratio was not intentionally weighted to create ineffectiveness.

Due to the fact that the terms of the hedging instrument and those of the expected cash flow closely matched and the low credit risk exposure to the counterparty of the cross-currency swap contract, it was concluded that the hedging instrument and the hedged item had values that would generally move in opposite directions. This conclusion was supported by a quantitative assessment, which consisted of one scenario analysis performed as follows. A EUR–USD spot rate increase by 10% occurring on the assessment date was simulated. The fair values of the hedging instrument and the hypothetical derivatives were calculated and compared to their initial fair values. As shown in the table below, the high degree of offset implied that the change in fair value of the hedged item was expected to largely be offset by the change in fair value of the hedging instrument, corroborating that both elements had values that would generally move in opposite directions.

Scenario analysis assessment		
	Hedging instrument	**Hypothetical derivative**
Initial fair value	-0-	-0-
Final fair value	<7,156,000>	<7,362,000>
Cumulative fair value change	<7,156,000>	<7,362,000>
	Degree of offset	**97.2%**

The following potential sources of ineffectiveness were identified:

- a substantial deterioration in credit risk of either the entity or the counterparty to the hedging instrument; and
- a change in the timing or amounts of the hedged highly expected cash flows.

The hedge ratio was set at 1:1.

ABC also performed assessments on each reporting date, yielding the same conclusions. These assessments have been omitted to avoid unnecessary repetition.

8.4.5 Fair Valuations, Effective/Ineffective Amounts and Cash Flow Calculations

Fair Valuations of the Hedging Instrument   The fair value of the hedging instrument on 15 July 20X0 was calculated as follows:

Hedging instrument fair valuation on 15-Jul-X0					
Cash flow date	**Implied interest rate**	**Discount factor**	**Fixed rate**	**Expected cash flow**	**Present value**
Cash flows of USD leg:					
31-Jul-X1	5.40%	0.9481	6.09%	6,175,000	5,855,000
31-Jul-X2	5.60%	0.8972	6.09%	6,175,000	5,540,000
					(*continued overleaf*)

31-Jul-X3	5.78%	0.8475	6.09%	106,175,000	89,983,000
			Total USD		**101,378,000**
			Total EUR (1.2500)		**81,102,000**
Cash flows of EUR leg:					
31-Jul-X1	4.50%	0.9564	5.19%	<4,210,000>	<4,026,000>
31-Jul-X2	4.71%	0.9128	5.19%	<4,210,000>	<3,843,000>
31-Jul-X3	4.89%	0.8697	5.19%	<84,210,000>	<73,237,000>
			Total EUR		<81,106,000>
			Fair value (before adjustments)		<4,000>
			Adjustments (CVA/DVA and basis)		4,000
			Fair value (including adjustments)		-0-

The expected cash flow of the USD leg was calculated as USD 100 mn × 6.09% × Days/360, where Days was the number of days in the interest period, and in respect of the 31 July 20X3 cash flow, the USD 100 million nominal was also added.

The expected cash flow of the EUR leg was calculated as EUR 80 mn × 5.19% × Days/360, where Days was the number of days in the interest period, and in respect of the 31 July 20X3 cash flow, the EUR 80 million nominal was also added.

The fair value of the hedging instrument on 31 December 20X0 was calculated as follows:

Hedging instrument fair valuation on 31-Dec-X0					
Cash flow date	Implied interest rate	Discount factor	Fixed rate	Expected cash flow	Present value
Cash flows of USD leg:					
31-Jul-X1	5.50%	0.9709	6.09%	3,316,000	3,220,000
31-Jul-X2	5.75%	0.9174	6.09%	6,175,000	5,665,000
31-Jul-X3	5.85%	0.8660	6.09%	106,175,000	91,948,000
			Total USD		100,833,000
			Total EUR (1.2800)		78,776,000
Cash flows of EUR leg:					
31-Jul-X1	4.60%	0.9756	5.19%	<2,261,000>	<2,206,000>
31-Jul-X2	4.80%	0.9303	5.19%	<4,210,000>	<3,917,000>
31-Jul-X3	4.95%	0.8858	5.19%	<84,210,000>	<74,593,000>
			Total EUR		<80,716,000>
			Fair value (before adjustments)		<1,940,000>
			Adjustments (CVA/DVA and basis)		58,000>
			Fair value (including adjustments)		<1,882,000>

The fair value of the hedging instrument on 31 December 20X1 was calculated as follows:

Hedging instrument fair valuation on 31-Dec-X1					
Cash flow date	Implied interest rate	Discount factor	Fixed rate	Expected cash flow	Present value
Cash flows of USD leg:					
31-Jul-X2	5.65%	0.9702	6.09%	3,316,000	3,217,000
31-Jul-X3	5.90%	0.9154	6.09%	106,175,000	97,193,000
			Total USD		**100,410,000**
			Total EUR (1.2200)		**82,303,000**
Cash flows of EUR leg:					
31-Jul-X2	4.80%	0.9745	5.19%	<2,261,000>	<2,203,000>
31-Jul-X3	4.95%	0.9279	5.19%	<84,210,000>	<78,138,000>
			Total EUR		<80,341,000>
			Fair value (before adjustments)		1,962,000
			Adjustments (CVA/DVA and basis)		<49,000>
			Fair value (including adjustments)		1,913,000

The fair value of the hedging instrument on 31 December 20X2 was calculated as follows:

Hedging instrument fair valuation on 31-Dec-X2					
Cash flow date	Implied interest rate	Discount factor	Fixed rate	Expected cash flow	Present value
Cash flows of USD leg:					
31-Jul-X3	5.90%	0.9689	6.09%	103,316,000	100,103,000
			Total USD		**100,103,000**
			Total EUR (1.1500)		**87,046,000**
Cash flows of EUR leg:					
31-Jul-X3	4.95%	0.9738	5.19%	<82,261,000>	<80,106,000>
			Total EUR		<80,106,000>
			Fair value (before adjustments)		6,940,000
			Adjustments (CVA/DVA and basis)		<69,000>
			Fair value (including adjustments)		6,871,000

The fair value of the hedging instrument on 15 July 20X3 was calculated as follows:

Hedging instrument fair valuation on 15-Jul-X3					
Cash flow date	Implied interest rate	Discount factor	Fixed rate	Expected cash flow	Present value
Cash flows of USD leg:					
31-Jul-X3	—	1.0000	—	100,000,000	100,000,000
			Total USD		**100,000,000**
			Total EUR (1.1100)		**90,909,000**
Cash flows of EUR leg:					
31-Jul-X3	—	1.0000	—	<80,000,000>	<80,000,000>
			Total EUR		<80,000,000>
			Fair value (before adjustments)		10,909,000
			Adjustments (CVA/DVA and basis)		-0-
			Fair value (including adjustments)		10,909,000

Fair Valuations of the Hypothetical Derivative   The fair value of the hypothetical derivative on 15 July 20X0 was calculated as follows:

Hypothetical derivative fair valuation on 15-Jul-X0					
Cash flow date	Implied interest rate	Discount factor	Fixed rate	Expected cash flow	**Present value**
Cash flows of USD leg:					
31-Jul-X1	5.40%	0.9481	6.09%	6,175,000	5,855,000
31-Jul-X2	5.60%	0.8972	6.09%	6,175,000	5,540,000
31-Jul-X3	5.78%	0.8475	6.09%	106,175,000	89,983,000
			Total USD		**101,378,000**
			Total EUR (1.2500)		**81,102,000**
Cash flows of EUR leg:					
31-Jul-X1	4.50%	0.9564	5.20%	<4,218,000>	<4,034,000>
31-Jul-X2	4.71%	0.9128	5.20%	<4,218,000>	<3,850,000>
31-Jul-X3	4.89%	0.8697	5.20%	<84,218,000>	<73,244,000>
			Total EUR		<81,128,000>
			Fair value (before adjustments)		<26,000>
			Adjustments (CVA/DVA and basis)		26,000
			Fair value (including adjustments)		-0-

The expected cash flow of the EUR leg was calculated as EUR 80 mn × 5.20% × Days/360, where Days was the number of days in the interest period, and in respect of the 31 July 20X3 cash flow, the EUR 80 million nominal was also added.

The fair value of the hypothetical derivative on 31 December 20X0 was calculated as follows:

		Hypothetical derivative fair valuation on 31-Dec-X0			
Cash flow date	Implied interest rate	Discount factor	Fixed rate	Expected cash flow	Present value
Cash flows of USD leg:					
31-Jul-X1	5.50%	0.9709	6.09%	3,316,000	3,220,000
31-Jul-X2	5.75%	0.9174	6.09%	6,175,000	5,665,000
31-Jul-X3	5.85%	0.8660	6.09%	106,175,000	91,948,000
			Total USD		**100,833,000**
			Total EUR (1.2800)		**78,776,000**
Cash flows of EUR leg:					
31-Jul-X1	4.60%	0.9756	5.20%	<2,265,000>	<2,210,000>
31-Jul-X2	4.80%	0.9303	5.20%	<4,218,000>	<3,924,000>
31-Jul-X3	4.95%	0.8858	5.20%	<84,218,000>	<74,600,000>
			Total EUR		<80,734,000>
			Fair value (before adjustments)		<1,958,000>
			Adjustments (CVA/DVA and basis)		20,000>
			Fair value (including adjustments)		<1,938,000>

The fair value of the hypothetical derivative on 31 December 20X1 was calculated as follows:

		Hypothetical derivative fair valuation on 31-Dec-X1			
Cash flow date	Implied interest rate	Discount factor	Fixed rate	Expected cash flow	Present value
Cash flows of USD leg:					
31-Jul-X2	5.65%	0.9702	6.09%	3,316,000	3,217,000
31-Jul-X3	5.90%	0.9154	6.09%	106,175,000	97,193,000
			Total USD		**100,410,000**
			Total EUR (1.2200)		**82,303,000**
Cash flows of EUR leg:					
31-Jul-X2	4.80%	0.9745	5.20%	<2,265,000>	<2,207,000>
31-Jul-X3	4.95%	0.9279	5.20%	<84,218,000>	<78,146,000>
			Total EUR		<80,353,000>
			Fair value (before adjustments)		1,950,000
			Adjustments (CVA/DVA and basis)		<10,000>
			Fair value (including adjustments)		1,940,000

The fair value of the hypothetical derivative on 31 December 20X2 was calculated as follows:

Hypothetical derivative fair valuation on 31-Dec-X2					
Cash flow date	Implied interest rate	Discount factor	Fixed rate	Expected cash flow	Present value
Cash flows of USD leg:					
31-Jul-X3	5.90%	0.9689	6.09%	103,316,000	100,103,000
			Total USD		**100,103,000**
			Total EUR (1.1500)		**87,046,000**
Cash flows of EUR leg:					
31-Jul-X3	4.95%	0.9738	5.20%	<82,265,000>	<80,110,000>
			Total EUR		<80,110,000>
			Fair value (before adjustments)		6,936,000
			Adjustments (CVA/DVA and basis)		<21,000>
			Fair value (including adjustments)		6,915,000

The fair value of the hypothetical derivative on 15 July 20X3 was calculated as follows:

Hypothetical derivative fair valuation on 15-Jul-X3					
Cash flow date	Implied interest rate	Discount factor	Fixed rate	Expected cash flow	Present value
Cash flows of USD leg:					
31-Jul-X3	—	1.0000	—	100,000,000	100,000,000
			Total USD		**100,000,000**
			Total EUR (1.1100)		**90,909,000**
Cash flows of EUR leg:					
31-Jul-X3	—	1.0000	—	<80,000,000>	<80,000,000>
			Total EUR		<80,000,000>
			Fair value (before adjustments)		10,909,000
			Adjustments (CVA/DVA and basis)		-0-
			Fair value (including adjustments)		10,909,000

Calculation of Effective and Ineffective Amounts   The ineffective part of the change in fair value of the hedging instrument was the excess of its cumulative change in fair value over that of the hypothetical derivative. The fair values of the hedging instrument and the hypothetical derivative at each relevant date were as follows:

Date	Hedging instrument fair value	Period change	Cumulative change	Hypothetical derivative fair value	Cumulative change
15-Jul-X0	-0-	—	—	-0-	—
31-Dec-X0	<1,882,000>	<1,882,000>	<1,882,000>	<1,938,000>	<1,938,000>
31-Dec-X1	1,913,000	3,795,000	1,913,000	1,940,000	1,940,000
31-Dec-X2	6,871,000	4,958,000	6,871,000	6,915,000	6,915,000
15-Jul-X3	10,909,000	4,038,000	10,909,000	10,909,000	10,909,000

The effective and ineffective parts of the change in fair value of the hedging instrument were the following (see Section 5.5.6 for an explanation of the calculations):

Effective and ineffective amounts				
	31-Dec-X0	**31-Dec-X1**	**31-Dec-X2**	**15-Jul-X3**
Cumulative change in fair value of hedging instrument	<1,882,000>	1,913,000	6,871,000	10,909,000
Cumulative change in fair value of hypothetical derivative	<1,938,000>	1,940,000	6,915,000	10,909,000
Lower amount	<1,882,000>	1,913,000	6,871,000	10,909,000
Previous cumulative effective amount	-0-	<1,882,000>	1,913,000	6,871,000
Available amount	<1,882,000>	3,795,000	4,958,000	4,038,000
Period change in fair value of hedging instrument	<1,882,000>	3,795,000	4,958,000	4,038,000
Effective part	<1,882,000>	3,795,000	4,958,000	4,038,000
Ineffective part	-0-	-0-	-0-	-0-

Fair value hedges of foreign currency debt were covered in Sections 8.1 and 8.2. Fair value hedges require a fair valuation of the bond (i.e., the hedged item) for the risk(s) being hedged. There was no need to retranslate into EUR the USD carrying amount of the bond, as it was already included in the fair valuation of the hedged item. Otherwise a double counting would occur.

In a cash flow hedge, the recognition of the hedged item is not affected by the application of hedge accounting. Since the foreign currency bond is a monetary item, IAS 21 requires its carrying amount to be retranslated at each reporting date using the spot rate prevailing on such date. The adjustments to the cash flow hedge reserve of equity have to take into account the hedged item retranslation gains or losses. In other words, the effective parts of the hedge are recognised in the cash flow hedge reserve of equity after the hedged item's retranslation gains/losses. The following table summarises the amounts of retranslation gains/losses and the amounts recognised in the cash flow hedge reserve:

Retranslation gains/losses and amounts in cash flow hedge reserve				
	31-Dec-X0	**31-Dec-X1**	**31-Dec-X2**	**15-Jul-X3**
Bond USD carrying amount	100,000,000	100,000,000	100,000,000	100,000,000
EUR–USD spot rate	1.28	1.22	1.15	1.10
EUR translated amount	78,125,000	81,967,000	86,957,000	90.909.000
Retranslation gain/loss	1,875,000	<3,842,000>	<4,990,000>	<3,952,000>
Effective part	<1,882,000>	3,795,000	4,958,000	4,038,000
Difference	<7,000>	<47,000>	<32,000>	86,000
Amount to be recognised in cash flow hedge reserve	<7,000>	<47,000>	<32,000>	86,000
Cumulative amounts in cash flow hedge reserve	<7,000>	<54,000>	<86,000>	-0-

For the sake of clarity, let us look at the 31 December 20X0 figures. The effective part indicated that, in theory, EUR <1,882,000> would be added to the cash flow hedge reserve. However, EUR <1,875,000> was reclassified from this reserve to profit or loss to offset the bond's EUR 1,875,000 retranslation gain. As a result, EUR 7,000 was subtracted from the cash flow hedge reserve on that date.

Accruals and Payable/Receivable Amounts   The following table summarises the accruals and payables related to the bond:

	Average EUR–USD	Spot EUR–USD	EUR coupon accrual (1)	EUR payable amount (2)	Retranslation payable (3)
31-Dec-X0	1.2630	1.2800	<2,264,000>	<2,234,000>	
15-Jul-X1	1.2680	1.2400	<2,615,000>	<2,674,000>	<72,000>
31-Dec-X1	1.2320	1.2200	<2,321,000>	<2,343,000>	
15-Jul-X2	1.2170	1.2100	<2,725,000>	<2,740,000>	<19,000>
31-Dec-X2	1.1680	1.1500	<2,448,000>	<2,486,000>	
15-Jul-X3	1.1240	1.1000	<2,950,000>	<3,015,000>	<113,000>

Notes:

(1) USD 100 mn × 6.09% × (Days/360)/Average EUR–USD, where Days was the number of calendar days in the accrual period (i.e., 169 for accrual periods ending on 31 December and 196 for accrual periods ending on 15 July)

(2) USD 100 mn × 6.09% × (Days/360)/Spot EUR–USD

(3) USD payable amount × (1/previous Spot EUR–USD – 1/current Spot EUR–USD), where USD payable amount was the USD 100 mn × 6.09% × Days/360 corresponding to the previous accrual period

The accruals and payables related to the USD leg of the CCS were identical to those of the bond, but with opposite sign. The following table summarises the accruals and payables related to the EUR leg of the CCS:

CCS EUR leg accruals and payables

	Fixed rate	Days	EUR leg accrual (*)	Payable amount
31-Dec-X0	5.19%	169	1,949,000	1,949,000
15-Jul-X1	5.19%	196	2,261,000	2,261,000
31-Dec-X1	5.19%	169	1,949,000	1,949,000
15-Jul-X2	5.19%	196	2,261,000	2,261,000
31-Dec-X2	5.19%	169	1,949,000	1,949,000
15-Jul-X3	5.19%	196	2,261,000	2,261,000

(*) 100 mn × 5.19% × Days/360, where Days was the number of calendar days in the accruing period

8.4.6 Accounting Entries

The required journal entries were as follows.

1) Journal entries on 15 July 20X0.
The bond was issued.

Cash (Asset)	80,000,000	
Financial debt (Liability)		80,000,000

No entries were required to record the CCS as its initial fair value was zero.
2) Journal entries on 31 December 20X0
The accrued interest of the bond was EUR <2,264,000>. The payable related to this accrued interest was EUR <2,234,000>.

Interest expense (Profit or loss)	2,264,000	
Interest payable (Liability)		2,234,000
Other financial income (Profit or loss)		30,000

The accrual of the USD leg of the CCS was EUR 2,264,000. The receivable related to this accrued interest was EUR 2,234,000.

Interest receivable (Asset)	2,234,000	
Other financial expenses (Profit or loss)	30,000	
Interest income (Profit or loss)		2,264,000

The accrual of the EUR leg was EUR <1,949,000>.

Interest expense (Profit or loss)	1,949,000	
Interest payable (Liability)		1,949,000

The retranslation of the bond's carrying amount into EUR resulted in a EUR 1,875,000 gain. The change in fair value of the CCS produced a EUR 1,882,000 loss, fully deemed to be effective. The difference between these two amounts was recognised in the cash flow hedge reserve of equity.

Financial debt (Liability)	1,875,000	
Other financial income (Profit or loss)		1,875,000
Other financial expenses (Profit or loss)	1,875,000	30,000
Cash flow hedge reserve (Equity)	7,000	
Derivative contract (Liability)		1,882,000

3) Journal entries on 15 July 20X1
The accrued interest of the bond was EUR <2,615,000>. The payable related to this accrued interest was EUR <2,674,000>.

Interest expense (Profit or loss)	2,615,000	
Other financial expenses (Profit or loss)	59,000	
Interest payable (Liability)		2,674,000

The interest payable corresponding to the bond's previous accrued interest was retranslated, producing a EUR 72,000 loss.

Other financial expenses (Profit or loss)	72,000	
Interest payable (Liability)		72,000

The bond coupon was paid using the amount received under the USD leg of the CCS.

Interest payable (Liability)	4,980,000	
Cash (Asset)		4,980,000

The accrued interest of the USD leg was EUR 2,615,000. The receivable related to this accrued interest was EUR 2,674,000.

Interest receivable (Asset)	2,674,000	
Interest income (Profit or loss)		2,615,000
Other financial income (Profit or loss)		59,000

The interest receivable corresponding to the USD leg's previous accrued interest was retranslated, producing a EUR 72,000 gain.

Interest receivable (Asset)	72,000	
Other financial income (Profit or loss)		72,000

The interest receivable corresponding to the USD leg was received.

Cash (Asset)	4,980,000	
Interest receivable (Asset)		4,980,000

The accrual of the EUR leg was EUR <2,261,000>.

Interest expense (Profit or loss)	2,261,000	
Interest payable (Liability)		2,261,000

The interest payable corresponding to the EUR leg was paid.

Interest payable (Liability)	4,210,000	
Cash (Asset)		4,210,000

4) Journal entries on 31 December 20X1

The accrued interest of the bond was EUR <2,321,000>. The payable related to this accrued interest was EUR <2,343,000>.

Interest expense (Profit or loss)	2,321,000	
Other financial expenses (Profit or loss)	22,000	
Interest payable (Liability)		2,343,000

The accrual of the USD leg of the CCS was EUR 2,321,000. The receivable related to this accrued interest was EUR 2,343,000.

Interest receivable (Asset)	2,343,000	
Interest income (Profit or loss)		2,321,000
Other financial income (Profit or loss)		22,000

The accrual of the EUR leg was EUR <1,949,000>.

Interest expense (Profit or loss)	1,949,000	
Interest payable (Liability)		1,949,000

The retranslation of the bond's carrying amount into EUR resulted in a EUR 3,842,000 loss. The change in fair value of the CCS produced a EUR 3,795,000 gain, fully deemed to be effective. The difference between these two amounts was recognised in the cash flow hedge reserve of equity.

Other financial expenses (Profit or loss)	3,842,000	
Financial debt (Liability)		3,842,000
Derivative contract (Liability)	3,795,000	
Cash flow hedge reserve (Equity)	47,000	
Other financial income (Profit or loss)		3,842,000

5) Journal entries on 15 July 20X2
The accrued interest of the bond was EUR <2,725,000>. The payable related to this accrued interest was EUR <2,740,000>.

Interest expense (Profit or loss)	2,725,000	
Other financial expenses (Profit or loss)	15,000	
Interest payable (Liability)		2,740,000

The interest payable corresponding to the bond's previous accrued interest was retranslated, producing a EUR 19,000 loss.

Other financial expenses (Profit or loss)	19,000	
Interest payable (Liability)		19,000

The bond coupon was paid using the USD amounts received under the USD leg of the CCS.

Interest payable (Liability)	5,102,000	
Cash (Asset)		5,102,000

The accrued interest of the USD leg was EUR 2,725,000. The receivable related to this accrued interest was EUR 2,740,000.

Interest receivable (Asset)	2,740,000	
Interest income (Profit or loss)		2,725,000
Other financial income (Profit or loss)		15,000

The interest receivable corresponding to the USD leg's previous accrued interest was retranslated, producing a EUR 19,000 gain.

Interest receivable (Asset)	19,000	
Other financial income (Profit or loss)		19,000

The interest receivable corresponding to the USD leg was received.

Cash (Asset)	5,102,000	
Interest receivable (Asset)		5,102,000

The accrual of the EUR leg was EUR <2,261,000>.

Interest expense (Profit or loss)	2,261,000	
Interest payable (Liability)		2,261,000

The interest payable corresponding to the EUR leg was paid.

Interest payable (Liability)	4,210,000	
Cash (Asset)		4,210,000

6) Journal entries on 31 December 20X2

The accrued interest of the bond was EUR <2,448,000>. The payable related to this accrued interest was EUR <2,486,000>.

Interest expense (Profit or loss)	2,448,000	
Other financial expenses (Profit or loss)	38,000	
Interest payable (Liability)		2,486,000

The accrual of the USD leg of the CCS was EUR 2,448,000. The receivable related to this accrued interest was EUR 2,486,000.

Interest receivable (Asset)	2,486,000	
Interest income (Profit or loss)		2,448,000
Other financial income (Profit or loss)		38,000

The accrual of the EUR leg was EUR <1,949,000>.

Interest expense (Profit or loss)	1,949,000	
Interest payable (Liability)		1,949,000

The retranslation of the bond's carrying amount into EUR resulted in a EUR 4,990,000 loss. The change in fair value of the CCS produced a EUR 4,958,000 gain, fully deemed to be effective. The difference between these two amounts was recognised in the cash flow hedge reserve of equity.

Other financial expenses (Profit or loss)	4,990,000	
Financial debt (Liability)		4,990,000
Derivative contract (Liability)	4,958,000	
Cash flow hedge reserve (Equity)	32,000	
Other financial income (Profit or loss)		4,990,000

7) Journal entries on 15 July 20X3

The accrued interest of the bond was EUR <2,950,000>. The payable related to this accrued interest was EUR <3,015,000>.

Interest expense (Profit or loss)	2,950,000	
Other financial expenses (Profit or loss)	65,000	
Interest payable (Liability)		3,015,000

The interest payable corresponding to the bond's previous accrued interest was retranslated, producing a EUR 113,000 loss.

Other financial expenses (Profit or loss)	113,000	
Interest payable (Liability)		113,000

The bond coupon and principal were paid/repaid using the amounts received under the USD leg of the CCS. The bond principal represented EUR 90,909,000 (= USD 100 mn/1.1000).

Interest payable (Liability)	5,614,000	
Financial debt (Liability)	90,909,000	
Cash (Asset)		96,523,000

The accrued interest of the USD leg was EUR 2,950,000. The receivable related to this accrued interest was EUR 3,015,000.

Interest receivable (Asset)	3,015,000	
Interest income (Profit or loss)		2,950,000
Other financial income (Profit or loss)		65,000

The interest receivable corresponding to the USD leg's previous accrued interest was retranslated, producing a EUR 113,000 gain.

Interest receivable (Asset)	113,000	
Other financial income (Profit or loss)		113,000

The interest receivable corresponding to the USD leg was received.

Cash (Asset)	5,614,000	
Interest receivable (Asset)		5,614,000

The accrual of the EUR leg was EUR <2,261,000>.

Interest expense (Profit or loss)	2,261,000	
Interest payable (Liability)		2,261,000

The interest payable corresponding to the EUR leg was paid.

Interest payable (Liability)	4,210,000	
Cash (Asset)		4,210,000

The retranslation of the bond's carrying amount into EUR resulted in a EUR 3,952,000 loss. The change in fair value of the CCS produced a EUR 4,038,000 gain, fully deemed to be effective. The difference between these two amounts was recognised in the cash flow hedge reserve of equity.

Other financial expenses (Profit or loss)	3,952,000	
Financial debt (Liability)		3,952,000
Derivative contract (Liability)	4,038,000	
Cash flow hedge reserve (Equity)		86,000
Other financial income (Profit or loss)		3,952,000

The CCS notionals were exchanged. ABC paid EUR 80 million and received USD 100 million (worth EUR 90,909,000). The difference was worth EUR 10,909,000 (= 90,909,000 – 80 mn).

Cash (Asset)	10,909,000	
Derivative contract (Asset)		10,909,000

The following table gives a summary of the accounting entries:

	Cash	Interest receivable	Derivative contract	Financial debt	Interest payable	Cash flow hedge reserve	Profit or loss
15-Jul-X0							
Bond issuance	80,000,000			80,000,000			
31-Dec-X0							
Bond accrued coupon					2,234,000		<2,234,000>
CCS accrual USD leg		2,234,000					2,234,000
CCS accrual EUR leg					1,949,000		<1,949,000>
Bond retranslation				<1,875,000>			1,875,000
CCS revaluation			<1,882,000>			<7,000>	<1,875,000>
15-Jul-X1							
Bond accrued coupon					2,674,000		<2,674,000>
Bond accrual retranslation					72,000		<72,000>
Bond coupon payment	<4,980,000>				<4,980,000>		
CCS accrual USD leg		2,674,000					2,674,000
CCS interest receivable retranslation		72,000					72,000
CCS USD leg receipt	4,980,000	<4,980,000>					
CCS EUR leg	<4,210,000>				2,261,000		<2,261,000>
CCS EUR leg payment	<4,210,000>				<4,210,000>		
31-Dec-X1							
Bond accrued coupon					2,343,000		<2,343,000>
CCS accrual USD leg		2,343,000					2,343,000
CCS accrual EUR leg					1,949,000		<1,949,000>
Bond retranslation				3,842,000			<3,842,000>
CCS revaluation			3,795,000			<47,000>	3,842,000

(continued overleaf)

15-Jul-X2						
Bond accrued coupon					2,740,000	<2,740,000>
Bond accrual retranslation					19,000	<19,000>
Bond coupon payment	<5,102,000>				<5,102,000>	
CCS accrual USD leg				2,740,000		2,740,000
CCS interest receivable retranslation				19,000		19,000
CCS USD leg receipt	5,102,000			<5,102,000>		
CCS accrual EUR leg					2,261,000	<2,261,000>
CCS EUR leg payment	<4,210,000>				<4,210,000>	
31-Dec-X2						
Bond accrued coupon					2,486,000	<2,486,000>
CCS accrual USD leg				2,486,000		2,486,000
CCS accrual EUR leg					1,949,000	<1,949,000>
Bond retranslation			4,958,000			<4,990,000>
CCS revaluation				<32,000>		4,990,000
15-Jul-X3						
Bond accrued coupon					3,015,000	<3,015,000>
Bond accrual retranslation					113,000	<113,000>
Bond coupon payment	<96,523,000>	<90,909,000>			<5,614,000>	
CCS accrual USD leg				3,015,000		3,015,000
CCS interest receivable retranslation				113,000		113,000
CCS USD leg receipt	5,614,000			<5,614,000>		
CCS accrual EUR leg					2,261,000	<2,261,000>
CCS EUR leg payment	<4,210,000>				<4,210,000>	
Bond retranslation		3,952,000				<3,952,000>
CCS revaluation			4,038,000		86,000	3,952,000
CCS exchange	10,909,000		<10,909,000>			
	12,630,000>	-0-	-0-	-0-	-0-	<12,630,000>

8.4.7 Concluding Remarks

ABC's objective when entering into the combination of the bond and the CCS was to incur an annual expense representing 5.19%, or EUR 4,210,000 (= 80 mn × 5.19% × 365/360).

During the first, second and third years of the term of the bond (and of the hedging relationship) the overall impact of the strategy on profit or loss was an annual expense of EUR 4,210,000. The annual net cash outflow was exactly EUR 4,210,000 as well. Therefore, ABC's objective was fully achieved.

This outcome occurred because there were no ineffective amounts. Otherwise, the target still would have been achieved from an annual net cash flow perspective, but not from an annual expense perspective. Even in the presence of inefficiencies, the overall 3-year expense would have been EUR 12,630,000 (= 4,210,000 × 3).

As mentioned in the previous case studies, the basis component of the CCS was part of the hedging instrument. A notably volatile behaviour of the basis could have created significant inefficiencies. When the basis component of a CCS is excluded from the hedging instrument, IFRS 9 allows an entity to recognise changes in the fair value of this component either in profit or loss or temporarily in OCI to the extent that those changes relate to the hedged item.

CHAPTER **9**

Hedging Equity Risk

This chapter focuses on the issues affecting equity recognition and hedging. Many of the concepts outlined herein are within the scope of IFRS 9 and IAS 32 *Financial Instruments: Disclosure and Presentation*. Besides the hedging of equity risk of investments in other companies, this chapter also covers the accounting treatment of preference shares, derivatives on own shares and convertibles (see Figure 9.1).

9.1 RECOGNITION OF EQUITY INVESTMENTS IN OTHER COMPANIES

In this section I will refer to investments in non-structured entities (i.e., entities that have sufficient equity and provide the equity investors voting rights that enable them to make significant decisions relating to the entity's operations). An investment in equity securities of another company is recognised according to the degree of influence over the investee (see Figure 9.2) as follows:

1) The group has control over the investee. Control is regarded as the power to govern the operating and financial policies of the investee so as to obtain benefits from its activities. Usually, control is presumed if the investor holds more than 50% of the voting rights of the investee. The existence and effect of potential voting rights are also considered when assessing whether the group controls the investee. Companies that are controlled by the group are usually called **subsidiaries**. Subsidiaries are **fully consolidated**.

2) The group has interests in a joint venture. A joint venture is a contractual arrangement whereby the group and other parties undertake an economic activity that is subject to joint control, that is, when the strategic operating and financial policies require the unanimous consent of the parties sharing control. Joint ventures are accounted for using the **equity consolidation** method (see below). In addition, under IFRS there is another type of joint arrangement called "joint operation" that is proportionally consolidated.

3) The group has **significant influence** over an investee but it is neither a subsidiary nor a joint venture. In this case, the investee is called an **associate**. Significant influence is the power to participate the operating and financial policies of the investee, but without

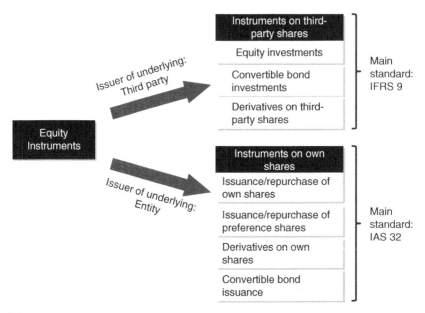

FIGURE 9.1   Equity instruments.

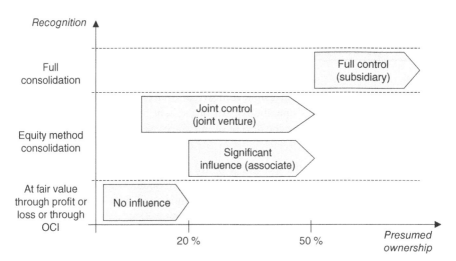

FIGURE 9.2   Recognition of equity investments.

control or joint control over those decisions. Usually significant influence is presumed when the group holds at least 20%, but no more than 50%, of the actual and potential voting rights of the investee. An associate is accounted for in the consolidated financial statements using the **equity method**. Under the equity method the investment is originally accounted for at cost. The investment carrying amount increases (decreases) with the profits (losses) of the associate and decreases with the dividends of the associate.

4) The group does not exercise significant influence or control over the investee. This is the usually case when the group holds less than 20% of the actual and potential voting rights of the investee. The investment is then classified as held at either fair value through profit and loss or fair value through other comprehensive income. This is an *irrevocable* choice.

(a) The equity investment is classified at FVTPL if it is acquired for the purpose of selling it in the near term (i.e., investment is held for trading). The investment is measured at fair value. Gains and losses arising from changes in fair value are included in profit or loss.

(b) The equity investment is classified at FVOCI if it is acquired for the purpose of not holding it for trading. The investment is measured at fair value. Gains and losses arising from changes in fair value are included in OCI. Dividends received from the investment are recognised in profit or loss.

9.1.1 Hedging Investments Consolidated under Equity Method

IFRS 9 prohibits designating an investment accounted for by the equity method as a hedged item to avoid conflicts with existing accounting requirements for that item. Under the equity method of accounting, the investor records its share of the investee's gains or losses from its investment. It does not account for changes in the price of the equity shares, which would become part of the basis of an equity method investment if fair value hedge accounting were permitted. Changes in earnings of an equity method investee presumably would affect the fair value of its equity shares. Applying fair value hedge accounting to an equity method investment thus could result in some amount of "double counting" of the investor's share of the investee's earnings. The IASB believed that result was inappropriate. In addition, the IASB was concerned that it would be difficult to develop a method of implementing fair value hedge accounting, including measuring hedge ineffectiveness, for equity method investments and that the results of any method would be difficult to understand. For similar reasons, IFRS 9 prohibits fair value hedge accounting for a firm commitment to acquire or dispose of an investment accounted for using the equity method.

9.1.2 Impairment of Equity Investments

Because unconsolidated equity investments are measured at fair value, there is no need to test them for impairment. If an investment has experienced a significant and prolonged decline in its fair value, such decline would already be presented in the entity's financial statements when fair valuing the asset.

9.2 DEBT VERSUS EQUITY CLASSIFICATION OF OWN INSTRUMENTS

IAS 32 establishes the principles for distinguishing between liabilities and equity. The appropriate classification is determined on initial recognition and is not subsequently changed unless the terms of the instrument are modified. The classification of financial instruments issued by the entity as debt or equity can be complex. The economic substance of a financial instrument, rather than its legal form, governs its classification. Liabilities within the scope of IFRS 9 are those that arise from present contractual obligations. Conversely, IAS 32 identifies a critical feature of an equity instrument as including no present contractual obligation to pay cash or to transfer another financial asset.

9.2.1 Recognition as a Liability

A fundamental characteristic of a financial liability is a present contractual obligation to transfer assets to the holder of the instrument, over which the issuer has no discretion. A financial instrument is a liability if there is a contractual obligation:

- to deliver cash or another financial asset to another entity; or
- to exchange financial assets or financial liabilities with another entity under conditions that are potentially unfavourable to the entity.

9.2.2 Recognition as an Equity Instrument

An equity instrument represents a residual interest in the net assets of the issuer. More precisely, a financial instrument is considered an equity instrument if either of the following conditions is met:

(i) There is no contractual obligation to deliver cash or another financial asset to another entity; or to exchange financial assets or liabilities under conditions that are potentially unfavourable to the issuer.

(ii) The instrument will or may be settled in the issuer's own equity shares: a non-derivative that includes no contractual obligation for the issuer to deliver a variable number of its own equity instruments; or a derivative that will be settled by the issuer exchanging a fixed amount of cash or another financial asset for a fixed number of its own equity instruments.

The IASB issued a remarkably narrow amendment in 2008 whereby certain instruments that would otherwise meet the definition of a liability (because of the obligation to redeem the instrument at the option of the holder) could be classified as equity if very strict criteria were met. One of those criteria is that the puttable share is the most subordinate instrument. A **puttable instrument** is one that requires the issuer to repurchase or redeem the instrument for cash or some other financial asset on exercise of the put.

Not all instruments are classified as either only debt or only equity. The following table summarises the classification of the most common hybrid and equity instruments:

Instrument	Classification
Ordinary shares	Equity
Redeemable preference shares with non-discretionary dividends	Liability
Redeemable preference shares with discretionary dividends	Liability for principal, and equity for dividends
Non-redeemable preference shares with discretionary dividends	Equity
Non-redeemable preference shares with non-discretionary dividends	Liability
Convertible bond which converts into a fixed number of shares only, if converted	Liability for bond and equity for conversion option
Convertible bond which converts into a variable number of shares to the value of the liability	Liability

9.3 HYBRID SECURITIES – PREFERENCE SHARES FROM AN ISSUER'S PERSPECTIVE

The financial capital markets have witnessed over the last several decades a strong development of different types of securities. Because some of these securities simultaneously have debt and equity elements, they are called "hybrid securities". In general there are three types of hybrid securities: preference shares, convertible debt and contingent convertible debt. The aim of preference shares is to optimise their equity treatment by the rating agencies, their dividend tax deductibility, their investor demand and their IFRS accounting impact. It is critical to understand all the terms and conditions of the preference shares to ensure their appropriate classification as debt or equity.

9.3.1 Contractual Discretion

An instrument will be considered an equity instrument if the entity has a contractual "discretion" over whether to make any cash payments. A strong economic incentive to make payments does not amount to a contractual obligation and is therefore not sufficient for liability classification. Anything outside the contractual terms is not considered when classifying an instrument under IAS 32. Therefore, contractual discretion is not affected by the following:

- a history of making distributions or an intention or ability to make distributions in the future;
- the amount of the issuer's reserves;
- the entity's expectation of a profit or loss for the period;
- the ability or inability of the issuer to influence the amount of its profit or loss for the period, any economic compulsion to make distribution or the ranking of the instrument on the liquidation of the entity;
- a possible negative impact on the price of ordinary shares of the issuer if dividends are not paid to ordinary shares (because of restrictions on paying dividends on the ordinary shares if dividends are not paid on the preference shares).

Example: Perpetual Instrument with Discretionary Interest

Suppose that an entity issues a perpetual debt instrument with annual interest, and that the entity has discretion over whether to pay the instrument's interest. Payment of interest is mandatory when the entity distributes dividends to its common shareholders. Unpaid interest does not accrue additional interest. Because the entity has no contractual obligation to deliver cash (or another financial asset), the instrument as a whole is classified as an equity instrument.

Example: Perpetual Instrument with Non-discretionary Interest

Suppose that an entity issues a perpetual debt instrument with annual interest, and that the entity is obliged to pay the instrument's interest. While the entity will never pay the instrument's principal, a perpetual instrument with a mandatory coupon is a liability in its entirety because the whole of its value is derived from the future string of interest payments.

9.3.2 Economic Compulsion

Economic compulsion takes place when an entity has an economic motivation, but is not obliged, to make a specific decision. For example, an issuer of a callable bond may have a strong motivation to call the bond on the call date if the bond pays a much higher than market interest rate.

In general, economic compulsion does not play a role in the classification decision under IAS 32. For example, a sold call option on an entity's own shares may be classified as either equity or liability depending on its form of settlement. The option will be considered as equity if upon exercise the issuer of the shares is obliged to deliver a fixed number of shares in exchange for a fixed amount of cash. The option will be considered as a liability if the option can only be settled in cash or if either of the two parties to the option has the right to choose between cash (or an equivalent variable number of shares) and physical settlement. Whilst there might be a strong economic compulsion to physically settle the option (e.g., because the entity owns sufficient treasury shares to meet the exercise), the existence of a right on the part of either of the two parties to choose cash settlement would cause it to be classified as a liability.

However, once a financial obligation has been established through the terms and conditions, economic compulsion may be relevant in special circumstances. One example in which economic compulsion may play a role in the instrument's classification would be an undated preference share issue with a contractually accelerating dividend, whereby in the foreseeable future the dividend yield was scheduled to be so large that the issuer would be economically compelled to redeem the instrument. In these circumstances, classification as a financial liability was appropriate because the issuer had little, if any, discretion to avoid redeeming the instrument.

9.3.3 Degree of Subordination

IAS 32 does not take into account the level of seniority of payment of the instrument when classifying it as equity or liability. For example, an instrument can be *pari passu* with all the senior debt and be classified as equity. Similarly, an instrument can be *pari passu* with all other preference shares and be classified as liability. The seniority of payment is only relevant on liquidation of the entity and does not play a role in indicating whether the issuer has discretion to make payments under the instrument.

9.3.4 Legal Form

When deciding the classification of a financial instrument between liability and equity, attention should be paid to the underlying substance and economic reality of the contractual obligation and not just its legal form. For example, the mere fact that a financial instrument has the legal title of "shares" does not mean that the instrument should be classified as equity.

In general, the rule of thumb regarding the classification of preference shares as a liability or as equity is as follows:

- Preference shares which are mandatorily redeemable on a specific date or at the option of the holder: the principal would be classified as a liability.
- Non-redeemable preference shares: the principal would be classified as equity.
- Preference shares which carry non-discretionary dividend obligations whether cumulative or non-cumulative: the dividends would be classified as a liability and would be taken to profit or loss as financial expenses.

9.3.5 Entity's Historical Trend or Ability to Make Distributions

The entity's history of making distributions in prior years or its ability to make distributions does not impact the classification of an instrument.

9.4 CONVERTIBLE BONDS – ISSUER'S PERSPECTIVE

In general, convertible bonds are instruments which give the holder the right to "convert" a bond into a fixed number of the issuer's common stock (i.e., ordinary shares) at a pre-specified price –the conversion price. Let us assume a convertible bond issued by ABC with a EUR 100 million notional and conversion price of EUR 10.00. The value of the convertible bond at maturity had the profile depicted in Figure 9.3:

- The convertible bondholders would exercise their conversion right if ABC's share price was higher than EUR 10.00, and receive 10 million shares (= 100 mn notional/10 mn shares) in exchange for EUR 100 million.
- If ABC's share price was equal to or below EUR 10.00, the convertible bondholders would not exercise their conversion right and would ask instead for a redemption of the bond in cash (i.e., they would receive EUR 100 million).

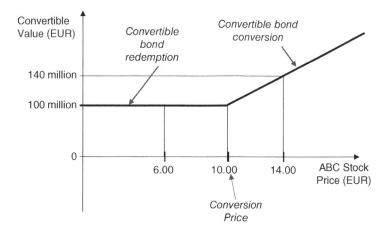

FIGURE 9.3 Convertible bond value at maturity.

Convertible bonds have both common stock and straight bond features. Like common stock, convertible bondholders benefit from an appreciation of the issuer's common stock (in our previous example, when ABC's share price was above EUR 10.00). Like straight bonds (i.e., non-convertible bonds), convertible bonds can have cash redemption at maturity (in our previous example, when ABC's share price was at or below EUR 10.00) and fixed coupon payments.

From an issuer's perspective, at inception a convertible bond is split into two components: a bond part (the host contract) and an embedded option part. The bond part represents the coupon payments and the potential redemption in cash at par. The option part represents the right to exchange the bond for a number of shares. The embedded option can be recognised as either a derivative (i.e., a liability) or an equity instrument.

9.4.1 Convertible Bonds Denominated in the Entity's Functional Currency – Fixed for Fixed

If a convertible bond allows the holder to convert the bond into a **fixed number** of the entity's equity instruments in exchange for a **fixed amount of cash** (or other assets), the written option is an equity instrument from an issuer's perspective. This instrument is called a **compound instrument** (Figure 9.4), and from an accounting standpoint is split into a liability component (the host contract) and an equity component.

On the issue date, the fair value of the liability component is determined using a market interest rate for an equivalent non-convertible bond. This amount is recorded as a liability on an amortised cost basis until extinguished on conversion or redemption of the bond. The remainder of the proceeds of the issue is allocated to the equity component (see Figure 9.5). No gain or loss arises from initially recognising the components of the instrument separately. The equity part is recognised in shareholders' equity, net of income tax effects.

FIGURE 9.4 Compound instruments.

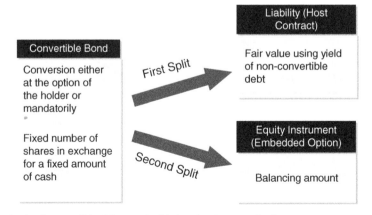

FIGURE 9.5 Split of convertible debt – embedded option is an equity instrument.

9.4.2 Convertible Bonds Denominated in the Entity's Functional Currency – Fixed for Variable

If a convertible bond allows the holder to convert the bond into anything *other than* a **fixed number** of the entity's equity instruments in exchange for a **fixed amount of cash** (or other assets), the written option is a derivative from the issuer's perspective. This instrument is called a "hybrid instrument" (Figure 9.6) and from an accounting standpoint is split into a liability component (the host contract) and a derivative component.

On the issue date, the fair value of the liability component is determined using a market interest rate for an equivalent non-convertible bond. This amount is recorded as a liability on an amortised cost basis until extinguished on conversion or redemption of the bond. The remainder of the proceeds of the issue is allocated to the derivative component (see Figure 9.7). No gain or loss arises from initially recognising the components of the instrument separately. The derivative part is recognised as a liability and fair valued at each reporting date.

9.4.3 Convertible Bonds Denominated in a Foreign Currency

Suppose that an entity whose functional currency is the EUR issues a USD-denominated convertible bond that can be converted into a fixed number of the entity's shares for a fixed amount of USD. Because the amount is fixed in USD, it is a variable in the *functional currency of the issuer* (EUR).

IAS 32 states that a contract that will be settled by the entity delivering a fixed number of its own equity instruments in exchange for a variable amount of cash is a financial liability. Consequently, the written option should be classified as a liability, from an issuer perspective.

FIGURE 9.6   Compound instruments.

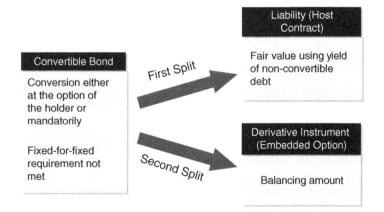

FIGURE 9.7   Split of convertible debt – embedded option is a derivative.

This treatment would result in reporting gains and losses arising from the entity's own equity through profit or loss, along with the currency gains and losses. Therefore, IFRS 9 permits cash flow hedges of such FX exposure.

9.5 CONVERTIBLE BONDS – INVESTOR'S PERSPECTIVE

From an investor's perspective, a convertible bond is recognised in its entirety at FVTPL because the host contract and the embedded derivative are not closely related. The host contract resembles a debt instrument while the embedded derivative resembles an equity derivative instrument. As a result, at each reporting date the convertible bond would be fair valued and the change in fair value since the last fair valuation would be recognised in profit or loss.

9.6 DERIVATIVES ON OWN EQUITY INSTRUMENTS

The term "own equity instruments" usually refers to equity instruments issued by the parent company. However, the term also refers to equity instruments issued by its fully consolidated subsidiaries, as these instruments are in substance equivalent to equity instruments of the parent company.

9.6.1 Hedging Own Equity Instruments

IFRS 9 prohibits an equity instrument classified by an entity in its shareholders' equity in the statement of financial position from being designated as a hedged item. For example, an equity instrument does not meet the following hedge accounting requirements: (a) that a hedged item is a firm commitment, a highly expected forecast transaction or an already recognised asset or liability (the equity instrument is not an asset or liability, but an element of shareholders' equity); and (b) that the hedged item represents an exposure to changes in fair value that could affect reported profit or loss, or OCI in the case of investments at FVOCI (an equity instrument is not fair valued, and its repurchase/reissuance does not affect profit or loss). This prohibition does not apply to the holder of the equity instrument.

9.6.2 Derivatives on Own Equity Instruments

A derivative on an own equity instrument may be accounted for as a derivative instrument or an equity instrument, depending on the type of derivative and method of settlement.

- Derivatives on own equity that result in the delivery of a fixed amount of cash or other financial assets for a fixed number of the entity's own equity instruments are classified as equity instruments. All other derivatives on the entity's own equity are treated as derivatives and accounted for as such under IFRS 9.
- Derivatives on own equity where the counterparty or the issuer has a choice between cash settlement and physical delivery) are recognised as derivatives.

The following table illustrates whether a derivative on own shares is a financial liability or an equity instrument:

	Physical delivery only *(1)*	**Physical delivery or cash settlement (at the discretion of the issuer or the holder)**	**Cash settlement only (or net share equivalent)** *(2)*
Forward contract to buy own shares	Equity plus recognition of a financial liability	Derivative plus recognition of a financial liability	Derivative
Forward contract to sell own shares	Equity	Derivative	Derivative
Purchased call on own shares	Equity	Derivative	Derivative
Written call on own shares	Equity	Derivative	Derivative
Purchased put on own shares	Equity	Derivative	Derivative
Written put on own shares	Equity plus recognition of a financial liability	Derivative plus recognition of a financial liability	Derivative

Notes:
(1) Assuming the settlement is made by exchanging a fixed amount of cash for a fixed number of the entity's own shares
(2) In a net share settlement, a variable number of shares is delivered/received having a fair value equivalent to the derivative's fair value at the time of exercise

9.7 CASE STUDY: ACCOUNTING FOR A STOCK LENDING TRANSACTION

This case study covers the accounting of securities lending transactions. Suppose that an entity has a large investment in equity shares of another company. If the entity wants to earn additional income, or to lower its cost of funding, it might lend those shares to a financial institution. The financial institution may need to borrow those instruments to cover a short position or to meet delivery obligations. Securities lending is a transaction where a lender (the entity in our case) transfers legal title to securities to a borrower (the financial institution) and the borrower is obliged to return the same type of securities to the lender at the end of the lending period.

Securities lending transactions are usually collateralised by receiving cash or low-risk securities. In the event of a default by the borrower, the securities lending agreement provides the entity with the right to liquidate the collateral held.

Suppose that, on 1 April 20X0, ABC had 40 million shares in DEF and that it lent those shares to XYZ Bank. As a consequence of the stock lending agreement, legal ownership of the shares was transferred to XYZ Bank. The shares were trading at EUR 10.00 on that date. To reduce its credit exposure to XYZ Bank, ABC received EUR 400 million cash from XYZ Bank as collateral at the beginning of the transaction. The lending agreement matured on 1 August 20X0 (usually there is no maturity to the agreement, and either the lender or the borrower can terminate the agreement at any time). Figure 9.8 highlights the initial flows of the transaction.

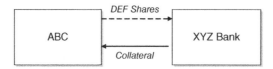

FIGURE 9.8   Lending agreement – initial flows.

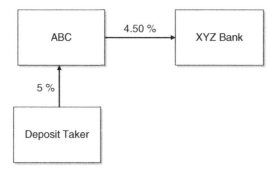

FIGURE 9.9   Lending agreement – interest flows.

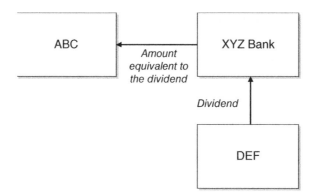

FIGURE 9.10   Lending agreement – dividend flows.

ABC derived income by investing the EUR 400 million cash collateral in a deposit yielding 5%. Normally, as in our case, this income would be paid over to the borrower, less a margin to represent a stock lending fee for providing securities to the financial institution. In our case, this interest was to be received (and passed to the borrower) on maturity of the lending agreement. The lending margin was 50 basis points, or 0.50%. Figure 9.9 shows the transaction's interest cash flows.

Suppose also that the DEF shares paid a EUR 0.50 dividend per share on 15 July 20X0. The dividend was received by XYZ Bank as it was the legal owner of the shares. Under the lending agreement, XYZ Bank was required to pass the dividend on a gross basis to ABC on the dividend payment date, as shown in Figure 9.10.

On maturity of the transaction (1 August 20X0), the initial flows were reversed as shown in Figure 9.11: XYZ Bank returned the shares to ABC in exchange for the repayment of the EUR 400 million collateral. ABC became the legal owner of the shares.

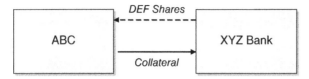

FIGURE 9.11   Lending agreement – final flows.

9.7.1 Accounting Entries

Suppose that ABC reported its financial statements quarterly, at the end of each March, June, September and December. The required journal entries were as follows:

1) To record the DEF share loan and the collateral received on 1 April 20X0
   The DEF shares were classified at FVTPL. The 40 million DEF shares were fair valued by ABC on the previous reporting date (31 March 20X0) at EUR 9.00 per share. When an entity lends its securities, it reports these securities as pledged assets in its statement of financial position (i.e., balance sheet). The shares remained on ABC's asset side.

Lent securities (Asset)	360,000,000	
Investment in DEF shares (Asset)		360,000,000

The cash collateral that ABC received on the securities lending transaction was recognised. Because the collateral had to be returned in the future, ABC also recognised a liability.

Cash (Asset)	400,000,000	
Collateral on securities lent (Liability)		400,000,000

2) To record the fair valuation and the accrued interest on 30 June 20X0
   The DEF shares were trading at EUR 11.00 on 30 June 20X0. ABC classified the investment in DEF shares at FVTPL. On the previous reporting date (30 March 20X0), the shares were fair valued at EUR 9.00 per share. The change in fair value of the shares represented a EUR 80 million (= 40 million × (11 − 9)) gain.

Lent securities (Asset)	80,000,000	
Other financial income (Profit or loss)		80,000,000

The collateral was invested in a deposit yielding 5% on an actual/360 basis. The interest to be received was recognised on an accrual basis and recorded as interest income. The number of days elapsed since 1 April 20X0 was 90. The accrued interest amount was EUR 5,000,000 (= 400 million × 5% × 90/360).

Interest receivable (Asset)	5,000,000	
Interest income (Profit or loss)		5,000,000

Under the lending agreement, ABC was obliged to pass the interest received less a margin of 50 bps. The interest to be paid to the financial institution was recognised on an accrual basis and recorded as interest expense. The number of days elapsed since 1 April 20X0 was 90. The accrued interest amount was EUR 4,500,000 (= 400 million × (5% − 0.50%) × 90/360).

Interest expense (Profit or loss)	4,500,000	
Interest payable (Liability)		4,500,000

3) To record the amount equivalent to the dividend received on 15 July 20X0
The DEF 40 million shares paid a EUR 20 million dividend (EUR 0.50 per share) on 15 July 20X0. Under the lending agreement, XYZ Bank was required to pass the dividend to ABC on the dividend payment date.

Cash (Asset)	20,000,000	
Other financial income (Profit or loss)		20,000,000

4) To record the end of the lending agreement on 1 August 20X0
The number of days elapsed since 30 June 20X0 was 32. Thus, the deposit accrued interest amount was EUR 1,778,000 (=400 million × 5% × 32/360).

Interest receivable (Asset)	1,778,000	
Interest income (Profit or loss)		1,778,000

On 1 August 20X0, the deposit paid 122 days' interest at an annual rate of 5% (122 days having elapsed since 1 April 20X0). The interest amount was EUR 6,778,000 (=400 million × 5% × 122/360).

Cash (Asset)	6,778,000	
Interest receivable (Asset)		6,778,000

The number of days elapsed since 30 June 20X0 was 32. Thus, the accrued amount of the interest to be paid by ABC to XYZ Bank was EUR 1,600,000 (=400 million × (5%-0.50%) × 32/360).

Interest expense (Profit or loss)	1,600,000	
Interest payable (Liability)		1,600,000

ABC had to pay 122 days' interest at an annual rate of 4.50% interest to XYZ Bank (122 days having elapsed since 1 April 20X0). The interest amount was EUR 6,100,000 (=400 million × (5% − 0.50%) × 122/360).

Interest payable (Liability)	6,100,000	
Cash (Asset)		6,100,000

XYZ bank returned to ABC the borrowed 40 million DEF shares.

Investment in DEF shares (Asset)	440,000,000	
Lent securities (Asset)		440,000,000

ABC returned the EUR 400 million cash collateral.

Collateral on securities lent (Liability)	400,000,000	
Cash (Asset)		400,000,000

9.7.2 Final Remarks

Looking at ABC's profit or loss statement during the life of the lending agreement, it can be noted that the rationale behind the lending of DEF shares was to enhance the yield on the investment. ABC obtained 50 basis points for lending DEF shares (or EUR 678,000). Figure 9.12 compares the pre-tax profit or loss statements of ABC without and with the lending agreement in place.

Without the lending agreement:

Profit or Loss	
Dividend Income:	20,000,000
Total Pre-Tax:	20,000,000

With the lending agreement:

Profit or Loss	
Interest Income:	6,778,000
Interest Expense:	<6,100,000>
Dividend Income:	20,000,000
Total Pre-Tax:	20,678,000

FIGURE 9.12 Comparison of profit or loss statements.

The transaction, however, had two major disadvantages. Firstly, ABC lost the voting rights on the DEF shares during the life of the transaction. Secondly, ABC received an interest amount equivalent to the gross dividend of DEF shares, but could not claim any tax deductions related to such dividend.

Finally, two particular comments are worth noting. Firstly, in our case study the amount of collateral was based on the market value of the DEF shares at the beginning of the lending agreement, and this amount remained unchanged during the life of the agreement. Commonly, the collateral amount changes in order to eliminate credit exposure of the lender (ABC) to the borrower (XYZ Bank). The lender monitors the market value of the shares lent on a daily basis and requests additional collateral or returns surplus collateral in accordance with the market value of the lent/borrowed shares. The corresponding accounting entries are then produced on a daily basis to record the additional collateral received or returned, a substantial operational burden. Secondly, lending agreements usually do not have a fixed maturity. At any time, either the lender or the borrower can terminate the agreement by providing notice to the other party.

9.8 CASE STUDY: ACCOUNTING FOR A MANDATORY CONVERTIBLE BOND FROM AN ISSUER'S PERSPECTIVE

This case study covers the accounting of both a bond mandatorily convertible into a fixed number of shares (a **fixed parity** mandatory convertible) and a bond mandatorily convertible into a variable number of shares (a **variable parity** mandatory convertible). A mandatorily convertible (or exchangeable) bond is an instrument that includes an unconditional obligation requiring the issuer to redeem the bond by delivering a specified number of shares of the issuer (or a third party in the case of an exchangeable bond) at a specified date or dates.

9.8.1 Accounting for a Fixed Parity Mandatory Convertible Bond

Let us assume that on 1 January 20X0 ABC issued a fixed-parity mandatory convertible bond on its own shares with the following terms:

Fixed Parity Mandatory Convertible Bond Terms	
Issue date	1 January 20X0
Issuer	ABC Corporation ("ABC")
Issue proceeds	EUR 99.5 million
Principal	EUR 100 million
Maturity	3 years
Interest	5%, annually payable each 31 December
Conversion	Obligatorily convertible on maturity into 10 million new shares of ABC

Let us also assume that, at bond maturity, ABC issued 10 million ordinary shares with a par value of EUR 1.00 each. The issue value was EUR 10.00 per share. Therefore, the share premium was EUR 9.00 per share.

Two are the potential accounting treatments of mandatory convertibles depending whether the conversion implies the delivery of a fixed number for a fixed amount of cash (or its equivalent in other assets).

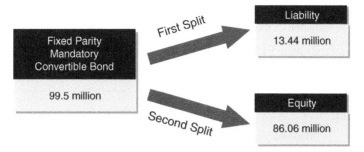

FIGURE 9.13   Split of fixed-parity mandatory convertible.

Mandatory convertibles which upon conversion the issuer has an obligation to deliver a **fixed number** of its own shares, are **compound** instruments that have both debt and equity characteristics. Under IFRS, the components of a mandatory convertible are bifurcated at the time of issuance into a debt component and an equity component. The initial carrying amount of the debt component is calculated as the present value of the bond cash flows for which the entity has a potential obligation to pay. The cash flows are discounted using the prevailing yield of similar debt without the conversion feature. The equity component represents the requirement to convert the mandatory convertible into ABC shares. Its initial value is calculated as the difference between the issue proceeds and the debt component. There is no subsequent fair valuation for either component, assuming that the debt component is recognised at amortised cost. This was the situation in our case.

Let us assume that when the mandatory convertible bond was issued, the prevailing yield of similar debt without the conversion feature was 5.70%. The debt component, EUR 98.12 million, was determined as the present value of the bond cash flows, assuming that the bond does not have the equity conversion feature. The calculation of the carrying amount of the debt component was performed as follows (amounts in EUR millions):

$$13.44 = \frac{5}{1+5.7\%} + \frac{5}{(1+5.7\%)^2} + \frac{5}{(1+5.7\%)^3}$$

As the proceeds of the mandatory convertible issue were EUR 99.5 million, the equity component represented EUR 86.06 million (= 99.5 mn − 13.44 mn), as shown in Figure 9.13. Therefore, the bifurcation resulted in a positive value being ascribed to the equity component and a lower value (discount) to the debt component. This discount was amortised as an adjustment (increase) to interest expense over the term of the mandatory convertible.

The amortised cost and interest expense of the liability component at each accounting date was determined as follows:

Year	Amortised cost Beginning Year (a)	Interest expense (b) = (a) × 5.7%	Cash payment (c)	Amortised cost at end of year (d) = (a) + (b) − (c)
1	13,440,000	766,000	5,000,000	9,206,000
2	9,206,000	525,000	5,000,000	4,731,000
3	4,731,000	271,000 (*)	5,000,000	-0-

(*) The calculation was in reality 270,000. The difference was due to rounding. The figure 271,000 was used to reach a EUR 100 million redemption amount

Accounting Entries   The required journal entries were as follows.

1) To record the issuance of the mandatory convertible on 1 January 20X0:

The issue proceeds were EUR 99.5 million. The initial fair value of the equity component was EUR 86.060,000. The initial value of the debt component was EUR 13,440,000.

Cash (Asset)	99,500,000	
Mandatory convertible (Liability)		13,440,000
Other equity instruments (Equity)		86,060,000

2) To record the interest expense and coupon payment on 31 December 20X0:

Interest expense (Profit or loss)	766,000	
Mandatory convertible (Liability)	4,234,000	
Cash (Asset)		5,000,000

3) To record the interest expense and payment on 31 December 20X1:

Interest expense (Profit or loss)	525,000	
Mandatory convertible (Liability)	4,475,000	
Cash (Asset)		5,000,000

4) Entries on 31 December 20X2:

To record the interest expense and payment:

Interest expense (Profit or loss)	270,000	
Mandatory convertible (Liability)	4,730,000	
Cash (Asset)		5,000,000

To record conversion of the mandatory convertible and the issuance of 10 million new shares with a par value of EUR 1.00 each:

Other equity instruments (Equity)	86,060,000	
Share capital (Equity)		10,000,000
Share premium (Equity)		76,060,000

9.8.2 Accounting for a Variable Parity Mandatory Convertible Bond

In the previous example, the embedded equity conversion was recognised as an equity instrument because the conversion feature implied the issuer delivering a fixed number of own shares in exchange for a fixed amount of cash (i.e., it met the "fixed-for-fixed" requirement for equity instruments). Next I will cover a mandatory convertible in which the number of own shares to be delivered was variable.

Suppose that on 1 January 20X0 ABC issued a mandatorily convertible bond on its own shares with the following terms:

Variable parity mandatory convertible bond terms	
Issue date	1 January 20X0
Issuer	ABC Corporation
Issue proceeds	EUR 99.5 million
Principal	EUR 100 million
Maturity	3 years
Interest	5.7% annually, payable 31 December
Conversion	Obligatorily convertible on maturity into the following number of shares the issuer: Number of shares = Bond principal/Share price at maturity

On maturity the issuer had the obligation to deliver a variable number of shares. The number of shares to be delivered was equal to the bond principal (i.e., EUR 100 million) divided by the share price at conversion (i.e., the bondholder had no equity price risk). The fair value of the embedded conversion was nil during the life of the mandatory convertible and, as result, the instrument was initially recognised as a liability without any embedded option (see Figure 9.14). In other words, the mandatory convertible was theoretically equivalent to (i) the issuance of a straight bond (i.e., a bond without any conversion features), (ii) the issuance of shares at maturity and (iii) the redemption of the straight bond using the proceeds from the share issuance.

The bond was recognised at amortised cost using the effective interest rate (EIR) method. The bond's EIR was 5.887%. The EIR was determined by taking into account the EUR 99.5 million issue proceeds and the EUR 5.7 million annual coupon, as follows:

$$\frac{5.7 \text{ mn}}{1+\text{EIR}} + \frac{5.7 \text{ mn}}{(1+\text{EIR})^2} + \frac{105.7 \text{ mn}}{(1+\text{EIR})^3} = 99.5 \text{ mn}$$

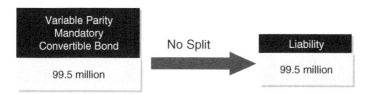

FIGURE 9.14 Initial recognition of variable parity mandatory convertible.

The liability's amortised cost and interest expense at each accounting date was deter-mined as follows:

Year	Amortised cost at beginning year (a)	Interest expense (b) = (a) × 5.887%	Cash payment (c)	Amortised cost at end of year (d) = (a) + (b) − (c)
1	99,500,000	5,858,000	5,700,000	99,658,000
2	99,658,000	5,867,000	5,700,000	99,825,000
3	99,825,000	5,875,000 (*)	5,700,000	100,000,000

(*) The calculation was in reality 5,880,000. The difference was due to rounding. The figure 5,875,000 was used to reach the EUR 100 million redemption amount

Accounting Entries The required accounting entries were as follows:
1) On the issue date (1 January 20X0)

Cash (Asset)	99,500,000	
Mandatory convertible (Liability)		99,500,000

2) On the first reporting and coupon payment date (31 December 20X0)

Interest expense (Profit or loss)	5,858,000	
Mandatory convertible (Liability)		158,000
Cash (Asset)		5,700,000

3) On the second reporting and coupon payment date (31 December 20X1)

Interest expense (Profit or loss)	5,867,000	
Mandatory convertible (Liability)		167,000
Cash (Asset)		5,700,000

4) On the third reporting and conversion date (31 December 20X2)
   Suppose that on maturity (31 December 20X2), ABC's share price was EUR 12.50. As a result, the bond converted into 8 million (= 100 mn/12.5) shares of ABC with a nominal value of EUR 1.00 per share. The bond also paid a EUR 5.7 million coupon on that date.

Interest expense (Profit or loss)	5,875,000	
Mandatory convertible (Liability)		175,000
Cash (Asset)		5,700,000

Mandatory convertible (Liability)	100,000,000	
Share capital (Equity)		10,000,000
Share premium (Equity)		90,000,000

Mandatory Convertibles with both Fixed and Variable Features The previous two examples covered mandatory convertibles with fixed parity and variable parity features. Mandatory convertibles that combine both features (e.g., a bond mandatorily convertible into a fixed number of shares plus an additional variable number of shares that is a function of the share price at maturity) are recognised as hybrid instruments. At the time of issuance the instrument is split into a debt component (the host contract) and a derivative component (see Figure 9.7). The initial carrying amount of the debt component is calculated as the present value of the bond cash flows assuming that the bond does not have the equity conversion feature. The cash flows are discounted using the prevailing yield of similar debt without the conversion feature. The derivative component represents the requirement to redeem the principal in shares. The derivative component is calculated as the difference between the issue proceeds and the debt component. There is a subsequent fair valuation of the derivative component at each reporting date and at maturity.

9.9 CASE STUDY: ACCOUNTING FOR A CONVERTIBLE BOND FROM AN ISSUER'S PERSPECTIVE

This case study covers the accounting of convertibles. A convertible bond is an instrument which can be converted into shares of the bond issuer at the holder's option. At specific dates (usually at any time during the life of the convertible), the bondholder can exercise his/her conversion right.

There are two potential accounting treatments of convertibles depending on their conversion characteristics. If the potential conversion implies the delivery of a fixed number of issuer shares for a fixed amount of cash (or its equivalent in other assets), the instrument is called a **compound instrument** and is recognised as a liability and an equity instrument. Otherwise, the instrument is called a **hybrid instrument** and is recognised as a liability and a derivative.

9.9.1 Accounting for a Fixed-for-Fixed Convertible Bond

In this first example, upon conversion the issuer would deliver a fixed number of the issuer's shares. Suppose that, on 1 January 20X0, ABC issued a convertible bond on its own shares with the following terms:

Convertible bond terms	
Issue date	1 January 20X0
Issuer	ABC
Issue proceeds	EUR 99.5 million
Principal	EUR 100 million
Maturity	3 years (31 December 20X2)

Interest	2% annually, payable 31 December
Conversion	At the holder's option on maturity. Convertible into 10 million new shares of ABC, to be issued on maturity
Conversion rate	EUR 10 per share
Price of ABC shares on the issue date	EUR 7 per share

At maturity the bondholders had the right to receive shares of ABC rather than receiving the EUR 100 million principal. Were the bondholders to exercise their conversion right, ABC would deliver 10 million (= Principal/Conversion rate = EUR 100 mn/EUR 10 per share) own shares. In the situation where, when exercised by the holder, the issuer has the obligation to deliver a fixed number of shares, convertibles are compound instruments that have both debt and equity characteristics. The fixed-for-fixed criterion is met as following conversion the holder receives a fixed number of shares in exchange for the bond's principal (i.e., in exchange for a fixed amount of cash – or other assets worth a fixed amount).

From an issuer's perspective, the components of fixed-for-fixed convertibles are bifurcated at the time of issuance into a debt component and an equity component (see Figure 9.7). The initial carrying amount of the debt component is calculated as the present value of the bond cash flows assuming that the bond's conversion right is not exercised. The cash flows are discounted using the prevailing yield of similar debt without the conversion feature (i.e., a straight bond issued by the issuer with similar maturity). The equity component represents the option to convert the bond into ABC shares. It is calculated as the difference between the issue proceeds and the debt component. There is no subsequent fair valuation for either component.

Suppose also that at the time of issuance, the prevailing yield for ABC debt with a 3-year term but without a conversion option was 5%. The initial carrying amount of debt component was EUR 91.83 million, calculated as the present value of the bond cash flows (i.e., the EUR 2 million annual coupons and the EUR 100 million redemption amount) discounted using the 5% yield for similar straight debt of the issuer, as follows:

$$\frac{2}{1+5\%} + \frac{2}{(1+5\%)^2} + \frac{102}{(1+5\%)^3} = 91.83$$

The remainder of the proceeds of the issue were allocated to the equity component. As the proceeds of the convertible issue were EUR 99.5 million, the equity component was EUR 7.67 million (= 99.5 mn – 91.83 mn), as shown in Figure 9.15. Therefore, the bifurcation resulted

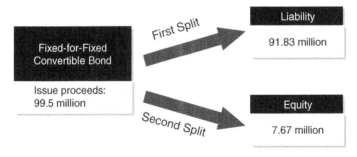

FIGURE 9.15   Split of fixed-for-fixed convertible bond.

in a positive value being ascribed to the equity component and a lower value (discount) to the debt component. This discount was amortised as an adjustment (increase) to interest expense over the term of the convertible bond.

The liability discount (i.e., the difference between the EUR 100 million redemption amount and the EUR 91.83 million initial carrying amount) was amortised as an adjustment (increase) to interest expense over the term of the convertible. The amortised cost and interest expense of the liability at each accounting date were calculated as follows:

Year	Amortised cost at beginning year (a)	Interest expense (b)=(a) × 5%	Cash payment (c)	Amortised cost at end of year (d) = (a) + (b) – (c)
1	91,830,000	4,592,000	2,000,000	94,422,000
2	94,422,000	4,721,000	2,000,000	97,143,000
3	97,143,000	4,857,000	2,000,000	100,000,000

Accounting Entries

1) Accounting entries on the issue date (1 January 20X0)

Cash (Asset)	99,500,000	
Convertible bond (Liability)		91,830,000
Share premium (Equity)		7,670,000

2) Accounting entries on the first reporting and coupon payment date (31 December 20X0)

Interest expense (Profit or loss)	4,592,000	
Convertible bond (Liability)		2,592,000
Cash (Asset)		2,000,000

3) Accounting entries on the next reporting and coupon payment date (31 December 20X1)

Interest expense (Profit or loss)	4,721,000	
Convertible bond (Liability)		2,721,000
Cash (Asset)		2,000,000

4) Accounting entries on the maturity date (31 December 20X2) to record the interest expense and coupon payment

Interest expense (Profit or loss)	4,857,000	
Convertible bond (Liability)		2,857,000
Cash (Asset)		2,000,000

At this point there are two different scenarios to consider, depending on the share price at maturity.

Scenario 1: Conversion. Suppose that at maturity, ABC shares were trading at EUR 13, above the EUR 10 conversion rate. As a consequence, the bondholders would exercise their conversion right and ABC would issue 10 million ordinary new shares with a par value of EUR 1.00 each. The share issue value was EUR 10.00 per share or EUR 100 million. Therefore, the share premium was EUR 9.00 per share or EUR 90 million. The related accounting entries would be as follows:

Convertible bond (Liability)	100,000,000	
Share capital (Equity)		10,000,000
Share premium (Equity)		90,000,000

Scenario 2: Redemption (i.e., no conversion). Suppose that at maturity, ABC shares were trading at EUR 8, below the EUR 10 conversion rate. As a consequence, the bond-holders would not exercise their conversion right and ABC would pay the EUR 100 million redemption amount. The related accounting entries would be as follows:

Convertible bond (Liability)	100,000,000	
Cash (Asset)		100,000,000

9.9.2 Accounting for a Fixed-for-Variable Convertible Bond

In a second example, I will cover a convertible bond in which, following conversion by the bond-holders, the issuer may deliver a fixed amount of shares (physical settlement), a cash amount (cash settlement) or a combination of cash and shares (net share settlement). Suppose that, on 1 January 20X0, ABC issued a convertible bond on its own shares with the following terms:

Convertible bond terms	
Issue date	1 January 20X0
Issuer	ABC
Issue proceeds	EUR 99.5 million

Principal	EUR 100 million
Redemption amount	100% of the principal amount
Maturity	3 years (31 December 20X2)
Interest	2% annually, payable on 31 December
Conversion	At the holder's option, on maturity. If holder exercises conversion right, issuer my choose to deliver either:
	a) 10 million new ABC shares (physical settlement);
	b) a cash amount equivalent to the market value of the convertible at maturity (cash settlement); or
	c) a cash amount equal to the redemption amount plus a number of shares such that the total consideration is equal to the market value of the convertible at maturity (net share settlement)
Conversion rate	EUR 10 per share
Current price of ABC shares	EUR 7 per share

In the situation where, upon conversion, the issuer is under no obligation to deliver a fixed number of its own shares, convertibles are hybrid instruments that have both debt and equity derivative characteristics. Under IFRS, the components of convertibles of this type are bifurcated at the time of issuance into a debt (liability) component and a derivative component.

- The debt (liability) component represents the bond's feature as a debt instrument if it is not converted. The initial carrying amount of the debt component is calculated as the present value of the bond cash flows assuming that the bond does not have the equity conversion feature. The cash flows are discounted using the prevailing yield of debt of the issuer with the same maturity and without the conversion feature. The liability component is commonly measured at amortised cost.
- The derivative component represents the conversion right. Its initial value is calculated as the difference between the issue proceeds and the debt component. There is a subsequent fair valuation of the derivative component at each reporting date.

The calculation of the debt (liability) component (EUR 91.83 million) was identical to that in the previous fixed-for-fixed convertible example. The remainder of the proceeds of the issue was allocated to a derivative component. As the proceeds of the convertible issue were EUR 99.5 million, the initial carrying amount of the derivative component was EUR 7.67 million (= 99.5 mm – 91.83 mn), as shown in Figure 9.16.

The amortised cost and interest expense of the liability component at each accounting date were identical to those of the previous fixed-for-fixed convertible example:

Year	Amortised cost at beginning year (a)	Interest expense (b) = (a) × 5%	Cash payment (c)	Amortised cost at end of year (d) = (a) + (b) – (c)
1	91,830,000	4,592,000	2,000,000	94,422,000
2	94,422,000	4,721,000	2,000,000	97,143,000
3	97,143,000	4,857,000	2,000,000	100,000,000

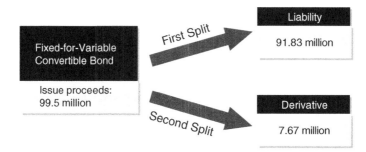

FIGURE 9.16   Split of fixed-for-variable convertible bond.

The derivative component had to be fair valued at each reporting date. The change in fair value was recognised in profit or loss. Suppose that the derivative's fair values were as follows:

Year	ABC's share price	Derivative component fair value	Change in fair value
Inception	7.00	7,670,000	
1	9.00	8,380,000	710,000
2	10.00	9,450,000	1,070,000
3	13.00	30,000,000	20,550,000

Accounting Entries

1) Accounting entries on the issue date (1 January 20X0)

Cash (Asset)	99,500,000	
Convertible bond (Liability)		91,830,000
Derivative (Liability)		7,670,000

2) Accounting entries on the first reporting and coupon payment date (31 December 20X0)

Interest expense (Profit or loss)	4,592,000	
Convertible bond (Liability)		2,592,000
Cash (Asset)		2,000,000
Other financial expenses (Profit or loss)	710,000	
Derivative (Liability)		710,000

3) Accounting entries on the next reporting and coupon payment date (31 December 20X1)

Interest expense (Profit or loss)	4,721,000	
Convertible bond (Liability)		2,721,000
Cash (Asset)		2,000,000
Other financial expenses (Profit or loss)	1,070,000	
Derivative (Liability)		1,070,000

4) Accounting entries on maturity date (31 December 20X2) to record the interest expense, coupon payment and derivative revaluation:

Interest expense (Profit or loss)	4,857,000	
Convertible bond (Liability)		2,857,000
Cash (Asset)		2,000,000
Other financial expenses (Profit or loss)	20,550,000	
Derivative (Liability)		20,550,000

At maturity ABC shares were trading at EUR 13, above the EUR 10 conversion rate. As a result, the bondholders exercised their conversion right. Let us cover next three different scenarios, one for each type of conversion.

Scenario 1: Conversion in shares only. Under this scenario, ABC issued 10 million ordinary new shares with a par value of EUR 1.00 each. The share issue value was EUR 13.00 per share or EUR 130 million. Therefore, the share premium was EUR 12.00 per share or EUR 120 million. The related accounting entries would be as follows:

Convertible bond (Liability)	100,000,000	
Derivative (Liability)	30,000,000	
Share capital (Equity)		10,000,000
Share premium (Equity)		120,000,000

Scenario 2: Conversion in cash only. Under this scenario, ABC paid the market value of the convertible bond (i.e., EUR 130 million) in cash. The related accounting entries would be as follows:

Convertible bond (Liability)	100,000,000	
Derivative (Liability)	30,000,000	
Cash (Asset)		130,000,000

Scenario 3: Conversion in cash and shares (net share settlement). Under this scenario, ABC paid bondholders a mixture of cash and shares. The amount of cash paid was EUR 100 million, representing the redemption amount. The number of new shares delivered was 2,308,000 (= 30 mn/13.00 per share) representing the excess of the bond's EUR 130 million market value over its redemption amount. The related accounting entries were as follows:

Convertible bond (Liability)	100,000,000	
Derivative (Liability)	30,000,000	
Cash (Asset)		100,000,000
Share capital (Equity)		2,308,000
Share premium (Equity)		27,692,000

9.10 CASE STUDY: HEDGING STEP-UP CALLABLE PERPETUAL PREFERENCE SHARES

The aim of this case study is to illustrate the process of deciding whether an instrument, a **step-up callable perpetual preference share**, is classified as equity or as a liability. It also highlights the challenge of hedging equity instruments.

A perpetual step-up instrument is an irredeemable callable financial instrument with fixed or floating dividend payments. The instrument includes a "step-up" dividend clause that would increase the dividend at a predetermined date in the future unless the instrument has previously been called by the issuer. Suppose that on 1 January 20X0, ABC issued the following step-up callable perpetual preference shares:

Step-up callable preference shares – terms	
Issue date	1 January 20X0
Issuer	ABC
Principal	EUR 200 million
Maturity	Perpetual, subject to call right
Call Right	The issuer has the right, but not the obligation, to redeem the shares on 31-Dec-X2 and every 3 years thereafter
Dividend (annually)	Euribor 12M + 100 bps up to and including 31-Dec-X2. Euribor 12M + 500 bps, thereafter
Dividend payment	Payment of dividend is mandatory only if dividends are paid on ABC's ordinary shares
Seniority	Upon liquidation of the issuer, principal is paid out ahead of ordinary shares, but subordinated to other senior and subordinated claims of the issuer

First of all, let us analyse whether the elements of the instrument were classified as debt or equity. In our preference shares, ABC had potentially two types of payments to the holder of the preference shares: principal and dividends.

- Regarding the principal, ABC had no contractual obligation to redeem the instrument. The fact that ABC was expected to call the instrument in December 20X2 so as to avoid the above market payments (this is commonly referred to as "economic compulsion") was not considered relevant in the classification. Therefore, the principal was not considered a liability as ABC had no contractual obligation to deliver cash, or any other financial asset, to the holder under conditions that were potentially unfavourable to the entity. Thus, the principal was classified as equity.
- Regarding the dividends, they were payable only if dividends were paid on ordinary shares (which themselves were payable at the discretion of ABC). As a consequence, ABC had no contractual obligation to ever pay a dividend. Thus, the dividends were classified as equity.

IAS 32 considers that the seniority of payment of an obligation, which arises only on liquidation of the entity, does not affect the classification of the financial instrument. So in our case, the seniority of the preference shares between subordinated debt and ordinary shares did not affect the liability/equity classification. Similarly, the legal definition of the instrument as "shares" had no impact on the classification. Substance rather than legal form rules the liability/equity classification.

The instrument was classified as equity under IAS 32, as the entity could choose not to redeem the instrument and to pay no distributions on it in perpetuity. Whilst a consequence of a non-payment of interest was that the entity could not pay an ordinary dividend, this restriction did not amount to a contractual obligation.

9.10.1 Accounting versus Credit Impact

By issuing the step-up callable preference shares, ABC strengthened its capital base as the issue was deemed by the credit rating agencies to be an equity instrument. The accounting consideration of an instrument as equity or debt is not relevant for the rating agencies when assessing the impact of the instrument on the issuer's credit rating. Conversely, factors that are relevant for the credit rating agencies, such as the seniority of the instrument relative to other claims, may be irrelevant from an accounting viewpoint.

9.10.2 The Hedging Problem

The classification of the dividends as equity may cause a problem: dividends distributed by the entity cannot be considered a hedged item under IFRS 9. The fundamental principle under IFRS 9 is that, in a hedging relationship, the hedged item creates an exposure to risk that could affect the profit or loss statement (or permanently OCI, for equity investments at fair value through OCI). In our case, any paid dividends were considered a distribution of profits, and thus were not recorded in profit or loss. As a consequence, the dividends of ABC's step-up callable preference shares were not eligible for designation as a hedged item in a hedge accounting relationship.

If ABC wanted to hedge the dividends exposure to rising Euribor rates by entering into a pay-fixed receive-floating interest rate swap, it was left with three options:

1) To consider the swap as undesignated. ABC would recognise the changes in fair value of the swap in profit or loss, probably increasing profit or loss volatility.
2) To designate the swap as the hedging instrument of an existing floating rate liability that ABC had not yet hedged. Clearly this second alternative did not make much sense, as ABC would be better off just hedging the liability instead of the preference shares.
3) To embed the swap into a (hybrid) instrument that did not require the swap to be fair valued.

Suppose that ABC decided to pursue the third option. The strategy encompassed including the receive-floating pay-fixed interest rate swap in an asset or liability that could be recognised at amortised cost as a whole – that is, that did not require the whole instrument to be recognised at FVTPL (for an asset), or did not require the bifurcation of the swap from the host contract (for a liability).

One way to implement this strategy was the following. Suppose that, simultaneously with the preference shares issue, ABC issued a fixed rate bond. The bond was accounted for at amortised cost, and therefore, no fair valuing of the bond was required. The bond had the following terms:

Fixed rate bond – terms	
Issue date	1 January 20X0
Issuer	ABC
Principal	EUR 200 million
Maturity	3 years (31-Dec-X2)
Interest (annually)	4%, paid every 31 December

The proceeds of the bond were invested in a floating rate deposit. The deposit was accounted for at amortised cost. The deposit had the following terms:

Floating rate deposit – terms	
Issue date	1 January 20X0
Issuer	XYZ Bank
Investor	ABC
Principal	EUR 200 million
Maturity	3 years (31-Dec-X2)
Interest (annually)	Euribor 12-month minus 0.10%, paid on 31 December

In order to generate the strategy's accounting entries, suppose that the Euribor 12-month rates and the interest/dividend payments were as follows:

Payment date	Euribor 12-month	Pref. shares dividend rate	Deposit rate	Bond rate	Resulting rate
31-Dec-X0	3.00%	4.00%	2.90%	4.00%	5.10%
31-Dec-X1	3.40%	4.40%	3.30%	4.00%	5.10%
31-Dec-X2	3.70%	4.70%	3.60%	4.00%	5.10%

9.10.3 Accounting Entries

The required journal entries were the following.

1) To record the issuance of the three instruments on 1 January 20X0

The proceeds of the preference shares issue and the fixed rate bond issue were EUR 200 million. The investment in the bank deposit was EUR 200 million as well.

Cash (Asset)	200,000,000	
Preference shares (Equity)		200,000,000
Cash (Asset)	200,000,000	
Financial debt (Liability)		200,000,000
Bank deposit (Asset)	200,000,000	
Cash (Asset)		200,000,000

2) To record the interest and dividends on 31 December 20X0

Suppose that the ordinary shares paid a dividend, and as a result that the holders of the preference shares were entitled to receive a dividend payment. As the preference shares rate was 4%, the dividend was EUR 8 million (= 4% × 200 million). Note that the accounting entry shown below is simplified: in reality, and previously to 31 December 20X0, ABC would have declared a dividend and recognised its related payable that would be eliminated on dividend payment. The interest expense and payment on the fixed rate bond was EUR 8 million (= 4% × 200 million). Similarly, the interest income from the bank deposit was EUR 5.8 million (= 2.90% × 200 million).

Retained earnings (Equity)	8,000,000	
Cash (Asset)		8,000,000
Interest expense (Profit or loss)	8,000,000	
Cash (Asset)		8,000,000
Cash (Asset)	5,800,000	
Interest income (Profit or loss)		5,800,000

3) To record the interest and dividends on 31 December 20X1

Suppose that ABC paid a EUR 8.8 million (= 4.40% × 200 million) dividend to the holders of the preference shares. The interest expense and payment on the fixed rate bond was EUR 8 million (= 4% × 200 million). Similarly, the interest income from the bank deposit was EUR 6.6 million (= 3.3% × 200 million).

Retained earnings (Equity)	8,800,000	
Cash (Asset)		8,800,000
Interest expense (Profit or loss)	8,000,000	
Cash (Asset)		8,000,000
Cash (Asset)	6,600,000	
Interest income (Profit or loss)		6,600,000

4) To record the interest and dividends on 31 December 20X2

Suppose that ABC paid a EUR 9.4 million (= 4.7% × 200 million) dividend to the holders of the preference shares. The interest expense and payment on the fixed rate bond was EUR 8 million (= 4% × 200 million). Similarly, the interest income from the bank deposit was EUR 7.2 million (= 3.6% × 200 million).

Retained earnings (Equity)	9,400,000	
Cash (Asset)		9,400,000
Interest expense (Profit or loss)	8,000,000	
Cash (Asset)		8,000,000
Cash (Asset)	7,200,000	
Interest income (Profit or loss)		7,200,000

5) To record the redemption of the three instruments on 31 December 20X2

Suppose that ABC exercised its preference shares' call right on 31 December 20X2 to avoid paying the step-up dividend rate thereafter. The redemption amount of the preference shares was EUR 200 million. The redemption amounts of the fixed rate bond issue and the bank deposit were each EUR 200 million.

Preference shares (Equity)	200,000,000	
Cash (Asset)		200,000,000
Financial debt (Liability)	200,000,000	
Cash (Asset)		200,000,000

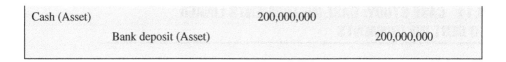

9.10.4 Concluding Remarks

The main objective of the hedge was to fix the expected cash flow to be paid each year under the preference shares. Figure 9.17 highlights the resulting cash flow from the strategy during the year ending on 31 December 20X2. ABC paid a combined EUR 10.2 million fixed amount (an overall yield of 5.1%).

The secondary objective was to avoid recording the mark-to-market of the hedging strategy in profit or loss. This objective was also achieved as none of the three instruments was marked-to-market.

Whilst the two objectives were achieved, there were some effects that made the hedging strategy far from optimal. Firstly, the balance sheet was notably enlarged and some ratios deteriorated because of the hedge (e.g., ABC's return on assets). Secondly, there was an additional cost because the funding level of the bond was higher than the yield of the deposit. Thirdly, there could be a potential mismatch of cash flows as the dividend payment may not be paid (e.g., because a dividend was not distributed to the ordinary shareholders) while the deposit and bond cash flows always took place. Finally, ABC's profit or loss statement showed an exposure to interest rate risk (see Figure 9.18), to rising Euribor 12-month rates when dividends were not distributed to the preference shareholders.

FIGURE 9.17 Cash flows on 31-Dec-X2.

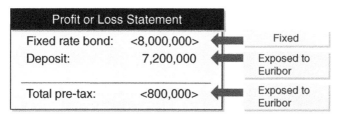

FIGURE 9.18 Profit or loss on 31-Dec-X2, assuming no dividend is paid to the preference shareholders.

9.11 CASE STUDY: BASE INSTRUMENTS LINKED TO DEBT INSTRUMENTS

This case study shows an *obsolete* strategy –a base instrument linked to a debt instrument – to achieve equity recognition for dividends of an instrument that otherwise would have been recognised as a liability, enhancing an entity's capital position. This loop was closed by the IFRS Interpretations Committee (IFRIC) but allows me to provide an interesting short example on debt versus equity classification.

Assume that a "base" instrument consisted of irredeemable (i.e., perpetual) callable preference shares with dividends that had to be paid if interest was paid on another (the "linked") instrument, as shown in Figure 9.19. The terms of the linked instrument obliged the issuer to make interest payments, and hence the "linked" instrument was classified as a liability. The linked instrument was callable by the issuer at any time, and had a small notional.

In the old days, this strategy's preference shares dividends were classified as equity because the base instrument (i.e., the preference shares) did not have a contractual obligation to deliver cash (or any other financial asset). After an opinion issued by the IFRIC, these dividends were classified as a liability because the linkage to the linked instrument created an *implicit* contractual obligation for the entity to pay dividends on the base instrument.

The linked instrument frequently had a small face value compared to the base instrument. This insignificant value did not impact the liability classification. It did not eliminate the fact that the issuer had no discretion over the payment of the dividend on the base instrument (i.e., the linking created a contractual obligation with regard to the base instrument).

If the linked instrument was callable by the issuer at any time, the issuer could avoid paying interest on the base instrument. However, until the linked instrument was called, a contractual obligation to pay interest on the base instrument existed.

9.12 CASE STUDY: PARKING SHARES THROUGH A TOTAL RETURN SWAP

This case study covers a transaction to monetise an existing investment in shares of another company. It may be used to finance the acquisition of shares as well. An equity total return swap (TRS) may allow for cash settlement, physical settlement or a combination of both. A TRS involves receiving the total return on a specified reference asset in exchange for a string of interest payments. The total return is the capital gain or loss on the reference asset, plus any interim dividends. The TRS allows an entity to derive the economic benefit of owning an asset without having to commit cash resources to it.

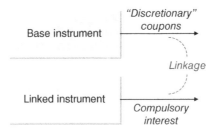

FIGURE 9.19 Base preference shares.

TRSs have many potential uses. For example, through a TRS an entity may postpone a monetary gain, may comply with ownership regulations, or may raise collateralised financing. A TRS can also be used as an investment tool to get exposure to the appreciation (and depreciation) of a group of shares. This last use of TRSs is quite uncommon among corporates but quite popular among hedge funds.

Suppose that ABC was a highly leveraged entity and did not want to use the debt capital markets to raise new financing. ABC had an investment in shares of DEF – an unrelated company – and decided to raise financing by monetising its investment in DEF. The investment was classified at fair value through OCI. As part of the strategy, ABC entered into the following TRS:

Total return swap terms	
Trade date	1 January 20X0
Counterparties	ABC and XYZ Bank
Underlying shares	Ordinary shares in DEF
Number shares	20 million
Initial price	EUR 10 per share
Notional amount	EUR 200 million
Maturity	2 years (31 December 20X1)
ABC receives on dividend payment date	An amount equal to the gross dividend distributed to the underlying shares. This amount is received on the date that the dividend is paid
ABC pays annually	Euribor 12-month plus 50 bps, on the notional amount, paid annually on 31 December
Settlement	At maturity, ABC has the right to choose between cash and physical settlement
Cash settlement	Final amount = Number shares × (Final price – Initial price) If the final amount is positive, ABC receives the final amount at maturity. If the final amount is negative, ABC pays the absolute value of the final amount at maturity
Final price	The closing price of the underlying shares at maturity

9.12.1 Asset Monetisation Strategy

At the beginning of the transaction, ABC sold 20 million DEF shares to XYZ Bank at market value. As DEF shares were trading at EUR 10 on that date, ABC received EUR 200 million for the sale. Figure 9.20 highlights the initial flows of the monetisation strategy. Legal ownership of the DEF shares was transferred to XYZ Bank.

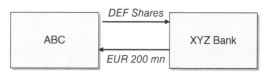

FIGURE 9.20 Monetisation strategy – initial flows.

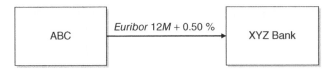

FIGURE 9.21   Monetisation strategy – interest flows.

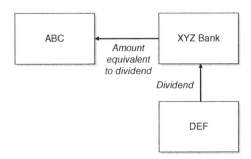

FIGURE 9.22   Monetisation strategy – dividend flows.

During the term of the TRS, ABC paid Euribor plus 50 bps annually on the notional amount, as shown in Figure 9.21.

DEF distributed a dividend periodically to its shareholders. Suppose that on 31 December 20X0 ABC declared and simultaneously paid a EUR 0.10 dividend per share, and on 31 December 20X1 a EUR 0.12 dividend per share. Because XYZ Bank was the legal owner of the shares, it received the dividends. Through the TRS, XYZ Bank was obliged to pass to ABC an amount equal to the dividends received on the underlying DEF shares. Figure 9.22 shows the cash flows related to the dividends.

At the end of the transaction, ABC could choose either to buy back the shares (physical settlement), or to cash settle the TRS. ABC would choose the latter if it were not interested in continuing to own the DEF shares. Under the cash settlement alternative, the closing price of the DEF shares prevailing on the TRS maturity date (the "final price") would be determined. If the final price was greater than the initial price, XYZ Bank would pay to ABC the appreciation of the shares. The cash settlement amount would be calculated as:

$$\text{Final amount} = \text{Number of shares} \times (\text{Final price} - \text{Initial price})$$

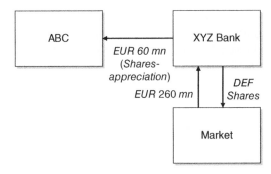

FIGURE 9.23   Monetisation strategy – Cash settlement flows.

If the final price was lower than the initial price, ABC would pay to XYZ Bank the deprecia-tion of the shares. The cash settlement amount would be calculated as:

$$\text{Final amount} = \text{Number of shares} \times (\text{Initial price} - \text{Final price})$$

Suppose that the closing price of DEF shares on 31 December 20X1 was EUR 13.00 and that ABC opted for cash settlement. As a consequence, XYZ Bank was obliged to pay to ABC the appreciation of the DEF shares, or EUR 60 million (= 20 million shares × (13 − 10)). In reality, and in order not to be exposed to the price of the DEF shares, XYZ Bank would have sold the shares in the market near the close of the trading session. As a consequence, XYZ Bank would have received EUR 260 million (=20 million shares × 13) for selling the shares in the market. Figure 9.23 shows the different flows taking place at maturity.

9.12.2 Accounting Entries

From an accounting standpoint, the key element was to assess whether ABC could derec-ognise the sold DEF shares at the beginning of the TRS. Whilst ABC physically sold the DEF shares to XYZ Bank and ABC had no obligation to repurchase the shares at maturity, it retained all risks and rewards on the shares. As a result, ABC continued to recognise the DEF shares in its statement of financial position (i.e., balance sheet). This accounting treatment made sense: in essence the TRS replicated the position of a secured financing transaction in which ABC borrowed EUR 200 million, paid a Euribor + 50 bps interest and posted the DEF shares as collateral. The required journal entries were as follows.

1) Entries on 1 January 20X0 to record the sale of the shares

Cash (Asset)	200,000,000	
DEF shares – collateralised (Asset)	200,000,000	
DEF shares (Asset)		200,000,000
Financial debt (Liability)		200,000,000

2) Entries on 31 December 20X0

Suppose that the DEF shares were trading at EUR 12.00 per share and that they were classified at FVOCI. Thus the change in their fair value since the last valuation was a gain of EUR 40 million (= 20 mn shares × (12 − 10)), recorded in OCI. To record the fair valuation of the shares:

DEF shares – collateralised (Asset)	40,000,000	
Equity instruments at FVOCI (Equity)		40,000,000

Assuming that the Euribor 12-month fixing for the interest period was 4.20%, ABC paid to XYZ Bank EUR 9,531,000 in interest (= 200 million × (4.20% + 0.50%) × 365/360):

Interest expense (Profit or loss)	9,531,000	
Cash (Asset)		9,531,000

Assuming that the DEF shares paid a dividend of EUR 0.10 per share, ABC received EUR 2,000,000 (= 20 million shares × 0.10) through the TRS:

Cash (Asset)	2,000,000	
Dividend income (Profit or loss)		2,000,000

3) Entries on 31 December 20X1

First, let us assume that the DEF shares were trading at EUR 13 per share. Thus the change in their fair value since the last valuation was a gain of EUR 20 million (= 20 mn shares × (13 – 12)). Second, assuming that the Euribor 12-month fixing for the interest period was 4.40%, ABC paid to XYZ Bank EUR 9,936,000 in interest (= 200 million × (4.40%+0.50%) × 365/360) under the TRS. Finally, assuming that the DEF shares paid a dividend of EUR 0.12 per share, ABC received EUR 2,400,000 (= 20 million shares × 0.12) through the TRS.

DEF shares – collateralised (Asset)	20,000,000	
Equity instruments at FVOCI (Equity)		20,000,000
Interest expense (Profit or loss)	9,936,000	
Cash (Asset)		9,936,000
Cash (Asset)	2,400,000	
Dividend income (Profit or loss)		2,400,000

Regarding the termination of the TRS on 31 December 20X1, I will cover the accounting entries for the two settlement alternatives available to ABC.

Under the cash settlement alternative, a final amount was calculated and paid by one party to the other. The DEF shares were trading at EUR 13 per share, above the EUR 10.00 initial value. As a result, ABC received EUR 60 million (= 20 mn shares × (13 – 10)) from XYZ Bank. Once the TRS was terminated, ABC was not exposed to the risks and rewards of the DEF shares, and as a result the DEF shares were derecognised from ABC's balance sheet and the amount accumulated in OCI was recycled within equity.

In this example, EUR 60 million was assumed to be the amount accumulated in OCI related to the derecognised 20 million DEF shares.

Cash (Asset)	60,000,000	
Financial debt (Liability)	200,000,000	
DEF shares – collateralised (Asset)		260,000,000
Equity instruments at FVOCI (Equity)	60,000,000	
Share premium (Equity)		60,000,000

Under the physical settlement alternative, ABC bought back the 20 million DEF shares at EUR 10 per share (the initial price). Once the TRS was terminated, ABC continued to be exposed to the risks and rewards of the DEF shares, and as a result the DEF shares remained on ABC's balance sheet. The amounts accumulated in OCI (EUR 60 million) remained until future derecognition of the DEF shares.

Financial debt (Liability)	200,000,000	
DEF shares (Asset)	260,000,000	
DEF shares – collateralised (Asset)		260,000,000
Cash (Asset)		200,000,000

9.13 CASE STUDY: HEDGING AN EQUITY INVESTMENT WITH A PUT OPTION

The aim of this case study is to illustrate the application of hedge accounting when hedging the market risk of an equity investment classified at FVOCI using a purchased put option.

Suppose that on 31 January 20X7, ABC purchased 10 million shares in DEF at EUR 10 per share. ABC classified this investment at FVOCI. To protect the investment from a decline in DEF's share price during the next 4 months, ABC purchased a put option on 31 January 20X7. The main terms of the put option were as follows:

Put option terms	
Trade date	31 January 20X7
Option type	Put option
Counterparties	ABC and XYZ Bank
Option buyer	ABC
Expiry	31 May 20X7 (4 months)
Strike	EUR 9.00

Nominal	10 million shares
Underlying	DEF ordinary shares
Premium	EUR 6 million
Settlement	Cash settlement

ABC designated the put option as the hedging instrument in a fair value hedge of its equity investment. Two alternatives are discussed below. In the first the time value of the put option was excluded from the hedging relationship (i.e., only the option's intrinsic value was designated as the hedging instrument), an alternative that was arguably inefficient from an operational perspective. In the second, the put option in its entirety was designated as the hedging instrument, the preferred choice.

9.13.1 Accounting Treatment of the Put Time Value when Excluded from the Hedging Relationship

When an entity designates only the intrinsic value of a purchased option (or an option combination) as the hedging instrument in a hedge accounting relationship, the change in fair value of an option's time value is recognised in OCI to the extent that it relates to the hedged item. Under IFRS 9, the accounting treatment of an option time value depends on whether the hedged item is transaction related or time-period related (see Section 2.10.3).

In this case, we are dealing with a time-period related hedged item because ABC hedged the fair value of the DEF shares over a period of time (4 months). As a result, the accounting for the time value of the put option was recorded in a two-step process:

- The first step encompassed amortising the "aligned" initial time value over the life of the hedging relationship. The aligned time value was determined using the valuation of an option that had critical terms (nominal, term and underlying) that perfectly matched the hedged item. In this case the terms of the "aligned" option were identical to those of the hedging instrument, except that the counterparty to the aligned option was assumed not to expose ABC to credit risk. We assume that because derivative transactions between ABC and XYZ Bank were fully collateralised, both the actual and aligned time values were EUR 6 million at inception of the hedging relationship. Whilst IFRS 9 does not prescribe an accounting method when both time values are identical, ABC decided to use the guidelines for when an actual time value exceeds an aligned time value, amortising the initial time value based on the aligned time value. IFRS 9 does not prescribe the amortisation method to be used; commonly entities use a straight-line amortisation.
- In this case, both the aligned and actual time values were identical. The second step consisted in deferring in the time value reserve of OCI the excess/deficit of the change in time value of the hedging instrument over/below the period amortised amount. Were the initial aligned time value to exceed the actual time value, the initial actual time value would have been amortised to the extent that it related to the aligned time value, the deviation of the aligned time value relative to the amortised amount, and any difference between the actual and the aligned time values would have been recorded in equity (e.g., in retained earnings).

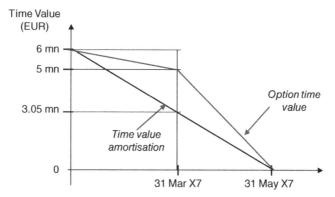

FIGURE 9.24   Aligned time value amortisation.

The following table and Figure 9.24 detail the amortisation of the aligned time value:

Date	Days in period	Time value amortisation (a)	Change in time value (b)	Time value reserve entry (a) – (b)
31 January 20X7	—			
31 March 20X7	59	<2,950,000> (1)	<1,000,000>	1,950,000 (2)
31 May 20X7	61	<3,050,000>	<5,000,000>	<1,950,000>
Total	120	<6,000,000>	<6,000,000>	0

Notes:
(1) <2,950,000> = 59/120 × <6,000,000>
(2) 1,950,000 = <1,000,000> – <2,950,000>

Hedging Relationship Documentation   At its inception, the hedging relationship was documented as follows:

Hedging relationship documentation	
Risk management objective and strategy for undertaking the hedge	The objective of the hedge is to protect the EUR value of 10 million shares of DEF against unfavourable movements in DEF's share price below EUR 9.00. This hedging objective is consistent with ABC's overall risk management policy of reducing the variability of its profit or loss statement using options
Type of hedge	Fair value hedge
Hedged item	10 million DEF shares classified at FVOCI
Hedging instrument	The cash settled put option contract with reference number 023547, traded on 31 January 20X7 with strike EUR 9.00 on 10 million DEF shares. The counterparty to the option is XYZ Bank
Hedge effectiveness assessment See below	

Hedge Effectiveness Assessment   Only the intrinsic value of the hedging instrument is designated in the hedging relationship. Hence, the time value of the hedging instrument is excluded
from the hedging relationship.

- The change in intrinsic value of the hedging instrument will be recognised in OCI to the
extent that it relates to the hedged item.
- The change in fair value of the hedged item for price decreases below the protected price
of EUR 9.00 per share will also be recognised in OCI.
- The change in time value of the option will be amortised to retained earnings in equity to
the extent that they relate to an aligned time value.

The "aligned" option would be an option with terms identical to those of the hedging
instrument, except that the counterparty to the aligned option is assumed not to expose the
entity to credit risk. Because both the actual and aligned time values were identical at inception of the hedging relationship, the entity has decided to use the guidelines for cases in which
actual time values exceed aligned time values, amortising the initial time value based on the
aligned time value. The amortisation method to be used is the straight-line amortisation.

Hedge effectiveness will be assessed prospectively at hedging relationship inception and
on an ongoing basis at least upon each reporting date and upon occurrence of a significant
change in the circumstances affecting the hedge effectiveness requirements.

The hedging relationship will qualify for hedge accounting only if all the following criteria are met:

1) The hedging relationship consists only of eligible hedge items and hedging instruments.
The hedge item is eligible as it is an asset that exposes the entity to fair value risk, impacts
OCI and it is reliably measurable. The hedging instrument is eligible as it is a derivative
and it does not result in a net written option.
2) At hedge inception there is a formal designation and documentation of the hedging relationship and the entity's risk management objective and strategy for undertaking the hedge.
3) The hedging relationship is considered effective.

The hedging relationship will be considered effective if the following three requirements
are met:

1) There is an economic relationship between the hedged item and the hedging instrument.
2) The effect of credit risk does not dominate the value changes that result from that economic relationship.
3) The hedge ratio of the hedging relationship is the same as that resulting from the quantity
of hedged item that the entity actually hedges and the quantity of the hedging instrument
that the entity actually uses to hedge that quantity of hedged item. The hedge ratio should
not be intentionally weighted to create ineffectiveness

Whether there is an economic relationship between the hedged item and the hedging
instrument would be assessed on a qualitative basis by comparing the critical terms of the
hedging instrument and the hedged item. The critical terms considered would be the number
of shares, the strike price, the term and the underlying.

Because the hedging instrument will only have intrinsic value when the share price of
DEF shares is below EUR 9.00, effectiveness will be assessed only during those periods
in which the put option has an intrinsic value. The effective and ineffective amounts of the

change in intrinsic value of the hedging instrument would be computed by comparing the cumulative change in intrinsic value of the hedging instrument with that of the hedged item. Any part of the cumulative change in intrinsic value of the hedging instrument that does not offset a corresponding cumulative change in the fair value of the hedged item would be treated as ineffective and recorded in OCI.

Fair Valuations of Hedging instrument and Hedged Item DEF share prices, in EUR, on the relevant dates were as follows:

Date	DEF share price
31 January 20X7	10
31 March 20X7	8
31 May 20X7	6

The fair value of the hedging instrument was calculated using the Black–Scholes model, ignoring counterparty credit risk. The option intrinsic value was calculated using the spot rates. The time value of the option was calculated as the difference between the option fair value and the option intrinsic value. This fair valuation did not take into account XYZ Bank's credit risk.

Option fair values (EUR)	31-Jan-X7	31-Mar-X7	31-May-X7
Share price	10	8	6
Fair value	6,000,000	15,000,000	30,000,000
Undiscounted intrinsic value	-0- *(1)*	10,000,000 *(2)*	30,000,000 *(3)*
Discount factor		1.00 *(4)*	1.00
Intrinsic value (discounted)	-0-	10,000,000	30,000,000
Time value	6,000,000	5,000,000 *(5)*	-0-
Change in intrinsic value	—	10,000,000 *(6)*	20,000,000
Change in time value	—	<1,000,000>	<5,000,000> *(7)*

Notes:

(1) 10 million shares × max [0, Strike − Spot] = 10 million × max [0; 9 − 10] = 0
(2) 10 million shares × max [0, Strike − Spot] = 10 million × max [0; 9 − 8] = 10,000,000
(3) 10 million shares × max [0, Strike − Spot] = 10 million × max [0, 9 − 6] = 30,000,000
(4) Assumed to be 1.00 due to the notably short term remaining life
(5) Fair value − Intrinsic value = 15,000,000 − 10,000,000 = 5,000,000
(6) Intrinsic value$_{Current}$ − Intrinsic value$_{Previous}$ = 10,000,000 − 0 = 10,000,000
(7) Time value$_{Current}$ − Time value$_{Previous}$ = 0 − 5,000,000 = <5,000,000>

According to the previous table, on 31 March 20X7 the fair value of the put option was EUR 15 million. This fair value did not take into account XYZ Bank's credit risk because the transaction was fully collateralised.

Suppose as an exercise that the transaction was uncollateralised and that on 31 March 20X7 ABC assessed whether the adjustment for counterparty credit risk had a material impact on the option fair valuation. The EUR 15 million fair value was the present value of the option's expected payoff discounted at Euribor. The option had two months (i.e., 61 days) to expiry and Euribor for such maturity was trading at 3.10%. Therefore, the expected payoff of the option was calculated as the future value of the EUR 15 million:

$$\text{Expected payoff} = 15 \text{ million} \times (1 + 3.10\% \times 61/360) = 15{,}079{,}000 \text{ (rounded)}$$

Two-month EUR-denominated CDs issued by XYZ Bank were trading at 20 bps over 2-month Euribor. The option's credit adjusted fair value was calculated as the present value of the expected payoff using XYZ Bank's credit spread:

$$\text{Credit adjusted fair value} = 15{,}079{,}000/[1 + (3.10\%+0.20\%) \times 61/360]$$
$$= 14{,}995{,}000 \text{ (rounded)}$$

The difference between the credit adjusted and the unadjusted fair values was an immaterial EUR 5,000 (= 15,000,000 − 14,995,000). Therefore, even in the case of an uncollateralised transaction, assumption of identical actual and aligned time values would have been reasonable.

The share fair value calculation was as follows:

Share fair values (EUR)	31-Jan-X7	31-Mar-X7	31-May-X7
Share price	10	8	6
Number of shares	10,000,000	10,000,000	10,000,000
Fair value	100,000,000	80,000,000 (1)	60,000,000
Change in fair value	—	<20,000,000>	<20,000,000> (2)

Notes:
    (1) 10 million shares × EUR 8 per share = 80,000,000
    (2) Fair value$_{\text{Current}}$ − Fair value$_{\text{Previous}}$ = 60,000,000 − 80,000,000 = <20,000,000>

Hedge Effectiveness Assessment Performed at Inception of the Hedging Relationship The hedge qualified for hedge accounting as it met the three effectiveness requirements:

1) Because the critical terms (such as number of shares, strike price, maturity and underlying) of the hedging instrument and the hedged item matched the entity concluded that the hedging instrument and the hedged item had values that would generally move in opposite directions (for share prices below or at EUR 9.00 per share), and hence that an economic relationship existed between the hedged item and the hedging instrument.
2) Because the credit rating of entity and the counterparty to the hedging instrument was relatively strong (XYZ Bank is rated A+ by Standard & Poor's) and the transaction was fully collateralised, the effect of credit risk did not dominate the value changes that result from that economic relationship.
3) The hedge ratio designated (1:1) was the one actually used for risk management and it did not attempt to avoid recognising ineffectiveness. Therefore, it was determined that a hedge ratio of 1:1 was appropriate.

Potential sources of ineffectiveness are a change in the credit collateral agreement generating substantial credit risk, or a change in the holding of the shares below the number of shares underlying the put option.

Another effectiveness assessment was also performed on 31 March 20X7, yielding similar conclusions.

Accounting Entries

1) To record the share and option purchases for EUR 100 million and EUR 6 million respectively, on 31 January 20X7

DEF shares (Asset)	100,000,000	
Cash (Asset)		100,000,000
Put option (Asset)	6,000,000	
Cash (Asset)		6,000,000

2) To record the closing of the accounting period on 31 March 20X7

The change in the fair value of the shares represented a EUR 20 million loss, split between an effective part and an excess part. The effective part, EUR 10 million, was recognised in retained earnings. The excess, EUR 10 million, was recognised in OCI as the equity investment was recognised at FVOCI.

The change in fair value of the option produced a EUR 9 million gain. Of this amount, a EUR 10 million gain and a EUR 1 million loss were related to the option's intrinsic value and time value, respectively. The change in intrinsic value was 100% effective because the hedged item's fair value for share prices below EUR 9.00 had an identical behaviour to the put option's change in intrinsic value. The change in time value produced a EUR 1 million loss, split between a EUR <2,950,000> amortisation and a EUR 1,950,000 excess. The latter amount was recognised in the time value reserve in OCI.

Gains/losses on equity investments at FVOCI (Equity)	10,000,000	
Retained earnings (Equity)	10,000,000	
DEF shares (Asset)		20,000,000
Put option (Asset)	9,000,000	
Retained earnings (Equity)		10,000,000
Retained earnings (Equity)	2,950,000	
Time value reserve (Equity)		1,950,000

3) To record the expiry of the option and the end of the hedging relationship on 31 May 20X7

The change in the fair value of the shares produced a EUR 20 million loss, split between an effective part and an excess part. The effective part, EUR 20 million, was recognised in retained earnings. There was no excess amount.

The change in fair value of the option produced a EUR 15 million gain. Of this amount, a EUR 20 million gain and a EUR 5 million loss were related to the option's intrinsic value and time value, respectively. The change in intrinsic value was 100% effective because the hedged item's fair value for share prices below EUR 9.00 had an identical behaviour to the put option's change in intrinsic value. The change in time value produced a EUR 5 million loss, split between a EUR <3,050,000> amortisation and a EUR <1,950,000> excess. This latter amount was recognised in the time value reserve in OCI.

The put option was cash settled. XYZ Bank paid to ABC the option's EUR 30 million fair value (i.e., its intrinsic value).

Retained earnings (Equity)	20,000,000	
DEF shares (Asset)		20,000,000
Put option (Asset)	15,000,000	
Retained earnings (Equity)		20,000,000
Retained earnings (Equity)	3,050,000	
Time value reserve (Equity)	1,950,000	
Cash (Asset)	30,000,000	
Put option (Asset)		30,000,000

As the hedging relationship ended on 31 May 20X7, any subsequent changes in the fair value of DEF shares were recognised in OCI.

Concluding Remarks   ABC's investment in DEF shares did not expose the entity to a more volatile profit or loss because the shares were recognised at FVOCI. However, the volatility of ABC's OCI could potentially increase due to the revaluation of the equity investment at each reporting date. If the shares had a prolonged decline, ABC's OCI position could suffer a severe decline.

In our example, had ABC not hedged its investment, the equity investments reserve account in OCI would have shown a EUR 40 million decline (see Figure 9.25).

Fortunately, ABC was cautious and hedged its investment. At the end of the hedge term, the equity investments reserve account showed a EUR 10 million decline, an amount considerably lower than EUR 40 million. However, because ABC wanted to benefit from full appreciation of the shares, the EUR 6 million cost of the protection ended up reducing ABC's capital position.

Note that ABC used the retained earnings account to record the effects of the hedge. IFRS 9 does not specify which equity account to use for this purpose. ABC could have chosen a capital account such as "share premium".

My final comment is to question the decision to exclude the option time value from the hedging relationship that caused an arguably "unnecessary" operational burden. In the next subsection I will cover the accounting mechanics when an option time value is included in the hedging relationship, an operationally easier approach.

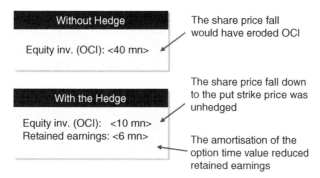

FIGURE 9.25 Summary of accounting effects.

9.13.2 Accounting Treatment of the Put Time Value when Included in a Hedging Relationship

In the case just covered, the put time value was excluded from the hedging relationship and amortised through retained earnings. That accounting process required ABC to calculate and post special entries related to the time value. Next, I will take a look at the strategy's accounting entries when the option in its entirety is designated as the hedging instrument.

1) To record the shares and the option purchases for EUR 100 million and EUR 6 million respectively, on 31 January 20X7

DEF shares (Asset)	100,000,000	
Cash (Asset)		100,000,000
Put option (Asset)	6,000,000	
Cash (Asset)		6,000,000

2) To record the closing of the accounting period on 31 March 20X7
   The change in the fair value of the shares was a loss of EUR 20 million, split between an effective part and an excess part. The effective part, EUR 10 million (i.e., the part fully offset by change in the option's intrinsic value), was recognised in retained earnings. The excess, EUR 10 million, was recognised in OCI as the equity investment was recognised at FVOCI.
   The change in fair value of the option was a gain of EUR 9 million, to be recognised in retained earnings. The option in its entirety constituted the hedging instrument, and as a result there was no need to split the option change in fair value between the change in its intrinsic and time values.

Gains/losses on equity investments at FVOCI (OCI)	10,000,000	
Retained earnings (Equity)	10,000,000	
DEF shares (Asset)		20,000,000
Put option (Asset)	9,000,000	
Retained earnings (Equity)		9,000,000

3) To record the expiry of the option and the end of the hedging relationship on 31 May 20X7 The change in the fair value of the shares was a loss of EUR 20 million, split between an effective part and an excess part. The effective part, EUR 20 million (related to the change in the option's intrinsic value), was recognised in retained earnings. There was no excess amount. The change in fair value of the option was a gain of EUR 15 million. The put option was cash settled. XYZ Bank paid to ABC the option's EUR 30 million fair and intrinsic value.

Retained earnings (Equity)	20,000,000	
DEF shares (Asset)		20,000,000
Put option (Asset)	15,000,000	
Retained earnings (Equity)		15,000,000
Cash (Asset)	30,000,000	
Put option (Asset)		30,000,000

The reader may notice that by designating the option in its entirety as the hedging instrument, the accounting process was greatly simplified. However, ABC still had to compute the cumulative change in the option intrinsic value to determine the effective part of the hedge item's change in fair value. The effective part was recorded in retained earnings as opposed to OCI. The overall final result was identical to that of the previous case (see Figure 9.25).

9.14 CASE STUDY: SELLING A FORWARD ON OWN SHARES

The aim of this case study is to illustrate the accounting implications of selling a forward on own shares. I begin with a forward that allows for physical settlement only, which is recognised as an equity instrument. Then I will turn to a forward that can be other than physically settled, which is recognised as a derivative.

9.14.1 Accounting Treatment of a Physically Settled Only Forward on Own Shares

Suppose that on 1 January 20X0 ABC entered into a forward purchase on its own shares that allowed for physical settlement only with the following terms:

Physically settled forward terms	
Start date	1 January 20X0
Counterparties	ABC and XYZ Bank
Maturity date	31 December 20X2 (3 years)
Reference price	EUR 10.00
Number of shares	10 million
Nominal amount	EUR 100 million
Underlying	ABC ordinary shares
Settlement	Physical delivery only

At maturity (i.e., 31 December 20X2) ABC was obliged to acquire 10 million own shares and to pay EUR 100 million. Because in all scenarios the instrument implied the exchange of a fixed number of shares for a fixed amount of cash (i.e., it met the fixed-for-fixed requirement), it was classified as an equity instrument.

The forward was initially recognised as deduction of equity and a liability. The initial carrying amount of the liability represented the present value of the final consideration, discounted using the yield of debt issued by ABC with the same term. Suppose that 3-year straight bonds issued by ABC were trading at a 5% yield on 1 January 20X0. The present value of the final consideration was EUR 86,384,000 (= 100 mn/(1+5%)^3). The liability component was recognised at amortised cost using the effective interest rate method. During the life of the forward the carrying value of the liability would be increasing to reach the final EUR 100 million consideration as follows:

Date	Interest expense	Liability carrying value
1-Jan-X0		86,384,000
31-Dec-X0	4,319,000 *(1)*	90,703,000
31-Dec-X1	4,535,000 *(2)*	95,238,000 *(3)*
31-Dec-X2	4,762,000	100,000,000

Notes:
  (1) 4,319,000 = 86,384,000 × 5%
  (2) 4,535,000 = 90,703,000 × 5%
  (3) 95,238,000 = 90,703,000 + 4,535,000

The following accounting entries were required:

On 1 January 20X0:		
Forward on own shares (Equity)	86,384,000	
Forward obligation (Liability)		86,384,000
On 31 December 20X0:		
Interest expense (Profit or loss)	4,319,000	
Forward obligation (Liability)		4,319,000
On 31 December 20X1:		
Interest expense (Profit or loss)	4,535,000	
Forward obligation (Liability)		4,535,000
On 31 December 20X2:		
Interest expense (Profit or loss)	4,762,000	
Forward obligation (Liability)		4,762,000

Additionally, on 31 December 20X2 the forward was physically settled. ABC received 10 million own shares and paid to XYZ Bank EUR 100 million. The related accounting entries were as follows:

Forward obligation (Liability)	100,000,000	
Cash (Asset)		100,000,000
Treasury shares (Equity)	86,384,000	
Forward on own shares (Equity)		86,384,000

9.14.2 Accounting Treatment of a Forward on Own Shares Treated as a Derivative

Suppose that on 1 January 20X0 ABC entered into a forward purchase on its own shares with the following terms:

Forward terms	
Start date	1 January 20X0
Counterparties	ABC and XYZ Bank
Maturity date	31 December 20X2 (3 years)
Reference price	EUR 10.00
Number of shares	10 million shares
Nominal amount	EUR 100 million
Underlying	ABC ordinary shares
Settlement	Physical delivery, cash settlement or net share settlement (at ABC's election)

At maturity (i.e., 31 December 20X2) ABC could choose the type of settlement:

- Physical delivery. ABC would acquire 10 million of its own shares and pay EUR 100 million.
- Cash settlement. ABC would receive or pay the fair value of the forward at maturity. In other words, ABC would receive the appreciation (pay the depreciation) of the shares above (below) the EUR 10.00 reference price.
- Net share settlement. ABC would receive a number of shares with a market value equal to the fair value of the forward at maturity.

Because the forward could be settled other than by physical settlement (i.e., the forward allowed the choice of cash or net share settlement), it did not comply with the fixed-for-fixed requirement for equity treatment and therefore was recognised as a derivative. The derivative had to be fair valued at each reporting date. Suppose that the fair valuation of the forward at each reporting date and at maturity was as follows:

Date	ABC share price	Forward fair value	Change in fair value
1-Jan-X0	9.44	Nil	—
31-Dec-X0	8.50	<14,418,000>	<14,418,000>
31-Dec-X1	11.00	9,804,000	24,222,000
31-Dec-X2	13.00	30,000,000	20,196,000

At inception, on 1 January 20X0, the forward fair value was nil. Nonetheless, ABC had to recognise a liability to take into account the potential payment of EUR 100 million were ABC to choose physical settlement. As in our previous example, the liability was initially recognised at its present value and accrued to the EUR 100 million final amount:

Date	Interest expense	Liability carrying value
1-Jan-X0		86,384,000
31-Dec-X0	4,319,000	90,703,000
31-Dec-X1	4,535,000	95,238,000
31-Dec-X2	4,762,000	100,000,000

The following accounting entries were required:

On 1 January 20X0:		
Forward on own shares (Equity)	86,384,000	
Forward obligation (Liability)		86,384,000
On 31 December 20X0:		
Interest expense (Profit or loss)	4,319,000	
Forward obligation (Liability)		4,319,000
Other financial expenses (Profit or loss)	14,418,000	
Derivative (Liability)		14,418,000
On 31 December 20X1:		
Interest expense (Profit or loss)	4,535,000	
Forward obligation (Liability)		4,535,000
Derivative (Asset)	24,222,000	
Other financial income (Profit or loss)		24,222,000

On 31 December 20X2:

Interest expense (Profit or loss)	4,762,000	
Forward obligation (Liability)		4,762,000
Derivative (Asset)	20,196,000	
Other financial income (Profit or loss)		20,196,000

Additionally, on 31 December 20X2 the forward was settled. The related accounting entries depended on the type of settlement elected by ABC. ABC could choose among physical settlement, cash settlement and net share settlement.

If ABC chose physical settlement, it received 10 million of its own shares and paid EUR 100 million to XYZ Bank. The related accounting entries were as follows:

Treasury shares (Equity)	130,000,000	
Derivative (Asset)		30,000,000
Cash (Asset)		100,000,000
Forward obligation (Liability)	100,000,000	
Share premium (Equity)		13,616,000
Forward on own shares (Equity)		86,384,000

If ABC elected cash settlement, it received from XYZ Bank EUR 30 million in cash (the forward's fair value at maturity). The related accounting entries were as follows:

Cash (Asset)	30,000,000	
Derivative (Asset)		30,000,000
Forward obligation (Liability)	100,000,000	
Share premium (Equity)		13,616,000
Forward on own shares (Equity)		86,384,000

If ABC elected net share settlement, it received from XYZ Bank own shares worth EUR 30 million (the forward's fair value at maturity). Because ABC shares were trading at 13.00, ABC received 2,307,692 (= 30 mn/13) own shares. The related accounting entries were as follows:

Treasury shares (Equity)	30,000,000	
Derivative (Asset)		30,000,000
Forward obligation (Liability)	100,000,000	
Share premium (Equity)		13,616,000
Forward on own shares (Equity)		86,384,000

CHAPTER 10

Hedging Stock-Based Compensation Plans

This chapter briefly describes the main stock-based compensation plans. These plans include all arrangements by which employees receive shares of stock or other equity instruments of the employer or the employer incurs liabilities to employees in amounts based on the price of the employer's stock. I first describe the main plans. I then review the IFRS accounting for these plans. Finally, I describe a case that covers the hedging of equity-settled stock option plans with equity swaps.

10.1 TYPES AND TERMINOLOGY OF STOCK-BASED COMPENSATION PLANS

Equity-based compensations plans are a tool to further align employee interests with those of the company's shareholders by enhancing the link between pay and long-term performance. These compensation plans are typically discretionary, providing flexibility to reward particular achievements or exceptional performance. As a result, most compensation plans are granted to key senior executives who are actively leading the drive to achieve sustained profitability at the company and who are expected to contribute most significantly to its long-term future and economic success.

10.1.1 Main Equity-Based Compensation Plans

In this section I will briefly describe the most common share-based compensation plans. Human resources consulting firms are constantly developing new types of plans. Additionally, changes in tax regimes usually bring new types of plans. However, most plans can be classified under one of the following categories.

Stock Option Plans An employee **stock option plan** (SOP) represents the right awarded to certain employees to purchase a number of common shares of the company at a pre-agreed exercise price, commonly subject to certain conditions. The exercise price is usually set at the market price of the underlying shares on the date of the award or an average of the stock price during a period up to the date of the award.

Stock Appreciation Rights   A **stock appreciation rights** (SAR) plan provides eligible employees of the company with the right to receive cash equal to the appreciation of the company's common shares over a pre-established strike price. Therefore, an SAR is a cash-settled SOP.

Share Plans   There are many kinds of **share plan**. In general, employees of the company either voluntarily buy shares of the company on advantageous terms, or are granted a number of shares for free.

The most common type of share plan, so-called "equity plus plan" or "leverage share savings plan", is a voluntary plan that gives eligible employees the opportunity to purchase shares of the company at the stock price on the purchase date and generally to receive at no additional cost a number of shares for each share purchased, up to a maximum annual limit, after a certain vesting period of several years. Commonly, the free shares to be received are forfeitable in certain circumstances.

Another typical design of a share plan is the so-called "discounted purchase plan", a voluntary plan that gives eligible employees the opportunity to purchase shares of the company at a discount to the stock price on the purchase date. Shares purchased under the share plan cannot be sold for a certain period from the time of purchase.

As mentioned earlier, there are all sorts of variations to the two previous designs. At the end of this chapter, share plan awarded by HSBC is covered, which in my view is remarkably complex.

Employee Stock Ownership Plans   An **employee stock ownership plan** (ESOP) is a retirement plan in which the company contributes its stock to a trust for the benefit of the company's employees. This type of plan should not be confused with employee stock option plans, also called ESOPs, described earlier. The structures of trust ESOPs vary, but typically a trust is set up by the company to acquire shares in the company for the benefit of the employees. Therefore, in a trust ESOP, its beneficiaries do not hold the stock directly (i.e., beneficiaries do not actually buy shares). Instead, the company contributes its own shares to the trust, contributes cash to buy its own stock, or, quite commonly, the trust borrows money from the company to buy stock. The structure of the plan is designed to benefit from significant tax advantages for the company, the employees, and the sellers. Employees gradually vest in their accounts and receive their benefits when they leave the company (although there may be distributions prior to that).

10.1.2 Terminology

There are specific terms used in relation to SOPs and SARs. The main terms are the following:

Beneficiary. The award recipient.

Grant date (see Figure 10.1). The date on which the entity and the beneficiary agree to the share-based payment arrangement, being when the entity and the counterparty have a shared understanding of the terms and conditions of the arrangement. If that agreement is subject to an approval process (e.g., by shareholders), the grant date is the date when that approval is obtained.

Vesting conditions. The conditions that must be satisfied for the beneficiary to become entitled to receive the award. Vesting conditions include service conditions, which require

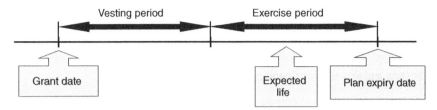

FIGURE 10.1 SOP/SAR main dates.

the other party to complete a specified period of service, and performance conditions, which require specified performance targets to be met (such as a specified increase in the entity's profit over a specified period of time). Vesting conditions are classified as either market conditions or non-market conditions.

Vesting period (see Figure 10.1). The waiting period under an equity-based incentive plan that must expire before the beneficiary becomes irrevocably entitled to the options involved. The beneficiary cannot sell or exercise unvested stock options. Vesting usually continues after termination of employment in cases such as redundancy or retirement. Vesting is commonly accelerated if the recipient's termination of employment is due to death or disability.

Exercise period (see Figure 10.1). The period in which the beneficiary may exercise his or her rights. Commonly, the exercise period starts just after the end of the vesting period.

Exercise price. The price at which the beneficiary can acquire the award underlying shares in the case of an SOP. In the case of an SAR, the exercise price is the price over which the appreciation of the shares would be calculated, and therefore, paid to the beneficiary.

Expected life. The best estimate as to when the beneficiary likely to exercise his or her options. In order to estimate the expected life, the company takes into account the vesting period, the past exercise history, the price of the underlying stock relative to its historical averages, the employee's level within the organisation and the underlying stock expected volatility.

Forfeiture. The potential cancellation of an award during the vesting period. An award, or portions of it, may be subject to forfeiture in certain circumstances. For example, an award may be forfeited if the recipient voluntarily terminates employment before the end of the relevant vesting period, or if the beneficiary is involved in certain harmful acts, such as breaches of legal, regulatory and compliance standards.

Dividends distributed to the underlying shares. Commonly, the beneficiary is not entitled to receive dividends before the settlement of the award.

10.2 ACCOUNTING FOR EQUITY-BASED COMPENSATION PLANS

This section reviews the accounting under IFRS for equity-based plans. The accounting standard that guides the recognition of share-based payments is IFRS 2 *Share-Based Payment*. IFRS 2 defines a share-based payment as a transaction in which the entity receives or acquires goods and services either as consideration for its equity instruments or by incurring liabilities for amounts based on the price of the entity's shares or other equity instruments of the entity. The accounting requirements for the share-based payment depend on how the transaction will be settled:

- the issuance/delivery of equity (SOPs, share purchase plans);
- the delivery of cash (SARs), or the issuance/delivery of equity with a cash alternative.

10.2.1 Vesting and Non-vesting Conditions

Frequently, an option right may only be exercised if specific performance targets, called conditions, are met during the vesting period (see Figure 10.2). IFRS 2 classifies all conditions as either vesting conditions or non-vesting conditions:

- **Non-vesting conditions** are conditions that determine whether the company receives the services that entitle the counterparty to the share-based payment. If a non-vesting condition is not met, the company is not receiving the "work" that entitles a beneficiary to the share-based payment. For example, a company may grant stock options to a board member on the condition that the member does not compete with the company during the vesting period. If the board member leaves to work for a competitor during the vesting period, the award is terminated. Another example of a non-vesting condition, for share plans, is a requirement for the employee to make investments in the company shares.
- **Vesting conditions** are conditions other than non-vesting conditions.

Vesting conditions are further divided into service and performance vesting conditions:

- **Service vesting conditions** are conditions that if not achieved result in forfeiture, such as the beneficiary's employment during the vesting period.
- **Performance vesting conditions** are vesting conditions other than service conditions.

Performance vesting targets are in turn divided into market and non-market vesting conditions:

- **A market vesting condition** is defined by IFRS 2 as "a condition upon which the exercise price, vesting or exercisability of an equity instrument depends that is related to the market price of the entity's equity instruments, such as attaining a specified share price or a specified amount of intrinsic value of a share option, or achieving a specified target that is based on the market price of the entity's equity instruments relative to an index of market prices of equity instruments of other entities". In summary, market vesting conditions are linked to the equity markets.
- **A non-market vesting condition** is a performance vesting condition other than a market condition. For example, an award may be exercised only if a certain earnings level per share is met, or a certain EBITDA growth is achieved.

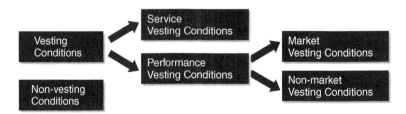

FIGURE 10.2   IFRS share-based award conditions.

10.2.2 Accounting for Stock Option Plans

Recall that SOPs can only be settled by delivering shares to the beneficiary. The settlement exclusively in shares establishes the rules for the plan's recognition, as follows.

Accounting Entries on Grant Date On grant date, the fair value of the award is estimated. An important ingredient in this estimate is the fair value of the equity option embedded in the award (see Figure 10.3), which is determined using an option pricing model, typically the Black–Scholes model.

The model takes into account the stock price at the grant date, the exercise price, the expected life of the option, the volatility of the underlying stock, its expected dividends and the risk-free interest rate over the expected life of the option. The expected life of the option is estimated using various behavioural assumptions, such as exercise patterns of similar plans.

Market vesting conditions and non-vesting conditions are taken into account when estimating the fair value of the equity option. Non-market vesting conditions and service conditions are not taken into account.

No accounting entries take place on grant date.

Accounting Entries at Each Reporting Date during the Life of the Award At each reporting date, the total compensation expense associated with the award is calculated (see Figure 10.4). The expense is measured by adjusting the fair value of the equity option that was calculated on the grant date for the expected likelihood of meeting the non-market vesting and service conditions. For example, if there is an 80% chance of achieving the non-market vesting and service conditions, the number of options is adjusted by multiplying the equity option fair value by 80%. Consequently, the compensation expense takes into account the expected number of options that

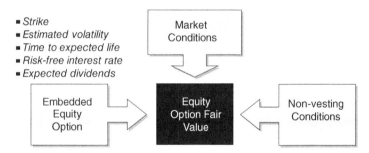

FIGURE 10.3 Equity option fair value estimation.

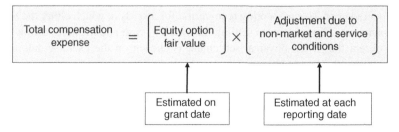

FIGURE 10.4 SOP compensation expense calculation.

are expected to vest. One of the ingredients of this adjustment is the estimation of the forfeiture rate for service conditions. Based on historical employee turnover data, the company estimates the percentage of beneficiaries who will leave the company before the vesting period lapses.

The total compensation expense is evenly allocated over the expected life of the award. For example, suppose that a company reports its financial statements on an annual basis. If at the first reporting date the total compensation was estimated to be EUR 16 million and the vesting period of the award was 4 years, the yearly compensation expense to be recognised on this date would be EUR 4 million (= 16 mn/4). The compensation expense allocated to the first year would be charged to the profit or loss statement and a corresponding increase in equity recognised.

IFRS 2 is not prescriptive on the accounting required for the credit to equity in respect of an SOP. Practice varies, depending on local regulatory requirements. One approach that is common in some jurisdictions is to credit a share-based payment reserve until the award has been settled and at a later stage to reclassify the amounts in that reserve to share capital (however, this may not be permitted in some jurisdictions) or other reserves. In other jurisdictions, the credit entry may be directly applied to retained earnings. In our example, the credit to equity was made to a share-based payment reserve (SOP reserve), as follows:

Personnel expense (Profit or loss)	4,000,000	
SOP reserve (Equity)		4,000,000

At each subsequent reporting date, the adjustment due to non-market and service vesting conditions was re-estimated. Using our previous example, suppose that the total compensation was revised upwards at the second yearly reporting date from EUR 16 million to EUR 20 million. The yearly compensation expense to be allocated over the 4-year vesting period would become EUR 5 million (= 20 mn/4). The compensation expense allocated to the second yearly period would be as follows:

Personnel expense (Profit or loss)	5,000,000	
SOP reserve (Equity)		5,000,000

10.2.3 Accounting for Stock Appreciation Rights

As mentioned previously, if exercised, SAR plans are settled by paying to the beneficiary the intrinsic value of the underlying option in cash. The accounting recognition of cash settled awards is covered next. The accounting recognition for awards in which either the beneficiary or the company can choose between settling the award in cash and in shares follows a similar procedure, except that if the physical settlement is chosen on the exercise date there is an additional accounting entry to recognise the physical delivery of the shares.

Required Actions on Grant Date No actions take place on the grant date.

Accounting Entries at Each Reporting Date during the Life of the Award At each reporting date, the total compensation expense associated with the award is calculated (see Figure 10.5).

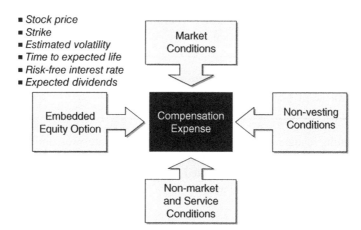

FIGURE 10.5   SAR compensation expense calculation.

The expense is measured by fair valuing the embedded equity option and adjusting it for the likelihood of achievement of all the vesting (market, non-market and service) and non-vesting conditions.

The total compensation expense is evenly allocated over the expected life of the award. For example, suppose that a company reports its financial statements on an annual basis. If at the first reporting date the total compensation was estimated to be EUR 16 million and the expected life of the award is 4 years, the yearly compensation expense to be recognised on this date would be EUR 4 million (= 16 mn/4). The compensation expense allocated to the first year would be charged to the profit or loss statement and a corresponding increase in liabilities recognised, as follows:

Personnel expense (Profit or loss)	4,000,000	
SAR award (Liability)		4,000,000

At each subsequent reporting date, the compensation expense was re-estimated. Using our previous example, suppose that the total compensation was revised upwards at the second yearly reporting date to EUR 20 million from EUR 16 million. The yearly compensation expense to be allocated over the 4-year expected life of the award became EUR 5 million (= 20 mn/4). The compensation expense allocated to the second yearly period would be as follows:

Personnel expense (Profit or loss)	5,000,000	
SAR award (Liability)		5,000,000

Also on the second reporting date an adjustment was made to the previous compensation expense to take into account the revised total compensation figure. This adjustment brought the already recognised compensation expense in line with the new total compensation estimate. As the company already had recognised a EUR 4 million expense at the first yearly reporting date, it would need to make a EUR 1 million adjustment to bring it in line with the new EUR 5 million yearly compensation expense, as follows:

Personnel expense (Profit or loss)	1,000,000	
SAR award (Liability)		1,000,000

The accounting recognition at the subsequent reporting dates was similar to the recognition outlined for the second yearly reporting date. Therefore, on a cumulative basis, no amount is recognised if the equity instruments granted do not vest because of a failure to satisfy market and/or non-market vesting conditions.

10.3 CASE STUDY: ABC'S SHARE-BASED PLANS

10.3.1 Main Terms

In order to illustrate the hedging and accounting of SOPs and SARs, let us look at an example. Suppose that ABC, a European company, on 1 January 20X1 granted two share-based plans, an SOP and an SAR, with identical terms (except the settlement feature) to its top management. The main terms of the SOP were the following (see Figure 10.6):

- Grant date: 1 January 20X1
- Number of options: 2 million
- Number of beneficiaries: 50
- Exercise price: EUR 50.00 (ABC's stock price on grant date)
- Vesting period: From 1 January 20X1 to 31 December 20X3 (i.e., 3 years' duration)
- Exercise period: At any time from 1 January 20X4 to 31 December 20X4
- Settlement: Upon exercise, beneficiaries will receive one share per option and pay the strike amount (i.e., the number of options times the strike price)
- Market vesting conditions: ABC's stock total return, including dividends, has to outperform the Euro Stoxx 50 index
- Service conditions: Each grant is conditional upon the beneficiary remaining in service over the vesting period
- Non-market vesting conditions: Each grant is conditional upon ABC's EBITDA achieving a 10% annual growth rate during the vesting period

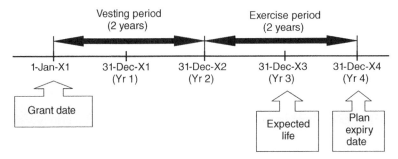

FIGURE 10.6 SOP/SAR main dates.

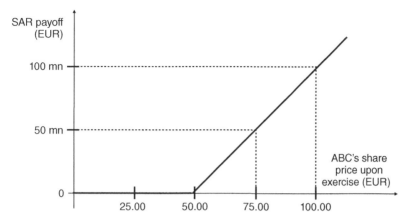

FIGURE 10.7   SAR payoff as a function of the price upon exercise.

Under the SOP, if a beneficiary exercised his/her options, he/she would pay the exercise amount (i.e., the EUR 50.00 strike times the number of options exercised) and receive his/her options' underlying ABC shares. The SOP had a 3-year vesting period. After completion of the vesting period, each beneficiary could exercise his/her vested options during the year commencing on the end date of the vesting period, subject to the achievement of three vesting conditions: (i) that ABC's stock price outperformed the European most liquid stock index, the Euro Stoxx 50; (ii) that the beneficiary remained an employee during the vesting period; and (iii) that during the vesting period ABC's EBITDA grew at least 10% annually.

Under the SAR, the mechanics were the same except for its payoff upon exercise. If a beneficiary exercised his/her options, he/she would receive in cash the intrinsic value of his/her options. The intrinsic value of the options was defined as the difference between the value of ABC's stock at expiry and the EUR 50.00 award exercise price, for the number of options the beneficiary had exercised. Figure 10.7 depicts the SAR payoff as a function of the stock price on exercise date (the volume-weighted average price on that date).

10.3.2 Accounting for ABC's Stock Option Plan

ABC's embedded equity stock option (including the market conditions) was fair valued only when the SOP was granted. The compensation expense was calculated at each balance sheet date by adjusting the fair value of the embedded equity option for the likelihood of achievement of the non-market and service conditions. The total fair value was recognised as a personnel compensation expense spread over the vesting period of the plan and an equity reserve.

Actions Required on Grant Date   On grant date, ABC estimated the fair value of the equity option, ignoring the non-market and service vesting conditions, but taking into account the non-vesting conditions (in this case there were no non-vesting conditions). Based on historical data, ABC estimated that on average the beneficiaries would exercise the fair value of the option at the end of the first 6 months of the exercise period (i.e., 3.5 years after the grant date). Thus, the best estimation of the expected life of the award was 3.5 years. The fair value of the equity option was calculated by pricing a call option on ABC stock with a strike of EUR 50.00 (i.e., at-the-money), an expiry of 3.5 years, a volatility equal to the implied volatility for such options on ABC stock, and a 2% expected dividend yield of ABC stock during its life. The option valuation also included the market vesting condition (the outperformance of the Euro Stoxx50 index), assuming a 60% correlation between ABC's stock price and the index. ABC used the Monte Carlo simulation method to estimate the fair value of this option, coming up with a fair value of EUR 21 million. Note that the fair value of the option did not include any estimates regarding the non-market and service conditions.

No accounting entries took place on grant date.

Accounting Entries at Each Reporting Date during the Life of the Award   At each reporting date, the total compensation expense associated with the award was calculated (see Figure 10.8). The expense was measured by adjusting the equity option fair value (which was calculated on the grant date) for the expected likelihood of meeting the non-market and service vesting conditions. Consequently, the compensation expense took into account the expected number of options that were expected to vest. Based on historical top employee turnover data, ABC estimated the percentage of the beneficiaries expected to leave the company before the vesting period lapsed. Also ABC estimated the likelihood of ABC's EBITDA achieving a 10% annual growth rate during the vesting period.

The total compensation (i.e., personnel) expense was evenly allocated over the 3-year vesting period of the award. The following table shows the personnel expense at each reporting date, assuming that ABC reported its financial statements on an annual basis.

Date	Equity option fair value (EUR mn)	Adjustment due to non-market conditions	Total personnel expense (EUR mn)	Period personnel expense (EUR mn)	Adjustments to previous entries (EUR mn)
31-Dec-X1	21.0	80%	16.8	5.6	—
31-Dec-X2	21.0 (1)	70% (2)	14.7 (3)	4.9 (4)	< 0.7 > (5)
31-Dec-X3	21.0	75%	15.8	5.3	0.8 (6)

Notes:
(1) Calculated on grant date, and fixed during the life of the award
(2) Estimated at each reporting date
(3) Calculated as (1) × (2) = 21 mn × 70%
(4) Calculated as (3)/Number of accounting periods = 14.7 mn/3
(5) 4.9 mn − 5.6 mn
(6) (5.3 mn × 2) − (4.9 mn × 2)

On 31 December 20X1, ABC estimated the expected likelihood of meeting the non-market vesting conditions to be 80%. A EUR 16.8 million total compensation expense was calculated by multiplying the EUR 21 million equity option fair value by the 80% estimate. The compensation expense allocated to the first year was charged to profit or loss and a corresponding increase in equity recognised as follows (amounts in EUR million):

Personnel expense (Profit or loss)	5.6
SOP reserve (Equity)	5.6

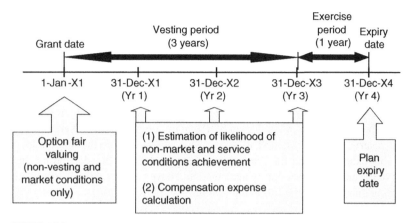

FIGURE 10.8 SOP compensation expense calculation dates.

On 31 December 20X2, the expected likelihood of meeting the non-market and service vesting conditions was re-estimated to be 70%. A EUR 14.7 million total compensation expense was calculated by multiplying the EUR 21 million equity option fair value by the 70% estimate. The compensation expense allocated to the second year was charged to profit or loss and a corresponding increase in equity recognised as follows (amounts in EUR million):

Personnel expense (Profit or loss)	4.9	
SOP reserve (Equity)		4.9

Also on 31 December 20X2, a EUR 0.7 million adjustment to the compensation expense was implemented as the new annual expense was EUR 4.9 million while the personnel expense recognised on 31 December 20X1 was EUR 5.6 million. The adjustment was recorded as follows (amounts in EUR million):

SOP reserve (Equity)	0.7	
Personnel expense (Profit or loss)		0.7

Following the same reasoning, and using the numbers in the table above, the accounting entries on 31 December 20X3 were the following (amounts in EUR million):

Personnel expense (Profit or loss)	5.3	
SOP reserve (Equity)		5.3
Personnel expense (Profit or loss)	0.8	
SOP reserve (Equity)		0.8

Accounting Entries upon Exercised/Unexercised Expiry   Following each exercise and at maturity of the SOP, the balance of the SOP reserve was recycled to another account of the shareholders' equity section. There were two scenarios to consider: (i) all (or part of) the plan options expired unexercised; and (ii) all (or part of) the plan options were exercised.

In order to describe the accounting entries under the first scenario, suppose that under ABC's SOP all the beneficiaries behaved identically and that on the SOP's expiration date on 31 December 20X4 no beneficiaries exercised their options. On that date, the SOP reserve had a carrying amount of EUR 15.8 million. Therefore, a compensation expense of EUR 15.8 million was recognised during the SOP's vesting period. It would have been illogical to leave an amount on the SOP reserve related to an SOP that no longer existed. Therefore, the balance of the SOP reserve was reclassified to some other account(s) of the shareholders' equity section. In this example I use the "retained earnings" account, but depending on the legal jurisdiction of the entity another equity account could have been used (e.g., "share premium"). The accounting entries were the following (amounts in EUR million):

SOP reserve (Equity)	15.8	
Retained earnings (Equity)		15.8

Under the second scenario, exercise of the SOP, there was also a transfer within the shareholders' equity section, but the accounts affected depended on the action taken by the company. Suppose that upon exercise of the SOP, the company could either (i) issue new shares or (ii) deliver treasury shares.

Suppose that the SOP was exercised simultaneously by all the beneficiaries at the end of the fourth year and that ABC issued 2 million new shares, with a nominal value of EUR 2 million. Upon exercise of the SOP the beneficiaries paid the EUR 100 million (= 2 mn × 50.00) strike amount in exchange for the new shares. The accounting entries were the following (amounts in EUR million):

Cash (Assets)	100	
SOP reserve (Equity)	15.8	
Share capital (Equity)		2
Share premium (Equity)		98
Retained earnings (Equity)		15.8

If the company delivered treasury shares instead, the accounting entries would be the following (amounts in EUR million), assuming that the treasury shares delivered were previously recognised at EUR 15 million:

Cash (Assets)	100	
SOP reserve (Equity)	15.8	
Treasury shares (Equity)		15
Share premium (Equity)		85
Retained earnings (Equity)		15.8

Conclusions If at the end of the vesting period, the non-market condition (i.e., a 10% growth in EBITDA) had not been achieved, a reversal of the SOP's personnel expense already recognised would have taken place. Thus, on a cumulative basis no amount of personnel expense would not be recognised if the equity instruments granted did not vest because of a failure to satisfy non-market vesting conditions or service conditions.

If the non-market vesting conditions and the service conditions were satisfied while an SOP's market and non-vesting conditions (in our case there were no non-vesting conditions) were met, the personnel expense would not be reversed, and the total expense would end up increasing shareholders' equity, even if the SOP expired unexercised. Thus, if an SOP has a market vesting condition or a non-vesting condition, the company might still recognise an expense even if that condition is not attained and the option does not vest.

From the grant date ABC knew the maximum amount of compensation expense that it could end up recognising in profit or loss. This maximum amount was the fair value of the equity option on grant date (i.e., EUR 21 million).

10.3.3 Accounting for ABC's Stock Appreciation Rights

The whole SAR award was fair valued periodically at each balance sheet date. The fair value was recognised as a personnel expense spread over the life of the plan and a liability.

Actions Required on Grant Date No actions and no accounting entries took place on the grant date.

Accounting Entries at Each Reporting Date during the Life of the Award At each reporting date and at maturity, the total compensation expense associated with the award was calculated (see Figure 10.9) by estimating the fair value of the embedded equity option expense and adjusting it for the expected likelihood of meeting the non-market and service vesting conditions. Consequently, the compensation expense took into account the expected number of options that were expected to vest.

The total compensation (i.e., personnel) expense was evenly allocated over the 3-year vesting period. The following table shows the personnel expense at each reporting date, assuming that ABC reported its financial statements on an annual basis.

Date	Equity option fair value (EUR mn)	Adjustment due to non-market conditions	Total personnel expense (EUR mn)	Period personnel expense (EUR mn)	Adjustments to previous entries (EUR mn)
31-Dec-X1	20.0	80%	16.0	5.3	—
31-Dec-X2	26.0 *(1)*	70% *(1)*	18.2 *(2)*	6.1 *(3)*	0.8 *(4)*
31-Dec-X3	29.0	75%	21.8	7.3	2.4 *(5)*

Notes:

(1) Calculated at each reporting date
(2) 26.0 mn × 70%
(3) Calculated as (2)/Number of accounting periods = 18.2 mn/3, assuming a 3-year vesting period
(4) 6.1 mn − 5.3 mn
(5) (7.3 mn × 2) − (6.1 mn × 2), assuming a 3-year expected life of the SAR

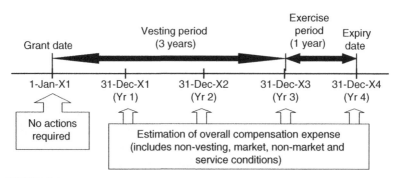

FIGURE 10.9 SAR compensation expense calculation dates.

On 31 December 20X1, ABC estimated both (i) the fair value of the embedded equity option (EUR 20 million) and (ii) the expected likelihood of meeting the non-market and service vesting conditions (80%). A EUR 16 million total compensation expense was calculated by multiplying the EUR 20 million equity option fair value by the 80% estimate. The compensation expense allocated to the first year was charged to profit or loss and a corresponding increase in liabilities recognised as follows (amounts in EUR million):

Personnel expense (Profit or loss)	5.3	
SAR award (Liability)		5.3

Repeating the process executed on the previous reporting date, on 31 December 20X2 ABC estimated a EUR 18.2 million compensation expense. Of this expense, EUR 6.1 million was allocated to the second year, charged to profit or loss and to liabilities as follows (amounts in EUR million):

Personnel expense (Profit or loss)	6.1	
SAR award (Liability)		6.1

Also on 31 December 20X2, a EUR 0.8 million adjustment to the compensation expense was implemented as the new annual expense was EUR 6.1 million while the personnel expense recognised on 31 December 20X1 was EUR 5.3 million. The adjustment was recorded as follows (amounts in EUR million):

Personnel expense (Profit or loss)	0.8	
SAR award (Liability)		0.8

Following the same reasoning, and using the numbers in the table above, the accounting entries on 31 December 20X3 were the following (amounts in EUR million):

Personnel expense (Profit or loss)	7.3	
SAR award (Liability)		7.3
Personnel expense (Profit or loss)	2.4	
SAR award (Liability)		2.4

Accounting Entries upon Exercise/Unexercised Expiry Suppose that no beneficiaries exercised their rights prior to the SAR's expiry date. Suppose further that at expiry, on 31 December 20X4, all the beneficiaries behaved identically. As a consequence, there were two scenarios to consider: (i) that all the SAR options expired unexercised; and (ii) that all the SAR options were exercised.

Under the first scenario, the SAR lapsed fully unexercised. Thus, the SAR's fair value was zero. At the previous reporting dates a total EUR 21.8 million compensation expense was recognised. Therefore, this compensation expense had to be reversed on 31 December 20X4. The accounting entries were the following (amounts in EUR million):

SAR award (Liability)	21.8	
Personnel expense (Profit or loss)		21.8

Under the second scenario, the SAR was fully exercised. Suppose that on 31 December 20X4 ABC's share price was EUR 68. The SAR's fair value was EUR 36 million (= 2 mn × (68 − 50)). As ABC had already recognised a total EUR 21.8 million compensation expense, an additional EUR 14.2 million (= 36 mn − 21.8 mn) expense was recognised as follows (amounts in EUR million):

Personnel expense (Profit or loss)	14.2	
SAR award (Liability)		14.2

Additionally, the EUR 36 million cash award payment to the beneficiaries was recognised as follows (amounts in EUR million):

SAR award (Liability)	36	
Cash (Assets)		36

Conclusions   At each reporting date ABC had to fair value the SAR award. This had several implications:

- ABC's profit or loss statement was exposed to a rising stock price, potentially increasing its volatility.
- Overall, ABC did not have to recognise a compensation expense were the SAR to expire worthless.
- On the grant date ABC did not know the maximum amount of compensation expense that could end up recognised in profit or loss. Similarly on the grant date, ABC did not know the amount of cash it would need to meet the SAR award.

10.4 MAIN SOP/SAR HEDGING STRATEGIES

In this section I cover the main strategies to hedge SOPs and SARs, based on ABC's share awards (see Figure 10.10).

10.4.1 Underlying Risks in SOPs and SARs

One not unusual hedging strategy is to do nothing. ABC would be exposed to the risk inherent in the plans. The risks in an SOP and in an SAR differ due to their accounting and settlement differences. Thus, hedging strategies for an SOP may not work for an SAR, and vice versa.

Main Risks in an SOP   Under its SOP, ABC was not exposed to **equity market risk**. Remember that from an accounting perspective, the equity option embedded in the SOP award was estimated at grant date. During the expected life of the award, the equity option was not further fair valued. Only the expectations of meeting the non-market conditions were reassessed at each reporting date. Therefore, ABC's profit or loss statement was not exposed to changes in ABC's stock price or changes in the likelihood of meeting the market conditions (i.e., ABC stock had to outperform the Euro Stoxx 50 index). In other words, ABC's profit or loss was not exposed to equity risk. While ABC's profit or loss was exposed to non-market risk (i.e., a 10% average EBITDA growth), its hedge was unavailable in the market.

ABC's shareholders were exposed to **dilution risk**. If the SOP ended up being exercised, ABC needed to deliver shares to the beneficiaries. Probably these shares would be newly

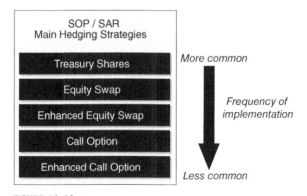

FIGURE 10.10   Main SOP/SAR hedging strategies.

issued, increasing the number of shares outstanding, and thus diluting existing shareholders. Nonetheless, the dilution risk was limited as new shares would be issued at a pre-established fixed price (EUR 50.00 per share).

Main Risks in an SAR   ABC was exposed to **equity market risk**. Remember that, from an accounting perspective, under the SAR the equity option was fair valued at each reporting date. Therefore, ABC's profit or loss was exposed to changes in ABC's stock price and to changes in the likelihood of meeting the market conditions (i.e., ABC stock had to outperform the Euro Stoxx 50 index).

ABC's profit or loss was exposed as well to the achievement of a non-market condition (i.e., a 10% average EBITDA growth). However, hedging this risk was unavailable in the market.

ABC was also exposed to **liquidity risk**. Upon exercise, ABC needed to pay a cash amount to the beneficiaries. A large amount of cash may require ABC to use precious liquidity resources or/and to raise financing.

ABC was not exposed to **dilution risk** as upon exercise no shares were delivered to the beneficiaries.

10.4.2 Hedging with Treasury Shares

Hedging with treasury shares is the most common way to hedge SOPs and SARs. In order to fully hedge the SOP/SAR with treasury shares, on 1 January 20X1 ABC needed to acquire 4 million shares in the market, investing EUR 100 million. The treasury shares were held on its balance sheet in a quantity that coincided with the number of unexercised stock options. Each time a beneficiary exercised his/her option rights:

- related to the SAR, ABC sold in the market the shares corresponding to the exercised options at the then prevailing share price. ABC paid the beneficiary the intrinsic value of the exercised stock options;
- related to the SOP, ABC delivered the shares to the beneficiary in exchange for the exercise amount.

At maturity of the plan, ABC needed to decide what to do with the remaining shares. In theory, ABC sold the shares in the market, but alternatively it could retain any remaining shares for future SOPs/SARs.

This strategy can be optimised by taking into account the likelihood of meeting the non-market conditions and the market conditions not directly related to ABC's stock price. As a result, ABC would acquire a number of shares equivalent to the number of options expected to vest.

Strengths of the Strategy   The strategy had the following strengths:

- If the plan options were fully exercised, ABC would effectively meet the settlement commitments under both plans.
- Ignoring the financing costs related to the treasury shares, this hedging alternative was cheaper than hedging with calls if the plans were fully exercised. If the stock options were exercised, ABC would have saved the call premium, which could be substantial.
- The initial acquisition of the shares could have a positive effect on ABC's stock price.
- The hedge was not revalued during the life of the plan. Thus, there is a parallel accounting treatment in equity of the SOP's embedded equity option and the treasury shares as none of them are revalued after the grant date.

Weaknesses of the Strategy   The strategy had the following drawbacks:

- The acquisition of treasury shares used liquidity resources from the company. ABC could have needed to raise financing to fund the own shares acquisition.
- The acquisition of treasury shares had a negative impact on ABC's debt-to-equity ratio. Treasury shares were deducted from equity, increasing ABC's leverage.
- The hedge was not revalued. This was a weakness only for the SAR award. The SAR award was revalued periodically while the hedge was not. As a result, ABC was not able to apply hedge accounting.
- At maturity of the plan the shares hedging unexercised options were no longer needed. ABC could sell the shares in the market at a price below the acquisition price (i.e., at a loss), permanently reducing equity.
- ABC did not receive the treasury shares dividends, as an entity cannot distribute dividends to its own shares.
- The acquisition of treasury shares could affect ABC's flexibility in managing its treasury shares. Legally there is a limit (e.g., 10%) on the maximum percentage of voting capital that companies can hold in their own shares. Buying a substantial amount of treasury shares could bring the company close to the legal limit, restricting potential acquisition of more shares.
- Although the shares acquired to hedge a plan in theory remained on ABC's balance sheet until expiration, there was a potential temptation to manage these shares like the rest of the treasury shares. Some companies dynamically manage their holdings of treasury shares to alleviate potential disruptions in its stock market trading. For example, a company may acquire treasury shares to provide liquidity when there is a large selling order in the market and sell them later when its stock shows excessive strength.

10.4.3 Hedging with Equity Swaps

One relatively common hedging strategy is to enter into an equity swap. Due to their significantly different effects, I will separate the analysis for each type of award.

Hedging an SOP with an Equity Swap   Suppose that ABC hedged its SOP plan with an equity swap. The strategy was in a way similar to a combination of a financing and an acquisition of treasury shares. Suppose that ABC entered into a total return equity swap with the following terms:

- Trade date: 1 January 20X1 (the award grant date)
- Termination date: 31 December 20X4 (the award maturity date)
- Number of shares: 2 million (the SOP number of options)
- Shares: ABC's ordinary shares
- Initial price: EUR 50.00 (ABC's share price on trade date)
- Initial equity notional: EUR 100 million
- Equity amount receiver: ABC
- ABC could partially/totally early terminate the equity swap at any time from 1 January 20X3 to 31 December 20X4
- ABC paid quarterly Euribor 3M plus 150 bps on the equity notional amount
- ABC received 100% of the gross dividends distributed to the underlying shares
- Settlement: physical settlement only

The strategy was executed as follows:

1) ABC entered into the equity swap on the award grant date. No up-front premium was paid.
2) During the life of the equity swap, ABC paid the equity swap floating amount, Euribor plus 150 bps on the equity swap notional. The equity swap notional was initially EUR 100 million, and was adjusted to take into account partial early terminations of the swap.
3) During the life of the equity swap, ABC received any dividends distributed to the underlying shares.
4) Upon each exercise of the SOP, ABC would terminate a number of shares of the equity swap equivalent to the number of options exercised under the plan. For example, if 200,000 options were exercised by the SOP beneficiaries, ABC would terminate 200,000 shares of the equity swap. Under the equity swap, ABC paid EUR 10 million (= 0.2 mn × 50) and received 200,000 of its own shares, which in turn were delivered to the beneficiaries in exchange for a EUR 10 million payment.
5) If at the end of the vesting period the non-market conditions were not achieved, ABC faced two main alternatives: either to maintain the equity swap until its maturity or to terminate it early and in full. In either case, under the equity swap ABC would end up buying 50 million own shares and paying EUR 100 million. ABC then would need to decide whether to hold the treasury shares for future share-based award or to sell them in the market.
6) If at expiry of the SOP there were options that remained unexercised, ABC would buy through the equity swap the remaining shares and pay EUR 50 per share. ABC then would need to decide what to do with the own shares: whether to hold them for future share-based plans or to sell them onto the market.

The equity swap was classified for accounting purposes as an equity instrument. The initial accounting entry under IFRS was to recognise a liability for an amount equal to the present value of the equity swap notional, with a debit to an equity account.

The equity swap was not fair valued during its life. As a result, the equity swap did not add volatility to ABC's profit or loss statement as both the plan (ignoring service conditions) and the equity swap did not require fair valuing after the grant date. However, a liability was recognised, increasing ABC's leverage metrics.

Hedging an SAR with an Equity Swap   Suppose that ABC hedged its SAR plan with an equity swap. The terms were identical to those of the equity swap traded to hedge the SOP, except its settlement terms. The equity swap hedging the SAR allowed for cash settlement only. Therefore, at each partial early termination and/or at maturity, ABC received, if its stock price was above EUR 50.00, an amount equal to

$$\text{Number of shares terminated} \times (\text{Stock price} - 50.00)$$

or paid, if its stock price was below EUR 50.00, an amount equal to

$$\text{Number of shares terminated} \times (50.00 - \text{Stock price}).$$

Figure 10.11 shows the equity swap settlement amount as a function of the final price at maturity (i.e., the volume-weighted average price on that date). It can be seen that if the final price was above EUR 50.00 and ignoring the SAR's service conditions, ABC perfectly hedged its commitment under the SAR. However, if the final price was below EUR 50.00, ABC lost a substantial amount.

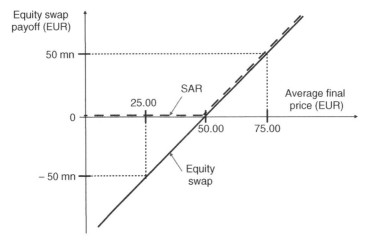

FIGURE 10.11 Equity swap settlement amount.

The strategy was executed as follows:

1) ABC entered into the equity swap on the award grant date. No up-front premium was paid.
2) During the life of the equity swap, ABC paid the equity swap floating amount, Euribor plus 150 basis points on the equity swap notional. The equity swap notional was initially EUR 100 million, and was subsequently adjusted to take into account partial early terminations of the swap.
3) During the life of the equity swap, ABC received any dividends distributed to the underlying shares.
4) Upon exercise of the SAR, ABC terminated a number of shares of the equity swap equal to the number of options exercised under the plan. For example, if 200,000 options were exercised by the SAR beneficiaries, ABC would terminate 200,000 shares of the equity swap. Assuming that ABC's share price was EUR 60 at the time of the exercise, under the equity swap, ABC received a EUR 2 million (= 0.2 mn × (60 – 50)) settlement amount. This amount was paid in turn to the SAR beneficiaries.
5) If at the end of the vesting period the non-market conditions were not achieved, ABC faced two main alternatives: either to maintain the equity swap or to terminate it early and in full. In order to avoid further exposure to ABC's stock price, ABC would probably terminate it early. ABC would either (i) receive the appreciation of the underlying shares above EUR 50, or (ii) pay the depreciation of the underlying shares below EUR 50.
6) If at expiry of the SAR there were options that remain unexercised, the equity swap would terminate. ABC would either (i) receive the appreciation of the remaining underlying shares above EUR 50, or (ii) pay the depreciation of the remaining underlying shares below EUR 50.

The equity swap was classified for accounting purposes as a derivative. It was unlikely that ABC could apply hedge accounting as the payoffs of the SAR (a call option) and the equity swap (a forward like) were very different when ABC's stock price was below EUR 50.00.

Assuming that the equity swap was undesignated, it was fair valued through profit or loss at each reporting date. Remember that the SAR was also fair valued at each reporting date, but the change in fair value was allocated over the 3-year vesting period. Therefore:

- If ABC's share price were above 50.00, the change in fair value of the SAR and of the equity swap would be similar (ignoring the time value of the equity option underlying the SAR and the adjustments due to the service condition). However, an accounting mismatch would occur in profit or loss, as the whole change in fair value of the swap would be recognised in profit or loss while just one third of the change in fair value of the SAR would be recognised in profit or loss.
- If ABC's share price were below 50.00, the change in fair value of the equity swap would be rather different from that of the SAR. To make things worse, only one third of the change in fair value of the SAR would be recognised in profit or loss. As a result a substantial mismatch in profit or loss would result, potentially increasing the volatility of ABC's profit or loss.

In summary, hedging an SAR with an equity swap may cause substantial distortions in an entity's financial statements. In the next subsection I will discuss a friendlier variation on the equity swap.

Strengths of the Strategy   The strategy had the following strengths:

- If the plan options were exercised, ABC effectively met the settlement commitments under both awards.
- ABC was not using cash resources, in contrast to a hedge with treasury shares.
- Ignoring the financing costs related to the equity swap, this hedging alternative was cheaper than hedging with calls if the plans were exercised. If the award's options were exercised, ABC saved the call premium, which was substantial due to the medium-term life of the award.
- The bank counterparty to the equity swap needed to buy the underlying shares in the market at inception. This initial acquisition had a positive effect on ABC's stock price.
- Regarding the SOP, the hedge was not revalued during the life of the award. Thus, there was a similar accounting treatment in equity as neither the SOP's embedded equity option nor the equity swap were fair valued subsequent to their commencement.

Weaknesses of the Strategy   The strategy had the following drawbacks:

- If the plans were unexercised because ABC shares traded below EUR 50.00, ABC would end up with either unwanted treasury shares (in case of the SOP) or a loss (in case of the SAR).
- Regarding the SAR, if the shares traded below EUR 50.00, there could be a substantial increase in the volatility of ABC's profit or loss statement due to the accounting recognition mismatch in profit or loss between the equity swap and the SAR.
- Regarding the SOP, the equity swap had a negative effect on ABC's leverage metrics, for example on its debt-to-equity ratio. On the one hand, there was a liability recognised from inception. On the other hand, there was an equity entry that reduced the balance of the shareholders' equity section of ABC's balance sheet.

- The equity swap consumed credit lines with its counterparty, reducing its flexibility to deal with this party. If the equity swap was collateralised and the share price fell, ABC would need to post collateral to the equity swap counterparty.
- In some jurisdictions, an equity swap may be treated as treasury shares from a legal perspective. This treatment could affect ABC's flexibility in managing its treasury shares, as they were subject to a maximum legal limit.

10.4.4 Hedging with an Enhanced Equity Swap

It was concluded in the previous subsection that hedging an SAR with an equity swap can create substantial distortions in an entity's financial statements, especially in profit or loss. In this subsection I will discuss a friendlier variation on the equity swap.

A long position in an equity swap can be viewed as the combination of a purchased call option and a sold a put option, with a strike equal to the equity swap's reference price (see Figure 10.12).

In our case, ABC bought a call option and sold a put option with the following common terms to hedge the SAR:

- Trade date: 1 January 20X1 (the award grant date)
- Counterparties: ABC and Gigabank
- Number of options: 2 million
- Shares: ABC's ordinary shares
- Exercise price: EUR 50.00 (ABC's share price on trade date)
- Exercise period: At any time from 1 January 20X3 to 31 December 20X4
- Partial exercise: The buyer can partially/totally exercise the options during the exercise period. An exercise of a call option will automatically exercise the put for the same number of underlying shares
- Settlement: Cash settlement only
- Additional condition: The option can only be exercised if ABC's stock total return (i.e., including dividend reinvestment) has outperformed the Euro Stoxx 50 index from trade date to 31 December 20X2
- Up-front premium: EUR 42 million (i.e., 21% of ABC's stock price on trade date), to be paid two currency business days following the trade date
- Dividends: Gigabank will pay ABC an amount equal to the delta times the gross dividends distributed to the underlying shares.

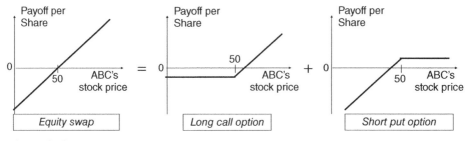

FIGURE 10.12　Split of an equity swap into a call option and a put option.

Now, from an accounting point of view, ABC would be likely to apply hedge accounting for the call option. As a result, the change in the fair value of the SAR (excluding the effect of the service conditions) and that of the call option, after both have been allocated to the vesting period, would cancel each other in profit or loss (see Section 10.4.5). The put would be recognised as a speculative derivative, and therefore, the full change in its fair value would be recognised in profit or loss. This way, the accounting mismatch between the SAR and its hedge would be caused only by the put. For example, if the put became deeper out-of-the-money, the accounting mismatch would gradually disappear.

10.4.5 Hedging with Standard Call Options

One relatively uncommon hedging strategy is to acquire from a bank a call option that perfectly mirrors the equity option embedded in an SOP/SAR plan. Therefore, ABC would buy two call options with the following common terms:

- Trade date: 1 January 20X1 (the award grant date)
- Number of options: 4 million (2 million per plan)
- Buyer: ABC
- Shares: ABC's ordinary shares
- Exercise price: EUR 50.00 (ABC's share price on trade date)
- Exercise period: At any time from 1 January 20X3 to 31 December 20X4
- Partial exercise: ABC can partially/totally exercise the options during the exercise period
- Settlement: For 2 million options (i.e., those hedging the SOP) physical settlement only. For the remaining 2 million options (i.e., those hedging the SAR) cash settlement only
- Additional condition: The options could only be exercised if ABC's stock total return (i.e., including dividend reinvestment) has outperformed the Eurstoxx50 index from trade date to 31 December 20X2
- Up-front premium: EUR 42 million (i.e., 21% of ABC's stock price on trade date), to be paid two currency business days following the trade date

The strategy was executed as follows:

1) ABC bought the call options on the awards' grant date, paying a EUR 42 million premium two currency business days following the trade date.
2) Upon exercise of the awards, ABC exercised a number of call options equivalent to the number of options exercised under the plan. For example, if 200,000 options were exercised by the SOP beneficiaries, ABC would exercise 200,000 physically settled call options, paying EUR 10 million (= 0.2 mn × 50) and receiving 200,000 own shares. These shares would be delivered to the beneficiaries in exchange for a EUR 10 million payment. If, for example, there were 200,000 options exercised by the SAR plan beneficiaries when ABC's stock was trading at EUR 60, ABC would exercise 200,000 cash settled call options, receiving EUR 2 million (= 0.2 mn × (60 − 50)). ABC would in turn pay EUR 2 million to the SAR beneficiaries.

3) If at the end of the vesting period, the non-market conditions had not been achieved, ABC would sell the options in the market.

4) If at expiry of the plans there were options remaining unexercised, ABC would exercise the corresponding call options if they were in-the-money, keeping the gains.

As we can see, the exercises under the awards were perfectly hedged by the call options exercises. From an accounting point of view:

- Due to their physical settlement term, the call options hedging the SOP plan were recognised in equity and no subsequent fair valuing was required. Therefore, the hedge had no impact on profit or loss. Remember, however, that the potential effects on profit or loss volatility due to non-market vesting conditions remained.
- Regarding the call options hedging the SAR plan, ABC needed to apply hedge accounting in order to minimise any mismatch with the award's accounting recognition. Therefore, the hedge eliminated the award's impact on profit or loss due to market vesting conditions. Remember, however, that the potential effects on profit or loss volatility due to non-market vesting conditions remained.

Strengths of the Strategy   The strategy had the following strengths:

- If the plan options were exercised, ABC would have effectively met the settlement commitments under both plans.
- ABC was not exposed to a share price lower than the strike price.
- In the case of the SAR, the hedge eliminated the award's profit or loss impact due to changes in market conditions as ABC was able to apply hedge accounting.
- The accounting treatment of the hedge was similar to that of the awards, not creating accounting mismatches.
- The implementation of the hedge had a positive effect on ABC's stock price as the bank supplying the call options needed to acquire ABC shares in the market at inception to hedge its position under the calls.
- ABC could sell the options at the end of the vesting period if the non-market conditions were not achieved. The sale would effectively reduce the hedge cost.

Weaknesses of the Strategy   The strategy had the following drawbacks:

- ABC paid a substantial premium up-front, as the SOP/SAR had medium-term maturities, using liquidity resources from the company. Financing might need to be raised to fund the premium. However, the premium was considerably lower than the initial outflow incurred when hedging the awards with treasury shares.
- The acquisition of call had a negative impact on ABC's debt-to-equity ratio. The premium of the call options hedging the SOP was deducted from equity, increasing ABC's leverage. However, the effect on leverage was considerably lower than the effect when hedging the awards with treasury shares.

10.5 CASE STUDY: HEDGING A STOCK OPTION PLAN WITH AN EQUITY SWAP

This case study covers the accounting of SOPs hedged with equity swaps. Suppose that on 1 January 20X0 ABC granted an SOP to its executives with the following terms:

Stock option plan terms	
Grant date	1 January 20X0
Vesting period	3 years (from 1 January 20X0 until 31 December 20X2)
Exercise date	31 December 20X2
Strike	EUR 10.00
Underlying shares	Ordinary shares of ABC
Number of options	10 million (each option was on one ABC share)
Settlement	Physical delivery
Service conditions	Each grant was conditional upon the beneficiary remaining in service over the vesting period
Non-market vesting conditions	Each grant was conditional upon ABC's EBITDA achieving a 10% annual growth rate during the vesting period
Other	ABC was committed to meet the potential exercises by delivering its own treasury shares (i.e., by not issuing new shares)

In order to hedge future exercises under the plan, ABC considered the following possibilities:

1) Not to hedge the plan. As ABC committed itself to deliver existing shares, upon exercise of the options ABC would have to buy 10 million shares in the market. From a cash flow perspective, ABC would then be exposed to rises in its share price: the higher the share price, the larger the disbursement to buy back its own shares. This was not acceptable to ABC management.

2) To buy a call option. The terms of the call option would be identical to those of the SOP's underlying equity option. ABC contacted an investment bank that quoted a EUR 14 million premium for the required call option. This was the best hedge possible: if the SOP was exercised ABC would exercise the hedging call option, and conversely, if the SOP was not exercised then ABC would not exercise the call option. Whilst recognising the merits of this course of action, ABC discarded it due to its high cost.

3) To hold the underlying shares. Under this choice, ABC would buy 10 million own shares in the market on the SOP grant date. If the SOP was exercised, ABC would deliver the shares to the SOP beneficiaries. If the plan was not exercised, ABC would sell the shares in the market. This choice was discarded by ABC due to its unwillingness to finance the purchase of the shares.

4) To enter into an equity swap. This course of action was similar to the previous one, but without using ABC's own funds to purchase the underlying shares. Under the equity swap, ABC would be obliged to buy 10 million of its own shares at maturity. The purchased shares would be then delivered to the SOP beneficiaries following their exercise.

The main disadvantage of this choice was that in the event of SOP beneficiaries not exercising their options, ABC would end up owning 10 million of its own shares and would probably have to sell them in the market at a (cash flow) loss. In other words, this hedge only worked if the options became exercised. ABC decided to pursue this course of action, due to the company's positive prospects and the use of external financing to purchase the shares. The terms of the equity swap were as follows:

Equity swap terms	
Start date	1 January 20X0
Counterparties	ABC and XYZ Bank
Maturity date	31 December 20X2 (3 years)
Reference price	EUR 10.00
Number of shares	10 million shares
Nominal amount	EUR 100 million
Underlying	ABC ordinary shares
Settlement	Physical delivery (ABC was obliged to buy on maturity date the number of shares at the reference price)
ABC paid	Euribor 12-month plus 0.50% annually, actual/360 basis, on the nominal amount
ABC received	100% of the gross dividend distributed to the underlying shares. ABC received these amounts on dividend payment date

Fair Valuation of the SOP at Each Reporting Date   On the SOP grant date, ABC had to value the award granted, excluding the service and non-market vesting conditions. ABC used the Black–Scholes valuation model with the following inputs: a 3-year time to expiry, a EUR 10 strike, a 20% volatility, a 10 million share nominal, a 4.50% interest rate and a 3% dividend yield. The value of the equity option underlying the SOP using this model, excluding the non-market conditions, was EUR 14 million.

At each reporting date, ABC calculated the adjusted fair value of the SOP (i.e., also including the service and non-market conditions). The SOP's EUR 14 million initial value had to be adjusted to incorporate only the expected number of options that would vest. Vesting was conditional on the beneficiary's continual employment and the achievement of a 50% growth in ABC's EBITDA during the SOP term. ABC's estimates at each reporting date are shown in the following table:

Date	Expected number of options to vest	Adjusted fair value of plan	Annual expense
31-Dec-X0	8.5 million	EUR 11.9 million (=8.5 mn/10 mn × 14 mn)	EUR 3,967,000
31-Dec-X1	8 million	EUR 11.2 million (=8 mn/10 mn × 14 mn)	EUR 3,733,000
31-Dec-X2	8.2 million	EUR 11.48 million (=8.2 mn/10 mn × 14 mn)	EUR 3,827,000

Under the equity swap, on 31 December 20X2 ABC was obliged to pay EUR 100 million to XYZ Bank, and in exchange XYZ Bank was obliged to deliver 10 million shares to ABC. This obligation to purchase a fixed number of shares for a fixed amount of cash represented a forward on ABC's own shares. The present value of the consideration to be paid was initially recognised as a liability and an equity instrument. Assuming that at the beginning of the transaction 3-year straight debt issued by ABC yielded 4.50%, the present value of the EUR 100 million was EUR 87,630,000 ($= 100$ mn$/(1 + 4.5\%)^3$). The liability carrying value increased at each reporting date to reach a final EUR 100 million consideration, as follows:

Date	Interest expense	Liability carrying value
1-Jan-X0		87,630,000
31-Dec-X0	3,943,000	91,573,000
31-Dec-X1	4,121,000	95,694,000
31-Dec-X2	4,306,000	100,000,000

Accounting Entries   The required journal entries were as follows.

1) Entries on 1 January 20X0

ABC recognised a EUR 87,630,000 liability representing the present value of ABC's future commitment to pay EUR 100 million.

Forward on own shares (Equity)	87,630,000	
Forward obligation (Liability)		87,630,000

2) Entries on 31 December 20X0

The estimated fair value of the SOP on 31 December 20X0 was EUR 11.9 million to be spread over the 3-year vesting period (i.e., EUR 3,967,000 per annum). Thus, ABC recognised a EUR 3,967,000 employee benefits annual expense.

Compensation expense (Profit or loss)	3,967,000	
SOP reserve (Equity)		3,967,000

Through the equity swap, ABC paid an annual interest of Euribor 12-month plus 50 bps. Suppose that the Euribor 12-month rate was 4.00% and that there were 365 days in the interest period. The interest expense for the period was EUR 4,563,000 ($=100$ million $\times$ (4%+0.50%) $\times$ 365/360).

Interest expense (Profit or loss)	4,563,000	
Cash (Asset)		4,563,000

Through the equity swap, ABC received an amount equivalent to the dividends distributed to the underlying shares –a manufactured dividend. Suppose that ABC distributed a EUR 0.30 dividend per share. For simplicity, suppose further that the dividend was paid on 31 December 20X0. Thus, ABC recognised a EUR 3 million manufactured dividend.

Cash (Asset)	3,000,000	
Interest income (Profit or loss)		3,000,000

ABC recognised the liability interest accrual.

Interest expense (Profit or loss)	3,943,000	
Forward obligation (Liability)		3,943,000

3) Entries on 31 December 20X1

The estimated fair value of the SOP on 31 December 20X1 was EUR 11.2 million, to be spread over the 3-year vesting period (or EUR 3,733,000 per annum). As EUR 3,967,000 was already recognised on 31 December 20X0, a EUR 3,500,000 (=3,733,000 × 2 – 3,967,000) amount was recognised as employee benefits compensation expense.

Through the equity swap, ABC paid an annual interest of Euribor 12-month plus 50 bps. Suppose that the Euribor 12-month rate was 4.20% and that there were 365 days in the interest period. The interest expense for the period was EUR 4,765,000 (=100 million × (4.2%+0.50%) × 365/360). This interest was paid on 31 December 20X1 as well.

Through the equity swap, ABC received an amount equivalent to the dividends distributed to the underlying shares. Suppose that ABC distributed a EUR 0.32 dividend per share on 31 December 20X1. As a result ABC received a EUR 3,200,000 manufactured dividend which was recognised as income in profit or loss.

Finally, ABC had to recognise the liability's EUR 4,121,000 interest accrual.

Compensation expense (Profit or loss)	3,500,000	
SOP reserve (Equity)		3,500,000
Interest expense (Profit or loss)	4,765,000	
Cash (Asset)		4,765,000
Cash (Asset)	3,200,000	
Interest income (Profit or loss)		3,200,000
Interest expense (Profit or loss)	4,121,000	
Forward obligation (Liability)		4,121,000

4) Entries on 31 December 20X2

The estimated fair value of the plan on 31 December 20X2 was EUR 11.48 million, to be spread over the 3-year vesting period. As a total of EUR 7,467,000 was already recognised, a EUR 4,013,000 (=11,480,000–7,467,000) amount was recognised as employee benefits compensation expense.

Through the equity swap, ABC paid an annual interest of Euribor 12-month plus 50 bps. Suppose that the Euribor 12-month rate was 4.40% and that there were 365 days in the interest period. The interest expense for the period was EUR 4,968,000 (=100 mn × (4.4% + 0.50%) × 365/360). This interest was paid on 31 December 20X2 as well.

Suppose that ABC distributed a EUR 0.34 dividend per share on 31 December 20X2. As a result, a EUR 3,400,000 manufactured dividend was recognised.

Additionally, ABC recognised the liability's EUR 4,306,000 interest accrual.

Compensation expense (Profit or loss)	4,013,000	
SOP reserve (Equity)		4,013,000
Interest expense (Profit or loss)	4,968,000	
Cash (Asset)		4,968,000
Cash (Asset)	3,400,000	
Interest income (Profit or loss)		3,400,000
Interest expense (Profit or loss)	4,306,000	
Forward obligation (Liability)		4,306,000

At the equity swap maturity ABC was obliged to purchase 10 million of its own shares at EUR 10.00 per share.

Forward obligation (Liability)	100,000,000	
Treasury Shares (Equity)	87,630,000	
Forward on own shares (Equity)		87,630,000
Cash (Asset)		100,000,000

Suppose that all the beneficiaries exercised their options, paying EUR 100 million and receiving 10 million ABC shares.

Cash (Asset)	100,000,000	
Treasury shares (Equity)		3,943,000
Share premium (Equity)		12,370,000

Finally, the amount in the SOP reserve was reclassified to share premium.

SOP reserve (Equity)	11,480,000	
Share premium (Equity)		11,480,000

Concluding Remarks The hedge via the equity swap worked very well because the SOP ended up being exercised. The combined effect on ABC's financial statements of the SOP and the equity swap during the 3 years was as follows:

- ABC's profit or loss statement showed the fair value of the SOP, the equity swap interest payments, and the equity swap dividend income. The equity swap increased the overall expense as its interest rate exceeded the dividend yield of ABC's shares (see Figure 10.13).
- ABC's cash position showed the difference between the equity swap interest and dividend flows (see Figure 10.14). Thanks to hedge, ABC paid for the shares the same amount it received from the participants. At the same time, ABC's shareholders' equity showed an increase in share premium equal to the fair value of the SOP plus the difference between (i) the liability final value and (ii) the liability initial value (see Figure 10.14).

Nevertheless, the hedge was imperfect and exposed ABC from a cash flow perspective (although not from a profit or loss perspective) to a decline in its share price. Suppose that on exercise date the shares were trading at EUR 8.00 per share and, as a consequence, that the SOP beneficiaries did not exercise their options. Suppose further that ABC decided to sell in

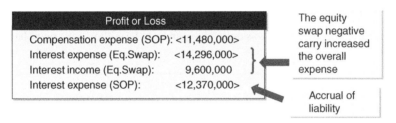

FIGURE 10.13 SOP and equity swap – combined effects on profit or loss (SOP exercised).

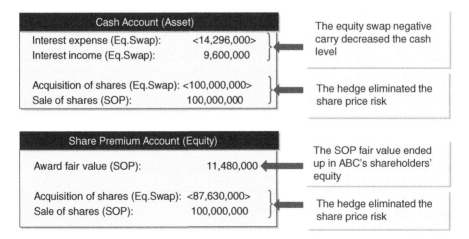

FIGURE 10.14 SOP and equity swap – combined effects on balance sheet (SOP exercised).

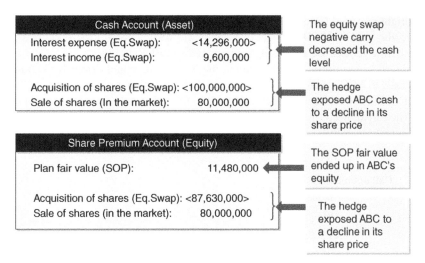

FIGURE 10.15 SOP and equity swap – Combined effects on balance sheet (SOP not exercised).

the market (at EUR 8.00 per share) the shares it acquired through the equity swap. The effects on ABC's financial statements would have been (see Figure 10.15) as follows:

- ABC's profit or loss statement would have been the same as if the beneficiaries had exercised their awards (see Figure 10.13).
- However, ABC's cash and equity positions would have been exposed to a decline in ABC's share price. The difference between the shares acquisition price and sale price would have affected negatively both the cash and equity levels, as shown in Figure 10.15.

10.6 CASE STUDY: HEDGING AN SAR PLAN WITH A CALL

This case study covers the accounting of an SAR plan when hedged with a call option on own shares. As explained previously in this chapter, an SAR is an award entitling beneficiaries to receive cash in an amount equivalent to any excess of the fair value of a stated number of shares of the employer's common shares over a stated price. Suppose that on 1 January 20X0 ABC granted an SAR to its executives with the following terms:

Share appreciation rights plan terms	
Grant date	1 January 20X0
Vesting period	3 years (from 1 January 20X0 until 31 December 20X2)
Exercise date	31 December 20X2
Strike	EUR 10.00
Number of rights	10 million (each right was for one ABC share)
Settlement	Cash settlement
Vesting conditions	Beneficiary being in continual employment and achievement of a 50% growth of ABC's EBITDA during the SAR term

Each right provided for a cash amount payment equivalent to the appreciation of ABC's share price above EUR 10.00. Subject to meeting the vesting conditions, ABC was exposed from a cash flow perspective to a rising share price from EUR 10.00.

In order to hedge future exercises under the SAR, ABC bought from XYZ Bank a call option indexed to ABC's own stock and paid a EUR 11.9 million up-front premium. The number of call options equalled the number of SAR options that ABC expected would vest (8.5 million). The call allowed for cash settlement only, to match the cash payment under the SAR. The remaining terms of the call option were identical to those of the SAR:

Call option terms	
Trade date	1 January 20X0
Option buyer	ABC
Option seller	XYZ Bank
Underlying	ABC ordinary shares
Expiry date	31 December 20X2
Strike	EUR 10.00
Number of options	8.5 million
Up-front premium	EUR 11.9 million
Settlement	Cash settlement

Ignoring the up-front premium, this was the best hedge possible: if the SAR was exercised ABC would exercise the hedging call option, and conversely, if the plan was not exercised then the call option would not be exercised. If the SAR vesting conditions were not met, a potential call payoff would be kept by ABC and not passed on to the SAR beneficiaries.

The call was designated as the hedging instrument in a cash flow hedge of the highly expected cash flow stemming from the SAR. I have not included the hedge documentation or the effectiveness assessment performed at hedge inception and at each reporting date to avoid unnecessary repetition (see the cash flow hedges in other chapters).

When defining the hedging relationship, ABC had to make several key decisions:

- To define the risk being hedged. In this case, ABC defined the risk being hedged as the cash flow variability of the expected future obligation associated with the SAR due to changes in the entity's share price.
- To decide whether to designate the option in its entirety or just its intrinsic value as the hedging instrument. This matter is covered next.

Fair Value in its Entirety versus Intrinsic Value Under IFRS 9, when hedging with an option, and entity may choose to assess hedge effectiveness on either (i) changes in the entire value (i.e., both intrinsic value and time value) of the purchased call option or (ii) changes in the intrinsic value of the option. Commonly, designating only the intrinsic value as the hedging instrument enhances effectiveness as in most instances the hedged item does not have time value. This common rule does not hold in this case. An SAR's resulting liability is adjusted to fair value each reporting period rather than to an amount equivalent to the excess of the then current fair value of the stated number of shares over a stated price (i.e., the SAR's intrinsic value). In other words, the fair valuation of an SAR consists of a time value portion and an intrinsic value portion. Therefore when the hedge item is an SAR, hedge effectiveness would be assessed based on changes in the entire fair value of the purchased call option, rather than just the intrinsic value. As a result, ABC designated the call option in its entirety as the hedging instrument in a cash flow hedge.

Fair Valuation of the Call option at Each Reporting Date   The fair values of the call option at each reporting date are shown in the following table:

Date	ABC share price	Call fair value	Period change	Call intrinsic value	Call time value
1-Jan-X0	10.00	11.9 mn	—	-0-	11.9 mn
31-Dec-X0	9.00	3.4 mn	<8.5> mn	-0-	3.4 mn
31-Dec-X1	11.00	11.05 mn	7.65 mn	8.5 mn	2.55 mn
31-Dec-X2	13.00	25.5 mn	14.45 mn	25.5 mn	-0-

Fair Valuation of the SAR at Each Reporting Date   At each reporting date and on the SAR maturity date, ABC had to fair value the granted rights:

- Firstly, ABC fair valued the SAR excluding the service and non-market vesting conditions. ABC used the Black–Scholes valuation model with the following inputs: the remaining time to expiry, a EUR 10 strike, the implied volatility of ABC's share price for such time to expiry and strike, a 10 million share nominal, the interest rate for such time-to-expiry term and ABC shares' expected dividend yield.
- Secondly, ABC adjusted the above mentioned fair valuation to include only the expected number of options that would vest (i.e., to take into account the expected achievement of service and non-market conditions). Vesting was conditional on the beneficiary's continual employment and the achievement of a 50% growth in ABC's EBITDA during the SAR term.

Date	Unadjusted fair value of SAR (EUR)	Expected number of options to vest	Adjusted fair value of plan	Annual expense
31-Dec-X0	4 million	8.5 million	EUR 3.4 million (=8.5 mn/10 mn × 4 mn)	EUR 1,133,000
31-Dec-X1	13 million	8 million	EUR 10.4 million (=8 mn/10 mn × 13 mn)	EUR 3,467,000
31-Dec-X2	30 million	8.2 million	EUR 24.6 million (=8.2 mn/10 mn × 30 mn)	EUR 8,200,000

Accounting Entries

1) Accounting entries on 1 January 20X0

The SAR was granted, no accounting entries were needed to record the award. The call purchase was recognised. ABC paid EUR 11.9 million.

Call option (Asset)	11,900,000	
Cash (Asset)		11,900,000

2) Accounting entries on 31 December 20X0

The adjusted fair value of the SAR was EUR 3.4 million, which corresponded to an annual expense of EUR 1,133,000 (= 3.4 mn/3) over the SAR's 3-year term.

Compensation expense (Profit or loss)	1,133,000	
SAR award (Liability)		1,133,000

Because (i) the terms of the call exactly replicated the SAR exercise right and (ii) the entity expected 8.5 million rights to vest (i.e., there was no overhedging), the full change in fair value of the call, a EUR 8,500,000 loss, was deemed to be effective and recorded in the cash flow hedge reserve. However, one third of that amount (EUR <2,833,000>) was reclassified to profit or loss.

Compensation expense (Profit or loss)	2,833,000	
Cash flow hedge reserve (Equity)	5,667,000	
Call option (Asset)		8,500,000

3) Accounting entries on 31 December 20X1

The adjusted fair value of the SAR was EUR 10.4 million, which corresponded to an annual expense of EUR 3,467,000 (= 10.4 mn/3) over the SAR's 3-year term. This amount represented a total EUR 6,934,000 (=3,467,000 × 2) to be expensed over the first 2 years. Because EUR 1,133,000 had already been expensed, a EUR 5,801,000 (=6,934,000 − 1,133,000) personnel expense was recognised during the period.

Compensation expense (Profit or loss)	5,801,000	
SAR award (Liability)		5,801,000

The change in fair value of the call produced a EUR 7,650,000 gain. Because (i) the terms of the call exactly replicated the SAR exercise right and (ii) the entity expected 8.0 million rights to vest (while the call underlying number of shares was 8.5 million), the effective part of the change in fair value of the call corresponded to an underlying 8.0 million shares. Therefore, EUR 7,200,000 (= 7,650,000 × 8 mn/8.5 mn) was deemed to be effective and recorded in the cash flow hedge reserve of equity and EUR 450,000 (= 7,650,000 − 7,200,000) was considered to be ineffective and recorded in profit or loss. Because two thirds of the hedged item had already impacted profit or loss, two thirds of the effective part (EUR 4,800,000) was reclassified from the cash flow hedge reserve to profit or loss, adjusting the compensation expense related to the SAR.

Call option (Asset)	7,650,000	
Cash flow hedge reserve (Equity)		2,400,000
Compensation expense (Profit or loss)		4,800,000
Other financial income (Profit or loss)		450,000

In addition, one third of the amount recorded in the cash flow hedge reserve on 31 December 20X0 (EUR <2,833,000> = <8,500,000>/3) was reclassified from the cash flow hedge reserve to profit or loss.

Compensation expense (Profit or loss)	2,833,000	
Cash flow hedge reserve (Equity)		2,833,000

3) Accounting entries on 31 December 20X2

The adjusted fair value of the SAR was EUR 24.6 million, which corresponded to an annual expense of EUR 8,200,000 (= 24.6 mn/3) over the SAR 3-year term. Because EUR 6,934,000 had already been expensed, a EUR 17,666,000 (=24,600,000 − 6,934,000) personnel expense was recognised.

Compensation expense (Profit or loss)	17,666,000	
SAR award (Liability)		17,666,000

The change in fair value of the call produced a EUR 14,450,000 gain. Because (i) the terms of the call exactly replicated the SAR exercise right and (ii) the entity expected 8.2 million rights to vest (while the call underlying number of shares was 8.5 million), the effective part of the change in fair value of the call corresponded to an underlying 8.2 million shares. Therefore, EUR 13,940,000 (= 14,450,000 × 8.2 mn/8.5 mn) was deemed to be effective and recorded in the cash flow hedge reserve of equity, and EUR 510,000 (= 14,450,000 − 13,940,000) was considered to be ineffective and recorded in profit or loss. Because the entire hedged item had already impacted profit or loss, all the effective part (EUR 13,940,000) was reclassified from the cash flow hedge reserve to profit or loss, adjusting the compensation expense related to the SAR.

Call option (Asset)	14,450,000	
Compensation expense (Profit or loss)		13,940,000
Other financial income (Profit or loss)		510,000

In addition, one third of the amounts recorded in the cash flow hedge reserve on 31 December 20X0 and on 31 December 20X1 (EUR <2,833,000> (= <8,500,000> × 1/3) and EUR 2,400,000 (=7,200,000 × 1/3)), totalling EUR <433,000>, was reclassified from the cash flow hedge reserve to profit or loss, adjusting the compensation expense related to the SAR.

| Compensation expense (Profit or loss) | 433,000 | |
| Cash flow hedge reserve (Equity) | | 433,000 |

All the beneficiaries exercised their awards, resulting in the entity paying EUR 24.6 million in cash.

| SAR award (Liability) | 24,600,000 | |
| Cash (Asset) | | 24,600,000 |

ABC exercised the call, receiving EUR 25.5 million in cash.

| Cash (Asset) | 25,500,000 | |
| Call option | | 25,500,000 |

Concluding Remarks The hedge worked reasonable well. The entity spent EUR 11.9 million buying the call, which corresponded to an expected EUR 3,966,000 annual compensation expense. As shown in the following table, there was a relatively small total deviation of EUR <61,000> (= 132,000 + <193,000>) from that target.

Reporting date	31-Dec-X0	31-Dec-X1	31-Dec-X2
SAR compensation expense	<1,133,000>	<5,801,000>	<17,666,000>
Call compensation expense	<2,833,000>	1,967,000	13,507,000
Total compensation expense	<3,966,000>	<3,834,000>	<4,159,000>
Target compensation expense	<3,966,000>	<3,966,000>	<3,966,000>
Deviation	-0-	132,000	<193,000>

In addition, ABC recognised in profit or loss a EUR 960,000 other financial income stemming from the ineffective part of the hedge.

The hedge worked reasonably well in part because the amount of underlying shares in the call (8.5 million) was relatively similar to the amounts of SAR awards being exercised. The hedging instrument must be constructed in such a manner as to consider the vesting provisions of the hedged SAR. A larger than expected achievement of an SAR's vesting conditions would result in underhedging, leaving the entity exposed to its own share price. Conversely, too optimistic an expectation of vesting conditions achievement would result in overhedging, implying that the entity paid a higher than needed premium to hedge the SAR.

A call option indexed to own shares has to be classified as a derivative in order to be eligible for designation as the hedging instrument in a hedge accounting relationship. In other words, a call option classified as an equity instrument would not be eligible as the hedging instrument in a hedge accounting relationship. Remember that a contract indexed to a company's own shares is classified as a derivative if its settlement may result in other than the entity paying/receiving a fixed number of shares in exchange for a fixed amount of cash (or other financial assets) – the fixed-for-fixed requirement. In our case, the call's cash settlement provision contravened the fixed-for-fixed requirement, allowing its designation as the hedging instrument in a hedging relationship. A similar result would have been achieved were a net share settlement alternative included or an election right between physical settlement and cash settlement (or net share settlement).

Ignoring vesting conditions, an SAR exposes an entity to its own share price risk. The higher its share price relative to the SAR's strike price, the greater the amount of cash that the entity would be required to pay to the SAR beneficiaries. This exposure starts as soon as the SAR is granted.

CHAPTER 11

Hedging Commodity Risk

This chapter focuses on the accounting challenges faced by entities when hedging commodity risk. For many industries, commodity contracts are an integral part of day-to-day business. For example, for companies in the oil, gas, utilities, mining and airline sectors, prices of certain commodities have a significant impact on their profitability and competitive position. Whilst each of these industries has its own accounting peculiarities, in this chapter I try to cover the most common accounting issues arising from their hedging of commodity risks.

11.1 MAIN COMMODITY UNDERLYINGS

The world of commodities includes a large number of different products. Underlyings of the most common commodity derivatives contracts can be grouped into the following categories:

- oil products – crude oil, diesel, fuel oil, gas oil, gasoline, jet fuel and naphtha;
- natural gas;
- coal;
- power;
- carbon emissions;
- base metals – aluminium, copper, lead, nickel, steel, tin and zinc;
- precious metals – gold, silver, palladium and platinum;
- agricultural (or soft commodities) – corn, soy complex, sugar and wheat.

11.2 LEASE, DERIVATIVE AND OWN-USE CONTRACTS

A contract to purchase or sell a commodity brings together a breadth of accounting standards – leases, derivatives, revenue recognition, and consolidation – which are individually among the most complicated areas of accounting. For example, a gas company may manage its gas on an integral basis, buying, storing and selling gas so as to optimise its overall portfolio.

Gas is an asset that flows through the organisation, and it can be extraordinarily complex to track the flow of gas from a particular contract, as shown in Figure 11.1. To identify the appropriate accounting treatment for each contract requires careful analysis and a deep understanding of the principles underlying the relevant IFRS standards.

11.2.1 Definitions of Lease, Derivative and Own-Use Contracts

In general, from an accounting perspective a commodity contract is treated as a lease contract, a derivative contract or an own-use instrument (see Figure 10.2).

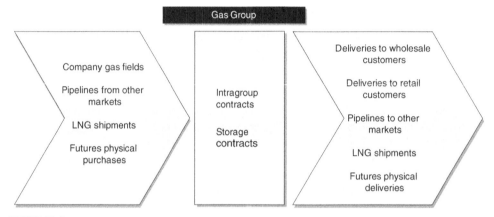

FIGURE 11.1   Gas group – gas purchase and sales contracts.

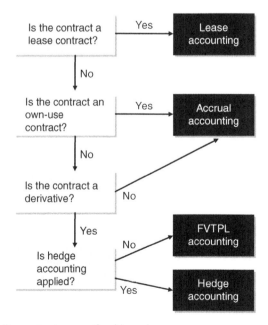

FIGURE 11.2   Commodity contract accounting hierarchy.

Lease Accounting   The first step in analysing a contract is to assess whether the contract meets the definition of a lease contract. IFRS defines a **lease contract** as "a contract that conveys the right to use an asset (the underlying asset) for a period of time in exchange for consideration". The right to use an identified asset is conveyed only if the purchaser (i.e., lessee) has the ability to both direct the use of the asset and receive the benefit from its use. For example, electricity suppliers often purchase carbon emission rights (CERs) from third-party owners of renewable energy generation facilities. Frequently, the underlying renewable energy is also sold to the electricity supplier, and it is fairly common for a purchaser to acquire 100% of the electricity and CERs associated with the facility.

Derivative Accounting   Commodity contracts that are not lease contracts fall within the non-financial items category. A contract to buy or sell a non-financial item may meet the definition of a **derivative**, even though non-financial items themselves fall outside the scope of IFRS 9.

A commodity contract is treated as an IFRS 9 instrument if any of the three following conditions is met:

1) The entity has a practice of settling similar contracts net in cash, or by entering into offsetting contracts, or by selling the contracts.
2) The entity has a practice of taking delivery and selling shortly after so as to profit from short-term fluctuations in price or a dealer's margin.
3) Where the contract permits either party to settle net in cash, or another financial instrument, or by exchanging financial instruments, or by selling the contracts, or where the non-financial item that is the subject of the contract is readily convertible to cash; unless the contract was entered into, and continues to be held, for the purpose of receipt or delivery in accordance with the entity's normal purchase, sale or usage requirements.

Under IFRS 9, a derivative is a financial instrument (or other contract within the scope of IFRS 9) with all the following characteristics:

1) Its value changes in response to changes in an underlying price or index (e.g., commodity price index).
2) It requires no initial investment, or significantly less than the investment required to purchase the underlying instrument.
3) It is settled at a future date.

Commodity contracts that fall within the scope of IFRS 9 are recognised at fair value. The fair value changes are recognised in profit or loss, unless cash flow hedge accounting is applied (fair value hedge accounting requires the change in fair value of the hedging instrument to be recognised in profit or loss).

Own-Use Accounting   Commodity contracts that are neither considered lease contracts nor derivative contracts are called **own-use contracts** (or "normal purchase and normal sale" under US generally accepted accounting principles). These contracts are not fair valued, but accounted for using the accrual method. Hence, revenues and expenses from these contracts are reported on a gross basis in the appropriate revenue and expense categories as the commodities are received or delivered. The "own use" exception is mandatory under IFRS (i.e., it is not elective).

11.2.2 Use of Similar Contracts for both Own-Use and Trading Purposes

In theory, a contract is treated as an own-use contract only if the entity intends to take delivery of the underlying to meet its purchase, sale or usage requirements. In practice, these conditions may be difficult to interpret.

Entities in the energy and utility sectors frequently engage in trading activities to benefit from market opportunities by buying and selling commodity contracts (e.g., futures on natural gas), profiting from short-term price fluctuations or from bid–offer spreads.

These entities may also engage in the purchase and/or sale of identical, or similar, commodity contracts for their own needs, taking physical delivery. For example, a utility may sell expected electricity generation or buy natural gas for its own consumption in its generation business.

The distinction between these two purposes is essential in defining own-use contract treatment. If this distinction cannot be made and all commodity contracts are deemed to be similar, then own-use contract treatment will not be possible. From this perspective the problem stems from interpreting what the standard means by "similar" contracts.

The market practice is to consider "similar" on a substance rather than form basis. Therefore, management intention and actual use of the contracts, rather than their legal form, are key ingredients in assessing whether to apply derivative or own-use accounting treatment. It is possible to apply, within the same entity, both derivatives and own-use accounting for contracts with identical legal form when the intended and actual usages of the contracts differ. The key issue is therefore being able to demonstrate the separation of both activities: trades for physical purposes and those for the purpose of short-term profit-making. This can be demonstrated through the use of appropriate organisational and portfolio structures, covering risk management policies and procedures.

11.3 CATEGORISATION ACCORDING TO SETTLEMENT TERMS

Whilst its legal form is not the main factor when deciding whether a contract is accounted for as a derivative or an own-use contract (assuming it is not a lease contract), sometimes its settlement terms may provide helpful arguments to assess its classification. In general, there are three types of commodity contract according to their settlement provisions: (i) contracts that are settled by physical delivery of the commodity; (ii) contracts that are settled net (i.e., in cash, by exchanging financial instruments or by exchanging financial assets); and (iii) contracts that are a combination of (i) and (ii).

11.3.1 Physically Settled Commodity Contracts

A commodity contract entered into, and continuing to be held, for the purpose of the physical delivery of the underlying commodity, in accordance with the entity's expected purchase, sale or usage requirements, does not fall within the scope of IFRS 9, and is therefore treated as an own-use contract (or executory contract). An exception would be when for similar contracts, the entity has a practice of taking delivery of the underlying and selling it within a short period after delivery for the purpose of generating a profit from short-term fluctuations in price or from a dealer's margin.

11.3.2 Net Settled Commodity Contracts

A commodity contract is net settled, if it may be settled in cash, or by the delivery of another financial asset or by exchanging financial assets. There are various ways in which a contract to buy or sell a non-financial item can be net settled. These include:

1) When the terms of the contract may permit either party to settle it net in cash or another financial instrument or by exchanging financial instruments.
2) When the ability to settle net in cash or another financial instrument, or by exchanging financial instruments, is not explicit in the terms of the contract, but the entity has a practice of settling similar contracts net in cash or another financial instrument or by exchanging financial instruments (whether with the counterparty, by entering into offsetting contracts or by selling the contract before its exercise or lapse).
3) When, for similar contracts, the entity has a practice of taking delivery of the underlying and selling it within a short period after delivery for the purpose of generating a profit from short-term fluctuations in price or dealer's margin.
4) When the non-financial item that is the subject of the contract is readily convertible to cash.

11.3.3 Commodity Contracts with Choice of Physical Delivery or Net Settlement

If the commodity contract allows the entity to choose between physical settlement and net settlement, it would need to assess whether:

- it has the stated intention of delivering the commodity;
- it will be able to meet the delivery requirements under the physical settlement alternative, based on its inventory levels and its production capacity.
- its past sales practices indicated that it would be choosing and meeting the delivery requirements.

11.4 CASE STUDY: HEDGING GOLD PRODUCTION WITH A FORWARD – OWN-USE APPLICATION

This case study covers the hedge of gold production with a forward contract using the own-use exception. Imagine that ABC, a gold producer with mines in the United States, South Africa and Australia and with the USD as functional and presentation currency, was assessing its market risk exposures. ABC's profit or loss statement was exposed to the following market risks (see Figure 11.3):

- commodities – gold, diesel fuel, natural gas and propane;
- foreign exchange – USD/AUD and USD/ZAR;
- interest rate – USD Libor.

The timeframe and manner in which the company managed these risks varied for each item based upon its market expectations and their relevance. Under its risk management policy, ABC sought to mitigate the impact of the gold price risk in order to achieve certainty for a portion of its revenues and enable it to plan its business with greater reliability.

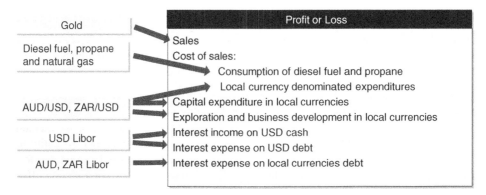

FIGURE 11.3   ABC's profit or loss exposure to market risks.

The market price for gold can fluctuate widely, often subject to sharp, short-term changes resulting from speculative activities. While the overall supply/demand for gold can affect its market price, because of the considerable size of above-ground stocks of the metal in comparison to other commodities, these factors typically do not affect the price of gold in the same manner or degree as supply/demand affects the market price for other commodities. These fluctuations are caused by numerous factors beyond an entity's control, including:

- speculative positions taken by investors or traders in gold;
- changes in the demand for gold as an investment;
- changes in the demand for gold used in jewellery and for other industrial uses;
- changes in the supply of gold from production, disinvestment, scrap and hedging;
- financial markets' expectations regarding the rate of inflation;
- the strength of the USD (the currency in which the gold price trades internationally) relative to other currencies;
- changes in interest rates;
- actual or expected gold sales by central banks and the IMF;
- gold sales by gold producers in forward transactions;
- global or regional political or economic events; and
- costs of gold production in major gold-producing nations, such as South Africa, the United States and Australia.

Following an assessment of its gold price risk exposure and the available alternatives for mitigating it, ABC decided to enter into a gold forward sales contract on 1 January 20X0. The forward was to be settled by physical delivery of 100,000 ounces of ABC's future gold production. The main terms of the forward contract were as follows:

Gold forward terms	
Start date	1 January 20X1
Counterparties	ABC and Megabank
Maturity	31 January 20X2
ABC sells	100,000 ounces of gold
ABC buys	USD 100 million
Forward rate	USD 1,000.00 per gold ounce
Settlement	Physical settlement

Next ABC had to assess the accounting treatment of the gold forward. The contract met the definition of a derivative because:

- the value of the contract varied with the price of gold;
- there was no initial investment to enter into the contract; and
- it was to be settled at a future date – the company planned to take delivery of the gold at the forward maturity.

Whilst the forward contract met the requirements for treatment as a derivative, ABC had to assess whether the non-financial contract was excluded from the scope of IFRS 9. This assessment would have strong implications for ABC's financial statements:

- If the contract was deemed to be a derivative (i.e., under the scope of IFRS 9), it would be recorded on ABC's statement of financial position (i.e., balance sheet) at fair value.
- Alternatively, if the contract was considered to be an own-use contract (i.e., outside the scope of IFRS 9), it would be recorded on a historical cost basis, without requiring further fair valuation. After initial recognition, the contract would be re-recognised in ABC's financial statements when the gold was delivered.

ABC concluded that the contract met the own-use requirements due to the following:

- It was entered into, and continued to be held, for the purpose of the physical delivery of the entity's production, in accordance with the entity's expected productive capacity and delivery intentions.
- Its past sales practices indicated that the company would be meeting the delivery requirements. In other words, there was no past history of unwinding similar contracts before maturity with a view to making a short-term profit.
- For similar contracts, the entity did not have a practice of taking delivery of the underlying and selling it within a short period after delivery for the purpose of generating a profit from short-term fluctuations in price or dealer's margin.

The absence of an obligation to fair value the forward made its accounting recognition relatively simple. Assuming that ABC reported on an annual basis on 31 December, the accounting entries were as follows:

1) Accounting entries on 1 January 20X1

No entries were required as there were no cash flows at inception of the forward contract.

2) Accounting entries on 31 December 20X1

No entries were required as there was no requirement to fair value the forward contract.

3) Accounting entries on 31 January 20X2

The forward contract was settled and ABC delivered 100,000 ounces of gold in exchange for USD 100 million. Assuming that ABC's gold inventory was valued at USD 800 per ounce, the delivered gold was worth USD 80 million (=100,000 ounces × 800).

Cash (Asset)	100,000,000	
Sales (Profit or loss)		100,000,000
Cost of goods sold (Profit or loss)	80,000,000	
Gold inventory (Asset)		80,000,000

We conclude this case study with some final remarks:

- The classification of the forward contract as an own-use instrument allowed ABC to avoid fair valuing it during its life. Whilst the forward was off balance sheet until its settlement, it was not hidden from investors: ABC was required to disclose it under IFRS guidelines.
- The forward allowed ABC to lock in a USD 20 million gross margin.

11.5 CASE STUDY: RAISING FINANCING THROUGH A GOLD LOAN

In this case study I cover a financial settlement using a commodity. Suppose that in order to protect the level of income in future years, ABC – a gold producer with the USD as functional and presentation currency – raised finance to be repaid using future gold production. This loan did not require any cash interest payments. Interest was embedded in the future gold to be delivered. The main terms of the gold loan were as follows:

Gold loan terms	
Start date	1 January 20X1
Borrower	ABC
Loan proceeds	USD 160 million
Maturity	31 December 20X4 (4 years)
Delivery schedule	31-Dec-X1: 100,000 ounces of gold
	31-Dec-X2: 100,000 ounces of gold
	31-Dec-X3: 100,000 ounces of gold
	31-Dec-X4: 100,000 ounces of gold
Interest	None
Implied forward rate	USD 400.00 per gold ounce
Repayment	Physical settlement according to the Delivery schedule

Next, ABC had to assess the accounting treatment of the gold loan. Whilst the gold loan contained an embedded derivative (i.e., the forward sale of gold) and would ordinarily be subject to fair valuation, it was accounted for as borrowings on a historical cost basis, an exception within IFRS 9, due to the subsequent repayment by physical delivery of gold ounces. Another way to look at this is as follows: the instrument was equivalent to a string of four prepaid forwards, each recognised under the own-use exception.

On 15 February 20X3, when the gold spot price reached USD 600 per ounce, ABC management expected gold prices to continue rising and decided to repay the loan early by delivering the remaining 200,000 ounces of gold. In this case, I look at the accounting impact of two alternatives: (i) that ABC delivered gold from its own production; and (ii) that ABC delivered gold purchased on a spot basis in the gold market.

Assuming that ABC reported on an annual basis on 31 December, the accounting entries were as follows.

1) Accounting entries on 1 January 20X1

ABC borrowed USD 160 million through the gold loan. The loan was recognised initially at the proceeds received, net of transaction costs incurred.

Cash (Asset)	160,000,000	
Gold loan (Liability)		160,000,000

2) Accounting entries on 31 December 20X1

ABC repaid a quarter of the gold loan by delivering 100,000 ounces of gold. The loan was recognised at cost and accordingly a quarter of the loan carrying value was reduced. Assuming that the delivered gold was valued at USD 300.00 per ounce in ABC's inventory, the "cost of goods sold" figure amounted to USD 30 million (100,000 ounces × 300.00).

Gold loan (Liability)	40,000,000	
Sales (Profit or loss)		40,000,000
Cost of goods sold (Profit or loss)	30,000,000	
Gold inventory (Asset)		30,000,000

3) Accounting entries on 31 December 20X2

ABC repaid another quarter of the gold loan by delivering 100,000 ounces of gold. The loan was recognised at cost and accordingly a quarter of the loan carrying value was reduced. Assuming that the delivered gold was valued at USD 320.00 per ounce in ABC's inventory, the "cost of goods sold" figure amounted to USD 32 million (100,000 ounces × 320.00).

Gold loan (Liability)	40,000,000	
Sales (Profit or loss)		40,000,000
Cost of goods sold (Profit or loss)	32,000,000	
Gold inventory (Asset)		32,000,000

4a) Accounting entries on 15 February 20X3, assuming that ABC delivered gold from its own mines

ABC repaid the outstanding balance of the gold loan (i.e., USD 80 million) by delivering 200,000 ounces of gold. This gold was delivered from ABC's mine production. Assuming that the delivered gold was valued at USD 370.00 per ounce in ABC's inventory, the "cost of goods sold" figure amounted to USD 74 million (200,000 ounces × 370.00).

Gold loan (Liability)	80,000,000	
Sales (Profit or loss)		80,000,000
Cost of goods sold (Profit or loss)	74,000,000	
Gold inventory (Asset)		74,000,000

4b) Accounting entries on 15 February 20X3, assuming that ABC acquired the gold in the spot market

ABC repaid the outstanding balance of the gold loan (i.e., USD 80 million) by delivering 200,000 ounces of gold. This gold was acquired from the gold spot market at USD 600.00 per ounce. Hence, ABC paid in the market USD 120 million (= 200,000 ounces × 600.00) for the gold and crystallised a USD 40 million loss (= USD 80 mn – USD 120 mn).

Gold loan (Liability)	80,000,000	
Other financial expense (Profit or loss)	40,000,000	
Cash (Asset)		120,000,000

We close this case study with some final remarks:

- The gold loan was recognised on a historical cost basis, recognised initially at the proceeds received, net of transaction costs incurred, and reduced as the future deliveries of gold settlements repaid the loan.
- ABC did not recognise an interest expense related to the gold loan. Because interest applicable to the loan was paid in gold, it was valued at cost of sales.
- There was no need to separate the embedded derivative. If instead the loan had been recognised as a liability and an embedded derivative, ABC could have applied cash flow hedge accounting.

As noted above, on 15 February 20X3, when the gold spot price reached USD 600 per ounce, ABC management expected the gold price to continue rising and decided to repay the loan early by delivering the remaining 200,000 ounces of gold. ABC had two alternatives: either (i) to deliver gold from its own mines, or (ii) to deliver gold purchased on a spot basis from the gold market.

In the scenario where ABC repaid the borrowing using gold from its own mines, no loss crystallised on ABC's profit or loss statement. However, a loss was implicitly recognised as an opportunity cost: a resulting sales figure (and sales margin) much lower than if, instead, the produced gold had been sold in the market. Another implication of such a decision was that ABC could not benefit, relative to the delivered gold, from potentially future higher gold prices, but also was not exposed to potentially future lower gold prices.

In the scenario where ABC repaid the loan by purchasing gold on the market, a loss was crystallised resulting in a one-off loss of USD 40 million before tax. This loss was recorded in profit or loss as a finance cost. If the gold prices continued to rise, ABC's undelivered inventory could benefit from a higher selling price, resulting in a rising sales figure. However, this undelivered gold exposed ABC's sales figure to potentially future lower gold prices.

11.6 CASE STUDY: HEDGING A SILVER PURCHASE FIRM COMMITMENT WITH A FORWARD – FAIR VALUE HEDGE

This case study is an example of a fair value hedge of a commodity firm commitment using a forward. I cover in detail each step in the application of hedge accounting.

ABC was a European wholesaler of silver, buying silver from mining companies and selling it to silver end-users, primarily in the electronics industry. On 1 February 20X7, ABC signed a contract to sell to an electronics company 10 million troy ounces of silver at a price of EUR 5.00 per ounce to be delivered and paid for on 31 May 20X7. ABC expected to meet this delivery with an agreed purchase from a mining company to be priced at the prevailing spot rate on the purchase delivery date.

11.6.1 Hedging Strategy

The sale at a fixed price exposed ABC to rising silver prices, as it could end up paying a price to acquire the 10 million troy ounces of silver higher than the EUR 5 per ounce selling price. In order to avoid being exposed to changes in silver prices, ABC's hedging policy was to pay and receive fixed prices in all its contracts.

To protect the sale from rising silver prices, on 1 February 20X7 ABC entered into a forward with the following terms (see Figure 11.4):

Silver forward terms	
Start date	1 February 20X7
Counterparties	ABC and Megabank
Maturity	31 May 20X7
ABC receives	EUR 45 million
ABC delivers	10 million troy ounces of silver
Forward rate	EUR 4.50 per ounce
Settlement	Cash settlement based on the EUR/ounce price of silver at maturity taking both the BCE's EUR–USD rate and the LME's USD/oz fixing Settlement amount = 10 mn × (USD/oz fixing)/(EUR–USD fixing) – EUR 45 million If the settlement amount is positive, ABC receives the settlement amount If the settlement amount is negative, ABC pays the absolute value of the settlement amount

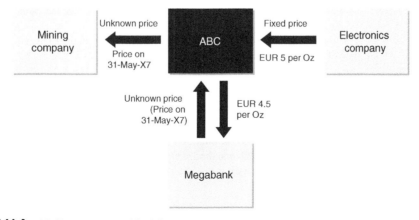

FIGURE 11.4   ABC's exposure and hedging strategy.

The instrument's EUR 4.50 per ounce forward rate was the forward rate for 31 May 20X7 prevailing on 1 February 20X7. Thus, ABC did not have to pay any premium for entering into the hedge. In other words, because it was an on-market forward, it had a nil fair value at inception.

The forward contract was a derivative because there was no initial net investment, it was linked to the price of silver and it was to be settled at a future date. First, ABC needed to evaluate whether the forward fell within the own-use exception of IFRS 9. At its maturity, the contract could only be settled in cash based on the silver spot price at maturity. A net settled commodity contract was treated as an IFRS 9 instrument (as a derivative in our case), and as a result, it was recognised in ABC's statement of financial position at fair value.

Next, ABC had to decide whether to apply hedge accounting to avoid mismatches in profit or loss.

- If the firm commitment (i.e., the planned sale of silver) was classified as a derivative contract, a hedging relationship would not be needed as both the firm commitment and the forward would be fair valued with changes in their fair value recognised in profit or loss. Both changes in fair value would be expected to almost fully offset.
- However, in our case ABC classified the firm commitment as an "own-use" commitment. Therefore, the firm commitment would not be fair valued unless it was designated as hedged item in a fair value hedge. Without hedge accounting application, only the forward contract would be fair valued through profit or loss, potentially increasing ABC's profit or loss volatility. Thus, ABC designated the commodity forward in a fair value hedge of the firm commitment.

11.6.2 Hedging Relationship Documentation

ABC designated the forward contract as the hedging instrument in a fair value hedge of its forecasted silver sale. At its inception, ABC documented the hedging relationship as follows:

Hedging relationship documentation	
Risk management objective and strategy for undertaking the hedge	The objective of the hedge is to protect the EUR fair value of the firm commitment to sell 10 million silver troy ounces against unfavourable movements in the silver price in EUR. This hedging objective is consistent with the entity's overall risk management strategy of fair valuing all its purchases and sales to reduce the variability of its profit or loss statement. The designated risk being hedged is the risk of changes in the EUR fair value of the firm commitment
Type of hedge	Fair value hedge
Hedged item	The firm commitment to sell 10 million ounces of silver signed with Chuan Electronics on 1 February 20X7
Hedging instrument	The forward contract with reference number 011895 to sell 10 million ounces of silver at EUR 5.00 per ounce on 31 May 20X7. The counterparty to the forward is Megabank and the credit risk associated with this counterparty is considered to be very low
Hedge effectiveness assessment	See below

11.6.3 Hedge Effectiveness Assessment

Hedge effectiveness will be assessed by comparing changes in the fair value of the hedging instrument to changes in the fair value of the hedged item. The hedged item will be valued at the silver EUR/oz forward price for 31 May 20X7.

- The change in fair value of the hedging instrument will be recognised in profit or loss.
- The change in fair value of the hedged item will also be recognised in profit or loss and adjusting the carrying amount of the hedged item.

Hedge effectiveness will be assessed prospectively at hedging relationship inception and on an ongoing basis at least upon each reporting date and upon occurrence of a significant change in the circumstances affecting the hedge effectiveness requirements.

The hedging relationship will qualify for hedge accounting only if all the following criteria are met:

1) The hedging relationship consists only of eligible hedge items and hedging instruments. The hedge item is eligible as it is a firm commitment that exposes the entity to fair value risk, affects profit or loss and is reliably measurable. The hedging instrument is eligible as it is a derivative and it does not result in a net written option.
2) At hedge inception there is a formal designation and documentation of the hedging relationship and the entity's risk management objective and strategy for undertaking the hedge.
3) The hedging relationship is considered effective.

The hedging relationship will be considered effective if the following three requirements are met:

1) There is an economic relationship between the hedged item and the hedging instrument.
2) The effect of credit risk does not dominate the value changes that result from that economic relationship.
3) The hedge ratio of the hedging relationship is the same as that resulting from the quantity of hedged item that the entity actually hedges and the quantity of the hedging instrument that the entity actually uses to hedge that quantity of hedged item. The hedge ratio should not be intentionally weighted to create ineffectiveness.

Whether there is an economic relationship between the hedged item and the hedging instrument will be assessed on a quantitative basis using the scenario analysis method for two scenarios in which the EUR/oz silver spot price at the end of the hedging relationship (31 May 20X7) will be calculated by shifting the spot price prevailing on the assessment date by +10% and −10%, and the change in fair value of both the hedge item and the hedging instrument compared.

11.6.4 Hedge Effectiveness Assessment Performed at the Start of the Hedging Relationship

Suppose that the silver spot price at hedge inception (1 February 20X7) was EUR 4.47 per ounce. The hedge effectiveness assessment at inception was performed by analysing the change in fair value of both the hedge item and the hedging instrument under two scenarios:

1) The silver price at the end of the hedging relationship was calculated by shifting the spot price by +10% to EUR 4.92 per ounce. The change in fair value of the hedging instrument was EUR 4.2 million (= 10 mn × (4.92 – 4.50) – 0). The change in fair value of the hedge item was EUR <4.15 million> (= 10 million × (5.00 – 4.92) – 4,950,000). The degree of offset was 101.2% (= 4.2 mn/4.15 mn).

2) The silver price at the end of the hedging relationship was calculated by shifting the spot price by −10% to EUR 4.02 per ounce. The change in fair value of the hedging instrument was EUR <4.8 million> (= 10 mn × (4.02 – 4.50) – 0). The change in fair value of the hedge item was EUR 4.85 million (= 10 mn × (5.00 – 4.02) – 4,950,000). The degree of offset was 99.0% (= <4.8 mn>/<4.85 mn>).

Based on these results (see Figure 11.5), ABC concluded that there was an economic relationship between the hedged item and the hedging instrument that gave rise to offset: the fair values of both elements moved in opposite directions and in relatively similar absolute magnitudes.

The assessment also included the determination of the relationship hedge ratio and the identification of the sources of potential ineffectiveness.

Regarding the hedge ratio and based on the results of the quantitative assessment, ABC concluded that the notional of the hedging instrument, 10 million silver ounces, was the quantity necessary to meet the risk management objective to hedge 10 million silver ounces of hedged item. As a result the hedge ratio was set to 1:1.

$$\text{Hedge ratio} = \frac{\text{Hedged item notional}}{\text{Hedging instrument notional}} = \frac{\text{10 mn silver ounces}}{\text{10 mn silver ounces}} = 1:1$$

ABC identified the following as the main sources of potential ineffectiveness: firstly, a significant deterioration in the creditworthiness of the counterparty to the hedging instrument (Megabank); and secondly, a restructuring of the terms of the firm commitment.

ABC concluded that the hedge qualified for hedge accounting as it met all the qualifying criteria (see Figure 11.6):

- The firm commitment and the silver forward contract were an eligible hedged item and hedging instrument respectively.
- There was a formal designation and documentation of the hedge.

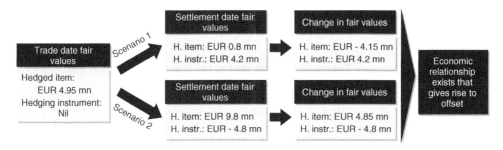

FIGURE 11.5 Economic relationship assessment results at hedge inception.

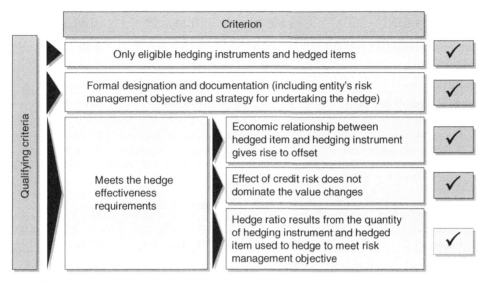

FIGURE 11.6   Effectiveness assessment results at inception.

- There was an economic relationship between the hedged item and the hedging instrument that gave rise to offset.
- The hedge's short-term tenor and Megabank's strong credit standing led ABC to conclude that the effect of credit did not dominate the hedge fair value changes. Moreover, there was a collateral agreement with daily margin calls that noticeably reduced credit exposure between the two parties to the hedging instrument.
- The hedge ratio resulted from the quantity of hedging instrument and hedged item used to hedge to meet risk management objectives, and it did not attempt to avoid recognising ineffectiveness.

There was another effectiveness assessment performed on 31 March 20X7. The process followed by ABC was very similar to that performed at hedge inception. It has been omitted to avoid unnecessary repetition.

11.6.5 Fair Valuations of Hedging Instrument and Hedged Item

The forward silver prices and the discount factor on the relevant dates were as follows:

Date	Forward rate for 31 May 20X7	Discount factor for 31 May 20X7
1 February 20X7	4.50	0.9900
31 March 20X7	4.60	0.9950
31 May 20X7	4.80	1.0000

The following table outlines the fair value calculation of the hedging instrument. Due to the short-term maturity of the forward contract and the existence of a collateral agreement with Megabank, there were no credit valuation adjustments on the hedging instrument.

Fair values (EUR)	1-Feb-X7	31-Mar-X7	31-May-X7
Silver forward price to 31-May-X7	4.50	4.60	4.80
Discount factor	0.9900	0.9950	1.0000
Forward fair value	-0- *(1)*	995,000*(2)*	3,000,000 *(3)*
Change in forward fair value	—	**995,000**	**2,005,000 (4)**

Notes:
   (1) 10 mn ounces × (forward price – 4.50) × Discount factor = 10 mn × (4.50 – 4.50) × 0.9900
   (2) 10 mn ounces × (forward price – 4.50) × Discount factor = 10 mn × (4.60 – 4.50) × 0.9950
   (3) 10 mn ounces × (forward price – 4.50) × Discount factor = 10 mn × (4.80 – 4.50) × 1.0000
   (4) 3,000,000 – 995,000

   The following table outlines the fair value calculation of the hedged item:

Fair values (EUR)	1-Feb-X7	31-Mar-X7	31-May-X7
Silver forward price to 31-May-X7	4.50	4.60	4.80
Discount factor	0.9900	0.9950	1.0000
Firm commitment fair value	4,950,000 *(1)*	3,980,000*(2)*	2,000,000 *(3)*
Change in forward fair value	—	**<970,000> *(4)***	**<1,980,000> *(5)***

Notes:
   (1) 10 mn ounces × (5.00 – forward price) × Discount factor = 10 mn × (5.00 – 4.50) × 0.9900
   (2) 10 mn ounces × (forward price – 4.50) × Discount factor = 10 mn × (5.00 – 4.60) × 0.9950
   (3) 10 mn ounces × (forward price – 4.50) × Discount factor = 10 mn × (5.00 – 4.80) × 1.0000
   (4) 3,980,000 – 4,950,000
   (5) 2,000,000 – 3,980,000

11.6.6 Accounting Entries

The required journal entries were as follows.

1) To record the forward contract on 1 February 20X7

No journal entries were required as the fair value of the forward contract was zero.

2) To record the closing of the accounting period on 31 March 20X7

The change in fair value of the forward contract produced a EUR 995,000 gain. The change in fair value of the firm commitment was EUR <970,000>.

Forward contract (Asset)	995,000	
Fair value hedge gains/losses (Profit or loss)		995,000
Fair value hedge gains/losses (Profit or loss)	970,000	
Firm commitment (Liability)		970,000

3) To record the end of the hedging relationship and the sale of the silver on 31 May 20X7

The change in fair value of the forward contract produced a EUR 2,005,000 gain. The change in fair value of the firm commitment was EUR <1,980,000>. On this date, the forward contract matured and ABC received from Megabank EUR 3 million in cash.

Forward contract (Asset)	2,005,000	
Fair value hedge gains/losses (Profit or loss)		2,005,000
Fair value hedge gains/losses (Profit or loss)	1,980,000	
Firm commitment (Liability)		1,980,000
Cash (Asset)	3,000,000	
Forward contract (Asset)		3,000,000

ABC acquired 10 million silver ounces from a mining company at the spot on 31 May 20X7, or EUR 4.80 per ounce, paying EUR 48 million. Simultaneously, ABC sold 10 million silver ounces to the electronics company at EUR 5.00 per ounce, receiving EUR 50 million, derecognising the firm commitment and that quantity of its inventory. The derecognition of the silver inventory (EUR 43 million) was recorded at the average price of such inventory in ABC's balance sheet, which was assumed to be EUR 4.30 per ounce.

Silver inventory (Asset)	48,000,000	
Cash (Asset)		48,000,000
Cash (Asset)	50,000,000	
Firm commitment (Liability)	2,950,000	
Sales (Profit or loss)		52,950,000
Cost of goods sold (Profit or loss)	43,000,000	
Silver inventory (Asset)		43,000,000

In this case, the loss on the firm commitment was almost fully offset by the gain on the forward contract. The sales proceeds were the original EUR 50 million plus the EUR 2.95 million change in fair value of the firm commitment. There was an additional EUR 50,000 gain stemming from the difference between the change in fair value of the forward and that of the firm commitment. The hedge preserved ABC's EBITDA from changes in the silver price, as

Without the hedge: *With the hedge:*

Profit or Loss
Sales: 50,000,000
COGS: 43,000,000
EBITDA:7,000,000

Profit or Loss
Sales: 52,950,000
COGS: 43,000,000
EBITDA: 9,950,000
Other financial income : 50,000

FIGURE 11.7   Summary of effects on ABC's profit or loss.

shown in Figure 11.7. ABC effectively sold the silver at the spot price prevailing on 31 May 20X7, even though the sales price was fixed on 1 February 20X7.

11.7 CASE STUDY: HEDGING COMMODITY INVENTORY WITH FUTURES

The aim of this case study is to illustrate the application of a commodity inventory hedge using futures contracts. Futures contracts are settled daily and any daily gain (loss) is deposited (withdrawn) in the entity's margin account at the futures exchange, what is referred to as **variation margin**. As a consequence, the futures position is reset at the end of each day so that the fair value of the combination of futures position and the margin is zero and the counterparty credit risk is almost zero.

11.7.1 Recognition of Inventories according to IAS 2

In the mining industry, inventories of metal are physically measured or estimated and valued at the lower of (i) cost and (ii) net realisable value (NRV). Costs of finished products are measured in terms of raw material cost, labour cost and a proportion of manufacturing overhead expenses. NRV is the amount estimated to be obtained from the sale of the item of inventory in the normal course of business, less any anticipated costs to be incurred to complete their production and those necessary to carry out the sale.

A write-down of an inventory is required if the NRV is lower than cost. The amount of any write-down of inventories from cost to NRV and all losses of inventories are recognised as an expense in the period the write-down or loss occurs.

A write-down may be reversed if the NRV recovers. The amount of any reversal of any write-down of inventories, arising from an increase in NRV, is recognised as a reduction in the amount of inventories recognised as an expense in the period in which the reversal occurs. Because an inventory valuation cannot exceed its cost, the maximum amount of reversal is the amount that revalues the inventory to cost.

When inventories are sold, the carrying amount of those inventories is recognised as an expense (i.e., as "cost of goods sold") in the period in which the related ordinary revenue is recognised.

11.7.2 Applying Hedge Accounting to Inventory

Even though an inventory is held at the lower of cost and net realisable value under IAS 2, an entity can apply hedge accounting (assuming that all other requirements are met) because the change in fair value of the inventory will affect profit or loss (as cost of goods sold) when the inventories are sold or their carrying amount is written down. Hence an entity can in theory apply a fair value hedge when hedging an inventory.

The adjusted carrying amount following the fair value adjustments becomes the cost basis for the purpose of applying the lower of cost and NRV under IAS 2.

11.7.3 Background Information

On 1 February 20X7 ABC, a gold mining company, held 100,000 ounces of gold of inventory carried at an average cost of USD 600 per ounce. The presentation and functional currency of ABC was the USD. To protect the inventory from a decline in gold prices, ABC hedged its position by selling 1,000 gold June futures contracts on the COMEX futures exchange on 1 February 20X7. Each contract was for 100 ounces of gold at USD 700 per ounce. The futures contracts matured on 21 June 20X7. The main terms of the futures contracts were:

Gold futures contracts terms	
Trade date	1 February 20X7
Futures exchange	COMEX
Maturity	21 June 20X7
Contract seller	ABC
Number of contracts	1,000
Contract size	100 gold troy ounces
Contract price	USD 700 per ounce
Delivery month	June 20X7
Settlement	Physical settlement. Delivery may take place on any business day beginning on the first business day of the delivery month or any subsequent business day of the delivery month, but not later than the last business day of the current delivery month

To avoid physical delivery of the gold, ABC planned to repurchase the futures position on 20 June 20X7, just prior to its expiry.

11.7.4 Hedging Relationship Documentation

ABC designated the futures contracts as the hedging instrument in a fair value hedge of its gold inventory. At its inception, ABC documented the hedging relationship as follows:

Hedging relationship documentation	
Risk management objective and strategy for undertaking the hedge	The objective of the hedge is to protect the USD value of 100,000 gold ounces of inventory held in Colorado against unfavourable movements of the gold price in USD.
	This hedging objective is consistent with ABC's overall risk management strategy of reducing the variability of its profit or loss statement by matching on a variable basis inventories and sales with gold futures and swaps.
	The designated risk being hedged is the risk of changes in the fair value of the entire hedged inventory (reflecting its actual location and including storage and directly related costs)
Type of hedge	Fair value hedge
Hedged item	The first 100,000 ounces of gold of the entity's finished goods inventory
Hedging instrument	The short 1,000 future contracts position for delivery in June 20X7 at a price of USD 700 per troy ounce, with trade number 56789. Because it is an exchange traded instrument, the credit risk associated with the instrument is considered to be very low
Hedge effectiveness assessment	See below

11.7.5 Hedge Effectiveness Assessment

Hedge effectiveness will be assessed by comparing changes in the fair value of the hedging instrument to changes in the fair value of the hedged item. The hedged item will be valued at the gold USD/oz spot rate rather than at the futures price.

- The change in fair value of the hedging instrument will be recognised in profit or loss.
- The change in fair value of the hedged item will also be recognised in profit or loss and adjusting the carrying amount of the hedged item.

Hedge effectiveness will be assessed prospectively (i.e., forward looking) at hedging relationship inception and on an ongoing basis at least upon each reporting date and upon occurrence of a significant change in the circumstances affecting the hedge effectiveness requirements.

The hedging relationship will qualify for hedge accounting only if all the following criteria are met:

1) The hedging relationship consists only of eligible hedge items and hedging instruments. The hedge item is eligible as it is an inventory item that exposes the entity to fair value risk and is reliably measurable. The hedging instrument is eligible as it is a derivative and does not result in a net written option.
2) At hedge inception there is a formal designation and documentation of the hedging relationship and the entity's risk management objective and strategy for undertaking the hedge.
3) The hedging relationship is considered effective.

The hedging relationship will be considered effective if the following three requirements are met:

1) There is an economic relationship between the hedged item and the hedging instrument.
2) The effect of credit risk does not dominate the value changes that result from that economic relationship.
3) The hedge ratio of the hedging relationship is the same as that resulting from the quantity of hedged item that the entity actually hedges and the quantity of the hedging instrument that the entity actually uses to hedge that quantity of hedged item. The hedge ratio should not be intentionally weighted to create ineffectiveness.

Whether there is an economic relationship between the hedged item and the hedging instrument will be assessed on a quantitative basis using the regression analysis method.

11.7.6 Hedge Effectiveness Assessment Performed at the Start of the Hedging Relationship

A regression analysis (see Figure 11.8) was performed by measuring the cumulative change in the fair value of 100,000 gold ounces in Colorado during a hedging period of 4 months and comparing it with that of the nearest gold futures contract on the COMEX. Each observation assumed that a 4-month hedge was put in place each month during the previous 15 years. The sign of the change in the fair value of the hedged item has been inverted to provide a clearer view. The results of the regression provided a R-squared coefficient of 98.8%. The t-statistic showed that the regression results were statistically valid.

Based on the results of the regression analysis using historical data, ABC determined that the spot price of gold in Colorado and the spot price of gold on the COMEX had a strong positive correlation. Accordingly, ABC concluded that the changes in the fair value of the futures contracts related to changes in the spot price of gold at the COMEX and the changes in the fair value of the gold inventory located in Colorado generally moved in opposite

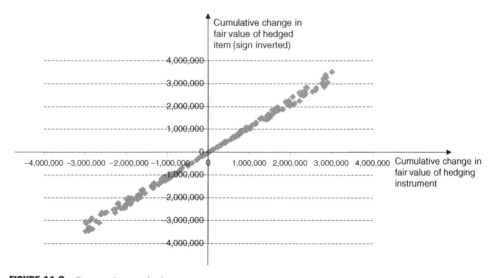

FIGURE 11.8 Regression analysis.

directions, and hence that an economic relationship existed between the hedged item and the hedging instrument.

The assessment also included the determination of the relationship hedge ratio and the identification of the sources of potential ineffectiveness.

Regarding the hedge ratio and based on the results of the quantitative assessment, ABC concluded that the notional of the hedging instrument, 100,000 gold troy ounces, was the quantity necessary to meet the risk management objective to hedge 100,000 gold troy ounces of hedged item. As a result the hedge ratio was set to 1:1.

$$\text{Hedge ratio} = \frac{\text{Hedged item notional}}{\text{Hedging instrument notional}} = \frac{100{,}000 \text{ gold troy ounces}}{100{,}000 \text{ gold troy ounces}} = 1{:}1$$

ABC identified the following as the main sources of potential ineffectiveness: firstly, a significant deterioration in the creditworthiness of the counterparty to the hedging instrument (the COMEX); and secondly, a reduction of ABC's gold inventory levels below the hedging instrument notional.

ABC concluded that the hedge qualified for hedge accounting as it met all the qualifying criteria (see Figure 11.9):

- The firm commitment and the gold futures contracts were an eligible hedged item and hedging instrument, respectively.
- There was a formal designation and documentation of the hedge,
- There was an economic relationship between the hedged item and the hedging instrument that gave rise to offset,

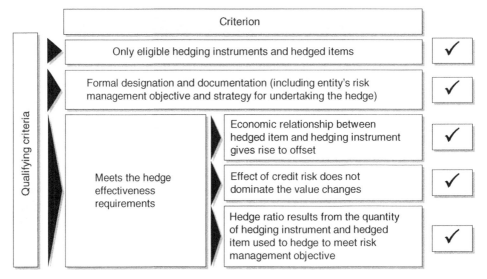

FIGURE 11.9 Effectiveness assessment results at inception.

- Despite ABC being exposed to the initial margin posted to the COMEX, the hedge's short-term tenor and the COMEX's strong credit standing led ABC to conclude that the effect of credit did not dominate the hedge fair value changes.
- The hedge ratio resulted from the quantity of hedging instrument and hedged item used to hedge to meet risk management objective, and it did not attempt to avoid recognising ineffectiveness.

There was another effectiveness assessment performed on 31 March 20X7. The process followed by ABC was very similar to that performed at hedge inception. It has been omitted to avoid unnecessary repetition.

11.7.7 Fair Valuations of Hedging Instrument and Hedged Item

Fair Valuations of the Hedged Item ABC estimated the fair value of the gold inventory using the COMEX spot price and adjusting it to reflect the differences that were due to changes in storage costs. The inventory was fair valued as follows:

Inventory fair value	1-Feb-X7	31-Mar-X7	20-Jun-X7
Spot price	690	644	607
Inventory theoretical value	69,000,000 *(1)*	64,400,000	60,700,000
Storage costs *(2)*	—	100,000	200,000
Inventory fair value	69,000,000	64,500,000 *(3)*	60,900,000
Change in inventory fair value	—	<4,500,000> *(4)*	<3,600,000>

Notes:
   (1) 100,000 ounces × 690
   (2) Storage costs incurred since 1-Feb-X7
   (3) Inventory theoretical value + Storage costs = 64,400,000 + 100,000
   (4) 64,500,000 – 69,000,000

Fair Valuations of the Hedging Instrument The spot and futures gold prices in USD per ounce on the relevant dates were as follows:

Date	Spot price	Futures price for 21 June 20X7
1 February 20X7	690	700
31 March 20X7	644	650.35
31 May 20X7	607	610.18

Due to daily settlement, the futures contract was fair valued by taking the expected cash flow at maturity on an undiscounted basis (i.e., ignoring the discount factor from valuation date to the contract maturity date) as follows, ignoring any counterparty credit risk:

Futures contracts fair values	1-Feb-X7	31-Mar-X7	20-Jun-X7
Futures price on 1-Feb-X7	700	700	700
Futures price	700	650.35	610.18
Futures fair value	-0- *(1)*	4,965,000 *(2)*	8,982,000 *(3)*
Change in futures fair value	—	4,965,000 *(4)*	4,017,000 *(5)*

Notes:

(1) 1,000 contracts × 100 ounces × (700 – 700)
(2) 1,000 contracts × 100 ounces × (700 – 650.35)
(3) 1,000 contracts × 100 ounces × (700 – 610.18)
(4) 4,965,000 – 0
(5) 8,982,000 – 4,965,000

11.7.8 Accounting Entries

The required journal entries were as follows.

1) To record the futures contracts trade on 1 February 20X7

In theory, no entries in the financial statements were required as the fair value of the futures contracts was zero. However, ABC had to post a margin in the futures exchange to guarantee the futures position. Suppose that the initial margin was 10% of the position, or USD 7,000,000 in cash.

Futures contracts margin (Asset)	7,000,000	
Cash (Asset)		7,000,000

2) To record the closing of the accounting period on 31 March 20X7

The futures contracts were revalued daily. When the futures position showed a gain from the previous day, the gain was posted in ABC's margin account with the broker (the broker in its capacity as member of the exchange). Conversely, when the futures position showed a loss, ABC had to post the lost amount in ABC's margin account with the broker. Therefore, at the end of each day the futures position was reset to keep its fair value at nil. The futures contracts did not appear on ABC's statement of financial position as assets or liabilities due to their nil fair value. Income earned on the margin account has been ignored for the purposes of this case.

For the sake of simplicity, I will summarise all the daily journal entries since 1 February 20X7 in one entry. The change in fair value of the futures contracts since 1 February 20X7 was a gain of USD 4,965,000. Because it was a fair value hedge, this amount was recorded in profit or loss.

Futures contracts margin (Asset)	4,965,000	
Fair value hedge gain/loss (Profit or loss)		4,965,000

As noted above, the margin account was updated daily to take into account the daily profit or loss of the futures position. Suppose that ABC maintained a USD 7,000,000 initial margin at all times and withdrew any excess (or deposited any deficit). As the futures position showed a gain of USD 4,965,000, the exchange through the futures broker deposited this amount in ABC's margin account at the broker, and this amount was transferred immediately to another bank account of the entity.

Cash (Asset)	4,965,000	
Futures contracts margin (Asset)		4,965,000

The gold inventory was revalued according to the change in fair value of the hedged item for the risk being hedged (a USD 4,500,000 loss).

Fair value hedge gain/loss (Profit or loss)	4,500,000	
Gold inventory (Asset)		4,500,000

3) To record the end of the hedging relationship and the repurchase of the futures contracts on 20 June 20X7

For the sake of simplicity, I will summarise all the daily journal entries since 31 March 20X7 in one. The change in fair value of the futures contracts since 31 March 20X7 was a gain of USD 4,017,000, recorded in profit or loss.

Suppose that ABC bought back its futures position, effectively closing its position. The margin account showed a balance of USD 11,017,000 (=7,000,000+4,017,000) and ABC immediately transferred this amount. The change in fair value of the hedged item (i.e., the inventory) represented a USD 3,600,000 gain recognised in profit or loss.

Futures contracts margin (Asset)	4,017,000	
Fair value hedge gain/loss (Profit or loss)		4,017,000
Cash (Asset)	11,017,000	
Futures contracts margin (Asset)		11,017,000
Fair value hedge gain/loss (Profit or loss)	3,600,000	
Gold inventory (Asset)		3,600,000

4) To record the sale of the gold inventory on 31 July 20X7

Suppose that the 100,000 ounces of gold were sold to a metal refining customer external to the ABC group on 31 July 20X7 at the spot price prevailing on that date. Assuming that the gold spot price on 31 July 20X7 was USD 720 per ounce, the sale proceeds were USD 72 million (= 100,000 ounces × 720). The inventory was valued at cost plus the inventory fair value gains/losses since hedge inception, or USD 51,900,000 (= 60,000,000 − 4,500,000 − 3,600,000).

Cash (Asset)	72,000,000	
Sales (Profit or loss)		72,000,000
Cost of goods sold (Profit or loss)	51,900,000	
Gold inventory (Asset)		51,900,000

Gold prices can be highly volatile. By entering into the gold futures contracts, ABC essentially protected its price exposure associated with its gold inventory until the hedge maturity. The hedge protected ABC's EBITDA as well (see Figure 11.10). Had ABC not hedged its inventory, its EBITDA and its pre-tax profit would have been USD 8,100,000 and USD 8,982,000 lower, respectively.

Because there was some ineffectiveness, ABC recognised an unexpected additional gain of USD 882,000 (= 8,982,000 − 8,100,000). This ineffectiveness arose due to the basis differential between COMEX gold prices and Colorado gold prices. To the extent the variability in the price of gold for these two locations was exactly the same (the basis differential remained constant), ABC would have offset its entire exposure to the variability in the price of gold associated with its inventory. Ineffectiveness caused by futures contracts can be substantial, as the futures price relates to a commodity with specific characteristics and for delivery in specific locations, which may differ considerably from the inventory being hedged. Similarly, actively traded ("liquid") futures contracts can be denominated in a currency different from that of the entity, creating additional hedging challenges for non-USD-based entities.

11.8 CASE STUDY: HEDGING A HIGHLY EXPECTED PURCHASE OF OIL WITH FUTURES AND AN FX FORWARD – CASH FLOW HEDGE

The aim of this case study is to illustrate the commodity hedge of a highly expected purchase using futures contracts and an FX forward. Recall, from our previous case study, that to enter into exchange traded futures (and options) entities have to post an initial margin. In addition,

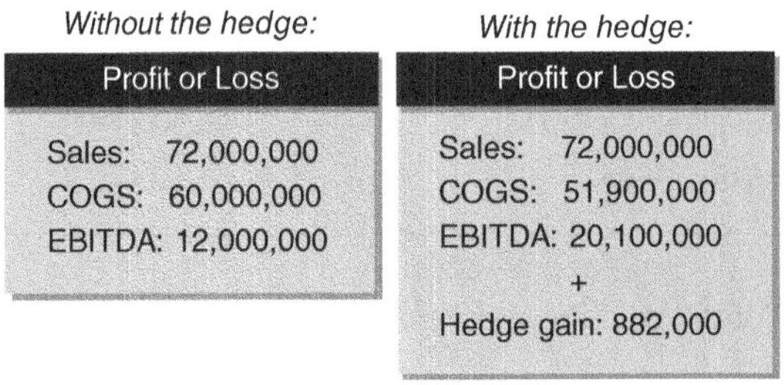

FIGURE 11.10 Summary of effects in ABC's profit or loss.

futures contracts are settled daily and any daily loss (gain) is posted to (taken from) the entity's margin account at the broker acting as intermediary with the exchange. As a consequence, the futures position is reset daily to keep its fair value at nil at the end of the day.

A second point to take into account is that the hedging instrument may not be treated as a derivative within the scope of IFRS 9, and instead be considered as an "own-use" instrument. In this case, because the entity was looking to unwind its futures position when the purchase price of another transaction was set, the futures contract was within the scope of IFRS 9.

11.8.1 Background Information

On 1 February 20X7, ABC, a European oil refining company, forecasted the purchase of 2 million barrels of Brent crude oil from an oil producer, expected to be priced on 31 May 20X7 at the USD/barrel spot price of Brent crude oil prevailing on this date. Delivery and payment would take place simultaneously on 7 June 20X7. ABC's presentation and functional currency was the EUR. ABC was worried that the EUR value of the oil purchase might increase before the oil purchase price was set. To hedge its exposure, ABC entered into an ICE long June futures position on the Intercontinental Exchange (ICE) for 2 million barrels at a price of USD 51 per barrel. The futures contracts were to expire on 21 June 20X7. The main terms of the futures contracts were as follows:

Crude oil futures contracts terms	
Trade date	1 February 20X7
Futures exchange	ICE
Maturity	15 June 20X7
Contract buyer	ABC
Number of contracts	2,000
Contract size	1,000 barrels of Brent crude oil
Contract price	USD 51/barrel
Delivery month	June 20X7
Settlement	(Exchange for) physical or cash settlement. Cash settlement based on the ICE Brent Index price for the day following the last trading day of the futures contract.

Simultaneously, ABC entered into an FX forward to buy USD 100 million at an exchange rate of 1.2500 on 31 May 20X7, and to be cash settled, as follows:

FX forward terms	
Trade date	1 February 20X7
Counterparties	ABC and Megabank
Maturity	31 May 20X7
ABC buys	USD 100 million
ABC sells	EUR 80 million

(continued overleaf)

FX forward terms	
Forward Rate	1.2500
Settlement	Cash settlement.
	On maturity date, there is a EUR cash settlement based on the EUR–USD fixing prevailing on that date
	Settlement amount = 100 mn/Fixing – EUR 80 mn
	If the settlement amount is positive ABC receives the settlement amount
	If the settlement amount is negative, ABC pays the absolute value of the settlement amount

11.8.2 Hedging Relationship Documentation

ABC designated the combination of the oil futures contracts and the FX forward as the hedging instrument in a cash flow hedge of its highly expected purchase. At its inception, ABC documented the hedging relationship as follows:

Hedging relationship documentation	
Risk management objective and strategy for undertaking the hedge	The objective of the hedge is to protect the EUR value of cash flow stemming from a highly expected purchase of 2 million barrels of Brent crude oil against unfavourable movements of the oil price in EUR.
	This hedging objective is consistent with ABC's overall risk management strategy of reducing the variability of its profit or loss statement by entering into commodities futures and swaps, and FX forwards and options.
	The designated risk being hedged is the risk of changes in the cash flow of the highly expected purchase
Type of hedge	Cash flow hedge
Hedged item	The first 2 million barrels of Brent crude oil denominated in USD. The forecast purchase transaction is expected to be settled and received on 7 June 20X7. The purchase price is expected to be set on 31 May 20X7.
	The forecast purchase transaction is highly probable to occur. The negotiation of the purchase transaction is at an advanced stage, and the entity has several years of history of similar purchases that have been executed according to plan. In addition, the oil supplier has a strong reputation in the market of being highly reliable
Hedging instrument	The combination of:
	1) Contract number 145678: a long ICE Brent crude oil futures contract position of 2 million barrels for expiry on 15 June 20X7 at a price of USD 51 per barrel. Because it is an exchange traded instrument, the credit risk associated with the instrument is considered to be very low.
	2) Contract number 145679: an FX forward to buy USD 100 million and sell EUR 80 million at an exchange rate of 1.2500, value date 31 May 20X7, and cash settlement. The credit risk associated with the counterparty to the FX forward is considered to be very low
Hedge effectiveness assessment	See below

11.8.3 Hedge Effectiveness Assessment

Hedge effectiveness will be assessed by comparing changes in the fair value of the hedging instrument to changes in the fair value of the hedged item. The hedged item will be valued at the Brent crude oil spot price on the ICE rather than at the futures price and at the EUR–USD FX forward rate with maturity 31 May 20X7. The hedge will be accounted as follows:

- The portion of the change in fair value of the hedging instrument that is determined to be an effective hedge will be recognised directly in the cash flow hedge reserve of OCI.
- The ineffective portion of the change in fair value of the hedging instrument will be recognised in profit or loss.

The effective portion would be the lesser of the following (taking into account their signs):

- The cumulative change in fair value of the hedging instrument from hedging relationship inception.
- The cumulative change in fair value of the hedged item from hedging relationship inception.

Hedge effectiveness will be assessed prospectively (i.e., forward looking) at hedging relationship inception and on an ongoing basis at least upon each reporting date and upon occurrence of a significant change in the circumstances affecting the hedge effectiveness requirements.

The hedging relationship will qualify for hedge accounting only if all the following criteria are met:

1) The hedging relationship consists only of eligible hedge items and hedging instruments. The hedge item is eligible as it is a highly expected forecast transaction that exposes the entity to fair value risk, affects profit or loss and is reliably measurable. The hedging instrument is eligible as it is a combination of derivatives that does not result in a net written option.
2) At hedge inception there is a formal designation and documentation of the hedging relationship and the entity's risk management objective and strategy for undertaking the hedge.
3) The hedging relationship is considered effective.

The hedging relationship will be considered effective if the following three requirements are met:

1) There is an economic relationship between the hedged item and the hedging instrument.
2) The effect of credit risk does not dominate the value changes that result from that economic relationship.
3) The hedge ratio of the hedging relationship is the same as that resulting from the quantity of hedged item that the entity actually hedges and the quantity of the hedging instrument that the entity actually uses to hedge that quantity of hedged item. The hedge ratio should not be intentionally weighted to create ineffectiveness

Whether there is an economic relationship between the hedged item and the hedging instrument will be assessed on a quantitative basis using the regression analysis method.

11.8.4 Hedge Effectiveness Assessment Performed at Hedging Relationship Inception

An effectiveness assessment was performed at inception of the hedging relationship and at each reporting date. The assessment also included the relationship hedge ratio and an identification of the sources of potential ineffectiveness.

A regression analysis (see Figure 11.11) was performed measuring the cumulative change in the EUR fair value of 2 million barrels of Brent crude oil during a hedging period of 4 months. Each observation assumes that a new hedge was put in place each month during the previous 5 years. The results of the regression provided an R-squared coefficient of 99.9%. The t-statistic showed that the regression results were statistically valid. The correlation coefficient was not 100% because the USD/barrel portion of the hedged item was valued using ICE's Brent crude oil spot prices and the EUR–USD spot prices using the European Central Bank fixing, while the hedging instrument was valued using the ICE futures prices and the EUR–USD forward prices.

Based on the results of the regression analysis using historical data, ABC determined that the EUR spot price of the Brent crude oil to be purchased and the combination of the long 4-month USD futures price of ICE Brent crude oil and the 4-month EUR–USD FX forward rate had a strong negative correlation. Accordingly, ABC concluded that the changes in the fair value of these variables will generally move in opposite directions, and hence that an economic relationship existed between the hedged item and the hedging instrument.

ABC concluded that the hedge qualified for hedge accounting as it met all the qualifying criteria (see Figure 11.12):

- The highly probable forecasted purchase transaction and the combination of crude oil futures contracts and the EUR–USD FX forward were an eligible hedged item and hedging instrument, respectively.
- There was a formal designation and documentation of the hedge.
- There was an economic relationship between the hedged item and the hedging instrument that gave rise to offset.

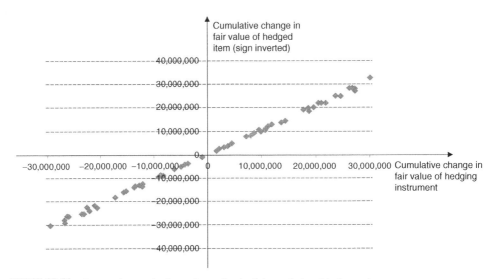

FIGURE 11.11 Regression analysis performed at hedging relationship inception.

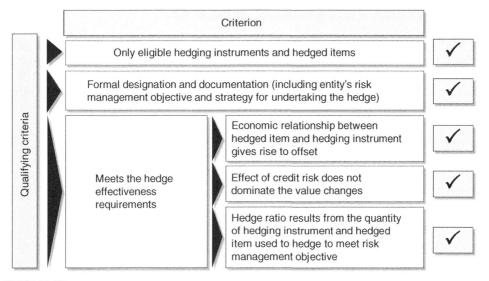

FIGURE 11.12   Effectiveness assessment results at inception.

- Despite being exposed to the initial margin posted to the ICE, the hedge's short-term tenor and the strong credit standing of ICE and Megabank led ABC to conclude that the effect of credit did not dominate the hedge fair value changes.
- The hedge ratio resulted from the quantity of hedging instrument and hedged item used to hedge to meet risk management objectives, and it did not attempt to avoid recognising ineffectiveness.

Regarding the hedge ratio and based on the results of the quantitative assessment, ABC concluded that the notional of the hedging instrument, 2 million crude oil barrels and USD 100 million, was the quantity necessary to meet the risk management objective to hedge 2 million crude oil barrels of hedged item. As a result the hedge ratio was set to 1:1.

$$\text{Hedge ratio} = \frac{\text{Hedged item notional}}{\text{Hedging instrument notional}} = \frac{\text{2 mn crude oil barrels}}{\text{2 mn crude oil barrels}} = 1:1$$

There were two main sources of potential ineffectiveness: firstly, a significant credit deterioration of the counterparties to the hedging instrument (the ICE and Megabank); and secondly, a change in the notional, date or probability of occurrence of the forecasted purchase.

There was another effectiveness assessment performed on 31 March 20X7. The process followed by ABC was very similar to that performed at hedge inception. It has been omitted to avoid unnecessary repetition.

11.8.5 Fair Valuations of Hedging Instrument and Hedged Item

Fair Valuations of the Hedged Item The hedged item – the cash flows associated with the highly probable forecasted purchase of crude oil – was fair valued at each relevant date in two stages. Firstly, the purchase of crude oil was fair valued in its currency of denomination (i.e., in USD) using the ICE Brent spot price. Then the calculated fair value was translated into EUR using the EUR–USD spot rate prevailing on fair valuation date.

Oil component: fair values	1-Feb-X7	31-Mar-X7	31-May-X7
Barrels hedged	2,000,000	2,000,000	2,000,000
ICE spot price (USD/barrel)	50	55	62
Fair value in USD	100,000,000 *(1)*	110,000,000 *(2)*	124,000,000 *(3)*
EUR–USD spot rate	1.2400	1.2750	1.3000
Fair value in EUR	80,645,000 *(4)*	86,275,000 *(5)*	95,385,000 *(6)*
Change in fair value	—	<5,630,000> *(7)*	<9,110,000> *(8)*

Notes:
> *(1)* 2,000,000 × 50
> *(2)* 2,000,000 × 55
> *(3)* 2,000,000 × 62
> *(4)* 100,000,000/1.2400
> *(5)* 110,000,000/1.2750
> *(6)* 124,000,000/1.30000
> *(7)* 80,645,000 – 86,275,000
> *(8)* 86,275,000 – 95,385,000

Fair Valuations of the Hedging Instrument The hedging instrument – the combination of the crude oil futures contracts and the EUR–USD FX forward – was fair valued at each relevant date using the ICE Brent futures price and the EUR–USD forward rate.

The fair valuation of the crude oil futures contracts on the relevant dates were as follows:

Oil futures fair values	1-Feb-X7	31-Mar-X7	31-May-X7
Barrels hedged	2,000,000	2,000,000	2,000,000
ICE futures price (USD/barrel)	51	55.5	62.1
Contracts position (USD)	102,000,000 *(1)*	111,000,000 *(2)*	124,200,000 *(3)*
Fair value (USD)	—	9,000,000 *(4)*	22,200,000 *(5)*
EUR–USD spot	1.2400	1.2750	1.3000
Fair value (EUR)	—	7,059,000 *(6)*	17,077,000 *(7)*
Change in fair value (EUR)	—	7,059,000 *(8)*	10,018,000 *(9)*

Notes:

(1) 2,000,000 × 51
(2) 2,000,000 × 55.5
(3) 2,000,000 × 62.1
(4) 111,000,000 – 102,000,000
(5) 124,200,000 – 102,000,000
(6) 9,000,000/1.2750
(7) 22,200,000/1.3000
(8) 7,059,000 – 0
(9) 17,077,000 – 7,059,000

The spot and forward EUR–USD rates on the relevant dates were as follows:

Date	Spot EUR–USD	Forward for 31 May 20X7	Discount factor for 31 May 20X7
1 February 20X7	1.2400	1.2500	0.9900
31 March 20X7	1.2750	1.2800	0.9930
31 May 20X7	1.3000	1.3000	1.0000

The fair value calculation of the FX forward was as follows:

FX forward fair values	1-Feb-X7	31-Mar-X7	31-May-X7
Forward rate to 31-May-X7 (on 1-Feb-X7)	1.2500	1.2500	1.2500
Forward rate to 31-May-X7 (on specified date)	1.2500	1.2800	1.3000
FX forward fair value	-0- *(1)*	<1,862,000> *(2)*	<3,077,000> *(3)*
Change in forward fair value	—	<1,862,000> *(4)*	<1,215,000> *(5)*

Notes:

(1) 100 mn USD × (1/1.2500 – 1/1.2500) × 0.9900
(2) 100 mn USD × (1/1.2500 – 1/1.2800) × 0.9930
(3) 100 mn USD × (1/1.2500 – 1/1.3000) × 1.0000
(4) <1,862,000> – 0
(5) <3,077,000> – <1,862,000>

The fair valuation of the hedging instrument – the combination of the crude oil futures contracts and the FX forward – was as follows:

Hedging instrument fair value changes	1-Feb-X7	31-Mar-X7	31-May-X7
Change in crude oil futures	—	7,059,000	10,018,000
Change in FX forward	—	<1,862,000>	<1,215,000>
Total change in fair value	—	5,197,000	8,803,000

Effective and Ineffective Amounts The following table details the effective and ineffective amounts. The effective amounts were calculated based on the lower of the cumulative changes in fair value of the hedging instrument and the hedged item. The ineffective part of the change in fair value of the hedging instrument was the excess of its cumulative change in fair value over that of the hedged item (see Section 5.5.6 for an explanation of the calculations):

	31-Mar-X7	31-May-X7
Cumulative change in fair value of hedging instrument	5,197,000	14,000,000
Cumulative change in fair value of hedged item (opposite sign)	5,630,000	14,740,000
Lower amount	5,197,000	14,000,000
Previous cumulative effective amount	—	5,197,000
Available amount	5,197,000	8,803,000
Period change in fair value of hedging instrument	5,197,000	8,803,000
Effective part	5,197,000	8,803,000
Ineffective part	-0-	-0-

11.8.6 Accounting Entries

1) To record the futures contracts on 1 February 20X7

ABC had to post a margin in the futures exchange to guarantee the futures position. Suppose that the initial margin was 10% of the USD 102 million initial position, or USD 10,200,000 in cash. As the EUR–USD spot exchange rate on that date was 1.2400, the equivalent EUR amount was EUR 8,226,000 (=10.2 mn/1.2400). The FX forward was not recognised on ABC's statement of financial position as its initial fair value was nil.

Futures contracts margin (Asset)	8,226,000	
Cash (Asset)		8,226,000

2) To record the closing of the accounting period on 31 March 20X7

The futures contracts were revalued daily. When the futures position showed a gain from the previous day, the gain was posted in ABC's margin account at the broker acting as intermediary to the futures exchange. Conversely, when the futures position showed a loss, ABC had to post the lost amount in its margin account at the futures exchange. Therefore, at the end of each day the futures position was reset to keep its fair value at nil.

For the sake of simplicity, I have summarised all the daily journal entries since 1 February 20X7 in one entry on 31 March 20X7. The change in fair value of the hedging instrument since 1 February 20X7 was a gain of EUR 5,197,000, split between a gain of EUR 7,059,000 related to the futures contracts and a loss of EUR 1,862,000 related to the FX forward. The effective part of the change in fair value of the hedging instrument was EUR 5,197,000, while the ineffective part was nil. The effective part was recognised in the cash flow hedge reserve in OCI. As there was no ineffective part, no amount was recorded in profit or loss.

The USD cash received in the futures contracts margin account was immediately converted into EUR and deposited in ABC's EUR bank deposit account, to avoid being exposed to the EUR–USD rate.

Futures contracts margin (Asset)	7,059,000	
FX forward (Liability)		1,862,000
Cash flow hedge reserve (Equity)		5,197,000
Cash (Asset)	7,059,000	
Futures contracts margin (Asset)		7,059,000

I am assuming that the initial cash margin did not change during the position's life of the position (in reality, it was adjusted on a daily basis to equal 10% of the contract position). The initial cash margin of USD 10,200,000 had an initial value of EUR 8,226,000. This was a monetary item and, therefore, had to be revalued at the EUR–USD spot rate on 31 March 20X7 (1.2750). The margin new value was EUR 8,000,000 (=USD 10,200,000/1.2750), showing a loss of EUR 226,000 (= 8,000,000 – 8,226,000):

Other financial gain/loss (Profit or loss)	226,000	
Futures contracts margin (Asset)		226,000

3) To record the end of the hedging relationship and the oil purchase on 31 May 20X7

For the sake of simplicity, I have summarised all the daily journal entries of the futures contracts since 31 March 20X7 in just one entry. The change in fair value of the hedging instrument since 31 March 20X7 was a gain of EUR 8,803,000, split between a gain of EUR 10,018,000 related to the futures contract and a loss of EUR 1,215,000 related to the FX forward. The effective part of the change in fair value of the hedging instrument was EUR 8,803,000, while the ineffective part was nil. The effective part was recognised in the cash flow hedge reserve in OCI. As there was no ineffective part, no amount was recorded in profit or loss.

The USD 13,200,000 cash received in the futures contract margin account was converted into EUR 10,154,000 (= 13,200,000/1.3000) at the 1.3000 FX spot rate and deposited in ABC's EUR bank deposit account, to avoid being exposed to the EUR–USD rate.

The initial cash margin of USD 10,200,000 had a value of EUR 8,000,000 on 31 March 20X7. This was a monetary item and, therefore, had to be revalued at the EUR–USD spot rate on 31 May 20X7 (1.3000). The margin new value was EUR 7,846,000 (=USD 10,200,000/1.3000), showing a loss of EUR 154,000 (= 7,846,000 – 8,000,000).

Futures contracts margin (Asset)	10,018,000	
FX forward (Liability)		1,215,000
Cash flow hedge reserve (Equity)		8,803,000
Cash (Asset)	10,154,000	
Futures contracts margin (Asset)		10,154,000
Other financial gain/loss (Profit or loss)	154,000	
Futures contracts margin (Asset)		154,000

ABC resold the futures contracts and received the initial USD 10,200,000 margin, which was immediately converted into EUR 7,846,000 at the 1.3000 EUR–USD spot rate on that date. Simultaneously, ABC settled the FX forward paying EUR 3,077,000.

Cash (Asset)	7,846,000	
Futures contracts margin (Asset)		7,846,000
FX forward (Liability)	3,077,000	
Cash (Asset)		3,077,000

The purchase of the 2 million barrels of Brent crude oil was agreed at the ICE Brent crude oil spot price (USD 62.00 per barrel), or a total of USD 124 million. As a result, from 31 May 20X7 the highly expected purchase became a firm commitment until its receipt. The hedging relationship was terminated.

4) To record the payment and receipt of the crude oil on 7 June 20X7
Suppose that the EUR–USD spot rate was 1.3050 on 7 June 20X7. The amount in EUR to exchange for USD 124,000,000 was EUR 95,019,000 (=124 million/1.3050). ABC paid this amount in exchange for the crude oil.

Crude oil inventory (Asset)	95,019,000	
Cash (Asset)		95,019,000

The cash flow hedge reserve showed a carrying amount of EUR 14 million (= 5,197,000 + 8,803,000). If a forecast transaction subsequently results in the recognition of a non-financial asset or liability, IFRS 9 requires an entity to adjust the initial cost (or the carrying amount) of the asset/liability, what is known as **basis adjustment**. Therefore, in our case the amount accumulated in the cash flow hedge reserve was adjusted out of equity and offset against the carrying amount of the crude oil inventory.

Cash flow hedge reserve (Equity)	14,000,000	
Crude oil inventory (Asset)		14,000,000

We conclude this section by observing, regarding the EUR–USD FX forward, that while retaining the determination of the settlement amount on 31 May 20X7, ABC probably should have included a settlement date on 7 June 20X7, to coincide with the oil payment.

11.9 CASE STUDY: AIRLINE JET FUEL CONSUMPTION HEDGE WITH JET FUEL AND CRUDE OIL – RISK COMPONENT

The aim of this case study is to illustrate the commodity hedging issues faced by airlines using a rolling hedging strategy that combines jet fuel swaps and crude oil futures. This case also shows how to apply hedge accounting when hedging a risk component.

11.9.1 Background Information

ABC Airlines, an entity with the USD as functional currency, planned to consume around 2.4 million tonnes of jet fuel (jet kerosene) over the next 24 months, on a uniform consumption basis. Jet fuel consumption was a major item of expenditure, making up over 20% of its operating expenses. Severe fluctuations in fuel prices could therefore have a considerable effect on the company's operating results.

ABC's procurement department bought jet fuel through long-term supply contracts or "term contracts" with several oil companies, based upon a projected volume for a given period. The purchase price was indexed to Platts spot prices (jet fuel price North West Europe (NWE) CIF Rotterdam barge) plus a fixed cost (USD 36 per tonne). This fixed cost included the cost of logistics, charges, the supplier margin and an amount that incorporated ABC's credit history, rating, and the volume it used at the location.

ABC's hedging policy of anticipated jet fuel requirements, as approved by its Board, was a rolling hedging programme of its consumption forecast up to 24 months before delivery, increasing the volume that it hedged over time (see Figure 11.13). ABC used crude oil futures to hedge the longer-term horizon (6–24 months) and switched from oil futures to jet fuel swaps in the short term (0–6 months) once these swaps became reasonably liquid. At the end of each quarter, the following hedging strategy was in place:

- 100% of fuel consumption was hedged for the time horizon within 6 months to delivery using jet fuel swaps on the NWE jet fuel;
- 50% of fuel consumption was hedged for the time horizon between 6 and 15 months using Brent crude oil futures;
- 10% of fuel consumption was hedged for the time horizon between 15 and 24 months using Brent crude oil futures;
- not to enter into any jet fuel hedging contracts with respect to its expected fuel purchases beyond the eighth quarter.

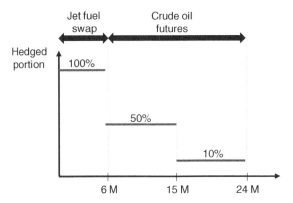

FIGURE 11.13   ABC's rolling hedging strategy.

This strategy took into account that jet fuel swap prices were only sufficiently liquid within 6 months of delivery. In contrast, Brent crude oil was one of the world's most widely-used commodities and among the most actively hedged and traded products worldwide. Whilst ABC took advantage of the high liquidity of Brent crude oil futures, it was exposed to the jet fuel crack spread (i.e., the difference between the price of oil and the price of jet fuel) for the time horizon between 6 and 24 months.

It is worth noting that there were several "jet fuel crack spreads" throughout the world. For example, the crack between the US Gulf Coast jet fuel price and the WTI crude oil price behaved differently than the crack between the NWE jet fuel price and the Brent crude oil price. Additionally, there were crack spread variations over time (see Figure 11.14).

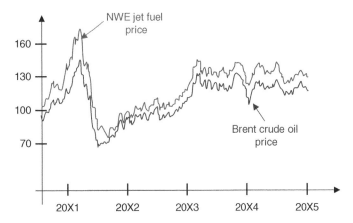

FIGURE 11.14   NWE jet fuel versus Brent crude oil (1-Jan-X0 prices rebased to 100).

On 1 April 20X5 ABC entered into a jet fuel swap with Megabank as follows:

Jet fuel swap terms	
Trade date	1 April 20X5
Counterparties	ABC Airlines and Megabank
Maturity	30 September 20X5
Total notional quantity	600,000 tonnes
Notional quantity	100,000 tonnes Apr-20X5
	100,000 tonnes May-20X5
	100,000 tonnes Jun-20X5
	100,000 tonnes Jul-20X5
	100,000 tonnes Aug-20X5
	100,000 tonnes Sep-20X5
Calculation period	Monthly during the term of the transaction
Fixed price payer	ABC Airlines
Fixed price	USD 900 per tonne
Floating price payer	Megabank
Commodity reference price	Jet fuel NWE (cargoes CIF), Platts European Marketscan
Floating price	The unweighted arithmetic mean of the relevant high and low prices for jet fuel published under the heading "JET CIF NWE/ BASIS ARA" as quoted in Platts European Marketscan for each successive day of the Calculation Period during which such prices are quoted
Payment date(s)	The last day of the calculation period (note: in practice, payment date is five New York business days later, but I have changed this for the sake of simplicity)
Pricing date(s)	Each commodity business day from and including 1 April 20X5 up to and including 30 September 20X5

Pursuant to the terms of the jet fuel swap, ABC and Megabank agreed to exchange monthly payments equal to the difference between a fixed price (USD 900) for a given monthly quantity of jet fuel (100,000 tonnes) and the monthly average market price for such quantity of jet fuel, with ABC receiving the amount of any excess of such market price over such fixed price and paying to Megabank the amount of any deficit of such fixed price under such market price. For example, on 30 April 20X5 there was a USD cash settlement based on the average NWE jet fuel price per tonne from 1 April 20X5 to 30 April 20X5 (the "floating price").

$$\text{Settlement amount} = 100{,}000 \text{ tonnes} \times (\text{floating price} - 900)$$

If the settlement amount was positive, ABC received the settlement amount; if it was negative, ABC paid the absolute value of the settlement amount.

Additionally, on 1 April 20X5 ABC entered into the following Brent crude oil futures contracts:

Crude oil futures contracts terms	
Trade date	1 April 20X5
Futures exchange	ICE
Contract buyer	ABC Airlines
Contracts	1) 1,198,500 barrels (bbl), contract expiring on 15 December 20X5, futures price USD 98/bbl
	2) 1,198,500 bbl, contract expiring on 15 March 20X6, futures price USD 98.30/bbl
	3) 1,198,500 bbl, contract expiring on 15 June 20X6, futures price USD 98.60/bbl
	4) 239,700 bbl, contract expiring on 15 September 20X6, futures price USD 99/bbl
	5) 239,700 bbl, contract expiring on 15 December 20X6, futures price USD 99.30/bbl
	6) 239,700 bbl, contract expiring on 15 Mar 20X7, futures price USD 99.70/bbl
Underlying	Brent crude oil

11.9.2 Hedging Risk Components

Under IFRS 9 an entity may hedge a specific risk (or risk component) in a financial and non-financial item provided the component is separately identifiable and reliably measurable.

Risk components can be (see Chapter 2):

- contractually specified (i.e., the risk component is explicitly specified in a contract);
- non-contractually specified (i.e., the risk component is only implicit in the fair value or cash flows of an items of which they are a part).

Therefore, a risk component does not necessarily have to be contractually specified for it to be separately identifiable. However, if the risk component is not contractually specified it may be more difficult to isolate parts of the market price into identifiable and measurable risk components. An entity would need to demonstrate whether a risk component is separately identifiable and reliably measurable.

Although the crude oil price was not a contractually specified component of its jet fuel purchase price, ABC determined that, based on the analysis of the market structure for oil and oil products, there was a relationship between crude oil and jet fuel prices. Its evaluation of the relevant facts and circumstances was as follows.

ABC operated in a geographical area in which Brent was the crude oil benchmark. Crude oil was the main driver of the price of jet fuel because of the production process for oil products: jet fuel was obtained through refining (i.e., converting crude oil into jet fuel), as shown in Figure 11.15. Moreover, the pricing of refined oil products did not depend on which particular crude oil was processed by a particular refinery because jet fuel was a standardised product.

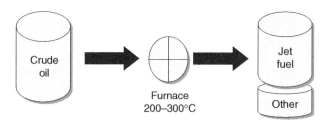

FIGURE 11.15 Jet fuel production process.

Thus, jet fuel purchase prices could be separated into two components:

- A crude component that represented the raw material cost a refiner incurred when producing jet fuel. Crude oil was unrefined and its price excluded any cracking spread.
- A jet fuel crack spread, or refining margin, component that represented the sum of the operational and fixed costs of operating a refinery, refiners' profit margins, and demand–supply imbalances in refining capacity and storages volumes. This component could be traded in the derivatives market as jet fuel crack spread. The benchmark in the geographical area in which ABC operated was indexed to Brent crude oil.

Based on these considerations, ABC concluded that, despite not being specified in any contractual arrangement, the crude oil component was a separately identifiable component of its forecast jet fuel purchases.

ABC determined that the crude oil component was **reliably measurable** due to the existence of an observable liquid forward market for crude oil for the entire relevant period for which ABC planned to hedge.

11.9.3 Hedging Relationship Documentation

ABC designated the jet fuel swap and the crude oil futures contracts as the hedging instrument in a cash flow hedge of its highly probable forecast purchase of jet fuel. At its inception, ABC documented the hedging relationship as follows:

Hedging relationship documentation	
Risk management objective and strategy for undertaking the hedge	The objective of the hedge is to protect the USD value of specific number of tonnes (see "hedged item" section) of highly expected purchase of jet fuel against unfavourable movements of jet fuel or crude oil prices in USD.
	This hedging objective is consistent with ABC's overall risk management strategy of reducing the variability of its profit or loss statement using jet fuel swaps and options, and crude oil futures, swaps and options.
	The designated risk being hedged is the risk of changes in the cash flow amounts related to a highly probable string of forecast jet fuel purchases.

(continued overleaf)

	Hedging relationship documentation
	The hedging strategy is a rolling one that consists of a 6-month hedge of the highly expected purchase of 600,000 tonnes of jet fuel. The crude oil component of another 540,000 tonnes of jet fuel highly expected to be consumed during the subsequent 18 months (450,000 tonnes during the subsequent 9 months and 90,000 tonnes during the last 9 months) will be hedged with six crude oil futures contracts. Each crude oil contract will be replaced with a 3-month jet fuel swap when their time to expiry becomes 6 months. Each time a futures contract is replaced with a jet fuel swap of 100,000 tonnes, the risk being hedged for the corresponding 3-month quantity is the jet fuel price risk in its entirety as opposed to the crude oil component of such price risk. Additionally, each time a futures contract is replaced with a jet fuel swap, new crude oil futures contracts will be purchased to maintain the hedge objective over the 24 months the hedging profile is kept
Type of hedge	Cash flow hedge
Hedged item	The initial hedge items are:
	1) The first 600,000 tonnes of jet fuel highly expected to be purchased during the next 6 months
	2) The crude oil component of the first 450,000 tonnes and 90,000 tonnes of jet fuel highly expected to be purchased during the 9 months following the next 6 months (i.e., months 7–15) and the 9 months following the next 15 months (i.e., months 16–24), respectively.
	The forecast purchases are considered to have a high probability of occurring because the entity has a consistent history of actually purchasing the forecasted quantities of jet fuel for the up-front 6 months.
	Regarding the forecasted purchase quantities being hedged for the periods beyond the initial 6 months are well below historical consumption levels
Hedging instrument	The initial hedging instruments are:
	1) The rolling 6-month jet fuel swap on 600,000 tonnes in which on a monthly basis ABC Airlines pays a fixed USD price per tonne and receives the monthly average spot jet fuel price. The main terms of the initial jet fuel swap are: a 56797 trade number, a fixed price of USD 900 per tonne and Megabank as the swap counterparty
	2) The purchased futures contracts on Brent crude oil with six subsequent quarterly expiries. Initially, with trade numbers 56797, 56798, 56799, 56800, 56801 and 56802, the first three trades on 1,198,500 barrels of Brent crude oil each and with expiries in December 20X5, March 20X6 and June 20X6, and the other three trades on 239,700 barrels of Brent crude oil each and with expiries in September 20X6, December 20X6 and March 20X7. Each futures contract will be replaced with a forward starting 3-month jet fuel swap when its time to expiry reaches 6 months, and new futures contracts will be bought to maintain the hedge's objective over 24 months
Hedge effectiveness assessment	See below

11.9.4 Hedge Effectiveness Assessment

Hedge effectiveness will be assessed prospectively (i.e., forward looking) at hedging relationship inception and on an ongoing basis at least at each reporting date and upon occurrence of a significant change in the circumstances affecting the hedge effectiveness requirements. For effectiveness assessment purposes, the hedged item will be replaced with a hypothetical derivative that exactly matches the critical terms of the hedged item.

Hedge effectiveness will be assessed by comparing changes in the fair value of the hedging instrument to changes in the fair value of the hypothetical derivative. The hypothetical derivative will be valued at spot prices rather than at forward prices.

The effective part of the change in fair value of the hedging instrument will be determined as the lower, taking into account their signs, of this fair value change and that of the hedged item.

- The effective part of the change in fair value of the hedging instrument will be recognised in the cash flow hedge reserve of OCI. This amount will be reclassified to adjust the carrying amount of the jet fuel inventory when the purchased hedged jet fuel is recorded.
- The ineffective part of the change in fair value of the hedging instrument will be recognised in profit or loss.

The hedging relationship will qualify for hedge accounting only if all the following criteria are met:

1) The hedging relationship consists only of eligible hedge items and hedging instruments. The hedge item is eligible as it is an inventory item that exposes the entity to fair value risk, impacts profit or loss and is reliably measurable. The hedging instrument is eligible as it is a combination of derivatives that does not result in a net written option.
2) At hedge inception there is a formal designation and documentation of the hedging relationship and the entity's risk management objective and strategy for undertaking the hedge.
3) The hedging relationship is considered effective.

The hedging relationship will be considered effective if the following three requirements are met:

1) There is an economic relationship between the hedged item and the hedging instrument.
2) The effect of credit risk does not dominate the value changes that result from that economic relationship.
3) The hedge ratio of the hedging relationship is the same as that resulting from the quantity of hedged item that the entity actually hedges and the quantity of the hedging instrument that the entity actually uses to hedge that quantity of hedged item. The hedge ratio should not be intentionally weighted to create ineffectiveness.

Regarding the first hedging relationship, whether there is an economic relationship between the hedged item and the hedging instrument will be assessed on a qualitative basis.

Regarding the second hedging relationship, whether there is an economic relationship between the hedged item and the hedging instrument will be assessed on a quantitative basis using the scenario analysis method. On each assessment date, the change in fair value of both the hedged item and the hedging instrument will be compared under two scenarios in which the Brent crude oil spot price of the risk being hedged will be shifted upwards and downwards by 10%.

11.9.5 Hedge Effectiveness Assessment Performed at the Start of the Hedging Relationship

First Hedging Relationship Regarding the first hedging relationship, the hypothetical derivative was a jet fuel swap with critical terms identical to those of hedging instrument 1. In theory the fixed price of the hypothetical derivative should have taken into account that the "perfect hedge" would involve a credit risk-free counterparty, resulting in an immaterially higher fixed price (e.g., USD 900.10 per tonne) as the credit and debit valuation adjustments would be zero. In practice, due to the hedge's short-term tenor and the immateriality of the CVA, the entity assumed that the hypothetical derivative's fixed price was identical to that of the hedging instrument (i.e., USD 900 per tonne). Because the critical terms of both the hypothetical derivative and the hedging instrument matched, the entity concluded that the changes in the fair value of the hedged item and the hedging instrument generally moved in opposite directions, and hence that an economic relationship existed between the hedged item and the hedging instrument.

The assessment also included the determination of the relationship hedge ratio and the identification of the sources of potential ineffectiveness.

Regarding the hedge ratio for the first hedging relationship, ABC concluded that quantity necessary to hedge 1 tonne of jet fuel uplift was 1 tonne of jet fuel of the hedging instrument. As a result the hedge ratio was set to 1:1.

ABC identified the following as the main sources of potential ineffectiveness: firstly, a significant deterioration in the creditworthiness of the counterparty to the hedging instrument (Megabank); and secondly, a change in the (timing of) highly probable forecasted quantities and actual uplift of jet fuel by the entity below the hedging instrument notional.

Second Hedging Relationship Regarding the second hedging relationship, the hypothetical derivative was a crude oil swap with the following terms:

Hypothetical derivative terms	
Trade date	1 April 20X5
Counterparties	ABC Airlines and credit risk-free counterparty
Effective date	1 October 20X5
Maturity	31 March 20X7
Notional quantity	3,595,500 bbl for the 9-month period from October 20X5 to June 20X6 (i.e., 399,500 bbl per month) 719,100 bbl for the 9-month period from July 20X6 to March 20X7 (i.e., 79,900 bbl per month)
Calculation period	Quarterly during the term of the transaction
Fixed price payer	ABC Airlines
Fixed price	USD 99.00 per bbl
Floating price payer	Counterparty

Hypothetical derivative terms	
Commodity reference price	The closing price of the first nearby futures contract of Brent crude oil as quoted in USD/bbl on the International Petroleum Exchange
Floating price	The unweighted arithmetic mean of the commodity reference price for each successive day of the calculation period during which such prices are quoted
Payment date(s)	The last day of the calculation period
Pricing date(s)	Each commodity business day from and including 1-Oct-X5 up to and including 31-Mar-X7

When designating a risk component as a hedged item, the hedge accounting requirements apply to that risk component in the same way as they apply to other hedged items that are not risk components. For example, the qualifying criteria apply, including that the hedging relationship must meet the hedge effectiveness requirements, and any hedge ineffectiveness must be measured and recognised.

To assess whether there was an economic relationship between the hedged item and the hedging instrument that gave rise to offset, a scenario analysis (see Figure 11.16) was performed by measuring the cumulative change in the fair value of the hypothetical derivative and the hedging instrument (i.e., the string of futures contracts) under two scenarios:

- Under a first scenario, the price of the first nearby futures contract of Brent crude oil in 6 months' time was assumed to have increased by 10% to from USD 97.4 per barrel to USD 107.1 per barrel. The cumulative change in fair value of the hedging instrument over that of the hypothetical derivative resulted in a degree of offset of 104% (= 39.1 mn/37.6 mn).
- Under a second scenario, the price of the first nearby futures contract of Brent crude oil in 6 months' time was assumed to have declined by 10% to from USD 97.4 per barrel to USD 87.7 per barrel. The cumulative change in fair value of the hedging instrument over that of the hypothetical derivative resulted in a degree of offset of 96% (= <42.4 mn>/<44.3 mn>).

Based on the results of the scenario analysis, ABC concluded that an economic relationship existed between the hedged item and the hedging instrument.

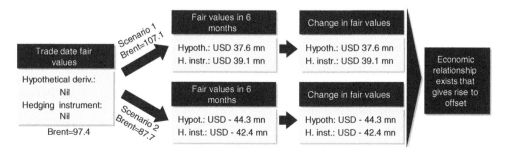

FIGURE 11.16 Economic relationship assessment for the second hedging relationship at hedging relationship inception.

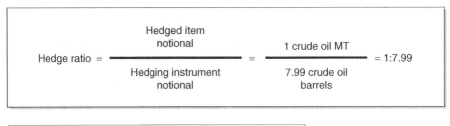

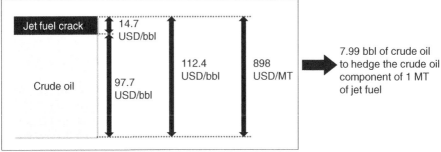

FIGURE 11.17   Hedge ratio estimation for the second hedging relationship performed at its inception.

The assessment also included the determination of the relationship hedge ratio and the identification of the sources of potential ineffectiveness.

Regarding the hedge ratio for the second hedging relationship and based on the spot prices of jet fuel and crude oil (see Figure 11.17), ABC concluded that the quantity necessary to hedge the crude oil component of 1 tonne of jet fuel was 7.99 (= 898/112.4) barrels of crude oil. As a result the hedge ratio was set to 1:7.99.

ABC identified the following as the main sources of potential ineffectiveness: firstly, a significant deterioration in the creditworthiness of the counterparty to the hedging instrument (the ICE Futures Exchange); and secondly, a change in the (timing of) highly probable forecasted quantities and actual uplift of jet fuel by the entity below the hedging instrument notional.

ABC concluded that both hedges qualified for hedge accounting as they met all the qualifying criteria (see Figure 11.18):

- The forecast purchases of jet fuel, and the jet fuel swap and the crude oil futures were an eligible hedged item and hedging instruments, respectively.
- There was a formal designation and documentation of the hedges.
- There was an economic relationship between the hedged item and the hedging instruments that gave rise to offset.
- Despite ABC being exposed to Megabank through the jet fuel swap and the initial margin posted to the ICE to secure the crude oil futures contracts, the jet fuel's short-term tenor and the ICE's strong credit standing led ABC to conclude that the effect of credit did not dominate the hedge fair value changes.

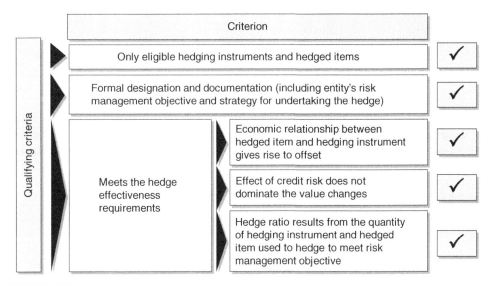

FIGURE 11.18 Effectiveness assessment results at inception.

- The hedge ratio resulted from the quantity of hedging instruments and hedged item used to hedge to meet risk management objectives, and it did not attempt to avoid recognising ineffectiveness.

There were other effectiveness assessments performed at each reporting date. The processes followed by ABC were very similar to that at hedge inception. They have been omitted to avoid unnecessary repetition.

11.9.6 Fair Valuations and Accounting Entries on 30 June 20X5

Suppose that ABC reported its financial statements on a half-yearly basis, on 30 June and 31 December.

Accounting Entries Related to Fuel Consumption Each day ABC consumed 3,280 tonnes of jet fuel (i.e., 100,000 tonnes per month). Each tonne consumed was priced using the jet fuel spot price (i.e., the arithmetic mean of the high and low prices for jet fuel published under the heading "CIF NWE/Basis ARA" as quoted in Platts European Marketscan) prevailing on the loading day plus USD 36 per tonne. At the end of each month ABC paid the suppliers a cash amount representing the monthly consumption.

Suppose that the average spot price during the period from 1 April 20X5 to 30 June 20X5 was 975.00 per tonne and that the jet fuel purchased was directly loaded onto ABC's airplanes for immediate consumption, so that no inventory was held. The accounting entries on 30 June 20X5 related to the jet fuel consumption during this period (300,000 tonnes at USD 975.00 plus 36.00 per tonne) were as follows (in USD):

Jet fuel cost (Profit or loss)	303,300,000	
Cash (Asset)		303,300,000

Fair Valuation and Accounting Entries Related to the Jet Fuel Swap Recall that hypothetical derivative 1 was a jet fuel swap with terms identical to those of the contracted jet fuel swap but without any counterparty credit risk. The main terms of hedging instrument 1 were as follows:

Hedging instrument	Notional	Fixed price	Expiry date
Jet fuel swap	600,000 tonnes	USD 900/tonne	30-Sep-X5

Therefore, the jet fuel swap had three periods already settled (corresponding to 30 April, 31 May and 30 June 20X5) and three upcoming settlement periods outstanding (corresponding to 31 July, 30 August and 30 September 20X5). The credit risk-free fair valuation of the jet fuel swap on 30 June 20X5, assuming that the then prevailing swap rate was USD 1,020 per tonne, was as follows:

Settlement date	Market swap rate	Jet fuel swap rate	Interest rate	Days from 30-Jun-X5	Expected settlement amount	Present value
31-Jul-X5	1,020	900	5%	31	12 mn	11,949,000
30-Aug-X5 *(1)*	1,020	900	5.10%	61	12 mn *(2)*	11,897,000 *(3)*
30-Sep-X5	1,020	900	5.20%	91	12 mn	11,844,000
				Total	36 mn	35,690,000

Notes:
(1) Assuming 31-Aug-X5 is a non-business day
(2) $12,000,000 = [100,000 \times (1,020 - 900)]$
(3) $11,897,000 = [12,000,000 /(1 + 5.10\% \times 61/360)]$

The change in fair value of the hypothetical derivative was thus a gain of 35,690,000, as its initial fair value was nil.

USD 12 million was the expected credit risk-free settlement amount to be received each remaining month by ABC under the jet swap. ABC had to subtract the CVA. Let us go over the CVA calculation for the 31-Sep-X5 settlement amount. Recall from Chapter 3 that the exponential CDS default method was as follows:

$$CVA = \text{Credit risk - free settlement amount} \times PD \times LGD$$

$$PD = 1 - \exp\left(\frac{-CDS \times Maturity}{LGD}\right)$$

where PD is the probability of default, CDS is the credit default swap spread or bond spread (in our case 1-, 2- and 3-month CDS protection on Megabank was trading at 30 basis points), LGD is the loss given default (in our case LGD was assumed to be 45%, constant over the remaining life of the swap) and Maturity is the time to settlement date, in years (in our case this is 91 days out of 365, or 0.25). Therefore PD was 0.17% (= $1 - \exp(-0.003 \times 0.25/0.45)$). The CVA was USD 9,000 (=12,000,000 × 0.17% × 45%).

The fair valuation of the jet fuel swap on 30 June 20X5, including CVA, was as follows:

Settlement date	Market swap rate	Jet fuel swap rate	Interest rate	Days from 30-Jun-X5	Expected settlement amount	CVA	Present value
31-Jul-X5	1,020	900	5%	31	12 mn	3,000	11,946,000
30-Aug-X5	1,020	900	5.10%	61	12 mn	6,000 *(1)*	11,891,000 *(2)*
30-Sep-X5	1,020	900	5.20%	91	12 mn	9,000	11,835,000
				Total	36 mn		35,672,000

Notes:
(1) 6,000 = 12,000,000 × [1 − exp((−0.003 × (61/365)/0.45)]× 0.45
(2) 11,891,000 = [(12,000,000 − 6,000)/(1 + 5.10% × 61/360)]

The change in fair value of the jet swap – hedging instrument 1 – from inception until the reporting date was then USD 35,672,000, as its initial fair value was nil.

The effective part of this fair value change was USD 35,672,000, the minimum of the fair value change of the hypothetical derivative (USD 35,690,000) and that of the hedging instrument (USD 35,672,000). The effective part was recognised in the cash flow hedge reserve of OCI.

The ineffective part was nil, the difference between the fair value change of the hedging instrument (USD 35,672,000) and the effective part (USD 35,672,000 as well). The ineffective part would have been recognised in profit or loss.

The accounting entries to record the change in fair value of the jet fuel swap were as follows (in USD):

Jet fuel swap (Asset)	35,672,000	
Cash flow hedge reserve (OCI)		35,672,000

On the last day of each month (i.e., 30 April 20X5, 31 May 20X5 and 30 June 20X5) ABC and Megabank settled the jet fuel swap. The settlement amounts totalled USD 22.5 million:

Period start	Period end	Average jet fuel	Settlement amount
1-Apr-X5	30-Apr-X5	939	3,900,000
1-May-X5	31-May-X5	978	7,800,000
1-Jun-X5	30-Jun-X5	1,008	10,800,000
	Total		22,500,000

Cash (Asset)	22,500,000	
Jet fuel cost (Profit or loss)		22,500,000

This amount was recognised in profit or loss ("jet fuel cost") rather than adjusting an inventory account (i.e., a basis adjustment), as the jet fuel purchased went straight into ABC's airplanes rather than into storage.

Fair Valuation of the Crude Oil Hypothetical Derivative The hypothetical derivative was an 18-month crude oil swap, with quarterly settlement periods, starting on 1 October 20X5, and with a USD 99 per barrel swap rate. Suppose that the crude oil swap rate prevailing on 30 June 20X5 for an 18-month swap forward starting on 1 October 20X5 was USD 113 per barrel. The fair valuation of the hypothetical derivative was as follows:

Settlement date	Notional (bbl)	Market swap rate	Hyp. der. rate	Interest rate	Days/years from 30-Jun-X5	Expected settlement amount	Present value
31-Dec-X5	1,198,500	113	99	5.30%	183 D	16,779,000	16,339,000
31-Mar-X6	1,198,500	113	99	5.40%	274 D	16,779,000 *(1)*	16,117,000 *(2)*
30-Jun-X6	1,198,500	113	99	5.50%	365 D	16,779,000	15,893,000
30-Sep-X6	239,700	113	99	5.60%	1.25 Y	3,355,800	3,135,000
31-Dec-X6	239,700	113	99	5.70%	1.5 Y	3,355,800	3,088,000 *(3)*
31-Mar-X7	239,700	113	99	5.80%	1.75 Y	3,355,800	3,041,000
						Total	57,613,000

Notes:
(1) $16,779,000 = [1,198,500 \times (113 - 99)]$
(2) $16,117,000 = [16,779,000 / (1 + 5.40\% \times 274/360)]$
(3) $3,088,000 = [3,355,800/(1 + 5.70\%)^{1.5}]$

Therefore, the change in fair value of the hypothetical derivative during the period was a USD 57,613,000 gain.

Fair Valuation and Accounting Entries Related to the Crude Oil Futures On 1 April 20X5 (the start date of the hedging relationship) the main terms of the initial crude oil hedging instruments were as follows:

Hedging instrument	Notional	Price	Expiry date
Crude oil futures	1,198,500 bbl	USD 98/bbl	15-Dec-X5
Crude oil futures	1,198,500 bbl	USD 98.3/bbl	15-Mar-X6
Crude oil futures	1,198,500 bbl	USD 98.6/bbl	15-Jun-X6
Crude oil futures	239,700 bbl	USD 99/bbl	15-Sep-X6
Crude oil futures	239,700 bbl	USD 99.3/bbl	15-Dec-X6
Crude oil futures	239,700 bbl	USD 99.7/bbl	15-Mar-X7

The fair valuation of the string of futures contracts on 30 June 20X5, assuming CVA to be insignificant as the counterparty was an exchange and the position was margined, was as follows:

Settlement date	Notional (bbl)	Market futures rate	Traded futures rate	Interest rate	Days/years from 30-Jun-X5	Expected settlement amount	Present value
15-Dec-X5	1,198,500	112.1	98	5.30%	183 D	16,899,000	16,456,000
15-Mar-X6	1,198,500	112.5	98.3	5.40%	274 D	17,019,000 (1)	16,347,000 (2)
15-Jun-X6	1,198,500	112.8	98.6	5.50%	365 D	17,019,000	16,120,000
15-Sep-X6	239,700	113.1	99	5.60%	1.25 Y	3,380,000	3,157,000
15-Dec-X6	239,700	113.3	99.3	5.70%	1.5 Y	3,356,000	3,088,000 (3)
15-Mar-X7	239,700	113.5	99.7	5.80%	1.75 Y	3,332,000	3,019,000
						Total	58,187,000

Notes:
(1) $17,019,000 = [1,198,500 \times (112.5 - 98.3)]$
(2) $16,347,000 = [17,019,000 / (1 + 5.40\% \times 274/360)]$
(3) $3,088,000 = [3,356,000 / (1 + 5.70\%)^{1.5}]$

Due to the rolling hedging strategy, in which each quarter a crude oil futures contract was replaced with a 3-month jet fuel swap, ABC kept a record of the cash flow hedge reserve amounts related to each futures contract separately:

Futures settlement date	Futures change in fair value	Hyp. der. Change in fair value	Effective part	Ineffective part
15-Dec-X5	16,456,000	16,339,000	16,339,000	117,000
15-Mar-X6	16,347,000	16,117,000	16,117,000	230,000
15-Jun-X6	16,120,000	15,893,000	15,893,000	227,000
15-Sep-X6	3,157,000	3,135,000	3,135,000	22,000
15-Dec-X6	3,088,000	3,088,000	3,088,000	0
15-Mar-X7	3,019,000	3,041,000	3,019,000	0
		Total	57,591,000	596,000

The effective and ineffective parts of the change in fair value of the crude oil future were recorded in OCI and profit or loss respectively. The accounting entries to record the change in fair value of the crude oil futures were as follows:

Crude oil futures (Asset)	58,187,000	
Cash flow hedge reserve (OCI)		57,591,000
Other financial income (Profit or loss)		596,000

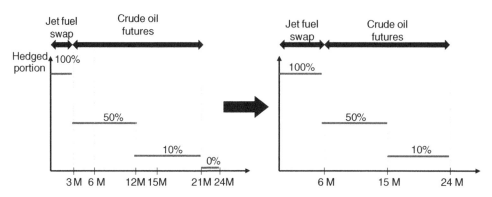

FIGURE 11.19   Hedge rollover strategy on 30 June 20X5.

Hedge Adjustment to Maintain Rolling Hedging Strategy   On 30 June 20X5 ABC's hedging strategy had the profile shown in Figure 11.19 (left). Because at the end of each quarter ABC's target hedging profile was as shown in Figure 11.19 (right) ABC had to do the following:

1) Replace the crude oil futures contracts expiring on 15 December 20X5 with a 3-month jet fuel swap with a notional of 100,000 tonnes per month (i.e., a total notional of 300,000 tonnes). Thus, ABC sold all its 15 December 20X5 crude oil futures contracts, locking in a USD 16,456,000 gain. The jet fuel swap had a start date of 1 October 20X5, a maturity date of 31 December 20X5, and a USD 1,023 per tonne swap rate.
2) Purchase an additional 958,800 bbl (= 1,198,500 – 239,700) of crude oil futures contracts expiring on 15 September 20X6 at USD 113.1 per barrel. The overall position crude oil futures position expiring on this date became 1,198,500 bbl at an average price of USD 110.30 (=239,700 bbl at USD 99/bbl and 958,800 bbl at USD 113.1/bbl).
3) Purchase 239,700 bbl of crude oil futures contracts expiring on 15 June 20X7 at USD 113.7 per barrel.

The accounting entries to record the sale of the crude oil futures expiring on 15 December 20X5 were as follows (in reality, due to the daily margining mechanism, any daily gain/loss was realised by adjusting the margin amount posted by ABC at the exchange, but to keep the calculations simple I have assumed a lump-sum receipt from the ICE on 30 June 20X5):

Cash (Asset)	16,456,000	
Crude oil futures (Asset)		16,456,000

The new 3-month jet fuel swap and the newly purchased futures contracts remained off the balance sheet as I assume they were traded at market rates (i.e., their initial fair value was nil).

Following the execution of the rollover strategy the outstanding hedging instruments as of 30 June 20X5 were as follows:

Hedging instrument	Notional	Price	Expiry date
Jet fuel swap	300,000 tonnes	USD 900/tonne	30-Sep-X5
Jet fuel swap	300,000 tonnes	USD 1,023/tonne	31-Dec-X5
Crude oil futures	1,198,500 bbl	USD 98.3/bbl	15-Mar-X6
Crude oil futures	1,198,500 bbl	USD 98.6/bbl	15-Jun-X6
Crude oil futures	1,198,500 bbl	USD 110.3/bbl	15-Sep-X6
Crude oil futures	239,700 bbl	USD 99.3/bbl	15-Dec-X6
Crude oil futures	239,700 bbl	USD 99.7/bbl	15-Mar-X7
Crude oil futures	239,700 bbl	USD 113.7/bbl	15-Jun-X7

Additionally on 30 June 20X5, ABC had to recalculate the hedge ratio, using a process similar to that of 1 April 20X5.

The fair valuations and accounting entries on the subsequent reporting dates followed a similar process and have been omitted to avoid unnecessary repetition.

11.9.7 Concluding Remarks

In this case, the benchmark variables used to set the purchased jet fuel price and that of the jet fuel swap were identical – the CIF NWE/Basis ARA jet fuel price. It is not uncommon for European airlines to purchase jet fuel at prices linked to variables (e.g., NWE barges FOB Rotterdam jet fuel price) different from that of the hedging instrument. For example, some airports price relative to a CIF benchmark price (which excludes transport costs), whereas other airports rely on a FOB benchmark price (which includes transport costs). Having different benchmark variables would mean that the hypothetical derivative was different from the hedging instrument, bringing another layer of operational complexity.

Similarly, while jet fuel was a standardised product not dependent on which particular crude oil was processed by a particular refinery, the benchmark jet fuel crack spread derivatives market in the geographical area in which ABC operated was indexed to Brent crude oil. Moreover, ABC operated in a geographical area in which Brent was the crude oil benchmark. This meant that if, for example, ABC used crude oil futures based on WTI crude oil as the hedging instrument of the crude oil component, changes in the price differential between Brent crude oil and WTI crude oil would cause hedge ineffectiveness. In other words, the hypothetical derivative would be linked to Brent crude oil, while the hedging instrument would be linked to WTI crude oil.

CHAPTER 12

Hedging Inflation Risk

This chapter covers the main issues affecting inflation risk hedging. Inflation-linked contracts are an integral part of the day-to-day business of many industries. For example, inflation may have a significant impact on the profitability and competitive position of highway companies. Inflation-linked instruments make it possible to manage inflation risk.

Before I address the accounting effects of inflation hedging decisions, I provide a basic understanding of the inflation markets.

12.1 INFLATION MARKETS – MAIN PARTICIPANTS AND INDICES

This section introduces the reader to the inflation markets by presenting an overview of the market's main participants and indices.

12.1.1 Inflation Market Participants

Inflation markets attract a diverse group of participants. In general, these participants can be categorised as inflation payers or receivers (see Figure 12.1).

Inflation Payers Inflation payers are typically entities with direct or indirect inflation-linked revenues. Inflation is paid predominantly for the purpose of creating financial expenses that match these revenues. Inflation payers include the following:

- **Sovereigns**. Theoretically, paying inflation can smooth the cash flows of governments as a substantial proportion of governments' incomes are at least partially inflation-linked. For example, value added taxes on gasoline are a function of the price and demand for this commodity. By matching the mix of income and payments, a government can reduce the volatility of its cash flows and, in theory at least, reduce the need to adjust its fiscal policy. In practice sovereigns with large borrowing requirements are the largest issuers of inflation-linked bonds tapping an investor base different from that of fixed rate and floating rate bonds.

- **Utility and infrastructure companies.** These typically have pricing structures that are statutorily linked to inflation.
- **Real estate companies**. Rents on commercial investment properties are often periodically adjusted to incorporate inflation. Real estate companies may want to shed some of their revenues' natural exposure to inflation risk by paying inflation.

Inflation Receivers   Inflation receivers have typically been entities aiming to achieve a specific return over inflation and entities incurring costs (e.g., wages) linked to inflation. Inflation receivers include asset managers and pension funds with specific inflation benchmarks and pension funds with pension schemes' liabilities linked to inflation.

- **Pension funds and insurance companies**. Often these institutional investors offer additional retirement coverage investments and are interested in real returns rather than nominal returns. Investing in inflation-paying securities on their assets side can substantially reduce their liabilities' natural exposure to inflation risk.
- **Asset managers**. Inflation-linked funds offer investors an asset class that traditionally has shown low correlation to other asset classes such as equities and fixed rates.
- **Retail investors**. Although most individuals invest in inflation-linked cash flows via their pension schemes, many wealthy investors prefer to additionally invest directly in inflation-linked securities.

Other Market Participants   There are other market participants that do not have a natural exposure to either pay or receive inflation. These include investment banks taking inflation positions to accommodate their clients' inflation hedging needs and hedge funds willing to pay (or receive) inflation when in their view inflation expectations are too high (or low).

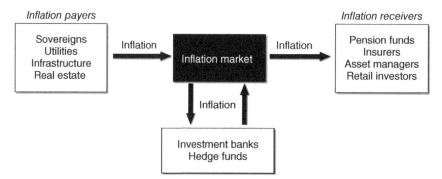

FIGURE 12.1   Inflation market – main participants.

12.1.2 Measuring Inflation from Indices

Any inflation-linked instrument needs a reference measure of inflation – a so-called **inflation index**. This subsection explains what an inflation figure represents and how it is measured from inflation indices.

A (retail) inflation index tries to measure the price of a representative basket of consumer goods and services in a specific country. Every month officials in that country publish a new index level, based on the prices of a basket encompassing hundreds of components. The components of inflation indices and their weights vary from country to country, and include transportation, food and non-alcoholic beverages, clothing and footwear, education, restaurants and hotels, alcohol and tobacco, housing and household goods.

Whilst housing represents one of the largest sources of expenditure for most people, it is much harder to observe than other areas of the index that are directly purchased. For example, the housing component of the UK's Retail Price Index (RPI) tries to incorporate all costs incurred by a homeowner, from mortgage costs to depreciation and council tax.

In itself the level of an inflation index is meaningless, unless it is compared with a previous level. When the price levels of two dates of the same inflation index are compared, a measurement of the increase (or decrease) of the prices in that economy between the two dates is obtained (what is commonly termed as **inflation**).

A base date is chosen at which the value of the index is set to, say, 100. An index value represents the value of the underlying basket at a point in time (i.e., a certain month/year) assuming that the basket was worth 100 on the base date.

Suppose that the levels of an inflation index associated with March 20X0 and March 20X1 were 130.15 and 135.66, respectively. The annualised inflation rate between those two periods was therefore 4.23% (= 135.66/130.15 − 1).

Suppose further that the officials in the country to which the inflation index related reported an inflation figure related for April 20X1 of 4.05%. The published value of the index corresponding to April 20X1 was 136.12 (= 135.66 × (1 + 4.05%/12)).

In general, the change in purchasing power between times 0 and t is given by $\text{Index}_t / \text{Index}_0$, where Index_t is the value of the index at time t and Index_0 is its value at time 0.

12.1.3 Main Inflation Indices

In this subsection I briefly describe the most important inflation indices.

Eurozone Inflation Index   The euro-area inflation derivatives market is arguably the most liquid, active and transparent inflation market. The benchmark index for the eurozone is the Harmonised Index of Consumer Prices (HICP) which measures the price levels of the different eurozone countries. The HICP is a weighted sum of the euro-area countries' HICP indices, weighted to take into account the share of GDP of each country in the overall GDP of the eurozone. The country weights are adapted on an annual basis based on GDP. The item weights of the HICP also vary as a consequence of varying country weights due to the fact that the individual HICP indices have varying item weights. As countries accede to the monetary union, they will be included in the index. Each member state uses the same methodology.

The unrevised HICP excluding tobacco (HICPxT) is used as the reference index in most bonds and derivatives linked to European inflation. HICP is published monthly by Eurostat (www.europa.eu.int/comm/eurostat/). The base year for HICP is 1996, meaning that the average index value of HICP equalled 100 during 1996. HICP is typically published 2 weeks after the end of the month. For instance, the HICPxT index value for March is announced on about 15 April. The index announced is called the unrevised index. Eurostat might revise the index if after gathering more data its officials believe their initial announcement was inaccurate.

Although the value of the index can be revised, the unrevised version is used in both the cash and the derivatives market. The HICPxT index is published by Bloomberg under the ticker CPTFEMU<Index>.

France   When France originally decided to issue inflation-linked debt, there was considerable debate about which index the issues should be linked to. A national index was likely to be a better match to the government's liabilities, while the eurozone HICPxT index appealed to international investors. Given the fact that the latter index was relatively new, the non-seasonally adjusted French Consumer Price Index (CPI) was chosen. The index for each month is published by INSEE (www.insee.fr/en/indicateur/indic_cons/indic_cons.asp) on about the 22nd of the subsequent month. Again the unrevised index is used for both bonds and derivatives. The French CPI is published by Bloomberg under the ticker FRCPXTOB<Index>. The base year is 1998.

United Kingdom   In the UK market, inflation-linked securities are linked to the RPI. The unrevised version is used for inflation swaps. The Office for National Statistics (www.statistics.gov.uk/) publishes the RPI index value for each month on about the 15th of the following month. The Bloomberg ticker for RPI is UKRPI<Index>. The base reference date is January 1987.

United States   The All Items Consumer Price Index for all urban consumers (CPI-U) published by the Bureau of Labor Statistics is used as the reference index for most US inflation-linked bonds and derivatives. The index can be found on Bloomberg under the ticker CPURNSA<Index>. The base is given by the average index of 1982–1984.

12.1.4 Components of a Bond Yield and the Fisher Equation

The value of a debt instrument is driven by its associated yield, which for a currency is a function of the term to maturity of the instrument. Normally for an issuer and a currency, the longer the term to maturity, the higher the yield. The yield of a debt instrument has a number of components (see Figure 12.2):

- A **credit risk premium** that takes into account the creditworthiness of the issuer. Normally, longer-term maturities are viewed to have more credit risk than shorter-term maturities.
- A **liquidity risk premium** that takes into account how deep the market is for the debt instrument. Normally, longer-term maturities are viewed to have more liquidity risk than shorter-term maturities.
- A **nominal interest rate** which represents a risk-free rate adjusted for expectations and risks related to future inflation during the term of the debt instrument. In theory all bonds of all issuers with the same term to maturity and denominated in the same currency have an identical nominal interest rate.

In turn, a nominal interest rate can be broken down into two parts:

- A **real interest rate** which represents the interest rate in an economy after the effects of inflation have been removed.
- A **breakeven inflation** component. The breakeven inflation represents the **expected inflation** during the term of the bond and a premium that compensates investors for the risk of potential changes in inflation expectations.

The Fischer Equation   Because the yield and the sum of the credit risk premium and the liquidity premium of a bond can be directly observed from active markets (e.g., independent quotes may be obtained in the market for credit derivatives), nominal interest rates can be inferred. An interesting debate within the economic community concerns whether real interest rates can be reliably determined. The **Fisher equation** provides a relationship between nominal interest rates, real interest rates and inflation:

$$(1 + \text{nominal interest rate}) = (1 + \text{real interest}) \times (1 + \text{inflation})$$

This formula can be approximated as:

$$n \approx r + i$$

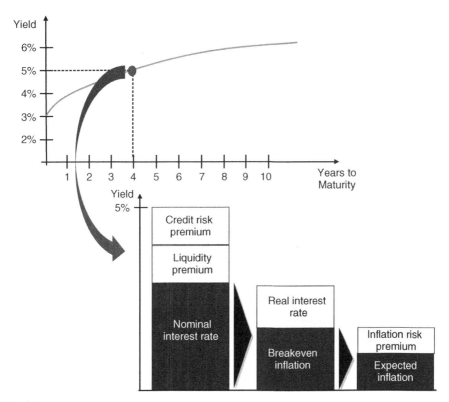

FIGURE 12.2   Components of a bond yield.

where n is the nominal interest rate, r is the real interest rate, and i represents inflation expectations and inflation risk premium.

12.1.5 Breakeven Inflation

As noted previously, the breakeven inflation rate (BEI) in a bond's yield represents the sum of the expected inflation and the inflation risk premium, two components of nominal yields that on their own are not always easily quantifiable. Assuming an inflation risk premium much lower than the expected inflation, a BEI provides a rough measure of inflation expectations.

Assuming an inflation-linked bond (ILB) and a comparable fixed rate bond of the same issuer and liquidity, the BEI equals the difference between the yields of these bonds. If actual inflation is greater than breakeven inflation, the ILB is likely to outperform the fixed rate bond. If actual inflation is lower than breakeven inflation, the fixed rate bond is likely to outperform the ILB. In other words, breakeven inflation is the future inflation rate required for an ILB to achieve the same return as a comparable fixed rate bond, if held to maturity. Thus, investors who wish to take a view on the path of inflation have a choice. If they believe that inflation will be higher than the level priced in by the market, they will sell fixed rate bonds and buy ILBs. If lower, they will do the opposite.

12.2 INFLATION-LINKED BONDS

This section discusses the basics of inflation-linked bonds. It explains key concepts such as real rates and breakeven inflation. ILBs, sometimes known as "linkers" or "real bonds", are an attractive asset class for investors whose liabilities are linked to inflation, such as insurance companies and pension funds. ILBs are predominantly issued by governments and provide income and total return which adjusts to keep up with the pace of inflation. The UK was the first major market to issue these bonds in 1981 and the US government followed suit by issuing Treasury inflation-protected securities (TIPS) in 1997. Inflation-indexed government bonds are also available in many other countries including Australia, Canada, France, Germany, Italy and Sweden.

The main cash flows in a ILB are as follows (see Figure 12.3):

- On the issue date, the ILB investors pay the bond's initial notional to the issuer (or to the banks intermediating the issuance).

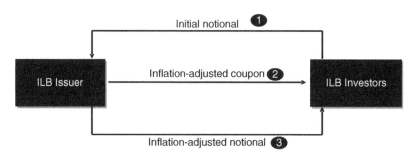

FIGURE 12.3   Inflation-linked bond cash flows.

- Periodically, the issuer pays to the investors a fixed coupon on an inflation-adjusted notional amount.
- At maturity, the issuer pays to the investors the initial notional adjusted for inflation.

A new ILB is typically issued with an initial notional and a real yield determined through the auction process. Imagine that on 1 January 20X0 a new ILB was issued with a real semiannual coupon of 2%, a initial notional of 100 and a 2-year maturity. The initial consumer price index ($Index_0$) was set at 200, the CPI for October 20W9, 3 months prior to the issue date.

Over time, the notional adjusts according to changes in the CPI from the time the bond is issued. In our example, the adjusted notional amount at time t equalled $100 \times Index_t/Index_0$, where $Index_t$ is the value of the CPI at time t. Thus, as time passes the redemption value increases in such a way as to keep its inflation-adjusted value at 100. In our example, the redemption amount at maturity was 105.55, calculated adjusting the initial notional of 100 for the change in inflation from its issue date (CPI was 200) to maturity (CPI was 211.1 in October 20X1), or $100 \times 211.11/200$. In theory, in a deflationary environment the principal repayment amount at maturity could decline below the initial notional. In practice, many ILBs guarantee a "deflation floor" with which they will repay at least the initial notional amount at maturity, no matter what the inflation environment.

The coupon paid in an ILB is the real coupon multiplied by the adjusted notional value. As a result, coupon payments increase over time in an inflationary environment and decrease in a deflationary environment. In our example, the ILB paid a semiannual coupon of 1% (= 2%/2) of the adjusted notional amount. Because the adjusted notional on 30 June 20X0 was 101.25, the semiannual coupon paid on that date was 1.01 (=101.25 × 2% /2).

The following table and Figure 12.4 summarise the main cash flows under the ILB.

	1-Jan-X0	30-Jun-X0	31-Dec-X0	30-Jun-X1	31-Dec-X1
Indext	200	202.5	205.3	208.4	211.1
Index0	200	200	200	200	200
Index/Index0		1.0125	1.0265	1.042	1.0555 (1)
Adj. notional	100	101.25	102.65	104.2	105.55 (2)
Coupon payment		1.01	1.03	1.04	1.06 (3)
Principal repayment					105.55 (4)
Total cash flow		1.01	1.03	1.04	106.61 (5)

Notes:
(1) $Index_t/Index_0 = 211.11/200$
(2) *Initial notional* × $Index_t/Index_0$= *100* × *1.0555*
(3) *Adjusted notional* × *Coupon rate/2 = 105.55 × 2%/2*
(4) *Adjusted notional at maturity date*
(5) *Coupon + Principal repayment = 1.06 + 105.55*

With the inflation-adjusted value of both the coupon and the notional always preserved, the bond hedged the risk of rising inflation. However, the hedge was slightly imperfect, since the inflation index lagged 3 months.

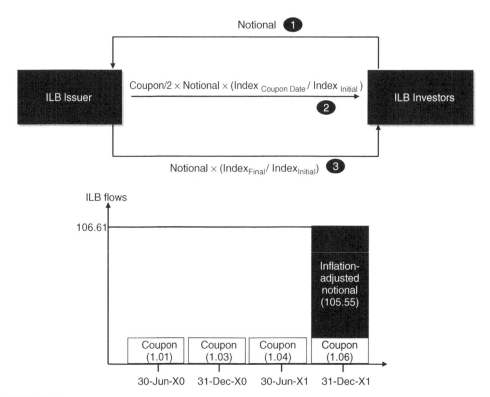

FIGURE 12.4   ILB cash flows.

The accreting nature of ILBs heightens the credit exposure of the investor to the bond issuer. Consequently, the longer the term of the ILB and the larger the inflation, the larger the credit exposure is.

The return on an ILB has two sources of yield: the real yield and a yield representing actual trailing inflation. ILBs are unique in that their real yields are clearly identifiable, and they provide a predictable real return.

12.3 INFLATION DERIVATIVES

The primary purpose of inflation derivatives is the transfer of inflation risk. The advantage of inflation derivative contracts over inflation bonds is that derivatives can be tailored to fit particular client demand more precisely than bonds. Their flexibility also allows them to replicate in derivative form the inflation risks embedded in other instruments such as standard cash instruments (i.e., inflation-linked bonds).

Inflation swaps are the most common inflation derivatives. An inflation swap is a bilateral contract involving the exchange of inflation-linked payments for predetermined fixed or floating payments. It is typically used to hedge inflation risk as it allows entities to swap inflation-linked payments for fixed payments, and vice versa. For example, an entity having inflation-linked revenue streams could swap fixed payments for inflation-linked payments over a predetermined period, effectively creating inflation-linked borrowing. There are a number of instruments that can be classified as inflation derivatives, ranging from zero-coupon inflation swaps to structured inflation products.

There are many types of periodic inflation swaps, and in Sections 12.3.1–12.3.3 I will describe the most common ones, which I have termed zero-coupon, non-cumulative periodic and cumulative periodic inflation swaps. In Section 12.3.4 I turn to inflation caps and floors.

12.3.1 Zero-Coupon Inflation Swaps

Zero-coupon inflation swaps are simple structures that account for a large proportion of the inflation derivatives market, due to their simplicity. These swaps provide a direct measurement of breakeven inflation.

A zero-coupon inflation swap is an agreement between two counterparties in which one party agrees to pay an inflation-linked flow versus a fixed amount, for a given notional amount and period of time. The only cash flows in a zero-coupon swap are paid at maturity (see Figure 12.5): a compounded fixed amount

$$\text{Notional} \times [(1 + X\%)^t - 1]$$

where $X\%$ is the market quoted zero-coupon rate, representing the expected average annual inflation rate over the period, and t is the number of years to maturity; and a realised inflation amount

$$\text{Notional} \times \left(\frac{\text{Index}_{\text{final}}}{\text{Index}_{\text{final}}} - 1 \right)$$

where $\text{Index}_{\text{Final}}$ and $\text{Index}_{\text{Initial}}$ are jointly defined by the payment date, start date and the lag, which is the number of months between the payment date and the month in which $\text{Index}_{\text{Final}}$ is observed. For example, if the payment date is in May, and the lag is 3 months, then $\text{Index}_{\text{Final}}$ is for the month of February.

The following table provides an example of the main terms in a 5-year zero-coupon inflation swap:

Zero-coupon inflation swap terms	
Trade date	28 October 20X2
Effective date	1 November 20X2
Maturity date	1 November 20X7 (5 years)
Notional	EUR 100 million
Party A receives from party B	Notional × [(1 + 2.50%)⁵ – 1], paid at maturity date
Party A pays to party B	Notional × [(Index$_{\text{Final}}$/Index$_{\text{Initial}}$) – 1], paid at maturity date
Index	HICPxT for the eurozone, non-revised, published by Eurostat. For information purposes only, this index is published on Bloomberg page CPTFEMU<Index>
Index$_{\text{Initial}}$	HICP corresponding to the month of August 20X2. Index$_{\text{Initial}}$ was set at 234.5
Index$_{\text{Final}}$	HICP corresponding to the month of August 20X7

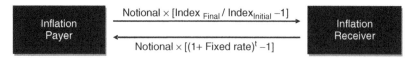

FIGURE 12.5   Zero-coupon inflation swap – cash flows.

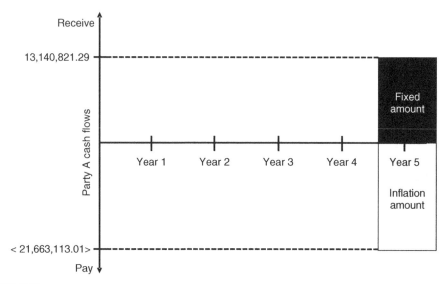

FIGURE 12.6   Zero-coupon inflation swap – cash flows.

Party A received the fixed amount and paid the inflation amount. The fixed rate was 2.50%, representing the expected annual inflation over the 5-year period. A realised annual inflation rate lower than 2.50%, would result in A receiving a settlement amount at maturity. Conversely, a realised annual inflation rate higher than 2.50% would result in A paying a settlement amount at maturity. The position of B was the opposite of that of A. Party A probably had inflation-linked revenues and through the zero-coupon inflation swap it was protecting itself against an annual European inflation rate lower than 2.50% over the next 5 years, while not benefiting from a potential rise in such inflation above 2.50%. Zero-coupon inflation swaps are also interesting for investors (like B) looking to protect an investment over a certain period against rising inflation rates.

Suppose that the HICP level corresponding to August 20X7 was 285.3. The settlement amount on 1 November 20X7 was calculated as follows: A was due to receive EUR 13,140,821.29 (= 100 mn × ((1 + 2.50%)^5 − 1)) from B, while A was due to pay EUR 21,663,113.01 (= 100 mn × (285.3/234.5 − 1)) to B. Therefore, A paid to B the difference, EUR 8,522,291.72 (= 21,663,113.01 − 13,140,821.29), as shown in Figure 12.6.

It is important to note that the accreting nature of zero-coupon inflation swaps heightens credit exposure, in the absence of other credit risk mitigants like a collateralised ISDA agreement. In our previous numerical example, A was expected to pay to B over EUR 8.5 million, a substantial amount relative to the notional amount.

12.3.2 Non-cumulative Periodic Inflation Swaps

A **periodic inflation swap** is an agreement between two counterparties in which one party agrees to periodically swap fixed payments (or floating payments linked to Libor/Euribor rates) for floating payments linked to an inflation rate, for a given notional amount and period of time.

In a **non-cumulative periodic inflation swap** the notional is not adjusted and as a result the periodic cash flows are calculated over the initial notional (see Figure 12.7), as follows. One party to the swap periodically pays a fixed amount (or a Euribor/Libor based amount)

$$\text{Notional} \times X\%$$

where $X\%$ is a fixed rate, representing the expected average annual inflation rate over the life of the swap. The other party to the swap periodically pays the realised inflation amount during the interest period

$$\text{Notional} \times \left(\frac{\text{Index}_t}{\text{Index}_{t-1}} - 1 \right)$$

where Index_t is the inflation index corresponding to the end date of the interest period (taking into account the time lag between such date and the month in which the inflation index is observed) and Index_{t-1} is the inflation index corresponding to the end date of the previous interest period.

The following table provides an example of the main terms of a 5-year non-cumulative inflation swap with a 3% fixed rate and a notional amount.

Periodic non-cumulative inflation swap terms	
Trade date	28 October 20X2
Effective date	1 November 20X2
Maturity date	1 November 20X7 (5 years)
Notional	EUR 100 million
Party A pays	Notional × 3.00%, paid annually on 1 November
Party B pays	Notional × [(Index$_t$/Index$_{t-1}$) – 1], paid annually on 1 November
Index	HICPxT for the eurozone, non-revised, published by Eurostat. For information purposes only, this index is published on Bloomberg page CPTFEMU<Index>
Index$_t$	HICP corresponding to the month of August of the year of the Party B payment date
Index$_{t-1}$	Index$_t$ corresponding to the previous payment date. For the initial payment date, Index$_{t-1}$ shall be Index$_{\text{Initial}}$
Index$_{\text{Initial}}$	234.5

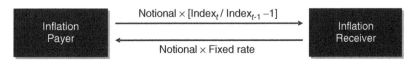

FIGURE 12.7 Non-cumulative inflation swap – cash flows.

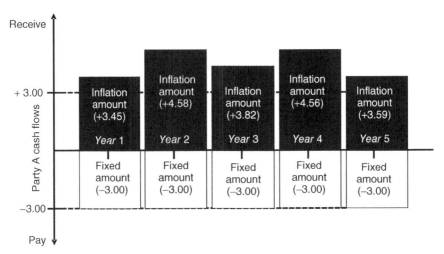

FIGURE 12.8   Non-cumulative periodic inflation swap – cash flows.

The following table provides a numerical example of the inflation swap settlement amounts, from party A's perspective, based on an assumed scenario of the inflation index (amounts in EUR millions). Because each year the annual inflation was larger than the 3% fixed rate, A received each year a settlement amount that represented the excess of the annual inflation relative to the 3% fixed rate (see Figure 12.8).

	1-Nov-X3	1-Nov-X4	1-Nov-X5	1-Nov-X6	1-Nov-X7
$Index_t$	242.6	253.7	263.4	275.4	285.3
$Index_{t-1}$	234.5	242.6	253.7	263.4	275.4
$Index_t/Index_{t-1} - 1$	0.0345	0.0458	0.0382	0.0456	0.0359
Inflation leg amount	3.45	4.58	3.82	4.56	3.59
Fixed leg amount	<3>	<3>	<3>	<3>	<3>
Settlement amount	**0.45**	**1.58**	**0.82**	**1.56**	**0.59**

12.3.3 Cumulative Periodic Inflation Swaps

In a **cumulative inflation swap** the notional on the inflation leg is adjusted and as a result the periodic cash flows are calculated over the initial notional (see Figure 12.9). A cumulative inflation swap is equivalent to a string of zero-coupon inflation swaps, as follows. One party to the swap periodically pays a fixed amount (or a Euribor/Libor based amount):

$$\text{Notional} \times [(1 + X\%)^t - 1]$$

where $X\%$ is a fixed rate. The other party periodically pays the realised inflation amount during the interest period:

$$\text{Notional} \times \left(\frac{Index_t}{Index_{Initial}} - 1 \right)$$

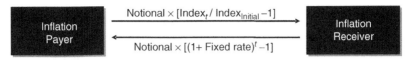

FIGURE 12.9 Cumulative periodic inflation swap – cash flows.

where $Index_t$ is the inflation index corresponding to the end date of the interest period (taking into account the time lag between such date and the month in which the inflation index is observed) and $Index_{Initial}$ is the inflation index corresponding to the effective date (taking into account the corresponding time lag).

The following table provides an example of the main terms in a 5-year cumulative inflation swap with a 3% fixed rate.

Periodic cumulative inflation swap terms	
Trade date	28 October 20X2
Effective date	1 November 20X2
Maturity date	1 November 20X7 (5 years)
Notional	EUR 100 million
Party A pays	Notional $\times [(1 + 3.00\%)^t - 1]$, paid annually on 1 November t: number of years between the effective date and party A payment date
Party B pays	Notional $\times [(Index_t/Index_{Initial}) - 1]$, paid annually each 1 November
Index	HICPxT for the eurozone, non-revised, published by Eurostat. For information purposes only, this index is published on Bloomberg page CPTFEMU<Index>
$Index_{Initial}$	HICP corresponding to the month of August 20X2 $Index_{Initial}$ was set at 234.5
$Index_t$	HICP corresponding to the month of August of the year of the party B payment date

The following table provides a numerical example of the inflation swap settlement amounts, from party A's perspective, based on an assumed scenario of the inflation index (amounts in EUR millions). Because each year the annual inflation was higher than the 3% fixed rate, A received each year a settlement amount that represented the excess of the cumulative annual inflation relative to the 3% fixed rate (see Figure 12.10). The compounding effect amplified the difference over time, resulting in an increasing settlement amount.

	1-Nov-X3	1-Nov-X4	1-Nov-X5	1-Nov-X6	1-Nov-X7
$Index_t$	242.6	253.7	263.4	275.4	285.3
$Index_{Initial}$	234.5	234.5	234.5	234.5	234.5
$Index_t/Index_{Initial} - 1$	0.034542	0.081876	0.123241	0.174414	0.216631
Inflation leg amount	3.45	8.19	12.32	17.44	21.66
Fixed leg amount	<3.00>	<6.09>	<9.27>	<12.55>	<15.93>
Settlement amount	0.45	2.10	3.05	4.89	5.73

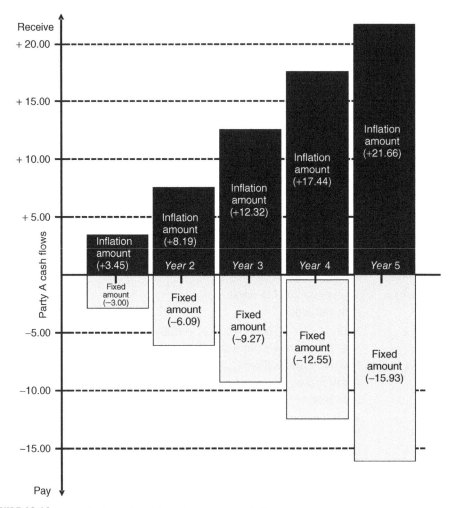

FIGURE 12.10 Cumulative periodic inflation swap – cash flows.

12.3.4 Inflation Caps and Floors

Besides swaps, options can also be traded on inflation indices. An **inflation cap** is an option (or a string of options, called caplets) that provides a cash flow equal to the difference between inflation and a pre-agreed strike rate if this difference is positive. An **inflation floor** is an option (or a string of options, called floorlets) that provides a cash flow equal to the difference between a pre-agreed strike rate and inflation if this difference is positive. Caps and floors play a natural role in hedges of an interval of inflation exposures. For instance, a floor on the principal is often included in inflation-linked bonds in order to protect investors against deflation and/or low inflation rates.

Cumulative or Zero-Coupon Inflation Caps and Floors

Before moving on to periodic caps and floors I cover the simplest of the inflation options: caps and floors on cumulative (also called zero-coupon) inflation. A cumulative inflation floor pays the difference with respect to a (compounded) strike in case inflation turns out to be lower than a pre-specified strike. Floors on cumulative inflation are often embedded in inflation-linked bonds or swaps where principal redemption is floored at par. For instance, all the US TIPS and French government OATis bonds have a redemption-protecting floor guaranteeing redemption equal to par. The following table highlights the main terms of a 3-year 1% cumulative inflation floor that protected the buyer against a 3-year average inflation (i.e., the cumulative inflation over 3 years) below 1%:

Cumulative inflation floor terms	
Trade date	28 October 20X2
Effective date	1 November 20X2
End date	1 November 20X5 (3 years)
Notional	EUR 100 million
Buyer	Party A
Up-front premium	Party A pays 0.21% of the notional (i.e., EUR 210,000) on the effective date
Party B pays	Notional $\times \max[(1+1.00\%)^3 - (\text{Index}_{Final}/\text{Index}_{Initial}), 0)]$, paid on end date
Index	HICPxT for the eurozone, non-revised, published by Eurostat. For information purposes only, this index is published on Bloomberg page CPTFEMU<Index>
$\text{Index}_{Initial}$	HICP corresponding to the month of August 20X2 $\text{Index}_{Initial}$ was set at 234.5
Index_{Final}	HICP corresponding to the month of August 20X5

The following table provides an example of the payoff under the floor after a deflationary 3-year period. In this example the average annual inflation was negative (−2.5%), and as a result, party A was compensated for the deficit relative to a 1% average inflation. Thus, on 1 November 20X5 party B paid EUR 10,365,000 to party A.

	1-Nov-X5
Index_{Final}	217.3
$\text{Index}_{Initial}$	234.5
$\text{Index}_{Final}/\text{Index}_{Initial}$	0.92665 *(1)*
$\max(1.01^3 - \text{Index}_{Final}/\text{Index}_{Initial}, 0)$	10.365% *(2)*
Party B payment to Party A (EUR)	10,365,000 *(3)*

Notes:
> *(1) 217.3/234.5*
> *(2) Maximum of $(1.01^3 - 0.92665)$ and zero*
> *(3) 10.365% × 100,000,000*

Periodic Inflation Caps and Floors In a periodic inflation cap (floor) the buyer is protected periodically against inflation exceeding (underperforming) a certain level, the cap rate (floor rate). A cap (floor) that has more than one exercise date is a combination of several single options called caplets (floorlets). The following table summarises the main terms of a 3-year 4%

On the effective date:

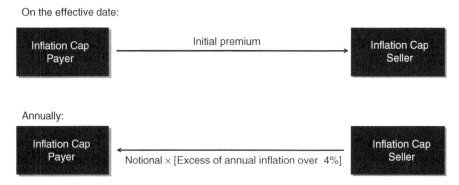

FIGURE 12.11 Annual inflation cap – cash flows.

inflation cap that protected the buyer against an annual inflation rate above 4% (see Figure 12.11). For the protection, party A paid on 1 November 20X2 a EUR 210,000 premium.

Annual inflation cap terms	
Trade date	28 October 20X2
Effective date	1 November 20X2
End date	1 November 20X5 (3 years)
Notional	EUR 100 million
Buyer	Party A
Up-front premium	Party A pays 0.21% of the notional (i.e., EUR 210,000) on the Effective date
Party B pays	Notional $\times$ max$[($Index$_t/$Index$_{t-1}) - (1+4.00\%), 0)]$
Party B payment dates	Every 1 November from, and including, 1 November 20X3 up to, and including, the end date
Index	HICPxT for the eurozone, non-revised, published by Eurostat. For information purposes only, this index is published on Bloomberg page CPTFEMU<Index>
Index$_{t-1}$	Index$_t$ corresponding to the party B previous payment date Index$_{t-1}$ for the party B first payment date was set at 234.5 (HICP corresponding to the month of August 20X2)
Index$_t$	HICP corresponding to the month of August of the year of the party B payment date

The following table provides an example of the payoffs under the cap. In this example the year-on-year inflation for the first year was 4.733% (= 245.6/234.5 – 1), and, as a result, the excess of the annual inflation over 4% was 0.733%. Thus, on 1 November 20X3 party B paid EUR 733,000 (i.e., the 0.733% excess inflation over the EUR 100 million notional) to party A. During the second year, annual inflation was 3.094% (= 253.2/245.6 – 1), below 4%, and therefore A did not receive any compensation under the cap. During the third year, annual inflation was 6.003% (= 268.4/253.2 − 1) exceeding 4%, and thus A received EUR 2,003,000 in compensation.

	1-Nov-X3	1-Nov-X4	1-Nov-X5
$Index_t$	245.6	253.2	268.4
$Index_{t-1}$	234.5	245.6	253.2
$Index_t/Index_{t-1}$	1.04733	1.03094	1.06003 *(1)*
$max(Index_t/Index_{t-1} − 1.04 , 0)$	0.733%	0%	2.003% *(2)*
Party B payment (EUR)	733,000	-0-	2,003,000 *(3)*

Notes:
> *(1) 268.4/253.2*
> *(2) Maximum of (1.06003 − 1.04) and zero*
> *(3) 2.003% × 100,000,000*

12.4 INFLATION RISK UNDER IFRS 9

This section explains some of the accounting issues when inflation is involved.

12.4.1 Hybrid Instruments

Suppose that ABC is Germany-based company with the EUR as its functional (and presentation) currency. ABC issued inflation-linked debt denominated in EUR in which payments of principal and interest are linked to an inflation index. The inflation link is not leveraged and the principal is protected.

Recall from Section 1.6 that when a financial liability encompasses a combination of a host contract and an embedded derivative (a "hybrid instrument"), the issuer needs to assess whether the embedded derivative should be accounted for separately. IFRS 9 does not require the separation of the embedded derivative (see Figure 1.7):

1) If the derivative does not qualify as a derivative if it were free-standing. In our example, the inflation-linked feature qualified as a derivative if it was separated from the liability; or
2) If the host contract is accounted for at fair value, with changes in fair value recorded in profit and loss. In our example, the host contract was recognised at amortised cost; or
3) If the economic characteristics and risks of the embedded derivative are closely related to those of the host contract. This was the key element affecting the assessment. Let us take a look to different inflation underlyings:

- **European** CPI. This inflation index is the one commonly used in the EUR currency economic environment. Therefore there was no need to separate (the instrument was treated as a liability in its entirety).
- **German** CPI. Same conclusion as for the European CPI if a sufficiently high correlation can be demonstrated between European and German inflation.
- **British** RPI. The inflation index relates to a different economic environment. Thus, ABC would need to split the bond into a host contract and a derivative.

In our example, the bond was principal protected. IFRS 9 does not address whether an inflation-linked bond not requiring separation must be principal protected to be eligible for amortised cost recognition. A prolonged deflationary economy may cause a principal unprotected bond to be redeemed below its initial nominal amount, and the accounting community regards the bond as having cash flows that are solely payments of principal and interest on the principal outstanding.

Also, in our example the inflation adjustment was not leveraged. Imagine that instead the adjustment each year was for three times the CPI. In this case, the embedded inflation derivative would be accounted for separately. However, it is less clear whether the separation is the three-times adjustment or just the leveraged part (i.e., a two-times adjustment). However, it is generally understood that splitting the embedded derivative into two derivatives is not generally permitted under IFRS 9, and as a result, the full inflation adjustment (i.e., three times CPI) should be separated.

12.4.2 Hedging Inflation as a Risk Component

Can the inflation component (or "risk portion") of a fixed or variable interest rate instrument be designated as the risk being hedged in a hedging relationship? Whilst the main requirement is that the portion of a risk has to be identifiable and separately measurable, answering this question may require careful judgement of relevant facts and circumstances.

In principle, inflation may only be hedged when changes in inflation constitute a contractually specified portion of cash flows of a recognised financial instrument. This may be the case where an entity acquires or issues inflation-linked debt. In such circumstances, the entity has a cash flow exposure to changes in future inflation that may be cash flow hedged.

In principle, an entity is not permitted to designate an inflation component which is not contractually specified. For example, IFRS 9 does not deem separately identifiably and reliably measurable the inflation component of issued or acquired fixed rate debt in a fair value hedge. However, for financial instruments, IFRS 9 introduces a rebuttable presumption, meaning that there are limited cases under which it is possible to identify a risk component for inflation and designate that inflation component in a hedging relationship, even though the inflation component is not contractually specified. The assessment is based on the particular circumstances in the related debt market. The following is taken from the application guidance of IFRS 9 (B6.3.14):

> *For example, an entity issues debt in an environment in which inflation-linked bonds have a volume and term structure that results in a sufficiently liquid market that allows constructing a term structure of zero-coupon real interest rates. This means that for the respective currency, inflation is a relevant factor that is separately considered by the debt markets. In those circumstances the inflation risk component could be determined by discounting the cash flows of the hedged debt instrument using the term structure of zero-coupon real interest rates (i.e., in a manner similar to how a risk-free (nominal) interest rate component can be determined).*

In the case of eurozone countries, IFRS 9 does not provide guidance on whether the analysis of inflation as eligible risk component has to be done by analysing the inflation market of the country or the overall inflation for the currency. In my opinion, when a bond is denominated in EUR, the relevant market structure for inflation should be eurozone inflation.

12.5 CASE STUDY: HEDGING REVENUES LINKED TO INFLATION

One of the uses of inflation derivatives is to match inflation-linked revenues with fixed rate funding. Entities exposed to inflation risk and with substantial funding needs may access different investor bases and hedge their inflation risk separately, lowering their cost of funding. The aim of this case study is to illustrate the application of a cash flow hedge of a string of highly expected inflation-linked revenues.

12.5.1 Background

Imagine that in 20X0, ABC – a British toll road operator – signed a 15-year contract with the British government to operate from 1 January 20X1 a highway that had just been constructed. Although both parties to the contract expected their collaboration to last 15 years, every 5 years the British government had the right to renegotiate the contract if the quality of maintenance of the highway was considered to be below a certain standard.

The contract established a cash cost price per vehicle of GBP 4.00 for the calendar year 20X1. The contract included a price adjustment mechanism that provided customers with a fixed "real" price. The price that ABC charged vehicles travelling through its highway was adjusted every 1 January to incorporate the most recent yearly inflation using the British RPI. For example, as shown in Figure 12.12, the price for the year 20X2 would be set by taking the price set for year 20X0 (GBP 4.00) and adjusting it for the inflation rate from October 20X0 to October 20X1. Assuming that the levels of the RPI corresponding to October 20X0 and October 20X1 were 134.1 and 139.8 respectively, implying a 4.28% annualised inflation rate, the price for the year 20X2 would be GBP 4.17 ($= 4.00 \times (1 + 139.8/134.1)$).

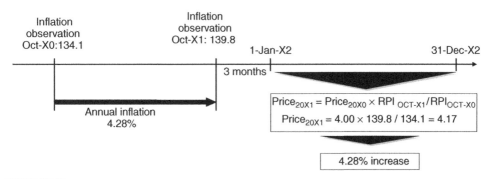

FIGURE 12.12 Annual reset mechanism of toll price.

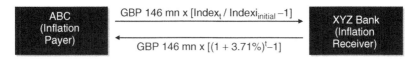

FIGURE 12.13   Inflation-linked swap annual cash flows.

By far the largest item affecting ABC's costs was financing expense, which stemmed from interest payments under a 15-year fixed rate loan. Because the revenues were linked to inflation while costs were fixed, ABC hedged the mismatch by entering into a 4-year inflation-linked swap (ILS) with the following terms:

Inflation swap terms	
Trade date	1 January 20X1
Effective date	31 December 20X1
Counterparties	ABC and XYZ Bank
Nominal amount	GBP 146 million
Termination date	31 December 20X5 (4 years)
ABC receives	Notional $\times [(1 + 3.71\%)^t - 1]$, paid annually on 31 December, starting on 31 December 20X2 t: number of years between the effective date and ABC payment date
ABC pays	Notional $\times [(\text{Index}_t/\text{Index}_{\text{Initial}}) - 1]$, paid annually on 31 December, starting on 31 December 20X2
Index	British non-revised RPI
$\text{Index}_{\text{Initial}}$	The index for the month of October 20X0 which was 134.1
$\text{Index}_{\text{Final}}$	The index for the reference month of October preceding ABC payment date

Under the ILS, each year ABC paid the realised inflation and received a fixed rate of 3.71%, accrued since the effective date (see Figure 12.13). Thus, on a notional of GBP 146 million and assuming a constant amount of traffic, ABC locked in revenues growing at a 3.71% annual rate. The GBP 146 million notional represented the expected revenues for the year 20X1 (i.e., 36.5 million vehicles times GBP 4.00). Whilst ABC was exposed to a lower than expected volume of traffic, it concluded that 36.5 million vehicles was a reliable estimate.

12.5.2 Hedging Relationship Documentation

ABC designated the ILS as the hedging instrument in a cash flow hedging relationship of a string of four highly expected cash flows. In order to justify the high probability of occurrence of the cash flows ABC produced an analysis in which it substantiated that traffic of 36.5 million vehicles was a conservative estimate and described the pricing mechanism formalised under the contract with the British authorities.

Hedging relationship documentation	
Risk management objective and strategy for undertaking the hedge	The objective of the hedge is to protect the GBP value of the highly expected cash flows stemming from the operation of a toll road for 4 years.
	This hedging objective is consistent with the entity's risk management strategy of reducing the variability of its profit or loss statement caused by inflation-linked revenues with inflation-linked swaps and debt.
	The designated risk being hedged is the risk of changes in the GBP value of the highly expected cash flows due to unfavourable movements in the British RPI rate
Type of hedge	Cash flow hedge
Hedged item	The hedged item is the yearly high expected cash flows stemming from the contract to operate highway E-106, from 1 January 20X2 to 31 December 20X5, corresponding to a forecasted annual traffic of 36.5 million vehicles.
	These cash flows are highly probable as the forecasted annual traffic is considered to be very conservative, and the pricing mechanism has been formalised through a contract with the British government
Hedging instrument	The inflation-linked swap contract with reference number 012845. The counterparty to the ILS is XYZ Bank and the credit risk associated with this counterparty is considered to be very low. The ILS contract has a GBP 146 million notional, an effective date of 31 December 20X1 and a maturity date of 31 December 20X5. Yearly settlement amounts will be paid/received as the net of (i) the entity paying the cumulative inflation since the effective date on the notional and (ii) the entity receiving a cumulative amount yielding an annual 3.71% fixed rate since the effective date on the notional
Hedge effectiveness assessment	See below

12.5.3 Hedge Effectiveness Assessment – Hypothetical Derivative

Although the cash flows take place almost evenly during the year, for assessment purposes they will be grouped into one flow taking place at the end of the year. Hedge effectiveness will be assessed by comparing changes in the fair value of the hedging instrument to changes in the fair value of a hypothetical derivative. The terms of the hypothetical derivative – an ILS with nil fair value at the start of the hedging relationship – reflected the terms of the hedged item. The terms of the hypothetical derivative were identical to those of the hedging instrument except the counterparty to ILS which was assumed to be credit risk-free and a fixed rate of 3.70%.

Note that the fixed rate of the hypothetical derivative (3.70%) was different from that of the hedging instrument (3.71%) due to the absence of CVA in the hypothetical derivative (the counterparty to the hypothetical derivative was assumed to be credit risk-free).

Changes in the fair value of the hedging instrument will be recognised as follows:

- The effective part of the gain or loss on the hedging instrument will be recognised in the cash flow hedge reserve of OCI. The accumulated amount in equity will be reclassified to profit or loss in the same period during which the hedged expected future cash flow affects profit or loss, adjusting the sales amount.
- The ineffective part of the gain or loss on the hedging instrument will be recognised immediately in profit or loss.

Hedge effectiveness will be assessed prospectively at hedging relationship inception, on an ongoing basis at each reporting date and upon occurrence of a significant change in the circumstances affecting the hedge effectiveness requirements.

The hedging relationship will qualify for hedge accounting only if all the following criteria are met:

1) The hedging relationship consists only of eligible hedge items and hedging instruments. The hedge item is eligible as it is a string of highly expected forecast transactions exposing the entity's profit or loss to fair value risk and is reliably measurable. The hedging instrument is eligible as it is a derivative and it does not result in a net written option.
2) At hedge inception there is a formal designation and documentation of the hedging relationship and the entity's risk management objective and strategy for undertaking the hedge.
3) The hedging relationship is considered effective.

The hedging relationship will be considered effective if all the following requirements are met:

1) There is an economic relationship between the hedged item and the hedging instrument.
2) The effect of credit risk does not dominate the value changes that result from that economic relationship.
3) The hedge ratio of the hedging relationship is the same as that resulting from the quantity of hedged item that the entity actually hedges and the quantity of the hedging instrument that the entity actually uses to hedge that quantity of hedged item. The hedge ratio should not be intentionally weighted to create ineffectiveness.

Whether there is an economic relationship between the hedged item and the hedging instrument will be assessed on a qualitative basis. The assessment will be complemented by a quantitative assessment using the scenario analysis method for one scenario in which the expected inflation rates will be calculated by shifting the expected inflation rates prevailing on the assessment date by +2%, and the change in fair value of both the hypothetical derivative and the hedging instrument compared.

12.5.4 Hedge Effectiveness Assessment Performed at Start of the Hedging Relationship

ABC performed an effectiveness assessment on 1 January 20X1, the start date of the hedging relationship, which was documented as follows.

The hedging relationship was considered effective as all the following requirements were met:

1) There was an economic relationship between the hedged item and the hedging instrument. Based on the qualitative assessment performed supported by a quantitative analysis, the entity concluded that the change in fair value of the hedged item was expected to be substantially offset by the change in fair value of the hedging instrument, corroborating that both elements had values that would generally move in opposite directions.

2) The effect of credit risk did not dominate the value changes resulting from that economic relationship as the credit ratings of both the entity and XYZ Bank were considered sufficiently strong.

3) The 1:1 hedge ratio of the hedging relationship was the same as that resulting from the quantity of hedged item that the entity actually hedged and the quantity of the hedging instrument that the entity actually used to hedge that quantity of hedged item. The hedge ratio was not intentionally weighted to create ineffectiveness.

Due to the fact that the main terms of the hedging instrument and those of the expected cash flow closely matched and the low credit risk exposure to the counterparty of the ILS contract, it was concluded that the hedging instrument and the hedged item had values that would generally move in opposite directions. This conclusion was supported by a quantitative assessment, which consisted of one scenario analysis performed as follows. The expected inflation rates on the assessment date were simulated by shifting on a parallel basis the expected inflation rates prevailing on the assessment date by +2%. As shown in the table below, the change in fair value of the hedged item was expected to largely be offset by the change in fair value of the hedging instrument, corroborating that both elements had values that would generally move in opposite directions.

Scenario analysis assessment		
	Hedging instrument	Hypothetical derivative
Initial fair value	Nil	Nil
Final fair value	<24,472,000>	<24,592,000>
Cumulative fair value change	<24,472,000>	<24,592,000>
	Degree of offset	**99.5%**

The hedge ratio was set at 1:1, resulting from the GBP 146 million quantity of hedged item that the entity actually hedged and the GBP 146 million quantity of the hedging instrument that the entity actually used to hedge that quantity of hedged item. The hedge ratio was not intentionally weighted to create ineffectiveness.

The following sources of ineffectiveness were identified: a change in the estimated cash flows below the hedged notional, a substantial deterioration of the creditworthiness of the counterparty to the ILS and changes in the agreement with the British government.

ABC also performed an effectiveness assessment on each reporting date, yielding very similar results, which have been omitted to avoid unnecessary repetition.

12.5.5 Fair Valuations of the ILS and the Hypothetical Derivative

The following table details the fair valuation of the hedging instrument on 1 January 20X1:

Hedging instrument fair valuation on 1 January 20X1

Cash flow date	Discount factor (1)	Expected inflation rate (2)	Expected RPI (3)	Inflation leg cash flow (4)	Fixed leg cash flow (5)	Expected settlement amount (6)	Present value (7)
31-Dec-X2	0.8972	4.22%	139.8	<6,206,000>	5,417,000	<789,000>	<708,000>
31-Dec-X3	0.8458	3.45%	144.6	<11,432,000>	11,034,000	<398,000>	<337,000>
31-Dec-X4	0.7950	3.30%	149.4	<16,658,000>	16,860,000	202,000	161,000
31-Dec-X5	0.7466	3.10%	154.0	<21,666,000>	22,902,000	1,236,000	923,000
CVA/DVA							<39,000>
Total							-0-

Notes:

(1) Discount factor, between 31-Jan-X1 (valuation date) and the cash flow date calculated using the GBP Libor curve

(2) Expected inflation rate from previous year's October to October of the year of the cash flow. For example, 4.22% was the expected inflation rate from October 20X0 to October 20X1

(3) The level of the British RPI index assuming a level of 134.1 for the month of October 20X0. For example, $139.8 = 134.1 \times (1 + 4.22\%)$, rounded to one decimal place

(4) <GBP 146 mn> × (Previous RPI/Current RPI – 1). For example, <6,206,000> = <146 mn> × (139.8/134.1 – 1)

(5) GBP 146 mn × [(1+3.71%)Years – 1], where Years was the number of calendar years since the effective date (31 December 20X1). For example, $11,034,000 = 146 \text{ mn} \times [(1+3.71\%)2 – 1]$

(6) Inflation leg cash flow + Fixed leg cash flow. For example, <789,000> = <6,206,000> + 5,417,000

(7) Settlement amount × Discount factor. For example, <708,000> = <789,000> × 0.8972

The following table details the fair valuation of the hedging instrument on 31 December 20X1:

Hedging instrument fair valuation on 31 December 20X1

Cash flow date	Discount factor	Expected inflation rate	Expected RPI (*)	Inflation leg cash flow	Fixed leg cash flow	Expected settlement amount	Present value
31-Dec-X2	0.9481	4.28%	139.8	<6,206,000	5,417,000	<789,000>	<748,000>
31-Dec-X3	0.8963	3.60%	144.8	<11,650,000>	11,034,000	<616,000>	<552,000>
31-Dec-X4	0.8449	3.45%	149.8	<17,093,000>	16,860,000	<233,000>	<197,000>
31-Dec-X5	0.7934	3.25%	154.7	<22,428,000>	22,902,000	474,000	376,000
DVA							34,000
Total							<1,087,000>

(*) RPI corresponding to October 20X1 was 139.8

The following table details the fair valuation of the hedging instrument on 31 December 20X2:

Hedging instrument fair valuation on 31 December 20X2

Cash flow date	Discount factor	Expected inflation rate	Expected RPI (*)	Inflation leg cash flow	Fixed leg cash flow	Expected settlement amount	Present value
31-Dec-X3	0.9554	4.70%	145.0	<11,867,000>	11,034,000	<833,000>	<796,000>
31-Dec-X4	0.9115	3.30%	149.8	<17,093,000>	16,860,000	<233,000>	<212,000>
31-Dec-X5	0.8675	3.20%	154.6	<22,319,000>	22,902,000	583,000	506,000>
DVA							8,000
Total							<494,000>

(*) RPI corresponding to October 20X2 was 145.0

The following table details the fair valuation of the hedging instrument on 31 December 20X3:

Hedging instrument fair valuation on 31 December 20X3

Cash flow date	Discount factor	Expected inflation rate	Expected RPI (*)	Inflation leg cash flow	Fixed leg cash flow	Expected settlement amount	Present value
31-Dec-X4	0.9700	2.10%	148.0	<15,133,000>	16,860,000	1,727,000	1,675,000
31-Dec-X5	0.9404	2.20%	151.3	<18,726,000>	22,902,000	4,176,000	3,927,000
CVA							<56,000>
Total							5,546,000

(*) RPI corresponding to October 20X3 was 148.0

The following table details the fair valuation of the hedging instrument on 31 December 20X4:

Hedging instrument fair valuation on 31 December 20X4

Cash flow date	Discount factor	Expected inflation rate	Expected RPI (*)	Inflation leg cash flow	Fixed leg cash flow	Expected settlement amount	Present value
31-Dec-X5	0.9772	1.80%	150.7	<18,073,000>	22,902,000	4,829,000	4,719,000
CVA							<24,000>
Total							4,695,000

(*) RPI corresponding to October 20X4 was 150.7

The fair valuation of the hypothetical derivative was similar to that of the hedging instrument. The only differences were the fixed leg cash flows (which were computed based on a 3.70% fixed rate) and the absence of CVA (DVA remained present).

The following table summarises the fair values of the hedging instrument and the hypothetical derivative at each relevant date:

Date	Hedging instrument fair value	Period change	Cumulative change	Hypothetical derivative value	Cumulative change
1-Jan-X1	-0-	—	—	-0-	—
31-Dec-X1	<1,087,000>	<1,087,000>	<1,087,000>	<1,215,000>	<1,215,000>
31-Dec-X2	<494,000>	593,000	<494,000>	<622,000>	<622,000>
31-Dec-X3	5,546,000	6,040,000	5,546,000	5,496,000	5,496,000
31-Dec-X4	4,695,000	<851,000>	4,695,000	4,655,000	4,655,000
31-Dec-X5	-0-	<4,695,000>	-0-	-0-	-0-

The ineffective part of the change in fair value of the hedging instrument was the excess of its cumulative change in fair value over that of the hypothetical derivative. The effective and ineffective parts of the period change in fair value of the ILS were the following (see Section 5.5.6 for an explanation of the calculations):

	31-Dec-X1	31-Dec-X2	31-Dec-X3	31-Dec-X4	31-Dec-X5
Cumulative change in fair value of hedging instrument	<1,087,000>	<494,000>	5,546,000	4,695,000	-0-
Cumulative change in fair value of hypothetical derivative	<1,215,000>	<622,000>	5,496,000	4,655,000	-0-
Lower amount	<1,087,000>	<494,000>	5,496,000	4,655,000	-0-
Sum of previous effective parts	—	<1,087,000>	<494,000>	5,496,000	4,655,000
Available amount	<1,087,000>	593,000	5,990,000	<841,000>	<4,655,000>
Period change in fair value of hedging instrument	<1,087,000>	593,000	6,040,000	<851,000>	<4,695,000>
Effective part	<1,087,000>	593,000	5,990,000	<841,000>	<4,655,000>
Ineffective part	-0-	-0-	50,000	<10,000>	<40,000>

The following table summarises the settlement amounts under the ILS:

Date	Actual inflation	RPI level	ILS settlement amount
31-Dec-X2	4.28%	139.8	<789,000>
31-Dec-X3	4.70%	145.0	<833,000>
31-Dec-X4	2.10%	148.0	1,727,000
31-Dec-X5	1.80%	150.7	4,829,000

The following table summarises the revenues generated by ABC, assuming that the actual annual traffic was exactly 36.5 million vehicles:

Year Ending	Traffic	Price	Revenue
31-Dec-X1	36.5 mn	4.000	146,000,000
31-Dec-X2	36.5 mn	4.170	152,205,000
31-Dec-X3	36.5 mn	4.325	157,863,000
31-Dec-X4	36.5 mn	4.414	161,111,000
31-Dec-X5	36.5 mn	4.495	164,068,000

12.5.6 Accounting Entries

Suppose that ABC reported financially every 31 December.

1) Accounting entries on 1 January 20X1

No entries were required as the fair value of the swap was nil on trade date.

2) Accounting entries on 31 December 20X1

ABC recognised GBP 146 million revenues for the year, which were received in cash. The change in fair value of the ILS produced a GBP 1,087,000 loss, fully deemed to be effective and recorded in the cash flow hedge reserve of OCI.

Cash (Asset)	146,000,000	
Sales (Profit or loss)		146,000,000
Cash flow hedge reserve (Equity)	1,087,000	
Inflation swap (Liability)		1,087,000

3) Accounting entries on 31 December 20X2

ABC recognised GBP 152,205,000 revenues for the year, which were received in cash. ABC paid GBP 789,000 under the ILS and adjusted the revenues figure. The change in fair value of the ILS produced a GBP 593,000 gain, fully deemed to be effective and recorded in the cash flow hedge reserve of OCI.

Cash (Asset)	152,205,000	
Sales (Profit or loss)		152,205,000
Sales (Profit or loss)	789,000	
Cash (Asset)		789,000
Inflation swap (Liability)	593,000	
Cash flow hedge reserve (Equity)		593,000

4) Accounting entries on 31 December 20X3

ABC recognised GBP 157,863,000 revenues for the year, which were received in cash. ABC paid GBP 833,000 under the ILS and adjusted the revenues figure. The change in fair value of the ILS produced a GBP 6,040,000 gain, of which GBP 5,990,000 was deemed to be effective and recorded in the cash flow hedge reserve of OCI, while GBP 50,000 was considered to be ineffective and recorded in profit or loss.

Cash (Asset)	157,863,000	
Sales (Profit or loss)		157,863,000
Sales (Profit or loss)	833,000	
Cash (Asset)		833,000
Inflation swap (Asset)	6,040,000	
Cash flow hedge reserve (Equity)		5,990,000
Other financial income (Profit or loss)		50,000

5) Accounting entries on 31 December 20X4

ABC recognised GBP 161,111,000 revenues for the year, which were received in cash. ABC received GBP 1,727,000 under the ILS and adjusted the revenues figure. The change in fair value of the ILS produced a GBP 851,000 loss, of which GBP <841,000> was deemed to be effective and recorded in the cash flow hedge reserve of OCI, while GBP <10,000> was considered to be ineffective and recorded in profit or loss.

Cash (Asset)	161,111,000	
Sales (Profit or loss)		161,111,000

Cash (Asset)	1,727,000	
Sales (Profit or loss)		1,727,000
Cash flow hedge reserve (Equity)	841,000	
Other financial expenses (Profit or loss)	10,000	
Inflation swap (Asset)		851,000

6) Accounting entries on 31 December 20X5

ABC recognised GBP 164,068,000 revenues for the year, which were received in cash. ABC received GBP 4,829,000 under the ILS and adjusted the revenues figure. The change in fair value of the ILS produced a GBP 4,695,000 loss, of which GBP <4,655,000> was deemed to be effective and recorded in the cash flow hedge reserve of OCI, while GBP <40,000> was considered to be ineffective and recorded in profit or loss.

Cash (Asset)	164,068,000	
Sales (Profit or loss)		164,068,000
Cash (Asset)	4,829,000	
Sales (Profit or loss)		4,829,000
Cash flow hedge reserve (Equity)	4,655,000	
Other financial expenses (Profit or loss)	40,000	
Inflation swap (Asset)		4,695,000

12.5.7 Concluding Remarks

The objective of the hedge was to generate revenues, assuming a constant 36.5 million annual traffic, growing at a rate of 3.71%. The following table details the target revenues:

Year ending	Traffic	Target price (*)	Target revenue
31-Dec-X1	36.5 mn	4.000	146,000,000
31-Dec-X2	36.5 mn	4.148	151,402,000
31-Dec-X3	36.5 mn	4.302	157,023,000
31-Dec-X4	36.5 mn	4.462	162,863,000
31-Dec-X5	36.5 mn	4.627	168,885,500

(*) $4.000 \times (1 + 3.70\%)^{Years}$, where Years was the number of years elapsed since 31-Dec-X1. For example, $4.302 = 4.000 \times (1 + 3.70\%)^2$

The hedge worked very well, each year almost reaching the target revenues. The following table compares the realised revenues (the sum of the traffic revenues generated plus the ILS settlement amounts) with the target revenues:

Year ending	Traffic revenues	ILS settlement amounts	Total realised revenues	Target revenue	Deviation
31-Dec-X1	146,000,000	-0-	146,000,000	146,000,000	0
31-Dec-X2	152,205,000	<789,000>	151,416,000	151,402,000	14,000
31-Dec-X3	157,863,000	<833,000>	157,030,000	157,023,000	7,000
31-Dec-X4	161,111,000	1,727,000	162,838,000	162,863,000	<25,000>
31-Dec-X5	164,068,000	4,829,000	168,897,000	168,886,000	11,000

In our example, ABC reported financially on an annual basis and the amounts under the ILS were settled coinciding with the reporting. In practice, it is likely that both reporting periods differ and accruals of the ILS settlement amounts need to be calculated. It is crucial to exclude accrual amounts when fair valuing an ILS to avoid double counting.

ABC was exposed to a lower than expected traffic, having concluded that 36.5 million vehicles was a sufficiently conservative estimate. If the British economy experienced a prolonged recession causing traffic figures to be below the hedged figure, ABC would be overhedged and ineffectiveness would be present, potentially adding volatility to the entity's profit or loss.

The ILS term was relatively short compared to the agreement. Normally ABC would have hedged a term coinciding with the term of the fixed finance. If for example the debt has a 15-year maturity, ABC would have taken out a 15-year ILS. However, the existence of the 5-year break clause in the agreement may have prevented the entity from applying hedge accounting for a term longer than 5 years.

12.6 MATCHING AN INFLATION-LINKED ASSET WITH A FLOATING RATE LIABILITY

Suppose that investors have heavily sold bonds of CDN Corporation after a suit was filed with a US court. ABC, a competitor of CDN, with the EUR as its functional currency, considered that CDN's inflation bonds were trading at "irrational" levels and decided to invest in a CDN inflation-linked bond with a maturity of 4 years. To fund the investment, ABC issued a 4-year floating rate bond in which it paid a Euribor 12-month plus 100 basis points interest on a constant notional of EUR 100 million.

In order to lock in a 250 bps positive carry between both bonds, ABC entered into a 4-year inflation-linked swap in which ABC paid the inflation-linked coupons and principal related to the CDN bond, and received Euribor 12-month plus 350 bps on a EUR 100 million notional.

In order to avoid fair valuing the derivative through profit or loss, ABC decided to apply hedge accounting. ABC considered the following two choices:

- designating the swap as an instrument hedging the variability of the cash flows pertaining to both bonds;
- designating the swap as an instrument hedging the fair value of the inflation-linked bond.

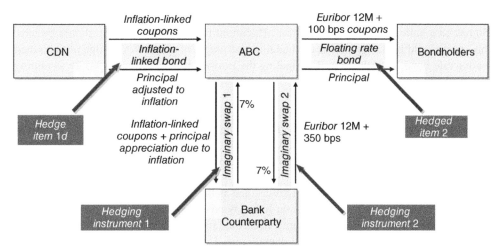

FIGURE 12.14 Alternative 1 – simultaneous cash flow hedging.

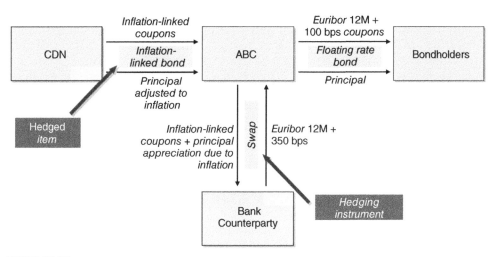

FIGURE 12.15 Alternative 2 – fair value hedging of the inflation-linked swap.

Suppose that it designated the swap as a simultaneous hedge of the cash flows of both bonds. Under this alternative (see Figure 12.14), the swap from a theoretical perspective was split into two "imaginary" swaps. Each swap would be designated as the hedging instrument in a separate cash flow hedging relationship.

In a first imaginary swap, ABC would pay CDN's inflation-linked coupons and the appreciation of the principal due to inflation, and receive a fixed rate on a notional of EUR 100 million. The fixed rate would be calculated to result in a zero fair value. Suppose that the calculated fixed rate was 7%. This swap would be designated as the hedging instrument in a cash flow hedge of the purchased inflation-linked bond, with the aim of mitigating the inflation risk exposure stemming from the bond's cash flows.

In a second imaginary swap, ABC would pay 7% and receive Euribor 12-month plus 250 bps on a notional of EUR 100 million. The initial fair value of this swap should be zero. This swap would be designated as the hedging instrument in a cash flow hedge of the issued floating rate bond, with the aim of mitigating the Euribor 12-month risk exposure stemming from the bond's cash flows.

Now suppose that it designated the swap in its entirety as a fair value hedge of the inflation-linked bond (see Figure 12.15). The hedged item would be the cash flows pertaining to that bond, excluding credit risk. In my view this alternative is preferable as it is operationally simpler than the previous one, in which ABC would need to keep track of two hedging relationships, with their related documentations, effectiveness assessments, fair valuations and accounting entries.

Another key element to be taken into account is the greater flexibility provided by this alternative. Imagine that the CDN inflation-linked bond experienced a strong rally following a better than expected settlement of the suit, ABC could just sell the bond and unwind the swap, recognising in profit or loss the related overall gain. Under the first alternative, ABC would do the same but it would need to reclassify the amounts recognised under the second hedging relationship (the cash flow hedge of the liability) as their coupons impact profit or loss, an additional operational burden.

CHAPTER **13**

Hedge Accounting: A Double-Edged Sword

Hedge accounting is optional: it is a choice made by the management of an entity. Hedge accounting is a special accounting treatment available to ensure that the timing of profit or loss recognition on the hedging instrument matches that of the hedged item. When hedging, corporations face the decision between entering into hedge accounting compliant hedges and pure economic hedges (see Figure 13.1). At first glance, it seems a straight-forward decision as the reduction in profit or loss volatility stemming from applying hedge accounting provides a powerful argument for adopting hedge accounting compliant hedges. However, in reality the decision whether or not to implement hedge accounting compliant hedges can be a difficult one: applying hedge accounting may be operationally complex and accounting compliant hedges are relatively limited (forwards/swaps and standard options).

The decision whether or not to adopt hedge accounting compliant hedges requires an in-depth analysis at both the entity level and the consolidated level as it may affect earnings, earnings per share, cash flows, gearing, interest cover, dividend cover, covenants, margins, bonuses and staff payment schemes. In my view it does not make sense to discard an attractive hedging strategy just because of the volatility it may add to profit or loss. Shareholders may punish executives for short-term volatility, but will certainly penalise underperforming companies. I believe that a well-designed disclosure to investors and analysts in which the merits and the drawbacks of a weak hedge accounting compliant strategy should be sufficient.

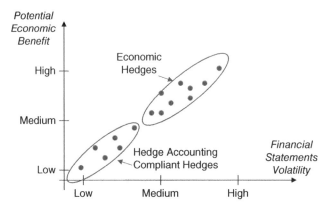

FIGURE 13.1   Economic hedges versus hedge accounting compliant hedges.

ERICSSON: Change of Accounting Policy

Ericsson, a Swedish electronics group, hedged highly probable forecast transactions related to sales and purchases with the purpose of limiting the impact related to currency fluctuations on these forecasted transactions. In 2013, Ericsson decided to discontinue applying hedge accounting for this type of hedge for **cost efficiency** reasons.

Prior to the decision, Ericsson applied cash flow hedge accounting for highly probable forecast transactions. Revaluation of these hedges was reported under "other comprehensive income" and was at release recycled to sales, cost of sales and R&D expenses, respectively.

After the decision, revaluation of new hedges were reported under "other operating income and expenses" in the profit or loss statement.

Ericsson disclosed such accounting policy change in a presentation to analysts.

13.1   POSITIVE INFLUENCE ON THE PROFIT OR LOSS STATEMENT

The application, or not, of hedge accounting treatment may have important effects on the profit or loss statement (see Figure 13.2), especially when hedging highly expected sales or purchases. Usually these hedges are implemented to mitigate commodity and/or FX risk.

Suppose that an entity is considering hedging a highly expected foreign currency denominated sale of finished goods with a derivative. The expected sale will not be recorded in profit or loss until the sale finally takes place. The sale will be recorded in the EBITDA section of the profit or loss statement.

If the entity applies hedge accounting, the hedge will be treated as a cash flow hedge. The effective part of the change in fair value of the derivative will be recorded in OCI. When the hedged item (i.e., the highly expected sale) affects profit or loss, the accumulated amount in equity (i.e., in OCI) will be reclassified from OCI to profit or loss, on the same EBITDA line as the hedged item entry. This is relevant as EBITDA is a key indicator for financial analysts and investors. Thus, the application of hedge accounting in this example has two benefits:

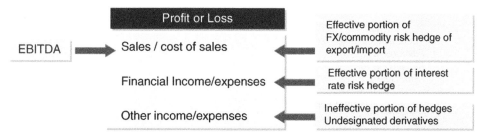

FIGURE 13.2 Influence of hedges on profit or loss.

firstly, it ensures that the recognitions in profit or loss of the hedged item and the hedging instrument take place simultaneously; and secondly, that the recognitions are made on the same profit or loss line (e.g., sales).

If the entity does not apply hedge accounting, the change in fair value of the derivative for the period will be recognised in the "other financial gains and losses" item of profit or loss since the derivative's inception. Therefore, there will be a recognition mismatch between the hedged item and the hedging instrument in terms of not only timing but also profit or loss lines.

Thus, the use of hedge accounting may reduce not only profit or loss volatility, but also EBITDA volatility. The decision to use hedge accounting can be especially relevant to companies for which the price of raw materials is a very important component of their finished products sale price.

13.2 SUBSTANTIAL OPERATIONAL RESOURCES

Implementing hedge accounting is a big challenge as the requirements are far reaching. The administrative load needed to prepare disclosure and presentation requirements, to produce hedge documentation and to assess effectiveness can be substantial. A good deal of training is also needed for accounting and treasury personnel to achieve a sufficiently high level of competence. Additionally, strong information systems capabilities are needed to adequately process information flows and reporting. Also modelling tools are frequently needed to be able to correctly evaluate financial instruments and hedged items. Finally, supervision and appropriate policies and procedures are required to determine whether all hedge accounting requirements are properly met. Lack of appropriate controls can have a real and visible impact on the reported results of an organisation.

America West Weak Controls

In 2005, the external auditors of America West Airlines Inc. concluded that America West's fuel hedging transactions did not qualify for hedge accounting under US generally accepted accounting principles and that its financial statements for prior periods required restatement to reflect the fair value of fuel hedging contracts in the balance sheets and statements of shareholders' equity of America West. These accounting errors were the result of deficiencies in its internal control over financial reporting from the lack of effective reviews of hedge transaction documentation and of quarterly mark-to-market accounting entries on open fuel hedging contracts by personnel at an appropriate level.

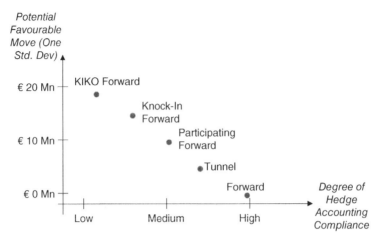

FIGURE 13.3   Economic upside versus degree of hedge accounting compliance.

13.3 LIMITED ACCESS TO HEDGING ALTERNATIVES

Widespread adoption of hedge accounting compliant hedges may lead entities to undertake hedging instruments that are sub-optimal from an economic perspective. Usually hedging instruments that provide more potential room for economic benefit tend to show a lower degree of applicability of hedge accounting.

A good many hedging strategies are neither fully hedge accounting compliant nor completely non-compliant. As discussed in some of the case studies in Chapter 5, there are hedging instruments that can be split into a part that meets the requirements of hedge accounting and a part that does not meet these requirements. Figure 13.3 depicts the usual negative relationship between the potential economic upside (measured as the participation in potentially favourable market movements) and the degree of hedge accounting compliance in FX hedges of highly expected sales or purchases.

13.4 RISK OF REASSESSMENT OF HIGHLY PROBABLE TRANSACTIONS

One potential problem with using hedge accounting occurs when the originally highly probable cash flow being hedged is suddenly no longer expected to take place. In a cash flow hedge of a highly expected cash flow, the change in fair value of the hedging instrument is recorded in equity until the underlying cash flow affects profit or loss. If the underlying cash flow is no longer expected to take place, the hedging instrument gain or loss deferred in equity has to be transferred to profit or loss immediately. This transfer can have a devastating effect on profit or loss if the deferred amount in equity represented a very large loss.

Airbus and the Delivery Delay for the Airbus 380 Superjumbo

In June 2006, Airbus – a European airplane manufacturer – reported that it would delay delivery of the A380 superjumbo for a second time. At that time EADS had 159 orders for its A380 planes, listed at USD 100 million each, for 16 airlines. Some airlines had clauses in their purchase contracts that allowed them to cancel their orders if the aircraft delivery were more than a year late.

Suppose that Airbus hedged one of its USD denominated highly expected sales, and that it applied hedge accounting. The changes in fair value of the hedging instrument were then recorded in equity. Suppose further, that due to the delay, the airline cancelled the plane order. A cancellation may have had two different outcomes:

1) If Airbus still reasonably expected the sale to take place: the deferred gain or loss that was previously accumulated in equity remained in equity until the sale finally occurred.

2) If Airbus no longer expected the sale to take place: the deferred gain or loss that was accumulated in equity was immediately transferred to profit or loss.

This second outcome could have a devastating impact on Airbus's earnings if the deferred amount in equity represented a very large loss.

13.5 LOW COMPATIBILITY WITH PORTFOLIO HEDGING

Most large multinationals centralise their financial risk management in a treasury centre, which is responsible for risk and liquidity management, and funding for the whole group. Frequently, the treasury centre applies a portfolio approach to hedging. This means that it does not consider individual exposures, but combines different exposures together, and only enters into hedges with third parties when the residual risk in the portfolio may compromise the delivery of corporate objectives.

The overall risk is usually measured using the **value at risk** (VaR). The VaR approach attempts to measure the probability that the portfolio does not lose more than a specific amount within a specific time horizon. The hedging strategy then involves limiting the portfolio exposures so that the financial and other business targets are not endangered by financial risks. Figure 13.4 depicts the hedging process on a portfolio basis.

Unless macrohedging (i.e., portfolio hedge accounting) is applied, when a derivative is taken out to hedge a net group position the application of hedge accounting (microhedging) often requires assigning the hedging instrument to an individual transaction between an entity of the group and an outside party, an assignment that may sometimes not be feasible as shown in Section 5.17. As a consequence, an entity may end up not applying for hedge accounting for many of the hedging transactions with outside parties.

At the time of writing, the IFRS 9 macrohedging project was at a preliminary stage. If the macrohedging project ends up providing rigid application of portfolio hedging, there is likely

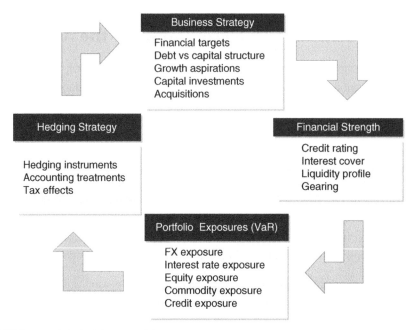

FIGURE 13.4   Portfolio hedging – decision process.

to be a gap between risk management and hedge accounting, which may deter companies from applying hedge accounting for their dynamic or portfolio hedging strategies.

13.6 FINAL REMARKS

When a company is contemplating hedge accounting for a specific hedge, careful analysis is required of the costs and benefits of its application. This can be a complex decision because the main benefit – the added value that comes from reduced earnings volatility – is difficult to measure in practice.

Although most companies try to maximise the use of hedge accounting, it is important not to exclude attractive hedging strategies just because of an unfavourable accounting treatment. Let us not forget that risk management can be a competitive weapon: companies can gain advantage over competitors who fail to optimise risk management.

The following table summarises the pros and cons of applying hedge accounting to a specific hedge:

Strengths	Weaknesses
Reduced volatility in earnings	Limited availability of hedging alternatives
Reduced volatility of EBITDA	Low compatibility with portfolio hedging techniques(*)
Improved cash flow forecasting	Systems and human resources to meet hedge documentation, effectiveness assessment and disclosure requirements
Reduced risk of breaching covenants	Potential volatility in reserves (if cash flow or net investment hedge)
Reduced risk of credit rating downgrades	Risk of accounting restatements

(*) The IFRS 9 macrohedging project was not finalised at the time of writing

Index

Printed and bound by CPI Group (UK) Ltd, Croydon, CR0 4YY

23/04/2025